Stalking Crimes and Victim Protection

Prevention, Intervention, Threat Assessment, and Case Management

Stalking Crimes and Victim Protection

Prevention, Intervention, Threat Assessment, and Case Management

Edited by
Joseph A. Davis

CRC Press
Boca Raton London New York Washington, D.C.

Library of Congress Cataloging-in-Publication Data

Stalking crimes and victim protection: prevention, intervention, threat assessment, and case management / edited by Joseph A. Davis
    p. cm.
    Includes bibliographical references and index.
    ISBN 0-8493-0811-9 (alk. paper)
    1. Stalking. 2. Stalkers—Psychology. 3. Stalking victims. 4. Criminology psychology.
I. Davis, Joseph A.

HV6594.S73 2001
362.88—dc21   2001025361
                                                                                         CIP
        Catalog record is available from the Library of Congress

Visit the CRC Press Web site at www.crcpress.com

© 2001 by CRC Press LLC

No claim to original U.S. Government works
International Standard Book Number 0-8493-0811-9
Library of Congress Card Number 2001025361
Printed in the United States of America   3 4 5 6 7 8 9 0
Printed on acid-free paper

Dedication

To my two wonderful children: Meghan and Haley. Thank you for your patience and for forgiving me for all the times and many hours you missed playing with Dad while he was coordinating, researching, writing, and editing this book.

To the fond memory of Bruce L. Danto, M.D. — mentor, colleague, and friend. As an early pioneer on the subject of the psychiatry of stalking, stalker–victim relationships, threat assessment, and personal safety and security, your legacy will not be forgotten. Your memory will continue to live on in your teachings, writings, and with your former students — this editor, fortunately, having been one of them.

To my colleagues, who are, without question, a highly dedicated group of professionals who dedicate their time and expertise and who comprise the San Diego "Stalking Strike Force" and "Stalking Case Assessment Team" (SCAT). Your work and continuous efforts on stalking and related cases are highly appreciated.

To Bonita F. Hammell, Ph.D., my colleague, who unexpectedly passed away at the age of 48 on March 24, 1999. Bonnie, your friendship, engaging personality, humor, compassion, dedication, and talents are greatly missed by all.

Finally, to all of the countless numbers of victims of domestic violence and workplace violence and to those victims of relentless stalking and related unwanted pursuit, may the criminal justice system always prevail on your behalf.

Foreword

I have had the honor and privilege of associating with thousands of remarkable psychologists during my more than three-decade involvement in criminal psychology. Few have the background and expertise comparable to Dr. Joseph Davis in the fields of public safety and forensic psychology. With his unique combination of psychology and law, together with his unequaled background and experience, he is a natural to edit as well as co-author several chapters in this most comprehensive text. The book represents an exceptionally diligent and thorough effort to shed light on an increasingly troublesome and persistent societal problem — stalking.

Stalking is a long-standing civil and criminal enigma and many who deal directly with this act, as well as those who deal with victims and the stalkers themselves, have virtually no information regarding the crime or the criminal. They go into investigations and interviews with little or no information. This book will be of inestimable value to them.

The importance of each author's efforts in the creation of this book cannot be underestimated. This information is of practical value, the quality of the research is excellent, and the significance of this book as a contribution to the literature regarding the act of stalking is unequaled. I am convinced that the number of times this text will be read, referenced, and cited will be innumerable.

As the contributing authors scan the horizons of knowledge for clues and solutions in their particular areas of expertise, each chapter becomes eye opening and exciting as they attempt to uncover the core causes of stalking, the personalities and characteristics of stalkers, the risks associated with being a victim of stalking, and possible remedies.

The majority of Americans live with the belief that people are basically good. On occasion, however, we fail and we are prone to make mistakes. For the most part, we are able to take responsibility for our actions. Our dilemma, then, is to determine why some choose to live outside the rules of human decency — why some choose to stalk. Therefore, if we are to survive in the 21st century, an understanding of crime and criminals is essential.

When Joe Davis asked me to provide a foreword to this book, without any hesitation, I agreed. His work ethic, competence, and tenacity were enough to assure anyone that this text would become a reality. It is the most complete, multifaceted manuscript on this topic to date. As a former FBI agent and behavioral scientist, I understand the dangers of making assumptions about the criminal mind. The best safeguard is gathering as much information as possible about a particular crime or criminal and staying focused. As the gap between stalking cases and solutions to these cases widens, efforts must be made to accelerate our knowledge and thus increase our solution rate. This book helps the reader to understand the frequency, impact, and motives of stalkers. It represents a complete commitment by the editor and contributing authors to provide the best text possible for a complete understanding of this crime and the criminal stalker.

No stone has been left unturned in this impeccably researched and impressively footnoted academic work and practical search for truth. In 30 years as a behavioral scientist and criminologist, I have not found a more profound or exhaustive text or work on a specific crime or criminal such as this one.

Finally, this text is written and edited with a sense of cooperation, not competition. It is my hope that this extraordinary effort on the parts of all the contributing authors will be of lasting value to those who have the task of identifying, diagnosing, prosecuting, and ultimately reducing the act of stalking in America.

James T. Reese, Ph.D. (F.B.I., retired)
Editorial Board, *Journal of Threat Assessment*
James T. Reese and Associates, Lake Ridge, Virginia
Diplomate, Society for Police and Criminal Psychology
Fellow, American Academy of Experts in Traumatic Stress

Preface

This is a book of extreme overriding importance. As stalking cases continue to seriously increase in growing numbers in our society, an even greater responsibility is placed on those who not only assess and evaluate stalkers, but also who work to prevent, intervene, manage, and educate the victims of stalking, and who train public safety personnel and our communities on this matter of growing issue.

Emphasizing a multidisciplinary approach to dealing with stalkers and their victims, *Stalking Crimes and Victim Protection: Prevention, Intervention, and Threat Assessment* is a complete and comprehensive work to date. Professionals contributing to this book who are researchers, mental health clinicians, psychologists, psychiatrists, criminologists, sociologists, academics and university professors, security experts, investigators, and security practitioners in the field have lent their special talents and expertise to the making of this book. A much needed resource in the field, anyone who currently provides services to victims, evaluates the mental state of the stalker, investigates stalking and related cases, or who provides threat assessments or consults on security issues and safety planning can and will benefit from this book.

From the editor's experience, stalking, stalker, and victim cases are best evaluated and managed using a multidisciplinary approach. Therefore, the editor and contributing authors have ambitiously undertaken this important work with the hopeful intent to educate, inform, and raise public awareness as to this growing phenomenon. Many current changes and trends as well as cutting-edge research by nationally and internationally recognized experts on the subject are taking place in the field today in the following areas: psychology, psychiatry, and criminology of stalkers, stalking laws, statutes and anti-stalking legislation, public policy, stalking victims, victim services, stalking recognition, stalking investigation, stalker typologies and profiles, case management, use and caveats of temporary restraining orders (TROs), domestic violence and stalkers, workplace violence and stalkers, security issues and personal protection, electronic stalking, cyberstalking and the Internet, stalking prevalence on college campuses, stalking evidence and documentation, and intervention and prevention strategies, along with approaches to the assessment of potential threats of dangerousness by establishing threat assessment and risk management units.

This book provides highlights regarding several stalking and stalker case examples and analysis for clinical-forensic study and comparison. Finally, this book provides some helpful guidelines and suggestions for training purposes, as well as how to develop and establish threat assessment and case management teams for the purposes of investigating, evaluating, managing, and prosecuting stalkers and stalking cases, and for security planning, and victim assistance purposes.

Acknowledgments

Stalking Crimes and Victim Protection: Prevention, Intervention, and Threat Assessment was prepared with the helpful assistance of many dedicated professionals. From the editor's perspective, when examining and managing any stalking case, a balance of personnel representing a "team approach" oftentimes provides the most effective results. The many contributing authors to this book represent that balance from a multidisciplinary perspective.

Overall, I would like to thank the following individuals for their generous input and contributions to this project. I am indebted to all for their assistance, for without them, this book could not have been completed. First and foremost to my talented wife, Eileen (a University of California magna cum laude in English with a Master's degree in education), for her patience, literary skills, and talents, where mine as a scientist are occasionally missing. To Bretton S. Pelphrey, MFS, my former graduate student, for his masterful suggestions on design and related artwork; to Georgia Spiropoulos, M.A., assistant to Dr. Bonnie S. Fisher, Division of Criminal Justice, University of Cincinnati, for her research support on Professor Fisher's chapter and contribution to "Campus Stalking"; to Erika Stevens, J.D., and Bonnie D. Lucks, M.A., Ph.D. candidate, my former graduate students, who are now doctoral psychology students at U.S. International University. To Lisa M. Stewart, M.A., my former extern from the John Jay College of Criminal Justice, Graduate Program in Forensic Psychology, now a doctoral student in psychology at the Fielding Institute; to Tzaddi Bondi, Veronica Huberman, and Jennifer Hackbarth, my former teaching and research assistants at California State University; and to Toby M. Finnie, director and founder of the High Tech Crime Consortium (HTCC), Tacoma, Washington. Furthermore, I would also like to thank Dr. Glenn S. Lipson, psychologist and adjunct professor of psychology at the California School of Professional Psychology (CSPP), and my stalking case assessment team colleague in San Diego, for his clinical and forensic perspective on stalking; and to Dr. J. Reid Meloy, associate professor of psychiatry at University of California at San Diego, also a colleague in San Diego, for his talents, valuable input over the years, and for his many contributions to the field; to Dr. Kaye DiFrancesca, psychologist and adjunct professor of psychology, also at CSPP, for her overall support and professional brilliance over the years; to Dr. Nicholas C. Allioti, clinical, school, and family psychologist, my former research supervisor, dissertation chair, and friend. Additionally, I would like to thank Dr. Fred Clemens, Dr. Bob Wildman, Dr. Carroll Smith, Dr. Joseph King, Dr. Barry Malinger, Dr. Tom Mullis, Dr. Alistar V. E. Harris, Dr. Angelo "Angie" Gadeleto, Dr. Charles Neal, Dr. Chuck Kugler, and Dr. Melinda Wagoner, all who are very talented university educators in their respective fields who were my former mentors during my undergraduate and graduate years of study; to senior criminologist and professor emeritus, Dr. John "Jack" Kinney, my mentor, colleague, and friend; to Dr. Park E. Dietz, Dr. John Monahan, and Professor Larry Fitch, J.D., former director of the Institute of Law, Psychiatry and Public Policy (ILP&PP), all my psychology-law professors while at the University of Virginia where I gained a great deal of knowledge about forensic assessment and the mentally ill offender — all three have influenced my thinking as a former student in forensic psychology, law, and public policy while at the ILP&PP in the mid-1980s. And, to Dr. David T. Susman and Kathy M. Susman, M.A., my longtime friends and former forensic mental health colleagues and forensic assessment team members with the Virginia Department of Mental Health at CMCS. Your support over the years has been immeasurable! A simple thanks to both of you is just not enough. Also, I would like to thank my CRC editor, Becky McEldowney, and my production staff, Naomi Rosen and Naomi Lynch, for all their kind support and feedback on this project. And finally, to four individuals (posthumously): Dr. Eleanor Kemp, my first experimental psychology professor, Dr. Herbert Babb, a brilliant psychologist who was my first clinical-forensic psychology supervisor and former mentor at CMCS, Dr. Bruce L. Danto, forensic psychiatrist, my former mentor, colleague, and friend, and Dr. Bonita F. Hammell, my former colleague, who unexpectedly passed away March 24, 1998. All of your wisdom, knowledge, and compassion for the field of science, research, psychology, and human behavior still continue as a legacy with those you have influenced so greatly. Thank you.

Joseph A. Davis
San Diego, California

About the Editor

Joseph A. Davis, Ph.D., LL.D

A subject matter expert in the areas of public safety psychology, clinical and forensic psychology, psychology of trauma and crisis intervention, critical incident debriefing, mental health law, and public policy, the editor of *Stalking Crimes and Victim Protection: Prevention, Intervention, and Threat Assessment* is Joseph A. Davis, Ph.D., LL.D. Dr. Davis earned a B.S. in psychology with honors with a minor in biology, a M.S. in psychology, a Doctor of Philosophy (Ph.D.) in clinical psychology, and a Doctor of Laws (LL.D) in law and public policy (honoris causa). A member of the Phi Kappa Phi, Psi Chi, Pi Gamma Mu, and Omicron Delta Kappa honorary societies, Dr. Davis completed his post-graduate forensic psychology and forensic mental health assessment, education, and training at the University of Virginia at the Institute of Law, Psychiatry and Public Policy (ILP&PP) in 1985. He further went on to complete his post-graduate inpatient forensic assessment training at Central State Forensic Hospital and Western State Hospital, and his pre-doctoral clinical psychology assessment and psychotherapy training at the Veterans Administration Medical Center (VAMC) on the inpatient psychiatry and psychology service. He also completed an additional elective post-graduate training in clinical neuropsychology at Sharp Cabrillo Hospital in San Diego.

Dr. Davis has served as a consultant and expert on a wide variety of issues for private, criminal, and civil justice agencies that include the U.S. Government, the California Department of Justice, and district, municipal, and superior state courts. Formally educated and trained in clinical and forensic psychology, law and public policy, he began his career as a full-time psychologist in public service to the Commonwealth of Virginia assigned to the State Department of Mental Health Outpatient and Forensic Assessment Services. During his tenure as a Commonwealth psychologist, for several years Dr. Davis provided full-time outpatient on-call mental health emergency and crisis intervention services, outpatient clinical assessment and evaluation, psychotherapy, case management, disability determination assessment, forensic assessment, and court consultation services to the local community, general and psychiatric hospitals, county district attorney, and county sheriff's office, as well as to schools and other criminal/civil justice systems and entities. An editorial board member and subject matter peer-reviewer for several national scientific journals and textbook publishers, he also holds several adjunct faculty appointments to many major universities in California and abroad. Dr. Davis has published over 50 peer-reviewed articles over the past 17 years, and has been recognized and testified as a court expert in five U.S. states and Canada in several subject areas, primarily focusing on and covering the disciplines of forensic psychology, public safety psychology, traumatology (psychology of trauma), critical incidents, debriefing and post-traumatic stress, mental health law and public policy, stalking and criminal psychopathology, violence, and aggression.

A former workplace violence prevention and threat assessment consultant to the Scripps Center for Quality Management, Inc. in San Diego, Dr. Davis has been the medical and allied health editor-in-chief and a member of the editorial advisory board to the *Canadian Journal of Clinical Medicine* in Edmonton, Alberta, Canada for the past 6 years. He is now the executive director to the Institute of Law, Psychology and Public Policy Studies and founder of both the Center for the Advancement of Trauma Studies (CATS) and the Center for Applied Forensic-Behavioral Sciences (CAFBS) in San Diego. Additionally, he is a senior partner with The TAP Group, Inc., a consortium of security, threat assessment, prevention, and intervention experts located in San Diego and Long Beach, California; and vice president of the High Tech Crime Consortium (HTCC), a non-profit organization dedicated to assisting public and private industry regarding technology and cybercrime, located in Tacoma, Washington (www.hightechcrimecops.org). A long-standing member to the first multidisciplinary based "Stalking Strike Force" and "Stalking Case Assessment Team" (SCAT), he is a respected researcher, clinician, educator, trainer, presenter, and speaker. In addition to devoting his time to university-level teaching on the subjects of abnormal psychology and psychopathology, personality psychology, social psychology, and psychology and law, he also advises undergraduate, graduate, and doctoral students on various research projects in psychology, behavioral sciences, law, and criminal justice.

With an active teaching, research, and training agenda, he is a consultant to many state agencies and is an on-call service provider to several federal agencies. He maintains a private office devoted to education, research, development, and training involving the prevention of violence, threat assessment, risk management, and stalking in the workplace, violence in the school setting, pre-incident education, post-incident stress debriefing and training, and case management. Dr. Davis is married and the father to two daughters. A native of Virginia, he and his family reside in San Diego, California.

The Contributors

Contributing Authors

Steven F. Albrecht, DBA, CPP, PHR
President
The Baron Center, Inc.
San Diego, California

S. Anthony Baron, Ph.D., Psy.D.
Chief Executive Officer
The Baron Center, Inc.
San Diego, California

Gregory S. Boles (Det. III, ret.)
LAPD Threat Management Unit
and
Current Director
Global Threat Management Division
Kroll Associates
Los Angeles, California

Marcella A. Chipman, J.D.
Private Law Practice
San Diego, California

Melissa J. Collins, B.A.
Victim Service Provider
Anti-Stalking Program
New York, New York

William R. Cupach, Ph.D.
Department of Communications
Illinois State University
Normal, Illinois

Bruce L. Danto, M.D. (deceased)
Forensic Psychiatrist
Fullerton, California

Joseph A. Davis, Ph.D., LL.D.
Senior Partner
The TAP Group, Inc.
and
San Diego State University
Department of Psychology
San Diego, California

Denise R. Emer, Ph.D.
Daeman College
Department of Psychology and Social Work
Amherst, New York

Bonnie S. Fisher, Ph.D.
University of Cincinnati
Department of Criminal Justice
Cincinnati, Ohio

Suzanne Hoffman, Ph.D.
Executive Vice President
The Baron Center, Inc.
San Diego, California

Ronald M. Holmes, Ed.D.
Vice President and Co-Founder
Center for Unresolved Homicides
Department of Administration of Justice
University of Louisville
Louisville, Kentucky

Detective Sergeant Robert L. Jones
Public Safety Division
University of California
San Diego, California

Kim Kelly, B.A.
Investigator
Office of Personnel Management
San Diego, California

Lois M. Kosch, J.D.
Wilson, Petty, Kosmo & Turner, LLP
San Diego, California

Glenn S. Lipson, Ph.D., ABPP
Private Clinical Practice
and
Department of Psychology
California School of Professional Psychology
San Diego, California

Bonnie D. Lucks, M.A.
Ph.D. candidate (clinical psychology)
U.S. International University
San Diego, California

Wayne Maxey, B.S.
Investigator
Special Operations Division
District Attorney's Office
San Diego, California

Neal Miller, J.D.
Principle Associate
Institute of Law and Justice
Washington, D.C.

Doreen Orion, M.D.
Private Clinical Practice
and
Medical Faculty
University of Colorado Health Sciences Center
Colorado Springs, Colorado

Regina A. Petty, J.D.
Wilson, Petty, Kosmo & Turner, LLP
San Diego, California

Robin Siota, Psy.D.
Private Research Consultant
San Diego, California

Brian H. Spitzberg, Ph.D.
San Diego State University
Department of Communications
San Diego, California

Lisa M. Stewart, M.A.
Doctoral student in clinical psychology
The Fielding Institute
San Diego, California

Jo Ann Ugolini, M.B.A.
Private Security Consultant
Los Angeles, California

Kerry Wells, J.D.
Deputy District Attorney
Special Operations Division
San Diego, California

Mary Beth Wilkas, M.A.
Private Security Consultant
San Diego, California
and
Dallas, Texas

Digital Arts

Bretton S. Pelphrey, MFS

Research Assistants

Georgia Spiropoulos, M.A.

Erika Stevens, J.D.

Lisa M. Stewart, M.A.

Veronica Huberman, B.A.

Jennifer Hackbarth, B.A.

Kelli Kottkamp, B.A.

Tzaddi Bondi, B.A.

Dan Foster, B.S.

Teri Caperton

Cyrus Madavi

Tonia Tran

Stephanie Hoagland

Table of Contents

Part X
Educating and Training Those Who Stalk the Stalker 487

21   Staying One Step Ahead of Stalkers and Stalking Crimes: Personnel Development, Training, and Ongoing Education   489

Joseph A. Davis

Appendix
Educating Those Who Stalk the Stalker: A Training Perspective   495

Kerry Wells and Wayne Maxey

PART I

Stalking and Stalkers:
Theories, Research, and Typologies

Stalkers and Other Obsessional Types: A Review and Forensic Psychological Typology of Those Who Stalk*

1

JOSEPH A. DAVIS
MARCELLA A. CHIPMAN

Contents

Introduction

Stalking, an age-old phenomenon, was discussed in the ancient writings of Hippocrates, researched extensively in the early 20th century by French psychiatrist G.G. de Clerambault, given notoriety with the tragic death of former Beatle John Lennon, and viewed as *Fatal Attraction* in local theaters across the nation. Stalking is unique as the repetitive, harassing, long-term course

* *Source:* Davis, J. A. and Chipman, M. A. *Journal of Clinical Forensic Medicine*, 4, 166–172. Copyright © 1997. APS and Harcourt Brace & Company, Ltd. Reprinted with permission.

3

of conduct and behavior reflects the internal dynamics of the stalker's motivating mental disorder. Furthermore, the investigation of stalking can be very complex and quite difficult.

The numerous and progressive acts comprising the intentional course of conduct require a continuity of purpose: harassment designed to control the victim. A multidisciplinary approach, utilizing law enforcement, legal, medical, and mental health professionals, is necessary to effectively eradicate this encroaching behavior. In 1990, the first anti-stalking legislation was passed in California. In just 6 years, all 50 states have followed suit. Public awareness has encouraged federal legislation to stop stalking behavior as a course of conduct crime and to give victims a measure of protection. This research is a compilation of the many periodicals, law review articles, studies, and projects of law enforcement, legal counsel, medical professionals, forensic mental health professionals, forensic examiners, and criminologists generated since 1992. The study of stalkers and stalking behavior is a work in progress. As questions are answered, statutes are amended, and diagnoses are distinguished, it becomes a mere steppingstone to the future understanding of the pervasive stalking phenomenon facing our culture and society today.

Stalking behavior, historically characterized as romantic, obsessive advances, has recently been identified as psychopathological by the mental health, law enforcement, and legal communities. Stalking behavior is broad in scope and can be evaluated as to potential threat as well as charted on a continuum with gradient variations of mental disorder and resultant injury to the victim (Sapp, 1996; Hammell, 1996; Davis, 1996a, b; Zona et al., 1993; Dietz et al., 1991).

Erotomania, the delusional belief that the stalker is passionately loved by an unattainable victim, generally a celebrity, is classified diagnostically as a delusional disorder, known as "de Clerambault's syndrome" (Zona et al., 1993) (see *Diagnostic and Statistical Manual of Mental Disorders, Fourth Edition*, DSM-IV. Axis-I, Clinical Disorders: Delusional Disorder, Erotomanic Type — Diagnostic Features). The subject goes to extreme lengths to contact or make his or her presence known to the victim. However, the incidence of physical injury is anecdotal (Davis, 1996; Menzies et al., 1995; Zona et al., 1993; Meloy, 1992; Dietz et al., 1991).

Press coverage of these rare occurrences of injury has dramatically increased the public awareness of stalking behavior. Media attention directed toward a high profile target, such as Rebecca Schaeffer (killed by convicted stalker Robert John Bardo) or David Letterman, pursued relentlessly by Mary Margaret Ray, has publicly exposed the devastating fears, injury, and pain of the celebrity, opening the floodgates for numerous victims recoiling in fear behind bolted doors, drawn curtains, and unanswered telephones of the homes and offices of ordinary people.

Press coverage of celebrity victims and their families has given a rever-
berating voice to the thousands of unrecognized victims who were forced
into hiding, terrorized into silence, and ignored or disbelieved when they
finally summoned the courage to seek help (Davis, 1997; Chipman, 1996;
Zona et al., 1993; Dietz et al., 1991).

"Simple obsessional" stalking of the most common, yet least protected,
victim generally begins when the relationship between the two people has
gone bad or there is a perception of mistreatment (Wells, 1996). It is usually
preceded by domestic violence or other assaultive behavior. Often rational-
ized, excused, or denied until the victim has suffered irreparable harm, this
behavior is not limited to the poor, the uneducated, or the incompetent. The
"simple obsessional" stalker may reveal indices of personality disorder; however, the stalking is more often the result of the power struggle of the insecure
stalker following his or her perceived rejection by the helpless victim. In fact,
schizophrenia, hallucinations, or bizarre behavior, if more than incidental,
removes the behavior from classification within the stalking continuum
(Zona et al., 1993). The stalker's life from all outward appearances is seemingly normal (Edwards, 1992).

The middle ground of the stalking spectrum is that held by the "love
obsessional." This stalking behavior type orchestrates a calculated and relentless
harassment campaign intended to make the victim aware of the stalker's existence. The victim is generally known by the stalker, perhaps as a co-worker, a
friend of a friend, a bank teller, or grocery store clerk. The communication
efforts of the stalker are creative yet unintelligible from the perception of the
victim: a cellophane-wrapped rat for Valentine's Day, severed fingernails of a
stranger, or assorted issues of *Texas Monthly Magazine* (Dietz et al., 1991).

The recognition and identification of stalking behavior as criminal are
difficult, because from all outward appearances, most of the stalker's acts are
considered normal behavior (Edwards, 1992). Some of the conduct may
involve criminal activity such as trespassing, vandalism, threatening phone
calls, petty theft offenses, or domestic violence. However, these offenses, if
charged at all, are generally not dealt with severely. The nominal punishments
— credit for time served or brief probationary periods — are minimal
deterrents to obsessional behavior. Until the recent media blitz following the
murder of television actress Rebecca Schaeffer by Robert John Bardo in 1990,
and resultant public awareness as to the seriousness and degree of stalking
in our society, the law enforcement and legal communities failed to look far
beyond isolated misdemeanor convictions. The heightened awareness and
increased understanding of stalking behavior have presented the criminal
history of the stalker in a focused perspective to empirically demonstrate the
escalation of the violence. The stalker does not stop until he or she is stopped.
Stalking involves certain elements of control, manipulation, fear, and

psychological power over the victim (Sapp, 1996; Davis, 1996; Hammell, 1996; Zona et al., 1993; Dietz et al., 1991).

California was the first state to enact anti-stalking legislation in 1990, Penal Code 646.9, after the murder of stalking victim, actress Rebecca Schaeffer. Since that time, all 50 states have enacted similar statutes (Walsh, 1996). The National Institute of Justice (NIJ) has developed a Model Anti-Stalking code (National Institute of Justice, 1993). Security expert Gavin de Becker and psychiatrists Park Dietz and Michael Zona were instrumental in establishing the Threat Management Unit (TMU) of the Los Angeles Police Department (LAPD).

There is an important distinction between making a threat and posing a threat (Fein et al., 1995). These concepts are not mutually exclusive. Within the overlap, constitutional issues arise for the protection of the stalker's First Amendment rights. Current California cases, including *People v. Halgren*, Cal. App. 4th, filed September 28, 1996 by the Fourth District Court of Appeal, uphold the constitutionality of Penal Code 646.9 (Chipman, 1996; Wells, 1996).

This research will first examine research findings on stalkers: who they are, what they do, and why they do it, why they select, and when they stalk their chosen victims. Next, this paper will review the development of threat management and assessment which both monitors the stalker and educates the victim in order to modify behavior and arrest the progression and escalation of the stalker's violent behavior. Finally, a brief study of the California statute, Penal Code 646.9 as amended, will reveal the efforts of the legal community to stop the stalker while protecting the victim (Wells, 1996; Jordan, 1995).

Who, What, Where, When, and Why of Stalkers and Stalking? No One Particular Profile of a Stalker

Since 1990, there has been an increasing interest in the subject of stalkers, threat assessment, risk management, and victimology from many different disciplines such as psychiatry, psychology, criminology, sociology, public policy, and law. Furthermore, this has subsequently stimulated the amount and quality of contributed clinical, empirical, and case study research data at the local, state, and federal levels defining the characteristics of stalking from both legal and behavioral standpoints (Davis, 1997; Hammell, 1996; Sapp, 1996).

More Than One Type of Stalker

Stalkers come from all walks of life and intelligence levels. They may be devoid of any criminal recidivism, include persons with diagnosable mental illnesses, as well as individuals with socially maladaptive behaviors. Many possess dependent or controlling personalities (Wells, 1996). Empirical studies of behavioral characteristics used to determine motive or to predict violence are in the developmental stages. There has not been enough time since recognition of stalking as criminal to answer many key questions (Chipman, 1996).

To date, several researchers have attempted to isolate from the literature various key behavioral and cognitive elements that potentially identify a typology of the stalker. Several researchers such as Sapp (1996), Davis and Chipman (1997), Zona et al. (1993), Holmes (1993), and Meloy (1992) have contributed to the literature on the typology of stalkers. Sapp (1996) suggested that there are at least seven different typologies of stalkers, such as random, celebrity, single agenda, casual acquaintance, and domestic stalkers (Sapp, 1996). Holmes (1998, 1993) suggested that there are at least six different types of stalkers, such as celebrity, lust, hit, love-scorned, domestic, and the political stalkers. Davis and Chipman (1997) found that stalkers fell into several categories, such as public figure (attentional seeking and status-seeking stalkers attaching to high-profile individuals in the public or media), fixated-focus (contested issues of special importance to the stalkers), violent and non-violent (stalkers who are outwardly focused and who threaten to do harm to a targeted victim, i.e., "I will kill you if you don't fulfill my request" vs. the inwardly focused stalker, i.e., "I will kill myself if you don't go out with me," etc.), domestic relational, work relational, first-time encounter and random chance encounter, therapeutic relational stalkers (healthcare provider and current patient or former patient who has some fixation with the provider or has developed a dependency relationship with the provider stemming from problems with personal boundaries, like in borderline personality disorder treatment cases), electronic, and, finally, a subset of the electronic-type online stalker such as the cyberstalker.

Geberth (1996) suggested that stalkers can fall into two broad categories: psychopathic personality and psychotic personality stalkers. In a research study conducted by Harmon et al. (1995), she suggested that stalkers fall into such categories as affectionate/amorous or persecutory/angry. Dietz et al. (1991) suggested from his research that stalkers comprise at least six categories, such as jilted lover, narcissistic, over-idealized romantic, batterer, perverted, and, finally, the psychotic.

Michael Zona (1993), a psychiatrist and now a consultant with the Omega Threat Management Group, and reserve officer with the Los Angeles Police Department, has classified stalkers in three broad categories. Erotomanics diagnostically are those who falsely believe that the victim is in love with them, comprising only about 10% of those who stalk. The 'love obsessional' stalkers, generally strangers to the victim, who employ harassment to gain their victim's attention, constitute 43% of those who stalk. The commonest types, yet the most injurious of all, are the 'simple obsessional' stalkers, the ex-spouses or

Table 1.1   Threat Assessment of Stalkers as Series of Continuums

Type	Relationship to Victim	Problematic	Likelihood of Violence
I	None	High	"Limited"
II	None	High	"Limited"
III	None/slight	Moderate	Moderate
IV	Slight	Moderate	Moderate[a]
V	Moderate	Moderate	Moderate
VI	Intimate	Slight	High
VII	Extended/intimate	Slight	Very high

[a] When children or adolescents are targeted by these stalkers, the likelihood of physical harm and violence is considerably higher.

Excerpted from A. Sapp, 1996; presentation to the Academy of Criminal Justice Sciences, Las Vegas, NV.

ex-lovers, who account for about 47% of all stalking cases. As with other domestic violence or abuse situations, this type of incident is frequently unreported until irreparable harm or even death occurs (Johnson, 1993).

Zona has also classified the stalking victims into four groups: 38% are ordinary citizens, 13% are former employers or supervisors, 32% are lesser-known entertainment or community figures, and only 17% are recognized celebrities (Zona et al., 1993; Johnson, 1993).

San Diego County Deputy District Attorney, Paul Johnson, pointed out that Zona's statistical base comes from the Los Angeles area where nationally known celebrities abound, yet the residency of stalkers is not limited to Southern California. Nationally, the percentage of celebrity stalking is lower. The category percentages would dramatically change if the stalked domestic violence victim came forward with greater frequency (Zona et al., 1993; Johnson, 1993).

Statistical percentage reports aside, stalking is a matter of major concern today. It is estimated that more than 200,000 women are currently being stalked. One in 20 women will be stalked during their lives (Wells, 1996; National Institute of Justice, 1993).

Probably the most critical observation of consequence is the relationship of the stalker to the victim. Sapp (1996), in a presentation to the Academy of Criminal Justice Sciences (ACJS), has developed a dimensional stalker typologies formulation (Table 1.1). This typology examines specific stalking behaviors along a potential "credible threat profile continuum." The "credible threat continuum" has been divided into minimally three general stalking classifications and into seven types, based upon a progressive degree of relationship. Application of the diagnostic features of obsessional mental dysfunctions described in DSM-IV (American Psychiatric Association, 1994) and the statistical likelihood of threat and violence demonstrate a direct correlation between the degree of relationship between the stalker and his victim and the incidence or likelihood of physical and psychological injury (Davis, 1997; Wells, 1996; Sapp, 1996; Meloy, 1992).

In contrast, an inverse proportion of the degree of mental disorder is observable; the more distant or unattainable the relationship, the more acute the delusional disorder, and the less likelihood of injury to the victim (Sapp, 1996).

Erotomania-Type Stalker

"Types I, II, and III" are typological categories which define stalkers who choose an unknown victim. Delusions of "destiny" exist, and "but for some insurmountable obstacle or unawareness," the stalker and the victim would be united (Sapp, 1996). *Random stalker* selects a complete stranger, who nevertheless meets the stalker's requirements. The type II *celebrity stalker* pursues an unattainable celebrity or public figure, given the victim's notoriety, economic, or social status (Sapp, 1996).

The stalker engages in repetitive, harassing conduct which is generally limited to extensive communication and threats through the mail or by telephone (Sapp, 1996; Morin, 1994). The type III *single agenda stalker* chooses victims who are involved with a topic of particular concern to the stalker: economic or environmental matters etc. (Sapp, 1996). The selected agenda or issue is the perceived source of the concern, psychopathological attachment, problem, or relationship issue between the stalker and the intended victim or business (Davis, 1997; Sapp, 1996; Morin, 1994).

Contrary to popular misconception due to extensive press coverage of celebrities, these three types of stalkers rarely engage in face-to-face contact with their victims. Actual attempts to harm either the victim's person or property are virtually non-existent (Zona et al., 1993). Delusional erotomanic stalkers steadfastly believe that they are passionately loved by the object of their delusion. They focus on a spiritual union rather than a sexual attraction. If they are violent, they may direct the violence to a third party they presume to interfere with the relationship (Meloy, 1992; Dietz et al., 1991).

The difficulty of classification and identification of any type of stalker is highlighted by the case of John Hinckley, Jr., the would-be assassin of President Reagan. Hinckley has been described as a particularly dangerous case of erotomania (Goldstein, 1987). The opinion of the prosecution expert at Hinckley's trial was a diagnosis of personality disorder, while the defense expert opinion found paranoid schizophrenia: none of the psychiatrists involved in Hinckley's trial mentioned erotomania (Clarke, 1990). Less than 2 hours before his assault on President Reagan, Hinckley had written a letter to Jodie Foster. The second paragraph began: "As you well know by now I love you very much. Over the past seven months I've left you dozens of poems, letters and love messages *in the faint hope that you could develop an interest in me*" [emphasis added]

(Clarke, 1990). Such a statement refutes any delusional erotomanic conviction Hinckley might have possessed that he was passionately loved by Foster. The statement more accurately reflects the unrealistic hopes of a disturbed and immature fan suffering from unrequited love (Menzies et al., 1995).

According to Park Dietz, a psychiatrist who researches and investigates celebrity-type stalkers, there is no composite of "star" stalkers, although their letters share common delusions communicated to their victims: sharing a life of love (e.g., Rebecca Schaeffer, Theresa Saldana); or a business relationship (e.g., Johnny Carson, Monica Seles, and Steffi Graf); or rescue from harm or miserable fate (e.g., John Lennon, Michael J. Fox, etc.). Generally, non-threatened celebrities are often the object of obsessive fixation. The stalker is more likely to ruminate on the approachable "girl next-door" such as Olivia Newton-John as opposed to an actress who plays cold and ruthless characters as did Joan Collins (Dietz et al., 1991).

Love Obsessional-Type Stalker

Stalkers of the second general category choose victims they have previously met, no matter how fleeting the acquaintance, or victims who are co-workers with whom the stalkers interact on a regular basis. The chance-met victim could be a grocery store clerk, a bank teller, or a friend of a friend. Often healthcare professionals are targeted, due to the intensity of medical appointments (Wells, 1996). The type IV *acquaintance stalker* perceives and builds a fantasy relationship from passing casual interaction with the victim. However, the type V *co-worker stalker* targets a co-worker with whom he or she interacts on a daily basis. The stalker misconstrues every contact or interaction as an affirmation of the purported relationship, no matter how innocent or accidental the conduct of the victim (Sapp, 1996; Morin, 1994).

Often, these stalkers are affluent, well-educated, high-strung professionals with no personal life except their out-of-control obsession with the corporate colleague who is barely known to this new breed of 1980s-driven American sociopath (Edwards, 1992). Dietz (1991) has worked with the LAPD and developed a personality character profile of the workplace-type stalker: Dietz (1991) states this type of stalker is a workaholic who feels cheated out of his personal and professional aspirations, and who perceives proof of reciprocal interaction with the victim through innocuous circumstances. Although generally intelligent, he or she is angry, paranoid, deceitful, and without remorse, taking no responsibility for his or her actions. Stuart Fischoff, a professor at California State University, Los Angeles (UCLA), believes many single professional men no longer differentiate between their social and personal lives (Edwards, 1992).

The rigid boundaries between "work friends," "social friends," and "intimates" have been warped by networking, power lunching, and corporate retreats designed with the expected, albeit tacit, requirement for the employees to interface emotionally. Business lunches and office functions have become a substitute for courtship (Edwards, 1992).

The Threat Management Unit (TMU) within the LAPD currently charts this unexplored territory. "The workplace stalker generally does not conceal his relentless pursuit. The stalker's co-workers are aware of his odd behavior, but it is generally water cooler gossip and viewed as quirky, because he talks rationally on any other topic and he competently does his job" (Edwards, 1992).

Stalkers, Threats, and Dangerous Stalking Days

The TMU pays particular attention to the so-called "dangerous days": Valentine's Day, Mother's Day, July 4th, Easter, and Christmas. Brainstorming is necessary. Victims rarely understand the significance of the "gifts" the stalker sends; they try to learn the nuances of the obsession — a mind game, a contest of wits that becomes a race. No one knows what triggers the anger of the stalker. What is the cause of his or her sudden decision that it is time for the victim to die? Justice Department studies of stalker mentality have noted the stalker imputes great power to the victim. Paranoid, the stalker lives in an emotionally charged universe, a dream world full of perceived signs and symbols generated by the victim.

A stalker aims for more than friendship or true love: he or she seeks to become the most important thing in the victim's life. And by terrorizing the victim, the stalker tries to make this wish come true (Edwards, 1992).

Simple Obsessional-Type Stalker

The largest and by far the most dangerous type of stalker, the "simple obsessional" (Zona et al., 1993) has been categorized by Sapp (1996) as type VI, the *intimate partner stalker,* and type VII, the *domestic violence stalker.* The common threads of power and control over the victim, who is viewed by the stalker as valuable property, are exacerbated by denial the relationship has terminated. Rejection is unacceptable. The difference between the two subtypes is the existence of prior domestic violence in the type VII relationship. Repetitious physical assaults of the past relationship are accelerated and even justified because of the termination. "What's past is prologue" (William Shakespeare, *The Tempest,* Act II, Scene 1).

This most problematic group stems from domestic violence which is emerging in epidemic proportions. On a national scale, FBI statistics reveal that acts of domestic violence occur at least once every 15 seconds and also that 30% of murdered women were killed by their boyfriends or husbands (American Medical Association, 1992). Surveys indicate that law enforcement is contacted in fewer than 50% of the San Diego stalking cases. Of the reported cases, 57% culminate in temporary restraining orders, but such judicial action augments the risk of violence to the victim (Hammell, 1996).

Intimate partner and the domestic violence stalker motivations may be exhibited by contrasting feelings: intense affection or extreme disdain for the victim. The stalker's behavior may be irrational, and even violent, or may manifest in benign acts such as flattery (National Institute of Justice, 1993). But the single, unifying issue of stalking intimates is control. Psychological and physical terrorism permeate the stalker's behavior and depend substantially upon the perceived inequality of power and control between the stalker and the intended victim. From the victim's perspective, stalking is "a nightmare which I am unable to stop" (Sapp, 1996; Davis, 1996; Walsh, 1996).

Due to the prior intimate relationship, stalking behavior is not readily recognized until a serious pattern has emerged. Often excusing or dismissing stalking as retaliatory behavior coincidental to child custody battles or bitter divorce actions, victims are reluctant to report the conduct because their fears have not often been taken seriously by friends, family, or law enforcement (Sapp, 1996). The victim may be in complete denial of the harassing conduct, particularly if there are codependency issues. By the same token, a "vindictive victim" may cry "wolf," encouraged by the exposure given stalking on radio–television talk shows and the television or daytime media "soaps" (Chipman, 1996; Davis, 1996).

Former close contact and intimate knowledge afford the stalker easy access to the victim. Unnoticed for a time by neighbors and co-workers of the victim, the stalker's harassing behavior includes annoying phone calls, unwanted letters, unauthorized removal or address diversion of the victim's mail, arrival at the victim's home or workplace, or vandalism and trespass by tampering with the victim's answering machine or automobile (Wells, 1996).

Law enforcement and the legal system respond to harassment which violates criminal statutes. However, conduct short of such violations cloaks the stalker with perceived immunity. The 1996 presentation of "Stalking the Stalker" by the San Diego District Attorney's Stalking Strike Force included an opening statement by "Jodi" (the victim's real identity is protected), a stalking victim: "The loss is more than just time out of your day to fight it. It's your soul, it's your privacy, it's your being, it's your emotions — everything is taken away from you. You are robbed of everything" (Chipman, 1996; Davis, 1996).

Threat Assessment and Evaluation: Prevention, Prediction, and Intervention

Stalking is extremely complex and it can be very volatile. For successful management, and intervention in stalking cases, the stalker's profile requires accurate assessment. Designed to modify, control, or eliminate inappropriate behavior, the focus of intervention is doubly directed to stopping the suspect and to educating the victim, utilizing methods dictated by the specific case variables. In some instances, suspect intervention would be devastating. But more often than not, an aggressive approach is required, particularly with multiple and progressively harmful criminal violations (Sapp, 1996; Williams et al., 1996).

Stalking is an evolving, continual, or progressive crime. By definition, it is not static. California Penal Code section 646.9 defines stalking: *"Any person who willfully, maliciously, and repeatedly follows or harasses another person and who makes a credible threat with the intent to place that person in reasonable fear for his or her safety, or the safety of his or her immediate family, is guilty of the crime of stalking."*

The elements require actions to occur on multiple occasions. This requires a "course of conduct" involving a behavioral pattern composed of a series of acts over a period of time, which demonstrate a "continuity of purpose."

The credible threat must be expressed or implied from the course of conduct, and made with the intent to place the victim in fear for his or her safety. There must also be an apparent ability of the perpetrator to carry out the credible threat (Hammell, 1996; Davis, 1996; Wells, 1996).

Contrary to the twin traditional law enforcement goals of apprehension and prosecution, threat evaluation and assessment entail investigative and operational techniques used to identify, assess, and manage the risks of targeted violence and potential perpetrators. The distinction between *making* and *posing* a threat is important: some people who make threats ultimately pose them; many persons who make threats do not pose threats, while some persons who pose threats never make threats. Violence is a process, an incremental development of problems, conflicts, disputes, and failures which results in a physical act (Davis, 1996; Hammell, 1996).

Threat Assessment of Potential Harm

Threat assessment identifies the "attack-related" behaviors and attempts to move the suspect away from employing violence as a viable option (Sapp, 1996; Fein et al., 1995). Once the suspect is identified, the possible risks posed to the potential target are assessed. Investigation focuses on both the suspect and the target. The suspect's behavior, interests, and state of mind are evaluated. Multiple sources of information are utilized; personal interviews are conducted with the suspect, paying particular attention to body language, gestures, and eye contact. Interviews with family, friends, neighbors, or previous victims are conducted. Prior criminal history, medical and mental health records, letters, books, journals, and diaries of the suspect are identified and evaluated. From the information gathered, the factors indicating risk to the victim are assessed.

Were there past or present threats to kill this victim? Is there a history of violence against this victim or others? Weapons, violations of temporary restraining orders (TROs), possessiveness, jealousy, and depression are all factors predictive of future violence. Substance abuse, irrational mood swings, and past history of stalking behavior are additional factors for consideration (Sapp, 1996; Hammell, 1996; Davis, 1996; Wells, 1996; Dietz et al., 1991).

Information regarding the potential target is equally important. How well does the suspect know the victim and his or her personal lifestyle including daily work patterns? Is the victim vulnerable to attack or afraid of the suspect? Is he or she sufficiently sophisticated to grasp the need for caution and avoidance of contact? The victim must be educated about the phenomenon of stalking. The predicament and problem are the victim's. Law enforcement can only operate within the scope of its limited powers. The victim must explore his or her options for additional security — modify behavior by employing unlisted phone numbers and post office boxes. He or she must also consider the possibility of relocation and steps to secure absolute anonymity. Ultimately, the victim must develop a tolerance level for some of the stalker's behavior in order to avoid becoming dysfunctional (Sapp, 1996; Wells, 1996; Davis, 1996; Williams et al., 1996).

The third component of an actual threat evaluation and assessment is actual case management. First, a plan is developed to manage the subject and the risk, whether through detective contact, restraining orders, arrest and detention, or aggressive prosecution. Second, the plan is implemented and executed by meticulous documentation and consultation with the assessment team and the external experts. Unanswered questions must be confronted and answered. Redirection may be required. When it is determined the suspect's possible violent action toward the victim no longer poses appreciable concern, consideration may be given to closing the case (Sapp, 1996; Wells, 1996; Davis, 1996; Fein et al., 1995; Dietz et al., 1991).

Legislative Statutes
Stalking the Stalker in His Tracks

In 1990, California "created" a new crime by passing the first anti-stalking legislation in the United States. With unprecedented speed, all 50 states plus the District of Columbia have passed similar protective measures, acting as a catalyst for federal Canadian anti-stalking laws (Walsh, 1996). On September 25, 1996, President Bill Clinton signed a stricter and aggressive anti-stalking bill into law, validating nationwide restraining orders and extending protection to the victim's family. This law also made it a federal crime for a stalker to cross state lines with the intention of harassing a victim (*West's Legal News*, October 8, 1996).

During the past 6 years, the remaining 50 states drafted individual anti-stalking legislation, while California amended Penal Code section 646.9 three times (Jordan, 1995). The amendments have specifically addressed, expanded, and redefined "threat." Threats relating to family members are covered. Threats made in any manner causing reasonable fear for the victim's safety are within the protection of the law. Threats, implied by a pattern of conduct or made with the apparent ability to be carried out, and causing reasonable fear for the safety of the victim, are statutorily prohibited (California Penal Code section 646.9 (a).

Punishments have been increased by each amendment. A second stalking conviction is now a felony. TRO violations are no longer necessary to make a first offense a felony. An initial stalking conviction in violation of a TRO is now punishable in state prison for up to 4 years, as is a second conviction, not necessarily against the same victim, within 7 years (California Penal Code section 646.9 (a).

Effective January 1996, Assembly Bill 985 (AB 985) amended Californian Penal Code section P.C. 646.9 (a), removing the specific intent requirement and establishing an objective standard of fear on the part of the victim (California Penal Code section 646.9 (a).

In 1993, at the request of Congress, the National Institute of Justice (NIJ) developed a Model Anti-Stalking Code. In 1994, Congress added subtitle F, "National Stalker and Domestic Violence Reduction," under Title IV Violence against Women in the Violent Crime Control and Law Enforcement Act of 1994.

Under these provisions, states or local government units are eligible to receive grants to establish programs designed to improve stalking and domestic violence data entry processes in state and local databases which are integrated with the National Crime Information Center (NCIC). Pursuant to 42 U.S.C. 14038, the Attorney General, in conjunction with the states, shall compile data regarding domestic violence and intimidation (including stalking) as part of the National Incident-Based Reporting System (NIBRS).

The daily utilization of these databases is critically important. Prior to felony arraignment, state criminal history research is linked to these key interstate sources, the primary tracking tools of prior convictions and outstanding warrants for interstate offenders (Chipman, 1996).

Conclusion

By definition, stalking research has no conclusion. It is an evolving process, ever changing with each level of understanding. Those who understand it best are perhaps the stalkers and their victims. We are on the outside, looking in at incomprehensible behavior, inconceivable terror, and debilitating fear. Perhaps the best conclusions are observations of the victims (Chipman, 1996).

Kathleen Tobin Krueger, stalking victim and wife of former Texas Senator Bob Krueger, spoke before the Senate Judiciary Committee, relating the horrifying experiences she and her family suffered because of a stalker: "I'm convinced that stalking is the most under-reported and fastest growing crime in America today ... maybe, just maybe, by coming forward and putting a face on the victimization of stalking, I can, in some small measure, help to bring us all relief from within the legal system. But I need your help. Yes, we all must help."

Bibliography

American Medical Association (1992). *Diagnostic and Treatment Guidelines on Domestic Violence.* Washington, D.C.: American Medical Association.

American Psychiatric Association (1994). *Diagnostic Criteria from DSM-IV.* Washington, D.C.: American Psychiatric Association.

Chipman, M. A. (1996). Reality of a Nightmare. Thomas Jefferson School of Law, course in scientific evidence, unpublished research paper, San Diego.

Clarke, J. W. (1990). *On Being Mad or Merely Angry: John W. Hinckley, Jr. and Other Dangerous People.* Princeton, NJ: Princeton University Press.

Davis, J. (1996a). Stalking and Stalkers: A Legal and Psychological Analysis. Presentation, Thomas Jefferson School of Law, Course in Scientific Evidence and Expert Testimony, San Diego.

Davis, J. (1996b). Elements of Psychological Personality Profiling and Behavioral Assessment, San Diego. Presentation, California State University, Los Angeles.

Davis, J. (1997). A Developing a Threat Assessment and Risk Analysis of Those Who Stalk. Presentation, Second Annual Stalking the Stalkers Conference, San Diego.

Davis, J. (1997). A Psychological and Legal Analysis of Those Who Stalk. Unpublished manuscript, San Diego.

Davis, J. and Chipman, M. A. (1997). A forensic psychological typology of stalkers and other obsessive types, *Journal of Clinical Forensic Medicine* (U.K.), 4, 166–172.

Dietz, P., Matthews, D., Van Duyne, C., Martell, D., Parry, C., Stewart, T., Warren, J., and Crowder, J. (1991). Threatening and otherwise inappropriate letters to Hollywood celebrities, *Journal of Forensic Sciences,* 36(1), 185–209.

Edwards, L. (1992). Trespassers of the heart, *Eyewitness,* December, 34–40.

Fein, R. A., Vosskuil, B., and Holden, G. A. (1995). Threat assessment: an approach to prevent targeted violence, *National Institute of Justice — Research in Action,* September 1–7.

Geberth, V. (October 1992). Stalkers, *Law and Order,* 40(10), 138–143.

Geberth, V. (1996). *Practical Homicide Investigation: Tactics, Procedures, and Forensic Techniques*, 3rd ed. (pp. 683–688). Boca Raton, FL: CRC Press.

Goldstein, R. L. (1987). More forensic romances: De Clerambault's syndrome in men, *Bulletin of the American Academy of Psychiatry and Law*, 15, 267–274.

Hammell, B. F. (1996). Stalking: The Torment of Obsession: The STOP Program (Stalking Treatment Options Program). San Diego District Attorney Anti-Stalking Case Conference, San Diego.

Harmon, R. (1998). Anti-Stalking Legislation: A New Answer for an Age Old Problem. Conference presentation, American Academy of Forensic Sciences 50th Anniversary Meeting, San Francisco, CA.

Harmon, R., Rosner, R., and Owens, H. (1995). Obsessional harassment and erotomania in a criminal court population, *Journal of Forensic Sciences*, 40(2), 188–196.

Holmes, R. M. (1993). Stalking in America: types and methods of criminal stalkers, *Journal of Contemporary Criminal Justice*, 9, 317–327.

Holmes, R. M. and Holmes, S. (Eds.) (1998). *Contemporary Perspectives on Serial Murder* (pp. 137–148). Thousand Oaks, CA: Sage Publications.

Johnson, P. (1993). When creeps come calling, *Law Enforcement Quarterly*, February–April, 9–10, 32.

Jordan, T. J. (1995). The efficacy of the California stalking law: surveying its evolution, extracting insights from domestic violence cases, *Hastings Women's Law Journal*, 6, 363–383.

Meloy, J. R. (1992). *Violent Attachments*. Northvale, NJ: Jason-Aronson Publishers.

Menzies, R. P. D., Federoff, J. P., Green, C. M., and Isaackson, K. (1995). Prediction of dangerous behavior in male erotomania, *British Journal of Psychiatry*, 166, 529–536.

Morin, K. (1994). The phenomenon of stalking: do existing state statutes provide adequate protection? *San Diego Justice Journal*, 1, 123.

National Institute of Criminal Justice (October 1993). A project to develop a model anti-stalking code for states. Final Summary Report presented to the National Institute of Justice, 92.

Sapp, A. (1996). Stalking Typologies. Conference presentation, Academy of Criminal Justice Sciences, March 12–16, Las Vegas.

Walsh, K. L. (1996). Safe and sound at last? Federalized anti-stalking legislation in the United States and Canada, *Dickinson Journal of International Law*, 14, 373–402.

Wells, K. (1996). California's anti-stalking law — a first, *Law Enforcement Quarterly*, August–October, 9–12.

Williams, W. L., Lane, J., and Zona, M. A. (1996). Stalking: successful intervention strategies, Alexandria, Virginia, *The Police Chief Magazine*, February.

Zona, M. A., Kaushal, K. S., and Lane, J. (1993). A comparative study of erotomanic and obsessional subjects in a forensic sample, *Journal of Forensic Sciences*, 38(4), 894–903.

About the Contributing Authors

Joseph A. Davis, Ph.D., LL.D.

A subject matter expert in the area of public safety psychology, the editor of *Stalking Crimes and Victim Protection: Prevention, Intervention, Threat Assessment, and Case Management* is Joseph A. Davis, Ph.D., LL.D. With a B.S. in psychology with honors, M.S. in psychology, Ph.D. in clinical psychology, and LL.D. (Doctor of Laws) in law and public policy (honoris causa), Dr. Davis completed his post-graduate forensic mental health assessment, education, and training at the University of Virginia at the Institute of Law, Psychiatry and Public Policy in 1985. He is the executive director of the Institute of Law, Psychology and Public Policy Studies and is a partner with The TAP Group, Inc. (threat assessment and prevention) in San Diego and Long Beach, California. With adjunct faculty appointments at several major universities in California and abroad, he has published extensively over the past 17 years in five academic areas covering the disciplines of clinical-forensic, police/public safety psychology, criminology, traumatology, and law and public policy. Over the past 6 years, he has been the Medical and Allied Health editor-in-chief and a member of the editorial advisory board to the *Canadian Journal of Clinical Medicine* in Edmonton, Alberta. In addition to devoting his time to university-level teaching and clinical research, he maintains a private office devoted to management and organizational consulting, training, research and development, critical incidents and trauma response, and public safety psychology. He is married and the father of two daughters. A native of Virginia, he and his family reside in San Diego, California.

Marcella A. Chipman, MLS, J.D.

Marcella A. Chipman, MLS, J.D. holds a Master of Library Science degree and is a 1997 graduate of the Juris Doctor ABA Law Program at the Thomas Jefferson School of Law in San Diego. She was a former 3rd-year scientific evidence law student of the editor, Joseph A. Davis, where Dr. Davis held a former adjunct law faculty appointment from 1996–1998. Ms. Chipman is an attorney-at-law with a private criminal law practice in San Diego specializing in legal research and criminal defense law.

Criminal Stalking: An Analysis of the Various Typologies of Stalkers

2

RONALD M. HOLMES

Contents

Introduction

As actress Rebecca Lynn Schaeffer opened her door, she was greeted and then fatally shot by Robert John Bardo. This one act of criminal stalking galvanized the attention of American society to the dangers of such predators and led states across the nation to enact stalker laws. Only a few years earlier, Arthur Jackson, a carpenter from Aberdeen, Scotland, stalked and stabbed actress Theresa Saldana in broad daylight on a residential street in Los Angeles. John Hinckley, Jr. shot President Ronald Reagan in an attempt to impress actress Jodie Foster. He is in prison although released periodically on furloughs. Anne Murray, the pop singer, has been a victim of a continuous letter-writing campaign that contained threatening remarks. Martina Hingis, an internationally recognized professional tennis player, is allegedly currently stalked by

Dunravko Rajcevic. He claims a romantic relationship with Ms. Hingis, a claim she denies.

Not all stalkers seek the attention of the rich and famous. Many estranged husbands and wives seek out former mates to terrorize. The troubled and disturbed send letters, make telephone calls, and send e-mail messages for purposes of terrorizing. Many follow up these acts with sexual assaults and murder. There are few people truly safe from a predatory stalker.

Relatively little is known about the mind and mentality of the stalker. Law enforcement has long been exposed to cases that result in murder. But social scientists know little about the mental condition of the stalker. This lack of information is changing, however. New literature is making its way into the arena. In Fuller and Hickey's book, *Controversial Issues in Criminology* (1999), a debate rages over the effectiveness of the new stalking laws. No definitive answer is forthcoming (Fuller and Hickey, 1999). Another publication is J. Reid Meloy's *The Psychology of Stalking* (Meloy, 1998). Meloy examines various types of stalkers as well as looks into the psychology of the predator. Both are important works that shed insight into the mental condition of the stalker and contribute to our understanding of the stalker problem. Nevertheless, we are in a beginning stage of this serious personal concern. One step in understanding the stalker is to understand his behavior. This is the purpose of this endeavor.

What Constitutes the Crime of Stalking?

In viewing many definitions of stalking, it appears there are several components:

- A deliberate course of action.
- A repeated course of action.
- This action causes a "reasonable" person to feel threatened, terrorized, harassed, or intimidated.
- This action actually causes the victims to feel threatened, terrorized, harassed, or intimidated.

Many states have initiated laws to combat stalking. Kentucky, for example, has passed House Bill 445, which defines the crime of stalking (Kentucky Revised Statutes Section 508.130, 1) as:

- An intentional course of conduct
- Directed at a specific person or persons
- Which seriously alarms, annoys, intimidates or harasses the person or persons
- Which serves no legitimate purpose

The crime of stalking in California is

> Any person who willfully, maliciously, and repeatedly follows or harasses another person and who makes a credible threat with the intent to place that person in reasonable fear for his or her safety, or the safety of his or her immediate family (California's Penal Code Section 646.9, a).

Florida's definition of stalking is similar to California's statute:

> Any person who willfully, maliciously, and repeatedly follows or harasses another person, and makes a credible threat with the intent to place that person in reasonable fear of death or bodily injury, commits the offense of aggravated stalking (Florida's Penal Code, Section 784.048. 3).

Of course there are other definitions of stalking with similar language. As varied as the laws or definitions, just as divergent are the persons and the behaviors involved in these predatory acts.

Stalking takes many forms: phone calls, letters, e-mail correspondence, personal confrontations, etc. For example, in Oregon, a 24-year-old man sent letters and presents to an 11-year-old girl. Professing his lasting love for the child, the man wrote letters to her that said, "When I seen (sic) her, when I look into her eyes, my mind goes blank … I will wait for ten years. I will and about sex I don't want none until our honeymoon." The man is now serving a sentence at the Oregon State Correctional Institute (Hallman, 1992).

Literature Review on Stalking

Methods within the stalking process have become an important and integral part. Norris and Birnes (1998) discuss the process of the stalker. Drs. Ronald and Stephen Holmes (1996) examine the stalking of the sexual predator. They list "the stalk" as one of the five steps in the selection of a victim and the execution of serial murder.

Criminal stalking has recently become an area of serious examination. Park Dietz and associates (Dietz, 1991) analyzed threatening letters sent to members of the U.S. Congress. This study attempted to gauge the seriousness of the threats. The numbers of such letters range in the hundreds each year and are rising, thus a need was realized to develop an index of personal safety to these public servants. The content, style, and compositions of the letters were elements of examination and interpretation.

Vernon Geberth, a retired New York homicide detective, lists two different types of stalkers (Geberth, 1992). One is the psychopathic personality stalker. Invariably a male, and representing the largest population of stalkers,

Table 2.1 Notable Selected Stalkers and Their Celebrity Victims

Stalker	Selected Victim
Joni Penn	Sharon Gless, actress
Mark Chapman	John Lennon, musician
Arthur Jackson	Theresa Saldana, actress
John Hinckley, Jr.	Jodie Foster, actress
Tina Ledbetter	Michael J. Fox, actor
Stephen Stillabower	Madonna, singer and actress
Robert Hoskins	Madonna, singer and actress
Nathan Trupp	Michael Landon, actor
Ralph Nau	Olivia Newton-John, singer
Robert Bardo	Rebecca Schaeffer, actress
Billie Jackson	Michael Jackson, singer
Mary Margaret Ray	David Letterman, talk show host
Roger Davis	Vanna White, TV game show hostess
Brook Hull	Terri Garr, actress
Ruth Steinhagen	Eddie Waitkus, baseball player
Daniel Vega	Donna Mills, actress
Robert Keiling	Anne Murray, singer
Dubravko Rajevic	Martina Hingis, tennis player
Jonathon Norman	Steven Spielberg, movie director
Edwin Carlson	Barbara Mandrell, singer
Tina Ledbetter	Scott Bakula, actor

Information for the stalkers and the victims in this table was obtained from sources including Geberth's article on stalkers in *Law and Order*, 1992; *U.S. News and World Report*, *People Weekly*, *Los Angeles Magazine*, and *The New Statesman and Society*.

he comes from a dysfunctional family; violence is the norm. He stalks because he has lost control over a subject, e.g., a former girlfriend or a wife, and exercises too frequently fatal violence.

The list of stalkers who target celebrities continued to increase in 2000. Table 2.1 is only a brief list to date as to the number of high profile celebrities who have been relentlessly pursued or harassed in the 1990s.

The psychotic personality stalker is the second type. Regardless of gender, this stalker becomes obsessed with a seemingly unobtainable love. Suffering from a delusional belief that he or she is passionately loved by the person stalked, if the victim only knew the stalker the victim would grow to love the predator. The stalker mounts a campaign of harassment to make the victim aware of the stalker's existence, and thus his or her personal feeling of love or affection (Geberth, 1992).

Regardless of the number of articles that appear in both the professional and popular literature (such as *Time*, *The Los Angeles Magazine*, *People Weekly*, and *U.S. News & World Report*), stalking is a formidable problem. It is only now that serious efforts are made to examine stalking as a major social enigma.

Various Typologies of Stalkers

Behavior stems from many constitutional and/or experiential factors. People behave differently arising from diverse motivational factors and anticipated gains. It is likely that the unique combination of biology, environment, or personal chemistry accounts for the behavior of a personality. This combination is not understood at this time. While many have their theories regarding behavior, what is true is that we do not understand the human condition, criminal or not.

One initial effort toward understanding the stalker mentality is to develop a typology of stalkers. Holmes and Holmes (1998a) did this with serial murderers in their book, *Serial Murder*, listing four types of serial killers: visionary, mission, hedonistic, and power/control. From this exercise, a better understanding was gained to investigate crimes of sequential killers.

Next a typology of stalkers will be described based upon the motives and anticipated gains: celebrity, lust, hit, love-scorned, domestic, and political stalker types. Much of this work is based on the groundbreaking research of Dietz et al. (1991), Geberth (1992), and Zona et al. (1993).

The Celebrity Stalker

The celebrity stalker is one who stalks someone typically in the entertainment profession: recording artist, actor or actress, or athlete (football, baseball, tennis, etc.). Although this victim is well known on an impersonal level, for example a famous TV star, the target is personally unknown. For example, Robert Bardo mailed Rebecca Schaeffer love letters 2 years before he killed her. At one time he traveled by bus from Arizona to Hollywood to personally deliver flowers and a giant teddy bear. Refused admittance to the studio, he obtained her address. Bardo wrote his sister months before and confessed a love for Schaeffer.

The victim is selected carefully by the celebrity stalker. The motivation is personal; the anticipated gain is psychological. As with the case of Bardo, violence is often fatal. Sometimes it is not. This is illustrated by the case of Arthur Jackson's knife-wielding assault on Theresa Saldana. A deliveryman just happened to come upon the attack and wrestled the knife away from Jackson only after he had repeatedly stabbed Saldana. His intent was to kill; the interdiction of a stranger circumvented his intent. With the celebrity stalker, there is no personal affinity, no lines of bloodship, and, of course, no sexual motivation.

The Lust Stalker

The lust stalker is impelled by a depraved sense of sexual lust. This type of sexual offender is typically a serialist. The victims are typically strangers but possess certain traits or characteristics that identify them as ideal victim types.

The hunt itself may be quite involved or a spur-of-the-moment occasion. The anticipated gain is sexual predation. Too often the lust stalker will undergo an escalation into violence which includes the murder of the victim.

Jerome (Jerry) Brudos, a serial murderer from Oregon, is an excellent example of the lust stalker. In Stack's book, *The Lust Killer* (1983), the author stated that Brudos used a ruse to "arrest" his victims, taking them to his home. He killed at least four women. He cut off an ankle of one woman; he cut off a breast of another; a third, both breasts; and finally with the fourth victim, he sent electrical shocks through her body while she hung from a rafter in his garage. Brudos was arrested while stalking his fifth victim, a young college woman.

The Hit Stalker

An example of a stalker is the professional killer. Such a stalker would be the "murderer for hire." The victims are strangers selected carefully by the employer of the professional killer. What the hit stalker desires is monetary reward or other material goods to be realized from successful predation. Fatal violence is the norm; no sexual acts are demanded. Again, there is no personal relationship.

An example of the hit stalker is Richard Kuklinski. In a HBO special entitled *The Iceman Tapes*, this admitted professional killer (a hired Mafia hitman) coldly and dispassionately described his murders of pre-selected victims. He even relates leaving his home on Christmas Eve while assembling toys for his children to go into town to kill a man for pay.

The Love-Scorned Stalker

Unlike most stalkers, the love-scorned stalker intends violence, usually not fatal violence, against someone known. The victim, therefore, is personally known. Realizing a psychological gain, this predator asserts the victim; once realizing how much the stalker really cares, the victim will return that affection. A personal relationship exists between the stalker and the victim, though not by blood or marriage. It is through this relationship that the stalker makes the victim aware of his deep and abiding love for her. There may have been at one time a personal relationship in which the stalker has misunderstood that relationship. There is no sexual component to the stalking although the act of the assault may take on a sexual element.

A young 18-year-old college coed went to the police for protection. She said a young man, also a freshman at the same university, had written her letters and followed her to her part-time job, walking behind her, darting behind bushes and buildings on campus. She knew the stalker since high school. Later, it was discovered that the young man had broken into her house, went through her bedroom dresser, and had stolen panties and bras. Upon developing an analysis of the situation, the man was encouraged to seek hospitalization for his mistaken belief that the young woman was in love with him and wanted to have his babies.

The Domestic Stalker

The domestic stalker at one time shared an intimate part of the victim's everyday life. This relationship was inclusive of, but not necessarily limited to, love. The two people may have been married, lived together, or simply were a committed couple.

All too frequently a case is reported when an estranged husband hunts his former wife. Often the stalking is a long-termed affair, and the confrontation between the two results with tragic consequences. "Getting even" with that individual who once shared an important part of the stalker's life becomes a motivational factor in his reasoning for not only the stalk, but also the perpetration of violence.

Recently an estranged husband was stalking his wife for days. He finally approached her outside a daycare center where she had dropped off their only child. While she was getting into her car to go to work, he ran up to her car, shot her in the face, and then shot himself. He died at the scene. The anticipated gain is perversely psychological; fatal violence is too often the goal. The target was one with whom he shared an intimate relationship. Again, there is no sexual motivating factor involved in the stalking episode.

The Political Stalker

The intended victim of the political stalker is a personal stranger. It may be the President of the United States, the mayor of a large city, a minor town leader, or someone else in the citizens' eyes. The history of this country has more than its share of those who have stalked public officials including our presidents. In many cases, the public officials have been wounded. Unfortunately, in too many other cases, the victims have been murdered.

The victims of the political stalker are selected carefully, and the stalking is planned. There is usually a public appearance that precipitates the stalking and the intended fatal violence which ensues. As noted, sexual motivations are missing in this form of predation. When Lee Harvey Oswald shot President Kennedy, the President was not acquainted with the assassin. They were strangers. There was no money exchanged between a terrorist organization and Oswald for killing the President. Apparently it was a political ideology that accounted for the motivation to murder. John Wilkes Booth killed Lincoln because of political ideologies which were different from those espoused by the President. Lynette "Squeaky" Fromme shot President Gerald Ford. She

Table 2.2 Presidential Stalkers

Year	President	Stalker	Age	Location	Weapon	Injury
1835	Andrew Jackson	Richard Law	35	U.S. Capitol	Handgun	None
1865	Abraham Lincoln	John Wilkes Booth	26	Ford Theater	Handgun	Death
1881	John Garfield	Charles Guiteau	38	Train station	Handgun	Death
1901	William McKinley	Leon Czolgosz	28	U.S. Expo	Handgun	Death
1912	Teddy Roosevelt	John Shrank	36	Hotel	Handgun	Injury
1933	Franklin Roosevelt	Guiseppe Zangara	32	Public park	Handgun	None
1950	Harry S. Truman	Griselio Torresola	25	Blair House	Handgun	None
1960	John Kennedy	Richard R. Pavlick	69	Motorcade	Explosives	None
1963	John Kennedy	Lee Harvey Oswald	24	Motorcade	Rifle	Death
1974	Richard Nixon	Samuel Byck	44	Airport	Handgun	None
1975	Gerald Ford	Lynette Fromme	26	Public park	Handgun	None
1975	Gerald Ford	Sarah Moore	45	Hotel	Handgun	None
1981	Ronald Reagan	John Hinckley, Jr.	25	Sidewalk	Handgun	Wound

Adapted from Sifakis, C. (1991). *Encyclopedia of Assassinations*, Facts on File, New York.

was almost certainly motivated by the influence of the relationship with Charles Manson (see Table 2.2).

The political stalker is fundamentally different from other stalkers. The lust stalker is motivated by a predatory sense of sex as conquest. The hit stalker anticipates a material gain. The celebrity stalker hopes to bask in the reflected glory of the celebrity or believes the target shares the affectionate relationship that is in his mind only.

Implications for Law Enforcement Interdiction

In recent years, stalking laws have become popular with advocates of "get tough" crime prevention measures. They provide the criminal justice system with a means of taking action against a growing problem of harassment, intimidation, and domestic violence. The diversity in the language of stalker laws in various states (approximately 26) is reflective of the myriad of perceptions legislators have concerning the seriousness of stalkers. Some limit the definition of stalking to the continued threat of violence by one spouse to another. Yet other statutes are more definitive and offer protection against harassment, threat, etc. by most anyone against another. These diversities and limitations can be confusing and frustrating for law enforcement and the courts.

The diversity and limitations placed by some statutes can be frustrating for law enforcement. The intent of the stalker as defined in the legislation is an example of how difficult legislation is to enforce. Additionally, the proof of intent of a stalker to harm someone is very difficult. Most stalking statutes are very limited in their scope or too complex to be practical. Proof of the intent to do harm by one who professes great love of the victim is certainly difficult at best. Designing or refining state statutes to be inclusive of many of the unique problems associated with stalking is a challenge.

Legislators should consider that anti-stalking legislation is unique in that it attempts to criminalize stalking conduct in order that future, more serious, violent conduct may be prevented. Designing legislation that allows the apprehension and prosecution for events that preclude a possibility of future violent events is a formidable task. These statutes must include provisions that equip law enforcement officers and the courts with the discretion in enforcement and furnish a suitable deterrent to discourage and stop further action by the stalker. The author most certainly agrees with this focus and supports its implementation and intention.

Conclusion

Stalking is a social condition that is attracting more attention in the law enforcement community. Like those in law enforcement, we should be concerned with the early identification of stalkers. Gaining insight into the mentality of the stalker may be the first step. It is commonly believed that if the actions and motivations of the stalker can be understood and identified, it is possible that early intervention may hold the key in preventing future and needless acts of violence.

For too long, this type of behavior has been overlooked and the potential for future violence underestimated. While many states across the country do not have anti-stalking legislation in place, many of the penalties ascribed to these statutes lack the teeth needed to fully protect the stalker's target. Only when we understand the trials and tribulations of the victims, and the psychology of the offender, may we be fully in a position to prevent these types of offenses and the oftentimes violent episodes that accompany the "final confrontation."

There must be an effort at early identification of the stalkers. One initial step is to make differential judgments concerning various types of stalkers. This has been the focus of this article.

Bibliography

Dietz, P., Matthews, D., Martell, D., Stewart, T., Hrouda, D., and Warren, J. (1991). Erotomania, *New Statesman and Society*, 3(July 27), 31–32.

Fuller, J. and Hickey, E. (1999). *Controversial Issues in Criminology.* Boston: Allyn and Bacon.

Geberth, V. (1992). Stalkers. *Law and Order*, 40(10), October, 138–143.

Geberth, V. (1993). *Practical Homicide Investigation: Tactics, Procedures, and Forensic Techniques,* 2nd ed. Boca Raton, FL: CRC Press.

Hallman, T. (1992). Stalker robs girl of innocence, *The Oregonian,* Monday, March 9, A1–A8.

Hickey, E. (1997). *Serial Killers and Their Victims.* Belmont, CA: Wadsworth Publishing.

Holmes, R. and DeBurger, J. (1988). *Serial Murder.* Thousand Oaks, CA: Sage Publications.

Holmes, R. and Holmes, S. (1996). *Profiling Violent Crimes: A Viable Investigative Tool.* Thousand Oaks, CA: Sage Publications.

Holmes, R. and Holmes. S. (1998a). *Serial Murder.* Thousand Oaks, CA: Sage Publications.

Holmes, R. and Holmes, S. (1998b). *Contemporary Perspectives on Serial Murder.* Thousand Oaks, CA: Sage Publications.

Holmes, R. and Holmes, S. (2001). *Mass Murder in America.* Thousand Oaks, CA: Sage Publications.

Meloy, J. (1998). *The Psychology of Stalking.* San Diego, CA: Academic Press.

Norris, J. and Birnes, W. (1988). *Serial Killers: The Growing Menace.* New York: Dolphin Books.

Sifakis, C. (1991). *Encyclopedia of Assassinations.* New York: Facts on File.

Stack, A. (1983). *The Lust Killer.* New York: Signet Books.

Zona, M. A., Kaushal, K. S., and Lane, J. (1993). A comparative study of erotomanic and obsessional subjects in a forensic sample, *Journal of Forensic Sciences,* 38(4), 894–903.

About the Contributing Author

Ronald M. Holmes, Ed.D.

Ronald M. Holmes, Ed.D. is an internationally recognized and very respected criminologist and professor of justice administration at the University of Louisville. Dr. Holmes has published 19 books dealing with topics such as serial murder, psychological profiling, sex crimes, sexual behaviors, criminology, mass murder, and other related topics. His pioneering book, *Profiling Violent Crimes: A Viable Investigative Tool,* with co-author Stephen Holmes (1996), and *Mass Murder in America* (2001) are both leading books on the subject in the fields of applied criminology and criminal psychology. He also has a leading textbook in criminology and has three more textbooks to be released this year, one as an introduction to criminal justice and two others, an introduction to policing as well as a book on mass murder in America.

Dr. Holmes has also authored more than 60 articles in peer-reviewed scholarly journals. Additionally, he has psychologically profiled more than 500 murder and sex-related crimes over the last 20 years.

Dr. Holmes is also the vice president of the American Institute of Criminal Justice and of the National Center for the Study of Unresolved Homicides in Lexington, Kentucky. He has lectured across the world on criminal justice topics including murder, serial and mass murder, psychological profiling, sex crimes, violence and aggression, and school shootings.

PART II

Erotomania, Obsession, Pursuit, and Relational Stalking

Obsessive Behavior and Relational Violence in Juvenile Populations: Stalking Case Analysis and Legal Implications

3

DENISE M. EMER

Contents

Introduction

In her senior year in a suburban Chicago high school, Valerie Curda was not enjoying the activities that most adolescents do before embarking on the next chapter of their young lives. While many of her contemporaries were studying hard to gain admittance to good colleges, working to make money for a last summer of fun, or spending summer days in the sun with friends, Valerie was living a nightmare. Valerie feared daily for her life, as she became a victim of a dangerous stalker, her ex-boyfriend. Valerie and her ex-boyfriend dated for 2 years in high school. After 1 year of dating, the boy became more protective, always wanting to know where Valerie was going and demanding that Valerie call him as soon as she arrived home. Eventually, her boyfriend insisted that Valerie not go out with anyone unless he was also going to be present. Initially, Valerie accepted her boyfriend's behavior, assuming it was an indication of his love for her. Valerie eventually ended the relationship when she met someone else and started dating him; this is when the following behaviors and subtle threats by her ex-boyfriend began. Valerie's ex-boyfriend began following Valerie and her friends home from work, sending Valerie letters, calling Valerie's home, and vandalizing Valerie's friend's car. Valerie couldn't complete her mandatory volunteer work hours for school, and had to avoid the public library because her ex-boyfriend and his friends pursued her relentlessly. One evening, Valerie's ex-boyfriend came to her workplace with a pair of handcuffs and a sawed-off shotgun. Thankfully, Valerie wasn't there that night (Gilbert, 1998).

Since the adoption of California's anti-stalking law, Penal Code 646.9 (1990), most states have responded to research suggesting that stalking may be an epidemic problem by instituting laws which make stalking and/or harassing behaviors criminal offenses (McAnaney and Curliss, 1993; Suarez, 1994). However, although stalking is currently recognized as a major social problem, concerns have been limited to adult populations (Meloy and Gothard, 1995). The statistics typically reported suggest that most of the targets of stalkers are between the ages of 20 and 45, and tend to arise from domestic problems, often marital (Simon, 1999). While it has been acknowledged that the crime of stalking can occur at all socioeconomic levels (Simon, 1999), the notion that adolescents could become predatory stalkers and victims of such individuals in their own peer group has been largely ignored. Adolescent obsessional behavior has generally been considered a normal phase through which all teenagers pass, a phase which quickly ends without posing serious danger to other adolescents. Society, by and large, accepts the "moonstruck adolescent" as a natural figure in teenage romantic encounters, and presumes that the behaviors of such individuals, unlike their adult counterparts, are innocuous. Simon (1999) wrote:

> It is not unusual for adolescents to become infatuated and romantically preoccupied with some person. Indeed, the relationship may be totally one-sided and exist only from afar because the idealized person of the adolescent's ardor may be unaware of his interest. Young romantics sit outside the person's house, hide in the bushes, follow his or her car to steal a glimpse, or telephone and hang up just to hear the voice of the person on the pedestal. Boys are acculturated through television and movies to pursue the woman of their desire. Unlike adult stalkers, adolescents usually do not make threats. (p. 54)

In recent years, society has been forced to revise its notion that juvenile behavior is generally harmless, and confront the reality that juveniles are capable of participating in violent crime; the national statistics attest to this fact (Allen-Hagen and Sickmund, 1993). Recent cases of adolescents involved in dating violence and obsessional behaviors suggest that the concept of the stalker may also need revision that includes adolescent populations.

A recent survey conducted by the National Institute of Justice (NIJ) and the Centers for Disease Control and Prevention (CDC) found that stalking is strongly linked to the controlling behavior and physical, emotional, and sexual abuse perpetrated against women by intimate partners (Tjaden and Thoennes, 1997). More specifically, the survey results revealed that most female victims knew their stalkers and were significantly more likely to be stalked by either a current spouse, a former spouse, a cohabitating partner, or a date. Furthermore, it was reported that "a clear relationship existed between stalking and other emotionally controlling and abusive behavior. About 81% of these women were, at some point in the relationship, physically assaulted by their partner, and 31% were sexually assaulted" (Tjaden and Thoennes, 1997, p. 2).

These given results link violence within an intimate relationship (both sexual and physical) with later stalking; the reality that juvenile males are increasingly entering the court system for commission of sexual offenses bears relevance to the potential for juveniles to become involved in stalking crimes (Barbaree et al., 1993; McCann, 1998). Recent research indicates that sexual harassment is a significant problem in adolescent populations. Moore et al. (1989) reported that 7% of respondents from a nationally representative sample of adolescents, primarily women between the ages of 18 and 22, have experienced at least one episode of non-voluntary sexual intercourse during childhood or adolescence.

Another study conducted with 250 senior high school students at a Minnesota secondary vocational education center that serves four school districts in a seven-county metropolitan area indicated that 50% of females have been sexually harassed at school (Strauss, 1993). A 1993 study conducted by the American Association of University Women (AAUW) with 1632 students in grades 8 through 11 from 79 schools revealed that four out of five students (81%) report having been the target of some form of sexual harassment, 47% of which were in grades 6 through 9. Thirty-two percent of victims reported a first experience of sexual harassment prior to seventh grade. The plethora of research on the increase in dating violence among teens also has important implications regarding the potential for adolescents to become involved in stalking (Barrett, 1998; National Coalition Against Domestic Violence [NCADV], 1997).

Recent studies indicate that dating violence occurs in at least one in ten teenage couples (Levy, 1991). Numerous facts about the current social milieu suggest that adolescent stalking is a problem in need of attention. Statistics support a general rise in juvenile violence, decreased ages for first sexual experiences (possessiveness often accompanies such entanglements), and an increase in sexual harassment, sexual offending, and dating violence in youth populations.

The remainder of this chapter will discuss cases that demonstrate that stalking is an adolescent problem. Furthermore, the relationship between the rise of dating violence in teens and stalking episodes will be analyzed, and potential reasons why teenagers may be particularly vulnerable to violence and stalking in adolescence will be discussed. Similarities and differences between adolescent and adult stalkers will also be addressed. Finally, some critical issues for legal consideration with regard to juvenile stalkers and their young victims will be examined.

Illustrative Cases

High School Students and Stalking Experiences

If Valerie Curda's experience was an anomaly, it might be easy to suggest that stalking is still largely an adult problem, save for a few adolescents with severe mental illness or cognitive impairment. However, obsessional behaviors among adolescents may be more common than is currently believed. In a 1996 edition of *Redbook*, Barbara Hansen, now 31 years old, discussed how her "life changed forever" when she "once smiled at a high school classmate" (O'Malley, 1996, p. 120). The student Barbara smiling at Charles Skoglund began a pattern of stalking which has, 15 years later, left Ms. Hansen terrified of revealing her address, how far she has moved from her home town, where her family lives, and where she plans to raise her family. Barbara's stalker, in spite of anti-stalking legislation, still roams free (O'Malley, 1996). The failure of such cases to receive widespread attention may be more a product of societal stereotypes about proper adolescent behavior than a lack of actual cases being perpetrated or reported.

In Skoglund's case, his initial response to Barbara's smile seemed to be a "passing teenage obsession" to those who knew the situation (O'Malley, 1996, p. 121). Skoglund stared at Hansen in class, followed her home from school, followed her to after-school activities, watched her from a distance through binoculars across the street from her parents' home, and once even watched her from a manhole on her street (O'Malley, 1996, p. 121). Hansen's case, however, was no passing phase of a lovesick teen — Skoglund became fixated on her and pursued her relentlessly following her high school years, even after she was married. Stalking cases that often continue into the adult years may have their roots in adolescence, but the significance of the behaviors being perpetrated in adolescence are underreported or not taken seriously. Even if overt stalking behaviors are not apparent in adolescence, deviant thought processes may be starting there, as is suggested by the case of Kathleen Baty. Ms. Baty was stalked by Lawrence Stager, a man she was briefly acquainted with in high school because the two were on the track team together (O'Malley, 1996). Stager finally received a prison sentence for holding Baty hostage at knifepoint in 1990 following 8 years of threats, including one incident in which Stager came to Baty's door with a .357 magnum with the firing pin removed (O'Malley, 1996).

A recent study conducted by the NCADV (1997) reported that of the total 582 teens surveyed, 45% reported severe jealousy by their partners, 28% reported verbal abuse, 27% reported partners who controlled who they spent their time with, 25% reported being shoved and pushed, 14% reported having partners who threatened to commit suicide if they did not comply with some relationship request, and 8% had been threatened with a weapon in a dating context. In Valerie Curda's case, four police reports were filed before a court date was even set, and the perpetrator was only given 6 months on supervision. Perhaps Valerie's own words stated it best when she wrote, "when people hear about a teenager being stalked, many think it is just an exaggeration. They may realize it is real after it is too late. I am hoping to make it known that this is also happening to teenagers" (Gilbert, 1998, p. 154).

Lynn's Case

In a recent chapter entitled "Young Stalkers, Young Victims" (Landau, 1996), the following case of a 16-year-old named Lynn (name changed) was discussed. Her case suggests that the prevailing belief that young stalkers are less dangerous than adult stalkers is certainly misguided and could potentially be lethal. As is the case in many adult stalking crimes, Lynn's boyfriend began stalking her after their relationship ended. The author wrote:

> He started by continually parking near her house and looking into her windows. Then came the phone calls — sometimes he would threaten to kill her, other times he would comment on some aspect of her appearance or behavior to assure Lynn that he knew her every move. Besides watching her home, Lynn's stalker constantly followed her. He trailed the young woman both on foot and in his car, and whether she went shopping or on a date, he would call later to discuss the outing with her. As a result, Lynn felt that her former boyfriend could harm her whenever he wished and that she wasn't safe anywhere (Landau, 1996, pp. 46–47).

Although Lynn filed a restraining order against her former boyfriend, nothing really changed. Lynn's family had to drastically alter their lifestyle in order to ensure that their daughter was protected at all times; this included always having their curtains drawn and never leaving Lynn alone.

Jody's Story

As suggested in "Young Stalkers, Young Victims," there are two important sides to the problem of adolescent stalking: adolescents can be victims, but they can also be perpetrators of the crime. A young woman named Jody, also interviewed for the chapter, discussed her horror when she realized her teenage brother had been stalking a girl for over 4 years. Jody remembers that her brother would dress up at night in black or camouflage and enter the wooded area near the home of the girl he was pursuing. He hid in the trees and in the bushes in order to watch the girl in her bedroom and in her basement. Other times he would call the girl and hang up after uttering a few obscenities. Over time, Jody's brother began to bring friends with him to watch the girl in her home. Although the victim's family knew who Jody's brother was, the police were unable to intervene without substantial proof. Jody's brother later committed rape and is currently wanted for the crime of rape in two counties (Landau, 1996, pp. 47–48).

Mindy's Tragedy

There is nothing more tragic than a young life cut short because a teenage stalker was not properly restrained. Mindy's story is perhaps the most tragic of all; in July of 1994 she was shot to death by her former boyfriend, whom she had dated since the age of 15 and hoped to marry someday. Prior to her death, Mindy had been stalked by her former boyfriend, whom she left because of his violent tendencies. Angered that Mindy ended the relationship, her ex-boyfriend began leaving her letters, following her, breaking into her home, and taking some of her possessions. Mindy's young life ended when her ex-boyfriend:

> … unexpectedly called Mindy and politely told her that he was finally willing to accept the breakup. Claiming that now he only wished her happiness, he asked that she stop by the following day to pick up the items he had taken from her home. Her mother warned her not to go, preferring to let him keep everything, but Mindy went anyway. As she drove up his driveway, he shot her to death (Landau, 1996, p. 50).

Andrea's Story

The NCADV recently constructed a manual entitled "Teen Dating Violence Resource Manual" (1997) in an attempt to both increase awareness of abusive adolescent relationships and provide resources to help teens who find themselves in such situations. One Iowa teen interviewed for the project presented her story of abuse and obsession:

At first it seemed like any "normal" high school relationship. We were considered a couple. "Going out" is the term used, which meant we had an exclusive relationship and commitment.

> But I didn't realize then what commitment meant to him. His definition was completely different than mine. His meant that he was the only person in my life, no friends, no family, nothing beyond him. I lost track of all my friends because I wasn't allowed to see them. I literally did everything he told me to so that he wouldn't yell at me or call me names or push me around ... It's been almost a year since we broke up and he's still harassing me. At first he tried to get me back but once he realized he couldn't have me and control me anymore he decided to get my friends and new boyfriend away from me. He started driving by my house and 'showing up' where I was. It got to be annoying and frightening. I started having nightmares and was scared to go anywhere alone ... I am now trying to get legal help to make this nightmare stop (NCADV, 1997, p. 104).

College Students and Stalking Experiences

The above cases suggest that stalking not only occurs in teenage populations, but has the potential to be as lethal as adult stalking crimes. One of the major consequences of failing to recognize the existence of stalking in teenagers is that such behaviors may continue and worsen as adolescent perpetrators embark on their college careers. Ms. Emily Spence-Diehl, the coordinator of Florida International University's Victim Advocacy Center, argued that college students may be particularly vulnerable to stalkers because college campuses are self-contained, closed environments, activities and services are centralized, and the majority of students are young, single people who are comfortable with casual opposite sex contacts; these characteristics make it relatively easy to obtain individuals' class schedules, gain exposure to numerous people repeatedly, blend into groups, and develop unrequited "crushes" ("Stalking: Is It Terrorism on Campus," 1997). Unfortunately, the same social conditioning that prevents adults from recognizing the gravity of psychological and physical abuse in teenage populations carries over into college environments (see Stacey et al., 1994 for an extensive discussion of dating violence at the University of Maine between 1982 and 1992).

The consequences of this kind of social conditioning became almost deadly for a Michigan State University freshman whose administration, parents, and friends attributed her boyfriend's controlling and dangerous behavior to the normal "growing pains" of young adults. However, the pattern of the adult intimate partner stalker (Davis, 1997, 1998, 1999; Davis and Chipman, 1997;

Davis and Emer, 1997; Mullen et al., 1999; "What Is Stalking?," 1997; Zona et al., 1993) was unfolding right before their eyes:

> Whenever we were out with a group of people, he'd say, 'I saw you looking at that guy'. He wouldn't let me pluck my eyebrows or wear lipstick. 'No more manicures', he insisted. Six months into our relationship, he wouldn't even let me go jogging anymore (Finkelstein, 1997, p. 321).

Over time, this young woman's boyfriend prohibited her from spending time with her roommate, whom he called a "whore" and a "slut." He demanded she rip up the money in her wallet to prove that he was more important to her than her material possessions, and bashed a chair into the wall until she did so. Eventually, the boy punished his girlfriend by shoving her into walls or slamming her body into doors if he thought she was looking at another male. Although the young woman tried to end the relationship over the summer when school was not in session, her ex-boyfriend began a pattern of harassment and physical violence the following year at school. He secured a room in her dorm, took the same classes as she did, followed her to work, and sat outside her dorm room. When she refused to remain in the relationship, he pressed a cigarette into her neck (Finkelstein, 1997). Unfortunately, this Michigan State University (MSU) student found out how difficult it was to get adult members of the college community and in her life to take the problem seriously. Like high school dating violence and stalking, the prevalence of college intimate partner violence and obsessive behaviors appears to be underestimated by adults who have the power to intervene.

There are other obstacles to ending patterns of abuse and harassment in college relationships; these obstacles involve characteristics of the victims and perpetrators themselves. The power of emotional blackmail used by a college offender might overpower his victim's resources, because the victim's identity is still forming, and she lacks a sense of what is appropriate in relationships. This was the problem in the case of a Brown University student, whose abuser hit her for the first time when she refused to reveal her answering machine code for screening her messages (Finkelstein, 1997). This victim was fighting a difficult battle between her fragile ego at the time and her belief that the black and blue marks on her stomach, face, and arms were the product of inappropriate and dangerous behavior; she knew the behavior was wrong, but she also enjoyed the security and status that came with having a steady partner. The student's boyfriend helped to allay her concerns that she wasn't smart enough to succeed at the university and made her believe she could make it. Also, as is the case in high school battering scenarios, college women romanticize and glamorize male violence. Numerous studies suggest that college women believe that violent fights actually improve their relationships (Finkelstein, 1997), and find controlling behavior to be indicative of their desirability as women. Amidst stereotypical college males who prefer to party with their friends and engage in fleeting encounters with several women, having a boyfriend who is highly concerned about his partner's whereabouts may make many college women feel special. Like the high school adolescent, the young woman in college may be particularly vulnerable to violent abuse in relationships and stalking behaviors because in addition to becoming involved with a troubled partner, she lacks the maturity, experience, and identity stability to evaluate the gravity of the situation.

Recent research suggests that stalking is occurring at disturbing rates in college undergraduates. Fremouw et al. (1997) reported that 17% of male undergraduates and 30% of female undergraduates studied in their sample have been stalked at some point during their undergraduate experiences. Researchers Spitzberg et al. (1998) measured obsessive relational intrusion (ORI) and stalking in college populations. ORI is defined as "repeated and unwanted pursuit and invasion of one's sense of physical or symbolic privacy by another person, either stranger or acquaintance, who desires and/or presumes an intimate relationship" (Cupach and Spitzberg,1998, p. 234; see also Meloy, 1996b on what he terms "obsessive following"). ORI and stalking are assumed to be components of the same behavior, with stalking being a more severe form of intrusion (Spitzberg and Cupach, 1996; Spitzberg et al., 1998). Spitzberg et al. reported that of the 69 male and 93 female undergraduates surveyed in their sample, 27% claim to have been victims of stalking.

Commensurate with findings of stalking and obsessive relational intrusion in research surveys are the number of cases being reported on college campuses in which students are being prosecuted through the legal system for stalking. In September of 1997, the University of Missouri reported 9 assaults, 21 trespassing arrests, and various incidents of stalking and "peeping" on campus just from the period through July of that year (Mehta and Wagman, 1997).

In April 1998, a Rutgers University football player was arrested and charged with three counts of making terrorist threats, and one count of stalking. The student was repeatedly calling his ex-girlfriend and leaving threatening messages on her answering machine, coming to her dorm room and making threats against residents, and reportedly perpetrating violent acts against her during their relationship (Barber, 1999). In February 2000, two New Mexico State University students were arrested and charged with one count of stalking and one count of libel. The two students had reportedly been stalking and harassing their victim, another university student, since the beginning of January, as well as posting fliers inviting individuals to enter the victim's residence for sex (Haussamen, 2000).

In January 2000, a Pennsylvania State University student was scheduled to stand trial for charges of aggravated assault, harassment, and stalking. The student reportedly grabbed a female friend by the mouth, causing severe bleeding and potential permanent damage to her salivary glands. The perpetrator had been arrested in October for two prior incidents involving disorderly conduct and harassment of the same victim (Xu, 2000).

As a result of increasing reports of cases of stalking and related crimes on campus, some colleges and universities are beginning to develop policies for dealing with such cases in an effort to both encourage reporting and discourage commission of these crimes. For example, the Association for Student Judicial Affairs (ASJA), a professional association with headquarters at Texas A & M University which represents over 750 institutions of higher education in the United States and Canada, passed a resolution to develop and enforce regulations to prohibit stalking on college and university campuses (Association for Student Judicial Affairs, 1994). In addition, some colleges and universities, such as Central Michigan University, are beginning to include explicit information about the legal definition of stalking and avenues to prosecute offenders in their campus' sexual harassment policy information (Central Michigan University Police Department, 1999). Other schools are conducting workshops on campus to increase awareness of the problem of stalking in college populations (e.g., University of South Florida's College of Public Health included stalking in its "Special Issues in Domestic Violence" Series, August 2000).

Some campuses are not only including explicit information in their student codes about the definitions of stalking and its related consequences for offenders, but are also raising awareness about the potential violence associated with stalking through education and training programs for campus faculty and staff. For example, in a report of the Committee on Campus Violence at Johns Hopkins University, four specific recommendations were made to train faculty, staff, resident advisors, and campus health workers to understand what stalking is, and to recognize warning signs of obsessive behavior (Knapp et al., 1997). Furthermore, the problem of dating violence and stalking on college campuses is reflected in current research being directed toward exploration of how widespread the problem is, and the characteristics of perpetrators and victims (see Blackburn, 1999; Craver, 1999). In addition, middle school and secondary educational systems are beginning to conduct research on the effectiveness of "Dating Violence Prevention Programs" (Macgowan, 1997; Simon, 1996).

Relationship between Adolescent Dating Violence and Stalking

Background Information

As McFarlane et al. (2000) noted, stalking is closely related to intimate partner violence (see also Coleman, 1997 for an investigation of the role stalking plays in domestic violence). Furthermore, when intimate partner violence and stalking co-occur, the chances of severe violence and/or victim death are high (Davis, 1997, 1998, 1999; Davis and Chipman, 1997; Davis and Emer, 1997; deBecker, 1997; Lingg, 1993; Palarea et al., 1999).

Research on stalking suggests that approximately 70 to 80% of all stalking cases are perpetrated by individuals who have had some prior personal relationship with the victim before the stalking began (Lemon, 1994; Meloy, 1998; "What is Stalking?," 1997). This prior relationship is often a romantic one, and tends to involve domestic violence ("What is Stalking?," 1997; Meloy, 1998). Coleman (1997) reported results from a sample of 141 college women which indicate that women who experienced significant abuse during their relationship were more likely to be stalked by former partners after the relationship ended. In the psychological literature, stalkers of this type have been categorized as "simple obsessional," also known as the intimate partner targeting stalker, the domestic violence targeting stalker, and the rejected stalker (Davis, 1997, 1998, 1999; Davis and Chipman, 1997; Davis and Emer, 1997; Mullen et al., 1999; "What is Stalking?," 1997; Zona et al., 1993).

These types of stalkers have been identified as persons who exhibit a number of specific characteristics, among them emotional immaturity, feelings of powerlessness, jealousy, extreme insecurity about themselves, and low self-esteem (Davis, 1997, 1998, 1999; Davis and Chipman, 1997; Davis and Emer, 1997; Mullen et al., 1999; "What is Stalking?," 1997). In the language of batterer typologies (Walker, 1996), the batterer in a domestic violence situation who fits this stalking profile has been labeled a "power and control batterer." This type of batterer is said to be predominantly motivated by a need for power and control; he also has trouble with anger management and distorted attitudes about appropriate sex role behaviors (Walker & Meloy, 1998).

Psychologists have also recently argued that there is an important relationship between stalking behaviors and obsessive thinking patterns (Meloy, 1996; Sonkin, 1997; Walker and Meloy, 1998; Walker and Sonkin, 1995). Furthermore, the self-esteem of the simple obsessional stalker is generally closely tied to his relationship with his significant other. As such, these types of stalkers are said to "bolster their own self-esteem by dominating and intimidating their mates. Exercising power over another gives them a sense of power in a world where they otherwise feel powerless" ("What is Stalking?," 1997, p. 3).

Case studies conducted on the simple obsessional stalker reveal that this type of stalker may be the most dangerous, because the victim (the intimate partner) is the major source of the stalker's sense of self-worth, such that loss of the partner becomes the stalker's greatest fear ("What is Stalking?," 1997; Palarea et al., 1999; Walker and Meloy, 1998). When the victim ends her relationship with this type of stalker, the stalker will often stop at nothing to regain his lost sense of worth; in practical terms, this means that the stalker will do whatever it takes, including physical violence, to regain possession of the ex-partner. Research findings and statistics suggest that stalking cases which involve prior intimate partners are by far the most dangerous. A recent article reported that "domestic violence victims who leave an abusive relationship run a 75% higher risk of being murdered by their partners" ("What is Stalking?," 1997, p. 3; see also Walker and Meloy, 1998 for a discussion of lethality risk in domestic violence stalking cases).

The pattern of stalking discussed above and its relationship to domestic violence might help to explain why more adolescents today are becoming victims of both dating violence and stalking, and are also becoming perpetrators of these dangerous crimes. Consider the psychological profile of the simple obsessional stalker. Many of these characteristics are typical components of so-called "adolescent angst" — intense emotions characterize the adolescent state, particularly in the context of first loves and initial sexual discovery. With the increase in sexual activity among teens today, particularly at younger ages than ever before, many teenagers might find themselves ill-equipped to deal with the powerful emotions which often accompany intimate, committed relationships (Levy, 1991; Papazian, 1999).

Teenage relationships often wax and wane, and in doing so might take a teen's self-esteem through a rollercoaster ride. College environments may exacerbate the problem.

As noted by Emiliano Diaz de Leon, a 21-year-old ex-abuser and current educator for the Dating Violence Project at the Center for Battered Women in Austin, Texas, students who go away to college may be enjoying unchecked sexual freedom for the first time, and engage in promiscuous sex without being mature enough to handle the myriad of powerful emotions that accompany intimacy (Finkelstein, 1997). Coupled with a still emerging identity and fragile ego, these emotions can be overwhelming and might propel young people toward violent means for making sure that their partners do not reject them.

As researcher Barry Lubetkin noted, teenage stalking may be particularly dangerous because the stalker is highly possessive, and the victim is not yet interpersonally skilled enough to screen potentially volatile partners (Landau, 1996). A teenager's premature commitment to an exclusive relationship could result in domestic violence, as maladaptive or underdeveloped coping resources pale in comparison to powerful emotions (see O'Keefe, 1997 for an analysis of predictors of dating violence in high school students).

The teenage years are fraught with insecurity, jealousy, and identity crises; teens rely heavily on their peers and their dating partners to feel a sense of worth, to feel attractive, and to feel powerful within their social groups. Sociologist Mary Riege-Laner surveyed 371 students at Arizona State

University and revealed that attitudes and emotions such as jealousy, guilt, fear, insecurity, and confusion created the greatest number of abusive incidents (reported in Morell, 1984). Molidor (1995) reported findings that suggest that jealousy may be a major factor leading to violence in youth dating. Like the simple obsessional stalker whose greatest fear is losing the symbol of his worth, the intimate partner, teenagers too fear that they will lose the symbol of their worth in the eyes of their peers — also the intimate partner. Teenagers rely on their peer groups for a sense of identity and esteem, and greatly fear the loss of peer group association (see also Craver, 1999 for a discussion of the relationship between dating violence, identity, and self-esteem among college women). In a recent study conducted by the NCADV (1997), 14% of the teenage respondents (582 total surveyed) reported that they remained in abusive dating relationships because of low self-esteem (or, in some cases, no self-esteem).

Rosen and Bezold (1996) presented data that suggest that low self-esteem and rigid gender role conceptions place young women at risk for dating abuse and violence. Furthermore, peer pressure arising from the current adolescent culture, including movies, magazines, and music (Papazian, 1999), might distort teen's cognitions about dating conventions and appropriate sex role behaviors. For example, in the teen culture, a girl's success is often judged, and her status achieved, by whether or not she has a boyfriend (Gardner, 1994; Suarez, 1994). As Barbara Bennett, executive director of the Women's Self Help Center in St. Louis, stated, "some girls think it is worth an occasional violent incident in order to keep the boyfriend. Like their fellow adult victims of violence, they think he'll change" (Gardner, 1994, p. 13).

Belinda Lafferty, coordinator of the teen domestic violence program at Youth East Side Services in Bellevue, Washington, noted other gender-role stereotypes that prevail in the adolescent culture which could serve to distort teens' perceptions of appropriate intimate behaviors. The common stereotype that males must be "strong, in charge, and macho" and that girls should be "beautiful and compliant" (Gardner, 1994) creates a cognitive schema which suggests that dating violence and harassment are acceptable, even expected behaviors (Hamberger and Ambuel, 1998). Boys are expected to be the sexual aggressors; their peers expect them to exercise almost overbearing control as a means of asserting their masculinity. Girls, on the other hand, rely on a boyfriend for esteem and social acceptance (Suarez, 1994); these expectations appear to be related to risks for dating violence. O'Leary et al. (1989) found that dating violence perpetrated by high school males was predicted by their beliefs of entitlement in relationships and sex-role socialization in the use of aggression. In other words, many teenage boys believe that they are entitled to get whatever they need or want from an intimate partner, and if she doesn't give it willingly, they have the right to demand it forcefully though whatever means necessary (this has also been termed "teenage territorialism," the notion that a teen has a right to completely possess that which he believes belongs to him [Landau, 1996, p. 50]).

This belief that one is entitled to attention and compliance from the female he desires is exemplified in the writing of an affidavit in a Massachusetts court, filed against a 14-year-old defendant. The teenage petitioner wrote, "...he said that if I did not go out with him then he would rape me if he had to" (Cochran et al., 1994).

In the NCADV survey, many female respondents reported that they remained in abusive dating relationships because of the extreme control their boyfriends exerted over them, and the fear it caused; respondents claimed that they "couldn't get out," "felt trapped," were "manipulated to stay," and were "scared to assert themselves" (National Coalition Against Domestic Violence, 1997). Perhaps the most disturbing observation made by adults who work with teenagers involved in domestic violence is the apparent widespread acceptance of interpersonal violence in teen groups (Gardner, 1994); teens think it is a normal expression of romantic feelings, and this belief is reinforced by their peer groups, who hold the same beliefs. In fact, studies suggest that knowledge that other peers have used dating violence predicts perpetration of such violence among college students (Tontodonato and Crew, 1992); thus, dating violence may in part result from social learning phenomena.

One of the reasons teenagers might accept interpersonal violence and obsessive behavior is that they hold a distorted schema for expressions of intimacy and love. Many teens equate violence with jealousy, and jealousy with love; some social scientists have termed this cognitive distortion "normative confusion" (Sugarman and Hotaling, 1989). What this means is that obsessive behaviors and violent means of control are viewed as appropriate expressions of love and commitment.

Research studies on perceptions of dating violence in teenagers support this notion of a distorted perspective. In a 1994 study conducted by Symons et al., only 12.7% (n = 71) of their sample of abused teenagers (n = 339) believed that the violent physical experiences they endured and described constituted abuse. In a nationwide survey of 582 teens conducted by the NCADV entitled the "Teen Dating Violence Project" (TDVP, 1995–1996), teens reported numerous misconceptions about abuse in relationships; 12 respondents said that they believed they deserved the abuse, 5 claimed abuse was a sign of love, and 8 responded that "abuse is a sign of caring" or that "abuse is supposed to happen."

Some teenage girls may also be reluctant to admit they are being abused because they rely heavily on their boyfriends for support they cannot get from their families. Teenagers may be especially vulnerable to dating violence because many are experiencing problems that they either hide from their families or cannot discuss with them, for example, drug- and alcohol-related involvement. This vulnerability makes it easier for an abusive boyfriend to exert control, either physical, sexual, or psychological, over his partner; this appears to have been the situation in the case of a New Jersey 15-year-old who was forced to have sex with her abusive boyfriend in return for his driving her to alcoholism counseling sessions ("Boy Meets Girl," 1993).

Other aspects of the social context in which adolescent relationships take place would seem to make teenagers particularly vulnerable to both perpetrating intimate violence and stalking behaviors, and become victims of these experiences. As Levy (1991) noted, adolescents might exaggerate their concept of proper gender role behaviors in an effort to avoid potential stigma from their judgmental peers; social demands include proof of heterosexual orientation, independence from parents, and total conformity.

In the NCADV survey, some of the teenage respondents reported that they endured abuse because "the abuser was popular," they "didn't want to disappoint others," they "needed to be accepted," and they "didn't want to lose friends." Furthermore, there is an expectation in adolescent peer groups that girls will make boyfriends their top priority, even if this means not speaking to anyone else, not pursuing individual interests, and not going anywhere without the boyfriend (Levy, 1991). Since a young woman's peer group status is based upon her having a boyfriend, and her esteem and identity are heavily tied to acceptance by her peer group, she becomes extremely vulnerable to victimization because she goes to great lengths to justify and rationalize violent, obsessive behavior (Swindle, 1992).

Prevalence and Cases

The above discussion suggests some potential ways in which the fragility of adolescence and the unique social environment in which adolescent dating occurs could conspire to create potentially violent and obsessive relationships within the youth population. Unfortunately, research on the prevalence of dating violence in adolescent populations suggests that violence in relationships between adolescent intimate partners is occurring at alarming rates, often with serious consequences. A recent report suggested that more than half of American teenagers might be involved in relationship violence, either as abusers or victims (Papazian, 1999).

Current statistics may in fact be conservative, because many cases of dating violence and stalking in adolescents are handled in juvenile court proceedings and never reach the attention of public safety and law enforcement (Papazian, 1999). Furthermore, research indicates that teenagers are both experiencing and perpetrating stalking behaviors; it seems that dating violence and stalking in adolescent intimate relationships are inextricably tied.

Consider the following findings regarding dating violence collected over the past two decades summarized in the report by the NCADV (1997): 12% of high school daters report experiencing some form of dating violence (Gelles and Pedrick-Cornell, 1990); 33% of teenage girls report physical violence from their dates (Lee, 1991); 26.9% of high school junior and senior students surveyed (out of a sample of 135 women and 121 men) report being perpetrators or victims of dating violence (O'Keefe et al., 1986); in one survey of college students, 165 (28.2%) of 585 dating students reported having been pushed, grabbed, or shoved by their partner, and 102 (17.4%) reported having been struck, slapped, or punched (Rouse et al., 1988); one study found that one out of five college students report at least one incident of premarital abuse in their relationships, ranging from slapping and hitting to more life-threatening violence; follow-up studies suggest that physical violence occurs at a rate of approximately 20 to 50% in college dating relationships (Jordan, 1987; O'Keefe et al., 1986); 16.8% of 2338 students from seven midwestern and western colleges and universities had either inflicted abuse or suffered abuse in a dating relationship (Morell, 1984); in surveys of American college students, 21 to 30% reported at least one occurrence of physical assault with a dating partner (Browne, 1987); O'Keefe et al. (1986) found that 35.5% of high school students had experienced violence in a dating relationship; Levy (1991) found that 28% of the teens in her study had experienced dating violence; Lloyd (1991) reported that between one in three and one in two college students, and one in ten high school students have been initiators or victims of dating violence; Symons et al. (1994) found that 60% of their sample of 561 teenagers ranging in age from 15 to 20 years old had been involved in at least one violent act during a relationship; an additional 25% had experienced two or more abusive behaviors; among the 60% who experienced violent behavior in the Symons study, 24% reported extremely violent experiences such as rape or weapon use.

Other recent studies conducted with teenage populations mirror the results reported above. The NCADV's "Teen Dating Violence Project" involved conducting a nationwide qualitative survey on teen dating violence between October 1995 and February 1996 (National Coalition Against Domestic Violence, 1997). Of the total 582 respondents, 45% reported knowing someone who had been in, or was currently in a violent dating relationship; 36% of the 45% noted that the person they knew in the violent relationship was a friend/peer. In addition, 60% of the teens surveyed reported having experienced some form of abuse in a dating relationship, and 47% reported having used some form of abuse against a partner in a dating relationship.

In Barrett's (1998) report entitled "Survival Tales: An Examination of High School Dating," numerous disturbing statistics are enumerated regarding both physical and emotional abuse by a partner. The findings summarized in Barrett's report are alarming: Makepeace (1981) found that 62% of the 202 college students surveyed knew someone in a violent dating relationship and 21% had direct experience with dating violence, many of whom reported multiple events; Billingham and Sack (1986) reported that of the 526 college students surveyed, one third had experienced violence in a dating relationship. In a comprehensive profile of adolescent restraining order defendants in Massachusetts, numerous statistics supporting the pervasiveness of dating violence, obsessional intrusion, and stalking among adolescents were reported.

The study included all adolescent defendants between the ages of 11 and 17 who had a restraining order issued against them from September 1992 through June 1993. Both the anecdotes provided by victims and the statistics presented in this report present a disturbing profile of adolescent relationships, a profile which suggests that society's belief that stalking is an adult crime is a dangerously outdated assumption.

Consider the following excerpts: the first is from the affidavit of the girlfriend of a 17-year-old defendant from a wealthy suburban community; the second is from an affidavit filed by an inner city girl against her 16-year-old boyfriend:

> Finally, he held the knife to his own wrist and I jumped in the car and started to leave. He sat on the trunk, but I kept driving and he showed me his bloody wrist. This is the 3rd time he pulls out a knife in my presence and threatens to kill himself (Cochran et al., 1994, p. 4). He stabbed me a couple of times once on my index finger, on my arms, twice on my legs and constantly just hitting me. He always thought I was cheating on him (Cochran et al., 1994, p. 4).

According to the Massachusetts report, between September 1992 and June 1993, 757 civil restraining orders were issued against adolescents between 11 and 17 years of age. Furthermore, the report reveals that over 1100 adolescents in Massachusetts alone annually commit domestic abuse (and this only represents the cases that are actually reported by victims).

This is astounding, as it seems consonant with research that suggests gross underreporting of dating violence in adolescent populations (estimated reporting ranges from 4 to 40% [Bergman, 1992; Gelles, 1987; Pagelow, 1988]). In addition, statistics gathered in the Massachusetts report suggest a pattern of violence in these defendants; 17% of them have a prior arraignment for violating a civil restraining order.

The majority of these adolescent defendants (56.9%) and the victims are currently in, or used to be in, a dating relationship with each other; more than half (57%) of the restraining orders issued against teenagers in Massachusetts concern a dating relationship between the defendant and the victim. The report indicates that in 10 months time, at least 369 restraining orders were issued against teenagers for abusing their boyfriend/girlfriend (in some cases, ex-boyfriend/girlfriend).

The characteristics of the adolescent defendants discussed in the Massachusetts report make it possible to compare and contrast adult simple obsessional stalkers with adolescent batterers. The following characteristics are discussed: most teenage batterers involved in dating violence (87%) are between 16 and 17 years of age (12.2% are between the ages of 14 and 15, with the youngest age reported being 13 at 0.8%). Most adolescent batterers are male (81%). Tactics used by batterers include both physical and psychological manipulation, as evidenced by the following affidavit excerpt filed by a parent on behalf of her teenage daughter:

> Threatened to kill my daughter and then take his own life if she ended their relationship. He has attempted to control her life by deciding who she should talk to, what she could wear, and wanting to know her whereabouts at all times (Cochran et al., 1994, p. 10).

Abuse characteristics enumerated in the Massachusetts report are reminiscent of reported cases of adult intimate partner stalking. These characteristics were based on analyses of plaintiffs' affidavits and reveal both the actions made by adolescent defendants as well as the psychological and physical consequences experienced by their victims.

Based on restraining order complaint forms, over 70% of victims reported being in fear of physical harm from the defendant. More than 48% reported that the defendant made an attempt to harm them physically, and 47% reported actually being physically abused in some way. Information gathered from restraining orders in which affidavits were available indicated that 73.4% of the victims reported experiencing some form of physical abuse. In these cases, 55% of the victims describe a pattern of behavior on the part of the defendant which suggests that the incident described by the affidavit was not the first threat or experience of violence.

Various tactics used by teenage defendants to threaten, harass, and control their victims are revealed by the Massachusetts report: 56% of the victims were threatened with physical violence and/or death, one third received repeated phone calls, and one fourth reported that the defendants harassed their families in an effort to reach them. In 17% of the affidavits, the use of a weapon is indicated (weapons include knives, other sharp instruments, and guns). The rationale that states if "I can't have you, no one will," frequently used to describe the adult simple obsessional stalker, is also operating in teenage abuse scenarios. Two teenagers' affidavits describe their experience of being threatened as follows:

> Telling me that if he can't have me no one can, then he preceded to put a gun up to my head and told me he would kill me (Cochran et al., 1994, p. 13). He repeatedly told me he loved me and he was going to kill me if I went out with anyone else, that if he couldn't have me no one could (Cochran et al., 1994, p. 15).

The final variable in the affidavits for which information was gathered involves the incident that preceded the onset of the most recent experience of abuse. The most common incident reported by victims was the recent breakup of a relationship between the victim and the defendant (48%), or the victim's refusal to talk with or date the defendant (11%). The similarity here to the profile of the simple obsessional adult stalker is clear; studies suggest that these stalkers are most dangerous when their victims decide to physically remove themselves from the presence of the offender permanently, generally by ending the romantic relationship or beginning a new relationship (Davis, 1997, 1998, and 1999; Davis and Chipman, 1997; Davis and Emer, 1997; Walker and Meloy, 1998).

Since stalking cases which grow out of domestic violence situations are said to be the most lethal, and there is clear documentation of both dating violence and obsessive intrusion in adolescent populations, the reality that stalking crimes are being perpetrated by adolescents cannot be denied. The problem may be that societal stereotypes about adolescent courtship behaviors have thus far prevented appropriate labeling of adolescent behaviors as examples of the crime of stalking. As such, the problem of adolescent stalking has been largely ignored.

Differences between Adolescent and Adult Offenders and Victims

The research presented thus far makes it clear that the archetype of the benign moonstruck adolescent may be dangerous insofar as it allows society and lawmakers to close their eyes to the potential lethality of adolescent intimacy. It is clear that adolescents can and do perpetrate violence in romantic relationships and appear to utilize various harassment techniques to control their partners and ex-partners, often with the effect of causing them to fear for their safety. Although the definition of stalking varies somewhat across states, with some requiring a more stringent "credible threat" standard and others broadening the definition to include any behavior which is considered to be threatening in its intent and/or evokes "a reasonable fear" of death or bodily harm to the victim (D'Amico, 1997; Landau, 1996; Simon, 1999; "Stalking Laws by State," 2000), most attempt to capture the pattern of conduct unique to stalking crimes. As noted in the "Project to Develop a Model Antistalking Code for States," "unique to stalking is the element of escalation that raises initially what may be bothersome and annoying — but legal — behavior to the level of obsessive, dangerous, and even violent acts" (Landau, 1996, p. 65). The prevailing societal notion of the stalker has been focused on an adult, who, as Landau puts it, becomes involved in "dangerously obsessive entanglements" (Landau, 1996, p. 46). Given the cases presented in this chapter, is there any question that the adolescent too can become involved in such entanglements? Is there any question that the adolescent intimate partner is capable of behavior that is threatening or causes a teenage partner to reasonably fear for her safety?

Contrary to popular belief, there appears to be considerable similarity between the profile of the adult intimate partner stalker and the profile of the adolescent stalker who often goes on to become an adolescent batterer. Adolescent offenders have been described as being motivated by "anger, jealousy, and a desire to retaliate against physical or emotional hurt" (Papazian, 1999, p. 2).

Like the adult simple obsessional follower, the adolescent batterer demonstrates a need to control his partner during their relationship, and exhibits signs of excessive jealousy. This is clear in the adolescent's desire to accompany his partner wherever she goes and his anger when he is not included, his constant commentary on what she should wear, who she should see, and what she should do, and demands for phone calls whenever she arrives home from an outing in which he is not present. Even as the relationship is still continuing, the adolescent offender begins a pattern of harassment, including, but not limited to, repeated phone calls to check his partner's whereabouts, inquisition of his partner's family members, and clinging behaviors. When his partner decides to end the relationship due to the obsessive and intrusive behaviors being exhibited, the adolescent offender begins both psychological and physical attempts to threaten and control, including threats to kill himself (often with a weapon visibly present), threats to physically harm or kill the ex-partner, vandalizing the property of his ex-partner and/or her friends and family, and relentless pursuit of his ex-partner, watching her at home, at school, and at work. Sadly, like in tragic cases involving adult intimate partner stalkers, cases of adolescent intimate partner stalkers sometimes end in death to the victim.

As noted by Landau, "anyone who thinks teenage stalking isn't as potentially lethal as the adult version is wrong — dead wrong" (Landau, 1996, p. 48). Recall Mindy's tragic story discussed earlier in the chapter, a case of a young woman whose life ended prematurely because a young stalker was not stopped.

In addition to similarities between the physical threats used by adolescent and adult intimate partner stalkers, there are also similarities in the psychological techniques aimed to control, manipulate, and frighten the victim. Many of the psychological techniques enumerated in comprehensive lists of coercive techniques used by adult batterers (see Sonkin, 1997) can be applied to the adolescent offender. Like adults, adolescent offenders attempt to (1) isolate their partners (primarily by controlled socialization with family and friends, and monitored use of communication techniques, such as the telephone); (2) engage in what Sonkin broadly labeled "monopolizing of perceptions" via pathological jealousy, controlled activities (including self-enhancing activities such as wearing makeup), and checking where the partner is/surveillance; and (3) degrade and humiliate their partners via cursing and name-calling, denial of power, private and public humiliation, forced sex, rejection through emotional, social, and affectional means, and threats (to kill a partner or family members, to commit suicide, and to use weapons). Furthermore, the stalking acts typical of adult domestic violence cases mirror the kinds of behaviors reported in adolescent battering and stalking cases (see Sonkin, 1997 for a full checklist).

Like adults, adolescents (1) break into their partners' homes or other private property, sometimes vandalizing them; (2) leave items for their partners at school, home, or work; (3) watch their partners from a distance; (4) follow their partners on car or on foot; (5) hide in the bushes or conduct other surveillance of their partners' homes; (6) engage in surveillance of their partners at work and at school; (7) vandalize their partners' or the partners' friends' properties; (8) destroy property to scare or intimidate their partners; (9) steal things from their partners; (10) break into their partners' homes or cars; (11) harass their partners and/or their partners' friends and family with phone calls or notes; (12) fail to respect visitation limitations; and (13) violate restraining orders. These similarities are clear from the numerous cases presented in this chapter, and from other systematic studies of adolescent relationship abuse (see Gamache, 1991; Sugarman and Hotaling, 1989).

Teen dating violence and adult battering are not confined to one particular socioeconomic class, ethnic group, or community (Suarez, 1994). The dynamics of intimate partner violence appear to be the same in teenage and adult experiences — both involve low self-esteem on the part of the victim, a need to assert power on the part of the batterer, and a batterer's belief that he is entitled to control his partner (Gamache, 1991; Shen, 1993). The teenage victim is made to lose her independence, experiences a diminished sense of self-esteem, feels "trapped" in the relationship, experiences terror at the thought of ending the relationship, believes she is in danger, and is at her greatest risk of injury when she tries to leave the relationship; attempts to end the relationship often result in an escalation of violence (Gamache, 1991; Suarez, 1994). All of these characteristics are reminiscent of the adult woman who experiences intimate partner violence and stalking. Furthermore, recent research suggests that there are similarities in the psychological profiles of adolescent stalkers and their adult counterparts. McCann (1998) reports a clinical case of adolescent stalking behavior which bears strong similarity to adult profiles, including abandonment rage, desperate attempts to repair the ego damage caused by rejection, and threats of violence. In addition, the case presented by McCann suggests that stereotypes about adolescent simple obsessional stalkers as differing from their adult counterparts due to a lack of contributing psychopathology or disturbances in identity and attachment are also misguided. McCann's adolescent case exhibited contributing psychopathological symptoms similar to adults with the same stalking profile.

It is clear that there are striking similarities between adolescent victims of relationship abuse and stalking, and adult victims of these same crimes. It is also clear that the danger adolescent women face needs to be taken more seriously. The differences that do exist between adolescent victims and their adult counterparts are important, because they may serve to intensify the risk of danger for the adolescents who find themselves in potentially deadly relationships. First, as young people continue to enter into sexual relationships at younger ages, the potential for intrusive behaviors, obsession, and violence may continue to grow. It has been documented that more dating violence is being reported than ever before; this may be due to the combination of two factors: (1) entering into sexual relationships before the requisite maturity to handle the emotional turmoil that accompanies them is reached and (2) the expanding media link between sex and violence in our current culture (Chandler, 1991). Second, the type of dependence that teenage victims have on their abusers is likely different than the major source of dependence adult victims experience; teenagers tend to rely on their abusers for emotional and social stability, whereas adult victims additionally rely on their abusers for financial support (Suarez, 1994). However, this difference should not cause social scientists, lawmakers, or educators to minimize the teenage victim's experience — social status, self-esteem, and identity formation are extremely powerful components of adolescent life and can exert significant pressure on teens to endure experiences they might not otherwise accept. Third, the fact that adolescent relationships typically involve unmarried partners is critical, because the abuser might have a lowered perception of control over his partner, and thus intensify his methods to control, harass, and threaten her. Studies suggest that dating couples seem to exhibit higher rates of violence than married couples do (Hamberger and Ambuel, 1998), perhaps because there is less commitment and thus more options or flexibility for leaving the relationship for another (Riggs et al., 1990). Fourth, while teenage victims and adult victims often get trapped in a cycle of violence and feel that they cannot leave the abuser, their reasons may be somewhat different, though not entirely; teenagers might be more likely to remain in a relationship that is clearly intrusive, harassing, and violent because of peer pressure, conformity to gender role stereotypes, and inexperience in dating relationships (Gamache, 1991). However, like adult victims, adolescent victims may also remain in abusive relationships because of learned helplessness (Walker, 1979), depression (Papazian, 1999), blaming themselves for "provoking" the offender (Papazian, 1999), beliefs that the offender will change (Papazian, 1999), beliefs that the offender needs them because no one else understands him (Papazian, 1999), and a form of Stockholm syndrome in which the teenager comes to view her abuser as a needed protector or provider of other survival needs, whether they be emotional or physical (Graham and Rawlings, 1991; but see Makepeace, 1981 for a view of dating violence as distinct from marital violence). In fact, some psychologists have argued that teenagers are more vulnerable to "Stockholm syndrome" because they are more likely to mistake violence as evidence of love and devotion ("Some Accept Violence," 1991). Last, since the adolescent is relatively inexperienced with intimate relationships, relies heavily on peer group standards for a sense of reality and normalcy, and is still in the process of identity formation, she may not recognize or be willing to accept that the experience she is having is inappropriate. As such, relative to her adult counterpart, an adolescent victim may more easily become an enabler for a pattern of intrusive and controlling behaviors which eventually escalate to a potentially lethal level. The cases and research findings presented in this chapter suggest that cognitive distortions which could lead to enabling are typical for adolescent victims.

It is imperative that physicians, social scientists, educators, law enforcement personnel, policy makers, and mental health providers begin to recognize not only the reality of adolescent stalking and battering, but also the signs and symptoms that such behavior is occurring. Also, it is important to develop criteria for determining which adolescents are at risk for becoming involved in such behaviors. The problem of adult partner violence and stalking likely has its roots in adolescent behavior patterns that are overlooked, downplayed, or continue without consequence; these patterns then surface again as the adolescent reaches adult status and embarks on intimate relationships (Hamberger and Ambuel, 1998).

Recent work has been aimed at uncovering predictor variables for adolescents who may be at risk for perpetrating stalking crimes and relationship abuse. Some researchers argue that stalking begins as the phenomenon discussed earlier, termed "obsessive relational intrusion" (Spitzberg and Cupach, 1994; Spitzberg et al., 1998; Spitzberg and Rhea, 1999) or "obsessive following" (Meloy, 1996b), which although not legally considered criminal behavior, involves activities which appear to be early forms of stalking. ORI behaviors include leaving notes on a car windshield, frequent phone calls, leaving or sending gifts, monitoring whereabouts, following behaviors, exaggerated expressions of affection relative to relationship context, invading personal property, physical restraint, threats to harm the self or a partner, and sexual coercion (Spitzberg et al., 1998). These precursor behaviors, which often progress to the level of criminal stalking, are a documented problem in adolescent and college populations; this is clear from the cases and research findings presented in this chapter, and has been documented elsewhere as well (Fremouw et al., 1997; McCann, 1998; Spitzberg and Cupach, 1994; Spitzberg et al., 1998). Furthermore, the affective experience of jealousy has been linked to ORI and stalking (Dutton et al., 1996; Guerrero et al., 1995). Specifically, excessive jealousy has been related to surveillance activities (Guerrerro et al., 1995), a predisposition to act in an aggressive fashion when one is angry, humiliated, and/or depressed (Guerrero and Andersen, 1998), and physical abuse and stalking of an intimate partner in order to maintain control (Dutton et al., 1996).

For an adolescent with a fragile ego and a strong dependence on social acceptance from peers to achieve self-esteem, the experience of jealousy is an inevitable reality. Without the cognitive and emotional maturity to deal with such a powerful emotion, the adolescent could become overwhelmed by it, and desperate to keep his partner in an effort to retain or regain an already frail self-esteem. The victim, herself battling with a fragile sense of self-worth and an underdeveloped identity, might allow such intrusions for fear that her social status and self-esteem will otherwise crumble.

Adolescents who enter prematurely into intimate relationships might become trapped in a vicious cycle which escalates over time — a jealous, controlling boyfriend attempts to assert his masculinity with ever-increasing intrusive demands, and a girlfriend who defines herself through him allows it to continue, perhaps not even recognizing due to her inexperience that the behaviors being made and demanded are not appropriate expressions of love.

Since teens are becoming involved in intimate relationships long before they have any understanding of the conventions of dating and appropriate boundaries (Gardner, 1996), adolescent relationships might be dangerous breeding grounds for violence and stalking. The consequences of premature intimacy may be twofold: (1) young people are at risk for being physically harmed, maybe even killed, and (2) even if they manage to leave the relationship unharmed, they form an intimacy schema which is distorted and will likely plague their future relationship experiences.

The question then remains, if it is clear from numerous case reports and systematic research that dating violence and stalking are realities of adolescent and college student life, why is there only one documented case of a simple obsessional adolescent stalker (McCann, 1998)? This case, like the multitudes presented here, involved a pattern of threatening letters sent by the offender to his ex-girlfriend following her decision to end the relationship, surveillance outside his girlfriend's home, and repeated violations of restraining and protection orders. The victim in this case, an adolescent female, experienced fear as a result of her ex-boyfriend's behavior, as did her parents.

Although McCann reported encountering adolescent obsessional followers in both his clinical and forensic experiences, he noted that research indicates that clinical evaluations are infrequent among adult obsessional followers, and that these individuals usually come to the attention of law enforcement before mental health personnel (McCann, 1998). In the case McCann presented, school officials were instrumental in confronting the stalking behavior and initiating clinical intervention. The take-home message might be that for whatever reason, educational systems have not been effective in identifying stalking and related violence in student relationships; this could be because of underreporting by student victims, prevailing stereotypes about teenage stalking as "teenage infatuation gone awry" (McCann, 1998), a lack of resources for dealing with these problems and thus a hesitation to identify them, or some combination of all of the above. Regardless of the reason, the result is the same: an aberrant, dangerous pattern of relating may be forming and setting the stage for future stalking and violence. Perhaps with greater identification and intervention, adult stalking and the violence that results from it could be minimized.

Legal Issues and Implications

In recent years, articles have begun to appear in the literature which discuss the need for legal protections for teenagers involved in violent relationships (see Sousa, 1999). Despite the fact that investigation and intervention for these offenses are being taken seriously in school systems across the country (see Sousa et al., 1997), legal protection for teenagers remains inadequate.

One of the barriers to early intervention for adolescent offenders is that adolescents cannot pursue the same legal avenues as adults do with regard to domestic violence and stalking. Suarez (1994) wrote, "while the dynamics of teen and adult intimate violence are quite similar, the protections provided by the law for these two classes of abuse are dramatically different. Most domestic violence laws explicitly or effectively define domestic violence as abuse against adults, and hence do not provide protection for teen victims" (Suarez, 1994, p. 435; see also Moak, 1996 for legal problems associated with teenage dating violence).

As Suarez concludes, this failure to include adolescents in the legal statutes reflects not only a social unwillingness to accept the reality of adolescent dating violence and harassment, but also prevents teenagers from receiving needed protection from dangerous individuals. Thirty-nine states and the

District of Columbia do not currently consider teenagers involved in dating violence to be victims of domestic abuse (Suarez, 1994; but see "Dating Violence: New Protections," 1995 for a discussion of new legal protections for teenage victims of domestic violence in Michigan, Minnesota, Oklahoma, and Rhode Island; also, Brustin, 1995).

Statutes that exclude teenagers from coverage under domestic violence statutes do so because of the way in which they define what domestic violence is. These definitions include: statutes that define the victim as a spouse/former spouse, cohabitant/former cohabitant, or co-parent; statutes that have a strict requirement that the victim and the abuser currently reside together; and statutes that have some kind of specific "adult" requirement, such as a requirement that abuse occurred between persons who are either over the age of 18 or have been legally emancipated from their parents (Suarez, 1994). These legal requirements make it virtually impossible for adolescents between the ages of 13 and 17 to receive protection from the law when they are being battered. Other than the obvious difficulty these legal definitions pose for teens in need of safety from ex-partners who become abusers and stalkers, these legal shortcomings also prevent teenage victims from participating in programs provided by the state to counsel and care for domestic violence survivors (Suarez, 1994).

Currently there are only 11 states that have defined their domestic violence laws loosely enough to allow adolescents to be covered under their statutes, but even these statutes do not explicitly include teenagers in their language, and the language used is ambiguous. For example, Colorado's Criminal Code defines domestic violence as "the infliction or threat of infliction of any bodily injury or harmful physical contact or the destruction of property or threat thereof as a method of coercion, control, revenge, or punishment upon a person with whom the actor is involved in an intimate relationship" (Colorado Review Statute, 18-6-800.3 (1) Supp. 1993).

In its definition of what constitutes an "intimate relationship," the statute includes "present or past unmarried couples," but as Suarez (1994) noted, the statute does not make clear what is required for two individuals to be considered a "couple" by law. Other statutes, such as those in Illinois, Massachusetts, New Hampshire, and New Mexico, have tried to utilize language that would allow for the inclusion of adolescent cases, but even these statutes are fraught with ambiguity and do not necessarily make the inclusion of adolescents explicit (Suarez, 1994).

Furthermore, even in states that define their domestic violence laws broadly enough to include teenagers under civil proceedings, criminal penal codes still exclude teenagers and thus make it difficult for them to seek legal recourse against their perpetrators. Although these teens might be able to obtain a generic civil restraining order against their perpetrators, they will not be able to benefit from additional legal protections that follow from domestic violence legislation (Suarez, 1994).

Anti-stalking legislation could provide a means of legal protection for adolescent victims, but these laws also have problems when applied to juveniles. The positive side of anti-stalking legislation for juveniles is that these statutes generally do not require a specific relationship between the perpetrator and the victim, and typically do not have age restrictions (Suarez, 1994). On the other hand, domestic violence codes and anti-stalking legislation are intimately tied, such that a lack of inclusion in domestic violence legislation may severely limit the benefit teens can receive from anti-stalking laws. Suarez wrote:

> Most anti-stalking laws are not prospective in their relief. In other words, only a few states specifically offer anti-stalking restraining orders. Even then, such anti-stalking restraining orders may be available only after a conviction for stalking. Thus, inclusion of teenage daters in domestic violence definitional statutes is vital. Only then will teen daters be able to obtain domestic violence restraining orders, which provide protection without a prior determination of criminal guilt. Second, under the rubric of "aggravated stalking", most anti-stalking laws impose higher penalties on stalkers who violate restraining orders. Hence, if it were made easier for teenagers to obtain restraining orders by way of inclusive domestic violence laws, then anti-stalking laws would afford them even greater protection. A teenager who merely has a generic civil restraining order may not be sufficiently protected by anti-stalking laws because some states will find aggravated stalking only if the order violated is a domestic violence restraining order (Suarez, 1994, p. 446).

Perhaps the most important limitation raised by Suarez regarding anti-stalking protections for adolescents involves the requirement that most states have for proof of the perpetrator's explicit "intent" to harm the victim. Considering society's general tendency to mistake a teenager's incessant following, phone calls, intimidating gestures, and manipulative ploys as the desperate actions of a typical lovesick teen, many boyfriends may not be deemed guilty of violating anti-stalking laws, in spite of their harassing behaviors.

The danger of not including adolescents in domestic violence statutes is multifaceted: it puts teens in danger of being psychologically and/or physically harmed, it prevents intervention for troubled teens who might otherwise continue and escalate their pattern of abuse (not only with their current partner, but in later relationships), and it sends a message to adolescents that their distorted schema for intimacy is in fact the correct one. As therapist and founder of the Southern California Coalition for Battered Women, Barrie Levy noted:

Once somebody finds that violence is the way to get what you want and feel powerful, it is hard to change unless you have some sense that there is something really wrong with it or you experience some sanctions like arrest … a lot of kids … say that getting caught made a difference (Abcarian, 1991).

Adolescents who abuse, harass, and stalk their intimate partners are likely motivated by jealousy, insecurity, fragile identities, and a need to assert their masculinity. If intervention does not occur at these early stages, alternative ways of coping with the powerful thoughts and feelings that motivate these behaviors will not be learned, and the pattern of behavior will carry over from adolescence to adulthood.

Conclusion

The cases, statistics, and research findings presented in this chapter make it clear that stalking, dating abuse, and relationship violence are as much a problem of adolescence as they are adulthood. So why hasn't the law caught up with the reality of adolescent battering and stalking, and why are there only a handful of educational awareness programs being instituted in school systems throughout the country?

Perhaps Suarez summarized it best in her account of opposition to expanding the definition of domestic violence legislation when she wrote, "topping the list may be the assertion that teen dating violence either does not exist, or is inherently different from adult intimate abuse. Some may argue that teens are too immature to be in serious relationships and that the law should not 'condone' such activity by recognizing its incident hazards" (Suarez, 1994, p. 450).

The legal system's unwillingness to address the reality of adolescent dating violence and stalking will not make it disappear, nor will the refusal of educators, policy makers, and parents to revise their stereotype of the lovesick teen. We may choose to close our eyes, but the danger teenagers face will remain, and if left unchecked, will threaten and perhaps end the lives of promising youth.

Perhaps acknowledgment of adolescent stalking patterns and dating violence would have saved the life of Amy Carnevale, a 14-year-old who was stabbed to death in 1991 by her 17-year-old boyfriend Jamie Fuller in Beverly, Massachusetts. When interviewed following Carnevale's death, school officials remarked, "Before Carnevale and Fuller, we knew there were some problems, but we didn't think it was very widespread" ("Boy Meets Girl," 1993). Following the tragic incident, the high school instituted a dating-violence education program, noting that prevention, rather than intervention, brings the greatest successes.

Ample studies have clarified the imminent need for more programs of this nature, and for legal reform that protects our youth as they embark on intimate relationships for the first time. All that remains is acknowledgment from adults who have the power to make these changes a reality.

Bibliography

Abcarian, R. (October 13, 1991). In Love, in danger: teen victims of dating abuse often are too immature and insecure to escape jealous, sometimes violent boyfriends. *Los Angeles Times,* pp. E1 and E14.

Allen-Hagen, B. and Sickmund, M. (July 1993). Juveniles and Violence: Juvenile Offending and Victimization. U.S. Department of Justice, OJJDP: Fact Sheet.

American Association of University Women (1993). *Hostile Hallways: The AAUW Survey on Sexual Harassment in America's Schools.* Washington, D.C.: American Association of University Women Educational Foundation and Harris/Scholastic Research.

Association for Student Judicial Affairs (February 12, 1994). *Stalking Resolution.* Website: http://asja.tamu.edu/about/stalking.htm.

Barbaree, H. E., Marshall, W. L., and Hudson, S. M. (1993). *The Juvenile Sex Offender.* New York: Guilford Press.

Barber, M. (April 28, 1999). Rutgers University athlete arrested for threatening woman, *Daily Targum.* Website: http://web.lexis-nexis.com/universe.

Barrett, A. E. (1998). Survival Tales: An Examination of High School Dating. M.S.S.W. thesis, University of Texas, Arlington.

Bergman, L. (1992). Dating violence among high school students, *Social Work,* 37, 21–27.

Billingham, R. E. and Sack, A. R. (1986). Courtship violence and the interactive status of the relationship, *Journal of Adolescent Research,* 1, 315–325.

Blackburn, E. J. (1999). Forever Yours: Rates of Stalking Victimization, Risk Factors, and Traumatic Responses among College Women. Doctoral dissertation, University of Massachusetts, Amherst.

Boy meets girl, boy beats girl (December 13, 1993). *Newsweek,* pp. 66–68.

Browne, A. (1987). *When Battered Women Kill.* New York: McMillan Free Press.

Brustin, S. L. (1995). Legal responses to teen dating violence, *Family Law Quarterly,* 29, 331–356.

Central Michigan University Police Department (1999), *Stalking.* Website: http://www.cmich.edu/STALK.htm.

Chandler, K. (November 18, 1991). Young love's dark side: schools seek to counter abuse, *Star Tribune* (Minneapolis/St. Paul), p. 1A.

Cochran, D., Brown, M. E., Adams, S. L., and Doherty, D. (April 14, 1994). Young Adolescent Batterers: A Profile of Restraining Order Defendants in Massachusetts. Massachusetts Trial Court, Office of the Commissioner of Probation.

Coleman, F. L. (1997). Stalking behavior and the cycle of domestic violence, *Journal of Interpersonal Violence*, 12, 420–432.

Colorado Review Statute, 18-6-800.3 (1) (Supp. 1993).

Craver, R. S. (1999). Dating Violence and Its Relation to Identity, Self-Esteem, and Silencing the Self among College Women. Doctoral dissertation, North Carolina State University, Raleigh.

Cupach, W. R. and Spitzberg, B. H. (1998). Obsessive relational intrusion and stalking, in B. H. Spitzberg and W. R. Cupach (Eds.) (pp. 233–263). *The Dark Side of Close Relationships*. Mahwah, NJ: Lawrence Erlbaum Associates.

D'Amico, M. (February 1997). *The Law vs. On-Line Stalking*. Website: http://www. madcapps.com/Writings/cybersta.htm.

Dating violence: new protections for abused teens (September 1995). *Women's Advocate*, 16, 1–2.

Davis, J. (December 1997). Psychological and Legal Analysis of Stalking and Stalkers, 5th Annual Scientific Conference, American College of Forensic Examiners, Coronado, CA.

Davis, J. (June 1998). Stalker and stalker typologies: forensic mental health and public safety implications, District Attorney Office of San Diego, Training Seminar and Workshop to Local Law Enforcement Agencies, San Diego.

Davis, J. (September 1999). Stalking identity encounter profiles: constructing a threat assessment profile, a safety plan and a case management strategy from a stalker typology, Break-out training session, Speaker and trainer, Third Annual District Attorney Stalking-the-Stalker Conference, Del Mar, CA, September 23–24, 1999.

Davis, J. and Chipman, M. (1997). Stalkers and other obsessional types: a review and forensic psychological typology of those who stalk, *Journal of Clinical–Forensic Medicine*, 4, 166–173.

Davis, J. and Emer, D. (1997). A psychological and legal analysis of stalkers and stalking, Professional presentation and training workshop, Peace Officers Research Associations of California (PORAC), Las Vegas, NV, April 13–17.

de Becker, G. (1997). *The Gift of Fear: Survival Signals that Protect Us from Violence*. Boston: Little, Brown.

Dutton, D. G., Van Ginkel, C., and Landolt, M. A. (1996). Jealousy, intimate abusiveness, and intrusiveness, *Journal of Family Violence*, 11, 411–423.

Finkelstein, K. E. (October 1997). Dating violence: the hidden danger college women face, *Glamour Magazine*, 95, 320–321, 337–339.

Fremouw, W., Westrup, D., and Pennypacker, J. (1997). Stalking on campus: the prevalence and strategies for coping with stalking, *Journal of Forensic Sciences*, 42, 664–667.

Gamache, D. (1991). Domination and control: the social context of dating violence, in B. Levy (Ed.), *Dating Violence: Young Women in Danger*. Seattle, WA: Seal Press.

Gardner, M. (June 30, 1994). A hidden fact of life for teens: dating violence, *Christian Science Monitor*, 12–13.

Gardner, M. (March 11, 1996). Teaching teens to put a stop to dating violence, *Christian Science Monitor*, 12–13.

Gelles, R. J. (1987). *Family Violence*. Newbury Park, CA: Sage Publications.

Gelles, R. and Pedrick-Cornell, C. (1990). *Intimate Violence in Families*. Newbury Park, CA: Sage Publications.

Gilbert, R. N. (1998). *Welcome to Our World: Realities of High School Students*. Thousand Oaks, CA: Sage Publications.

Graham, L. R. and Rawlings, E. I. (1991). Bonding with abusive dating partners: dynamics of Stockholm syndrome, in B. Levy (Ed.), *Dating Violence: Young Women in Danger*. Seattle, WA: Seal Press.

Guerrero, L. K. and Andersen, P. A. (1998). The dark side of jealousy and envy; desire, delusion, desperation, and destructive communication, in B. H. Spitzberg and W. R. Cupach (Eds.), *The Dark Side of Close Relationships*. Mahwah, NJ: Lawrence Erlbaum Associates.

Guerrero, L. K., Andersen, P. A., Jorgensen, P. F., Spitzberg, B. H., and Eloy, S. V. (1995). Coping with the green-eyed monster: conceptualizing and measuring communicative responses to romantic jealousy, *Western Journal of Communication*, 59, 270–304.

Hamberger, L. K. and Ambuel, B. (1998). Dating violence, *Violence among Children and Adolescents*, 45, 381–389.

Haussamen, H. (February 10, 2000). New Mexico State University students arrested for stalking, in *The Round Up*. Website: http://web.lexis-nexis.com/universe.

Jordan, C. E. (1987). The nature and extent of domestic violence in Domestic Violence Prevention and Services Plan. Department for Mental Health and Mental Retardation Services, New York.

Knapp, S. (March 27, 1997). *Report of the Committee on Campus Violence*. Baltimore, MD: The Johns Hopkins University, Committee on Campus Violence. Website: http://www.jhu.edu/news_info/reports/violence/members.html.

Landau, E. (1996). *Stalking*. New York: Franklin Watts.

Lee, R. (January 1991). *Love and Violence: Victims and Perpetrators*. New York: New York City Coalition for Women's Mental Health.

Lemon, N. K. D. (December 1994). Domestic violence and stalking: a comment on the model anti-stalking code proposed by the National Institute of Justice, in *Battered Women's Justice Project*, Duluth, MN. Website: http://www.vaw.umn.edu/stalk.asp.

Levy, B. (Ed.) (1991). *Dating Violence: Young Women in Danger*. Seattle, WA: Seal Press.

Levy, B. (1993). *In Love and in Danger; a Teen's Guide to Breaking Free of Abusive Relationships*. Seattle, WA: Seal Press.

Lingg, R. A. (1993). Stopping stalkers: a critical examination of anti-stalking statutes, *St. John's Law Review*, 67, 347–381.

Lloyd, S. (1991). The darkside of courtship: violence and sexual exploitation, *Family Relations*, 40, 14–20.

Macgowan, M. J. (1997). An evaluation of a dating violence prevention program for middle school students, *Violence and Victims*, 12, 223–235.

Makepeace, J. M. (1981). Courtship violence among college students, *Family Relations*, 30, 97–102.

McAnaney, K. G. and Curliss, L. A. (1993). From imprudence to crime: anti-stalking laws, *Notre Dame Law Review*, 68, 819–909.

McCann, J. T. (1998). Subtypes of stalking (obsessional following) in adolescents, *Journal of Adolescence*, 21, 667–675.

McFarlane, J., Willson, P., Malecha, A., and Lemmey, D. (2000). Intimate partner violence: a gender comparison, *Journal of Interpersonal Violence*, 15, 158–169.

Mehta, D. and Wagman, J. (September 8, 1997). Is this campus safe? in *The Maneater*. Website: http://web.lexis-nexis.com/universe.

Meloy, J. R. (1996a). A clinical investigation of the obsessional follower: "she loves me, she loves me not ...," in L. Schlesinger (Ed.), *Explorations in Criminal Psychopathology* (pp. 9–32). Springfield, IL: Charles C Thomas.

Meloy, J. R. (1996b). Stalking (obsessional following): a review of some preliminary studies, *Aggression and Violent Behavior*, 1, 147–162.

Meloy, J. R. (1998). The psychology of stalking, in J. R. Meloy (Ed.), *The Psychology of Stalking: Clinical and Forensic Perspectives*. San Diego, CA: Academic Press.

Meloy, J. R. and Gothard, S. (1995). A demographic and clinical comparison of obsessional followers and offenders with mental disorders, *American Journal of Psychiatry*, 152, 258–263.

Moak, D. P. (1996). Teenage dating violence: a problem without a legal solution, *Adelphia Law Journal*, 11, 39–61.

Molidor, C. E. (1995). Gender differences of psychological abuse in high school dating relationships, *Child & Adolescent Social Work Journal*, 12, 119–134.

Moore, K. A., Nord, C. W., and Peterson, J. L. (1989). Non-voluntary sexual activity among adolescents, *Family Planning Perspective*, 21, 110–114.

Morell, L. (Fall 1984). Violence in premarital relationships. Response to the victimization of women and children, *Journal of the Center for Women Policy Studies*, 7, 17–18.

Mullen, P. E., Pathé, M., Purcell, R., and Stewart, G. W. (1999). Study of stalkers, *American Journal of Psychiatry*, 156, 1244–1249.

National Coalition Against Domestic Violence (1997). *Teen Dating Violence Resource Manual*. Denver, CO.

National Teen Dating Violence Project (October 1995 to February 1996). *National Teen Relationship Violence Survey*. Denver, CO: National Coalition Against Domestic Violence.

O'Keefe, M. (1997). Predictors of dating violence among high school students, *Journal of Interpersonal Violence*, 12, 546–568.

O'Keefe, N. K., Brockopp, K., and Chew, E. (1986). Teen dating violence, *Social Work*, 31, 465–468.

O'Leary, K. D., Barling, J., Arias, I., Rosenbaum, A., Malone, J., and Tyree, A. (1989). Prevalence and stability of physical aggression between spouses: a longitudinal analysis, *Journal of Consulting and Clinical Psychology*, 57, 263–268.

O'Malley, S. (1996). Nowhere to hide: why the new stalking laws still don't protect women, *Redbook*, 188, 120–123.

Pagelow, M. D. (1988). The incidence and prevalence of criminal abuse of other family members in family violence, in L. E. Ohlin and M. Tonry (Eds.), *Family Violence: A Review of Research, Crime and Justice Series*, Vol. 11 (pp. 263–313). Chicago, IL: University of Chicago Press.

Palarea, R. E., Zona, M. A., Lane, J. C., and Langhrinchsen-Rohling, J. (1999). The dangerous nature of intimate relationship stalking: threats, violence, and associated risk factors, *Behavioral Sciences and the Law*, 17, 269–283.

Papazian, R. (September 9, 1999). *Teens Battering Teens: The National Problem of Dating Violence*. Website: http://www.apbnews.com/safetycenter/family/dateviolence.

Riggs, D. S., O'Leary, K. D., and Breslin, F. C. (1990). Multiple correlates of physical aggression in dating couples, *Journal of Interpersonal Violence*, 5, 61–73.

Rosen, K. H. and Bezold, A. (1996). Dating violence prevention: a didactic support group for young women, *Journal of Counseling and Development*, 74, 521–525.

Rouse, L. P., Breen, R., and Howell, M. (1988). Abuse in intimate relationships: a comparison of married and dating college students, *Journal of Interpersonal Violence*, 3, 414–429.

Shen, F. (July 18, 1993). Welts betray dark side of teen dating: specialists see a youthful version of battered spouse syndrome, *Washington Post*, A1, A16.

Simon, R. I. (1999). *Bad Men Do What Good Men Dream: A Forensic Psychiatrist Illuminates the Darker Side of Human Behavior*. Washington, D.C.: American Psychiatric Press.

Simon, T. B. (1996). *Dating: Peer Education for Reducing Sexual Harassment and Violence among Secondary Students*. Holmes Beach, FL: Learning Publications.

Some Accept Violence in the Dating Game (August 30, 1991). *Orlando Sentinel*, E5.

Sonkin, D. J. (1997). *Domestic Violence: The Perpetrator Assessment Handbook* (available from Daniel J. Sonkin, 1505 Bridgeway, Suite 105, Sausalito, CA 94965).

Sousa, C. A. (July 1, 1999). Teen dating violence: the hidden epidemic, *Family and Conciliation Courts Review*, 37, 356–374.

Sousa, C., Farrell, C., and Wilk, K. (August 1997). *Guidelines to School Districts on Addressing Teen Dating Violence*, Massachusetts Department of Education. Website: http://www.doe.mass.edu/doedocs/tvguide.html.

Special Issues in Domestic Violence (August 27, 2000). *University of South Florida College of Public Health News Release*. Website: http://www.med.usf.edu/publichealth/newsfile/news980825c.html.

Spitzberg, B. and Cupach, W. (1994). *The Dark Side of Close Relationships*. Mahwah, NJ: Lawrence Erlbaum Associates.

Spitzberg, B. H. and Cupach, W. R. (August 1996). Obsessive Relational Intrusion: Victimization and Coping. Paper presented at the meeting of the International Society for the Study of Personal Relationships, Banff, Canada.

Spitzberg, B. H. and Rhea, J. (1999). Obsessive relational intrusion and sexual coercion victimization, *Journal of Interpersonal Violence*, 14, 3–20.

Spitzberg, B. H., Nicastro, A. M., and Cousins, A. V. (1998). Exploring the interactional phenomenon of stalking and obsessive relational intrusion, *Communication Reports*, 11, 34–47.

Stacey, C. L., Schandel, L. M., Flannery, W. S., Conlon, M., and Milardo, R. H. (1994). It's not all moonlight and roses: dating violence at the University of Maine, 1982–1992, *College Student Journal*, 28, 2–9.

Stalking: Is It Terrorism on Campus? (April 7, 1997). *Stalking Laws by State*. Website: http://members.aol.com/lrfuzz1/StalkingLaws/StateLaws.html.

Strauss, S. (1993). Sexual harassment in the schools, *Vocational Education Journal*, 68, 29–31.

Suarez, K. (1994). Teenage dating violence: the need for expanded awareness and legislation, *California Law Review*, 82, 423–471.

Sugarman, D. B. and Hotaling, G. T. (1989). Dating violence: prevalence, context, and risk markers, in M. A. Pirog-Good and J. E. Stets (Eds.), *Violence in Dating Relationships* (pp. 1–32). New York: Praeger.

Swindle, K. (June 5, 1992). Beginnings of abuse: when boys strike their girlfriends, it's an early sign of big trouble, *Sacramento Bee*, Section 7.

Symons, P. Y., Groer, M. W., Kepler-Youngblood, P., and Slater, V. (1994). Prevalence and predictors of adolescent dating violence, *Journal of Child and Adolescent Psychiatric Nursing*, 7, 14–23.

Tjaden, P. and Thoennes, N. (1997). Stalking in America: Findings from the National Violence against Women Survey. Denver, CO: Center for Policy Research.

Tontodonato, P. and Crew, B. K. (1992). Dating violence, social learning theory, and gender: a multivariate analysis, *Violence and Victims*, 7, 3–14.

Walker, L. E. (1979). *The Battered Woman*. New York: Harper & Row.

Walker, L. E. A. (1996). Assessment of abusive spousal relationships, in F. Kaslow (Ed.), *Handbook of Relational Diagnosis* (pp. 338–356). New York: Wiley.

Walker, L. E. A. and Meloy, J. R. (1998). Stalking and domestic violence, in J. R. Meloy (Ed.), *The Psychology of Stalking: Clinical and Forensic Perspectives*. San Diego, CA: Academic Press.

Walker, L. E. A. and Sonkin, D. J. (1995). *Juris Monitor Stabilization and Empowerment Programs*. Denver, CO: Endolor Communications.

What is Stalking? (December 1997). Website: http://www.xs4all.nl/~cdirks/engfat1.html.

Xu, S. (January 10, 2000). Assault, Harassment Trial Date Set for Former Penn State Student, *Daily Collegian*. Website: http://web.lexis-nexis.com/universe.

Zona, M., Sharma, K., and Lane, J. (1993). A comparative study of erotomanic and obsessional subjects in a forensic sample, *Journal of Forensic Sciences*, 38, 894–903.

About the Contributing Author

Denise M. Emer, Ph.D.

Denise Emer, Ph.D. is currently an assistant professor of psychology at Daemen College in New York. Dr. Emer received her Ph.D. in developmental-cognitive psychology from the State University of New York at Buffalo. She has also completed post-doctoral training in the area of clinical-forensic psychology, including an externship at the state psychiatric hospital in Buffalo, NY, supervised training in the area of forensic psychology with Dr. Joseph Davis (San Diego, CA), consultation work with forensic psychologist Dr. Robert Demerath (Buffalo, NY), and continuing education in the use of REBT and the diagnosis, treatment, and forensic implications of dissociative identity disorder. Dr. Emer has also served as a co-presenter on the psychological and legal implications of stalking with Dr. Joseph Davis at a training workshop for the Peace Officers Research Association (PORAC) in 1997. Dr. Emer has received grants to conduct and present numerous research projects on psycholegal issues, including serial murder and the insanity defense, juvenile homicide, and, most recently, obsessive relationships and stalking experiences in youth populations. Dr. Emer teaches courses in the areas of forensic psychology, health psychology, abnormal psychology, pathological personality styles, and paraphilic disorders. She has also served as the director of fieldwork programs for undergraduate and master's level students in the human service professions.

Dr. Emer has also published research on the effectiveness of various treatment alternatives for mentally ill outpatients. Dr. Emer has conducted numerous workshops for youth populations and community organizations in the areas of health psychology, including the psychological, social, and professional consequences of perfectionism, and the psychological components of healthy aging in elderly populations. Dr. Emer has also served as a consultant to community organizations for the design and implementation of centers to promote healthy aging in elderly populations, and has helped to design interdisciplinary academic programs to promote the study of forensic psychology and criminal justice.

Dr. Emer's academic honors include being invited to become a member of Sigma Xi (Professional Scientific Society), receiving two research grants for continued work in the areas of forensic and personality psychology, being elected to Who's Who Among Graduate Students in American Universities and Colleges, receiving an NIH (National Institute of Health) Pre-doctoral Fellowship, and serving as the first recipient of the Robert Rice Memorial Award for Early Excellence in Research at SUNY Buffalo. She is currently a member of the American Psychological Association, the Eastern Psychological Association, the Psychological Association of Western New York, and the

American College of Forensic Examiners. Her prior faculty positions include serving as an assistant professor of psychology at St. Bonaventure University in Olean, NY.

Erotomania, Stalking, and Stalkers: A Personal Experience with a Professional Perspective

4

DOREEN ORION

Contents

Introduction

I am a psychiatrist who has been having a long-term love affair with a former patient — in her mind, that is. She has the diagnosis of erotomania. As of this writing, I have been stalked for over 11 years, across several state lines, and had restraining orders violated over 50 times — all by the same hopelessly delusional woman.

As a psychiatrist, I have spent most of my professional life studying and trying to understand mental illness and mental disorder. I have treated thousands of patients, most, I like to think, with some degree of success. Yet, extricating myself from this former patient's erotomanic mission has proven impossible to do.

The DSM-IV defines delusional disorder, erotomanic type, as "delusions that another person, usually of higher status, is in love with the individual" (American Psychiatric Association, 1994, p. 301). Although it is the only

DSM-IV diagnosis that specifically mentions "stalking" as a potential associated behavior, there are at least 20 other mental illnesses in which erotomanic delusions, and therefore stalking, can manifest. In addition, while
more than half of all stalkers have some form of mental illness, erotomania
is the only one in which stalking routinely occurs (Harmon et al., 1995).

Erotomania: A Historical Perspective

For centuries, erotomania was equated with nymphomania. It was not until
the psychiatric literature of the late 1800s that erotomania began to be conceptualized as a delusional, rather than libidinal, disorder. Yet, it was still
thought of as a mental illness almost exclusively of women, even though
many of the case histories reported by the alienists of the time were of men.
For most of the 20th century, erotomania continued to be considered a
disease almost solely of women, although it was apparent that the majority
of erotomanics in forensic populations are men.

Given the very few case histories reported in the psychiatric literature, it
is difficult to determine if this is a vestige of an earlier age, although the word
"erotomanic" is still used at times as a pejorative reference to women who
challenge men in positions of power. Two prominent if not infamous modern
examples are Anita Hill and Monica Lewinsky (Dowd, 1998).

What drives the truly deluded individuals to fixate on another, often
someone they do not even know? As erotomanics not only latch onto their
objects, but assign to them the belief that the object can "fix" every aspect
of the erotomanic's often lonely and unfulfilled life, "fixate" is the perfect
word for what they do and do so well.

Toward the latter part of the 20th century, a shift occurred in psychiatry
away from psychodynamic theory (usually associated with the philosophy of
Sigmund Freud) and decidedly toward the biologic theory, as more and more
mental illnesses were thought to have a biologic basis, if not a genetic component. Pharmaceutical companies have responded with a plethora of new
and often highly effective drugs that control debilitating psychiatric symptoms. Yet it is easy to imagine that this biological revolution will pass erotomanics by. These patients do not want to get well, because they simply feel
they do not have to. The "love" they feel from their objects is real. To them,
it is the object that seems to need medication for rebuffing their romantic
overtures. The recurring theme with erotomanics is that they just don't get
it: after being charged with one of her numerous restraining order violations,
the woman stalking me expressed her outrage and asked me to show some
Christmas spirit by dropping the charges, ending her letter with, "P.S. I love
you. I also have a [Christmas] gift for you."

A Psychoanalytic Perspective

There have been several modern hypotheses about the disorder's etiology, starting with Freud, who theorized that it developed as a defense against latent homosexual urges. Since there have been several cases of homosexual erotomania reported in the literature, Freud's assertion that the disorder "remains totally unintelligible on any other view" is likely to not withstand close scrutiny (Strachey, 1958).

Other psychodynamic theories abound, including the belief that erotomania arises out of a grandiose attempt to deal with narcissistic blows to the ego that it was a denied self-love projected onto another or that it represents the search for a safe, idealized father (Strachey, 1958; Cameron, 1959; Enoch et al., 1967).

Aside from the purely psychodynamic, purely organic etiologies have also been theorized: erotomania resulting from a medication reaction as part of a seizure disorder due to a meningioma, mental retardation childbirth, and senile dementia (Doust and Christie, 1978; Signer, 1987; Greyson, 1977; Murray et al., 1990; Drevets and Rubin, 1987). Like schizophrenia (a more global psychotic disorder), erotomania may have a strong biologic component. Although rare, there have also been tantalizing reports in the literature about delusional disorders running in families, as well as erotomania in identical twins (Berry and Haden, 1980; Menzies et al., 1995).

Cultural Factors

Finally, cultural factors have also been implicated, although these may have a greater influence on the content of the delusions, and thus the resulting behavior, than the actual development of delusions in the first place (Nadarajah et al., 1991; Rugeiyamu, 1980; Chiu, 1994). One study found a high percentage of erotomanics appeared to be foreign born (Zona et al., 1993). While this might be an artifact of the study's location, Los Angeles, which attracts many foreign-born celebrity stalkers, similarities between erotomanic delusions and the inability to adapt to a new culture have been noted: both are characterized by identity problems, impaired reality testing, and social isolation (Meyers, 1998).

It has been postulated that erotomania develops in those who are foreign born due to a disturbance in acculturation, and that when men with a certain pre-morbid personality emigrate from a sexually repressive culture to a more open Western society, they misinterpret the normal social behavior of Western women by attaching romantic meaning where there is none (Meyers and Meloy, 1994).

A New Model of Stalker and Stalking Causality

The author proposes a model which incorporates biologic, psychodynamic, and cultural factors. It may be that erotomanics are born with a predisposition to develop any one of a number of psychotic disorders, but that their early development tips the scales in favor of that particular delusional disorder or even erotomanic delusions as part of another form of psychosis.

Even patients who have other, more serious mental illnesses, such as schizophrenia and bipolar disorder, can suffer from erotomanic delusions as part of their overall illness. Such patients have been said to have "secondary" erotomania as opposed to the "pure" or "primary" disorder. Although this distinction is no longer in use, it does seem to have treatment implications, which will be discussed later. In this chapter, I use the terms erotomania and erotomanic without distinguishing between the "primary" or "secondary" forms. From my extensive review of the literature, as well as involvement in my own and other cases, the backgrounds of both types of erotomanics appear very similar indeed.

Erotomanics tend to come from emotionally distant, if not abusive, families. They feel worthless and the resulting lack of self-esteem contributes to their drive to find fulfillment through fantasy, as their reality is chronically wanting. In some predisposed individuals, the fantasies eventually cross the line into delusions, propelling the individual into a delusional abyss from which he or she rarely recovers, the focus of which is romance.

In adolescence and adulthood, these patients tend to keep to themselves and are often classified as "loners" by those who know them. If they are employed, it is often at a menial job, one that affords little in the way of emotional empowerment. Most erotomanics have never married and may never have been in any romantic relationship at all, although in a formal study, this would be hard to corroborate: how could one tell if a prior "relationship" claimed by the erotomanic was really one at all, or just an earlier delusional attachment? This is particularly true for "primary" erotomanics who do not suffer from the hallucinations or bizarre delusions of schizophrenics who might have "secondary" erotomania.

Erotomanics appear to be stunted at an adolescent level of relating to others. When they write letters to their objects, the missives often seem more age-appropriate to a teenager, rather than an adult. Emotionally and socially immature, they continue the adolescent-like fantasy of an ideal love that can somehow right all their wrongs and make their lives whole, well into adulthood. In adolescence, such love is not taken seriously; it is considered innocent, harmless, a "crush." In adulthood, that same love becomes menacing when, as an erotomanic delusion, it is attached to all the attendant rights and privileges of adulthood; there are no more restrictions on where one can drive, where one can move to, or how many phone calls one can make.

The erotomanic manner of relating to the object is very much like an adolescent crush. It has been reported that they tend to avoid face-to-face contact with their objects, preferring instead to write letters, and also to call and surreptitiously follow. In fact, the only type of contact erotomanics seem less likely to engage in than other stalkers is face-to-face (Zona et al., 1993). This appears to be another holdover from adolescence: a pubescent girl with a crush on the high school's football captain (there could certainly be no higher authority than that) loiters in the hallway watching him, never dreaming of actually making a direct approach to him. Yet, full of adolescent optimism, she might misinterpret his response to her, mistaking his effort to remove some lint in his eye for a flirtatious wink.

Similarly, erotomanics also misjudge their objects' responses, filtering them through their psychotic prism, grossly distorting even the clearest rejections into declarations of love. Likewise, if the football captain happens to drop a piece of paper, our adolescent girl might scoop it up to sleep with under her pillow. She might even "stalk" him, to find out where his homeroom is or when he has a free period. As an adolescent, it must almost always stop there: she cannot really follow him home (she doesn't drive), and if he moves away she's unlikely to convince her parents to follow. This same "crush," harmless in these formative years, becomes ominous in adulthood, which brings with it the means to pull off much more intrusive, aberrant, and potentially violent stalking behavior.

Once all the factors are in place, i.e., a genetic or biological predisposition, a lack of nurturing in early development, and later life experiences as an adolescent and young adult that reinforce poor self-esteem and loneliness, some form of loss may occur as a triggering event before the erotomanic illness actually manifests. Patients with secondary erotomania may already have shown the signs and symptoms of their major mental illness before erotomanic delusions become apparent. So what triggers the specific development of erotomanic delusions in susceptible individuals? Erotomania has been theorized to be a form of mourning, with approximately 25% of recorded cases occurring after a significant loss (Evans et al., 1982). The attachment that is lost (the death of a parent or a pet, the loss of a job) seems to be one of particular importance, one which generated whatever tenuous self-esteem the erotomanic was capable of feeling. Without it, he or she becomes truly alone. Less tangible, but no less devastating losses such as experiencing a rape have also been theorized to be triggering events (Orion, 1997).

de Clerambault's Classification

After the triggering event occurs, it is only a matter of time before an object is latched onto and the choice of object may be influenced by cultural factors.

Starting with the father of erotomania, G. G. de Clerambault, a French psychiatrist, who was the first to systematically classify the disorder, much emphasis has been placed in the literature on the higher status or social desirability of the objects, as it is through them that erotomanics believe their unhappy lives can be magically transformed (Davis and Chipman, 1997, p. 166; de Clerambault, 1942).

For female erotomanics, this seems to hold true in the traditional way, as doctors, priests, celebrities, and CEOs are all favorite targets. For male erotomanics, a traditional view of female desirability also appears to be at work. Male erotomanics are much more likely to fixate on younger, attractive women. Perhaps there is a Darwinian principle in effect here with females biologically programmed to select strong, powerful men and thus usually older men, while their male counterparts feel the drive to choose physically desirable women of childbearing age.

Other cultural factors, such as media influences, also appear to be at work. Although it seems we have only recently started hearing about stalking and particularly erotomania, both have been around for millennia. The great Roman physician, Soranus, known for his humane treatment of the mentally ill, was the first to describe cases of erotomania, including one in which a man threw himself into the ocean, believing his nymph-goddess-object was waiting for him there. Since then, cases have appeared from time to time in the medical literature, although it was not until 1921 when de Clerambault reported erotomania (or de Clerambault's syndrome as it is still sometimes called) as a distinct syndrome with clear, identifiable characteristics.

Clearly, then, erotomania has always been with us. So, why does it seem as if so many more people, most visibly celebrities, are being plagued by erotomanic stalkers? Are there really more stalkers around or are we just hearing more about them? The answer probably lies in a combination of both: while we've seen that there have always been erotomanics, erotomanics themselves, along with the rest of us, have never had access to the variety of resources we have today, namely, planes, trains, and automobiles.

Even as recently as early in the last century, if an erotomanic developed a fixation on a celebrity, what could he or she really do about it? Telephones were not widely available, the mail system was unreliable, and transportation over any significant distance took so long that the object would likely be long gone by the time the erotomanic arrived. If you lived in America, for example, and were convinced that Napoleon was in love with you, you would be very unlikely to ever meet him, no matter your resolve.

Non-celebrity objects of long ago also had some protections not in force today. As a society, we are much more mobile than ever before. It used to be that we tended to be born, live, and die in the same village or town, and live with or near our extended families for our entire lives. So, if Ivan had an erotomanic fixation on Brunhilde, the maid he saw at market one week, his family might try to keep him at home, rather than risk the public embarrassment of his continually seeking her out and showing up at her home uninvited.

Role of the Media in Perceived Stalking

The media has also played an important role in the perceived increased incidence of stalking. One can imagine how those who already have difficulty separating reality from fantasy view a television program with a celebrity talking directly into the camera, seemingly directly to them. Particularly with the advent of interview and gossip shows, and of magazines devoting so much space to articles about celebrities, their homes, and their families, we may very well know more about celebrities than we do about our next-door neighbors.

Technology and Stalking

Technology provides an intimacy with complete strangers that has never been known before. And such immediate access is stimulating in itself: with live television, we can know what a celebrity did or said in the very moment we were watching, rather than reading about a distant event. This confers a certain immediacy, which in itself is stimulating. Due to my own experience being stalked, I cannot help cringing whenever celebrities bring out their kids or talk in detail about their personal lives. It seems to me that such intimate details are simply grist for the erotomania/stalker mill: the more they know, the more they think they know and, ultimately, the more they think the object really knows them.

Messages in the media also give the impression that "no" does not necessarily mean "no" and that it is perfectly okay for a man to pursue a woman, even after she has repeatedly rebuffed him. The recent award-winning movie, *The Piano*, perfectly illustrated this point, for didn't she come around in the end? Movies like *There's Something About Mary* also give the message that, ultimately, it is the woman's fault for being stalked, a sentiment that unfortunately many stalking victims are all too familiar with.

It has been theorized that the celebrities who seem the most approachable, who are more like the girl-next-door, are the ones who are most likely to be targeted by erotomanics. It might also be that when non-celebrities are stalked by erotomanics, part of what goes into the equation, in addition to being in the wrong place at the wrong time, is a perceived approachability and warmth. Any one of us who is asked what our ideal mate would be like is unlikely to list "cold" or "aloof" as attributes. Why should erotomanics be any different? If anything, since they fully believe their objects really are perfect, they do not perceive anything less.

Perhaps it is for this reason that so many therapists seem to have been stalked. One study found that 56% of psychiatrists who responded to a survey reported being stalked (Buckley and Resnick, 1994). There have also been cases of lawsuits against clinicians and disciplinary actions by professional boards due to allegations of sexual misconduct made by erotomanics, frustrated at being constantly rebuffed.

Treatment of Erotomanic Disorder

Treatment of erotomania is, unfortunately, in its infancy. Separation of the object from the erotomanic seems to be of paramount importance, as any contact only further stimulates the delusional system. Psychotherapy has not proven to be effective, probably because there simply is no way to convince the erotomanic that the object does not reciprocate his or her love. Other approaches, such as encouraging any activities that improve self-esteem (such as getting a job, doing volunteer work, etc.) and decrease isolation (such as attending group and other therapies, joining clubs, etc.), should be attempted. Although these will in all likelihood not impact the basic delusion of being loved, at the very least, such interventions will decrease, albeit by a small percentage, the amount of time the erotomanic spends thinking about and/or contacting the object.

At this time, medications seem to offer the best hope for treatment. Conventional psychiatric wisdom is that if the erotomanic delusions are "secondary," i.e., a result of a more global psychiatric disorder, the primary illness (schizophrenia, bipolar disorder, etc.) should be treated. If the patient truly suffers from delusional disorder, erotomanic type, the anti-psychotic drug Pimozide has been reported to decrease the force of the erotomanic delusions.

With any medication treatment, however, it is important to understand that often the best result that can be achieved is that the erotomanic delusions endure, although the patient is less compelled to act on them. As erotomania is a relatively uncommon subtype of stalking, it is unlikely that clinical studies on treatment approaches will be forthcoming any time soon. Still, case reports in the literature continue to be published, providing at least some guidance for clinicians.

When trying to quantify how many erotomanics are out there, it is important to realize that there are probably many who never come to attention because they never stalk their objects, but rather obsess about them endlessly in private. Two studies have estimated that 10% of all stalkers had delusional disorder, erotomanic type (Meloy and Gothard, 1995). If all patients with erotomanic delusions are counted, the numbers would certainly be higher and almost impossible to quantify.

The DSM-IV estimates that 0.03% of the population, or 3 in 10,000, have one of the five delusional disorders (American Psychiatric Association, 1994). One 1983 study estimated that of all patients with delusional disorders, approximately 10%, or 3 in 100,000, have the erotomanic type (Rudden et al., 1983).

Recently, a Department of Justice survey reported that 8% of all American women have been stalked, 22% of them by strangers and 19% by acquaintances (Tjaden, 1998). Presumably, many of these strangers and acquaintances were erotomanic.

Ultimately, numbers mean nothing if you are a victim. Eleven years ago, I treated a patient who could not let go, forever changing my life. She has called my office repeatedly, peeked in my windows, had me paged in the middle of the night, and followed me to another state. She has violated restraining orders dozens of times and has cumulatively spent over a year in jail. Still, she does not stop. I truly believe that the crime of stalking exists at a level where the crime of domestic violence was 20 years ago: people do not take it seriously enough, police do not arrest perpetrators often enough, judges do not impose appropriate punishment consistently enough, and mental health providers do not render treatment effectively enough.

Conclusion

The solution for all of these inadequacies, just like with domestic violence, is education. From education comes better laws, better enforcement, and, through research, better treatment. Although erotomania is the least common type of stalking, it should not be neglected.

Erotomanics are mentally ill and do require intensive treatment. However, we have yet to determine just what that approach to treatment is.

Bibliography

American Psychiatric Association (1994). *Diagnostic and Statistical Manual of Mental Disorders (DSM-IV)*, 4th ed. (p. 301). Washington, D.C.: American Psychiatric Association.

Berry, J. and Haden, P. (1980). Psychose passionnelle in successive generations, *British Journal of Psychiatry*, 137, 574–575.

Buckley, R. and Resnick, M. (1994). Stalking Survey: Oregon Psychiatric Society, Portland, OR, March 4–5, 1994. Unpublished manuscript in Lion, J. and Herschler, J., The stalking of clinicians by their patients, in J.R. Meloy (Ed.), *The Psychology of Stalking*. San Diego, CA: Academic Press.

Cameron, N. (1959). Paranoid conditions and paranoia, in A. Arieti (Ed.), *American Handbook of Psychiatry* (pp. 525–526). New York: Basic Books.

Chiu, H. (1994). Case report: erotomania in the elderly, *International Journal of Geriatric Psychiatry*, 9, 674.

Davis, J. A. and Chipman, M. A. (1997). Stalkers and other obsessional types: a review and forensic psychological typology of those who stalk, *Journal of Clinical Forensic Medicine*, 4, 166–172.

de Clerambault, G. G. (1942). *Ouvre Psychiatrique*. Paris: Presses Universitaires.

Doust, J. W. L. and Christie, H. (1978). The pathology of love: some clinical variants of de Clerambault's syndrome, *Social Science and Medicine*, 12, 99–106.

Dowd, D. (January 2, 1998). The slander strategy, *The New York Times*, Op Ed.

Drevets, W. C. and Rubin, E. H. (1987). Erotomania and senile dementia, Alzheimer type, *British Journal of Psychiatry*, 151, 400–402.

Enoch, M. D., Trethowan, W. H., and Barker, J. C. (1967). *Some Uncommon Psychiatric Syndromes*. Bristol, England: John Wright & Sons Ltd.

Evans, D., Jecket, J., and Slott, N. (1982). Erotomania: a variant of pathological mourning, *Bulletin of the Menninger Clinic*, 46, 507–520.

Strachey, J., translator (1958). Freud, S. *The Standard Edition of the Complete Psychological Works of Sigmund Freud*, Vol. 12, *The Case of Schreber: Papers on Technique and Other Works* (p. 63). London: Hogarth Press.

Greyson, B. (1977). Erotomanic delusions in a mentally retarded patient, *American Journal of Psychiatry*, 134, 325–326.

Gross, L. (1994). Psychiatric and sociological aspects of criminal violence: an interview with Park Elliott Dietz, M.D., Ph.D. II. Currents in affective illnesses XI (May 1992), as reported in L. Gross, *To Have or to Harm* (p. 157). New York: Warner Books.

Harmon, R., Rosner, R., and Owens, H. (1995). Obsessional harassment and erotomania in a criminal court population, *Journal of Forensic Sciences*, 40, 188–196.

Meloy, J. R. and Gothard, S. (1995). Demographic and clinical comparison of obsessional followers and offenders with mental disorders, *American Journal of Psychiatry*, 152, 258–263.

Menzies, R., Fedoroff, J., Green, G., and Isaacson, K. (1995). Prediction of dangerous behaviour in male erotomania, *British Journal of Psychiatry*, 166, 530.

Meyers, J. (1998). Cultural factors in erotomania and obsessional following, in J. R. Meloy (Ed.), *The Psychology of Stalking: Clinical and Forensic Perspectives* (pp. 213–224). San Diego, CA: Academic Press.

Meyers, J. and Meloy, J. R. (1994). Discussion of a comparative study of erotomanic and obsessional subjects in a forensic sample, *Journal of Forensic Sciences*, JFSCA 39, 905–907.

Murray, D., Harwood, P., and Eapen, E. (1990). Erotomania in relation to childbirth, *British Journal of Psychiatry*, 156, 896–898.

Nadarajah, J., Kidderminster, K., and Denman, C. (1991). Erotomania in an Asian male, *British Journal of Hospital Medicine*, 45, 172.

Orion, D. (1997). *I Know You Really Love Me* (p. 68). New York: Macmillan.

Orion, D. (February 2, 1998). Old slander strategy. *The New York Times*, Letters to the Editor.

Rudden, M., Sweeney, J., Frances, A., and Gilmore, M. (1983). A comparison of delusional disorders in women and men, *American Journal of Psychiatry*, 140, 1575–1578.

Rugeiyamu, F. K. (1980). De Clerambault syndrome (erotomania) in Tanzania, *British Journal of Psychiatry*, 137, 102.

Signer, S. (1987). de Clerambault's syndrome in organic affective disorder: two cases, *British Journal of Psychiatry*, 151, 404–407.

Tjaden, P. (November 1998). Prevalence, incidence, and consequences of violence against women: findings from the National Violence Against Women Survey, in *Research in Brief*. Washington, D.C.: National Institute of Justice.

Zona, M., Sharma, K., and Lane, J. C. (1993). A comparative study of erotomanic and obsessional subjects in a forensic sample, *Journal of Forensic Sciences*, JFSCA 38, 894–903.

About the Contributing Author

Doreen Orion, M.D.

Doreen Orion, M.D. is a board certified forensic psychiatrist on the faculty of the University of Colorado, Colorado Health Sciences Center. She completed her undergraduate education at Cornell University where she graduated with distinction. She attended medical school at George Washington University (GWU) and completed internship and residency in psychiatry at the University of Arizona.

Dr. Orion lectures extensively on stalking and erotomania on a national level. Her popular book, *I Know You Really Love Me: A Psychiatrist's Journal of Erotomania, Stalking and Obsessive Love*, was published by Macmillan in 1997. She has been featured in articles by the Associated Press, Gannet News, and *People Magazine*, and interviewed on numerous television shows, including "48 Hours with Dan Rather" and "Larry King Live."

Stalking, Stalkers, and Domestic Violence: Relentless Fear and Obsessive Intimacy

5

STEVEN F. ALBRECHT

Contents

Introduction

The connection between stalking and domestic violence certainly seems obvious enough. The classic scenario persists in the minds of most people who see these related subjects from their periphery. One party (most often the female) in a husband–wife or boyfriend–girlfriend relationship breaks the connection and leaves or attempts to leave. The "wounded" party (which statistics, observers, scholars, and law enforcement agree is usually the male) attempts or succeeds in "wounding" the victim, using harassment, covert and overt threats, vandalism, battery, or even fatal violence. If the perpetrator in this event were ever posed with the question, "Why?" the simple answer would probably refer back to a well-trotted cliché: "If I can't have her, then nobody will!"

Domestic Relationships and Stalking Typologies

As for the psychiatric disorder known as erotomania, where the gender roles are curiously reversed, stalking can be divided into two distinct but related typologies: those in which the male perpetrator knows the victim from a past intimate relationship and those where the male perpetrator sees the victim from afar and wants to establish a physical, sexual, or romantic relationship, which starts by trying to get the victim to notice him (Davis, 1998, 1999; Davis and Chipman, 1997). This book chapter will focus on the former stalker typology.

This intimacy, either real or imagined, and the acts and events that follow between the victim and the perpetrator become evident along many levels of a stalking case investigation (Davis, 1998, 1999; Davis and Chipman, 1997).

Domestic Violence, Stalking, and the Law

The legal definition for the crime of stalking demands that the perpetrator's behavior is both unwanted and able to put the victim in fear. Yet state Penal Code stalking definitions are austere, purposely legal sounding, and lack the spirit of the human element that establishes the crime.

As the Supreme Court Justice who defined obscene material as, "I know it when I see it," stalking appears to be a readily identifiable behavior. Yet do we always recognize stalking behavior when we see it, hear of it, or witness the impact upon the victims?

One of the leading textbook authors in the field of criminology admits that the attention paid to stalking in terms of scholarly research has not matched the effort given to other crimes or criminal trends. Curtis Bartol, a criminal justice professor at Castelton State College in Vermont, states in his seminal text, *Criminal Behavior: A Psychosocial Approach*, "Systematic information on stalking in the U.S. is limited, despite the attention it receives from the media and the legislatures" (Bartol, 1999, p. 18).

J. Reid Meloy, Ph.D., an associate professor of psychiatry at the University of California at San Diego who researches stalking, notes the dearth of current research in the area of stalking:

> Stalking, clinically labeled 'obsessional following,' has received an enormous amount of legal attention. Clinical research, however, has been meager. I reviewed the extant studies published during the past 25 years — 10 scientific papers involving 180 subjects — and offered, in part, the following preliminary findings: Individuals who engaged in stalking were usually above average IQ, single or divorced males in their 30's, with prior criminal, psychiatric, and drug abuse histories. They pursued women about their age, the majority of whom were prior acquaintances (neither former

sexual intimates nor complete strangers). Pursuits usually were accompanied by threats and lasted for months or years, likely inducing psychiatric symptoms, such as anxiety and depression, in many victims. Face-to-face contact, phone calls, and letters were the most frequent means of approach, but most stalking cases did not result in personal violence. If it did, the victim was pushed, grabbed, hit, punched, or fondled. Homicide was rare — less than two percent (Meloy, 1998, pp. 177–178).

The subject of stalking as a human activity holds an interesting place in our history. From a legal and punitive perspective, it is a recent phenomenon, with cases drawing public, legislative, and law enforcement attention as recently as 10 years past. But in an anthropological sense, it is as primal as the first relationships between pre-historic men and the women they coveted.

Stalking Data Are Still Being Collected

Stalking data are at heart preliminary; the problem is a new one, with statistical studies and reports certainly less than 15 years old and, more likely, less than 10. It is a problem as old as human existence, yet it has only been listed formally as a state and federal "crime" within the last 10 years or so.

As recently as 5 years ago, many states had no penal code law that expressly defined and prohibited the crime of stalking. Today, all 50 states and the District of Columbia have enacted such laws, with most modeling the first one, which was created and enacted in 1990 in California. There is a now-standard definition for stalking, which is referred to legally as "obsessional following" which places the victim or his or her family into a psychological or physical feeling of threatened harm or actual injury.

As of January 1, 1999, California legislators added the so-called "electronic" violations to the stalking law, giving it more teeth against perpetrators who used such creative harassment methods as "personalized" videos, telephone, cellular phone, e-mail messages, and even pager messages. As an example, the California Penal Code section for homicide is "187." It is not unusual for perpetrators to leave a variety of "187"-related text messages for their victims. No training in cryptography is necessary for recipients of these "You're Dead" codes.

Notable Stalking Cases

The public's most familiar connection to stalking is through the unwanted following, letter-writing, or harassing of celebrities, athletes, or political figures. Examples of these cases abound. The public accounts of stalking cross from television and movie stars to politicians to athletes: David Letterman, actor

Michael J. Fox, actress Theresa Saldana, Madonna, Steven Spielberg, political pundit George Stephanopoulous, basketballer Dennis Rodman, and radio personality Howard Stern. The on-court stabbing of tennis player Monica Seles by a disturbed "fan" was an outrageous act, exceeded only by the German court system's inability to convict him of the crime.

Domestic Stalking and Issues of Safety and Security

According to security experts who work in Hollywood, New York, Washington, D.C., and for the professional sports leagues and media conglomerates, nearly every well-known television or movie actor, media figure (including Internet-driven celebrities like Cindy Margolis), or politician has had to deal with several overzealous critics or fans who feel they have the right to try and insert themselves into the lives of the famous.

In July 1997, the U.S. Secret Service revealed that President Clinton's daughter, Chelsea, was the target of a man's unwanted letter-writing and following campaign. While we can expect the President of the United States to receive this kind of threatening attention, it's disturbing to consider his child is also subject to stalking.

Within that same month, former San Diego resident and spree murderer Andrew Cunanan, the subject of one of the most intense FBI and local law enforcement manhunts in recent history, appeared to have stalked designer Gianni Versace prior to killing him.

Threat Management of Domestic Stalking

According to the Los Angeles Police Department Threat Management Unit (LAPD-TMU) and other research sources, only about 17% of all active stalking cases involve victims who might be described as "celebrities." This leaves a victim pool of non-famous people who must suffer this obsessional behavior at the hands of people they know, knew, or have no bonafide connection to whatsoever.

Worse yet, not only do the non-celebrity victims lack the notoriety to attract out-of-the-ordinary police attention, but they often lack the financial resources to hire bodyguards, consult with security experts, or employ screening mail and telephone services like the famous victims.

And yet, paradoxically, even the so-called "Hollywood" types, with their access to the best security devices, guards, and advice money can buy, still feel threatened, afraid, and "stalked" by their admirers. If money, equipment, and trained professionals do not do very much to deter the determined celebrity-stalker, consider how difficult, uncomfortable, or even life-threatening a stalker can make life for an average citizen-victim in the community.

The Scope of the Stalking Problem

To look at the stalking problem with specificity, it helps to start with the subject of domestic violence in particular. Recent data regarding "intimate partner violence" (as it's referred to by the Bureau of Justice Statistics) suggest some intriguing trends. While there are no surprises in the gender of the victims vs. the perpetrators (as noted previously throughout this text, females as victims encompass about 85% of the incidents), the trend in terms of domestic violence homicides continues to decline. It is difficult to point to one reason for this continually lowering rate, e.g., national domestic violence and stalking awareness, more community programs, legislative awareness, mandatory arrests by police, mandatory treatment for batterers, etc.

While the numbers of female victims of intimate partner homicide *fell* between 1993 and 1997, the statistics show a dismaying 8% *increase* in female murders from 1997 to 1998. White females, for example, represent the only category of victims for whom intimate partner homicide has not substantially decreased since 1976. The number of intimate partner homicides for all other racial and gender groups declined during the period. Between 1997 and 1998 the number of white females killed by an intimate partner increased by 15% (Rennison and Welchans, 2000, p. 3).

To move back to the arena of stalking, statistics from a similar BJS 1998 report by the National Institute of Justice suggest that 8% of all adult women will be stalked in their lifetimes, a figure approaching 1.5 million at any one time. The number of males being stalked is placed, from the same report, at 400,000. Currently, the number of active suspects attached to the crime of stalking is said to be over 200,000 (Tjaden and Thoennes, 1998).

To put this into the harsh black-and-white parlance of the responding law enforcement officer or detective, domestic violence cases involving stalkers are at once both easy and difficult to manage. The easy part refers to the clear fact that very little "detecting" must take place; the perpetrator is rarely anonymous and even less often a total stranger than a spouse or boyfriend. In terms of most state statutes, for any crime to fall under the broad heading of "domestic violence," some sort of relationship, however brief, mild, or innocuous, had to have taken place between victim and suspect.

Domestic Stalking and Stalkers
— Law Enforcement Perspective

From the police perspective, the crimes of domestic violence and/or stalking are simple to manage because we know the parties involved. Fingerprints and mugshots are rarely necessary because the victim usually knows her attacker. From there, however, all the case management simplicities dissolve into the difficult part of these crimes, which starts and ends with the relationship itself. The complex nature of any domestic violence-stalking case centers itself around the connection, intimacy, and longevity of the parties' interest in each other.

And so we can point to many cases along a spectrum of these possibilities:

- The woman who goes on one non-sexual date with a co-worker, only to have him assault her in the company parking lot when she refuses a second date
- The high school-age girl who breaks up with her teenage boyfriend, only to have him threaten her, stalk her, and in an amazingly callous act, set fire to a room in her home, thereby killing an infant being babysat by her mother (an actual Los Angeles case tried by O.J. Simpson's prosecutor Christopher Darden)
- The wife who has a "one-night stand" with a man she meets in a bar, only to have him stalk, kidnap, and sexually assault her later for getting back together with her husband
- The woman with two young children, who simply wants to get away from her battering, stalking ex-husband and start fresh

All of these cases speak to the complexity of the relationship between the victim and the perpetrator. Whether the stalking behavior started after one date or culminated after decades of spousal abuse, the issue is the same as we have seen throughout this textbook: an attempt to seek revenge for a failed relationship (on the part of the perpetrator), and a pattern of repetitive, unwanted behavior that makes reasonable people fear for their safety.

Thus, many women faced with the prospect of a "won't quit" suitor, lover, or spouse will stay in humiliating, degrading relationships just to avoid what they correctly perceive will be their partners' tremendously over-involved reactions at the threat of their departure. As they deal with this rising onslaught of psychological and physical injury, some women resign themselves to a faint hope that their partners will change, self-correct, or otherwise alter their growing range of destructive behaviors. Or, more accurately, they wait, in the often futile hope that the partners will get tired of them and move on, without them having to push the issue of a breakup to a potentially deadly close.

As a professor and author on domestic violence at the University of British Columbia, Dr. Donald Dutton has accurately used the term "conjugal paranoia" to suggest the perpetrator's inability to let his partner live a life separate from his own. This desire for power and control, interwoven with the rationalizing power of extreme jealousy, gives the perpetrator permission to say or do anything necessary to prevent this woman from leaving his side (Dutton, 1995).

The intimacy, either real or imagined, between the acts, the victim, and the perpetrator becomes evident along many levels of a stalking case investigation. The legal definition for the crime of stalking demands that the perpetrator's behavior is both unwanted and able to put the victim in fear. Yet state penal code stalking definitions are austere, purposely legal-sounding, and lack the spirit of the human element that establishes the crime.

Domestic Stalkers, Mental Illness, and Mental Disorder

In their published works and speeches, a number of methodical researchers, national experts, and case management practitioners (such as Drs. Donald Dutton, J. Reid Meloy, Michael Zona, Paul Mullen, and Joseph Davis) speak to a number of psychological, psychiatric, and behavioral issues found in the *Diagnostic and Statistical Manual of Mental Disorders* (DSM-IV) (American Psychiatric Association, 1994). These include: paranoid personality disorder, borderline personality disorder, and the antisocial personality disorder or ASPD.

Researchers should refer directly to the DSM-IV for the verbatim diagnostic criteria. Briefly, the paranoid personality has a "pervasive distrust and suspiciousness of others such that their motives are interpreted as malevolent, beginning by early adulthood" (American Psychiatric Association, 1994, p. 637). This connection to domestic violence and stalking behavior seems clear: the paranoid can't bear to see his current or former beloved with another man. Since loyalty by his partner is a powerful issue, he won't tolerate any sense that he is being demeaned, threatened, or "cuckolded" by another man. The possibilities of violence with this type of individual bear noting, especially when he rationalizes it as "counterattacking" behavior.

The borderline personality engages in highly counter-intuitive behavior; he seeks the comfort of relationships to support his sagging self-esteem and yet he often destroys those relationships with his jealous, controlling, or sabotage behavior. This disorder describes "a pervasive pattern of instability of interpersonal relationships, self-image, and affects, and marked impulsivity beginning by early adulthood" (American Psychiatric Association, 1994, p. 654).

As Dutton's research has suggested, the overwhelming nature of the jealousy behavior serves to prove the borderline correct: the harder he attempts to control his partner, the more he drives her away. Her subsequent departure only reaffirms his belief that he must seek her out and "rescue" the relationship using any means. Violence by these individuals is triggered by their inability to control their rising anger.

Finally, the diagnosis for ASPD speaks to "a pervasive pattern for and violation of the rights of others ..." (American Psychiatric Association, 1994,

p. 649). In short, ASPD is an *interpersonal* issue, where the perpetrator feels little if any remorse regarding his actions and continually tramples on the feelings and emotions of his partner. In more severe cases, these perpetrators can unleash immediate and tremendous violence against their target in one moment and easily justify it in the next. The hallmark of the ASPD domestic violence-stalker is his use of the "Big Four," e.g., minimize, deny, rationalize, and blame.

As an example, police investigators who arrest a woman's former boyfriend for stalking her, forcing entry into her apartment, breaking her jaw, and setting her car on fire (a common property target for many stalkers) might hear the "Big Four" in the following ways: "I wasn't stalking her, I was only trying to get her to talk to me about my stereo and other property she refuses to give me. Besides, I didn't hit her that hard. She must've fell after I left. She makes me crazy! You'd do the same thing if you had to deal with her. I didn't burn her car. That was someone else. Anyway, it's her fault. If she hadn't broken up with me, none of this ever would have happened. She's brought it all on herself."

For the pure ASPD perpetrator, treatment is either limited or completely ineffective. Many of these stalkers will go to their graves convinced they have done nothing wrong. And given the opportunity (release from jail, parole, probation, a rehab or treatment hospital, etc.), they will continue their behavior unabated.

The following case should serve to illustrate the ASPD perpetrator — a threatener, stalker, domestic violence attacker, and murderer in action.

Stalking and Domestic Violence Homicide — Case Study of Albert Petrosky

In the span of one week in April 1995, Albert Petrosky's wife told him that she no longer loved him, she was having an affair with a co-worker, and she wanted a divorce.

Within 6 days Terry Petrosky was dead, shot at her Jefferson County, Colorado workplace by her enraged husband, who also shot and wounded her female friend, shot at an off-duty law enforcement agent, shot and killed her boss, and shot and killed a responding sheriff's sergeant. We know what happened and why it may have happened; what we do not know is if it could have been prevented through more proactive security and/or law enforcement measures.

At age 35, Albert Leonard Petrosky, Jr. began to feel more and more like a failure. A beefy, rarely employed auto mechanic, he spent most of his time in a local Denver tavern, drinking, arguing, and often fighting with the other patrons. As he watched his life pass him by, he began to search for someone other than himself to blame. He chose his wife Terry, 37, as the target of his resentment.

She worked as a service deli manager at a Jefferson County, Colorado supermarket. She was well liked by her co-workers, friendly to her customers, and deemed competent by her supervisors. Each of these traits only increased her husband's anger toward her. And while she may have had a good life at work, her home problems — namely, those caused by Albert — began to mount.

On Saturday, April 22, 1995, Terry Petrosky reached her marital breaking point; what she would tell her husband would soon help him reach his as well.

Terry Petrosky began that afternoon by telling her husband that she was having an affair with a co-worker and wanted an immediate divorce. In a rage, he threw her on their bed and began choking her and hitting her with his fists. After he broke her nose, she tearfully agreed to sign a notarized paper that surrendered all rights to their community property and gave him full custody of their 8-year-old son. She then fled their house in terror and spent the next days with friends. She did not call police to report the spousal abuse. This was not the first time her husband had used his fists against her. (Anecdotal evidence suggests that throughout their stormy relationship, Albert may have sexually assaulted his wife on several occasions as well.)

By Monday, April 24, 1995, Terry Petrosky realized that although she had not reported his most recent domestic violence assault on her, it was time to take steps. She called in sick to work, and that day applied for and received a temporary restraining order (TRO) against Albert.

Getting the restraining order was one thing; finding Albert to serve him was quite another. During the week that passed, court officers attempted to serve Petrosky, to no avail. He had left his house, moved in with his mother, and begun to prepare for a final showdown with his wife.

Terry Petrosky returned to work on Wednesday, April 26, and those who saw her facial injuries suddenly knew that her problems with Albert had escalated. Albert had called the store over the past days and asked to speak with her. One of her co-workers lied to him and said she wasn't working, to which he made the death threat, "That's it. I'm gonna take her out."

When Terry was notified of these threats, she met with her store director Dan Suazo, 37, at the store and told him of the previous battery and the impending restraining order against her husband. They discussed her continuing problems with Albert and he suggested she intensify her efforts to have authorities serve him with the TRO (county officials had just intervened to help her get custody of their 8-year-old son).

At that time, the store chain had no formal training in how to effectively intervene in issues related to workplace violence or domestic violence at work. Since the company had no explicit policies or procedures regarding these events, the individual store directors relied on their own experiences and discretion to deal with unruly or violent customers, disgruntled current or former employees, or their spouses or partners.

In retrospect with the Albert Petrosky case and others that have ended in workplace violence or death, we often learn in hindsight using this wait-and-see mode. In law enforcement or threat assessment circles, this approach is sometimes referred to as the "observe and monitor" phase. What we know now is that while Terry Petrosky and her boss, Dan Suazo, were discussing what to do about Albert, he was preparing for a violent, final confrontation.

As other workplace, mass-murder, family, or domestic violence homicide cases have illustrated, it's not unusual for the suspect to begin putting his "ducks in a row." While Denver authorities searched for him in vain to serve Terry's TRO, Albert was busy selling his van, his tools, his clothing, and most of his other possessions. He called his sister in Alaska, at least twice, crying into the telephone and asking her to "take care of his son if anything happened to him."

He (Petrosky) bought a new van — one he knew his wife wouldn't recognize — and shaved his head — a look he knew she despised. He also gathered an arsenal of weapons, including a .32 caliber revolver, a 9-mm semi-automatic pistol, an SKS assault rifle, and .50 caliber rifle.

Petrosky could best be described as a neighborhood bully. He was loud, large, and obnoxiously opinionated in everything from his demeanor to his body language. His comments to others (including a marriage counselor, who captured an eerily prescient videotape of the Petrosky couple in session nearly 2 years before his rampage) included statements like: "Nobody can top me in an argument or a fight," "I'm a 'damaged unit'," and "I spend eighty to ninety percent of my energy keeping myself under control."

He had one arrest for assaulting another man in a bar (no charges filed) and one arrest for drunken driving (alcohol counseling, suspended license). In odd ways, Petrosky chose to obey certain laws certain ways. When faced with his driver's license suspension, he began riding his bicycle to the bar where he drank (atypical behavior for most people who lose their licenses yet continue to drive and hope not to get caught). And on the day of the shootings, Petrosky took the time to park his van *next* to the disabled parking place (perhaps so as not to get a citation on the day he killed three people).

In terms of the seven diagnostic criteria listed to assess individuals with antisocial personality disorder, J. Reid Meloy, who served as an expert witness for the prosecution, stated that "evidence was sufficient to strongly suggest a DSM-IV diagnosis of antisocial personality disorder " (Meloy, 1997).

On Friday, April 28, 1996, Albert Petrosky waited in the store's parking lot for his wife to arrive for work. His van was parked near the only driveway entrance. He had been in position, waiting for her, for nearly 4 hours.

He watched as his wife's car entered the lot and drove near the front of the store. She was sitting in the passenger seat of her car, having agreed to loan it for the day to her friend, Misty Hudnall, age 23.

As Hudnall stopped near the store's doorways to let Terry Petrosky out, Albert swerved his van near her and jumped out, armed with his revolver. He cursed threats at her and shot her in the lower back as she tried to flee inside. Half crawling and running into the store, Terry headed for cover near the store director's check-cashing booth near the doors.

Albert continued firing at her, now armed with his 9-mm. He fired eight more shots at her as she tried to crawl away. Store director Dan Suazo looked out from his crouched position inside the booth just as Petrosky fired three fatal shots at him.

Albert Petrosky took a few seconds to survey his work inside the store and said nothing. Leaving the store, he saw Misty Hudnall, still driving Terry's car after she had doubled-back through the parking lot on her way out to the only exit. He fired four more 9-mm rounds at her, striking the pregnant woman in the calf. As she sped away to head for a telephone to call the police, Petrosky got into his van and drove it to the highest point in the parking lot and to wait for their inevitable arrival.

Sgt. Timothy Mossbrucker, 36, a father of six and a deputy from the Jefferson County Sheriff's Office, drove into the store parking lot after witnesses relayed the news of Albert's attack. As he steered his police car toward Petrosky's position at the high point of the lot, Petrosky opened fire on him with the SKS model assault weapon, hitting him with a 7.62-mm shot in the jaw.

This shot traveled a distance of over 300 feet, and yet Petrosky was still not finished. After spraying the parking lot and nearby store buildings with at least 15 other SKS rounds, he switched to a .50 caliber scope-mounted rifle, attached to a bipod so he could fire it from a prone ground position. Petrosky fired three more .50 rounds at Sgt. Mossbrucker's patrol car as it slowly crashed to a stop.

An off-duty IRS agent, Robert O'Callaghan, was heading into the store when he saw Petrosky firing. He drew his own gun and after he exchanged several shots with the suspect, Petrosky quickly gave up and was subdued by a construction worker, who sat on him until more sheriff's deputies could arrive.

Police interrogation videotape following Petrosky's arrest (post-Miranda) shows a man externalizing the blame for his situation onto other people, and more specifically, his wife. On tape, he made no apologies for his actions, no admission of guilt, remorse, or sorrow, either toward his wife or the other victims. His mood swung from tears to anger to a subdued state, and back to anger.

At one point, he calmly described his actions to a female officer in the room, quite matter of factly, and with little affect. In short, there is much evidence of the "Big Four" on the video.

In the end, Albert Petrosky had threatened, stalked, shot, and killed his estranged wife. He killed her boss and a responding law enforcement officer. He had shot and wounded Terry's friend, and shot at an off-duty armed IRS agent.

After a lengthy and emotional trial, he was convicted of his crimes. In a footnote to this incident, only 2 weeks before he was to be sentenced to several life terms, Albert Petrosky hung himself in his jail cell.

With the usual understanding that we cannot perfectly predict the future and knowing in advance that our crystal ball is usually cloudy, we must ask and answer the question, "What should we learn from the Petrosky case?"

In some of the most current data collected on the subject of stalkers who actually commit violence, Dr. Paul E. Mullen, a psychiatrist and stalking researcher based in Australia, has suggested that the following "predictors" of violence (itself a topic of much scrutiny in threat assessment circles) may help law enforcement, mental health, security personnel, etc. to better intervene (consider the Albert Petrosky case in terms of these stalking–violence correlates):

- A prior history of drug and/or alcohol abuse and/or dependence;
- A prior history of assaultive behavior against others;
- And prior sexual intimacy with the victim (Mullen et al., 1999, p. 1249).

Domestic Violence and Stalking: A Future Outlook

The future of stalking, as a national, social, legislative, female, workplace, and law enforcement issue, is neither grim nor encouraging. To be a victim in the decade of the 2000s is to benefit, unfortunately, from the battered lives and hard deaths of stalking victims in the long and near past. This is a sad truth and certainly part of the evolutionary process as we learn more about stalkers, their behaviors, and their victims.

Yet on the hopeful side, there are far more resources available to victims, advocacy groups, and law enforcement than ever in our history of this problem. Law enforcement's response has changed from, "Call us when he gets there" or "We can't do anything until he actually puts his hands on you," to "We'll be right there with an Emergency Protective Order and a home–work safety plan."

But these resources can't be used if actual or potential stalking victims do not take steps to assist in their own protection, education, and recovery. By the time the victim is hiding on the floor of a darkened apartment, hoping the perpetrator will stop banging on the door and leave, or driving with a carload of personal belongings in an attempt to flee the state, or finally present at the scene of her own homicide, it is too late to have any impact.

Yet the issues of many victims of stalking and domestic violence remain primary: when and who do I call? How bad does it have to be before I involve the police? My boss? My family? If I take some action against this person, will it make the situation better or worse?

Particularly frightening and confusing for the stalking victim is that she often recognizes that something is not right long before those around her, sometimes including law enforcement. David Beatty, an attorney with extensive legislative experience who is acting executive director of the National Victim Center (NVC) in Bethesda, Maryland, points out that even though the legal definitions of stalking vary from state to state, one thing that remains constant in the experience of victims is that "stalking begins *before* the legal definition kicks in ... You can be harassing and you can be threatening before your actions reach the level of the legal definition" (Douglas and Olshaker, 1998, p. 227).

What anti-stalking groups, many of which are founded by former and current victims of stalkers, emphasize is that a pattern of this unwanted behavior must be stopped through appropriate intervention. Like acquaintance rape, stalking is also disturbing because we like to believe we can pick dangerous people out in a crowd: we can recognize the bad guys and steer clear and we'll be safe. But by their very nature and success, sexual predators often look just like us; they don't look like ogres (Douglas and Olshaker, 1998, p. 228).

In any case, it is as difficult to predict the *domestic violence* stalker as it is to predict who will stalk in general. One of the most confounding tasks is to differentiate between the lover who cannot relinquish the relationship and the dangerous domestic violence stalker (Walker, 1997, p. 149).

The relationship between stalking and domestic violence is a given. Yet our response to these life-threatening problems continues to be a growing concern for a number of constituencies. The solutions to these painful cases start and end with educating victims, providing them with educational tools and resources so we can help them protect themselves, and focusing on finding, barring, controlling, treating, or incarcerating the perpetrators.

Bibliography

American Psychiatric Association (1994). *Diagnostic and Statistical Manual of Mental Disorders*, 4th ed. (DSM-IV). Washington, D.C.: American Psychiatric Association.

Bartol, C. (1999). *Criminal Behavior: A Psychosocial Approach*, 5th ed. Englewood Cliffs, NJ: Prentice Hall.

Davis, J. (June 1998). Stalker and Stalker Types: Forensic Mental Health and Public Safety Implications, District Attorney's Office of San Diego, Training Seminar and Workshop to Local Law Enforcement Agencies, San Diego, CA.

Davis, J. (September 1999). Stalking identity encounters: constructing a threat assessment profile, a safety plan and a case management strategy from a stalker typology. Break-out training session, Speaker and trainer, Third Annual District Attorney Stalking-the-Stalker Conference, September 23–24, 1999, Del Mar, CA.

Davis, J. and Chipman, M. (1997). Stalkers and other obsessional types: a review and forensic psychological typology of those who stalk, *Journal of Clinical-Forensic Medicine*, 4, 166–173.

Douglas, J. and Olshaker, M. (1998). *Obsession*. New York: Scribner.

Dutton, D. G. (1995). *The Batterer: A Psychological Profile*. New York: Basic Books.

Meloy, J. R. (1997). Predatory violence during mass murder, *Journal of Forensic Sciences*, 42(2), 326–329.

Meloy, J. R. (1998). Stalking and domestic violence, in *The Psychology of Stalking* (pp. 177–178). San Diego, CA: Academic Press.

Mullen, P. E., Pathé, M., Purcell, R., and Stuart, G. W. (August 1999). Study of stalkers, *American Journal of Psychiatry*. 156, 8 and 1249.

Rennison, C. M. and Welchans, S. (May 2000). Intimate Partner Violence. Washington, D.C.: U.S. Department of Justice, Office of Justice Programs, Bureau of Justice Statistics, U.S. Government Printing Office.

Tjaden, P. and Thoennes, N. (April 1998). Stalking in America. Washington, D.C.: U.S. Department of Justice, National Institute of Justice Centers for Disease Control and Prevention, U.S. Government Printing Office.

Venneman, J. (July 30, 1996). Telephone interview (with Joe Venneman), Boise, ID.

Walker, L. (1997). Stalking and domestic violence, in J. R. Meloy (Ed.). *The Psychology of Stalking*. San Diego, CA: Academic Press.

West, R. (July 18, 1996). In-person interview (with Sgt. Randy West), Jefferson County Sheriff's Office, Golden, CO.

About the Contributing Author

Steven F. Albrecht, DBA, CPP, PHR

Dr. Steven Albrecht, DBA, CPP, PHR is nationally known for his writing, training, and consulting efforts on the prevention of workplace violence, domestic violence, and stalking. He has a B.A. degree in English, a Doctorate degree in business administration, and an M.A. degree with distinction in security management. He holds the certifications "Professional in Human Resources" (PHR) from the Society for Human Resource Management and "Certified Protection Professional" (CPP) from the American Society for Industrial Security (ASIS). His 12 books include *Ticking Bombs* and *Fear and Violence on the Job* (along with Michael Mantell, Ph.D.).

Dr. Albrecht recently retired after 15 years with the San Diego Police Department, where he had worked as fulltime officer, reserve sergeant, and Domestic Violence Unit investigator. With the editor, Dr. Joseph Davis, he formerly served as a senior partner and as the San Diego-based vice president for The TAP Group, Inc., a Long Beach, California threat management firm.

Dr. Albrecht is now the president of The Baron Center, Inc., a San Diego-based workplace violence prevention, intervention, training, and organizational development firm.

Paradoxes of Pursuit: Toward a Relational Model of Stalking-Related Phenomena

BRIAN H. SPITZBERG
WILLIAM R. CUPACH

Contents

Introduction

In the last decade of the 20th century, a crime was born in a social milieu that had, in the previous millennia, never thought to have been sanctioned legally. This crime was born in the matrix of individual rights to privacy vs. the culture of celebrity and rights to speech. Thus, when star-struck and obsessed individuals used public means of transit and communication to intrude unwanted into the lives of celebrities, a fragile balance between the right to secure one's privacy began to unravel between the rights of others to acquire access to facets of public and private life.

When such intrusions crossed the line of ambiguity and into the realm of murder, as with Rebecca Lynn Schaeffer and the attempt on Theresa Saldana's life, society jumped to the cause of privacy. In the span of less than a decade, all 50 states and the federal government passed some form of anti-stalking legislation. Such a rapid deployment of legislative momentum reveals to some extent the power of celebrity and media (Lowney and Best, 1995; Monaghan, 1998; Way, 1994), and to some extent the fear evoked by the image of the stalker: a person who can invade your life in the most personal and persistent manner.

As with any phenomenon that is so relatively new in its societal, legal, and political recognition, there has been relatively little opportunity to understand and explicate the complex activity. Stalking and its related phenomena are still largely unexplored scientifically. However, in the last few years, a critical mass of research has begun to illuminate the structures, if not yet the dynamics, of such unwanted intrusions.

The vast majority of research to date has focused on forensic or counseling populations, or on victims of stalking or unwanted intrusion. This chapter intends to summarize what is currently known about these intrusive processes, and outline an interactional perspective that has been underrepresented in the literature. This interactional perspective focuses on those forms of stalking in which there is a previous or desired relationship that the stalker wants to establish with the object of pursuit. The perspective conceptualizes a process we refer to as obsessive relational intrusion, and examines the process as a disjunctive relationship sustained through patterns of interaction, the effects of which the participants may only be vaguely aware. In articulating this interactional perspective, we attempt to provide insights that will be both theoretically heuristic and personally pragmatic. What we want to make clear at the outset, however, is our belief that an interactional perspective in no way absolves the intruder of legal or ethical responsibility for any threats or harms inflicted upon the persons they pursue.

The havoc wrought upon a person's sense of privacy and safety is not excused by the fact that this person, as an object of unwanted pursuit, sometimes attempts to behave in a civil or relationally responsible manner.

Nature of Stalking and Obsessive Relational Intrusion

"Stalking describes a constellation of behaviors in which one individual inflicts on another repeated unwanted intrusions and communications" (Pathé and Mullen, 1997, p. 12). Legally, stalking entails "the willful, malicious, and repeated following and harassing of another person that threatens his or her safety" (Meloy and Gothard, 1995, p. 258). Such a definition generally requires legal demonstration of intent to harass, persistence of harassment over time, and some degree of demonstrable threat to the safety of the pursued or the pursued object's family or property. Although early media and legislative accounts constructed the prototype of stalking as the crazed loner obsessively pursuing the public celebrity into the celebrity's private life, research has clearly indicated that the typical stalking victim is the reader of this chapter, or this reader's next-door neighbor.

For several years we have been conducting research on a phenomenon closely related to stalking. Obsessive relational intrusion (ORI) is the "repeated and unwanted pursuit and invasion of one's sense of physical or symbolic privacy by another person, either stranger or acquaintance, who desires and/or presumes an intimate relationship" (Cupach and Spitzberg, 1998, pp. 234–235). ORI and stalking are largely overlapping, but not identical, sets. There are two key differences between these sets of activities. First, to be considered stalking, behavior must be threatening, whereas some ORI behavior may be viewed as harassing, annoying, frustrating, or aggravating, but not necessarily threatening. Research shows that a wide range of obsessively intrusive behaviors, even those actions commonly associated with courtship and intimacy, are viewed as at least somewhat threatening when initiated persistently by someone whose attentions are unwanted (Cupach and Spitzberg, 1997). Nevertheless, ORI is not always threatening. Second, to be considered stalking, behavior does not need to be in the pursuit of intimacy, whereas ORI behavior pursues intimacy by definition.

Thus, for example, a political or underworld assassin does not need to pursue a relationship with his or her target in order to stalk the target. In contrast, ORI consists of the pursuit of a more intimate relationship with the object of pursuit. Despite this difference, research shows that most stalking begins in the context of an established or previous relationship (Brewster, 1998; Burgess et al., 1997; Fisher et al., 1999; Fremouw et al., 1997; Gill and Brockman, 1996; Hall, 1997; Hill and Taplin, 1998; Kienlen et al., 1997; Kong, 1996; McCreedy and Dennis, 1996; New Jersey State Police, 1997; Nicastro et al., 2000; Schwartz-Watts et al., 1997; Spitzberg and Rhea, 1999; Tjaden and Thoennes, 1998; Tucker, 1993).

Thus, although stalking and ORI are technically distinct concepts, the majority of stalking cases consist of obsessive relational intrusion, and many if not most of ORI cases can be considered forms of stalking, even if they might not meet strict legal tests as such in a court of law.

Stalking and ORI can be understood initially as consisting of structures and processes. Structures represent the basic units by which the phenomenon is classified. For example, who are the perpetrators, who are the victims, what are their demographics, what are the basic types of stalking, its motives, and predictors? Processes are the patterns and types of action over time, such as tactics, relationship types, frequency, duration, and types of coping initiated by the object of pursuit. Before a interactional model of ORI can be developed, it is important to specify what is currently known about the structure and processes of stalking and obsessive relational intrusion.

As of this writing, there have been at least 50 publicly available studies that in one way or another represent stalking or ORI. The review that follows is based primarily on abstractions across a selected set of these studies, the sample descriptions of which are summarized below:

- 187 recent former female stalking victims (Brewster, 1998)
- 120 felony domestic violence cases (Burgess et al., 1997)
- 356 domestic violence cases, of which 5 were charged with stalking (Buzawa et al., 1998)
- 141 college students, convenience sample (Coleman, 1997)
- 51 human resource or medical officer staff at government sites across the country reporting on a collective employee population of about 96,000 workers (Eisele et al., 1998)
- 1752 college students, convenience sample (Elliott and Brantley, 1997)
- 38 persons perpetrating 40 incidents of workplace violence in a medical setting (Feldman et al., 1997)
- Interview of nationally representative sample of 1000+ student colleges, comprising 4446 female respondents randomly selected from student lists (Fisher et al., 1999)
- Study 1: 294 college students; study 2: 299 college students, convenience sample (Fremouw et al., 1997)
- 504 Chief Student Affairs officers at 4-year North American universities (Gallagher et al., 1994)
- 601 criminal harassment Canadian cases from 1993–1996 (Gill and Brockman, 1996)
- 145 victims, convenience sample (Hall, 1997)
- 48 cases referred to clinic for harassment/menacing (Harmon et al., 1995)
- 175 forensic psychiatry clinic records of obsessional harassers (Harmon et al., 1998)
- 103 college females, convenience sample (Herold et al., 1979)
- 172 adults randomly selected from Perth, Australia (Hills and Taplin, 1998)

- 50 females recruited who had been harassed by a dumped paramour (Jason et al., 1984)
- 25 forensic stalking cases (Kienlen et al., 1997)
- 7472 cases charged with criminal harassment in Canada, 1994–1995, comprising 7462 incidents and 5382 perpetrators; most analyses based on sample of 5023 of incidents (Kong, 1996)
- 527 college students, faculty, and staff (Leonard et al., 1993)
- 343 college students, convenience sample (Levitt et al., 1996)
- 54 cases charged with criminal harassment in Canada (Lyon, 1997)
- 760 college students, convenience sample (McCreedy and Dennis, 1996)
- 141 femicide and 65 attempted femicide cases, based on proxy interviews and police records from 10 U.S. cities (McFarlane et al., 1999)
- Review of 10 previous studies of forensic or counseling case studies (Meloy, 1996)
- 20 obsessional followers compared to 30 non-stalking offenders (Meloy and Gothard, 1995)
- 586 North Carolina femicide case records (Moracco et al., 1998)
- 16 erotomanic cases (Mullen and Pathé, 1994a)
- 14 erotomanic cases (Mullen and Pathé, 1994b)
- 145 forensic psychiatric clinic referral stalkers (Mullen et al., 1999)
- 861 female college students, convenience sample (Mustaine and Tewksbury, 1999)
- All reported domestic violence stalking offenses, 1995–1997 (New Jersey State Police, 1997)
- 55 City Attorneys' Office domestic violence case files (Nicastro et al., 2000)
- 223 threat management cases from Los Angeles (Palarea et al., 1999)
- 100 victims of stalking (Pathé and Mullen, 1997)
- 178 counselors (Romans et al., 1996)
- 561 adolescent students, convenience sample (Roscoe et al., 1994)
- 17 psychiatric inpatients who had stalked, threatened, or harassed staff after discharge (Sandberg et al., 1998)
- 18 pretrial detainees charged with stalking compared with 18 matched non-stalker detainees (Schwartz-Watts et al., 1997)
- 242 stalking cases from Delaware's Criminal Justice Information files (Scocas et al., 1996)
- 240 stalking case files from Michigan, 1992–1997 (Spencer, 1998)
- 300 college students, convenience sample (Spitzberg and Cupach, 1996)
- 360 college students, convenience sample (Spitzberg and Rhea, 1999)
- 16,000 adults, national probability sample (Tjaden and Thoennes, 1998)
- 90 Florida agencies surveyed, including university police departments (Tucker, 1993)
- 36 college students, convenience sample (Westrup et al., 1998)

- 30 stalking cases (Wright et al., 1996)
- 74 Los Angeles Threat Management Unit cases (Zona et al., 1993)

Despite the diversity of samples, with a few notable exceptions (e.g., Hall, 1997; Hills and Taplin, 1998; Tjaden and Thoennes, 1998), most can be classified as forensic (criminal, suspect, case files), therapeutic (counseling, clinic patients), college (student), or workplace (employee) samples, and most of these employed available or convenience samples. Although some studies produce data on both suspected pursuers and victims, no study to date has elicited data from both the stalker and the stalker's object of pursuit simultaneously. That is, no study has yet treated the stalking process as a truly relational or dyadic phenomenon.

Structure of Stalking and Obsessive Relational Intrusion

Of incidence rate across a variety of studies employing convenience samples, approximately 15 to 20% of people report that they have been stalked (n = 7 studies). When the question is phrased more liberally, such as "followed," "harassed," "receiving persistent phone calls," or experiencing a troublesome "possessive relationship," the incidence rate tends to be substantially higher (approximately 28% across 4 studies). When people in positions to deal with large numbers of people (e.g., human resources managers, counselors, etc.) are asked whether any of their clients have been stalked or obsessively followed or harassed, as many as a third claim to have known or intervened in cases in the previous year (Gallagher et al., 1994), and as many as 15% have been stalked themselves (Romans et al., 1996). Certain populations seem rife with stalking, in which stalking seems to be one of the profile character-istics, such as domestic violence, sexual harassment experiences, and femicide (Leonard et al., 1993; McFarlane et al., 1999; Moracco et al., 1998). Finally, when the question is specifically asked in terms of obsessive relational intru-sion, between 2 and 50% of college students report prior victimization (Cupach and Spitzberg, 1998). The only large-scale nationally representative study to date reports an incidence of stalking of 8% for women and 2% for men (Tjaden and Thoennes, 1998).

The variability in duration of stalking relationships is extensive, ranging from days to 20 years (e.g., Brewster, 1998; Fisher et al., 1999; Hall, 1997; Jason et al., 1984; Mullen et al., 1999; Pathé and Mullen, 1997; Sandberg et al., 1998; Spitzberg and Cupach, 1996; Spitzberg and Rhea, 1999; Zona et al., 1993), with the Tjaden and Thoennes (1998) study reporting an average of 1.8 years per stalking relationship. The frequency with which such rela-tionships intrude into the object's life varies substantially as well. Some studies report one to several intrusions per week (e.g., Fisher et al., 1999; Jason et al., 1984), and other studies simply report the total numbers of intrusions, with a majority involving more than 20 contacts or intrusions (e.g., Gill and Brockman, 1996; Kienlen et al., 1997). Other studies simply report that 25 to 35% of cases have experienced prior incidents of stalking (e.g., Burgess et al., 1997; Nicastro et al., 2000).

Thus, the lower bounds of stalking incidence is approximately 2% for men and 8% for women, and the upper bounds appear to be between 25 and 50%. By either parameter, it is clear that obsessive, persistent following, harassing, and pursuit appear to be relatively common in our culture and certainly represent a problem of significant proportions. These incidence statistics lend credence to the notion that aggressive persistence in the pursuit of relational intimacy is a widely accepted cultural norm of courtship (Cupach and Spitzberg, 1998).

Gender Distribution

The general assumption seems to extend from domestic violence models of gender relations that women are the disproportionate victims of stalking. In general, however, this trend is more reflective of studies the more forensic, counseling-based, and the more legalistically formal their definition of stalking. Thus, such studies would indicate that approximately 80 to 90% of all victims of stalking are female (e.g., Burgess et al., 1997; Feldman et al., 1997; Fisher et al., 1999; Gill and Brockman, 1996; Hall, 1997; Kienlen et al, 1997; Kong, 1996; Lyon, 1997; McCreedy and Dennis, 1996; Meloy, 1996; Meloy and Gothard, 1995; New Jersey State Police, 1997; Nicastro et al., 2000; Palarea et al., 1999; Pathé and Mullen, 1997; Sandberg et al., 1998; Scocas et al., 1996; Schwartz-Watts et al., 1997; Spencer, 1998; Zona et al., 1993; cf. Hills and Taplin, 1998). In contrast, some studies of college populations, in which obsessive relational pursuit, harassment, or intrusion is the criterion, reveal non-existent or substantially less substantial sex differences in victimization (e.g., Fremouw et al., 1997; Harmon et al., 1995; Spitzberg and Cupach, 1996; Spitzberg and Rhea, 1999). The converse of these statistics also seems to follow. That is, most of these same studies show that the vast majority of pursuers are male, and this trend is more evident in the studies with more forensic, therapeutic, and legalistically oriented criteria (e.g., Harmon et al., 1998). Indeed, in an unexpected finding of the Tjaden and Thoennes (1998) study, even most of the pursuers of male victims were themselves reported as male.

Relationship Status

Evidence is relatively consensual that a majority of stalking relationships emerge as vestiges of some prior form of relationship, such as married, cohabiting, seriously dating or engaged, casual dating, friendships, or acquaintanceships, such as work colleagues or fellow students (Brewster, 1998; Burgess et al., 1997; Feldman et al., 1997; Fisher et al., 1999; Fremouw et al., 1997; Gill and Brockman, 1996; Hall, 1997; Harmon et al., 1995; Harmon et al., 1998; Hill and Taplin, 1998; Kienlen et al., 1997; Kong, 1996; Lyon, 1997; McCreedy and Dennis, 1996; McFarlane et al., 1999; Mullen and Pathé, 1994a; Mullen et al., 1999; New Jersey State Police, 1997; Nicastro et al., 2000; Pathé and Mullen, 1997; Sandberg et al., 1998; Schwartz-Watts et al., 1997; Spencer, 1998; Spitzberg and Rhea, 1999; Tjaden and Thoennes, 1998; Tucker, 1993). Unfortunately, studies tend to use non-comparable terms and filter questions in reporting relationships between victim and pursuer, so it is difficult to generalize across specific categories. However, the extent to which stalking emerges from previous or current relationships is suggestive that stalking tends to revolve around a fulcrum of motives to re-establish a prior relationship, create a preferred new relationship, or retaliate against a former partner for perceived transgressions in a previous relationship.

These motives are not necessarily mutually exclusive, as stalking and obsessive relational intrusion may well involve highly ambivalent and transient motive states on the part of the pursuer.

Motives

Perhaps nowhere is the relational nature of most stalking and ORI more evident than in the examination of attributed motives for pursuit. Given that pursuit occurs in the face of repeated rejection and failure to obtain the object of pursuit, the question of motive becomes particularly diagnostic. Jealousy is commonly attributed (14%, Brewster, 1998; 27%, Hall, 1997; 24% of non-psychotic stalkers, Kienlen et al., 1997; 18%, Nicastro et al., 2000), as are anger (31%, Harmon et al., 1995; 65% Kienlen et al., 1997; 16%, Nicastro et al., 2000), retaliation, or revenge (45%, Brewster, 1998; 32%, Hall, 1997; Mullen et al., 1999; Wright et al., 1996). All of these imply a sense of previous relational transgression. Other common motives attributed to the pursuer include trying to initiate intimacy (23%, Hall, 1997; 63%, Harmon et al., 1995; Mullen et al., 1999), refusing to accept the end of the relationship (Brewster, 1998; Hall, 1997), reconciliation (75%, Brewster, 1998; 40%, Nicastro et al., 2000), possessiveness (27%, Brewster, 1998; 33%, Wright et al., 1996), obsession, and infatuation (56%, Hall, 1997; 47%, Kienlen et al., 1997; 20%, Wright et al., 1996). Only a minority of cases are attributed with being purely power oriented, sexually oriented, intimidating, or predatory (Brewster, 1998; Kienlen et al., 1997; Mullen et al., 1999; Nicastro et al., 2000).

In short, the motive structure attributed to obsessive and unwanted pursuit tends, in the great majority of cases, to reflect a misguided desire for a type of relationship the object of pursuit does not want to reciprocate. Importantly, it is this very motive structure that helps to explain a paradox that love often begets aggressiveness in obsessive relational pursuit and stalking. The question often arises why people who care about and often idolize the object of their pursuit can simultaneously be so threatening and violent toward the same person. The answer, it seems, is in part because the object of pursuit is the source of so much frustration by denying the very thing that motivates the pursuer in the first place.

Thus, the pursuer seeks a new relationship, or to restore an old relationship, and this is precisely the state of affairs that the object of pursuit actively obstructs. Frustration and anger thereby serve to fuel obsessive pursuit that often turns threatening and injurious, even in the context of what the pursuer views as "courtship."

Types of Stalkers

One of the natural inclinations of clinicians and law enforcement scholars is to classify stalkers by certain characteristics. Such a classification system, if successful, helps to identify marker characteristics that both assist with diagnosis and prediction based on limited preliminary information, and also facilitate intervention efforts. To date, most typologies have tended to be based either on relatively clinical factors, such as the existence or non-existence of delusional states (e.g., believing the object of pursuit is in love with the pursuer), or on relatively structural factors such as whether or not there had been a previous relationship (e.g., Batza and Taylor, 1999; Cupach and Spitzberg, 1998; Emerson et al., 1998; McCann, 1998a; Roberts and Dziegielewski, 1996; Zona et al., 1998; Davis, 1998, 1999; Davis and Chipman, 1997; Holmes and Holmes, 1998; Holmes, 1993).

Other typologies identify stalkers by their underlying motive, such as amorous or persecutory (e.g., Harmon et al., 1998). Still other typologies use these characteristics, but also recognize variations on these themes, such as celebrity or public figure stalking (Batza and Taylor, 1999; Davis, 1999; Davis and Chipman, 1997; Holmes, 1993; Holmes and Holmes, 1998), scorned or rejection based (Batza and Taylor, 1999; Mullen et al., 1999), or purely strategic or predatory stalking (Holmes, 1993; Mullen et al., 1999; Davis, 1999; Davis and Chipman, 1997; Holmes and Holmes, 1998; Holmes, 1993).

Few typologies formulate stalker types based on the intersection between underlying characteristics and dimensional factors. However, Sapp (1996) as well as Davis and Chipman (1997) have attempted to base varying typologies on the type of relationship to the victim (none to intimate), mental health problems (slight to high), and the potential or likelihood of violence (limited to very high). Stalker types are identified in several broad categories.

First, *erotomanic: target unknown* stalkers include random-targeting stalkers (no relationship, high mental health problems, limited likelihood of violence), high profile or celebrity-targeting stalkers (no relationship, high mental health problems, limited likelihood of violence), and the isolated or single-issue targeting stalkers (no or slight relationship, moderate mental health problems, moderate likelihood of violence). The latter type reflects the person who links the object of his or her pursuit to a particular political or social issue or matter important to the stalker or pursuer.

Second, *love obsessional: target known* stalkers are either casual acquaintance (slight relationship, moderate mental health problems, moderate likelihood of violence) or co-worker-targeting (moderate relationship, moderate mental health problems, moderate likelihood of violence) stalkers.

Finally, *simple obsessional: target former intimate* stalkers include intimate partner-targeting stalkers (intimate relationship, slight mental health problems, high likelihood of violence) and domestic violence-targeting stalkers (extended/intimate relationship, slight mental health problems, very high likelihood of violence).

Furthermore, Davis and others (1998, 1999; Davis and Chipman, 1997), in their comprehensive review of the literature on stalking and stalkers, suggested that typologies should collectively represent a classification schema with a combination of several features and characteristics that involve the following: *geographic engagement and encounter* (work, recreational site, entertainment site, etc.), *style or type of communication approach* to the target victim or victims (written, verbal, non-verbal, electronic, internet, etc.), *behavioral indicators* (predatory, obsessive intrusional following, histrionic, manipulative, exploitative, voyeuristic, etc.), *psychiatric diagnosis* (erotomanic, delusional, antisocial personality, borderline personality disorder, paranoid schizophrenia, etc.), *relational status* (prior or former relation, current relation, non-existent relationship, fantasy-based relationship, etc.), as well as *threat assessment indicators* (threatening non-violent, threatening violent, etc.).

To date, stalker typologies generally have not been based on any formal system per se involving the intersection of specific underlying dimensions. However, an exception is a typology proffered by Wright et al. (1996), based on a small sample of law enforcement stalking files, in which they distinguished non-domestic and domestic (relationship dimension) and underlying motive structure (non-domestic organized and non-domestic delusional vs. domestic non-delusional and domestic delusional).

We find this typology wanting on several counts. First, the terminology "domestic" is anachronistic. Much stalking and ORI occur in dating and pre-dating contexts only remotely related to "domestic" contexts. Second, we believe the notion of delusion, while useful in a purely clinical sense, does not provide a very useful distinction in the context of the powerful rationalization

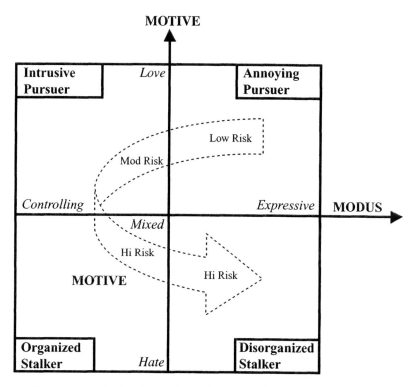

Figure 6.1 A Formal Typology of Stalker and Obsessive Relational Intrusion (ORI) Types

and paradoxical thought persistence that typify so much obsessional pursuit. In other words, virtually all stalking and ORI, by definition, imply distortions of thought processes that suggest at least a powerful capacity for self-deception, if not outright moments of delusion.

Finally, the Wright et al. typology is strangely asymmetric. The one dimension (relationship) distinguishes domestic from non-domestic cases, but it is unclear why there are organized non-domestic cases, but not organized domestic cases. In other words, the second dimension upon which the typology splits is ambivalent. We find the notion of the "organization" of stalking behavior to be more diagnostic than whether or not a stalker is delusional per se. Given these concerns, we believe a formal typology is possible, and needed.

Figure 6.1 illustrates a formal typology of stalkers and obsessive relational intruders. The typology is formed by the intersection of two underlying dimensions. The horizontal dimension, modus, distinguishes expressive from instrumental behavior as the character of the means of pursuit. This distinction is common in the violence literature (Tedeschi and Felson, 1994; Ressler et al., 1988; Wright et al., 1996) and concerns whether the pursuer is reacting primarily to emotional impulse or to strategic and intentional plans. The vertical dimension, motive, concerns the affective intentions of the pursuer, distinguishing between primarily amorous intentions vs. antagonistic intentions.

Presumably, these dimensions reflect a matrix of attributes and behavioral characteristics. The more characteristics, the more extreme the pursuer falls upon the continuum. At the extreme ends of these dimensions would be the more pure types, whereas people who fall more toward the intersection of these dimensions suggest a complex blend. We suspect that the unpredictable pursuers are unpredictable in large part because their underlying motive structure is ambivalent or mixed. Further, we predict that the types of pursuers defined by the top half of the typology are generally less of a threat than the pursuers defined by the bottom half of the typology. In other words, pursuers who have primarily antagonistic motives are likely to be more dangerous whether organized or disorganized in their actions. The organized pursuer carefully plans attacks that may be calculated to intimidate or otherwise harm, whereas the disorganized pursuer flies into unpredictable rages against the object of pursuit.

The types of pursuer defined by this typology are therefore labeled according to a sense of their characteristic mode and motive of pursuit. The *annoying pursuer* is someone who desires intimacy with someone, but merely selects ways of expressing this desire. This is the pursuer who is likely to pester a person with gifts, notes, calls, and a variety of misguided intimacy attempts. Given the fundamentally positive affective orientation, this person is unlikely to become much more than a nuisance to the object of pursuit.

Slightly more threatening is the *intrusive* pursuer, who is more calculating and strategic in attempting to engineer intimacy with the reluctant object of pursuit. Seeking ever new ways and contexts in which to manipulate an opportunity for the pursued person to "realize" how inevitable a relationship with the pursuer is, the pursuer concocts more intrusive situations in which to make his or her affections known. Such intrusiveness is likely to go beyond mere incompetence and awkwardness to brazen intrusions into the pursued person's life.

In making the transition from pursuit to stalking, the additional condition of "threat" must be fulfilled, and this seems far more likely when the motive structure underlying the pursuit has shifted from affection to antipathy. While relatively few stalkers are likely to feel purely antagonistic toward the object of their pursuit, the more often they feel hatred, frustration, anger, vengefulness, or embarrassment in regard to the object, the more antagonistic their motive structure is likely to become. When this occurs, the tone and nature of pursuit behavior are much more likely to be intermixed with activities designed to intimidate or threaten the object of pursuit.

By implying the potential hazards of *not* accepting the pursuer's defini-tion of the relationship, the pursuer hopes to persuade (i.e., coerce) the object of pursuit into the preferred relationship. In the case of the organized stalker, these acts of intimidation are more likely to display careful planning, prep-aration, management of time and place, and generally considerable informa-tion about the life of the person pursued. In contrast, the disorganized stalker is someone who by chance of encounter is more likely to simply lose control, to fly into a rage stimulated by a combination of anger and shame (Canary et al., 1998; Retzinger, 1991).

Such disorganized stalking is less likely to display the carefully managed scene, and more likely to be a product of jealousy of seeing the object with someone else, of anger resulting from an argument with the object, or of reaching the limit of patience and frustration and reacting on impulse. We admit that this "armchair" typology is at this point untested, but we also believe it is a more sensible typology than most currently available, and because it is based in large part on the diagnostic information available in pursuit behavior rather than personality or mental illness information, we anticipate that even-tually it may be more pragmatically useful in predicting threat.

Stalking and Stalker Tactics

Several studies have investigated the specific tactics of intrusion and stalking (Brewster, 1998; Burgess et al., 1997; Cupach and Spitzberg, 1998; Fisher et al., 1999; Gill and Brockman, 1996; Hall, 1997; Jason et al., 1984; Kienlen et al., 1997; McFarlane et al., 1999; Meloy and Gothard, 1995; Mullen and Pathé, 1994a; Mullen and Pathé, 1994b; Mullen et al., 1999; Nicastro et al., 2000; Palarea et al., 1999; Pathé and Mullen, 1997; Sandberg et al., 1998; Tjaden and Thoennes, 1998; Tucker, 1993). Unfortunately, there is relatively little commonality in the tactic phrasings employed across studies. For exam-ple, any given study may use the generic term "threat," whereas others may differentiate "threat against self," "threat against loved ones, family, or friends," and "threat against property or possessions." Some studies may examine "following" whereas others may distinguish "following in a car," "following to work or school," and "following home."

Consequently, specifying valid percentages of people experiencing spe-cific tactics of stalking and intrusion is difficult. However, Table 6.1 displays a representative cross section of tactics of both obsessive relational intrusion and cyberstalking activities, based on self-report surveys developed by Spitzberg and colleagues. These surveys were developed to reflect the breadth of both the "mundane" as well as the more horrifying aspects of unwanted intrusion, and yet be relatively parsimonious. Consequently, within each type

Table 6.1   Strategies and Tactics of Obsessive Relational Intrusion and Cyberstalking

Obsessive Relational Intrusion Strategies (Tactics)

- Leaving unwanted gifts (e.g., flowers, stuffed animals, photographs, jewelry, etc.)
- Leaving unwanted messages (e.g., notes, cards, letters, voice-mail, messages with friends, etc.)
- Making exaggerated expressions of affection (e.g., saying "I love you" after limited interaction, doing large and unsolicited favors for you, etc.)
- Following you around (e.g., following you to or from work, school, home, gym, daily activities, etc.)
- Intruding uninvited into your interactions (e.g., "hovers" around your conversations, offers unsolicited advice, initiates conversations when you are clearly busy, etc.)
- Invading your personal space (e.g., getting too close to you in conversation, touching you, etc.)
- Involving you in activities in unwanted ways (e.g., enrolling you in programs, putting you on mailing lists, using your name as a reference, etc.)
- Invading your personal property (e.g., handling your possessions, breaking and entering into your home, showing up at your door or car, etc.)
- Intruding upon your friends, family, or co-workers (e.g., trying to befriend your friends, family, or co-workers; seeking to be invited to social events, seeking employment at your work, etc.)
- Monitoring you and/or your behavior (e.g., calling at all hours to check on your whereabouts, checking up on you through mutual friends, etc.)
- Covertly obtaining private information (e.g., listening to your message machine, taking photos of you without your knowledge, stealing your mail or e-mail, etc.)
- Physically restraining you (e.g., grabbing your arm, blocking your progress, holding your car door while you're in the car, etc.)
- Engaging in regulatory harassment (e.g., filing official complaints, spreading false rumors to officials [boss, instructor, etc.], obtaining a restraining order on you, etc.)
- Stealing or damaging valued possessions (e.g., you found property vandalized; things missing, damaged, or hurt that only this person had access to, such as prior gifts, pets, etc.)
- Threatening to hurt him- or herself (e.g., vague threats that something bad will happen to him- or herself, threatening to commit suicide, etc.)
- Threatening others you care about (e.g., threatening harm to or making vague warnings about romantic partners, friends, family, pets, etc.)
- Verbally threatening you personally (e.g., threats or vague warnings that something bad will happen to you, threatening personally to hurt you, etc.)
- Leaving or sending you threatening objects (e.g., marked up photographs, photographs taken of you without your knowledge, pornography, weapons, etc.)
- Showing up at places in threatening ways (e.g., showing up at class, office, or work, from behind a corner, staring from across a street, being *inside* your home, etc.)
- Sexually coercing you (e.g., forcefully attempted/succeeded in kissing, feeling, or disrobing you, exposed him/herself, forced sexual behavior, etc.)
- Physically threatening you (e.g., throwing something at you, acting as if she/he will hit you, running finger across neck implying throat slitting, etc.)
- Physically hurting you (e.g., pushing or shoving you, slapping you, hitting you with fist, hitting you with an object, etc.)
- Kidnapping or physically constraining you (e.g., by force or threat of force, trapped you in a car or room; bound you; took you places against your will, etc.)

Table 6.1 (continued)   Strategies and Tactics of Obsessive Relational Intrusion and Cyberstalking

- Physically endangering your life (e.g., trying to run you off the road, displaying a weapon in front of you, using a weapon to subdue you, etc.)

Cyberstalking Strategies (Tactics)

- Sending tokens of affection (e.g., poetry, songs, electronic greeting cards, praise, etc.)
- Sending exaggerated messages of affection (e.g., expressions of affections implying a more intimate relationship than you actually have, etc.)
- Sending excessively disclosive messages (e.g., inappropriately giving private information about his/her life, body, family, hobbies, sexual experiences, etc.)
- Sending excessively "needy" or demanding messages (e.g., pressuring to see you, assertively requesting you go out on date, arguing with you to give him/her "another chance," etc.)
- Sending pornographic/obscene images or messages (e.g., photographs or cartoons of nude people, people or animals engaging in sexual acts, etc.)
- Sending threatening written messages (e.g., suggesting harming you, your property, family, friends, etc.)
- Sending sexually harassing messages (e.g., describing hypothetical sexual acts between you, making sexually demeaning remarks, etc.)
- Sending threatening pictures or images (e.g., images of actual or implied mutilation, blood, dismemberment, property destruction, weapons, etc.)
- Exposing private information about you to others (e.g., sending mail out to others regarding your secrets, embarrassing information, unlisted numbers, etc.)
- Pretending to be someone she or he wasn't (e.g., falsely representing him or herself as a different person or gender, claiming a false identity, status or position, pretending to be you, etc.)
- "Sabotaging" your private or social reputation (e.g., spreading rumors about you, your relationships, or activities to friends, family, partner, etc.)
- "Sabotaging" your work/school reputation (e.g., spreading rumors about you, your relationships, or activities in organizational networks, electronic bulletin boards, etc.)
- Attempting to disable your computer (e.g., downloading a virus, sending too many messages for your system to handle, etc.)
- Obtaining private information without permission (e.g., covertly entering your computer files, voicemail, or the files of co-worker, friend, or family member, etc.)
- Using your computer to get information on others (e.g., stealing information about your friends, family, co-workers, etc.)
- "Bugging" your car, home, or office (e.g., planting a hidden listening or recording device, etc.)
- Altering your electronic identity or persona (e.g., breaking into your system and changing your signature, personal information, or how you portray yourself electronically, etc.)
- Taking over your electronic identity or persona (e.g., representing him- or herself to others as you in chat rooms, bulletin boards, pornography or singles sites, etc.)
- Directing others to you in threatening ways (e.g., pretending to be you on chat lines and requesting risky sex acts, kidnapping fantasies, etc.)
- Meeting first on-line and then following you (e.g., following you while driving, around campus or work, to or from the gym or social activities, etc.)
- Meeting first on-line and then intruding in your life (e.g., showing up unexpectedly at work, front door, in parking lot, intruding in your conversations, etc.)
- Meeting first on-line and then threatening you (e.g., threatening to engage in sexual coercion, rape, physical restraint, or to harm him- or herself, your possessions, pets, family, or friends, etc.)

Table 6.1 (continued)   Strategies and Tactics of Obsessive Relational Intrusion and Cyberstalking

- Meeting first on-line and then harming you (e.g., corresponding with you through an on-line dating service and then following, harassing, or otherwise stalking you, etc.)
- First meeting you on-line and then stalking you (e.g., corresponding through an on-line dating service or as acquaintances and then following, harassing, or otherwise stalking you, etc.)

Adapted from the victim short forms of the ORI and COP questionnaires; Spitzberg et al., in press; Spitzberg and Rhea, 1999; Spitzberg and Hoobler, 2000.

of intrusion (i.e., "ordinary" pursuit, "computer"-based pursuit), each successive strategy tends to reflect a more serious breach of privacy or safety. Furthermore, it can probably be presumed that the more of any of these strategies and tactics that a person experiences, the more threatened, fearful, and at risk she or he will be (Nicastro et al., 2000).

Several conclusions can be derived from a consideration of the strategies and tactics in these and other studies. First, stalking and ORI are indeed highly interactional phenomena. Although stalkers may stalk from a distance, one of the purposes of stalking or ORI is to communicate something to the object of pursuit.

Second, to the extent that these tactics are sustained over time, they will elicit various responses from the pursued. This back and forth of intrusion and pursuit, and response and counter-response, in which both persons see their fulfillment of valued goals to be contingent in part upon the other's actions, constitutes a relationship. Unlike many or most relationships in life, in which there is some degree of mutuality of preferred future connection, stalking and ORI relationships are at least perceptually disjunctive. The pursuer wants one version of the relationship whereas the pursued wants a mutually exclusive alternative relationship, or no relationship at all.

Third, many (although certainly not all) of the strategies and tactics listed in Table 6.1 are behaviors that are perfectly acceptable in the context of mutually desired courtship. Thus, it is often not the behavior itself that is perceived as intrusive and unwanted, but the behavior in that particular context of a disjunctive relationship.

Fourth, and closely related, there is a strange ambivalence in the progression of strategies and tactics. That is, it seems paradoxical that a pursuer seeking a relationship with someone would be capable both of providing intimate gifts and physically abusing that person. This ambivalence suggests considerable conflict in the mind of the pursuer as to the appropriate means to the end of establishing a more intimate relationship with the pursued.

Whether this conflict is rooted in the pursuer's personality, social skills, contextual stresses, or the pathologies of a particular relationship, it is clear that both the pursuer and pursued engage the process of interaction, and that each person's actions will have effects on the evolution of that relationship.

Finally, one of the hallmarks of stalking is the notion of "threat." One of the ironies of ORI is that many tactics employed to pursue intimacy with a resistant object of pursuit become threatening because of their persistence and imperviousness to feedback indicating they are unwelcome. Thus, part of what makes intrusive behaviors threatening is their unresponsiveness to deterrence or negative reinforcement.

Relentlessness is scary to the extent that a recipient finds it difficult to exert any control over his or her privacy. Interestingly, therefore, the threat of ORI and stalking is often not due to the danger of actual threats, but of the threat of relatively mundane courtship activities that are no longer framed as courtship by the object of pursuit. Indeed, what little research has been done on the relationship between threats and violence indicates that the people likely to be violent are unlikely to threaten, and the people who threaten are unlikely to be violent (Calhoun, 1998). However, when threats are followed by violence, it is much more likely to occur in the context of a previously intimate relationship than in a non-intimate relationship (Harmon et al., 1998; Palarea, 1999).

Actual threats, in other words, are unlikely to be acted upon, whereas violence often emerges from a context in which the threat is not signaled by the prior relational behavior of the pursuer. Thus, while obsessive relational intrusions are often threatening in their impact (Cupach and Spitzberg, 1997), explicit threats appear to play a relatively circumscribed role in the fabric of intimidation and pursuit.

One of the sources of the fear and harassment associated with ORI and stalking is how resilient pursuit activity is to attempts by the object of pursuit to put a stop to the pursuit. Collectively, the actions that the object of pursuit engages in to manage pursuit can be referred to as coping responses. Research into coping responses has begun to map out the topography of resistance.

The Structure of Coping with Unwanted Intrusion

In order to understand the relationship that emerges, it is important to examine the structure of experience from the perspective of the pursued. The objects of pursuit often find themselves caught between the cultural imperatives of incompatible face concerns. Specifically, there are two basic criteria by which social actors' competence is evaluated: appropriateness and effectiveness. People want to obtain their personal objectives, but to do so, generally they need to behave in appropriate ways (Cupach et al., 2000; Cupach and Spitzberg, 1998).

These dual concerns of effectiveness and appropriateness are analogous to the culturally universal concerns of positive and negative face. Negative face is the desire to be free from imposition or constraint. Positive face is the desire to be liked (Brown and Levinson, 1987; Cupach and Metts, 1994).

In most social encounters and relationships, interactants are able to achieve these face concerns in ways that are perceived as acceptably appropriate and effective. Indeed, in most of everyday interaction, these concerns are interpersonally reinforcing in the sense that upholding each other's face facilitates the others' efforts to sustain your own face concerns (Athay and Darley, 1981).

When an interactant is faced with a face imposition, it is often difficult to know how to manage the transgression without losing further face and, thus, being viewed by self and other(s) as incompetent. When a person pursues a relationship too persistently or aggressively, for example, it is an imposition on one's negative face. Yet, to engage immediately in a bold-faced sanction of such pursuit is to impose upon the pursuer's face. Such sanctions may be viewed as overly harsh and risky to one's own self-perception of decorum.

Furthermore, being the object of attention is a cultural and interactional resource that is generally highly valued (Derber, 1981). Indeed, the social exclusion implicit in messages of rejection is considered extremely ego-threatening acts, fully capable of evoking diminished self-esteem and the onset of loneliness, anxiety, and depression (Leary, 1990).

The need to belong is itself viewed as a culturally universal and evolutionary need of the human condition (Baumeister and Leary, 1995). To attempt to deny these needs to another person based upon a set of activities that are also culturally reinforced in the various models of courtship, is to breach a basic norm of face negotiation. Consequently, many objects of pursuit may delay for some time engaging in actions to directly ward off the pursuits of another person.

There are many options available to the object of pursuit. In research virtually never integrated into the stalking literature, there are entire literatures concerned with distancing techniques, privacy restoration, and relationship disengagement (see, e.g., Aldwin and Revenson, 1987; Baxter, 1985; Beatty et al., 1999; Bouchard et al., 1997; Burgoon et al., 1989; Cody, 1982; Emmers, 1995; Gruber, 1989; Helgeson et al., 1987; Hess, 2000; Levitt et al., 1996; Maier, 1996; Metts et al., 1989; Nicastro et al., 2000; Rowatt et al., 1999; Stith et al., 1992; Werner and Haggard, 1992). In an attempt to bring some order to the structure of tactical options available for coping with unwanted pursuit, Table 6.2 was formulated by reviewing the distancing, privacy restoration, and stalking literatures. It identifies two domain levels of response: extra-relational and relational.

The extra-relational domain entails solipsist and unilateral responses on the one hand (moving inward), and dealings with people other than the

Table 6.2   A Taxonomy of Stalking and ORI Victim Coping Responses

Extra-Relational Responses

Moving Inward: Engaging in activities manages one's view of self, one's own world view, or the escape into one's self and one's own experiences. Mezzo (micro) exemplars are

Ignore problem (e.g., wait, assume problem is imaginary or will go away, etc.)

Ritual/symbolic closure (e.g., eliminate tokens or symbols of prior relationship, visualize life without pursuer, etc.)

Minimization (e.g., rationalize that problem is less significant than it is, etc.)

Denial (e.g., refuse to acknowledge the problem at all; rationalize alternative explanations for experiences, etc.)

Self-blame (e.g., attribute responsibility for problems to self-actions or perceptions, etc.)

Affective negativity (e.g., cry, be depressed, fatalistic, nihilistic, etc.)

Destructive escapism (e.g., invest time and effort into eating, smoking, drug abuse, sex, etc.)

Therapeutic escapism (e.g., invest time and effort into hobbies, music, writing, medicine, improve physical appearance, therapeutic activities, massage, meditation, exercise, etc.)

Seeking meaning (e.g., invest time and effort into religion, prayer, philosophy, etc.)

Destructive escapism (e.g., attempt suicide, become drug addict, etc.)

Moving Outward: Engaging the assistance, input, feedback, and/or support of third parties. Mezzo (micro) exemplars are

Mobilize information (e.g., seek information, research, read up on, etc.)

Mobilize relational involvement (e.g., seek protection or deterrence through tie signs and/or relationship with significant others, increase closeness with friends or family, etc.)

Mobilize social support (e.g., seek emotional and/or instrumental support from friends, family, counselor, etc.)

Mobilize legal/law enforcement input (e.g., seek input from victim's advocate, city or district attorney, police, domestic violence unit, etc.)

Mobilize independent/private assistance (e.g., private investigator, bodyguard, etc.)

Relational Responses

Moving Away: Engaging in activities to avoid interaction with the pursuer. Mezzo (micro) exemplars are

Cautiousness (e.g., make plans of action and escape, become more aware of environment, become more conservative in interactional choices, etc.)

Ignore person's behavior (e.g., avoid eye contact, be non-responsive to pursuer's talk and behaviors)

Hinting (e.g., mention busyness, significant other, etc. to suggest unavailability or disinterest)

Interaction control (e.g., avoid asking questions, closed body orientation, increase proximity with conversational partners other than pursuer, etc.)

Distancing (e.g., maintaining or increasing interactional physical distance, lean away during interaction, walking away, etc.)

Detachment/depersonalization (e.g., act impersonally, unemotionally, uninvolved, avoid jokes or intimate communication, behave ritualistically or strictly politely, avoid discussing relationship, etc.)

Verbal escape (e.g., making excuses, claiming prior commitments, claiming existing relational commitments, claiming role restrictions, etc.)

Restricting access (e.g., changing schedule, arriving earlier, leaving earlier, shifting activities to more public venues, avoiding familiar places, etc.)

Table 6.2 (continued)   A Taxonomy of Stalking and ORI Victim Coping Responses

Blocking access (e.g., arranging environment to avoid contact — closing office doors, hardening home security, changing locks, unlisting phone number(s), caller ID, *69, hang up when called, changing e-mail address, etc.)

Relocating (e.g., changing jobs, changing address, changing classes, changing hobby/recreational locations, etc.)

Relational termination (e.g., claim relationship is over, provide relationship ultimatum, or define boundaries, etc.)

Moving Toward/With: Engaging in activities to maintain relationship in a preferred relational form. Mezzo (micro) exemplars are

Diffusion (e.g., engaging in teasing, joking, humorously diminishing significance of pursuer's actions, etc.)

Positive face (i.e., make pursuer feel appreciated in hope this is all she/he needs; e.g., compliment, point out how fortunate pursuer is, etc.)

Seek sympathy/empathy (e.g., cry, explain personal problems, beg or plead, etc.)

Deception (e.g., flirt or hint at interest to get out of immediate situation, arrange or suggest future meeting with no intent to keep date, etc.)

Justification (i.e., specify rationale of acceptable relationship behavior, explain impossibility of reciprocity, etc.)

Relationship definition negotiation (i.e., discuss pursuer's and own preferred relationship objectives to arrive at a mutual definition; e.g., just be friends, just be colleagues, reconciliation of previous relationship, etc.)

Bargaining (e.g., offer compromises, promises, or other rewards to get pursuer to alter behavior, etc.)

Diversion (i.e., get pursuer interested in another object; e.g., introduce to someone she/he might be more compatible with, recommend to dating service, counseling, etc.)

Moving Against: Engaging in activities to end relationship, or harm, punish, retaliate against the pursuer. Mezzo (micro) exemplars are

Cost escalation (e.g., be unattractive, unpleasant, tedious, unpredictable, moody, difficult, unpleasant to be around, etc.)

Protective deterrence (e.g., self-defense training, air horn, mace, show weapon, put security stickers on car and home windows, etc.)

Proactive protection (e.g., call police, seek restraining order, press charges, sue, etc.)

"Turning the table" (e.g., flirt with pursuer's friend, call pursuer's parents, call and hang up on pursuer, invite an illegal act to get pursuer caught, etc.)

Guilt-tripping (e.g., elicit guilt or shame, explain problems caused by pursuer, etc.)

Nonverbal aggression (e.g., yell at, criticize, insult, make fun of, show anger, annoyance, antagonism, frustration, use harsh or hostile voice, etc.)

Verbal confrontation (e.g., tell pursuer you don't like him/her, don't want him/her, to stop, to stay away, etc.)

Warning/threat (e.g., articulate punishments/sanctions that pursuer will experience or object will invoke if pursuit continues, threaten with police, violence, retaliation, etc.)

Violence (e.g., hitting, shoving, using a weapon, throwing object, etc.)

Although many terms have been reinterpreted and exemplars often deduced or inferred, this taxonomy represents an exhaustive inclusion of coping tactics and responses from the following sources: Aldwin and Revenson, 1987; Baxter, 1985; Beatty et al., 1999; Bouchard et al., 1997; Burgoon et al., 1989; Cody, 1982; Emmers, 1995; Gruber, 1989; Helgeson et al., 1987; Hess, 2000; Levitt et al., 1996; Maier, 1996; Metts et al., 1989; Nicastro et al., 2000; Rowatt et al., 1999; Stith et al., 1992; Werner and Haggard, 1992.

pursuer on the other (moving outward). The second domain level is the relational, within which the object of pursuit attempts to deal more directly with the pursuer's actions. It consists of three levels of function (Horney, 1945): moving away, moving toward/with, and moving against. Moving away involves actions that attempt to remove oneself from the access of the pursuer. Moving toward or with entails actions that attempt to negotiate an acceptable mutual definition of the relationship, even if that definition is intended to be an end to the relationship entirely.

Finally, moving against consists of actions that attempt to punish or deter the pursuer. A variety of studies shows that objects of pursuit employ the full breadth of these coping responses (Brewster, 1998; Fisher et al., 1999; Fremouw et al., 1997; Gallagher et al., 1994; Gill and Brockman, 1996; Jason et al., 1984; Levitt et al., 1996; Nicastro et al., 2000; Tjaden and Thoennes, 1998).

One of the most widely discussed and least understood coping responses is the restraining order (e.g., Batza and Taylor, 1999; Gondolf et al., 1994; Fischer and Rose, 1995; Horton et al., 1987). There have been numerous studies of restraining orders in the context of domestic violence, but very few in the context of stalking specifically (e.g., Berk et al., 1983; Brewster, 1998; Chaudhuri and Daly, 1992; Gill and Brockman, 1996; Kaci, 1994; Keilitz et al., 1998; Hall, 1997; Harrell and Smith, 1996; Harrell et al., 1993; Meloy et al., 1997; Nicastro et al., 2000; Tjaden and Thoennes, 1998; Tucker, 1993).

The research to date has generally shown that restraining orders in general do not prevent subsequent violation of the order. In other words, in about half or more of cases in which a restraining order is in effect, the order is subsequently violated through some form of contact by the restrained party (e.g., Harmon et al., 1998). There is some evidence that mutual restraining orders do serve as an effective deterrent (Meloy et al., 1997), and that people who obtain restraining orders are generally satisfied with the decision to obtain an order (Horton et al., 1987; Keilitz et al., 1998). Thus far, only one study suggests the possibility that stalking activity may increase after the filing of restraining orders (Keilitz et al., 1998), although the increase was relatively small (from 4 to 7% of those surveyed).

Despite the rich array of options available to objects of pursuit, stalking and ORI are often viewed as intractable. Indeed, with an average duration of almost 2 years (Tjaden and Thoennes, 1998), it is easy to see why people become so frustrated with their seeming inability to stop the unwanted pursuit. This intractability and powerlessness may help to explain why stalking and ORI have such deleterious effects on victims of unwanted and persistent intrusion.

One of the paradoxes of pursuit is that there is a substantial correlation between the number of tactics of pursuit, the amount of fear and symptoms experienced by the object of pursuit, and the number of coping responses the object of pursuit uses (Nicastro et al., 2000; Spitzberg and Rhea, 1999). The intuitive resolution for this paradox is likely that the more victimized the person, the more coping responses the person attempts.

To date, therefore, there is little basis for suggesting that certain coping responses are likely to reduce or deter obsessive pursuit and intrusion.

Impact of Victimization

Victims of unwanted intrusion and pursuit experience a wide range of symptoms. High percentages of stalking victims report elevated levels of fear (57%, Brewster, 1998; 52%, Hall, 1997; 69%, Mullen and Pathé, 1994a; 80%, Nicastro et al., 2000; cf. McCreedy and Dennis, 1996; Romans et al., 1996), paranoia (36%, Brewster, 1998; 41%, Hall, 1997; 7%, Nicastro et al., 2000), and elevated levels of PTSD (Westrup et al., 1998). Most victims report significant disruptions in personality (83%, Hall, 1997), lifestyle or activity patterns (64%, Brewster, 1998; 82%, Pathé and Mullen, 1997), work (Mullen and Pathé, 1994a; Pathé and Mullen, 1997; Tjaden and Thoennes, 1998), and quality of life (99%, Brewster, 1998; 95% Fisher et al., 1999; 100%, Romans et al., 1996). In addition, significant proportions of stalking and ORI victims report having been physically (Burgess et al., 1997; Coleman, 1997; Feldman et al., 1997; Gallagher et al., 1994; Gill and Brockman, 1996; Kong, 1996; Palarea et al., 1999; Schwartz-Watts et al., 1997; Tjaden and Thoennes, 1998; Zona et al., 1993) or sexually (Scocas et al., 1996; Spitzberg and Rhea, 1999; Tjaden and Thoennes, 1998) assaulted or injured. In addition, many victims report heightened distrust of others, anxiety, depression, somatic difficulties, and anger or aggressiveness (Brewster, 1998; Hall, 1997; Nicastro et al., 2000; Pathé and Mullen, 1997).

Clearly, people who are stalked and obsessively pursued in unwanted ways tend to be victims; being the object of pursuit extols heavy economic, emotional, psychological, physical, and social costs. Such costs evidence the importance of a better understanding of the processes of stalking and obsessive relational intrusion.

Processes of Stalking and Obsessive Relational Intrusion

Stalking and obsessive pursuit of relationships are sometimes thought of as distinct, freakish, singular events. However, these phenomena actually are closely tied to ubiquitous, mundane, everyday interpersonal interactions.

Obsessive pursuit often represents an exaggeration and exacerbation of activities designed to create, develop, and maintain a social or personal relationship. Indeed, obsessive pursuit is grounded in the very activities that are considered normative in the everyday coupling and uncoupling of relational partners (Cupach and Spitzberg, 1998; Emerson et al., 1998).

Perils of Normal Relationship Construction and Deconstruction

Relationships are born out of the symbolic interactions that individuals share. Communication conveys what type of relationship the individuals share, as well as what type of relationship they desire. In other words, messages that are exchanged between people index the current relationship and can serve as bids for changing a relationship. At the same time, the definition of a relationship provides a context that guides how messages are to be interpreted, as well as what sorts of messages are deemed appropriate and relevant to the relationship.

Despite people's extensive experience in social interaction, the formation and maintenance of human relationships are fraught with difficulty. Although interactants share identical interaction episodes (i.e., they both participate in the same exchanges of behavior), they do not necessarily share the same relationship definition. Each individual digests the interactions and constructs his/her own interpretations, often assuming that the other shares the interpretation. Perhaps the most fundamental source of relational conflict, therefore, stems from non-mutuality of relationship definition (e.g., Morton et al., 1976).

For various reasons, the mismatch between relational intentions is quite common, and the discovery of mismatch is not immediate. Consequently, receiving unwanted relational attention is just as common as wanting attention from another that is not given.

One factor that contributes to non-mutuality of relationship definition is the fact that individuals do not always enter into interactions possessing clear-cut relational goals. Initial interactions are not always planned or anticipated, and sometimes they occur by chance. During such episodes, one person may quickly develop a relational goal, while the other person is content to experience the interaction spontaneously.

Even when individuals do plan their interactions, they may not consciously be pursuing a specific relational goal. Thus, an individual may abstractly anticipate the possibilities of future interactions, yet specific relational intentions may remain nebulous (e.g., "I like doing things together. I don't know how serious I want to get or how connected to this person I want to be"). Since neither person is likely to discuss explicitly his or her relational goal status, neither person is aware that there already is brewing a potential mismatch in relational intentions. Moreover, ambivalence about a relationship reflects the fact that an individual's relationship goal can fluctuate widely and frequently. It is not uncommon, for example, for some dating couples to go through multiple cycles of breaking-up and reconciling their relationship over and over again. In such cases, at least one person vacillates in the relational goal.

Relational Formation

Relationship formation occurs developmentally. In other words, relationships escalate incrementally in steps or stages, and they consequently evolve over time. Individuals seek each other's affinity (Bell and Daly, 1984; Bell et al., 1987) and reduce uncertainty about one another (Berger and Bradac, 1982) in gradual fashion. Since relationship building involves ongoing processes that require numerous interactions to accomplish, there is much opportunity for one or both individuals to change their relational goals. Ironically, the very features that lead one person initially to find another attractive can later be the sources of repulsion and relational dissatisfaction (e.g., the once spontaneous and novel person is now viewed as capricious and unpredictable) (Felmlee, 1998).

Although the passage of time would seem to facilitate mutual understanding, it also creates the opportunity for the once-compatible relational goals of partners to diverge. Individuals may fail to perceive this divergence because of the manner in which relationship definitions are constructed.

The negotiation of relationship definition is largely tacit in nature. Although it is said that persons "relate in talk," the relational content of interaction is much more analogic than digital (Watzlawick et al., 1967). That is, interaction, and especially courtship, tend to be series of "moves" rather than series of "declarations" (Sabini and Silver, 1982; Egland et al., 1996). Overt and explicit communication about relationship definition is more often the exception rather than the rule. Especially in nonromantic and undeveloped relationships, relational talk is awkward, and to an extent it is considered taboo as a topic of discussion (Baxter and Wilmot, 1995). Relationship definitions therefore develop via implicature. They are insinuated by and inferred from routine actions and reactions. This indirect negotiation of relationships affords much opportunity for miscommunication, misperception, and hence the mismatching of relational intentions (Metts and Spitzberg, 1996). As time passes, the gap between partners can grow larger, without the partners being aware of a mismatch.

Even when an individual realizes that she or he does not share another person's goal of escalating intimacy, rejection of the other person's attempt to escalate intimacy tends to be communicated indirectly and ambiguously. Objects of relational pursuit often find themselves caught between the cultural imperatives of incompatible face concerns. Specifically, there are two basic criteria by which social actors' competence is evaluated: appropriateness and effectiveness.

People want to obtain their personal objectives, but to do so, generally they need to behave in appropriate ways (Cupach and Spitzberg, 2000; Spitzberg and Cupach, 1996). These dual concerns of effectiveness and appropriateness are analogous to the culturally universal concerns of negative and positive face. Negative face is the desire to be free from imposition or constraint. Positive face is the desire to be liked and respected (Brown and Levinson, 1987; Cupach and Metts, 1994).

In most social encounters and relationships, interactants are able to achieve these face concerns in ways that are perceived as acceptably appropriate and effective. Indeed, in most everyday interaction, these concerns are interpersonally reinforcing in the sense that upholding each other's face facilitates the other's efforts to sustain your own face concerns (Athay and Darley, 1981; Brown and Levinson, 1987; Goffman, 1967).

When an interactant is faced with a face imposition, it is often difficult to know how to manage the transgression without losing further face and, thus, being viewed by self and other(s) as incompetent. When a person pursues a relationship too persistently or aggressively, for example, it threatens the object's negative face. Yet, to engage immediately in a bold-faced sanction of such pursuit obviously threatens the pursuer's face. At the same time, such sanctions may be viewed as overly harsh and risky to one's own self-perception of decorum, thereby threatening the object's face as well. Furthermore, being the object of attention is a cultural and interactional resource that is generally highly valued (Derber, 1981).

Indeed, the social exclusion implicit in messages of rejection is considered extremely ego-threatening acts, fully capable of evoking diminished self-esteem and the onset of loneliness, anxiety, and depression (Leary, 1990). The need to belong is itself viewed as a culturally universal and evolutionary need of the human condition (Baumeister and Leary, 1995).

To attempt to deny these needs to another person based upon a set of activities that are also culturally reinforced in the various models of courtship is to breach a basic norm of face negotiation. Consequently, social rejection (Folkes, 1982; Metts et al., 1992; Snow et al., 1991) and relational dissolution (Baxter, 1985; Cody, 1982) are communicated indirectly and, hence, ambiguously. Unfortunately, pursuers often interpret ambiguous messages as showing reciprocation and encouraging further pursuit (Bratslavsky et al., 1998; de Becker, 1997).

When relationship goals are mismatched and this becomes apparent to the pursuer, some persistence is viewed as normative by both pursuer and pursued. There exists in our culture a pervasive social script that promotes persistence, even in the face of rejection (Bratslavsky et al., 1998; Stith et al., 1992).

The stereotype of the ardent pursuer eventually winning over the object given sufficient effort is a familiar one, reinforced by the occasional experience of persistence paying off, as well as fictional portrayals in popular media. Certainly some of the relationship pursuit behaviors enacted by ardent and eventually successful suitors would be considered obsessive by some observers. Sometimes, the attention provided by excessive pursuit is desired and encouraged by objects.

Non-mutuality of relationship definition achieves crisis status when pursuit is unwanted and obsessive. Unfortunately, there is no objective and precise demarcation of where legitimate pursuit ends and where obsessive intrusion begins. As we have already indicated, many behaviors that comprise a stalking or obsessive intrusion profile are often a normal part of relationship development. Even in relationships considered to be "normal," individuals report spying on their partners, checking up on their whereabouts, using tie-signs to show possession and ward off potential rivals, and so forth (e.g., Guerrero et al., 1995; Patterson and Kim, 1991).

In some cases, behaviors that at the time were accepted as reasonable bids for friendship or romance are later reinterpreted as obsessive and/or threatening (Emerson et al., 1998). There also is considerable individual variation in the degree of tolerance for intrusion, and in judgments regarding how much and what types of pursuit are inappropriate. Nevertheless, most observers would agree that pursuit is excessive and inappropriate when it becomes obsessive (i.e., when pursuit persists in the face of repeated, overt, and explicit rejections by the object). In the next section, we briefly consider some of the dynamics that transform normal affinity-seeking into an obsession.

Processes That Foster the Escalation of Pursuit to the Level of Obsession

A number of distal predisposing factors have been proposed to explain why some persons may be more likely to escalate relational pursuit to obsessive levels more than others. For example, some obsessive pursuers may be characterized by an insecure attachment style (e.g., Dutton et al., 1996), pathological narcissism, and social incompetence (Meloy, 1996). However, even individuals who do not suffer from these problems or who are not generally prone to obsessive pursuit may become overly persistent under certain circumstances.

We propose that there are proximal processes that explain how otherwise normal (if annoying) pursuit escalates to obsession and threat. Specifically, we argue that processes of rumination, emotional flooding, and rationalization combine to disinhibit a pursuer's view of appropriate affinity-seeking behavior (see Cupach et al., 2000). Over time these processes lead to a gradual deficiency in the pursuer's ability to control his/her actions and comprehend the consequences of those actions.

Obsessive Rumination

Everyone ruminates, and in its most general sense, rumination can be positive or negative. Rumination occurs when one has repeated, distressing, intrusive, aversive thoughts regarding an unmet or thwarted goal (Millar et al., 1988). In the case of relational pursuit, the goal is to attain a certain kind of relationship with the object, or to re-establish a relationship that has been relinquished or redefined by the object. To the extent that the relational goal is unmet, the pursuer engages in excessive mulling.

In the absence of sufficient progress toward goal achievement, rumination intensifies over time and negative thoughts polarize. Paradoxically, attempts to suppress rumination exacerbate negative thought persistence (e.g., Wegner et al., 1987; Wegner and Zanakos, 1994; Wegner, 1994).

Not all unmet goals produce intense rumination. Relatively unimportant goals are abandoned rather than pursued after a modicum of effort is exerted. A person may feel sad about being rejected by a former relational partner, but does not obsessively ruminate about it because the relationship was not very high in the person's overall goal hierarchy. However, when lower-order goals are linked to other very important goals (i.e., goals that are high in one's goal hierarchy), then rumination persists (McIntosh et al., 1995; McIntosh and Martin, 1992).

Thus, when a pursuer believes that a higher-order goal such as life happiness or self-worth depends upon the fulfillment of the lower-order relationship goal, then rumination becomes pre-occupying. Rumination, in turn, leads the pursuer to (1) solidify commitment to the relational goal, and (2) redouble efforts to achieve the goal. As rumination persists and intensifies, attempts to develop or restore intimacy with the object persist and intensify. Relief from rumination comes only from goal achievement or goal abandonment. The importance of the goal, given its linkage to higher order goals for obsessive pursuers, renders goal abandonment unlikely.

Emotional Flooding

Because rumination is aversive and becomes increasingly negative over time, it is associated with negative arousal. When an important goal continues to be unmet, the person striving to attain the goal *feels* bad. As rumination becomes obsessive, the accompanying negative affect becomes absorbing and the individual feels flooded with arousal. The negative feelings constantly remind the individual that a crucial goal remains unmet and, consequently, fuel further rumination (Millar et al., 1988). In this way, the pursuer may get trapped into a vicious cycle of aversive rumination and affect.

"Rumination leads to greater negative affect, which in turn increases rumination, and so on, thereby perpetuating persistence in the recovery or development of the desired relationship" (Cupach et al., 2000, p. 141). Specific emotions such as guilt, shame, anger, and jealousy also motivate the pursuer to escalate efforts to secure the relationship, and eventually may lead to retaliation against the object when the pursuer finally realizes that the relationship goal is illusory (Carson and Cupach, 2000; Cupach et al., 2000).

Rationalization

As aversive rumination and emotional flooding intensify, concomitant rationalizations enable the pursuer's persistence and escalation of intimacy-seeking. The pursuer often distorts reality in a number of ways. Even in the face of evidence to the contrary, the pursuer exaggerates the object's sentiments regarding the pursuer, and tends to interpret signs of encouragement and reciprocation from the object, even when none are intended. Rejection by the object can go unnoticed, or even be misconstrued as showing signs of affection. The pursuer overlooks the annoyance and distress experienced by the object, and the pursuer fails to see the irrationality and obsessiveness of his/her behavior.

Finally, there are several normative, even noble, motives people can concoct for pursuing unreciprocated love (Aron et al., 1998; Baumeister et al., 1993; Bratslavsky et al., 1998). All of these sorts of rationalizations foster disinhibition in the pursuer's behavior, thereby allowing pursuit to escalate and persist.

The Paradoxes of Pursuit

Victims of obsessive pursuit are likely to feel a bit like Alice having fallen down the rabbit hole. Nothing seems to operate by the normal rules of social interaction and courtship, and yet, the pursuer may, paradoxically, believe it is the object of pursuit who is playing by the "wrong" set of rules. This paradoxical world might be illustrated by certain exemplars.

Pursuit Is Reinforced by Rejection

In ordinary life, rejecting the advances of a paramour tends to diminish the course of pursuit. In the world of the obsessive pursuer, rejection serves to arouse and thereby energize the pursuer. In addition, rejection triggers powerful cognitive processes of suppression, which paradoxically reinforces the fixation and rumination process.

These processes, in concert with the arousal and affective flooding in the face of rejection, lead to rationalization and disinhibition of normative constraints on threatening and excessive pursuit.

Enchantment Entices Enmity

In ordinary life, it is generally assumed that the purpose of an intimate relationship is to make oneself and another happy through the union. To discover that a course of action is causing the other harm or duress is a cause for altering one's path. In contrast, an obsessive pursuer is capable of subordinating the temporary discomfort caused the object of pursuit to the superordinate idealized vision of what the relationship *could* or *ought* to be.

Through sheer power of persistence, the pursuer intends to bring the object of intimacy under the spell of this vision or desire. However, the object's constant rejection of the pursuer will eventually seem like a defiling or disfiguring of the pursuer's face, and such rejection has consequences for anger, shame, and ultimately rage. Thus, the object of desire becomes the object of enmity and rage, often simultaneously. For example, Dunn (1999) reports her unpublished data from felony stalking cases that "36 percent of victims reported that the men charged with stalking intermingled declarations of love with their threats to commit mayhem" (p. 443). As the paradox unfolds further, she also found that the threatening nature of invasiveness in courtship to some extent can be counterbalanced by tokens of affection or previous relationship.

Such paradoxical or mixed messages were viewed as "*simultaneously* flattering or romantic as well as annoying and frightening" (p. 448). The danger of such ambivalence, which is likely nurtured quite by design of the pursuer, is that it can blind the object of pursuit to another paradox of pursuit. In its most extreme forms, the paradox that enchantment entices enmity leads to a paradoxical corollary: destruction of an object can fulfill the desire to possess the thing desired. By consuming the object of desire, it is owned and, furthermore, prevented from anyone else possessing the object.

Passion Begets Power

In ordinary relationships and interaction, the principle of least interest holds sway. The principle of least interest observes that the party who cares the least about the relationship has the most power. This power emanates from the power to do without or end the relationship with relatively little cost. Clearly, the party who wants the relationship more will have less motivation or need to deviate from his or her own objectives, given that there is relatively less to lose. But in obsessively pursued relationships, the lack of normative constraint on the pursuer's behavior permits the pursuer greater latitude in a campaign of intimate terror. Thus, the nightmare the object of pursuit faces is that she or he does not care for the relationship at all, and yet *cannot* end the relationship.

Such are some of the paradoxes faced in the wonderland of romance. Obsessive pursuers and stalkers live in a world that seems largely rational and sensible, except in the lack of possession of that which is most desired: the object of affection that would fulfill the pursuer's ideal of relational completion.

Perhaps the last paradox the stalker needs to comprehend is the hardest paradox to manage. As suggested in a poetic koan by T. S. Eliot in *East Coker*:

> *In order to possess what you do not possess,*
> *You must go by the way of dispossession.*

Bibliography

Aldwin, C. M. and Revenson, T. A. (1987). Does coping help? A reexamination of the relation between coping and mental health, *Journal of Personality and Social Psychology*, 53, 337–348.

Aron, A., Aron, E. N., and Allen, J. (1998). Motivations for unreciprocated love, *Personality and Social Psychology Bulletin*, 24, 787–796.

Athay, M. and Darley, J. M. (1981). Toward an interaction-centered theory of personality, in N. Cantor and J. F. Kihlstrom (Eds.), *Personality, Cognition, and Social Interaction* (pp. 281-308). Hillsdale, NJ: Lawrence Erlbaum Associates.

Batza, D. M. and Taylor, M. (1999). Stalking in the community and workplace, in E. K. Carll (Ed.), *Violence in Our Lives: Impact on Workplace, Home, and Community* (pp. 66–96). Boston: Allyn and Bacon.

Baumeister, R. F. and Leary, M. R. (1995). The need to belong: desire for interpersonal attachments as a fundamental human motivation, *Psychological Bulletin*, 117, 497–529.

Baumeister, R. F., Wotman, S. R., and Stillwell, A. M. (1993). Unrequited love: on heartbreak, anger, guilt, scriptlessness, and humiliation, *Journal of Personality and Social Psychology*, 64, 377–394.

Baxter, L. A. (1985). Accomplishing relationship disengagement, in S. Duck and D. Perlman (Eds.), *Understanding Personal Relationships* (pp. 243–265). London: Sage Publications.

Baxter, L. A. and Wilmot, W. W. (1995). Taboo topics in close relationships, *Journal of Social and Personal Relationships*, 2, 253–269.

Beatty, M. J., Valencic, K. M., Rudd, J. E., and Dobos, J. A. (1999). A "dark side" of communication avoidance: indirect interpersonal aggressiveness, *Communication Research Reports*, 16, 103–109.

Bell, R. A. and Daly, J. A. (1984). The affinity-seeking function of communication, *Communication Monographs*, 51, 91–115.

Bell, R.A., Tremblay, S.W., and Buerkel-Rothfuss, N.L. (1987). Interpersonal attraction as a communication accomplishment: development of a measure of affinity-seeking competence, *Western Journal of Speech Communication*, 51, 1-18.

Berger, C. R. and Bradac, J. J. (1982). *Language and Social Knowledge: Uncertainty in Interpersonal Relationships*. London: Edward Arnold.

Berk, R. A., Berk, S. F., Loseke, D. R., and Rauma, D. (1983). Mutual combat and other family violence myths, in D. Finkelhor, R. J. Gelles, G. T. Hotaling, and M. A. Straus (Eds.), *The Dark Side of Families: Current Family Violence Research* (pp. 197–212). Newbury Park, CA: Sage Publications.

Bouchard, G., Sabourin, S., Lussier, Y., Wright, J., and Richer, C. (1997). Testing the theoretical models underlying the ways of coping questionnaire, *Journal of Marriage and the Family*, 59, 409–418.

Bratslavsky, E., Baumeister, R. F., and Sommer, K. L. (1998). To love or be loved in vain: the trials and tribulations of unrequited love, in B. H. Spitzberg and W. R. Cupach (Eds.), *The Dark Side of Close Relationships* (pp. 307–326). Mahwah, NJ: Lawrence Erlbaum Associates.

Brewster, M. P. (1998). An Exploration of the Experiences and Needs of Former Intimate Stalking Victims, Final report submitted to the National Institute of Justice (NCJ 175475). Washington D.C.: U.S. Department of Justice.

Brown, P. and Levinson, S. (1987). *Politeness: Some Universals in Language Usage*. Cambridge: Cambridge University Press.

Burgess, A. W., Baker, T., Greening, D., Hartman, C. R., Burgess, A. G., Douglas, J. E., and Halloran, R. (1997). Stalking behaviors within domestic violence, *Journal of Family Violence*, 12, 389–403.

Burgoon, J. K., Parrott, R., Le Poire, B. A., Kelley, D. L., Walther, J. B., and Perry, D. (1989). Maintaining and restoring privacy through communication in different types of relationships, *Journal of Social and Personal Relationships*, 6, 131–158.

Buzawa, E., Hotaling, G., and Klein, A. (1998). The response to domestic violence in a model court: some initial findings and implications, *Behavioral Sciences and the Law*, 16, 185–206.

Calhoun, F. S. (1998). Hunters and Howlers: Threats and Violence against Federal Judicial Officials in the United States, 1789–1993 (USMS No. 80). Washington, D.C.: U.S. Marshall's Service, U.S. Department of Justice.

Canary, D. J., Spitzberg, B. H., and Semic, B. A. (1998). The experience and expression of anger in interpersonal settings, in P. A. Andersen and L. K. Guerrero (Eds.), *Communication and Emotion: Theory, Research and Applications* (pp. 189–213). San Diego, CA: Academic Press.

Carlson, M. J., Harris, S. D., and Holden, G. W. (1999). Protective orders and domestic violence: risk factors for re-abuse, *Journal of Family Violence*, 14, 205–226.

Carson, C. L. and Cupach, W. R. (2000). Fueling the flames of the green-eyed monster: the role of ruminative thought in reaction to romantic jealousy, *Western Journal of Communication*, 64, 308–329.

Chaudhuri, M. and Daly, K. (1992). Do restraining orders help? Battered women's experience with male violence and legal process, in E. S. Buzawa and C. G. Buzawa (Eds.), *Domestic Violence: The Changing Criminal Justice Response*, (pp. 227–252). Westport, CT: Greenwood.

Cody, M. J. (1982). A typology of disengagement strategies and an examination of the role intimacy, reactions to inequity and relational problems play in strategy selection, *Communication Monographs*, 49, 148–170.

Cody, M. J., Kersten, L., Braaten, D. O., and Dickson, R. (1992). Coping with relational dissolutions: attributions, account credibility, and plans for resolving conflicts, in J. L. Harvey, T. L. Orbuch, and A. L. Weber (Eds.), *Attributions, Accounts, and Close Relationships* (pp. 93–115). New York: Springer-Verlag.

Coleman, F. L. (1997). Stalking behavior and the cycle of domestic violence, *Journal of Interpersonal Violence*, 12, 420–433.

Cupach, W. R. and Metts, S. (1994). *Facework*. Thousand Oaks, CA: Sage Publications.

Cupach, W. R. and Spitzberg, B. H. (February 1997). The Incidence and Perceived Severity of Obsessive Relational Intrusion Behaviors, Paper presented at the Western States Communication Association Conference, Monterey, CA.

Cupach, W. R. and Spitzberg, B. H. (1998). Obsessive relational intrusion and stalking, in B. H. Spitzberg and W. R. Cupach (Eds.), *The Dark Side of Close Relationships* (pp. 233–263). Hillsdale, NJ: Lawrence Erlbaum Associates.

Cupach, W. R. and Spitzberg, B. H. (2000). The incidence and perceived severity of obsessive relational intrusion, *Violence and Victims*, 15, 357–372.

Cupach, W. R., Spitzberg, B. H., and Carson, C. L. (April 1999). Excessive Emotion: Toward a Theory of Obsessive Relational Intrusion and Stalking Perpetration, Paper presented at the Central States/Southern States Communication Joint Conference, St. Louis, MO.

Cupach, W. R., Spitzberg, B.H., and Carson, C. L. (2000). Toward a theory of obsessive relational intrusion and stalking, in K. Dindia and S. Duck (Eds.), *Communication and Personal Relationships* (pp. 131–146). New York: John Wiley & Sons.

Davis, J. (1998). *Psychological Typologies of Those Who Stalk*, Law Enforcement and Forensic Mental Health Seminar Presentation, San Diego, CA.

Davis, J. (October 1999). Stalker Typologies, Geographic Encounter Profiles (GEP), Crime and Intelligence Analysis: Examining the Mobility Patterns of Stalkers, and Victim Selection and Engagement, Conference presentation, Third Annual Stalking the Stalker Conference, San Diego, CA.

Davis, J. and Chipman, M. A. (1997). Stalkers and other obsessional types: a review and forensic psychological typology of those who stalk, *Journal of Clinical-Forensic Medicine*, 4, 166–173.

de Becker, G. (1997). *The Gift of Fear: Survival Signals that Protect Us from Violence.* Boston: Little, Brown.

Derber, C. (1981). *The Pursuit of Attention.* Boston: Schenkman.

Dunn, J. L. (1999). What love has to do with it: the cultural construction of emotion and sorority women's responses to forcible interaction, *Social Problems, 46,* 440–459.

Dutton, D. G., Ginkel, C. V., and Landolt, M. A. (1996). Jealousy, intimate abusiveness, and intrusiveness, *Journal of Family Violence,* 11, 411–423.

Egland, K. L., Spitzberg, B. H., and Zormeier, M. M. (1996). Flirtation and conversational competence in cross-sex platonic and romantic relationships, *Communication Reports,* 9, 105–118.

Eisele, G. R., Watkins, J. P., and Matthews, K. O. (1998). Workplace violence at government sites, *American Journal of Industrial Medicine,* 33, 485–492.

Elliott, L. and Brantley, C. (1997). *Sex on Campus: The Naked Truth about the Real Sex Lives of College Students.* New York: Random House.

Emerson, R. M., Ferris, K. O., and Gardner, C. B. (1998). On being stalked, *Social Problems,* 45, 289–314.

Emmers, T. M. (February 1995). Relational Rehabilitation: Rituals of Moving Out and Moving On, Paper presented at the Western States Communication Association Conference, Portland, OR.

Feldman, T. B., Holt, J., and Hellard, S. (1997). Violence in medical facilities: a review of 40 incidents, *Journal of the Kentucky Medical Association,* 95, 183–189.

Felmlee, D. H. (1998). Fatal attraction, in B. H. Spitzberg and W. R. Cupach (Eds.), *The Dark Side of Close Relationships* (pp. 3–31). Mahwah, NJ: Lawrence Erlbaum Associates.

Fischer, K. and Rose, M. (1995). When "enough is enough": battered women's decision making around court orders of protection, *Crime and Delinquency,* 41, 414–429.

Fisher, B. S., Cullen, F. T., and Turner, M. G. (1999), The Extent and Nature of the Sexual Victimization of College Women: A National-Level Analysis, Final Report submitted to the National Institute of Justice (NCJ 179977). Washington D.C.: U.S. Department of Justice.

Folkes, V. S. (1982). Communicating the causes of social rejection, *Journal of Experimental Social Psychology,* 18, 235–252.

Fremouw, W. J., Westrup, D., and Pennypacker, J. (1997). Stalking on campus: the prevalence and strategies for coping with stalking, *Journal of Forensic Sciences,* 42, 664–667.

Gallagher, R. P., Harmon, W. W., and Lingenfelter, C. O. (1994). CSAOs' perceptions of the changing incidence of problematic college student behavior, *NASPA Journal,* 32, 37–45.

Gill, R. and Brockman, J. (1996). A Review of Section 264 (Criminal Harassment) of the Criminal Code of Canada, Working document WD 1996-7e, Research, Statistics and Evaluation Directorate, Department of Justice, Canada.

Goffman, E. (1967). On face-work, in *Interaction Ritual: Essays on Face-to-Face Behavior* (pp. 5–45). New York: Pantheon Books.

Gondolf, E. W., McWilliams, J., Hart, B., and Stuehling, J. (1994). Court response to petitions for civil protection orders, *Journal of Interpersonal Violence*, 9, 503–517.

Gruber, J. E. (1989). How women handle sexual harassment: a literature review, *Sociology and Social Research*, 74, 3–9.

Guerrero, L. K., Andersen, P. A., Jorgensen, P. F., Spitzberg, B. H., and Eloy, S. V. (1995). Coping with the green-eyed monster: conceptualizing and measuring communicative responses to romantic jealousy, *Western Journal of Communication*, 59, 270–304.

Hall, D. M. (1997). Outside Looking In: Stalkers and Their Victims, Unpublished doctoral dissertation, Claremont Graduate School, Claremont, CA.

Harmon, R. B., Rosner, R., and Owens, H. (1995). Obsessional harassment and erotomania in a criminal court population, *Journal of Forensic Sciences*, 40, 188–196.

Harmon, R. B., Rosner, R., and Owens, H. (1998). Sex and violence in a forensic population of obsessional harassers, *Psychology, Public Policy, and Law*, 4, 236–249.

Harrell, A. and Smith, B. E. (1996). Effects of restraining orders on domestic violence victims, in E. S. Buzawa and C. G. Buzawa (Eds.), *Do Arrests and Restraining Orders Work?* (pp. 214–242). Thousand Oaks, CA: Sage Publications.

Harrell, A., Smith, B., and Newmark, L. (1993). Court Processing and the Effects of Restraining Orders for Domestic Violence Victims (Executive Summary), Washington, D.C.: Urban Institute.

Helgeson, V. S., Shaver, P., and Dyer, M. (1987). Prototypes of intimacy and distance in same-sex and opposite sex relationships, *Journal of Social and Personal Relationships*, 4, 195–233.

Herold, E. S., Mantle, D., and Zemitis, O. (1979). A study of sexual offenses against females, *Adolescence*, 14, 65–72.

Hess, J. A. (2000). Maintaining non-voluntary relationships with disliked partners: an investigation into the use of distancing behaviors, *Human Communication Research*, 26, 458–488.

Hill, A. M. and Taplin, J. L. (1998). Anticipated responses to stalking: effect of threat and target-stalker relationship, *Psychiatry, Psychiatry and Law*, 5, 139–146.

Holmes, R. M. (1993). Stalking in America: types and methods of criminal stalkers, *Journal of Contemporary Criminal Justice*, 9, 317–327.

Holmes, R. M. and Holmes, S. (1998). Stalking in America, in *Contemporary Perspectives on Serial Murder* (pp. 137–148). Thousand Oaks, CA: Sage Publications.

Horney, K. (1945). *Our Inner Conflicts: A Constructive Theory of Neurosis*. New York: Norton.

Horton, A. L., Simonidis, K. M., and Simonidis, L. L. (1987). Legal remedies for spousal abuse: victim characteristics, expectations, and satisfaction, *Journal of Family Violence*, 2, 265–279.

Hosman, L. A. and Siltanen, S. A. (1995). Relationship intimacy, need for privacy, and privacy restoration behaviors, *Communication Quarterly*, 43, 64–74.

Jason, L. A., Reichler, A., Easton, J., Neal, A., and Wilson, M. (1984). Female harassment after ending a relationship: a preliminary study, *Alternative Lifestyles*, 6, 259–269.

Kaci, J. H. (1994). Aftermath of seeking domestic violence protective orders: the victim's perspective, *Journal of Contemporary Criminal Justice*, 10, 204–219.

Keilitz, S. L., Davis, C., Efkeman, H. S., Flango, C., and Hannaford, P. L. (January 1998). Civil Protection Orders: Victims' Views on Effectiveness (National Institute of Justice Research Preview). Washington, D.C.: U.S. Department of Justice, U.S. Government Printing Office.

Kienlen, K. K., Birmingham, D. L., Solberg, K. B., O'Regan, J. T., and Meloy, J. R. (1997). A comparative study of psychotic and nonpsychotic stalking, *Journal of the American Academy of Psychiatry and Law*, 25, 317–334.

Kong, R. (1996). Criminal harassment, *Juristat*, 16 (12), Statistics Canada: Canadian Centre for Justice Statistics, 1–13.

Leary, M. R. (1990). Responses to social exclusion: social anxiety, jealousy, loneliness, depression, and low self-esteem, *Journal of Social and Clinical Psychology*, 9, 221–229.

Leonard, R., Ling, L. C., Hankins, G. A., Maidon, C. H., Potorti, P. F., and Rogers, J. M. (1993). Sexual harassment at North Carolina State University, in G. L. Kreps (Ed.), *Sexual Harassment: Communication Implications* (pp. 170–194). Cresskill, NJ: Hampton.

Levitt, M. J., Silver, M. E., and Franco, N. (1996). Troublesome relationships: a part of human experience, *Journal of Social and Personal Relationships*, 13, 523–536.

Lowney, K. S. and Best, J. (1995). Stalking strangers and lovers: Changing media typifications of a new crime problem, in J. Best (Ed.), *Images of Issues: Typifying Contemporary Social Problems*, 2nd ed., (pp. 33–57). New York: Aldine de Gruyter.

Lyon, D. R. (1997). The Characteristics of Stalkers in British Columbia: A Statistical Comparison of Persons Charged with Criminal Harassment and Persons Charged with Other Criminal Code Offences, Unpublished M.A. thesis, Simon Fraser University, B.C., Canada.

Maier, G. J. (1996). Managing threatening behavior: the role of talk down and talk up, *Journal of Psychosocial Nursing*, 34, 25–30.

McCann, J. T. (1998a). Risk of violence in stalking cases and legal case management, *Pennsylvania Bar Association Quarterly*, 69, 117–122.

McCann, J. T. (1998b). Subtypes of stalking (obsessional following) in adolescents, *Journal of Adolescence*, 21, 667–675.

McCreedy, K. R. and Dennis, B.G. (1996). Sex-related offenses and fear of crime on campus, *Journal of Contemporary Criminal Justice*, 12, 69–80.

McFarlane, J. M., Campbell, J. C., Wilt, S., Sachs, C. J., Ulrich, Y., and Xu, X. (1999). Stalking and intimate partner femicide, *Journal of Homicide Studies*, 3, 300–316.

McIntosh, W. D. and Martin, L. L. (1992). The cybernetics of happiness: the relation of goal attainment, rumination, and affect, in M. S. Clark (Ed.), *Emotion and Social Behavior* (pp. 222–246). Newbury Park, CA: Sage Publications.

McIntosh, W. D., Harlow, T. F., and Martin, L. L. (1995). Linkers and nonlinkers: goal beliefs as a moderator of the effects of everyday hassles on rumination, depression, and physical complaints, *Journal of Applied Social Psychology*, 25(14), 1231–1244.

Meloy, J. R. (1996). Stalking (obsessional following): a review of some preliminary studies, *Aggression and Violent Behavior*, 1, 147–162.

Meloy, J. R. and Gothard, S. (1995). Demographic and clinical comparison of obsessional followers and offenders with mental disorders, *American Journal of Psychiatry*, 152, 258–263.

Meloy, J. R., Cowett, P. Y., Parker, S. B., Hofland, B., and Friedland, A. (1997). Domestic protection orders and the prediction of subsequent criminality and violence toward protectees, *Psychotherapy*, 34, 447–458.

Metts, S. and Spitzberg, B. H. (1996). Sexual communication: a script-based approach, in B.R. Burleson (Ed.), *Communication Yearbook*, 19 (pp. 49–92). Thousand Oaks, CA: Sage Publications.

Metts, S., Cupach, W. R., and Bejlovec, R. A. (1989). 'I love you too much to ever start liking you': redefining romantic relationships, *Journal of Social and Personal Relationships*, 6, 259–274.

Metts, S., Cupach, W. R., and Imahori, T. T. (1992). Perceptions of sexual compliance-resisting messages in three types of cross-sex relationships, *Western Journal of Communication*, 56, 1–17.

Millar, K. U., Tesser, A., and Millar, M. (1988). The effects of a threatening life event on behavior sequences and intrusive thought: a self-disruption explanation, *Cognitive Therapy and Research*, 12, 441–457.

Monaghan, P. (March 6, 1998). Beyond the Hollywood myths: researchers examine stalkers and their victims, *Chronicle of Higher Education*, A17, A20.

Moracco, K. E., Runyan, C. W., and Butts, J. D. (1998). Femicide in North Carolina, 1991–1993, *Journal of Homicide Studies*, 2, 422–446.

Morton, T. L., Alexander, J. F., and Altman, I. (1976). Communication and relationship definition, in G. R. Miller (Ed.), *Explorations in Interpersonal Communication* (pp. 105–125). Beverly Hills, CA: Sage Publications.

Mullen, P. E. and Pathé, M. (1994a). The pathological extensions of love, *British Journal of Psychiatry*, 165, 614–623.

Mullen, P. E. and Pathé, M. (1994b). Stalking and the pathologies of love, *Australian and New Zealand Journal of Psychiatry*, 28, 469–477.

Mullen, P. E., Pathé, M., Purcell, R., and Stuart, G. W. (1999). Study of stalkers, *American Journal of Psychiatry*, 156, 1244–1249.

Mustaine, E. E. and Tewksbury, R. (1999). A routine activity theory explanation for women's stalking victimizations, *Violence Against Women*, 5, 43–62.

New Jersey State Police (1997). *Domestic Violence: Offense Report*, New Jersey Department of Law and Public Safety.

Nicastro, A. M., Cousins, A. V., and Spitzberg, B. H. (2000). The tactical face of stalking, *Journal of Criminal Justice*, 28, 69–82.

Palarea, R. E., Zona, M. A., Lane, J. C., and Langhinrichsen-Rohling, J. (1999). The dangerous nature of intimate relationship stalking: threats, violence, and associated risk factors, *Behavioral Sciences and the Law*, 17, 269–283.

Pathé, M. and Mullen, P. E. (1997). The impact of stalkers on their victims, *British Journal of Psychiatry*, 170, 12–17.

Patterson, J. and Kim, P. (1991). *The Day America Told the Truth*. New York: Prentice-Hall.

Ressler, R. K., Burgess, A. W., and Douglas, J. E. (1988). *Sexual Homicide: Patterns and Motives*. New York: Free Press.

Retzinger, S. M. (1991). *Violent Emotions: Shame and Rage in Marital Quarrels*. Newbury Park, CA: Sage Publications.

Roberts, A. R. and Dziegielewski, S. F. (1996). Assessment typology and intervention with the survivors of stalking, *Aggression and Violent Behavior*, 1, 359–368.

Romans, J. S. C., Hays, J. R., and White, T. K. (1996). Stalking and related behaviors experienced by counseling center staff members from current or former clients, *Professional Psychology: Research and Practice*, 27, 595–599.

Roscoe, B., Strouse, J. S., and Goodwin, M. P. (1994). Sexual harassment: early adolescent self-reports of experiences and acceptance, *Adolescence*, 29, 515–523.

Rowatt, T. J., Cunningham, M. R., and O'Hara, B. (June 1999). Let's Just Be Friends: The Communication of Social Rejection in Unrequited Love, Paper presented at the International Network on Personal Relationships/International Society for the Study of Personal Relationships Joint Conference, Louisville, KY.

Sabini, J. and Silver, M. (1982). *Moralities of Everyday Life*. Oxford: Oxford University Press.

Sandberg, D. A., McNiel, D. E., and Binder, R. L. (1998). Characteristics of psychiatric inpatients who stalk, threaten, or harass hospital staff after discharge, *American Journal of Psychiatry*, 155, 1102–1105.

Sapp, A. (1996). Stalker Typologies, Paper presented to the Academy of Criminal Justice Sciences, Las Vegas, NV.

Schwartz-Watts, D. and Morgan, D. W. (1998). Violent versus nonviolent stalkers, *Journal of the American Academy of Psychiatry and the Law*, 26, 241–245.

Schwartz-Watts, D., Morgan, D. W., and Barnes, C. J. (1997). Stalkers: the South Carolina experience, *Journal of the American Academy of Psychiatry and the Law*, 25, 541–545.

Scocas, E., O'Connell, J., Huenke, C., Nold, K., and Zoelker, E. (1996). *Domestic Violence in Delaware 1994: An Analysis of Victim to Offender Relationships with Special Focus on Stalking*. Dover, DE: Statistical Analysis Center.

Snow, D. A., Robinson, C., and McCall, P. L. (1991). "Cooling out" men in singles bars and nightclubs: observations on the interpersonal survival strategies of women in public places, *Journal of Contemporary Ethnography*, 19, 423–449.

Spencer, A. C. (1998). Stalking and the MMPI-2 in a Forensic Population, Ph.D. dissertation, University of Detroit Mercy, Detroit, MI.

Spitzberg, B. H. and Cupach, W. R. (August 1996). Obsessive Relational Intrusion: Victimization and Coping, Paper presented at the International Society for the Study of Personal Relationships Conference, Banff, Canada.

Spitzberg, B. H. and Hoobler, G. (2000). Cyberstalking and the Technologies of Interpersonal Terrorism, Paper presentation, Western States Communication Association, Coeur d'Alene, ID.

Spitzberg, B. H. and Rhea, J. (1999). Obsessive relational intrusion and sexual coercion victimization, *Journal of Interpersonal Violence*, 14, 3–20.

Spitzberg, B. H., Nicastro, A. M., and Cousins, A. V. (1998). Exploring the interactional phenomenon of stalking and obsessive relational intrusion, *Communication Reports*, 11, 33–48.

Spitzberg, B. H., Marshall, L., and Cupach, W. R. (2001). Obsessive relational intrusion, coping, and sexual coercion victimization, *Communication Reports*, 14, 19–30.

Stith, S. B., Jester, S. B., and Bird, G. W. (1992). A typology of college students who use violence in their dating relationships, *Journal of College Student Development*, 33, 411–421.

Tedeschi, J. T. and Felson, R. B. (1994). *Violence, Aggression, and Coercive Actions*. Washington, D.C.: American Psychological Association.

Tjaden, P. and Thoennes, N. (1998). *Stalking in America: Findings from the National Violence Against Women Survey*. Washington, D.C.: National Institute of Justice and Centers for Disease Control and Prevention (NCJ 169592).

Tucker, J. T. (1993). Stalking the problems with stalking laws, *Florida Law Review*, 45, 609–707.

Wallace, H. and Kelty, K. (1995). Stalking and restraining orders: a legal and psychological perspective, *Journal of Crime and Justice*, 18, 99–111.

Watzlawick, P., Beavin, J. H., and Jackson, D. D. (1967). *Pragmatics of Human Communication: A Study of Interactional Patterns, Pathologies, and Paradoxes*. New York: W.W. Norton.

Way, R. C. (1994). The criminalization of stalking: an exercise in media manipulation and political opportunism, *McGill Law Journal*, 39, 379–400.

Wegner, D. M. (1994). *White Bears and Other Unwanted Thoughts*. New York: Guilford Press.

Wegner, D. M. and Zanakos, S. (1994). Chronic thought suppression, *Journal of Personality*, 62, 615–640.

Wegner, D. M., Schneider, D. J., Carter, S. R., III, and White, L. (1987). Paradoxical effects of thought suppression, *Journal of Personality and Social Psychology*, 53, 5–13.

Werner, C. M. and Haggard, L. M. (1992). Avoiding intrusions at the office: privacy regulation on typical and high solitude days, *Basic and Applied Social Psychology*, 13, 181–193.

Westrup, D., Fremouw, W. J., Thompson, R. N., and Lewis, S. F. (1998). The psychological impact of stalking on female undergraduates, *Journal of Forensic Sciences*, 44, 554–557.

Wright, J. A., Burgess, A. G., Burgess, A. W., Laszlo, A. T., McCrary, G. O., and Douglas, J. E. (1996). A typology of interpersonal stalking, *Journal of Interpersonal Violence*, 11, 487–502.

Zona, M. A., Sharma, K. K., and Lane, J. C. (1993). A comparative study of erotomanic and obsessional subjects in a forensic sample, *Journal of Forensic Sciences*, 38, 894–903.

About the Contributing Authors

Brian H. Spitzberg, Ph.D.

Brian H. Spitzberg, Ph.D. received his B.A. (1978) in speech communication at the University of Texas at Arlington, and his M.A. (1980) and Ph.D. (1981) in communication arts and sciences at the University of Southern California. He is professor of communication in the School of Communication at San Diego State University. His areas of research are interpersonal competence, conflict, jealousy, courtship violence, sexual coercion, and stalking. He has co-authored two books on competence (*Interpersonal Communication Competence*, Sage Publications, 1984; *Handbook of Interpersonal Competence Research*, Springer-Verlag, 1989), co-edited two books on the "dark side" of communication (*The Dark Side of Interpersonal Communication*, LEA, 1994) and human relationships (*The Dark Side of Close Relationships*, LEA, 1998), and authored or co-authored numerous chapters in texts, on topics such as interpersonal competence, social skills assessment, anger, intimate violence, sexual coercion, stalking, and interpersonal conflict. He is author or co-author of over 50 scholarly publications and over 100 scholarly conference papers, including 8 "top-ranked" papers. His articles have appeared in journals such as *Human Communication Research, Communication Research, Communication Monographs, Western Journal of Communication, Communication Quarterly, Communication Education, Communication Reports, Journal of Social and Personal Relationships, Journal of Interpersonal Violence*, and *Violence and Victims*.

Dr. Spitzberg has been on the editorial board of *Western Journal of Communication, Communication Quarterly, Journal of Applied Communication Research, Journal of Social and Personal Relationships, Personal Relationships*, and *Communication Reports*, and is a frequent guest reviewer for a number of other interdisciplinary scholarly journals. He also serves in an advisory capacity for the San Diego City Attorney's Domestic Violence Unit and the San Diego District Attorney's intergovernmental Stalking Strike Force and Stalking Case Assessment Team (SCAT). He is a member of the Association of Threat Assessment Professionals (ATAP).

William R. Cupach, Ph.D.

William R. Cupach, Ph.D. received his B.A. in economics and communication arts from Loyola University of Chicago, and his Ph.D. in communication arts and sciences from the University of Southern California. Currently he is professor of communication at Illinois State University in Normal. His research pertains to problematic interactions in interpersonal relationships, including such contexts as embarrassing predicaments, relational transgressions, interpersonal conflict, and obsessive relational pursuit.

In addition to numerous monographs and journal articles, he has co-authored or co-edited eight scholarly books, including, most recently, *The Dark Side of Close Relationships* (LEA, 1998). He served as associate editor for the *Journal of Social and Personal Relationships*, and currently sits on the editorial board for seven scholarly journals.

PART III

Stalkers and Stalking in the Workplace and in Cyberspace

Stalkers, Stalking, and Violence in the Workplace Setting

7

SUZANNE HOFFMAN
S. ANTHONY BARON

Contents

0-8493-0811-9/01/$0.00+$1.50
© 2001 by CRC Press LLC

Introduction

The issue of violence in the workplace first came to national attention in the mid to late 1980s, when a rash of incidents involving the U.S. Postal Service (USPS) captured the public's attention. Since then, workplace violence has been the focus of various books (Mantell and Albrecht, 1994; Baron, 1993; Vanderbos and Bulateo, 1996), articles, and media programs. Many organizations have subsequently enacted specific workplace violence prevention programs which have included the implementation of "zero tolerance" threat policies, violence prevention training programs for human resource personnel, supervisors, managers, and employees, and the establishment of formal crisis management teams (Baron, 1993; Vanderbos and Bulateo, 1996) to assess and intervene in cases where threats and actual acts of violence have occurred within the work environment.

While much of the focus of the current literature on workplace violence has been on verbal harassment, communication of threats, physical assault, and homicide (Baron and Hoffman, 2000; Baron, 1993), relatively few authors have addressed the issue of stalking specifically as a component of workplace violence behavior. This chapter focuses on stalking as an element of workplace violence. We will attempt to provide a framework for understanding the types of stalking behavior that are likely to occur within the context of the work environment, outline the specific risks posed to the organizations where such behavior occurs, and discuss strategies for organizational case management.

Workplace Threats and Workplace Violence

For the purposes of this chapter, workplace violence is defined as a continuum of behaviors which constitute a direct or implied threat to the physical or emotional well-being of an individual within the context of his or her job or workplace. Threats of violence and acts of violence can be internal, as in the case of a current or former employee perpetrating an act of violence, and/or external, which occur when someone outside the organization such as a stranger, customer, spouse, or romantic partner of an employee poses a danger to the workplace. Behaviors range from "low-level" demonstrations of hostility (such as intimidation, belligerence, and the attempted sabotage of work products or the personal or professional relationships of the victim by the perpetrator) to "mid-level" behaviors (increased arguments, hostility, and/or the verbalization of threats) to "high-level" threats and/or acts of physical and sexual assault, suicide, and homicide (Baron, 1993).

Homicide has consistently been the second leading cause of death in the workplace since the Bureau of Labor Statistics (BLS) first measured the incidence of fatal occupational injuries in 1992 (Bureau of Labor Statistics, 1993–1998). For women specifically, homicide is and has been the leading cause of death in the workplace since 1992 (Bureau of Labor Statistics, 1993–1998). In 1998, homicides in the workplace fell to a 7-year low, with 12% of deaths attributed to homicide (Bureau of Labor Statistics, 1998).

Current data related to the number of non-fatal assaults at work are incomplete and difficult to estimate due primarily to issues of accurate reporting. However, it appears that the number of assaults that happen at work which result in physical or emotional injury, but are non-fatal, far exceed the number of reported homicides. The *National Crime Victimization Survey on Workplace Violence* (1992–1996) estimated that during that period of time more than 2 million U.S. residents were the victims of a violent crime while they were at work.

A startling figure, about 40% of the victims of non-fatal violent incidents in this study reported that they knew their offenders. Some of the most prevalent incidents involved threats, verbal harassment of the victim, and the sabotage of personal and company property. While stalking and domestic violence were not specifically addressed as elements of workplace violence in this report, intimates (defined as current and former spouses, girlfriends, and boyfriends) accounted for 2% of the workplace violence perpetrators identified by female victims and 1% of perpetrators identified by male victims.

Defining Stalking

Definitions of stalking vary, particularly when comparing clinical and legal definitions of the behavior. Westrup and Fremouw (1998) define stalking as "the unwelcome, repetitive and intrusive harassing and/or threatening behavior directed toward a specific individual." Meloy and Gothard (1995) suggested the term *obsessional following* as a corollary of stalking to describe "an abnormal or long-term pattern of threat or harassment directed toward a specific individual." Tjaden and Thoennes (1997) stated that stalking is "harassing or threatening behavior that an individual engages in repeatedly, such as following a person, appearing at a person's home or place of business, making harassing phone calls, leaving written messages or objects, or vandalizing a person's property."

Specific behaviors which constitute harassment in stalking cases are varied and can include such actions as following the victim, approaching the victim, making numerous phone calls, surveillance of the victim, harassing the victim's employer, significant others, children, or pets, interfering with personal property, and sending sexually explicit or threatening notes, e-mails, or gifts (Abrams and Robinson, 1998a). What is important to note is that from a clinical perspective, stalking behaviors may or may not be actually accompanied by a threat of serious harm, and they may or may not precipitate physical assault, sexual assault, or homicide (Meloy, 1998).

Conversely, in legal arenas stalking is defined by the current criminal code. Presently in the United States there are individual state laws but no one federal anti-stalking law. In fact, until 1990, no anti-stalking laws existed at all. However, as a result of several high-profile celebrity stalking cases, most notably the murder of actress Rebecca Lynn Schaeffer by Robert John Bardo and the physical attack on actress Theresa Saldana by Arthur Jackson, California passed the first anti-stalking law in the nation in 1990. By 1992, 30 additional states had passed anti-stalking or harassment laws and by 1993 all states, with the exception of Maine, had passed anti-stalking laws (Saunders, 1998).

Most current statutes require that the person following or harassing the victim has made a *credible threat of harm* to be prosecuted for the crime of stalking. California's stalking law was amended in 1994 and currently states that:

> Any person who willfully, maliciously, and repeatedly follows or harasses another person and who makes a credible threat with the intent to place that person in reasonable fear for his or her safety, or the safety of his or her immediate family, is guilty of the crime of stalking (Penal Code Section 646.9).

Additional sections of this penal code provide that the sentencing court may issue a restraining order for up to 10 years, require that the stalker obtain counseling, and, in some cases, order the stalker to register as a sex offender. The court can also recommend that the offender receive mental health treatment while incarcerated (Saunders, 1998).

Prevalence of Stalking

Few studies have assessed the prevalence of stalking in the United States. However, in 1998, the National Institute of Justice and Centers for Disease Control and Prevention published a research brief entitled *Stalking in America: Findings from the National Violence Against Women (NVAW) Survey* (Tjaden and Thoennes, 1997). In this survey, 8000 men and 8000 women were polled in a telephone survey about their experiences with stalking. In order to qualify as an experience of stalking, victims had to report that they felt a high degree of fear in combination with behaviorally specific questions about following and harassing behavior. Lifetime prevalence (referring to the number of individuals within a specific demographic group who were stalked at least once during some point in their lifetime) and annual prevalence (referring to the number of individuals who were stalked at some point during the previous 12 months) of stalking were measured.

Results of this survey indicated that 8% of women and 2% of men in the United States have been stalked at some point during their lifetime. The authors note that based on U.S. Census estimates, 1 out of every 12 women and 1 out of every 45 men have been stalked at some time during his or her life.

From an annual perspective, 1% of women and four tenths of 1% of men were stalked during the 12 months preceding the study. The study also reported that 74% of stalking victims were between the ages of 18 and 39 years old, and that women were significantly more likely to be stalked than men by intimate partners, half of whom stalked while the relationship was still intact. The study also confirmed previous research, which suggested that most stalking victims know their stalker. Of the respondents in this study, 38% were stalked by current or former husbands, 10% were stalked by current or former co-habitating partners, and 14% were stalked by current or former dates or boyfriends. Only 23% of female victims and 36% of male victims were stalked by strangers. Interestingly, this study also tested the assumption that women are most often stalked after leaving a relationship; 21% of participants said the stalking occurred before the relationship ended, 43% stated that the stalking occurred after the relationship ended, and 36% stated that the stalking occurred both before and after the relationship ended (Tjaden and Thoennes, 1997).

The results of this study indicate that, even with the fairly stringent definition of stalking which required the victim to report a high degree of fear, stalking is a significant criminal and social issue, and occurs more frequently than is evidenced by the number of actual criminal prosecutions for this crime. Additionally, the type of stalking that occurs most frequently is that which is perpetrated by current or former intimates. This is a finding that has been supported by various other researchers (Meloy, 1998; Abrams and Robinson, 1998b; Mullen and Pathé, 1994; National Institute of Justice Association, 1993) and suggests that prior intimates of current employees are likely to present the most tangible threat to the workplace in terms of stalking behavior and potential violence.

Stalking and Stalker Typologies

In an effort to create a typology of stalking, various researchers have focused on behavioral, relational, and psychiatric components (Davis and Chipman, 1997; Meloy, 1998; Zona et al., 1993; White and Cawood, 1998) of stalking. These typologies have been useful in predicting such factors as the types of stalking behaviors (i.e., letter-writing, approaching the victim, gift-giving, threats) the perpetrator is likely to engage in and whether or not the stalker is likely to become violent.

Davis and Chipman (1997) reviewed several studies of obsessional and intrusive following, stalkers, and stalking between 1992 and 1997 and found that no one particular psychological makeup or profile of a stalker existed. However, the researchers did find that various typologies did exist depending upon the variables studied across these studies, suggesting that certain characteristics were consistent such as pursuit behavior, psychiatric diagnosis or disorder, stalker–victim geographic encounter locations, and communication type (verbal vs. non-verbal patterns, electronic, other).

Meloy (1996) reviewed ten studies conducted by 19 different researchers published between 1978 and 1995. Typologies across studies were based on various characteristics and included patterns of pursuit, psychiatric characteristics, victim characteristics, and patterns of violence and threats. Notable findings across studies included the prominence of Axis I and Axis II psychiatric disorders in offenders, and patterns of pursuit of the victim which ranged from letter-writing, phoning, and visiting the home of the victim to achieving face-to-face meetings and threatening or physically attacking the victims.

Meloy (1996) reported several tentative findings with regard to threats and patterns of violence in stalking cases. Among these were that stalkers were more likely to threaten if there was a prior intimate relationship between the victim and the perpetrator. Three fourths of the stalkers in the studies reviewed who threatened their targets were not subsequently violent toward their victim's person or property. Those who made threats of violence prior to the actual violent act committed violent acts more often than those who did not threaten. Of particular note was the fact that while the most likely victim of violence that occurred was the object of the stalker's pursuit, those individuals who were seen as preventing or complicating access to the victim were the next most likely victim group.

Finally, with regard to victim characteristics, Meloy (1996) suggested that future research divide these individuals into three distinct and mutually exclusive groups: prior sexual intimates, prior acquaintances, and strangers.

Tjaden and Thoennes (1997) expanded upon the three relational categories described by Meloy, and created six categories to describe the relationship of the victim to the offender: spouse/ex-spouse, cohabiting partner/ex-partner, date/former date, relative other than spouse, acquaintance, and stranger. Consistent with previous studies, current and former intimates were responsible for the majority of the stalking behavior reported.

Mullen et al. (1999) divided a sample of 145 stalkers into five groups based upon the context and motivation of the perpetrator. *Intimacy-seekers* were identified as those seeking closeness with the object of their attention and identifying that individual as their "true love."

These subjects often idealized their victims and assigned them unique qualities, and frequently made claims that their feelings were reciprocated. *Rejected stalkers* were those who were estranged from a partner of other loved one. *Incompetent stalkers* acknowledged that the object of their attention did not reciprocate their feelings, but still hoped that their behavior would lead to intimacy. *Resentful stalkers* stalked with the specific purpose of frightening and distressing the victim, while *predatory stalkers* were those who were preparing to sexually assault the victim. Resentful and rejected stalkers were found to be most likely to threaten their victims; however, when controlled for confounding variables, only previous criminal convictions were found to be a statistically significant predictor of threats. In this study, assault was predicted by both previous convictions and substance abuse.

A retrospective study by Harmon et al. (1995) separated 48 stalking participants into two categories or axes: e.g., type of attachment and whether or not a prior relationship existed between the two participants. On the first axis, two attachment types were identified: affectionate/amorous and persecutory/angry. For the second axis, six subgroups to describe the prior relationship of the victim to the stalker were created. These included *personal, professional, employment, acquaintance,* and *none.*

While this study provided a useful and specific structure for conceptualizing subtypes of stalking relationships, no significant differences were found among the six subgroups on any of the variables tested. However, differences between similarly defined groups have been observed in other studies (Tjaden and Thoennes, 1997) and methodological problems likely contributed to lack of findings for this study.

Finally, psychiatric diagnoses have also provided a useful framework for understanding the perpetrators of stalking offenses. Zona et al. (1993) separated participants who had been identified as having engaged in stalking behaviors into three groups based upon 74 cases provided by the Threat Management Unit (TMU) of the Los Angeles Police Department. Seven of the participants were identified as having "primary erotomania"; that is, the stalker delusionally believes that he or she is loved by the victim. Thirty-two participants were labeled "love obsessional" and were characterized by the absence of a relationship between the stalker and the victim. In these cases, the stalkers do not hold the delusional belief that the objects of their obsession love them, as in the case of erotomania, but instead are convinced that if only they could make themselves known to the victims, those individuals would be attracted to them.

As time elapses with no positive response from the stalker's target, the feelings of attraction and love are often replaced with anger and rage. The third group in this study was comprised of 35 individuals who had experienced some type of prior relationships with their targets. These participants were labeled "simple obsessional" and included not only prior romantic or spousal relationships but also friendships, acquaintances, and work relationships. Results of this study suggested that those in the simple obsessional group were significantly more likely to engage in threats of violence and in violent behaviors, including harming the physical property of the target and the target itself (Zona et al., 1993).

Workplace Violence, Homicide, and Stalking

One of the most infamous cases of workplace violence and stalking occurred in 1988 in Sunnyvale, California. On February 16 of that year, Richard Wade Farley, a former employee of defense contractor ESL Corporation, shot and killed seven people and injured the victim of his obsessional pursuit, former co-worker Laura Black. Farley, age 39, had reportedly been infatuated with Black for approximately 4 years prior to the shootings. According to Black, Farley began to follow her and "manifested a strange obsession with me" (Downey, 1988) within 1 month of their meeting at ESL. Black maintained that they had only been introduced once prior to the onset of the behavior, and that she had never had a personal or romantic relationship with Farley.

Farley engaged in numerous types of stalking behaviors including parking across the street from her house, harassing her with letters and phone calls, sending strange gifts, and attending the company softball games where Black played for the ESL team. Farley followed Black to and from work, joined the gym where she worked out, and occasionally parked at a "7-11" store within sight of Black's house for extended periods of time. Black moved three times in an effort to discourage Farley and obtained an unlisted phone number. Relentless in his pursuit of Laura Black, Farley would continue to wait outside her workplace and follow her to her new address. By the time the shooting rampage occurred, Farley was sending threatening letters evidencing paranoid delusions to Black up to two times a week.

Farley was terminated from ESL Corporation in 1986 for "poor performance." Other employees stated that he had been terminated because of allegations of sexual harassment by Black. Farley obtained another job, enrolled in several college classes, and continued to harass Laura Black. In 1988, the threats escalated, and he began to accuse Black of sabotaging his career and ruining his life. In a November 13, 1988 letter to Black, Farley wrote "you cost me a job, $40,000 in equity taxes I can't pay and a foreclosure. I can't buy another house and yet I would like you and I to be friends. Don't you understand yet, you can't push me and do you have any idea what I'm willing to do if pushed beyond what I am willing to accept? I lost a job when I wouldn't bow to what they wanted. Why do you want to find out how far

I'll go? Is it so you can be right and win? Don't consider me a joke. I absolutely will not be pushed around and I'm beginning to get tired of trying to be nice." Farley repeatedly advised Black not to show the letters to anyone because they "might get the wrong impression and do something stupid which would make me do something stupid and it would spiral beyond any hope of recovery" (Morten, 1988).

Black hesitated to pursue a formal restraining order because she feared what Farley might do if she took formal action to stop the harassment. But at the beginning of 1988, Laura Black had enough. She hired an attorney and began the process of seeking a protective order against Richard Farley. Farley was served with a temporary restraining order on February 8, 1988.

On February 10, Black's lawyer received a letter from Farley recounting several "dates" he claimed to have had with her and claiming that he had physical evidence of their relationship. A court hearing was scheduled for Wednesday, February 17 to make the restraining order permanent. However, on February 16, one day before that hearing was to occur, Richard Farley stormed the offices of ESL Corporation where Laura Black continued to work and began shooting. When the rampage was over, seven of Black's co-workers lay dead or dying, and Black herself was injured, although not fatally. Farley was taken into custody and police searched his apartment. In it they found numerous firearms; none of the physical evidence of a relationship with Black that Farley claimed he had was discovered (Meloy, 1997). Following the killings, when Farley was asked what might have prevented the shooting spree, he stated, "if she would have just gone out with me."

Stalking and Stalkers in the Workplace Setting: A Typology

The incident that occurred at ESL Corporation is just one example of how stalking can affect the safety of the workplace and how these behaviors can escalate into incidents of workplace violence. See Table 7.1 for workplace stalker typologies.

The ESL Corporation workplace violence case involving Richard Farley endangered not only the victim of the intended stalking behavior (Laura Black), but those who worked with the victim as well as the integrity and security of the workplace itself.

Table 7.1 illustrates our formulation for understanding the types of stalking behavior that occur specifically within the workplace setting. This typology model is broken down along two separate dimensions: the first dimension, the *source* of the threat, can be conceptualized as either internal or external. The second dimension, divided into three (3) discrete categories based upon the work of previous researchers (Meloy, 1996; Harmon et al., 1995), describes

Table 7.1   Stalker and Stalking in the Workplace: A Typology

Relationship	Internal	External
Prior intimate	Former spouse, romantic or domestic partner or sexual partner who is a current co-worker, boss, or subordinate	Any former spouse, romantic, domestic, or sexual partner; can be former employee, supervisor, or subordinate no longer working in the same organization as the victim
Acquaintance	Current co-worker, supervisor, or subordinate with whom the victim is familiar	Customer, client, patient, or former co-worker, supervisor, or subordinate, or member of the community at large with whom the victim is known
Stranger	Co-worker, supervisor, or subordinate who works within the same organization but is unknown to the victim	Customer, patient, former co-worker, supervisor, or subordinate, client, or member of the community at large who is unknown to the victim

the nature of the *relationship* between the stalker and the victim. Of note is the fact that the first dimension is a dynamic one and can shift as a case progresses, while the second remains static.

For example, a stalker can begin as a co-worker of the victim (*internal, acquaintance*), but as a result of the stalking behavior be terminated and then move to being an *external* threat (as in the ESL case), which would require a somewhat different approach to risk management than would an internal case. The relationship with the victim is likely to remain static; the individual will remain an acquaintance of the victim.

No current research is available on the frequency and prevalence of each of these types of stalking as they occur exclusively within the workplace. However, based upon current epidemiological data (Tjaden and Thoennes, 1997), the most common type of stalking that occurs is that of prior intimates targeting their former partners.

Therefore, in the workplace, we would conclude that this is also the most common type of stalking that is likely to occur. Consequently, former spouses, partners, lovers, and/or boyfriends and girlfriends will likely pose the greatest risk in terms of workplace violence and stalking.

However, while employees are at greatest risk of being stalked and/or attacked by current or former intimates, they are also at risk of being targeted by acquaintances such as co-workers, customers, or community members who may develop an obsession with them. As illustrated by the case of Laura Black and Richard Farley, an individual can develop a relentless and sometimes delusional obsession with an employee that he/she has only seen or met briefly. Some perpetrators will fantasize that a special relationship exists between themselves and the victim; others will recognize that no relationship exists but will become obsessed with every detail of the victim's life and become convinced that if the victim really knew them, a relationship would be realized. This type of stalker can originate as either internal or external, and in the early stages of stalking some perpetrators may prefer to send anonymous gifts and communications, making it difficult in those cases to identify the source of the behavior.

Finally, employees are at risk of being stalked by strangers: an individual whom the employee believes that he or she has never met but one who has developed a specific fantasy about the employee and believes that a singular extraordinary relationship exists. Behaviors are likely to be similar to those described above; again, at times it may be difficult to identify the source of the behavior until numerous contacts have been made.

Employees who are being stalked by individuals who are also co-workers, whether they be prior intimates, acquaintances, or strangers, encounter a particularly difficult situation. When the stalker is a co-worker, he or she is provided ready access within the workplace to observe and approach the victim.

Unless the stalker has been barred from the workplace, it is unlikely that anyone will question the stalker's presence in the facility, and if the stalker chooses to become violent, he or she has the ability to enter the work site, even in workplaces where security measures such as key cards and access codes are in place.

Within the workplace, stalking victims are commonly harassed via letters, e-mails, gifts, and phone calls. Common workplace stalking behaviors also include driving through the parking lot looking for the victim's car, and watching for the victim to enter and leave the workplace each day. If the stalker works within the same organization as the victim (internal), behaviors may extend to monitoring the victim's workstation, leaving gifts on the victim's desk, or taking "souvenirs" from the victim's belongings.

The internal stalker often has the ability to observe many of the workplace social interactions of the victim and in some cases may even attempt to gain access to confidential personnel files to obtain more information about his or her target.

Violence Research on Stalking and Stalkers
— Stalking and Potential Workplace Violence

More recent studies report violence rates for stalking that range from 3 to 36% (Meloy and Gothard, 1995; Mullen and Pathé, 1994; Nakaso and Wykes, 1988). One recent review by White and Cawood (1998; as found in Meloy, 1998) of stalking studies reported that 50% of perpetrators in the studies reviewed threatened their victims, and 25% of those individuals acted on their threats. If the individual did become violent, the behavior was likely to consist of the stalker's attempt to kick, grab, punch, strike, or fondle the victim without seriously injuring the victim. The review further reported the homicide rate was less than 2% for the cases studied.

While the current research suggests that many individuals who engage in stalking behavior do not actually become violent with their targets, violent stalking occurs frequently enough to suggest that violence risk assessment should be conducted routinely in stalking cases (White and Cawood, 1998). This includes any cases that occur within the context of a workplace. When stalking behaviors occur at work, the significant implications for occupational safety become evident.

Further, safety issues extend not only to the employee victim; while the most likely victims of stalking violence are the targets themselves, the second most likely victim group is those whom the stalker believes are impeding his access to the victim (Meloy, 1996). Employees who are in relationships where stalking behavior is occurring, those who are leaving relationships in which they are being followed, surveilled, or threatened by current or former partners, and those who are being pursued or harassed by acquaintances or strangers are at risk not only for their own safety, but present a risk to the safety of those with whom they work.

From a workplace violence perspective, those who work with the victim (co-workers, supervisors, and customers) and/or those who intercede on behalf of the victim (human resources, EAP professionals, security personnel, legal representatives) are also at risk of being victimized by the stalker if he or she chooses to become violent.

In the next section, we will address specific threat management issues and the importance of including stalking behaviors as an integral component of a comprehensive workplace violence prevention program.

Violence and Stalking Behavior in the Workplace Setting

Concern for Organizational Case Management

For cases where stalking behavior extends to the workplace environment, strategic case management is essential in assessing risk for violence and for developing a structured intervention approach. In our experience, these cases are managed similarly to traditional workplace threat and violence cases, in that a crucial goal of threat management is the development of an estimation of potential violence risk to both the target and to any other involved individuals. Based on that estimation, a plan is then developed to thwart the unwanted behavior, assist the victim, and develop a plan to address any future threats, should they actually occur.

In most cases, the organizational case management of workplace violence and stalking cases involves a team approach; that is, professionals from a variety of disciplines are involved in assessing the case and in determining and implementing intervention strategies. Because there are typically a plethora of legal issues regarding employee safety and employer responsibility to this end, it is recommended that the organization's legal counsel typically be involved in determining case interventions. Additionally, individuals from human resources, risk management, employee assistance programs (i.e., mental health professionals), security, and law enforcement all play, at times, integral roles in case management, each bringing their own perspectives and areas of expertise to the table.

Following are some suggested guidelines and procedures for the case management of workplace violence cases that have stalking incorporated as a component of the threatening and potentially violent behavior. While the authors do not advocate a "cookbook" approach to case management, we offer these guidelines and procedures as a framework from which a situation-specific investigation and intervention plan can be constructed. In cases such as these where potential violence is at issue, we strongly recommend consultation with a threat assessment professional as part of a comprehensive intervention plan.

Further, although these guidelines and procedures are presented in the chronological order that they would often occur, some may be implemented concurrently. For example, one may interview the victim or witnesses while at the same time conducting a background check, collaborating with security regarding building access issues, and consulting legal counsel regarding relevant employment issues.

First Contact with the Victim

An organization typically becomes aware of stalking and potential workplace violence cases when the employee victim reports the behavior to a supervisor, security, or human resources professional. This can come about in a number of ways. Often, the employee will report the stalking behavior because he or she is fearful and is seeking assistance from the organization, either to protect himself or herself or, in cases of internal stalking, to stop the behavior of the perpetrator. These reports frequently occur after the verbalization of a threat or a significant increase in the frequency or intensity of contact with the victim. In other cases, particularly when the threat is external, employees will report the stalking to the organization after the perpetrator has voiced a threat or has extended the threatening behavior to the workplace. It is not uncommon for employee victims to also report the behavior when they are seeking or have obtained a protective order, putting the employer on notice about the potential threat. Finally, on occasion, concerned witnesses rather than the actual victim report stalking behaviors to the organization.

Whatever prompts the report of the stalking behavior, it is important to respond in an empathic manner while gathering as much information about the situation as possible. Immediate response and investigation are crucial in the threat assessment process. At this point, it is important to schedule or immediately conduct the victim interview.

Victim Impact and Interview

The victim interview can be one of the most important sources of information during the threat assessment process. Information must be obtained about the history of the behavior, from the first contact to the present, as well as information about the type of contact the stalker has engaged in, the frequency of contact, the intensity of the contact, the history of threats, if any, made by the perpetrator, and any known means for carrying out those threats. Additionally, the victim can often provide important information about potential risk and mitigating factors for the perpetrator, particularly when this individual is a former intimate or acquaintance.

During this interview, it is also important to understand the impact of the behavior on the victim; that is, how does he or she view the behavior? Is the victim fearful for his or her safety, and, if so, to what extent? What expectations does the victim have of the organization in response to his or her reporting this information? Does the victim have any suggestion for reducing the level of threat, and are these realistic and in fact likely to de-escalate the situation?

The authors recommend that a professional in threat assessment conduct the interview with the employee victim to assess the relevant risk factors and help determine an immediate safety plan if the risk of violence appears high or imminent. This individual can also discuss with the victim the security precautions that the organization can provide onsite, and emphasize the fact that the victim is primarily responsible for his or her own safety (White and Cawood, 1998). It may be important during this time to assist the employee in developing a "safety plan" (i.e., identifying safe places and people, when to call law enforcement) should an imminent threat to safety occur.

Consider the Need for Security

Based upon the information provided by the victim, an initial decision about whether to institute or increase security precautions at the worksite should be considered. We concur with White and Cawood (1998) who suggest that security precautions during the course of investigations are advisable in some cases to ensure safety when the level of risk remains unknown. Unless it is clear that there is little risk to the individual target(s) of stalking, competent security can provide a measure of containment in the workplace until a more definitive estimate of risk and corresponding intervention plan can be developed.

Leave of Absence Issues

When the perpetrator of stalking is internal (i.e., a current employee), it is often prudent to place that individual on a leave of absence pending the outcome of the investigation. The individual should be advised not to return to the worksite unless advised to do so by a designated company official, and should also be instructed not to contact anyone from the organization (except the designated contact person) until the investigation is complete. The organization can determine the pay status during this time. We often recommend continuing to pay the individual so as not to add to what may be severe levels of stress for the potentially violent perpetrator. If the individual is placed on a leave of absence, it is strongly suggested that all security cards and codes be confiscated so that the individual does not have access to the facility.

Interview Corroborating Witnesses

In some cases, there may be individuals at the workplace (co-workers, supervisors, vendors) who have witnessed the stalking behaviors, overheard threats made by the perpetrator, or who have observed other strange or aggressive behavior on the part of the perpetrator. These witnesses can play an important part in the threat assessment process by providing further information about potential risk factors, mitigating factors, and motivation for violence.

Review of Related Documentation

Legal records can provide important information about potential risk factors for violence. Background investigations can be obtained from investigative professionals, and important information about potential perpetrators can often be obtained within 2 to 3 days of the initial request.

In cases where potential violence is at issue, a thorough background check to determine whether the perpetrator has a record of previous threatening or violent behavior, substance abuse violations, registered weapons and/or weapons violations, and civil judgments can provide invaluable information about past behavior and history of violence. This information can also alert the organization to any recent stressors, or a pattern of deterioration of behavior, which could increase concern regarding potential risk for violence.

Employment records are also an important source of information when the perpetrator is internal. Information pertaining to work performance, productivity, absenteeism, disciplinary actions, and interpersonal relationships with co-workers and authority figures can help illustrate the current and historical functioning of the perpetrator. A significant deterioration in attendance and productivity could be associated with the preoccupation, mental and behavioral, that in part defines stalking (White and Cawood, 1998).

Assessment and Estimate of Level of Risk

An estimation of the level of risk of violence posed by the perpetrator is derived from the presence of certain risk factors associated with violence. These factors include, but are not limited to: history of violent behavior, history of stalking behavior, a history of threats and threatening behavior, significant social stressors, financial stressors, a history of interpersonal maladjustment, substance abuse or dependency, and an "obsession" with firearms and violence (Baron, 1993; Baron and Hoffman, 2000; Davis et al., 1999).

Factors which may mitigate, or inhibit, violent behavior are also considered. Examples of mitigating factors include an absence of violent behavior, serious psychopathology or substance abuse, strong social and familial support, community involvement, and capacity for empathy (Baron, 1993; Baron and Hoffman, 2000; Davis et al., 1999).

We conceptualize level of risk for stalking based upon a 5-point scale: no risk (level one), low risk (level two), moderate risk (level three), high risk (level four), and extreme risk (level five), taking into consideration the above-mentioned risk and mitigating factors. After an estimation of level of risk has been formulated, the next step in the threat management process is the development of a thorough intervention plan.

Develop a Plan and Strategy for Necessary Intervention

The goals for intervention are threefold: (1) to prevent an act of violence, (2) to end the stalking behavior, and (3) to assist the victim(s). The inherent risk in implementing any plan is that rather than de-escalating a potentially violent situation, it will actually escalate the situation and perhaps provide the "triggering event" (Baron, 1993; Baron and Hoffman, 2000; Davis et al., 1999) for the perpetrator in terms of committing a violent act. Therefore, as we have previously mentioned, prior to developing any intervention plan, we recommend consulting with an expert in threat assessment and stalking.

Intervention and Risk Assessment

Plans for intervention correspond to level of risk. For example, if an individual poses an imminent threat or extreme risk (level five), the intervention plan typically calls for immediate involvement of law enforcement. If level of risk is moderate (level three), intervention strategies may focus more on legal, organization, and victim-focused plans.

Interventions in the Workplace Setting

In cases of workplace violence and stalking, interventions will also depend upon the source of the threat (i.e., internal or external). If it is determined that the victim is being stalked or threatened by another employee, then intervention measures will likely focus at least in part on the employment status of the perpetrator. In most cases, perpetrators who stalk and threaten co-workers are in violation of organizational sexual harassment and workplace violence policies, and can be disciplined or terminated based upon these violations.

For both internal and external workplace stalking cases, an integral component of any intervention plan is determining the need for security based upon the level of risk posed by the perpetrator. While many larger organizations have internal, onsite security teams, few smaller organizations have such a resource. For these smaller companies, the retention of well-trained, professional, and unobtrusive outside security personnel can be a valuable asset in moderate to high-risk cases.

It is also important to consider whether to involve law enforcement as a part of the intervention plan, particularly if specific laws are being violated or if the perpetrator has voiced a plan or intent to harm the victim or others who may be associated with the victim. Additionally, the organization may wish to consider if a protective order may be useful in deterring the stalking behavior.

Finally, there are cases where the most appropriate intervention is to not intervene at all, because the intervention itself is likely to produce a violent outcome. In these cases, careful ongoing monitoring of the situation, defensive security measures, and victim assistance may be the most prudent actions that an organization can undertake (Mantell and Albrecht, 1994).

Providing Services to Victims — Referral and Follow-Up

An often-overlooked component of the intervention plan is the referral of the victim(s) for counseling, legal, or related kinds of services. In cases where the victim may benefit from obtaining a protective order, referral to the District Attorney's Office or a victim's advocacy group can be useful and also encourages the victim to seek outside resources to protect himself or herself. Referral for counseling, particularly if the organization has an Employee Assistance Program (EAP) in place, can assist the victim in addressing the psychological trauma often associated with being the target of a stalker.

Ongoing Assessment, Case Management, and Intervention

Once the initial intervention plan has been decided upon, it is important for the intervention team to determine how the case will be followed. A designated organization official should follow up with the victim on a regular basis to determine how the intervention plan has succeeded or not succeeded. The victim should be instructed to report any further contacts from the stalker should they occur and modifications in the intervention plan may be made if new information or behaviors become evident on the part of the stalker.

For example, if the contact from the stalker continues or if threats are initiated, continue, or escalate, it may be appropriate to re-evaluate current level of risk, as well as the initial intervention plan, and incorporate changes in strategy to reflect this new information.

Conclusion

As with traditional workplace violence cases, workplace stalking and violence situations present significant threats to organizational security and safety, not only for the targets of these behaviors, but for those who work in proximity with the victims. These cases require expertise in the areas of threat assessment and organizational intervention to appropriately manage and de-escalate threats. Organizations will most likely benefit from a comprehensive team approach to these cases, relying on expertise from psychological, legal, law enforcement, human resource, and management professionals to assess risk and develop a comprehensive response to potential workplace and stalking threats.

Bibliography

Abrams, K. M. and Robinson, G. E. (1998a). Stalking. I. An overview of the problem, *Canadian Journal of Psychiatry*, 43, 473.

Abrams, K. M. and Robinson, G. E. (1998b). Stalking. II. Victim's problems with the legal system and therapeutic considerations, *Canadian Journal of Psychiatry*, 43, 477.

Baron, S. A. (1993). *Violence in the Workplace: A Prevention Guide for Management and Businesses*. Oxnard: Pathfinder Publishing.

Baron, S. A. and Hoffman, S. J. (2000). *When Work Equals Life: The Next Stage of Workplace Violence*. Oxnard: Pathfinder Publishing.

Bureau of Justice Statistics (1992–1996). U.S. Department of Justice, Special Report: Workplace Violence, 1992–1996. Washington, D.C.: U.S. Government Printing Office.

Bureau of Labor Statistics (1993–1998). U.S. Department of Labor, National Census of Fatal Occupational Injuries. Washington, D.C.: U.S. Government Printing Office.

Bureau of Labor Statistics (1998). U.S. Department of Labor, National Census of Fatal Occupational Injuries. Washington, D.C.: U.S. Government Printing Office.

Davis, J. and Chipman, M. (1997). Stalkers and obsessional types: a review and forensic psychological typology of those who stalk, *Journal of Clinical-Forensic Medicine*, 4(4), 166–172.

Davis, J., Stewart, L. M., and Siota, R. (1999). Future prediction of dangerousness and violent behavior: psychological indicators and considerations for conducting an assessment of potential threat, *Canadian Journal of Clinical Medicine*, 6(3), 44–57.

Downey, K. (February 18, 1988). Richard Farley: trouble brewed beneath the surface, *San Jose Mercury News*, Section 1a.

Farnham, F. R. and Cantrell, P. (2000). Association between violence, psychosis and relationship to victim in stalkers, *Lancet*, 355, 199.

Fremouw, B., Westrup, D., and Pennypacker, J. (1996). Stalking on campus: the prevalence and strategies for coping with stalking, *Journal of Forensic Sciences*, 42, 666.

Harmon, R. B., Rosner, R., and Owens, H. (1995). Obsessional harassment and erotomania in a criminal court population, *Journal of Forensic Sciences*, 40, 188.

Mantell, M. M. and Albrecht, S. A. (1994). *Ticking Bombs: Defusing Violence in the Workplace*. New York: McGraw-Hill.

Mattman, J. W. and Kaufer, S. (1994). *The Complete Workplace Violence Prevention Manual*. Newport Beach, CA: The Workplace Violence Research Institute.

Meloy, J. R. (1996). Stalking (obsessional following): a review of some preliminary studies, *Aggression and Violent Behavior*, 1(2), 147.

Meloy, J. R. (1997). The clinical risk management of stalking: someone is watching over me, *American Journal of Psychotherapy*, 51, 175.

Meloy, J. R. (1998). Psychology of stalking, in J. Reid Meloy (Ed.), *The Psychology of Stalking*, chap. 1. New York: Academic Press.

Meloy, J. R. and Gothard, S. (1995). A demographic and clinical comparison of obsessional followers and offenders with mental disorders, *American Journal of Psychiatry*, 152, 258.

Morton, D. (February 18, 1988). Farley's letters reveal fantasy, *San Jose Mercury News*, Section 1a.

Mullen, P. E. and Pathé, M. (1994). Stalking and the pathologies of love, *Australian and New Zealand Journal of Psychiatry*, 28, 469.

Mullen, P. E., Pathé, M., Purcell, R., and Stuart, G. W. (1999). Study of stalkers, *American Journal of Psychiatry*, 156(8), 1244.

Nakaso, D. and Wykes, S. L. (February 18, 1988). Laura Black: she had to seek order to spell out rejection, *San Jose Mercury News*, Section 1a.

National Institute of Justice Association (1993). Project to Develop a Model Anti-Stalking Code for States, Washington, D.C.: U.S. Government Printing Office.

Saunders, R. (1998). The legal perspective on stalking, in J. Reid Meloy (Ed.), *The Psychology of Stalking*, chap. 2. New York: Academic Press.

Tjaden, P. and Thoennes, N. (1997). *Stalking in America: Findings from the National Violence Against Women Survey*, Denver, CO: Center for Policy Research.

Vanderbos, G. R. and Bulatao, E. Q. (1996). *Violence on the Job: Identifying Risks and Developing Solutions*. Washington, D.C.: American Psychological Association.

Westrup, D. and Fremouw, W. J. (1998). Stalking behavior: a literature review and suggested functional analytic assessment technology, *Aggression and Violent Behavior*, 3, 255.

White, S. G. and Cawood, J. S. (1998). Threat management of stalking cases, in J. Reid Meloy (Ed.), *The Psychology of Stalking*, chap. 15. New York: Academic Press.

Zona, M., Sharma, K., and Lane, J. (1993). A comparative study of erotomanic and obsessional subjects in a forensic sample, *Journal of Forensic Sciences*, 38, 894.

About the Contributing Authors

Suzanne Hoffman, Ph.D.

Suzanne Hoffman, Ph.D. is a California-based psychologist and organizational development consultant who specializes in the areas of workplace violence prevention and intervention, violence risk assessment, critical incident debriefing, and workplace sexual harassment. Dr. Hoffman's professional expertise includes consulting with a variety of organizations regarding difficult and potentially dangerous employees. Her experience includes post-trauma counseling and critical incident debriefing in organizations that have experienced incidents of workplace violence and other workplace tragedies.

Dr. Hoffman has worked with individuals from a variety of cultural and diagnostic backgrounds, and has interfaced with human resources and management teams to assist in the implementation of sexual harassment and workplace violence policies and procedures. Dr. Hoffman holds an undergraduate degree in psychology from San Diego State University (SDSU), and earned both a Master's degree and a Doctorate in clinical psychology from the California School of Professional Psychology (CSPP) in San Diego.

A member of both the American Psychological Association (APA) and the San Diego Psychological Association (SDPA), Dr. Hoffman is also a member of the Employee Assistance Program Association (EAPA) and The American College of Forensic Examiners (ACFE). She co-authored *When Work Equals Life: The Next Stage of Workplace Violence* (Pathfinder Publications, 2000) with Dr. S. Anthony Baron.

S. Anthony Baron, Ph.D., Psy.D.

S. Anthony Baron, Ph.D., Psy.D. is a noted author, speaker, and nationally recognized pioneer in workplace violence prevention, and has been described as "America's leading researcher into workplace violence" and the "most accurate" profiler by a recent definitive study of workplace violence entitled *New Arenas for Violence.* Working with clients in all areas of the public and private sectors, Dr. Baron has also been retained by the U.S. Postal Service (USPS) to provide workplace violence and threat assessment training throughout the United States.

He served on an executive committee for the postal service in Washington, D.C., which has implemented training based on his book for over 750,000 postal personnel. Dr. Baron is the author of *Violence in the Workplace: A Prevention and Management Guide for Businesses.* His second book is entitled *Violence in Our Schools, Hospitals, and Public Places,* and he co-authored two other books, *Occupational Medicine: Violence in the Workplace* and, most recently, *When Work Equals Life: The Next Stage of Workplace Violence* with Dr. Suzanne Hoffman (Pathfinder, 2000).

An active author on career transition, change management, downsizing, and emotional issues surrounding life and work performance, Dr. Baron is also an author of several workbooks and has been published in national business journals, leading national newspapers, and major publications.

An honors graduate of Biola University and United States International University (USIU), Dr. Baron holds graduate degrees in psychology, marriage and family therapy, and organizational development and has completed post-doctoral continuing education work at Harvard Medical School. Dr. Baron is a member of the American Psychological Association (APA), the California State Psychological Association (CSPA), and the Society of Human Resources Management (SHRM). He is board certified and a fellow of the American Academy of Experts in Traumatic Stress (AAETS).

Electronic Crime, Stalkers, and Stalking: Relentless Pursuit, Harassment, and Terror Online in Cyberspace

8

BONNIE D. LUCKS

The Internet is like a vault with a screen door on the back; I don't need jack hammers and atom bombs to get in when I can walk right through the door.

— **Anonymous, 2000**

Contents

Introduction

Cyberspace, the Global Internet System, or World Wide Web (a.k.a. cyberspace, Web, Net, or WWW) is an international system of new technology for communications in cyberspace. Not only is it profitable for private industry, businesses, and government agencies, it has opened up the door for a new type of crime, cybercrime, which has unlimited daunting consequences on a personal and global scale. Privacy and security are vulnerable as they are easily invaded by cybercriminals, who have the capability of maliciously hacking (McClure et al., 1999) into systems and software, presenting a challenge to network managers, security professionals, and high-tech computer investigators and crime units, which are now taking a prominent place in our law enforcement agencies. Crimes such as computer hacking, fraudulent business scams, spamming, e-mail bombing, releasing destructive viruses, child pornography, pedophilia, hate crimes, and cyberstalking now abound (Deirmenjian, 1999) (see Appendix 8.1).

Cyberstalking, in particular, presents unique issues and dilemmas for law enforcement agencies, mental health professionals, and their victims. Privacy laws may be broken as cyberstalkers obtain personal information about their victims on-line. First Amendment rights, the freedom of speech, need to be protected, as well as the victims of cyberstalkers. The victims may be threatened and harassed by their perpetrators who want "to kill, kidnap, or injure the person, reputation, or property of another, either on or offline" (U.S. Attorney General, 1999). Furthermore, the cyberstalkers have their victims terrorized right within the confines of their own homes.

The Stalking Law and Changes Accommodating Cyberstalking

The California Penal Code, Section 646.9, defines stalking as "any person who willfully, maliciously, and repeatedly follows or harasses another person and who makes a credible threat with the intent to place that person in reasonable fear for his or her safety, or the safety of his or her immediate family, is guilty of the crime of stalking." For the purposes of describing the law as it pertains to stalking and specifically cyberstalking, additional portions of the law are cited as such.

> (e) For the purposes of this section, "harasses" means a knowing and willful course of conduct directed at a specific person that seriously alarms, annoys, torments, or terrorizes the person, and that serves no legitimate purpose. This course of conduct must be such as would cause a reasonable person to suffer substantial emotional distress, and must actually cause substantial emotional distress to the person. (f) For the purposes of this section, "course of conduct" means a pattern of conduct composed of a series of acts over a period of time, however short, evidencing a continuity of purpose. (g) For the purposes of this section, "credible threat" means a verbal or written threat, including that performed through the use of an electronic communications device, or a threat implied by a pattern of conduct or a combination

of verbal, written, or electronically communicated statements and conduct made with the intent to place the person that is the target of the threat in reasonable fear for his or her safety or the safety of his or her family and made with the apparent ability to carry out the threat so as to cause the person who is the target of the threat to reasonably fear for his or her safety or the safety of his or her family. It is not necessary to prove that the defendant had the intent to actually carry out the threat. The present incarceration of a person making the threat shall not be a bar to prosecution under this section. (h) For the purposes of this section, the term, "electronic communication device" includes, but is not limited to, telephones, cellular phones, computers, video recorders, fax machines, or pagers (U.S. Attorney General, 1999; California Penal Code 646.9).

Specifically, there needs to be an established pattern of behaviors, with repetitive following or harassment, which constitutes a credible threat, and with the intent to place the victim in fear for his or her safety (Maxey, 1999). Additionally, Alaska, Arizona, Connecticut, New York, Oklahoma, and Wyoming have cyberstalking laws (Choney, 1999).

Stalking Statistics

According to Los Angeles Deputy District Attorney Scott Gordon (2000), "Most stalking victims are women between the ages of 18 and 26 ... and tend to be acquaintances, co-workers and short or long-term relationships." There are an estimated 200,000 Americans that are presently being stalked (D'Amico, 1997a). District Attorney Investigator Wayne Maxey of San Diego (1999) reports that 1 in 12 women will be stalked (8.2 million), 1 in 45 men will be stalked (2 million), which lasts on the average of 1.8 years, while 50% of the cases are not reported.

Additionally, according to the National Violence Against Women Survey (as cited in U.S. Department of Justice, 1998), race does not appear to be a factor, most victims know their stalker, especially when they are or were intimate partners, and most stalkers were motivated to control or instill fear in their victims.

Furthermore, in a recent study, Meloy (1998) has summarized factors that have currently been associated with stalking. Stalkers are more likely to have had a prior criminal history, a psychiatric diagnosis such as substance abuse or dependence, usually stimulants and/or alcohol, mood disorders, adjustment disorder, delusional disorder, paraphilia, and schizophrenia (Meloy and Gothard, 1995), and may have a personality disorder such as narcissistic, borderline, histrionic, antisocial, paranoid, or dependent disorder (Meloy, 1997). They may have had attachment problems (Meloy, 1992), particularly in their early childhood, and substance abuse or dependence histories; stalkers may be younger, more intelligent, and better educated, which is consistent with their resourcefulness and manipulativeness (Meloy and Gothard, 1995) than other criminals; they have had a failed intimate relationship with a maladaptive response to social incompetence, social isolation, and loneliness (Meloy, 1998).

Obsessional Relationship Intrusion to Stalking Typologies

Stalking is not an unfamiliar behavior within the law enforcement and mental health communities. Furthermore, there are many typologies described in the literature, with one end of the continuum beginning with obsessive relational intrusion (ORI), which is described as, "one person attempting to establish an interpersonal relationship with another person who does not want this relationship" (Cupach and Spitzberg, 1998).

The behaviors escalate in severity, culminating at the extreme end of the continuum with illegal behaviors known as stalking. Some of the possible contributing determinants of the pursuer have been proposed, specifically jealousy, betrayal, attachment style, possessiveness, domination/control, obsession, and co-dependency (Nicastro et al., 2000). Furthermore, the victim's "response to the intrusive event influences the pursuer's subsequent actions, which in turn affects the victim's subsequent actions, and so on" (Cupach and Spitzberg, 1998).

In a study by Nicastro et al. (2000) ORIs were found to be annoying. Furthermore, the more frequent the pursuit behaviors were, and the more types of pursuit a person was exposed to, the more various types of psychological symptoms were experienced by the victim. Symptoms included, but were not limited to, changes in their personalities, fright, anxiety, sleep disturbances, appetite disturbances, depression, and symptoms of posttraumatic syndrome, such as intrusive recollections and flashbacks (Nicastro et al., 2000). However, it was determined that "the best marker of victim trauma is the extent to which the victim feels compelled to resort to a greater number of coping responses" (Nicastro et al., 2000). "The more coping responses one employs, the worse the symptoms regardless of how much and what type of victimization one has experienced" (Spitzberg et al., 1998).

Studies have suggested that victims may engage in behaviors that reinforce their situation. Furthermore, restraining orders were found to be the cause of increased tactics by the pursuer and many restraining orders were violated. Mutual restraining orders, however, were associated with reduced risk of criminal offenses (Meloy et al., 1997).

As a relationship decays, according to studies by Walker and Meloy (1998), the frequency of pursuit behaviors increases in severity until they are

viewed as stalking, especially when the relationship was intimate and culminated in a form of domestic violence.

"There is no one psychological make-up or demographic profile of stalkers"
(Davis and Chipman, 1997). However, many typologies of stalkers have been
suggested. Zona et al. (1998) have proposed the categories of erotomania, love
obsessional, simple obsessional, and false victimization syndrome. "Erotomania
is the delusional belief that the stalker is passionately loved by an unattainable
victim, often a celebrity or a person of high status in society" (Davis and
Chipman, 1997). It has been classified as a delusional disorder, also known
as "de Clerambault's syndrome." In this case the stalker goes to great lengths
to contact or make his presence known to the victim (Zona et al., 1993; Davis
and Chipman, 1997; Cupach and Spitzberg, 1998; Meloy, 1998). Public
awareness through the media has singled out high profile targets such as
Rebecca Schaeffer, Jerry Lewis, and Michael J. Fox, to mention a few. This
category, however, comprises about 10% of all stalkers (Zona et al., 1993;
Davis and Chipman, 1997; Cupach and Spitzberg, 1998).

Davis and Chipman (1997) further differentiate stalkers by their relationships to their victims, as to whether the victim is known or unknown to the
stalker. Within the category of erotomania, all targets are unknown and are
random-targeting stalkers. These stalkers choose a complete stranger at random who meets the stalker's particular requirements. High profile or celebrity-targeting stalkers are those who choose a celebrity or public figure with
high economic or social status. Last, the single issue-type or "fixated focus"
stalker chooses victims that are involved in a particular topic of interest to
them (Davis and Chipman, 1997).

Love obsessional stalkers are usually known to the victim, whom they
relentlessly harass. The victim may be a co-worker, friend, or professional.
Davis and Chipman (1997) separate this category into the casual-, relational-
type stalker, where the stalker perceives a real or imagined fantasy relationship
with the victim, and the workplace or occupational setting-targeting stalker,
where the target is a co-worker with whom the stalker works and may mis-
construe the contents of his or her interactions. It is in this situation that
many people meet and do not have the time to nurture intimate relationships.
Therefore, the stalker may assume that business lunches and office functions
are a substitute for dating. Moreover, this situation tends to blur the behaviors
that constitute conventional courtship customs. When the stalker is spurned,
violence is one of the most common responses, particularly workplace violence. This typology consists of about 43% of all stalkers (Zona et al., 1993;
Davis and Chipman, 1997; Cupach and Spitzberg, 1998; Meloy, 1998).

Simple obsessional stalkers are the most common and the most violent.
The victims may be ex-spouses or ex-lovers with a relationship that may have
included a history of domestic violence. The stalker's behavior begins with

the intent to "restore or maintain the now unreciprocated relationship" (Cupach and Spitzberg, 1998).

The common goal of the stalker is power and control; thereby, the victim is viewed as a possession. Rejection is not an option for the stalker and his or her behaviors are exacerbated by the denial of the terminated relationship. If the relationship is continually rejected and cannot be restored, threats, retribution, and revenge become the primary goals of the stalker. Psychological and physical terrorism have no bounds as the victim lives in a nightmare. To complicate matters, child custody battles and acrimonious divorce proceedings intensify the stalker's retaliatory behaviors. This category of stalkers comprise 50% of stalking cases. They are, furthermore, sub-divided into the intimate partner-targeting stalker and the domestic violence-targeting stalker (Davis and Chipman, 1997; Cupach and Spitzberg, 1998; Meloy, 1998).

A study by Zona et al. (1993) examined cases from the Threat Management Unit of the Los Angeles Police Department (LAPD) that had involved stalkers whose victims were ex-partners. Their study found that the erotomanic and love obsessional offenders were delusional in their belief that the victims were passionately in love with them.

The offenders frequently attempted to contact their victims with the belief that there was some external force that prevented the victims to return their affection. Zona et al. (1993) found that the simple obsessional offenders did actually have prior relationships with the victims. With the ending of their intimate relationships, however, the offenders felt that they had been "wronged or mistreated" and it was this group of offenders that was more likely to cause bodily injury to their victims or destroy their property. The actions of the offenders' stalking behaviors were attributed to a "narcissistic rage" in reaction to the loss of the relationships (Zona et al., 1993).

False victimization syndrome (Zona et al., 1998; Mohandie et al., 1998) or falsely alleged victimization syndrome (Davis, 2000), although quite rare (2%) (Mohandie et al., 1998), involves someone who desires to be in the role of the victim. In this case, the victim convinces authorities that he or she is actually being pursued by a stalker. However, in actuality, there is no stalker, nor has one existed in reality — only in fantasy. The victim/stalker relationship usually has an elaborate deceptive story that the crime of stalking actually exists (Davis, 2000).

According to Mullen et al. (1999) other typologies have been introduced into the literature. One such classification system used two axes: "one, defining the nature of the attachment as either affectionate/amorous or persecutory/angry; the other defining the previous relationship" (Mullen et al., 1999). Simple dichotomies such as psychotic vs. non-psychotic have been suggested.

Security specialist Gavin de Becker (1997) proposed four categories based on the different types of pursuers and their motivations: attachment-seeking, identity-seeking, rejection-based, and delusion-based. Attachment seekers would like to have a relationship and select famous personalities as their romantic object. Identity-seekers pursue targets that might give them an identity. Rejection-based seekers are those who have been rejected and would like to renew the relationship or otherwise seek revenge. They usually remain focused on the people that they feel rejected them. Delusion-based seekers are those that are delusional and "their relationship is pre-ordained from God" (de Becker, 1999).

Mullen et al. (1999) has constructed five categories. The groups, although not mutually exclusive, are rejected, intimacy seeking, incompetent, resentful, and predatory. "Rejected stalkers," according to Mullen et al. (1999), "are a complex mixture of desire for both reconciliation and revenge." Their sense of loss in combination with "frustration, anger, jealousy, vindictiveness and sadness" are constantly in flux. Most have been found to be very persistent and have personality disorders, some delusional disorders, and morbid jealousy. This group is the largest group, containing ex-partners, and overlaps with the simple obsessional stalker (Zona et al., 1998). Due to their clinging nature and assertive entitlement, their personalities may include narcissism with persistent jealousy and paranoia. These stalkers were found to be the most difficult to engage due to the extent of their bitterness and extreme compulsion for revenge. Furthermore, they inflict damage to their victims' property with rare attacks to the victim. Some of these stalkers could be persuaded to cease their behaviors when fines or incarceration were imminent (Mullen et al., 1999).

"Intimacy-seeking stalkers" identify their victims as their "true love" and believe that their love is reciprocated. According to Mullen et al. (1999), these stalkers want to establish a relationship with their victims and become "jealous and enraged" when their efforts are to no avail. Most of these stalkers are similar to Zona et al. (1998) "erotomania type." They suffer from delusions, schizophrenia, and mania. Most of these stalkers are persistent and fanatically obsessed with their victims and appear to be isolated, lonely, and socially inept, with a pompous sense of entitlement. These stalkers are invulnerable to judicial sanctions, as this is the price they have to pay for "true love." Some can be violent and require psychiatric intervention (Mullen et al., 1999).

"Incompetent stalkers" are aware that their advances and affection are not reciprocated, however, they are hopeful that their efforts would be rewarded and ultimately lead to intimacy. This group is intellectually limited and lacks social skills necessary for courtship. They present with a sense of entitlement and have often stalked others. These stalkers abandon their victims with ease, however, since they do not attach any unique qualities to their victims, and there is a high probability that they would choose another victim (Mullen et al., 1999).

"Resentful stalkers" deliberately want to frighten and threaten their victims. Some have a vendetta against a victim in particular, however, most have a grievance and choose their victims at random. Their primary targets are young, attractive, wealthy, and happy women. The stalker, on the other hand, has recently been humiliated or professionally rejected. These stalkers have a sanctimonious attitude and legal sanctions only serve to infuriate them, which exacerbates their behaviors (Mullen et al., 1999).

"Predatory stalkers" take pride in their sense of power with the intent to sexually assault their victims. There may have been periods of time where they did get to know their victim. These stalkers consciously rehearse and fantasize their premeditated attack. Most use paraphilias and usually have had convictions of previous sexual offenses. These stalkers are the least intrusive and the most dangerous, sometimes lacking any forewarning prior to an assault. Since these stalkers have a high potential for calculated sexual violence they require criminal sanctions. Furthermore, due to their paraphilia disorder (see Appendix 8.1 for definitions), they may also require mental health treatment (Mullen et al., 1999).

Kristine K. Kielen (as cited in Brody, August 1998), a clinician who evaluates criminals who are mentally ill or dangerous, conducted a study wherein more than half of the male stalkers were found to have an attachment disorder. She has suggested that the attachment disorder stems from the loss or absence of a caring and consistent parent or guardian during childhood. She states that there usually is a precipitating factor, usually one of loss, that triggers their stalking behaviors. Kielen has suggested that there are three kinds of attachment disorders which describe stalkers: the "preoccupied," the "fearful," and the "dismissing" type.

The "preoccupied" stalker has "a poor self-image, but a positive view of others." This stalker will seek approval and validation from others to feel good about himself, and when he is rejected, will stalk to restore his sense of self. The "fearful" stalker has a poor self-image and tends to see others as "unreliable and unsupportive." He continually seeks others for their validation, however, since he does not trust others, rejects them, and then stalks due to the fact that there is the need to find someone for validation. The "dismissing" stalker thinks that other people are unworthy and he may remain distant in relationships. By keeping away, his sense of entitlement remains intact; however, when rejected he is angered and stalks for revenge (Brody, August 1998).

In a recent study by Knight (1999) on rapists' typology at the Massachusetts Treatment Center (MTC), he found that there were three forms of expressive aggression that were predicted by different developmental experiences. One form had expressive aggression with a mother that was emotionally unavailable, such as depression and psychological difficulties. In this case, the father was found to have a criminal history and sexual abuse in childhood. "Unsocialized general aggression" appeared to be predicted by an alcoholic father, a mother with a criminal history, and a poor family support system. "Sadism" was predicted by a father with a criminal history, poor family support, low intelligence, and less juvenile incarcerations (Knight, 1999). Apparently, early developmental childhood experiences impact other types of offenders in a similar fashion.

A recent study in Britain by Bennetto (2000) found that stalkers attempted to murder their victims in 25% of the cases. The study found that 3% of the victims were attacked by the offenders and 50% had threatened their victims with violence. Two out of five stalkers targeted the relatives and friends of the victims. In fact, 40% of the victims had reported that their stalkers had received help by their families and friends. Additionally, Bennetto's (2000) research found that the offenders were from a higher socioeconomic status, 50% were ex-partners of the victims, and 12% were strangers. Most of the victims were harassed several times each week, at home, at work, in public, and by electronic means such as the telephone. Furthermore, offenders sent messages to their victims from prison. Moreover, 33% of the victims attempted to deter their stalkers with a civil injunction which was ignored by most offenders.

Another study conducted by researchers Sheridan, Boon, and Davies (as cited in Bennetto, 2000) categorized the offenders into four types. They found that 25% of the offenders were of the "infatuation type" where the offender was obsessed and "in love" with the victim. These offenders lived in a fantasy world, believing that they should be together with their victims forever. Additionally, many of these cases found that attempts were made by the offenders to literally meet with their victims.

Second, the team of researchers determined that 50% were ex-partners and appeared to be bitter, hateful, angry, and hostile with a high potential for violence and verbal abuse in public. The offenders were found to be jealous of any new relationships that their former partners became involved with. In cases such as these, the victims were encouraged to move from their homes or jobs (as cited in Bennetto, 2000).

"Sadistic stalkers" in the study (Bennetto, 2000) made up 12.5%. In these cases, the relationship between the victim and the offender may have initially been a casual acquaintance that escalated to one where the offender sought control of the victim. The offender was found to vacillate between communicating his love, to those of threats, such as letting the victim know "we're going to die together." The offender had the capability of being cold and possibly psychopathic. Moreover, in these cases, the victim could not believe any assurances that were made by the offender and, therefore, due to the fact that the offender was unpredictable, the victim was advised to relocate (Bennetto et al., 2000).

Stalkers that were of the "delusional type" consisted of 12.5% and were found to have a history of previous sexual problems and offenses. This type of offender believes he has a relationship with the victim, however, in reality, it does not exist. These offenders continually harass the victims by telephone, letters, visits, and the sending of obscene materials (Bennetto et al., 2000).

Cybercrime

With the advent of the Internet and the growth of new technology comes the challenge of addressing old and new crimes. Stalkers, in particular, are contesting our conceptualization of traditional terrestrial crimes utilizing the new territory of cyberspace. Furthermore, as cyberspace becomes the everyday reality, or virtual reality (see Appendix 8.1 for definition of "cyber" terminology), of human existence, the number of deviant crimes or cybercrimes will increase as will the nature of their victimizations (Wall, 1998). The existence of cybercrimes has been acknowledged, with various offenses labeled as cyberstalking (Wall, 1998; Deirmenjian, 1999). Thus, distinctions in offenses will be clarified and cyberstalking differentiated.

According to Wall (1998) there are four groups of offenses that illustrate the range of activities of cybercrimes. These categories demonstrate the contested nature of the acts involved, the problems of identifying causality, and the particular victim or victim group, with the focus being the offense rather than the offenders or the victims. The four groups of cybercrimes are cybertrespass, cybertheft, cyberobscenity, and cyberviolence (Wall, 1998).

Cybertrespass acts involve crossing "established boundaries into spaces that have already been claimed" (Wall, 1998). These acts may be on an intellectual level at one end of the continuum, and at the extreme end escalate into an information warfare between nations. Other acts within this group are cybervandalism, cyberspying, and cyberterrorism (Wall, 1998).

Cybertheft may refer to traditional patterns of theft within cyberspace. Other forms would require a new understanding of property, especially pertaining to information that may be within a company's computer system or hard drive. In addition, cybercredit, cybercash, and cyberpiracy would be within this category (Wall, 1998).

Cyberobscenity refers to the trade of obscene materials within cyberspace. This category presently has no distinct components in terms of cyberlaw, as different individuals, institutions, and nations have different concepts and definitions of obscenity in cyberspace (Wall, 1998).

Cyberviolence describes the "violent impact of the cyberactivities of another upon an individual or social grouping" (Wall, 1998). Although the activities do not have to have a direct physical appearance, the victim feels the violence of the act resulting in long-term psychological ramifications. Activities within this group are cyberstalking, child exploitation, hate speech, and bomb-talk. In some situations there is no specific victim and the crime may be indirect as with cyberterrorism, while in other cases the crime is directed toward an individual, as it is in cyberstalking (D.S. Wall, personal communication, August 2000; Wall, 1998).

Cyberstalking

Offenders are atypical in terms of our traditional understanding of terrestrial crimes, although some of their behaviors appear similar. According to Meloy (1999), "stalking is an old behavior, a new crime" and now with a new tool. However, cyberspace with its unlimited access makes governance of freedom of speech, intellectual property, privacy, and safety more difficult to control (Deirmenjian, 1999). With billions of Internet users potentially reaching infinite numbers of people globally, "it is not just a case of 'old wine in new bottles,' or for that matter, 'new wine in new bottles,' rather many of its characteristics are so novel that the expression, 'new wine, but no bottles!'" appears to be a more appropriate description (Wall, 1999).

Cyberstalking, as with terrestrial stalkers, may include some of the same motives and typologies, such as the victims may be known, as a co-worker whose dating advances have been rejected. The ego-bruised offender retaliates with on-line sexual harassment and threats within the workplace, thus creating a hostile environment within the workplace (Anonymous, 2000). The U.S. Equal Employment Opportunity Commission and judicial decisions have been defining the Civil Rights Act, Title VII of 1964, specifically regulating the definition of "sexual harassment" and "hostile environment" as follows:

> Harassment on the basis of sex is a violation of the law. Unwelcome sexual advances, requests for sexual favor and other verbal or physical conduct of a sexual nature constitute sexual harassment when submission to such conduct is made either explicitly or implicitly a term or condition of an individual's employment. Submission to or rejection of such conduct by an individual is used as the basis for employment decisions affecting such individual; or such conduct has the purpose or effect of unreasonably interfering with the individual's work performance or creating an intimidating, hostile or offensive working environment (29 Code of Federal Regulations (CFR) 1604.11 (a)).

Studies by Sipior and Ward (1999) have identified two types of harassment. The first, "quid pro quo," is where employees receive sexual demands to retain their employment, obtain a promotion, or gain other considerations within the workplace. The second, "hostile environment," is where the harassment is less direct. The elements that are legally recognized as sexual harassment contain conduct that is "sexual in nature, unreasonable, severe or pervasive in the workplace and unwelcome" (Sipior and Ward, 1999).

In a study by Sproull and Kiesler (as cited in Sipior and Ward, 1999) it was found that since there was an absence of "social context cues," e-mails were more likely to be irresponsible, less constrained, include profanity, negative sentiment, and include extreme, revealing, and less desirable content. Along with flaming, criticism, and insults the study suggested that "inhibitions consistent with the norms of interpersonal communication are often relaxed" (Sproull and Kiesler as cited in Sipior and Ward, 1999).

E-mail-related litigation is one of the fastest growing areas in the workplace. Employers are financially liable over their employees' e-mail content, which in many cases are substantial. For example, the Chevron Corporation settled with four female employees for $2.2 million for sexual harassment. Some of the victims' symptoms were found to include depression, insomnia, loss of appetite, anxiety, and fatigue (Sipior and Ward, 1999).

In the situation where past intimate partners are involved, the offenders may remain on-line to harass, terrorize, and avenge their sense of loss, frustration, hatred, and anger, thereby establishing their power and control over their ex-partners. If the offenders have the intent to attack or terrestrially stalk their ex-partners, the computer may merely be a mechanism of convenience in addition to their arsenal of devices utilized to victimize their ex-partners (D. Parker, personal communication, August 2000). In this instance cyberstalking is another phase in the offender's overall pattern of stalking behavior using the new technology of the computer. Cyberstalking may therefore be combined with domestic violence cases (CyberGuards, 1998). Service victim providers concur, stating that "The internet is rapidly becoming another weapon used by batterers against their victims" (U.S. Department of Justice, 1998).

A study done on stalking behavior and the cycle of domestic violence by Coleman (1997) was conducted to access the presence of stalking behavior and domestic violence. Their study found that "those who reported more verbal and physical abuse during their relationship, were more likely to be stalked by their former partners after the relationship ended." The Director of Virginians Against Domestic Violence, Ruth Mickleim (as cited in Coleman, 1997), has estimated that approximately 90% of women who have been murdered by their former intimate partners may have been stalked prior to their deaths. It would not be inconceivable to speculate that their ex-partners would have been seeking revenge, power, or control when they could not reconcile the relationship (Coleman, 1997). This 90% research figure has since been questioned as to its factual accuracy (B. Spitzberg, personal communication, October 2000).

Business associates may become enraged when plans go awry or the offender feels deceived or cheated. President Clinton signed into law in 1996 the Interstate Stalking Act, 18 U.S.C. 2261A, which makes it a crime for any person to travel across state lines with the intent to injure or harass another person and, in the course thereof, places that person or a member of that person's family in a reasonable fear of death or serious bodily injury (CyberGuards, 1998).

For example, Keith Kosiewicz intended to extort money from a San Diego corporation. He sent threatening e-mails from Illinois to injure the executives of the business, violating Title 18, U.S. Code Section 875 (b), an anti-cyberstalking statute (U.S. Department of Justice, 1998). Kosiewicz claimed that he had been cheated by the San Diego corporation resulting in his rage. He sent approximately ten e-mail messages to the executives "demanding monetary compensation." His e-mails became hostile and terrorizing as his requests for settlement were unanswered. After a final warning and uncontrollable rage the offender arrived in San Diego to obtain his remuneration and was apprehended by the San Diego Police Department and the FBI (*United States of America v. Keith Christopher Kosiewicz*, 1999).

In 1997, Jane Hitchcock, a New York author, battled the Woodstock Literary Agency of New York for defamation of character and harassment. She asserts that this group of people utilized their internet skills to seek revenge for her reporting them to a New York attorney on unrelated fraud allegations. She received e-mail death threats, e-mail bombs, and had her name, address, and phone number posted on an internet pornography site which asked people to call her and share their fantasies with her (Deirmenjian, 1999; Hitchcock, 2000; Knott, 1999; Robinson, 1999).

After an on-line argument with a man about internet advertising, Armistead began receiving hundreds of e-mails from men responding to her "sex-wanted" ad. The ad included pictures of nude women with her photo and name attached. Although he was reported to his Internet service provider or ISP (see Appendix 8.1), the cyberstalker was able to continue his campaign against Armistead by using an anonymous re-mailer. Thereafter, Armistead's 5-year-old daughter became the cyberstalker's victim as she began receiving vulgar e-mails such as, "You're a little whore just like your mother" (Sherr, 2000). After receiving intimidating and threatening e-mails, she moved and changed her address to a post office box. The cyberstalker was not deterred and continued to e-mail her and claimed to have physically stalked her. Since the course of the case seemed to have become a terrestrial stalking situation, the cyberstalker could therefore be prosecuted, as the state of Georgia has no laws regarding cyberstalking per se. The cyberstalker, Hillyard, was charged with terrestrial stalking and was found "not guilty" (Deirmenjian, 1999; Hitchcock, 2000; Sherr, 2000).

Victims may be unknown to the offender, who is searching for a new relationship or friendship. The potential relationship may lead to intimacy or alienation; however, the relationship remains on-line. In this scenario, the offender is isolative, avoidant, awkward socially, narcissistic, paranoid, and would not make a connection with the victim without a computer.

Dwayne Comfort, a former USD student, sent over 100 threatening, harassing, terrorizing, and sexually explicit e-mails to five different victims, who were extremely vulnerable and had no way of protecting themselves from the onslaught of threats. The offender used personal information about the victims, causing them emotional distress, anxiety, fear, loss of sleep, and the inability to concentrate on their work or studies. According to the records, "He was preoccupied with his 'game' of power and intimidation to the point of obsession." The offender was intelligent and a "very savvy" computer expert who was able to avoid detection for 10 months (J. Davis, personal communication, June 2000; Choney, 1999; Maxey, 1999; *The People of the State of California v. Dwayne Comfort*, 1998).

Dating relationships may begin with alternative methods, such as meeting on a video dating service, with the intent of developing an intimate relationship. In one such case, the female decided that she was not interested in pursuing the relationship further. Spurned by her rejection, Andrew Archambeau continued to pursue the relationship by sending 20 e-mails in a 2-month period. The offender claimed that pursuing the romance via e-mails was nonthreatening as the victim could ignore them. The Michigan court did not agree (Carmody, 1994; Deirmenjian, 1999; *The Detroit News*, 1996).

Gary Dellapenta, a former security guard, had his romantic overtures rejected by a North Hollywood woman. Controlled by his inner rage, he harassed her by posting personal ads in her name on various Internet services. He posted the ads claiming that she had fantasies of being raped and gang-bang fantasies. The messages included her address and phone number. Men responded to the ad in the middle of the night offering to rape her. She posted a sign that stated that the ads were fake. The offender sent ads to respondents saying that the note was part of her fantasy. The victim did not even own a computer (Choney, 1999; Miller and Maharaj, 1999).

Predatory cyberstalkers attempt to befriend and romance their victims to arrange meetings. They may utilize a combination of coercion, violence, sexual deviance, sexual harassment, and threats. This category includes child exploitation or pedophilia. The offender may be compulsive, manipulative, exploitive, or self-absorbed and isolated. He may have a love obsession with a sense of entitlement and may have had multiple antecedent opportunities to rehearse his fantasy. While remaining in the domain of cyberspace, he may initially be annoying or helpful, until he becomes terrifying.

The use of Internet Relay Chat (IRC) lines are the easiest way for the predatory cyberstalkers to find their prey. They are computer savvy and are able to find the local users currently using chat, their channels, and nicknames (Mure, 1999). Predatory cyberstalkers frequent cybersex sites, pornographic sites, multi-interactive sites, and gaming sites, which may include the use of paraphilia, voyeurism, fetishism, and fantasy (see Appendix 8.1). When angered and irritated they utilize techniques such as spoofing, spamming, e-mail bombing, bulletin board ads, and attempts to defame their victims' characters (see Appendix 8.1 for definitions). With the use of bulletin board ads they have the capability to recruit and manipulate others to assist them in their exploits resulting in minimal effort on the part of the offender, while the victim suffers with symptoms of trauma.

The ultimate goal of some predatory cyberstalkers is to entice their victims into a face-to-face meeting. Their motivation is to exert power and control over their victims utilizing manipulation, fantasy, and any other tools possible to that end. Although, as above, the Internet provides ease of use, can be non-confrontational, impersonal, and anonymous, the removal of disincentives may keep the offender sending harassing, flaming (see Appendix 8.1), and threatening e-mails, or it may be a "prelude to more serious" and deviant behavior, "including physical violence" (CyberGuards, 1998). The predatory cyberstalkers may want to fulfill their sexual desires and fantasies. They may want the fantasy to be perfectly performed and may obsess about the details with little care for the victims. The offenders become lost in the world of fantasy; however, if a meeting occurs, the fantasy has crossed out of the realm of virtual reality, into reality.

According to a study by Malamuth (1986) on predictors of naturalistic sexual aggression, factors such as creating the "motivation to commit the act, those reducing internal and external inhibitions that might prevent it from being carried out, and those providing the opportunity for the act to occur" were essential to understanding the role of sexual aggression. The interaction of these factors was found to be the primary causal factor. Sexual arousal in response to aggression included power and the offender's desire to conquer and sexually dominate the victim. Hostility toward women was used in the study to determine its possible motivational functions. Malamuth (1986) suggests that there would be men who would not be "inhibited by women's suffering from and resistance to sexual aggression." For example, those offenders feeling low hostility to women may find the experience unpleasant if the victim is suffering and resistant. However, those offenders with feelings of high hostility toward women "may actually be reinforced and thereby encourage further aggression in the face of resistance" by the victim (Malamuth, 1986), essentially exhibiting a lack of empathy on the part of the offender (Grubin, 1999).

Malamuth's study (1986) considered the effects of sexual aggression stimulated by the mass media, wherein an attitude of aggression against women is accepted. The findings were consistent with the hypothesis that the media contributes to changes in attitudes regarding aggression which would "turn off social prohibitions against injuring or using others" (Malamuth, 1986). With multiple violent, sexually aggressive, and pornographic Websites available on the Internet, aggression is encouraged and practiced. Cyberstalkers have no social constraints that would suggest that their behavior is unacceptable, and with the utilization of anonymous personae, re-mailers, and sexually explicit chat rooms (see Appendix 8.1), their behaviors may appear to be accepted and encouraged.

Sub-categories within this group are those that stay within the realm of virtual reality, those that may become addicted to the excitement of virtual fantasy, and those that enter the terrestrial world leaving a path of destruction behind them, including those cases of pedophilia and child exploitation.

Kevin appeared to be a likable and responsible person with a job as a security guard at a hospital. The first time he logged onto the Internet from the hospital's library was the beginning of an addiction that ultimately led him on a path of destruction. As time went on, he progressed to spending hours on the Internet, and coincidently discovered on-line pornography. His on-line sexual world began to replace any contact with women in the real world, alleviating his loneliness. While on-line, he encountered a single woman looking for companionship. It wasn't long until their relationship blossomed and they were married. Concurrently, however, he had discovered lewd pornographic sites and was always on-line. Although he agreed that he had a problem and promised not to go on-line at home, he could not resist the urges to indulge in his addiction. He became transfixed to the cybersex world. The hospital noticed some "unusual" computer activity and installed cameras that recorded his actions. He was suspended for a short time from the hospital and ordered into therapy for his addiction. Presently, he lives under the constant observation of his wife and boss. "I think I can make it, but, if [she] goes, I know I'll head straight back to the computer" (Mannix et al., 2000).

Many "Net Junkies" spend hours on-line creating flawless identities to engage in "fabulous cyber-romances and lurid cybersex along with other high-tech escapists" (Focamp, 1999). They "cyber-engineer" a new persona as they are unhappy with who they really are. Individuals that are isolated and in need of physical human contact merge fantasy and reality, especially with the new virtual reality graphics that are available, and become completely mesmerized and addicted without face-to-face communications (Spitzberg and Hoobler, 2000; Focamp, 1999). Their playground is the world, and it is impervious to constraints of time and place.

Gaming communities provide violent social interactions and mass carnage as players destroy foes attempting to reach their goals. Most versions are multi-player and actual people control the animated software. Live opponents battle each other as they maneuver throughout the virtual world. The level of violence and suffering varies with the game and the level of its technology. LANs (local area networks) provide gamers the capability to link their computers together in order to engage in competitions, similar to the "all-night poker games" so popular in the past. These games sometimes go on for days, consistent with behaviors suggestive of a "non-substance form of addiction" (Simpson, 1999).

On-line gamers are technically sophisticated and write and download codes and weapons to modify popular games. They are affluent with the capacity to own the latest in technology, and may spend 72 hours in "the zone" on a game without a break. "It becomes almost subconscious," according to Higgins (as cited in Copeland, 2000). In the case of Barrysworld, players can log onto their chat room and interact with other players (Dempsey, 2000).

According to David Grossman (as cited in Simpson, 1999), a former West Point Academy psychology professor and author of *Stop Teaching Our Kids to Kill*, "People who live on those computers are so isolated from reality that they are able to convince themselves that their fantasy is reality. Violent computer games desensitize kids to real-life violence" (Simpson, 1999). Furthermore, Senator Joseph Lieberman states that, "Violent video games link screen violence and aggressive behavior in children and gives them a warped view that the world is more violent than it really is" (as cited in Saltzman, 2000). In games such as "Quake," training techniques teach one to "clear the room by moving quickly from target to target while aiming for the head" (Van Horn, 1999).

According to a survey by the National Institute on Media and the Family, 80% of high school kids were familiar with the shooter game "Duke Nukem," whereas only 5% of their parents had heard of the game (as cited in Simpson, 1999). Eric Harris, gunman in the 1999 Columbine High School shooting which left 15 dead, was found to have used his computer for game playing. The fact that he used gaming sites was not unusual for his age; however, it was "the possibility that he may have used the games to plot his rampage" that was problematic. He claimed to be a professional "Doom" and "DOOM 2" creator, designing different levels to the game, including one that supposedly represented Columbine High School (Simpson, 1999). "It's like playing tag, cyber-bullets don't hurt" (Simpson, 1999). Carolyn Klein, a child psychologist at the Lester B. Pearson School Board in Montreal (as cited in Saltzman, 2000), suggests that the reported brutality surrounding violent computer games conforms to Albert Bandura's social-cognitive learning theory, where vicarious learning takes place by watching someone else. The theory has been related to television and movies; however, with violent video games being interactive rather than passive, there may be an even greater chance that the behaviors may be copied (Saltzman, 2000).

Mike Merzenich (as cited in Copeland, 2000), a neuroscientist at the University of California, San Francisco, states that:

> ... video games give immediate feedback for every correct choice, prompting the release of neurotransmitters in the brain. That prompts direct learning, the type that occurs when a monkey gets food for pressing a lever. And because the learning is fast, focused and repetitive, games cause a great degree of limited learning in a little time. Which means that after two hours of gaming, you could know a heck of a lot about how to get a virtual car to the end of a racetrack without crashing. What's not clear, is whether you know anything else.

The problem that is suggested is that gaming teaches people to react quickly; however, there are circumstances where thinking slowly may be necessary. This power of advanced reasoning, according to Merzenich, is the basis of our species, to be able to consider various outcomes prior to making a decision (Copeland, 2000). Seymour Papert of MIT's Media Lab calls this a "grasshopper mind," where "there is a tendency to leap from one topic to another, relying on the ability to access information quickly rather than hold it in their heads" (as cited in Copeland, 2000). The generation will be one of fast-moving minds, with the expectation that information will be presented efficiently with the use of icons and images substituting for the written word (Copeland, 2000).

"Computer addicts," according to David Shenk (as cited in Sardar), writer on "data smog," suffer from "fragmentia," which includes symptoms of cardiovascular stress, weakened vision, impaired judgment, confusion, frustration, decreased benevolence, overconfidence, acute restlessness, boredom, and distraction (Sardar, 1998).

A study by the Media Analysis Laboratory at Simon Fraser University in Burnaby, British Columbia (as cited in Van Horn, 1999) found that the video game industry has 30% of the U.S. toy market, earning $8.8 billion in the United States, whereas the Hollywood box office gross was approximately $5.2 billion. They found that 80% of the users were between 13 and 15 years old with an average time on the computer of 5 hours per week. Heavy players spent more than 7 hours per week playing. Males were found to spend twice as much time as girls, and most were willing to give up various other activities in order to play the games (Van Horn, 1999).

A second study by Jean Funk, a clinical child psychologist at the University of Toledo (as cited in Van Horn, 1999), surprisingly found that parents recognized 9 out of 49 games presented in the study. Data suggest that parents do not have the information necessary to assist their children in making appropriate choices and are unlikely to supervise their child's electronic game playing (Van Horn, 1999).

Furthermore, Saltzman (2000) reports that recent findings from the Interactive Digital Software Association state that 71% of the most frequent users of computer games are over 18 years old, with 42% of the buyers averaging 36 years old. The average age for American gamers was found to be 28 years old. Female players were found to account for 43% of gamers (Saltzman, 2000).

"Under 18 U.S.C. 875(c), it is a federal crime, punishable by up to five years in prison and a fine of up to $250,000.00, to transmit any communication in interstate or foreign commerce containing a threat to injure the person of another" (CyberGuards, 1998). Additionally, Section 875(c) includes transmissions by e-mail, beepers, or the Internet (CyberGuards, 1998).

In 1995, a Michigan student, Jake Baker, posted four graphically violent stories on the Internet using the name of a female student. Although the story was erased from the Internet, others continued to post the stories. The threats were transmitted across state lines and received by Arthur Gonda. In their e-mails, they described their erotic fantasies of raping and torturing a female student.

Although the case was brought before the court, it was dismissed because Baker's words were protected under the First Amendment. Federal District Court Judge Avern Cohn said that "it was Baker's right to freedom of speech" and that the e-mail messages "did not constitute a credible threat" (Arnold, 1998; Deirmenjian, 1999; *United States of America v. Jake Baker and Arthur Gonda*, 1995).

The FBI later found provoking e-mail messages which describe their intentions in detail to abduct and abuse the female student. Despite the additional information, the case was dismissed and "Baker was assumed harmless" (Arnold, 1998; Deirmenjian, 1999; *United States of America v. Jake Baker and Arthur Gonda*, 1995).

According to MacKinnon (1993), "the legal system did not take action to protect Jane Doe" (the female student in the Baker case). "The District Court misapplied the First Amendment to "legitimate repeated threats of actions towards the victim though (Jane Doe) hadn't known at the time" (MacKinnon Web page, 2000). In this case, "the violation of a woman by slander was completely overlooked and dismissed" (Arnold, 1998; MacKinnon, 1993).

The case was considered fantasy and therefore the federal law was inapplicable, as it addresses "actual threats" as well as not including bulletin board postings or chat room assistance by others (CyberGuards, 1998).

Many Internet relay chat rooms, MUDs (see Appendix 8.1 for the definition), or other similar interactive spaces "have few boundaries or controls imposed upon them" (Michals,1997). Many people question whether these sites remain in the realm of fantasy or are preliminary trials that transform into reality. Sexual past deeds may be revisited and ultimately may blur the distinction between fantasy and reality. Since many of the sites feature male domination of female sexuality, the virtual world may reinforce behaviors in real life. Clearly, virtual rape is different than actual rapes that are experienced in the real world; however, erotic scenes may convert easily into graphic sexual violence from which women are reporting traumatization from these experiences. Many turn off their computers if they are feeling attacked; however, the memories linger (Michals, 1997).

A 27-year-old nurse from Georgia recalls her traumatic experience as she entered a chat room pretending to be a 15-year-old girl. Within moments she had seven to eight men sending her graphic pictures of women being raped and beaten. The men stated that, "They wanted to rape (her), spank (her) until (she) bled." According to the nurse, what was scary was that these men thought she was a 15-year-old girl (Michals, 1997).

Patti Britton, a counselor, sexologist, and spokeswoman for *Feminists for Free Expression*, suggests that "airing such violent inclinations freely and without reproach will merely normalize these tendencies, inuring society to the viciousness and inequality at its core" (as cited in Michals, 1997). Furthermore, the Internet emphasizes the link between on-line fantasy and real-life behavior. The violent role-playing on-line may be a reflection of male gender norms in an era of role re-definition, or it may be a function of men asserting their dominance and inevitably chasing women away from the Internet (Michals, 1997). Additionally, the Internet may allow women to act out their wildest dreams and fantasies in safety, procuring "an evening of anonymous sex" without some of the repercussions that would be experienced in real life. With the graphic depictions of sexual violence and pornography on-line, these images are brought into the home, but they are increasingly becoming common in the workplace reality (Michals, 1997).

Women have the choice to be a "victim" on-line and can empower themselves by changing chat rooms or turning off their computer, whereby they are taking responsibility for their own choices. However, according to Gilbert, co-author of *Surfergirls* (Seal Press), control and consent "become synonymous with feminine compliance or retreat" (as cited in Michals, 1997). Leaving the game may not be empowering, but rather it could be "damaging to a women's perception of herself and her sense of control." The presumption of power and freedom are an illusion in cases of on-line violence where women submit to their own violation. Although a woman may feel as though she has power, ultimately the "patriarchal cultural script validates the assumption that all women really want to be treated this way" (Michals, 1997).

New Websites such as "CUSeeMe" employ video cameras enabling each participant to watch the other play out fantasies in real time. According to Bill LeFurgy, editor of the weekly newsletter, *Culture in Cyberspace*, there is the possibility that within the next 5 to 10 years, sensory devices will probably be available for people to hook themselves up, enabling users to actually "feel their fantasies as they would if they were actually doing what they imagine on-line" (as cited in Michals, 1997).

Harassment on-line is like rape in that it is considered a power game. MacKinnon (1993) states that men use words that embody actions to abuse women. The words stimulate ideas and fantasies which are eventually acted upon. Words reflect attitudes. Words of violence can easily shape the feelings and opinions of others. "The process of empowerment of the perpetrator and traumatization of the victim occurs not because of the content of the words ... but because of the experiences they embody and convey" (MacKinnon, 1993). As MacKinnon (1993) states, "Unwelcome sex talk is an unwelcome sex act ... it works to exclude and segregate and subordinate and dehumanize, violating human dignity and denying equality of opportunity."

Stalking Law Legislation and the Internet

Although 50 states, the District of Columbia, and the federal government have passed laws criminalizing stalking, they presently need to reconsider precedents relating to new technology which "can transmit information around the world at the flick of a button" (Weaver, 1999); specifically the laws regarding cyberstalking that involve expressive conduct and speech which are protected by the First Amendment need revision (Weaver, 1999). There are laws which protect freedom of speech; however, there are laws which forbid harassment and protect individual privacy. An increase in one has a corresponding decrease in the other. The primary challenge is to find a balance between the two (CyberAngels, 2000; Spitzberg and Hoobler, 2000; Weaver, 1999). Additionally, on-line communications may be private, as in e-mails, or public, as with *Usenet* newsgroups. "Privacy protection from the cyberstalker is a major goal on-line for the cyberstalking target, just as privacy violation of the target is a major goal for the cyberstalker" (CyberAngels, 2000).

"The First Amendment does not prohibit any and all regulations that may involve or have an impact on speech" (U.S. Department of Justice, 1998). The U.S. Supreme Court has recognized that true threats may be criminalized without violating the First Amendment. The conduct, however, must be understood to constitute a "threat of violence," as in the case of *Watts v. United States*, wherein Watts was convicted of violating a 1917 statute which prohibits any person from "knowingly and willfully ... [making] any threat to take the life of or to inflict bodily harm upon the President of the United States." Watts was convicted of a felony by "knowingly and willfully threatening the President" (*Watts v. United States* 394 U.S. 705, 1969). It is understood, therefore, that the threats must be distinguishable from what is constitutionally protected speech, "such as political protest and other legitimate conduct" (U.S. Department of Justice, 1998).

The Liam Youens Case

Liam Youens fell in love with Amy Boyer in the 8th grade. He became obsessed with her and stalked her for approximately 2 years, although she had no idea she was being stalked. He had a Website dedicated to her and he felt rejected by her. He documented his desires and love for her, including her ultimate demise. Youens felt that if he couldn't have her, no one would, and that they could be together forever. On the Website he detailed her murder, including the gun he was to use. He obtained her social security number on-line for $40.00 and found her place of employment. As stated in his journal on-line, he drove up to her car as she was leaving work, opened his window next to her car window, shot her in the head, and followed by shooting himself. Amy Boyer was 20 years old (Rather, 2000; Boyer, 1999). Murder–suicide is the ultimate and last defiant act with total power and control.

The ease of purchasing someone's social security number for the purpose of malicious intent has come to the attention of the Justice Department. Senator Dianne Feinstein and Representative Ed Markey have introduced new legislation to Congress that will protect a citizen's personal privacy by prohibiting the sale of social security numbers. "The Social Security Number Protection Act of 2000" makes it a civil and criminal offense for a person to either sell or purchase someone else's social security number, except for legitimate purposes" (U.S. Newswire Staff, 2000; Roth, 2000). This proposal, which includes on-line or off-line sales for profit, hereafter, will become a federal crime. Former Vice President Al Gore remarked, "I believe that privacy is a basic American value. This new legislation will help Americans protect their social security numbers and as a result safeguard the privacy of their most sensitive information" (as cited in U.S. Newswire, 2000).

Chairman Robert Pitofsky of the Federal Trade Commission (FTC) states that privacy violations are so pervasive that it is time for Congress to take action. Internet companies openly trade information with marketeers that may contain personal and sensitive information. Furthermore, information is gathered creating consumer profiles without their consent, or their knowledge, while they are visiting certain Websites. Some of the information gathered contain recent purchases, travel plans, and medical information.

According to Senator Max Cleland, Democrat of Georgia, "Many see this tracking as being akin to stalking" (as cited in Safire, 2000). Information is gathered through "cookies" that are implanted in computers to track movements. Cookies are tiny strings of data, text files that are stored on a user's hard disk when visiting certain sites that track the Web-surfer's habits (Williams, 2000). According to Pitofsky, fewer than one in ten Internet sites that collect personal identifying data display the voluntary privacy seal. The FTC suggested that Websites offer consumers "the choice" of saying "no" to profiling. In reality, this appears as a viable option, however most people have neither the time nor understanding as to how their data will be used. Real privacy on-line is through written consent. This places the seller in a position to explain how their information is to be used (Safire, 2000; Lance, 2000; Lance and Scripps, 2000) rather than invading individual rights to privacy.

In *The Hound of the Baskervilles,* by author Sir Arthur Conan Doyle, there is a link between hunting and predatory sexuality. "From the perspective of the man hunting with hounds, the chase is hot, charged with phallic sexuality" (as cited in Luke, 1998). Contemporary hunting is structured and experienced as a sexual activity. There is a reciprocal relationship between the erotic nature of hunting animals and the predatory heterosexuality in the Western patriarchal society. Hunters describe their relationship with their prey in terms of sex and affection. According to Luke (1998) it is important to understand the vocabulary itself. "Love" means the desire to possess the creatures who excite the hunter. "Taking possession" entails killing the animal, perhaps eating it, and mounting the head. "Romance" refers to hunting. As Collard (as cited in Luke, 1989) comments,

> A romantic removes the "love object" from the reality of its being to the secret places of his mind and establishes a relationship of power/domination over it. There can be no reciprocity, no element of mutuality between the romantic lover and the "love object." The quest (chase) is all that matters as it provides a heightened sense of being through the exercise of power.

It is apparent that the prey is the inferior object, while the predator is powerful.

John Robinson was known on the Internet as "slavemaster" and arranged to meet women for sadomasochistic sex, according to Morrison (2000). Eight women and a child have been missing, with the remains of five women found in barrels on Robinson's property. Robinson has been charged with aggravated sexual battery and theft by two recent Internet chat pals. "If Robinson were charged and convicted in the killings, he would prove one of the worst murderers in the state history [of Kansas] and the first documented serial killer in the nation to use the Internet to recruit potential victims" (Morrison, 2000).

There are already an increasing number of physical abuse and violence cases that have been reported from the Internet. According to Robert Ressler, a former FBI criminologist, "These people are always there ... it's the technology and the tools they use that are changing." Many cases are adults targeting minors for sex or for use in pornography. In 1998, former President Clinton signed a bill into law that protects children against on-line stalking.

> The statute, 18 U.S.C. 2425, makes it a federal crime to use any means of interstate or foreign commerce (such as a telephone line or the Internet) to knowingly communicate with any person with the intent to solicit or entice a child into unlawful sexual activity. While this new statute provides important protections for children, it does not reach harassing phone calls to minors absent a showing of intent to entice or solicit the child for illicit purposes. (CyberGuards, 1998)

It is obvious that there are gaps in the laws and these are the changes that need to be addressed not only within the United States, but on a global scale as well.

Katie Tarbot, 13 years old, thought she had met the boy of her dreams in a chat room. His name was Mark and he claimed to be 23 years old. Within an hour he had requested her phone number, which she gave to him. They communicated frequently by e-mail and telephone. After months of chatting, he convinced Katie to meet him in Texas during a swim-team meet in 1996. She entered his hotel room where he began kissing her and grabbing her crotch. Fortunately, her mother suspected something was awry and followed Katie. Luckily the incident came to an end. Mark was a 40-year-old man and a "chat-room child molester" (Quart, 2000; Berst, 2000).

A 9-year-old girl and her family were harassed for 2½ years by someone sending out postings on the Internet soliciting sex with their phone number attached. Phone calls were received in the middle of the night asking to speak to the little girl. After moving and changing their telephone number, the police department's Computer Crime Unit was able to match Internet postings with a neighbor's telephone line always being connected with his ISP. After pleading guilty to transmitting obscene material, Charles Gary Rogers was charged with a misdemeanor and fined $750.00. However minimal the punishment was, many pedophiles were led to this 9-year-old girl (Sherr, 2000).

The FBI's undercover crime unit has arrested hundreds of sexual predators for soliciting minors on the Internet; however, many of those that are convicted serve little or no time. Apparently, judges may be reluctant to impose greater sentences on cyberstalkers as many of them are "highly educated, financially successful white men" (Baker, 1999). Currently federal sentencing guidelines allow for lenience with first-time offenders and those who show remorse. Furthermore, these cases are viewed as being "victimless" in nature. According to Jorges Martinez, a supervisory agent with Innocent Images (as cited in Baker, 1999), offenders have several traits in common:

Most are white males ages 25–45, few have criminal records, many have advanced degrees and come from a high socioeconomic background. Almost all are involved with children, either through their jobs or as volunteers. These guys are willing to travel distances. They have money. They have decent jobs. A lot of them are married.

The controversy reflects the discomfort of judges with these "sting" operations that just fall short of entrapment. It may be that the undercover agent posing as a child may serve as encouragement to those who would not otherwise act on their fantasies with children. Whereas an agent posing as a child would continue the conversation, the possibility remains that an actual child may terminate the correspondence. According to Martinez, "The FBI is tracking down a new breed of stalker who is able to flourish in the high-tech computer age" (as cited in Baker, 2000). Some children are being traded and sold over the Internet, which is not a victimless crime — it's not child pornography, it's child exploitation (Baker, 2000).

Senator Spencer Abraham plans to introduce to the Senate the "Just Punishment for Cyberstalkers Act of 2000." The bill will increase penalties for on-line sexual solicitation of children and make cyberstalking a federal crime. According to the bill, there would need to be a "justifiable belief on the part of victims that they are threatened with serious harm or death and would allow for law enforcement officials to pose as children online as part of a sting operation" (Barton and Deiters, 2000). The bill is in accordance with the action requested by former Vice President Al Gore in August 1999 in the report on cyberstalking by the U.S. Department of Justice (Barton and Deiters, 2000).

Hate crimes, including racism and civil rights violations, are easily committed in cyberspace. The victims are targets of opportunity. Multiple victims fitting the criteria for the vendetta are effortlessly threatened by e-mail with a single click on the computer (D'Amico, 1997).

Recently, Richard Machado, a 19-year-old Latino and a student at the University of California Irvine, e-mailed 59 Asian American students and staff threatening to "hunt them down and kill them." In his e-mails he accused them of being responsible for all the crimes on the campus and he ordered them to leave or he would personally make it his life career to "find and kill" every one of them. According to Assistant U.S. Attorney Michael Gennaco, this case may set a precedent for future prosecutions. Apparently this is the first civil rights charge where the crime was committed from a computer (Sciupac, 2000).

Furthermore, there are hate crimes where a single victim may be the intentional target, someone who appears vulnerable, receptive, and therefore easily lured, or he or she may be someone that unfortunately appears to fit the qualities of the offender's hate and vengeance. For the offender, the virtual world becomes a place where cyberstalking becomes a game where they can abuse their power and control over others (Anonymous, 2000).

The cyberstalkers may be young and clever, with the intention to "show off" their deeds "just for fun" or as a game. These young fun-seekers or hackers may be socially awkward within their peer group and rather than joining a gang, choose the Internet as their challenge and friend. Highly intelligent, these young hackers brag about their feats to their friends or to other hackers on-line, each trying to out-match the other in their antics. Most are innocent and take advantage of their experiences and knowledge to later become powerful highly paid computer security agents (D. Parker, personal communications, August 2000).

Malicious hackers, crackers, or cyberpunks begin as fun-seekers, on the other hand, and soon come to appreciate and enjoy criminal activity. Most are introverted and polite in the world of reality, however, they adopt a new persona once in cyberspace that is profane, crude, and threatening. "They are immoral, lie, cheat, steal, and exaggerate as a common activity and delight in deceiving 'the suits'" (D. Parker, personal communication, August 2000). Their goal is to wreak as much havoc and damage as they can. They have the capabilities of stealing access to corporate e-mail accounts, seizing control over entire systems, and setting damaging viruses which debilitate thousands of computers worldwide, such as the "I Love You" virus or the "Melissa" virus.

According to Donn Parker, computer crime author and security expert, "From interviews that I have conducted with cybercriminals, they may not be able to look their victim in the eye. They can only have relationships through non-personal means and therefore, they can abuse and misuse others through the computer. The significant factor is that they did not begin as crooks, murderers or thieves; to them they were just games" (D. Parker, personal communication, August 2000).

Ikenna Iffih, a quiet 20-year-old Nigerian immigrant and student at Northeastern University's College of Computer Science, "unleashed a trail of cybercrime from coast to coast" (Mannix et al., 2000). He penetrated NASA and Defense Department computers, compromised commercial Internet services, and stole access to a corporate e-mail account. Using telnet.proxy, he logged onto a computer system which provides supplies for U.S. troops worldwide. He effectively seized complete control over NASA's entire system. He used a "sniffer" (see Appendix 8.1) to acquire login names and passwords. He maliciously hacked into his own university's computer system and soon held the names, addresses, birth dates, and social security numbers of 9135 students. He renamed the password file of all accounts of Zebra Marketing Online Services, disenabling the use of the system by clients. Unfortunately, Iffih became careless and left clues daring the FBI to try to catch him. "They did"

(Mannix et al., 2000). According to Jonathan Zittrain, executive director of Harvard University's Berkman Center for Internet Society, "You'd have to be a pretty skilled and tenacious lawbreaker to avoid detection in the future" (as cited in Wallack, 2000).

Recently, the first hand-held computer device was infected with a virus, called *Phage*. The destructive virus has the capability to not only be shared among virus writers, but it has the ability to disguise itself and spread. This virus affects Personal Digital (data) Assistants (PDA), the *Palm OS*. However, unlike *Trojan horses* which has the capacity to affect hand-held devices, *Phage* appears to be spread easily.

According to Mikko Hermanni Hypponen (as cited in Reuters, 2000), the manager of anti-virus research at Finland-based F-Secure Corporation, *Phage* may be "disguised as computer games or pornographic images on Internet news groups and chat rooms." The virus can be downloaded in seconds and can attach itself to every program, although it does not affect database files. Hypponen has stated that in the future, it is not inconceivable that a similar virus would be "written for hand-held computers which send malicious programs over wireless internet connections" (as cited in Reuters, 2000). Along with PDAs, WAP Web-enabled phones have the capacity to send a "single message to up to 20 phones (an instant spaminator)" according to Schneider, a member of an Internet Crime Group. Tracking Mobile IPs from people committing crimes will prove to be problematic, unless the system administrators give out a static IP address.

Uniqueness of Cyberspace

The World Wide Web (WWW), however, possesses innovative techniques that are unique to the evolving technology of cyberspace, with detection next to impossible. Depending on the expertise and skills of the offender, the more complex and sophisticated strategies they employ, such as the use of chaining re-mailers, spoofing, spamming, sniffing, e-mail (electronic mail), chat rooms, bulletin boards, news groups, and the ability to easily obtain their victims' personal information. Indirect forms of harassment may consist of the cyberstalker impersonating his or her victim by sending fraudulent and abusive e-mails, spams, and bulletin board postings in the victim's name (Ellison, 1999). Unfortunately, warnings to cease and desist are ignored.

Additionally, cyberstalking is relatively easy due to new developments such as cable companies becoming ISPs. The cable modem access affords the user speed and vulnerability. Since the users are always "on-line," they are always exposed to hackers and cyberstalkers.

Furthermore, "The Cable Communications Policy Act of 1984 prohibits the disclosure of cable subscriber records to law enforcement without a court order and advanced notice to the subscriber" (Woodruff, 1999). Second, free e-mail accounts are readily available as are mail servers that strip the header and identifying information from the e-mail (re-mailer), affording the sender greater anonymity (see Appendix 8.1). Last, there are on-line services that provide "search services" which enable cyberstalkers to provide as little information as a person's name or state, and be able to ascertain the person's address, phone number, and a map to their home (Woodruff, 1999).

The spontaneous and instantaneous transmission features of the Internet are in accordance with the impulsive nature of some offenders. The element of surprise inherent in sending transmissions at will empowers the cyberstalkers, alluring them passionately into a narcissistic fantasy-based virtual reality. With anonymity, the offender's location is unknown; they often will create alternative personae affording them greater control over self-representation (Ellison, 1999). Utilizing characteristics that are unique to cyberspace, e-mails may be forged or spoofed (which changes the header); they may send communications under another user's name; they may gain access to computers and the Internet by using Trojan horse software (see Appendix 8.1), or through universities, Internet providers, local libraries, or computer coffee shops; they may capitalize on re-mailing networks with detection next to impossible to track down. Additionally, with the use of chat rooms and bulletin boards, cyberstalkers may entice other users' assistance by posting information about the victim, false or otherwise. Considering the multiple options available to the cyberstalkers, and their creativity, they have the capacity to terrorize and disrupt the lives of their victims.

Cyberstalkers and Fantasy

Cyberstalkers appear to be young, fairly lonely, perhaps isolated, highly intelligent, impulsive, cunning, resourceful, and appreciate the ease, anonymity, and privacy that cyberspace offers. They are unconstrained by social reality and thereby lack the normal social constraints inherent within face-to-face relationships. Without social anxiety, the cyberstalker is liberated and can enter a world of virtual reality, a world of fantasy where secret experiences, sexual or otherwise, may be arousing and motivating. "Cyberspace is a safe place in which to explore the forbidden and the taboo … it offers the possibility for genuine, unembarrassed conversation about accurate as well as fantasy images of sex" (as cited in MacKinnon, 2000). Furthermore, one can explore aberrant aspects of his or her sexuality without the endangerment of oneself to communicable diseases or public ridicule and opinion.

According to MacKinnon (Brooks-Szachta, 1995) there are ways to masturbate on-line. Burgess et al. (1986) proposed a fantasy-based motivational model for sexual homicide. Their study found a connection between daydreaming and compulsive masturbation. MacKinnon (as cited in Brooks-Szachta,1995) states that "when a social environment is created, such as the Internet, in which it becomes acceptable to share materials like the pornography of record, *United States v. Baker*, getting caught may appear less likely, perception of social disapprobation is reduced, controls disinherited and the possibility of aggressive acts increase" [italics added]. The Internet, similar to alcohol, acts as a disinhibiting stimulus that provides the cyberstalker a virtual domain of fantasy. Fantasies may be planned, rehearsed, and organized to perfection affording the cyberstalker unconstrained power.

Prentky et al. (1989) theorized that there was an underlying internal mechanism in the form of an intrusive fantasy life that drives the offender. It may be that the Internet offers the forum for playing out sexually violent fantasies in on-line chat rooms, that permits free and unquestioned expression with ease of accessibility (Michals, 1997) and, therefore, provides the tools for the offender's intrusive fantasy life and future offenses to be practiced and perhaps later realized.

> While it is unlikely that the translation of the fantasy into reality conforms precisely to a classical conditioning model, it does appear that the more the fantasy is rehearsed, the more power it acquires and the stronger the association between the fantasy content and sexual arousal. Indeed, the selective reinforcements of deviant fantasies through paired association with masturbation over a protracted period may help to explain not only the power of the fantasy but why they are so refractory to extinction (Prentky et al., 1989).

According to MacCulloch et al. (1983), the difference between men who act on their sexual fantasies and those who do not is that the former have a pervasive sense of their inability to control events in the real world. The offenders' "fantasy thereby acts as an operant that gives relief from their feelings of failure, with progression in both fantasy and behavior representing a form of habituation" (MacCulloch et al., 1983).

Behaviorists suggest that sexual deviance is learned and conditioned through masturbation fantasy. It is suggested that the early use of deviant sexual fantasies reinforces and strengthens their ideation, while deconditioning and weakening non-deviant sexual fantasies. Conversely, sexual urges may act as a precursor to fantasy (Langevin et al., 1998). Additionally, the law of contiguity holds that, "those events occurring close together temporally or spatially tend to be associated or learned" (Chaplin, 1985).

Many people have sexual fantasies; however, the sexual offender may have a different kind of fantasy prior to sexual violence. It is theorized that their fantasies are "deviant, repetitive, vivid and very important to the fantasizer" (Star Tribune, 1991). Their fantasies are paired with sexual arousal and release. Male offenders "repeatedly link fantasies of molesting children or rape with masturbation or intercourse, which establishes a link between their pleasure and other's pain." It is suggested that the stronger the link becomes, "the more likely the offender will act on those fantasies" (Star Tribune, 1991).

The Jeffrey Nelson Case

In 1991, Jeffrey Nelson was imprisoned for molesting a child. Six months after his release, he reported fantasizing about molesting young boys. He stated that his fantasy "grew in frequency and intensity" until he began to actually plan ways of acting on his fantasies. This case is illustrative in how fantasy is a key component in the escalation toward sexual violence (Star Tribune, 1991).

In a study by MacCulloch et al. (1983) at an English hospital, it was found that offenders had sadistic sexual fantasies which led to their behavioral practices similar to their fantasies. The behaviors and fantasies interacted and were linked by the offenders progressing to their sadistic sexual offending. The researchers found that the offenders "sought out or created situations in which they could gain control over their victims in a way that reflected their fantasy lives. The offenders' thoughts were found to influence their behaviors" (MacCulloch et al., 1983).

It is suggested that some victims, unknowingly, may engage the cyber-stalkers by their responses, which inadvertently encourages their aberrant behaviors (Cupach and Spitzberg, 1998). Maddi (1996) cites Bandura's concept of reciprocal determinism, in that the person and situation influence each other and, thereby, each changes the other. Thus, there is an interplay between the situation as the precursor, the environment, and the personalities involved. Furthermore, Maddi (1996) articulates the radical behaviorist's viewpoint which maintains that a reinforcing response pattern with an intermittent reinforcement schedule may produce response patterns that are difficult to unlearn even when no further reward is forthcoming, whereby extinguishing the behavior of the offender would be fraught with resistance.

According to Meloy (1997), "each victim contact with the offender is an intermittent positive reinforcement and predicts an increase in frequency of subsequent approach behavior." Victims may try to let the offenders down easily and thereby respond to their e-mails, even though law enforcement has requested otherwise. "Stalking is a pathology of attachment often driven by the force of fantasy" (Meloy, 1997). In studies of sexually deviant offenders by Prentky et al. (1989), offenders habitually left the crime scene in an organized fashion. According to Prentky et al. (1989), these behaviors are suggestive of the offenders' "reflecting, thinking and rehearsing the crime beforehand in fantasy."

In reality, anyone may have deviant sexual fantasies. Ressler (as cited in Brooks-Szachta, 1995), a retired FBI agent and criminologist who is an expert on the habits of killers, asserts that "while not all people who have sadistic fantasies act on them, every serial killer starts with fantasizing." It may be that with the combination and interaction of multiple factors — which may include impulsivity, anger, aggression, a basically unhealthy personality, multi-interactional Websites, pornographic Websites, cybersex Websites, MUDs, MOOs, the use of paraphilias, fetishism (Prentky et al., 1989), and/or voyeurism — that the Internet may actually function as a substitute for their behaviors, whereby anger may be discharged acceding the expression of sexual feelings.

Cyberspace, therefore, may have a therapeutic aspect in that it is an outlet for anxieties and emotions that otherwise would be inherently suppressed. However, the use of paraphilias suggests a preference for fantasy, with the paraphilias seen as a fantasy-stimulus, and thereby acts as a secret experience in the internal world of the cyberstalker. According to Prentky et al. (1989) these new "secret experiences" activate fantasy and provide the incentive for playing out the erotic fantasy so as to perceive it as an actual experience.

In a pornography study of sexual offenders at the Massachusetts Treatment Center (MTC), Carter et al. (1987) found that pornographic materials "relieved the urge to do a sexually violent act and that the materials also turned them on so much that it encouraged them to do a sexually violent act" (R. Knight, personal communication, August 2, 2000). By enhancing the computer with three-dimensional capabilities, virtual reinforcements, like other addictions, may create the obsession to increase the dosage and thereby compel the cyberstalker from the realm of virtual reality into reality (D. Vandervort, personal communication, August 2000).

FBI researchers have suggested that sadistic offenders have "histories of parental separation, physical or sexual abuse and paraphilic behaviors" (Grubin, 1999). Furthermore, "impaired early attachment, early trauma, a violent fantasy life and feedback between fantasy and behavior" reinforce their repetitive thinking patterns (Grubin, 1999). Zane Floyd, a 23-year-old, is currently being accused of killing four people in a Las Vegas supermarket. He stated that he was a loser, was forced out of the marines, and had a "love for his gun." After his arrest he reported that he had decided to act on his violent fantasies after losing at blackjack. Admitting there was "a sick fantasy inside of (his) head," he raped and terrorized a woman, donned his combat attire, and left her saying he "intended to kill the first 19 people that he encountered." He hoped that the police would then shoot him down. He later told an investigator that he "wondered what it would be like to kill someone." He stated that he had this fantasy since early childhood.

According to Kirby, a former FBI criminologist (as cited in O'Connell, 2000), "Floyd exhibited many characteristics common to people that commit multiple homicides." Kirby continues to elaborate that violent fantasies are developed as children, often to cope with some unpleasant psychological problem. Kirby states that they are able to control their fantasies through their teen years and are acted on in response to a triggering event, often of the opposite sex. Kirby states (as cited in O'Connell, 2000), "When these individuals finally act out their fantasy it is kind of like a script. They have gone over and over it so many times, that when they finally act it out, it is very familiar to them" (O'Connell, 2000).

Knight (1999) conducted a study to validate a typology for rapists at the Massachusetts Treatment Center. The results suggested that there was a relationship between sexual behavior, fantasy material, and aggressive behavior. One group distinguished itself as their "sexual drive was strongly related to pervasive anger, sadism and offense planning." A second group found that "pornography use was strongly related to both sexual drive and expressive aggression." The third group was defined by the use of paraphilias, although only "moderately related to expressive aggression, sexual drive, and offense planning." Knight's (1999) study suggested a strong positive relationship among sexual drive, violence, and offense planning or pre-offense planning.

In a meta-analysis of sexual offender recidivism, by Hanson and Bussiere (1998), it was found that the strongest predictors of sexual recidivism were those factors that related to sexual deviance, subjective distress, deviant sexual fantasies, and personality disorders. The extent to which the offenders experienced distress did not affect recidivism, however sexual offenders were found to obtain comfort in sexual thoughts and behaviors when confronted with stress. The fantasy afforded by the Internet, WWW, and multi-interactional sites of sex and violence would therefore provide the offenders multiple opportunities to practice and perfect their fantasies.

In a study conducted by Grubin (1999), it was found that isolation, social or emotional, was a feature consistently found in sadistic offenders. It was suggested that this "pervasive isolation" may not be a preference of the offenders, rather it may be indicative of an underlying disorder. Therefore, a previous history of offenses, deviant fantasy and behavioral rehearsals, and social and emotional isolation may be some of the factors of one who is at risk to repeat his or her offenses.

Additionally, Grubin (1999) suggests that early experiences of physical, sexual, or emotional abuse may impact the formation of attachment bonds and the normal development of empathy. Empathy may prevent one to form normal relationships and results in a feedback loop with further isolation (Grubin, 1999). The cyberstalker may therefore find comfort in relationships and contact with others within the confines of two-dimensional space, where anonymity may represent safety and emotions are expressed in a non-personal manner with the written word, whereby avoiding three-dimensional space which involves face-to-face interactions.

Since cyberspace lacks physical sensory cues, being constrained in two-dimensional space, boundaries are non-existent. For the most part, changes in body language, tone of voice, or facial expressions are lacking (Ellison, 1999) in the virtual environment as one is confined to letters, numbers, symbols, bits, and bytes (although some programs have video camera and microphone capabilities). Explicit, direct, bold, and deceptive verbalizations easily escalate into angry (flaming), harassing, abusive, hostile, and aggressive language. According to Meloy (1999) the offender perceives rejection of his narcissistic fantasy, which has been projected onto the victim, as stimulating shame and humiliation. This sense of pride is defended against with rage as the offender perceives abandonment and disillusionment. To re-establish his narcissistic fantasy, which maintains the rage and diminishes envy, the victim is thereby devalued, pursued, hurt, damaged, or destroyed and, ultimately, not worth having (Meloy, 1999).

Without physical boundaries, the cyberstalker does not need to be at the scene of the crime. The victim's perception is that the cyberstalker is always there, in cyberspace, with the ability to send multiple e-mails to one's home or workplace. Unlike terrestrial stalking, there is nowhere that the cyberstalker's victim feels safe. Hence, cyberstalking victims tend to experience more psychological symptoms such as paranoia, as the victim has no idea who the cyberstalker is and therefore is unable to trust others. The victims exhibit a decreased level of functioning in their daily lives, sleep, and eating patterns. The victims may be in a situation where there may be no escape fathomable (Anonymous, personal communication, June 2000). It may be implausible for the victims to change their e-mail addresses, as with a business or some employment environments, and therefore there is a sense of helplessness. Whereas in the case of the terrestrial stalker, the victims are afforded some choices to arrange for their safety, such as changing their places of residence (if they can manage the expenses involved), phone numbers, daily schedules, or setting up surveillance equipment. The victim of a cyberstalker constantly feels insecure as the cyberstalker "can break into your house without even walking in the front door. And they can send people into your life that can completely tear it apart" (Boehle as cited in Sherr, 2000).

Conclusion

Cyberspace has been likened to the age of the hippie, "from an obsession with pagan, psychedelic and new age spirituality to sexual neurosis and perversion, to plainly daft talk about free information, community and love" (Sardar, 1998). However, there is nothing of value on the Web that is free. The appearance of things that are free are actually invitations to entrapment, similar to the drug dealer's initial fixes. Cyberspace gives the appearance that communities are linked together, however "connection does not make a community" (Sardar, 1998). Computers give the false sense of being together, when in reality they divide, isolate, and fragment groups that define themselves by their fantasies.

Most Internet junkies are found to be isolative, sad, and desperate individuals motivated by lust and power. One can have cybersex with his computer, however, it is impossible to form a relationship with it. Cyberspace encourages individualism, where everyone is free to create his or her own world. This aspect of the Internet is an ideal environment for those incapable of facing people in reality, with the additional avenue for detailing, practicing, and perfecting their wildest fantasies with strangers. This new domain is the perfect tool for those with deviant behaviors and fantasies, intelligence, and the desire to control, threaten, and terrorize others (Sardar, 1998).

Those with unhealthy personalities utilize manipulation, exploitation, and isolation to corner their prey. Some are seeking revenge in an unjust world when sexual advances are rejected. They will attempt to regain their power and control while maintaining their fantasies through defamation of character, sexually deviant behaviors, and violence, including homicide and child exploitation. Others feel spurned and discriminated against seeking to viciously avenge their enemies, while there are some that find enjoyment in frightening others and wreaking as much havoc as possible to computer systems of individuals, corporations, and government agencies (Sardar, 1998).

Cyberstalking with its new innovative techniques, therefore, becomes the most viable modus operandi for perpetrators in this new phase of our human evolution.

Bibliography

American Psychiatric Association (1994). *Diagnostic and Statistical Manual of Mental Disorders*, 4th ed. Washington, D.C.

Anonymous (2000).

Anonymous (April 2000). Beware of cyberstalking — the latest workplace threat, *HR Focus*, p. S3.

Arnold, A. M. (February 1998). Rape in cyberspace: not just a fantasy, *Off Our Backs, Inc.* pp. 12–13.

Baker, D. (December 1999). When cyberstalkers walk, *American Bar Association Journal*, 50, 85.

Barton, J. and Deiters, B. (April 29, 2000). Abraham's bill targets internet pedophilias, *The Grand Rapids Press*, p. A5.

Beck, M., Rosenberg, D., Chideya, F., Miller, S., Foote, D., Manly, H., and Katel, P. (July 13, 1992). Murderous obsession, *Newsweek*, pp. 60–62.

Bennetto, J. (June 1, 2000). Families help stalkers to pursue their victims [Foreign Edition], *The Independent*, p. 13.

Bernstein, H. A. (1981). Survey of threats and assaults directed toward psychotherapists, *American Journal of Psychotherapy*, 35, 542–549.

Berst, J. (May 2, 2000). Look who's stalking now, new cases underline your vulnerability, *ZDNET*. Website: http://www.zdnet.com.

Best, J. (1999). *Random Violence: How We Talk about New Crimes and New Victims*. Berkeley, CA: University of California Press.

Boyer, A. (1999). Website: http://www.amyboyer.org.

Brody, J. (August 30, 1998). Stalkers exhibit psychiatric and personality disorders [2 Star Edition], *Houston Chronicle*, p. 9.

Brody, J. (September 27, 1998). Stalking the stalker — researchers try to unravel their motives [Final Edition], *Anchorage Daily News*, p. G1.

Brooks-Szachta, H. (1995). True threat analysis under 18 U.S.C. § 875 (c), The Role of Unique Features of Electronic Mail in a True Threat Analysis, *U.S. v. Jake Baker* 890 F Supp 1375 (E.D. Mich 1995) (testimony of Catherine MacKinnon and Robert Ressler).

Burgess, A. W., Hartman, C. R., Ressler, R. K., Douglas, J. E., and McCormack, A. (1986). Sexual homicide: a motivational model, *Journal of Interpersonal Violence*, 1, 251–272.

California Penal Code Section § 646.9. (Stalking).

Carmody, C. (1994). Deadly mistakes, *American Bar Association*, 80, 68–75.

Carter, D. L., Prentky, R. A., Knight, R. A., Vanderveer, P., and Boucher, R. (1987). Use of pornography in the criminal and developmental histories of sexual offenders, *Journal of Interpersonal Violence*, 2, 196–211.

Chaplin, J. P. (1985). *Dictionary of Psychology*, 2nd ed. New York: Dell Publishing.

Chapman, G. (April 10, 1995). Flamers, *The New Republic*.

Choney, S. (June 22, 1999). Stalking in cyberspace, cases start to grow, along with computer use, *The San Diego Union-Tribune*, p. 6.

Cohen, W. S. (1993). Anti-Stalking Proposals. Hearing before the Committee on the Judiciary, U.S. Senate (J-103-5). Washington, D.C.: U.S. Government Printing Office.

Coleman, F.L. (1997). Stalking behavior and the cycle of domestic violence, *Journal of Interpersonal Violence*, 12, 420–432.

Copeland, L. (April 13, 2000). Games people play; is interactive entertainment a fantasy come true or a bad dream? [Final Edition], *The Washington Post*, p. c.1.

Cupach, W. R. and Spitzberg, B. H. (1998). Obsessional relational intrusion and stalking, in B. H. Spitzberg and W. R. Cupach (Eds.), *The Dark Side of Close Relationships* (pp. 233–263). Hillsdale, NJ: Lawrence Erlbaum Associates.

CyberAngels (November 14, 1999). *Cyberstalking*. Website: http://www.cyberangels.org/safetyandprivacy/stalk5.html.

CyberAngels. (January 12, 2000). *Policy Concerns about* Cyberstalking. Website: http://cyberangels.com/safetyandprivacy/stalk3.html.

CyberGuards (1998). What is cyberstalking? From the U.S. Department of Justice, Interstate Stalking Act 18 U.S.C. § 875; Interstate Stalking Act applying to direct communications between the perpetrator and the victim, 47 U.S.C. § 223; Interstate Stalking Act revised by President Clinton (1996), 18 U.S.C. § 2261A, 2261, 2262; Interstate Child Protection Act that protects children from on-line stalking (1998), 18 U.S.C. § 2425. Website: http://www.usdoj.cog/criminal/cybercrime/cyberstalking.htm.

D'Amico, M. (February 1997a). *The Law vs. Online Stalking.* Website: http://www.madcapps.com/Writings/cybersta.htm.

D'Amico, M. (February 1997b). The law-abiding netizen–cyberstalking via the net, *CP Media,* p. 32.

Davis, J. (1998). Stalkers, Stalking and Their Victims: A Crime Behavioral Analysis Perspective. Conference presentation, The International Association of Crime Analysts (IACA), San Diego, CA.

Davis, J. (September 24, 1999). Stalking, Stalkers and Their Victims, 3rd Annual "Stalking the Stalker" Conference presentation, Del Mar Hilton, San Diego, CA.

Davis, J. (June 27, 2000). Personal communication, San Diego, CA.

Davis, J. and Chipman, M. (1997). Stalkers and other obsessional types: relentless fear, credible threat, violent behavior: a review and forensic psychological typology, *Journal of Clinical Forensic Medicine,* 4, 166–172.

de Becker, G. (1997). *The Gift of Fear.* New York: Bantam Doubleday Dell Publishing Group.

de Becker, G. (December 23–24, 1999). Intervention Decisions: The Value of Flexibility, 3rd Annual "Stalking the Stalker" Conference presentation, Del Mar Hilton, San Diego, CA.

Deirmenjian, J.M. (1999). Stalking in cyberspace, *Journal of American Academy of Psychiatry Law,* 27, 407–413.

Deiters, B. (April 29, 2000). Abraham's bill targets internet pedophiles, *The Grand Rapids Press,* p. A5.

Dempsey, M. (June 7, 2000). Fantasy landscapes lure affluent new consumers: online games [Surveys Edition], *Financial Times,* p. 04.

Ellison, L. (1999). Cyberstalking: Tackling Harassment on the Internet, Conference presentation, Cyberspace 1999: Crime Criminal Justice and the Internet — An International Conference, United Kingdom.

Focamp, P. (December 3, 1999). Reality bytes [1 Edition], *The Southland Times,* p. 5.

Gordon, S. (January 12, 2000). Personal communication, Los Angeles District Attorney.

Grubin, D. (1999). Actuarial and clinical assessment of risk in sex-offenders, *Journal of Interpersonal Violence,* 14, 331–343.

Hanson, R. K. and Bussiere, M. T. (1998). Predicting relapse: a meta-analysis of sexual offender recidivism studies, *Journal of Consulting and Clinical Psychology,* 66, 348–362.

Hitchcock, J. (January 10, 2000). *Cyberstalkers Arrested*. Website: http://www. federalcourts.com/federalcourt/News/Hitchcock_cyberstalkers_captured.html.

Jenson, B. (1996). Cyberstalking: Crime, Enforcement and Personal Responsibility in the On-Line World. Available e-mail: 10-04-00, 5:23 P.M.

Knight, R. A. (1999). Validation of a typology for rapists, *Journal of Interpersonal Violence*, 14, 303–330.

Knott, L. (December 12, 1999). Online stalkers corralled, *The Detroit News*. Website: http://www.metroactive.com/cruz/cyberstalkers-9945.html.

Lance, G. (May 26, 2000). Congress is asked to police online privacy [Final Edition], *Milwaukee Journal Sentinel*. p. 015.A.

Lance, G. and Scripps, H. (May 26, 2000). Internet privacy mostly a fig leaf, regulators charge [Final All Edition], *The Plain Dealer*, p. 11A.

Langevin, R., Lang, R. A., and Curnoe, S. (1998). The prevalence of sex offenders with deviant fantasies, *Journal of Interpersonal Violence*, 13, 315–327.

Luke, B. (1998). Violent love: hunting, heterosexuality, and the erotics of men's predation, *Feminist Studies*, 24, 627–655.

MacCulloch, M. J., Snowden, P. R., Wood, P. W., and Mills, H. E. (1983). Sadistic fantasy, sadistic behavior and offending, *British Journal of Psychiatry*, 143, 20–29.

MacKinnon, C.A. (1993). *Only Words*. Cambridge, MA: Harvard University Press.

MacKinnon, C. A. (2000). Website: http://www.cddc.vt.edu/feminism/MacKinnon.html.

Maddi, S. R. (1996). *Personality Theories: A Comparative Analysis*, 6th ed. (pp. 437–465). Pacific Grove, CA: Brooks/Cole Publishers.

Malamuth, N. M. (1986). Predictors of naturalistic sexual aggression, *Journal of Personality and Social Psychology*, 50, 953–962.

Mannix, M., Locy, T., Clark, K., Smith, A. K., Perry, J., McCoy, F., Fischer, J., Glasser, J., and Kap, D. E. (August 28, 2000). The web's dark side, *U.S. News & World Report*, p. 36.

Maxey, W. (September 23, 1999). Stalking, 3rd Annual "Stalking the Stalker" Case Conference presentation, Del Mar Hilton, San Diego, CA.

McClure, S., Scambray, J., and Kurtz, G. (1999). *Hacking Exposed: Network Security Secrets and Solutions* (p. XXV). Berkeley, CA: Osborne/McGraw-Hill.

Meloy, J. R. (1992). *Violent Attachments* (pp. 20–21, 70, 110–111). Northvale, NJ: Jason Aronson, Inc.

Meloy, J. R. (1997). The clinical risk management of stalking: "Someone is watching over me …," *American Journal of Psychotherapy*, 51, 174–184.

Meloy, J. R. (1998). *The Psychology of Stalking Clinical and Forensic Perspective*. San Diego, CA: Academic Press.

Meloy, J. R. (1999). Stalking: an old behavior, a new crime, *The Psychiatric Clinics of North America*, 22, 85–99.

Meloy J. R. and Gothard, S. (1995). Demographic and clinical comparison of obsessional followers and offenders with mental disorders, *American Journal of Psychiatry*, 152, 258–263.

Meloy, J.R., Cowett, P.Y., Parker, S.B., Hofland, B., and Friedland, A. (1997). Domestic protection orders and the prediction of subsequent criminality and violence toward protectees, *Psychotherapy*, 34, 447–458.

Michals, D. (March/April 1997). Cyber-rape: how virtual is it? *Ms. Magazine*, 7, 68–72.

Miller, G. (April 29, 1999). Man pleads guilty to using net to solicit rape [Home Edition], *The Los Angeles Times*, p. 5.

Miller, G. and Maharaj, D. (January 22, 1999). N. Hollywood man charged in 1st cyber-stalking case; internet: spurned suitor allegedly forged lurid e-mails, inviting would-be rapists to woman's home [Home Edition], *The Los Angeles Times*, p. 1.

Miller, G. and Maharaj, D. (January 27, 1999). Chilling cyberstalking case illustrates new breed of crime, *Los Angeles Times*, p. 1. Website: http://www.infowar.com/law/99/law_012799a_i.shtml.

Mohandie, K., Hatcher, C., and Raymond, D. (1998). False victimization syndrome in stalking, in Meloy, J. R. (Ed.), *The Psychology of Stalking Clinical and Forensic Perspective* (pp. 225–256). San Diego, CA: Academic Press.

Morrison, B. (June 9, 2000). Suspect may be first net serial killer, *USA Today*. Website: http://www.usatoday.com:80/life/cyber/tech/cti070.htm.

Mullen, P.E., Pathé, M., Purcell, R., and Stuart, G.W. (1999). Study of stalkers, *The American Journal of Psychiatry*, 156, 1244–1249.

Mure, J. (1999). Net stalkers, Klein Internet Services. Website: http://www.cyberstalking.doc.

Nicastro, A.M., Cousins, A.V., and Spitzberg, B.H. (2000). The tactical face of stalking, *Journal of Criminal Justice*, 28, 69–82.

O'Connell, P. (January 8, 2000). Suspect details grisly fantasies [Final Edition], *Las Vegas Review-Journal*, p. 1A.

Prentky, R.A., Burgess, A.W., Rokous, F., Lee, A., Hartman, C., Ressler, R., and Douglas, J. (1989). The presumptive role of fantasy in serial sexual homicide, *American Journal of Psychiatry*, 146, 887–891.

Quart, A. (2000). *Something Wicked This Way Comes*. Website: http://www.timedigital.com.

Rather, D. (March 30, 2000). *48 Hours: Cyberstalking* [Video-tape]. CBS, Incorporated. CBS Broadcasting Productions.

Reuters. (September 25, 2000). First palm virus spreads, killing programs, *Technology and Computing*. Website: http://home.netscape.cnn.com (retrieved September 25, 2000).

Robinson, G. (November 16, 1999). Screen fright [A Edition], *Evening Standard*, p. 59.

Roth, B. (June 9, 2000). Gore begins 'progress and prosperity tour' by warning about web [3 Star Edition], *Houston Chronicle*, p. 13.

Safire, W. (May 29, 2000). Erecting barriers against web stalkers [1 2 Edition], *The San Diego Union-Tribune*, p. B-6.

Safire, W. (May 29, 2000). Online privacy: an oxymoron [3 Star Edition], *Times Union*, p. A7.

Safire, W. (May 29, 2000). Stalking the internet [Op-Ed], *The New York Times*, p. 15.

Safire, W. (May 30, 2000). Stalking the internet — the neb noses of the net want to place the burden of privacy protection on the consumer [Region Edition], *Pittsburgh Post-Gazette*, p. A-13.

Safire, W., New York Times News Service (May 31, 2000). Congress to act against 'net' stalkers? Small chance, *The Grand Rapids Press*, p. A12.

Safire, W. (May 31, 2000). Stalking the internet [Final Edition], *The Commercial Appeal*, p. A8.

Safire, W. (June 2, 2000). Don't count on dot-coms to protect your privacy [Sunrise Edition], *The Oregonian*, p. C15.

Safire, W. (June 2, 2000). Internet companies let stalkers run wild [Orleans Edition], *Times-Picayune*, p. B07.

Safire, W. (June 2, 2000). Web snoopers could rip you off; stalking the internet [All Edition], *Cincinnati Enquirer*, p. A16.

Saltzman, M. (June 21, 2000). Virtual violence and real aggressiveness; is there correlation? [Final Edition], *Gannett News Service*, p. 1.

Sardar, Z. (January 2, 1998). The gods of cyberspace, *New Statesman*, 11, 48–49.

Sciupac, I. (January 25, 2000). Ex-UCI Student Indicted in Hate E-Mail Case, UC Irvine New University. Website: (http://members.tripod.com/alnguyen/new.htm).

Sherr, L. (February 24, 2000). (ABC News Producer) *20/20 Downtown*, Stalking in Cyberspace [Video-tape], American Broadcasting Companies, Inc. Website: http://more.abcnews.go.com/onair/2020/2020_000224_cyberstalker_feature.html.

Simpson, K. (November 28, 1999). Is it all doom & gloom? Computer gaming draws devotion and fire. Some see it as a healthy outlet and a way to socialize. Others say it inspires real-life violence [Rockies Edition], *Denver Post*, p. A, 1:1.

Sipior, J. C. and Ward, B. T. (1999). The dark side of employee email, *Association for Computing Machinery*, 42, 88–95.

Spitzberg, B. H. and Hoobler, G. (October 2000). Cyberstalking and the Technologies of Interpersonal Terrorism. Paper presentation to the Western States Communication Association, Coeur d'Alene, ID.

Spitzberg, B. H., Nicastro, A. M., and Cousins, A. V. (1998). Exploring the interactional phenomenon of stalking and obsessive relational intrusion, *Communication Reports*, 11, 33–48.

Star Tribune Newspaper of the Twin Cities Staff (October 18, 1991). Fantasy's role in sexual violence [Metro Edition], *Star Tribune*, p. 20A.

The Detroit News Staff (March 23, 1996). E-Mail Stalker Sentencing Likely Will Influence Future Cases. Associated Press.

The People of the State of California v. Dwayne Isaiah Comfort, SC No. 140412 (The Superior Court of the State of California for the County of San Diego, December 1, 1998).

Thompson, D. (Ed.) (1998). *The Oxford Dictionary of Current English*. New York: Oxford University Press.

U.S. Attorney General (August 1999). *Cyberstalking: A New Challenge for Law Enforcement and Industry.* A report from the Attorney General to the Vice President. Website: http://www.etracker.elibrary.com (retrieved December 12, 1999).

U.S. Department of Justice and Office of Justice Programs (1998). Stalking in America: findings from the national violence against women, *The Journal of State Government,* 71, 20–21.

U.S. Equal Employment Opportunity Civil Rights Act Title VII (1964). 29 Code of Federal Regulations § 1604.11.

U.S. Newswire Staff (June 8, 2000). Vice President Gore announces new legislation to prevent the sale of social security numbers, *U.S. Newswire,* p. 1.

United States of America v. Baker, 104 F.3d 1492 (1996).

United States of America v. Keith Christopher Kosiewicz, Title 18, U.S.C., § Sec. 875 (b), United States District Court Southern District of California, Grand Jury, August 1999.

Van Horn, R. (October 1999). Violence and video games, *Phi Delta Kappan,* 81, 173–174.

Walker, L.E. and Meloy, J. R. (1998). Stalking and domestic violence, in Meloy, J. R. (Ed.), *The Psychology of Stalking: Clinical and Forensic Perspectives* (pp. 139–161). San Diego, CA: Academic Press.

Wall, D. S. (1998). Catching cybercriminals: policing the internet, *International Review of Law, Computers & Technology,* 12, 201–218.

Wallack, T. (January 10, 2000). Top cops to tackle web crime [Final Edition], *San Francisco Chronicle,* p. B.1.

Watts v. United States, 394 U.S. 705 (1969).

Weaver, R. L. (1999). Free Speech, Crime, and the Challenge of Advancing Technology. Conference presentation, Cyberspace 1999: Crime, Criminal Justice and the Internet: An International Conference, United Kingdom.

Williams, J. (February 28, 2000). Personalization vs. privacy: the great online cookie debate, *Editor & Publisher,* 133, 26–27.

Woodruff, T. (September 27, 1999). Cyberstalking creeps into the political spotlight, *MSN MoneyCentral.* Website: http://moneycentral.msn.com/articles/news/capitol/4682.asp?special=msnnip.

Zona, M. A., Sharma, K. K., and Lane, J. L. (1993). A comparative study of erotomania and obsessional subjects in a forensic sample, *Journal of Forensic Sciences,* 65, 894–903.

Zona, M. A., Palarea, R. E., and Lane, J. C. (1998). Psychiatric diagnosis and the offender-victim typology of stalking, in Meloy, J. R. (Ed.), *The Psychology of Stalking Clinical and Forensic Perspectives* (pp. 69–84). San Diego, CA: Academic Press.

Appendix 8.1: Chapter Definitions and Terminology Related to Cyberstalking

BBS: Bulletin Board Systems enable messages to be left "in group forums to be read at a later time" which can be accessed by a large group of readers. (Jenson, 1996)

Chat rooms: Connections provided by online services and are available on the Internet. These connections allow people to communicate in real time via computer text and a modem. (Jenson, 1996)

Cookies: Tiny strings of data that are stored on a user's hard disk when visiting certain sites that track the Web-surfer's habits.

Cyberspace: "A consensual hallucination experienced daily by billions of legitimate operators, in every nation" — William Gibson (Quote, 2000). "A place where computer networking hardware, network software and people using them converge." — John Perry Barlow (Cyberangels' Website, 2000)

Cyberstalking: "The persistent unwanted and undeterred pursuit through the internet, or any other electronic medium or similar channel of communication involving a fascination, fixation, fantasy, or attachment to another that brings with it such behavior, oftentimes, a reasonable degree of concern or fear for one's own personal safety, their families' personal safety or both." (Davis, 1998)

E-mail: "Computer text sent instantaneously over telephone lines to another computer ready to receive the incoming message, or to an on-line service that stores the message in an electronic 'mail box' until the recipient collects it." (Jenson, 1996)

E-mail bomb: The act of sending massive amounts of e-mail to a single address with the malicious intent of disrupting the system of the recipient.

Fantasy: An elaborated set of cognitions (or thoughts) characterized by preoccupations (or rehearsal) anchored in emotion, and originating in daydreams. (Prentky et al., 1989)

Flaming: A public post or e-mail (electronic mail) message that expresses a strong opinion or criticism, which may be written with all capital letters and may use expletives. They are usually highly aggressive, offending, sarcastic, vulgar, or critical statements that are usually sent to someone that the sender disagrees with, or was upset by.

Internet: An international computer network that facilitates the World Wide Web, also known as the information highway.

ISP: Internet Service Provider.

MUDs: Multi-user dungeons where on-line fantasy role-playing game environment takes place in cyberspace. It occurs in text mode with the players assuming the identities of fictional characters and follows a series of rules that guide the adventure.

Paraphilia, fetishism type: The "recurrent, intense, sexually arousing fantasies, sexual urges, or behaviors involving the use of nonliving objects (e.g., female undergarments)." (American Psychiatric Association, 1994)

Paraphilia, pedophilia type: The "recurrent, intense sexually arousing fantasies, sexual urges, or behaviors involving sexual activity with a prepubescent child or children (generally age 13 years or younger)." (American Psychiatric Association, 1994)

Paraphilia, voyeurism type: The "recurrent, intense, sexually arousing fantasies, sexual urges or behaviors involving the act of observing an unsuspecting person who is naked, in the process of disrobing, or engaging in sexual activity." (American Psychiatric Association, 1994)

Re-mailer: Anonymous e-mail Web surfing, where borrowing an IP for one particular session is possible. Re-mailers cloak the identity of users who send messages through them by stripping all identifying information from an e-mail and allocating an anonymous ID (Ellison, 1999). "Re-mailers use public key cryptography, and by chaining together several re-mailers a user could create a trail so complex that it would be impossible to follow." (Ellison, 1999).

Shouting: Using all capital letters.

Sniffer: A program which allows one to watch data going through the network and looks for critical information. (D. Parker, personal communications, August 2000)

Spam: To send a message, like an ad, to many discussion groups without regard for its topical relevance. Also known as unsolicited advertisements.

Spoof: Changing the header information on an e-mail, such as the date, recipient, or sender in order to forge an e-mail. (R.H. Lee, personal communications, May 2000)

Trojan software: A program that can be planted on a victim's computer, which enables a stalker to have total access and control over a victim's computer, e.g., Back Oriface, SubSeven, and NetBus. (T. Finnie, Director, High Tech Crime Consortium, Tacoma, WA, personal communications, June 12, 2000)

Virtual reality: A simulation of the real world by a computer. (Thompson, 1998)

Appendix 8.2: Internet Resource Sites Related to Stalking and Victim Assistance Research on the Web

Anti-stalking Website: http://www.antistalking.com

Baron Center, Inc: http://www.baroncenter.com

Center for Successful Parenting (reviews video games and other media): http://www.moviereports.com/vgames.html

Michael Corcoran and Associates: http://www.corcoranassocates.com

CyberAngels: An on-line Internet safety organization: http://www. cyberangels.org

Firm of Batza and Taylor: http://www.batza&taylor.com

High Tech Crime Consortium: http://www.hightechcrimecops.com

Internet Tracker: http://www.pedowatch.org

More Stalking Information: http://www.p3p.com/features/stalker.shtml

Mr. Gavin de Becker Agency, Inc.: http://www.gdbinc.com

National Center for Victims of Crime: Stalking law information: http://www.nvc.org

National Criminal Justice Research Service: http://www.ncjrs.org/ victstlk.htm

National Domestic Violence Hotline: http://www.ndvh.org

National Organization for Victim Assistance (NOVA): http://www. try-nova.org

National Victim Center: http://www.ojp.usdoj.gov/ovc/help/stalk/ info44.htm

Other Helpful Web Sites: http://www.stalkingrescue.org

Privacy Rights Clearing House: http://www.privacyrights.org

Stalking Assistance Site: http://www.StalkingAssistance.com

Stalking Victim's Sanctuary: http://stalkingvictims.com

State Stalking Laws: http://www.nvc.org/hdir/statestk.htm

TAG, Inc.: http://www.TAGinc.com

TAP Group, Inc.: http://www.theTAPGroup.com

U.S. Department of Justice: http://www.ojp.usdoj.gov/nij

WHOA: Jane Hitchcock's Women Halting On-line Abuse: http://www. whoisshe.com

About the Contributing Author

Bonnie D. Lucks, M.A.

Bonnie D. Lucks, M.A. is a Ph.D. candidate in clinical psychology at the United States International University (USIU) in San Diego, California. Ms. Lucks also obtained a Master's degree in psychology from the United States International University and a Bachelor of Science degree in the biological sciences from the University of California, Los Angeles (UCLA).

Ms. Lucks is currently completing a pre-doctoral clinical psychology internship at San Diego State University in the Counseling and Psychological Services Center in La Mesa, California. She is also a Crisis Intervention Specialist for *Crisis House*, also in San Diego. Ms. Lucks' current interests are in clinical-forensic psychology, threat assessment, and the subject of stalkers, computer technology, network security systems, the Internet, and cyberstalking.

She is a member of several professional organizations including the Association for Threat Assessment Professionals (ATAP) and the San Diego Psychology-Law Society. She resides in San Diego, California.

PART IV

Stalking, Stalking Terror, and Unwanted Pursuit on Campus

Being Pursued and Pursuing during the College Years: Their Extent, Nature, and Impact of Stalking on College Campuses

9

BONNIE S. FISHER

Contents

0-8493-0811-9/01/$0.00+$1.50
© 2001 by CRC Press LLC

Introduction

Attention to the victimization of college and university students has been prompted by rising fears that campuses are not safe havens from criminal activity but instead hot spots for violence. The lobbying efforts of student advocacy groups, especially Security On Campus founded by the parents of Jeanne Ann Clery who was murdered in her Lehigh dormitory room in 1986, led to the passage of state-level and federal-level legislation to address college student victimization. In 1988, for example, Pennsylvania became the first state to pass a campus security reporting law (24 Pa. Cons. Stat. section 2501-3). Over a dozen states have since passed campus crime disclosure legislation (Bromley and Fisher, 2000).

Two years after Pennsylvania's action, Congress passed the Student Right-to-Know Act and Campus Security Act of 1990, the first federal-level campus reporting mandates (hereinafter referred to as the act) (20 U.S.C. 1092(f)). The act mandates that colleges and universities that participate in federal financial aid programs must "prepare, publish, and distribute" an annual security report that contains its campus security policies and campus crime statistics based on *Uniform Crime Report* (UCR) definitions. Crimes reported in the annual security report include: (1) sex offenses, (2) robbery, and (3) aggravated assaults.*

Throughout the 1990s, Congress maintained its interest in campus crime issues during several sessions. First, it authorized funding for three federal agencies — the General Accounting Office, the Department of Justice, and the Department of Education — to examine different aspects of campus crime: problems associated with the reporting requirements of the act, the state of campus law enforcement, and campus crime and security issues, respectively (General Accounting Office, 1997; U.S. Department of Education, National Center for Education Statistics, 1997; Reaves and Goldberg, 1996). Second, Congress passed several amendments to the act. For example, Congress amended the act in 1992 to include the Campus Sexual Assault Victims' Bill of Rights (Public Law 102-325, section 486(c)), which, among other mandates, requires schools to afford sexual assault victims certain basic rights. The act was amended again in 1998 to include additional reporting requirements (e.g., crime statistics broken down by four locations) and expand the disclosure of crime categories (e.g., murder, arson). The 1998 amendments also formally changed the name of the act to the Jeanne Clery Disclosure of Campus Security Policy and Campus Crime Statistics Act (www.soconline.org, 2000).

---

* Prior to August 1, 1992, rape statistics were mandated to be reported. On or after this date, sexual offenses (forcible or nonforcible) were required to be reported.

Coinciding with the attention by feminist scholars to college student victimization was interest in the sexual victimization and harassment of college women. The path-breaking national-level study by Koss and colleagues in the early 1980s established that the incidence of rape and other forms of sexual assault (e.g., sexual coercion) was common among college women (Koss et al., 1987).

Over the next two decades, numerous case studies and three national-level studies have broadened our understanding of the extent and nature of the sexual victimization, aggression, and violence against college women in the United States and Canada (see Belknap and Erez, 1995; Sellers and Bromley, 1996; Bohmer and Parrot, 1993; DeKeseredy and Schwartz, 1998; Fisher et al., 1998; Fisher et al., 2000; Fisher and Cullen, 1999; Muehlenhard and Linton, 1987). These studies have consistently revealed that rape, sexual assault, aggression and physical violence (e.g., hitting, slapping), and psychological abuse (e.g., insults, put-downs in front of friends) in dating and acquaintance relationships are experienced by a substantial number of college women.

To illustrate, a recent national-level study of college women estimated that nearly 5% of them experienced a rape or an attempted rape annually (Fisher et al., 2000). Studies of violence against college women in dating relationships estimate that between 20 and nearly 70% of the women have experienced some type of psychological or physical violence by their partner (see Belknap and Erez, 1995; Sellers and Bromley, 1996; Logan et al., 2000; Makepeace, 1981). Estimates of sexual harassment range between 30 and 70% depending on the definition of sexual harassment and the sample composition (e.g., only undergraduates, undergraduate and graduate students) (see Paludi, 1996).

Responding to lobbying pressures, Congress authorized a substantial amount of funding under the Violence Against Women Act to address sexual victimization among college women. First, in 1999, the U.S. Department of Justice awarded $8.1 million to 21 schools to develop, implement, and evaluate sexual assault, domestic violence, and stalking awareness and prevention programs and procedures, and provide and improve services for victims and training for service providers, including campus law enforcement. In a second round of funding, several grants were awarded during the fall of 2000 to additional schools. Second, the National Institute of Justice plans to announce the award of an $850,000 grant to perform a 3-year baseline, process, and impact evaluation of all the funded programs. Third, a national-level study to examine how colleges and universities respond to the report of a sexual victimization is now in the field, with results expected in mid-2001 (Educational Development Center Inc., University of Cincinnati, and Police Executive Research Forum, 2000).

Independent of the Congressional and research attention given to campus crime and the sexual victimization of college women, the media, women's advocate and victims' rights groups, and elected officials successfully labeled stalking a growing social, public health, and criminal justice problem.

As a result, stalking catapulted to the top of the policy agenda in all 50 state legislatures, the District of Columbia, and the federal government in the early 1990s. By 1995, all these governmental entities had passed anti-stalking legislation. Several constitutional challenges have been waged against anti-stalking legislation, and, overwhelmingly, the appellate courts have upheld the legislation as constitutional. In doing so, the courts have provided not only the criminal justice system with a means to arrest and prosecute criminal stalking behavior in a constitutionally acceptable manner, but they have also provided researchers with a means to legally define stalking to estimate (1) the extent, nature, and impact of being victimized, and (2) the numbers of people who are accused and convicted of stalking.

The research endeavors into stalking victimization and perpetration are in their infancy stage of development. To date, only a few studies have used a general population sample to examine the extent, nature, and impact of having been stalked. Of these studies, the majority have used a nonrandom sample of self-defined stalking victims which has known methodological limitations (Brewster, 2000; Hall, 1998). Other studies have relied on non-randomly selected clinical samples of stalking victims or have examined a limited number of cases where patients (or their relatives) have formed pathologic attachments to those in clinical practice (e.g., therapists, counselors) (Holmes et al., 2000; Lion and Herschler, 1998; Pathé and Mullen, 1997).

Tjaden and Thoennes' *National Violence Against Women Survey* provides the only legally defined (i.e., based on the model anti-stalking code for states) stalking estimates from a large, randomly selected sample of women and men in the United States. Using a legal definition of stalking that requires victims to feel a high level of fear, they estimated that 8.2 million women have been stalked at some time during their lives, and 2 million men have been stalked sometime in their lifetimes. They also estimated that 1,006,970 women and 370,990 men are stalked annually.

A few researchers are also in the first stages of developing new concepts and definitions for pursuit behaviors. These concepts are broader in coverage than those included in the statutes that define criminal stalking. For example, Langhinrichsen-Rohling et al. (2000) included "releasing harmful information" as part of their measure of pursuit behavior. Researchers also have developed names for these new concepts to distinguish them from criminal stalking. To illustrate, Cupach and Spitzberg's research (1996) on "obsessional relational intrusion" (or ORI) examines milder forms of intrusion whose characteristics include "repeated and unwanted behaviors."

The purpose of this chapter is to take stock in what we know about stalking and pursuit behaviors among college students from these first-generation studies. First, we discuss the demographic and lifestyle characteristics of college students that make them potentially vulnerable to becoming targets of stalking and pursuit behaviors. Second, before turning to the results of college student studies, a brief discussion of the various terms that researchers have developed to refer to the concept of pursuit behavior is required so that comparisons across studies can be made. Third, we review the studies that have attempted to "count" the number of students who (1) have been stalked or experienced pursuit behaviors and (2) have perpetrated these types of acts. Fourth, we provide insight into what we know about the nature of the types of behaviors used against college student victims and by pursuers, the victim–perpetrator relationship, and the duration and frequency of these behaviors. Fifth, we review what we know about the impact these experiences have on their victims. And last, we provide some guidance for college and university administrators in addressing stalking and pursuit behaviors among their students.

Are College Students Vulnerable?

Criminology and epidemiology researchers have produced a sizable body of research results that suggest that some individuals have a greater risk of victimization than others (see Crowell and Burgess, 1996). Researchers have shown that certain demographic and lifestyle/routine activity characteristics significantly predict an individual's risk of predatory victimization (see Fisher et al., 1998; Cohen and Felson, 1979; Hindelang et al., 1978; Miethe and Meier, 1994; Sampson and Lauritsen, 1990; Sampson and Wooldredge, 1987).

Researchers have also reported that individuals with certain demographic and lifestyle/routine activity characteristics are more likely to be criminally stalked than those individuals who do not exhibit these characteristics (Fisher et al., 2000; Mustaine and Tewksbury, 1999). College students' demographic and lifestyle/routine activities are characterized by high-risk factors identified by the general population stalking research.

First, Tjaden and Thoennes' (1998) study has shed much light on the demographic characteristics of stalking victims. They reported that young adults are the primary targets of stalkers; 52% of the stalking victims were 18 to 29 years old. Hall's (1998) results support their findings: the age category of 18 to 25 years had the largest percentage of victims, 24%.

As to who are the stalking victims, Tjaden and Thoennes (1998) concluded that stalking is gender neutral. Their results reveal that both males and females had been stalked: 78% of the stalking victims were females and 22% were males. Though stalking victims are both males and females, the primary victims are females and the primary perpetrators are males.

Westrup and Fremouw (1998) summarized the stalking studies that have examined offender populations. They concluded that the majority of stalkers have the following features: (1) they are single and never have been married, (2) they are better educated, and (3) they are intelligent.

The college population comprises a large number of youthful people. According to the Department of Education, just over 15 million students were enrolled in post-secondary institutions during the fall of 1997, of which 56% were females (U.S. Bureau of the Census, 1999). Of the full-time students enrolled during the fall of 1997, 82% of undergraduates, 41% of first-year professionals, and 25% of graduate students were under the age of 25 (U.S. Department of Education, 1997). Student enrollments are projected to steadily increased annually, thus adding to the number of potential attractive targets and would-be pursuers.

Second, one characteristic of criminal stalking behavior is that it is a repeated course of conduct or pattern of pursuit behavior. Obsessive relational intrusion has a similar "repeated" characteristic. For a pursuer to engage in a repeated course of conduct or pattern of pursuit behavior, that person must have access to the victim as well as time to behave in this manner. From a pursuer's perspective, access to the campus is relatively easy, especially if he or she is a fellow student. Many college campuses are park-like settings with permeable boundaries. Campuses are typically accessible during all hours; they are "open" 365 days a year, 7 days a week, and 24 hours a day to visitors and students alike, making access very easy.

Students' schedules and lifestyles are such that they typically are easy to locate, particularly when they are on campus, for several reasons. First, they routinely attend classes. Their course schedules usually change from term to term yet their schedules are very predictable with respect to the location of where each of their classes meets, the days of week the class meets, and the starting and ending time for the class. Their classes, coupled with ease of access to campus classroom buildings and the campus in general, would make surveillance, waiting for someone outside (or inside) their classroom, or leaving written messages or objects relatively simple acts. Second, a student's residential address, telephone number, and e-mail address are usually available in a printed school-sponsored directory, or more so now, via the Internet from the respective school's Website. If a would-be pursuer wanted to get this information, it would be quite easy.

This information could then be used by the pursuer to approach the victim by following or waiting for the victim outside his/her home or motor vehicle, or attempting to contact the victim by sending letters or gifts, making phone calls, or sending e-mail messages. These acts are relatively easy when a victim can be reached on campus because schools typically provide "no-cost" inter-campus and intra-campus mail, and telephone calls to on-campus numbers. Sending e-mail messages is easy, too, as many schools automatically assign e-mail addresses to new students and offer easy access to computer labs located throughout the campus.

Through these various means, a pursuer can pursue his/her target and be in a position to then threaten or harass the victim. And last, those students who live on campus or near campus in student housing or who work on campus or near campus may also be vulnerable targets, as the pursuer, especially if a fellow student, could have easy access to the target's dwelling or place of employment.

Third, several researchers have consistently found that in most pursuit behavior cases, the victim–pursuer relationship involved some type of prior relationship — former spouse, sexual intimates, professional, employment, or acquaintance (see Zona et al., 1998). In the majority of these cases, this relationship was a romantic one. The former intimate partner is the most common stalker of both female and male victims (Hall, 1998; Tjaden and Thoennes, 1998).

Complementing previous clinical studies of stalking victims, Tjaden and Thoennes (1998) provided compelling evidence that stalking is linked to violence and emotionally abusive behavior in intimate relationships (see Pathé and Mullen, 1997). Other recent research is supportive of their conclusion — stalking is a variant or extension of intimate partner violence that typically occurs after the relationship ends (Kurt, 1995; Logan et al., 2000). For example, Tjaden and Thoennes (1998) reported that "husbands and partners who stalk their partners are four times more likely than husbands or partners in the general population to physically assault their partners, and they are six times more likely than husbands and partners in the general population to sexually assault their partners" (p. 8).

The college years are a time when young adults come into contact with a variety of new people — fellow students and their friends, faculty, and staff. Some of these new contacts will develop into new friendships. Other contacts may evolve into dating and intimate relationships. Sometimes these relationships last a short time; other ones are more long term.

Dating in college is a popular social activity for the majority of students, primarily among undergraduates who are typically single (Elliot and Brantley, 1997). A recent survey reported that overall, 76% of college students tend to date only one person at a time; the remaining like to date several people at once (Elliot and Brantley, 1997). Spitzberg and Rhea (1999) suggested that "relational mobility" may be highest among young, college-aged populations (p. 7). In their study of intimate relationships, "college student respondents reported having dated an average of 4.7 persons since high school, and an average of 1.6 of these were considered 'steady.'"

Several studies have consistently shown that while involved in dating or in an intimate relationship acts of aggression, violence, and sexual assault occur frequently among college students (see Crowell and Burgess, 1996). For example, Makepeace (1981), using a nonrandom sample of students from one university, reported that 62% of the students personally knew someone who had been involved in courtship violence, and 21% had at least one personal experience with courtship violence. Nearly 36% of those students who had personally experienced courtship violence had more than one experience. Research has also shown that the majority of relationship aggression, violence, and sexual assault is committed by a fellow student (Fisher et al., 2000).

Last, for many people a terminated relationship may not end there. Typically, stalking and other pursuit behaviors tend to occur in response to the breakup of a relationship. Tjaden and Thoennes (1998) reported that 43% of women victims said that the stalking occurred before the relationship ended, and 36% said that it occurred both before and after the relationship ended. Research suggests that college students have such experiences. For example, Langhinrichsen-Rohling et al. (2000) concluded that unwanted pursuit behaviors are common following the termination of college students' dating relationships. Their survey results showed that 99% of the students who had been involved in a terminated relationship indicated perpetrating at least one form of unwanted pursuit behavior, and 89% reported that their ex-partner had engaged in at least one such behavior. There is reason to believe that characteristics of students and their lifestyle/routine activity can make them vulnerable to experiencing or initiating pursuit behaviors. We now turn to a discussion of the concepts that researchers have developed to measure the extent of various degrees of pursuit behavior between college student targets and pursuers.

Definition Issues: Clarifying Terms and Providing Definitions

Table 9.1 presents information about how researchers have named and defined the concept of pursuit behavior. Looking at column six of Table 9.1, there are three terms researchers have used to capture the concept of pursuit behaviors: (1) stalking, (2) obsessive relational intrusion, and (3) unwanted pursuit behaviors. A brief discussion of each is provided, as these concepts range from those identified by anti-stalking statutes, to those whose definitions are beyond the law but are deemed as pursuit behaviors.

The Nature of Stalking

While specific legal definitions of stalking vary widely from statute to statute and differ as to whether stalking is considered a misdemeanor or felony, all the statutes proscribe behavior that constitutes a pattern of conduct that seeks to harass and/or threaten the safety of another person. Three basic elements are needed to criminally charge and convict a defendant of stalking: (1) a course of conduct or pattern of behavior, (2) the presence of a threat, and (3) the criminal intent to cause fear in the victim. Briefly, the first element involves a course of conduct or behavior that is nonconsensual or intrusive upon another person.

Most statutes describe the course of conduct as repeated (usually two or more times) following, pursuing, or harassing of another person (e.g., lying in wait, surveillance, nonconsensual communications, telephone harassment, vandalism). Second, state anti-stalking statutes are divided as to the presence of a threat element. Some statutes do not explicitly require that the perpetrator make a threat; they require that the perpetrator act in a way that causes a reasonable person to feel fearful or frightened. Other statues specifically require that the perpetrator make a threat against the victim. Some states require that a "creditable" threat be made, that is, that the perpetrator must have the "apparent ability" to execute the threat, while other states omit the "apparent ability" requirement (Brewster, 2000). Third, for a defendant to be convicted of stalking, the stalker's course of conduct must be purposeful, willful, malicious, intentional, or knowingly cause fear, fright, terror with respect to death or serious bodily injury or harm, or substantial emotional distress in a reasonable person. Looking at Table 9.1, only three studies — Fisher et al. (2000), Coleman (1997), and Fremouw et al. (1997) — have used definitions of stalking that are derived from anti-stalking statutes.

The remaining studies that use the term "stalking" do not legally ground their definition of stalking. Some researchers such as Mustaine and Tewks-bury (1999) and McCreedy and Dennis (1996) allowed their respondents to define what the term meant when they answered their survey question about "being stalked." Other researchers such as Logan et al. (2000) adopted part of the legal criteria for stalking — repeated behavior — but not other criteria (e.g., intent to cause fear). Like Spitzberg and Rhea (1999), they also include broader pursuit behaviors into their stalking definition that may not meet the legal criteria.

Obsessive Relational Intrusion

Looking at Table 9.1, we can see that Spitzberg et al. (1998) defined obsessive relational intrusion as "repeated or unwanted pursuit and invasion of one's sense of physical or symbolic privacy by another person, either stranger or acquaintance, who desires and/or presumes an intimate relationship" (p. 34). When obsessive relational intrusion becomes threatening and when repeated over time, according to Spitzberg and Rhea (1999), it constitutes stalking (see also Spitzberg et al., 1998).

Spitzberg and Rhea (1999) argued that "obsessive relational intrusion and stalking are related but not isomorphic" (p. 6). There are important

Table 9.1 Summary of College Student Studies: Incidence and Prevalence Estimates of Experiencing Pursuit Behaviors

Study (publication date)	Characteristics of Sample Design			Context of Study	Name of the Concept and Definition Given to Pursuit Behavior	Perpetrator of Pursuit Behavior	Number of Pursuit Behaviors Measured	Reference Time Frame	Incidence or Prevalence Estimates of Experience	Most Commonly Experienced Types of Pursuit Behavior
	Type of Sampling Design	Participants	Response Rate							
National-Level Study										
Fisher et al. (2000)	Two-stage design: 1. Stratified random sample of 2 and 4-year institutions of higher education (n = 233) 2. Females randomly selected from chosen schools	Undergraduate and graduate female students (n = 4446)	86%	Estimate the extent and describe nature of the victimization of college women	Stalking: legally grounded in anti-stalking statutes Repeated behavior that seemed obsessive and made you afraid or concerned for your safety	Anyone — from a stranger to an ex-boyfriend	7	On average 7 months — since school began in the fall of current academic year (e.g., fall 1996)	13% — Stalked	Incidents: 1. 78% — telephoned 2. 52% — waited outside or inside places 3. 44% — watched from afar
Case Studies										
Langhinrichsen-Rohling et al. (2000)	Convenience: volunteers	Students who were enrolled in introductory psychology courses at a large public midwestern university (n = 160)	Not given	The termination of an important intimate relationship	Unwanted pursuit behaviors: activities that constitute ongoing and unwanted pursuit of a romantic relationship between individuals who are not currently involved in a consensual romantic relationship with each other	Ex-partner from a relationship that lasted at least 1 month	26	Lifetime	89%	1. 56% — asked friends about you 2. 40% — showed up at places 3. 36% — unwanted phone calls

Study	Sampling	Sample	Consent/participation	Definition	Situation	Number	Time frame	Prevalence	Details
Logan et al. (2000)	Convenience: volunteers	Students enrolled in an introductory communications class at a medium-sized southeastern university (n = 84 females; n = 46 males)	Study was described to the participants but what they were told is not included in article	Stalking: repeated behavior (once a day or more, and more than twice)	Situation following a difficult breakup with an intimate partner	26	Lifetime	Females — 29% Males — 24%	Females: 1. 63% — called you at home 2. 29% — talked to others to get information about you 3. 21% — drove by your house Males: 1. 55% — called you at home 2. 36% — came to your house 3. 36% — came to your work or school
Spitzberg and Rhea (1999)	Convenience: volunteers	Students enrolled in the basic communication course at a large public Texas university (n = 185 females; n = 178 males)	Not given	Investigation of relational intrusion behavior[b]	Relational intrusion behavior: repeated or unwanted pursuit and invasion of one's sense of physical or symbolic privacy by another person, either stranger or acquaintance, who desires and/or presumes an intimate relationship	Anyone — focusing on the worst relationship that the respondents had experienced	23[a]	Lifetime	Not reported	
Mustaine and Tewksbury (1999)	Convenience: volunteers	Female students in introductory-level sociology and criminal justice courses at nine post-secondary schools (including large and small universities, 4-year colleges, and community colleges) (n = 861)	"Very few, if any, students elected not to participate"	Not given	Stalking: self-defined by respondents	None explicitly	Prior 6 months	11%	

Table 9.1 (continued)   Summary of College Student Studies: Incidence and Prevalence Estimates of Experiencing Pursuit Behaviors

Study (publication date)	Characteristics of Sample Design			Name of the Concept and Definition Given to Pursuit Behavior	Perpetrator of Pursuit Behavior	Number of Pursuit Behaviors Measured	Reference Time Frame	Incidence or Prevalence Estimates of Experience	Most Commonly Experienced Types of Pursuit Behavior
	Type of Sampling Design	Participants	Response Rate	Context of Study					
Spitzberg et al. (1998)	Convenience: volunteers	Undergraduate students from a large southwestern public university (n=162: n = 93 females; n = 69 males)	Not given	Instructions explained "that people often pursue intimate relationships without realizing that the person being pursued does not want such a relationship. These pursuers may want friendship, or romantic intimacy, or perhaps just recognition. In addition, they often participate in activities or behaviors that do not appear in normal circumstances to be intimate, such as invading your privacy, intruding into your life, stalking, or refusing to let go."	Obsessive relational intrusion: repeated and unwanted pursuit and invasion of one's sense of physical or symbolic privacy by another person, either stranger or acquaintance, who desires and/or presumes an intimate relationship Stalking: self-defined by respondents	Anyone	Obsessive relational intrusion — 23 Stalking — none explicitly	Lifetime (forever)	Obsessive relational intrusion — not reported Stalking — 27%	

Study	Sampling	Sample		Study focus	Definition	Relationship	Number/Age	Time frame	Results
Coleman (1997)	Convenience: volunteers	Undergraduate heterosexual female psychology students (n = 141)	Not given	Study on the breakup of romantic relationships	Harassed: repeated, unwanted attention following the breakup. Stalking: legally grounded in Florida's anti-stalking statutes. Repeated, unwanted attention conducted in a malicious manner or becomes more threatening or violent over time, or former partner makes threats that caused you to fear for your physical safety	A dating or marital relationship that ended	29	Lifetime	Harassed — 27% Stalking — 9%
Fremouw et al. (1997)	Convenience: volunteers	Two studies: 1. West Virginia University undergraduates enrolled in psychology classes (n = 165 females; n = 129 males) 2. Additional subjects (n = 153 females; n = 146 males)	Not given	Frequency of stalking behavior	Stalking: legally grounded in West Virginia's anti-stalking statute. Having someone knowingly and repeatedly following, harassing, or threatening respondent	Anyone	Study 1–29 Study 2–22	Lifetime	Victimization: Overall — 24% Females — 31% Males — 17% Study 1: Females — 27% Males — 15% Study 2: Females — 35% Males — 18%
Dennis and McCreedy (1996)	Convenience: volunteers	Classes that enrolled primarily juniors and seniors in main campus of Eastern Carolina University	Not given	Crime survey	Stalking: self-defined by respondent	Someone (known or unknown) whom you thought might do you physical harm	None explicitly	Lifetime	6%

Table 9.1 (continued) Summary of College Student Studies: Incidence and Prevalence Estimates of Experiencing Pursuit Behaviors

Study (publication date)	Characteristics of Sample Design			Context of Study	Name of the Concept and Definition Given to Pursuit Behavior	Perpetrator of Pursuit Behavior	Number of Pursuit Behaviors Measured	Reference Time Frame	Incidence or Prevalence Estimates of Experience	Most Commonly Experienced Types of Pursuit Behavior
	Type of Sampling Design	Participants	Response Rate							
Levitt et al. (1996)	Students — convenience: volunteers	Students drawn from upper-level classes and employees at a southeastern university (n = 236 females; n = 107 males) (n = 273 students)	"Few students declined to participate and 23% of employee questionnaires never returned"	Assess frequency, nature, and precursors of negative relationship experiences	Troublesome behavior	Someone with whom the respondent had been involved with who had troubled him/her[c]	20-item troublesome behavior checklist of which "followed respondent" was one type of behavior	Previous 5 years	11%	
Unknown Level										
Elliot and Brantley (1997)	Not explicitly stated	College students (n = 1752)	9%	Student sexuality	Stalked or harassed with obscene phone calls	Anyone	1	Lifetime	Overall — 36% Females — 45% Males — 25%	

[a] Compared to Spitzberg et al.'s 1998 article, Spitzberg and Rhea in their 1999 article made slight wording changes in some of the 23 items and added another form of pursuit behavior (kidnapping and restraint). The 1999 article, however, does not contain an appendix like the one in the 1998 article that lists all the items. Consequently, we do not know which item was deleted. Note that both the 1998 and 1999 articles report results from a 23-item self-report measure; if one item was added another had to be deleted. Instructions given in this study were very similar to those used by Spitzberg et al. (1998) in their previous study.

[b] Two criteria had to be satisfied to be included in their study. First, the stalking questions referred to the situation following a difficult breakup with an intimate partner. Second, all the previously asked abuse victimization and perpetration questions had to be answered about the same partner as those from the stalking questions. When answering the abuse questions, respondents were asked to refer to the last relationship they had which lasted 1 year. If they had not had such a relationship, they were asked to refer to the relationship that lasted the longest.

differences between obsessive relational intrusion and stalking. First, among the purposes of pursuit behavior in obsessive relational intrusion is to establish a relationship. Unlike stalking, obsessive relational intrusion "is confined to relationships in which prior acquaintance of some degree is assumed by the pursuer, whether this acquaintance is real or delusional" (Spitzberg et al., 1998, p. 6). Second, not all obsessive relational intrusions can meet the legal criteria of creating fear of physical harm in the target or risk the safety of the target or their property. Third, the intrusions include not only forms of pursuit behavior (e.g., leaving unwanted messages), but they also can take forms that are broader than those that constitute stalking. Some types may even be considered another type of crime.

For example, grabbing, breaking and entering into the target's home, and kidnapping are included as forms of intrusion that Spitzberg and Rhea (1999) included in their 23-item measure of obsessive relational intrusion.

Unwanted Pursuit Behaviors

Other researchers have used the broad term "unwanted pursuit behaviors." Langhinrichsen-Rohling et al. (2000) use this term to refer to activities that constitute ongoing and unwanted pursuit of a romantic relationship between individuals who are not currently involved. Like Spitzberg and Rhea's (2000) definition, their definition is contingent on an aspect of a relationship.

From our discussion of the concepts and definitions used to measure pursuit behaviors, it is obvious that there are similarities and differences. Reading over the definitions in Table 9.1, it is apparent that there are two characteristics of pursuit behaviors that are common across the different concepts: (1) they are repeated or ongoing, and (2) they are unwanted by the target.

One difference between the types of pursuit behaviors is that criminal stalking includes elements of the presence of a threat and being in fear of bodily harm or feeling very frightened, whereas the other two types of pursuit behavior do not include these two elements. Other aspects differ; however, these differences can be used to develop a continuum of repeated and unwanted pursuit behavior. Although developing such a continuum is beyond the scope of this chapter, looking at Table 9.1, several dimensions could be included in this continuum: (1) types and number of pursuit behaviors (e.g., approach, surveillance, and intimidation behaviors), (2) frequency and duration of the behavior (e.g., once a day for a year, every week for 3 months), (3) type of perpetrator (e.g., ex-intimate partner, ex-dating partner, stranger, acquaintance), and (4) purpose of the behavior (e.g., ranging from the desire for a romantic relationship to the intent to make the target fearful for his/her personal safety).

The state of the current research points to the need for the research community to reach a consensus on how to define and operationalize pursuit behaviors. On one hand, a strict legal definition has practical and research limitations for the public health community: pursuit behavior estimates based on a narrow legal definition may be undercounting victims' needs of public health services.

In addition, pursuit behavior research based solely on legal criteria may limit our scientific investigation and clinical understanding of who has repeatedly experienced pursuit behaviors. On the other hand, a broader nonlegal definition does not serve the criminal justice community in terms of counting the violations of the law and the number of prosecutions of stalking. Researchers may want to consider definitions of pursuit behavior that once operationalized allow the researcher the opportunity to see how different legal and clinical or forensic criteria affect their pursuit behavior estimates.

As the author discusses in the next section, these similarities and differences in the definitions of pursuit behavior contribute to setting the parameters of understanding of "who counts" as having experienced or initiated pursuit behaviors. They also contribute to making comparisons between the estimates of pursuit behavior complicated.

Who Gets "Counted" as Having Experienced Pursuit Behaviors?

The measurement of "who counts" as having experienced pursuit behaviors is a young, yet daunting, enterprise because as the previous discussion revealed, no consensus exists among researchers or practitioners as to how to define and operationalize pursuit behaviors. Measuring the extent of who counts as having experienced pursuit behaviors, however, is important to researcher and practitioner communities. For example, campus administrators should know how many of their students have experienced these behaviors because it has implications for training campus law enforcement to identify high-risk relationships or at-risk students, respond to calls for service involving unwanted pursuit behavior, and provide prevention seminars, training counselors, and other medical-related service providers to respond to the psychological and physical needs of those who have experienced repeated and unwanted pursuit behaviors.

Table 9.1 presents a summary of the studies that have examined the incidence and prevalence of having experienced pursuit behaviors among college students. These studies are our only source of information as to the extent of criminal stalking against college students, as neither of the two major sources of victimization data in the United States, the *National Crime Victimization Survey* and the FBI's *Uniform Crime Reports*, collects criminal stalking data. In addition, schools covered under the Clery Act do not have to report their criminal stalking statistics.

There are several noteworthy points in Table 9.1. First, examining pursuit behaviors among college students has become a popular research topic. Over a 5-year period, at least ten published studies have examined these behaviors, including one study conducted by *Details* magazine and Random House and then published as a pop culture book (see Elliot and Brantley, 1997).

Second, quick popularity, however, has its methodological shortcomings. Similar to many new areas of social science research, the majority of these studies have used a nonrandom sample of college students from a single college or university (for exception as to the number of schools, see Mustaine and Tewksbury, 1999). Typically, the students who attend a large introductory-level class on the day the survey is administered or who volunteer for the study for part of a course requirement or extra credit comprise the sample (Coleman, 1997; Fremouw et al., 1997; Langhinrichsen-Rohling et al., 2000; Logan et al., 2000; Mustaine and Tewksbury, 1999; Sinclair and Frieze, 2000; Spitzberg and Rhea, 1999).

Case studies are well known for the limited generalizability of their results. Only one national-level study of stalking among college women has been done to date (Fisher et al., 2000). Nonetheless, conclusions from all these studies highlight the importance of examining repeated and unwanted pursuit behavior experiences for purposes of research, developing and implementing awareness and prevention education, training among staff, and providing medical and counseling services.

The question of how many college students have experienced pursuit behavior remains at best partially answered. As shown in Table 9.1, comparisons of the estimate of those who have experienced pursuit behaviors across the studies are complicated and limited for several methodological reasons. First, as already discussed in a previous section of this chapter, different definitions of pursuit behaviors have been employed. Second, researchers have used different selection criteria as to the pursuer of the pursuit behavior. For example, the majority of the studies explicitly limit the pursuer as someone with whom the respondent had a romantic relationship. Other studies use a broader definition of the pursuer that includes anyone from a stranger to an ex-intimate partner. To illustrate, Langhinrichsen-Rohling et al. (2000) qualified the pursuer in their survey to be an ex-partner from a relationship that lasted at least 1 month. In comparison, Fisher et al. (2000) do not place such a condition on who the perpetrator was. They explicitly refer to the perpetrator in their stalking survey question as "anyone from a stranger to an ex-boyfriend." Third, the number and types of pursuit behaviors vary from study to study. They range from none being explicitly referred to in the measure (e.g., Mustaine and Tewksbury, 1999; McCreedy and Dennis, 1996), to one type of pursuit behavior examined by Levitt et al. (1996), to 29 different types of pursuit behaviors examined by Coleman (1997) and Fremouw et al. (1997).

A methodological issue related to the number of pursuit behaviors measured is that many studies may not have employed the same types of behaviors. This hit-or-miss laundry list method of measurement limits the comparison of the types of pursuit behaviors that do overlap. For example, Fisher et al. (2000) explicitly measured sending letters and sending gifts as two separate types of behavior. However, other studies either did not explicitly include these two types or, like Langhinrichsen-Rohling et al. (2000), combined the two types into one type of behavior: "unwanted letters/gifts" and included "in-person gift" as a separate type of behavior. Fourth, the reference time frame varied from study to study. The majority of the studies used a lifetime reference. Only a few studies used a shorter reference period of 6 or 7 months. Despite these methodological differences across the studies, there is a common theme: a substantial percentage of college students reported having experienced pursuit behaviors in some form from the aforementioned list.

Fourth, examining the incidence and prevalence estimates from studies is complex given the methodological issues previously raised. There are, however, somewhat comparable studies that can shed some light on the extent of experiencing pursuit behaviors. As expected, those studies that use a broader definition of pursuit behaviors report a larger percent of students experiencing pursuit behaviors than studies that do not use a broad definition. Two studies that examined lifetime prevalence among male and female students illustrate this point. In Langhinrichsen-Rohling et al.'s (2000) study, of those who initiated the termination relationship, 89% reported that their ex-partners had engaged in at least one of the 26 pursuit behaviors that were measured. In comparison, in the Logan et al. (2000) study, of those who had been in a relationship that had a difficult breakup, 29% of the females and 24% of the males had experienced at least 1 of the 26 pursuit behaviors that were measured.

Two case studies, Fremouw et al. (1997) and McCreedy and Dennis (1996), estimated lifetime prevalence of stalking among male and female students. McCreedy and Dennis reported that 6% of their male and female sample reported being stalked. Fremouw and colleagues (1997) reported a much higher prevalence estimate — 24% of their male and female sample reported being stalked. Four studies examined stalking among female students. First, Fremouw et al. (1997) reported that 31% of the female college students indicated that they had ever experienced stalking — a concept that the respondents defined. Second, Coleman's lifetime estimate of criminal stalking among heterosexual undergraduates was 9%. Third, the Mustaine and Tewksbury (1999) study, in which respondents self-defined stalking, reported that within a 6-month reference period, 11% of the females reported being stalked. Fourth, Fisher et al.'s (2000) national-level study, employing a stalking question that provided a legally grounded description of the behavior, reported that 13% of the females reported being stalked over an average reference period of 7 months.

The discrepancy in the stalking estimates produced by these studies highlights the importance of taking into account the length of the reference period, the composition of the sample, and whether the concept of stalking is self-defined by the respondents or legally grounded when making any comparisons across studies (see also Tjadan et al., 2000).

Three studies compared the percentage of females and males that have experienced pursuit behaviors. Similar to Tjaden and Thoennes's stalking results (1998), every one of these studies reported that a larger percentage of female students had been stalked than male students (Elliot and Brantley, 1997; Fremouw et al., 1997; Logan et al., 2000). For example, Fremouw et al. (1997) found that 31% of the female students had ever been stalked compared to 17% of the male students. Logan et al. (2000) reported a similar difference among female and male student estimates of stalking following a breakup with an intimate partner — 29% compared to 24%.

Although there are a growing number of studies that have examined the extent to which college students have experienced pursuit behaviors, comparing the estimates is difficult, as the noted differences between the studies overshadow the number of studies.

These studies, however, have begun to develop our understanding as to the extent that college students have experienced pursuit behaviors. In doing so, they have raised methodological issues that researchers in this area need to consider. As we will see, some of these same measurement issues that plague studies that attempt to measure the extent of pursuit behavior are also evident in the perpetration of pursuit behavior research.

Who Gets "Counted" as Having Perpetrated Pursuit Behaviors?

Measuring who has engaged in pursuit behaviors has also captured researchers' attention. Several clinical researchers have attempted to isolate key cognitive and behavioral elements in order to develop a typological assessment of stalkers (see Davis and Chipman, Chapter 1, this book). Despite these attempts, counting who has perpetrated pursuit behaviors remains in its infancy stages of development. As can be seen in Table 9.2, the college student perpetration research is characterized by many of the same methodological and measurement issues that characterize the college student pursuit behavior experiences research.

Compared to the number of studies that have estimated the number of college students who have experienced pursuit behavior, the number of studies that has estimated the amount of perpetration behavior among college students is less. As Table 9.2 displays, only three studies (of which two also examined those who experienced pursuit behaviors) have examined the extent of perpetration among college students.

Table 9.2 Summary of College Student Studies: Prevalence Estimates of Perpetrator's Pursuit Behavior

| Study | Characteristics of Sample Design | | | Context of Study | Label and Definition of Pursuit Behavior | Target of Pursuit Behavior | Number of Pursuit Behaviors Measured | Reference Time Frame | Incidence or Prevalence Estimates of Having Perpetrated Pursuit Behaviors | Most Frequently Occurring Behaviors |
	Type of Sampling Design	Participants	Response Rate							
Case Studies										
Sinclair and Frieze (2000)	Convenience: volunteers	Students enrolled in an Introduction to Psychology course at University of Pittsburgh and who were heterosexuals and under 25 years old (n = 197 females; n = 44 males)	Not given	Study of "loving when your partner does not love back"	Stalking-related behaviors	The one person you liked the most	52	Lifetime		Females: 1. 92% — asked friends about him/her 2. 85% — tried to show up at social or recreational events where you'd know she/he would be 3. 75% — driven, ridden, or walked outside of class, school, home, or work Males: 1. 86% — asked friends about him/her 2. 79% — tried to show up at social or recreational events where you'd know she/he would be 3. 79% — sent or gave him/her notes, letters, e-mail, or other written communication

Langhinrichsen-Rohling et al. (2000)	Self-selected volunteers	Students who were enrolled in an introductory psychology course at a large public midwestern university (n = 120)	Not applicable	The termination of an important intimate relationship	Unwanted pursuit behaviors by respondent: activities that constitute ongoing and unwanted pursuit of a romantic relationship between individuals who are not currently involved in a consensual romantic relationship with each other	Ex-partner	26	Lifetime	99% perpetrated at least one unwanted behavior	1. 78% — unwanted phone call 2. 73% — in-person conversation 3. 55% — unwanted phone messages
Fremouw et al. (1997)	Convenience: volunteers	Two studies: 1. West Virginia University under-graduates enrolled in psychology classes (n = 165 females; n = 129 males)	Not applicable	Stalking behavior	Stalking; legally grounded in West Virginia's anti-stalking statute Always knowingly and repeatedly followed, harassed, or threatened someone	Someone	29	Lifetime (always)	Females — 0% Males — 2%

The paucity of research makes it difficult to answer the question of how many college students have perpetrated pursuit behavior. Further, a large discrepancy exists between the two estimates of how much perpetration of pursuit behaviors there is. To illustrate, Fremouw and colleagues (1997) reported that 2% of the males in their sample stalked someone. In contrast, Langhinrichsen-Rohling (2000) reported that 99% of the students in their sample had engaged in at least one pursuit behavior that was directed at an ex-partner. This wide discrepancy between the perpetration estimates clearly points to the need for more research to obtain a valid and reliable estimate of perpetration behavior among college students.

The Nature of Pursuit Behaviors

As shown in Tables 9.1 and 9.2, researchers have asked students about experiencing and perpetrating a number of different types of pursuit behaviors. In an attempt to make sense out of these different approaches to operationalizing pursuit behavior, researchers have developed categories of behaviors. To illustrate, Spitzberg et al. (1998) factor-analyzed their 23 items of different types of pursuit behavior and found these two factors: (1) general pursuit and (2) aggression. Using 41 different types of pursuit behavior, Sinclair and Frieze (2000) developed six categories of pursuit behavior. Also employing factor analytical techniques, they extracted the following categories of pursuit behavior: (1) approach (e.g., sending notes, asking person out on a date), (2) surveillance (e.g., showing up at events, spying), (3) intimidation (e.g., trying to scare the person, leaving unwanted items), (4) harm self (e.g., attempting to hurt self, physically hurting self), (5) verbal abuse and mild aggression (e.g., verbal abuse, harassing person), and (6) extreme harm (e.g., forcing sexual contact, damaging property).

As shown in the last column of Table 9.1, three studies have examined the types of pursuit behaviors that students have experienced. These studies suggest that the two most common types of behaviors are approach and surveillance. With respect to approach, a common type of behavior was reported by all the studies: the students indicated that the pursuer telephoned them.

For example, Fisher et al. (2000) reported that 78% of the stalking incidents involved telephone calls. Over a third of the students in the Langhinrichsen-Rohling (2000) study reported that they received unwanted telephone calls from an ex-partner after the relationship had ended. Logan et al. (2000) found that following the breakup of an intimate relationship, 63% of the females and 55% of the males experienced being called on the telephone.

Surveillance behaviors were also commonly experienced by the target. Students reported that the pursuer would try to get information from their friends about them and show up at places. For example, 29% of female students in the Logan et al. (2000) study reported the pursuer talked to others to get information about them and 21% drove by their homes. Male students reported experiences similar to female students — 36% of them reported that their pursuers, respectively, came to their houses and came to work or school.

With respect to gender differences in rates of pursuit behaviors, results presented by Langhinrichsen-Rohling et al. (2000) are consistent with data reported by Cupach and Spitzberg (1998) and others previously discussed and suggest that there are few gender differences in these rates. Langhinrichsen-Rohling et al. (2000) concluded that the primary difference is that females are more likely to leave telephone messages, whereas males are more likely to seek in-person communication with their ex-partners.

As should be expected, the pursuer research complements the target results. Looking at the last column in Table 9.2, common behaviors that pursuers reported engaging in were approach and surveillance behaviors. These results suggest that the majority of college student pursuers attempted to communicate with their targets by using various means. For example, Sinclair and Frieze (2000) reported that a large proportion of female and male students tried to show up at some social or recreational events where these "loved" were attending. Langhinrichsen-Rohling and colleagues reported that a sizable proportion of perpetrators called the targeted people, engaged in in-person conversations with these people, and left unwanted telephone messages for these people.

Those who have experienced pursuit behaviors have indicated that the duration of these experiences is not brief but rather persists for some time. Fisher et al. (2000) reported that the mean duration for the stalking incident, which is affected by the outlier cases, was 147 days; in contrast, the median duration for an incident was 60 days. Spitzberg and Rhea (1999) reported that the average case of obsessive relational pursuit lasted 4.8 months.

Stalking victims have also indicated that the stalker pursues them frequently. Fisher and colleagues (2000) reported that 41% of their respondents reported that the stalking occurred two to six times a week, while 13% stated that the incident occurred daily and 10% stated that it occurred more than once daily. In contrast, only 34% stated that the stalking incidents took place once a week or less, and of these victims, less than 4% reported the stalking incidents as being less than twice a month. Taken together, these results indicate that not only are pursuit behaviors somewhat long-lasting, but they are also consistently present in the lives of the victim.

An unanswered question concerning the relationship between pursuit behaviors and other forms of violence still remains. We now turn to a discussion of the research examining this relationship.

Pursuit Behaviors: Another Stage in the Cycle of Dating and Intimate Partner Violence

Clarifying the role that pursuit behaviors play in relationships, primarily dating and intimate partner relationships, has been the focus of a few college student studies.

Overall, the college student research suggests conclusions that are supportive of the results reported from general populations studies (Tjaden and Thoennes, 1998). In college student samples, the occurrence of abusive and aggressive behavior during a dating or intimate partner relationship appears to be related to the occurrence of pursuit behaviors after the breakup of the relationship. Coleman (1997) reported that "former partners not only committed hostile or aggressive acts *after* the breakup ... but also exhibited more abusive behavior *prior* to the breakup" (p. 430). Results from Logan et al.'s study of stalking after a difficult breakup (2000) complement Coleman's results. They reported that those who reported being stalked after breaking up experienced significantly more physical and psychological victimization during the relationship than those who reported no stalking victimization. Specifically, stalking was significantly associated with physical and psychological abuse victimization for women victims, and was associated with psychological abuse victimization for males. Given their results, Logan et al. (2000) conclude that "stalking is a continuation of intimate partner violence toward a partner after the relationship ends" (p. 102).

From the limited amount of research, it appears that college students are not immune from experiencing pursuit behaviors after a relationship ends. Those who have experienced abusive relationships are more at risk for experiencing pursuit behaviors after the relationship terminates. What is still unknown among college students is whether the stalking or other pursuit behaviors began before the relationship ended.

Impact of Pursuit Behaviors on Students

Clinical studies of victims suggest that stalking causes stress, fear, physical injury, and psychological trauma. Some of these life-damaging effects persist even after the stalking ceases. For example, Pathé and Mullen's results from their Australian study, using a nonrandom sample of 100 stalking victims, reported that 34% of the victims had been assaulted by their stalker — 31% physically and 7% sexually.

Physical injury is only one health-related consequence of being stalked; several clinical studies have consistently observed a range of psychological injuries that have devastating day-to-day and long-term impacts on the victim.

For example, Pathé and Mullen reported pronounced impacts on the victims: a sense of violation and inability to trust and heightened anxiety were common, as was powerlessness to change the situation. A quarter of the victims contemplated suicide, and most victims reported post-traumatic stress symptoms, with over a third meeting the criteria for a diagnosis of post-traumatic stress disorder. Research done in the United States supports Pathé and Mullen's results. For example, in her telephone survey of 145 self-defined stalking victims, Hall reported that the experience of being stalked is akin to psychological terrorism. Following a stalking experience, victims in her study became more cautious of others and aggressive, easily frightened or startled, paranoid, and less friendly.

These clinical studies have advanced our understanding of the different types of negative effects stalking can have on the victims; nonetheless, three critical questions are (1) what effects does experiencing pursuit behaviors have on student victims, (2) how do students cope with these experiences, and (3) is legal intervention used by student stalking victims?

Effects Pursuit Behaviors Have on Student Victims

Very few studies have examined the effects experiencing pursuit behaviors have on college students. Fisher et al. (2000) reported that in 95% of the stalking incidents, victims stated that they were "injured emotionally or psychologically." Spitzberg and Rhea (1999) further clarified the types of psychological effects that students may experience. They reported that experiencing obsessive relational intrusion significantly increases the experience of negative symptoms. These symptoms include general symptoms (e.g., helplessness, general stress, depression), loss of faith (e.g., loss of faith in the criminal justice system, blackouts, loss of income, loss of faith in the mental health system), and predicting resilience symptoms (e.g., greater safety awareness, stronger self-concept).

Coping Strategies

The research has shown that students adopt coping strategies in response to experiencing unwanted pursuit behaviors. Spitzberg and Cupach (1998) reported a five-factor structure of behavioral responses to obsessive relational instrusion. These included: (1) direct interaction (e.g., yell at person, have a serious discussion with person), (2) protection (e.g., call police, seek a restraining order), (3) avoidance (e.g, avoid eye contact, ignore person), (4) retaliation (e.g., threatened harm, hit the person), and (5) technology (e.g., obtain caller ID, obtain callback feature).

A few researchers have examined how students cope with being the target of pursuit behaviors. Most frequently student targets change their social environments by avoiding the stalker. To illustrate, the three most common responses among the females in Fisher et al.'s (2000) study were to avoid or try to avoid the stalker (43% of the incidents), confront the stalker (16%), and become less trusting of others (6%). Fremouw et al.'s (1997) results support the results of Fisher and colleagues. The coping strategies most frequently used by female students in their study were to ignore the stalker, confront the stalker, and change their schedules in order to avoid the stalker. In contrast, the male students most frequently confronted the stalker, ignored the stalker, and reconciled with the stalker (presuming a prior relationship). In both these studies, calling or reporting to the police was not a frequently used coping strategy.

The Use of Legal Interventions

Legal interventions are used by very few students. Similar to other victimization surveys, 83% of the stalking incidents in Fisher et al.'s (2000) study were not reported to the police or campus law enforcement officials.

Respondents were also very unlikely to use the legal system to address the stalker(s); in a little less than 4% of the incidents a respondent sought a restraining order, in only 2% of the incidents did the respondent file criminal charges, and in a little over 1% of the incidents did the respondent file civil charges. They were also not likely to use formal disciplinary processes available at the institutions; only 3% of the incidents involved a respondent filing a grievance or initiating disciplinary action. Complementing these results, Fremouw et al. (1997) found that very few students resort to legal interventions — either reporting to the police or having a restraint/warrant issued against the stalker.

In summary, very few studies have examined the toll that experiencing pursuit behaviors takes on students. What few have been done suggest that such behaviors have a negative toll on students. They also suggest that students rely on themselves to cope with these experiences. Rather than depend on legal interventions or school judicial processes to deter or stop the pursuer, students have adopted their own coping strategies in an attempt to stop the pursuit behaviors.

Implications for College-Level Intervention and Prevention

The results from college student studies as to the extent of pursuit behaviors suggest that college students do not exist in an ivory tower that insulates them from pursuit behaviors. There appears to be mounting evidence that a substantial number of college students have experienced pursuit behaviors that range from being simply unwanted to criminal stalking. There is also evidence that suggests that those who engage in pursuit behaviors directed at college students are not strangers to the target. Pursuers are typically fellow college students with whom the target has had a relationship. The studies further suggest that pursuit behaviors are part of the cycle of dating and intimate partner violence. And last, experiencing pursuit behaviors takes a negative toll on students emotionally and psychologically. In response to these negative effects, student victims have adopted non-confrontational coping strategies, including not using legal means to gain recourse on a stalker.

These empirical patterns have implications for college and university administrators. Below, two issues are addressed: first, getting campus administrators to recognize the extent and nature of pursuit behavior victimization and perpetration among college students; and second, providing suggestions for the content of pursuit behavior awareness and education.

Recognition of Pursuit Behavior — Victimization and Perpetration among College Students

Recognizing the extent that pursuit behaviors are experienced and perpetrated among their respective students is important to college and university administrators. This is the first step that they need to take to recognize that a substantial number of their students are targets and perpetrators of pursuit behaviors, including criminal stalking. Caution is needed at this step so that administrators do not blindly allocate resources to address the problem of pursuit behaviors among their students in an effort to "do something about the problem."

Campus administrators need to understand the nature of pursuit behaviors, especially those behaviors that can be facilitated by the operations of the campus (e.g., intra-campus mail, campus telephone calls), and the negative toll these experiences take on their students. Only in this way can administrators be judicious in their approaches to addressing the extent and nature of pursuit behaviors among their students. Among the challenges that administrators face in their efforts is balancing the "freedom" of the campus setting with the safety and security of the campus community.

Content of Pursuit Behavior Education and Anti-Pursuit Behavior Policy

A comprehensive approach to addressing the needs of those students (and faculty and staff, too) who have experienced "unwanted and repeated" pursuit behaviors is much overdue. College and university administrators are in a position to develop and implement policies and programs to enhance aware-ness and educate students as well as faculty and staff as to the extent, nature, and impact of pursuit behaviors, especially those behaviors that constitute criminal stalking.

One way to increase awareness and educate the campus community is to incorporate the topic of "unwanted and repeated" pursuit behaviors into sexual assault awareness and prevention and dating programs, especially given that these behaviors manifest after a relationship terminates. A separate "unwanted and repeated" pursuit behaviors or stalking program may be warranted to focus attention on the seriousness of the subject.

Another means to educate the campus community is to develop an anti-pursuit behavior or anti-stalking policy, similar to the sexual assault policy required by the Clery Act, or a sexual harassment policy. This policy could then be included in the student and faculty codes of conduct for a respective school. Like the required information for sexual assault policies, an anti-pursuit behavior could describe what pursuit behaviors are and provide a definition for criminal stalking. Details could be outlined as to what actions a victim can take to address the pursuer's behavior; for example, first having the victim document the behavior by saving all written communications, recording and saving all telephone messages, etc. Information can also be given telling the victim that he/she has the option of filing a formal grievance or complaint against the accused perpetrator and employing the university grievance or disciplinary process to sanction the perpetrator. In addition, the school should advise students that criminal stalking cases can be referred to the criminal justice system for further processing, and information as to how to contact the campus police and/or local police should be included in this policy. Also included in an anti-pursuit behavior policy should be contact information for counseling services and medical-related services.

Conclusion

Knowing when pursuit behavior happens during the course of any relation-ship is critical to the development of any intervention or prevention strategy. Students need to be educated as to what pursuit behavior entails, including the state-level definition of stalking. Included in this education should be identifying the "danger signs" of an unhealthy relationship in which pursuit behaviors may be exhibited by a dating, ex-dating partner, an intimate, ex-intimate partner, friend, or the signs of pursuit behavior from a professor, co-worker, and stranger. Others on campus need to be educated as well. Several different staff members on campus could be trained to identify high-risk relationships and pursuit behaviors. For example, housing staff, such as residential assistants who live in dormitories with students, should be trained to identify both high-risk relationships and targets and pursuers as they come in daily contact with many students.

Campus law enforcement officers need also to be trained as to how to respond to calls of service that include pursuit behaviors or criminal stalking. Counseling and other medical-service staff need to be trained to identify and treat those who are experiencing pursuit behaviors and those who are perpetrating these behaviors.

Bibliography

Belknap, J. and Erez, E. (1995). The victimization of women on college campuses: courtship violence, date rape and sexual harassment, in B. S. Fisher and J. J. Sloan (Eds.), *Campus Crime: Legal, Social, and Policy Perspectives.* Springfield, IL: Charles C Thomas.

Bohmer, C. and Parrot, A. (1993). *Sexual Assault on Campus: The Problem and the Solution.* New York: Lexington Books.

Brewster, M. P. (2000). Stalking by former intimates: verbal threats and other predictors of physical violence, *Violence and Victims,* 15(1), 41–54.

Bromley, M. and Fisher, B. S. (2000). Campus policing and victim services, in L. Moriarty (Ed.), *Policing and Victims.* Upper Saddle River, NJ: Prentice Hall.

Cohen, L. and Felson, M. (1979). Social change and crime rate trends: a routine activity approach, *American Sociological Review,* 44, 588–608.

Coleman, F. L. (1997). Stalking behavior and the cycle of domestic violence, *Journal of Interpersonal Violence,* 12 (3), 420–432.

Crowell, N. A. and Burgess, A. W. (1996). *Understanding Violence Against Women.* Washington, D.C.: National Academy Press.

Cupach, W. R. and Spitzberg, B. H. (1998). Obsessional relational intrusion and stalking, in W. R. Cupach and B. H. Spitzberg (Eds.), *The Dark Side of Close Relationships.* Mahwah, NJ: Lawrence Erlbaum.

Davis, J. A. and Chipman, M. A. (1997). Stalkers and other obsessional types: a review and forensic typology of those who stalk, *Journal of Clinical Forensic Medicine,* 4, 166–172.

DeKeseredy, W. S. and Schwartz, M. D. (1998). Woman abuse: results from the Canadian National Survey, in C. M. Renzetti and J. L. Edleson (Series Eds.), *Sage Series on Violence against Women,* Vol. 5. Thousand Oaks, CA: Sage Publications.

Educational Development Center Inc., University of Cincinnati, and Police Executive Research Forum (work in progress) (2000). Campus Sexual Assault: How American Colleges and Universities Respond. Washington, D.C.: National Institute of Justice, U.S. Department of Justice.

Elliot, L. and Brantley, C. (1997). *Sex on Campus: The Naked Truth about the Real Sex Lives of College Students.* New York: Random House.

Fisher, B. S. and Cullen, F. T. (1999). The Extent and Nature of Violence against College Women: Results from a National-Level Study. Washington, D.C.: Bureau of Justice Statistics, U.S. Government Printing Office.

Fisher, B. S. and Cullen, F. T. (2000). Measuring the Sexual Victimization of Women: Evolution, Current Controversies, Future Research. Washington, D.C.: National Institute of Justice, U.S. Government Printing Office.

Fisher, B. S., Cullen, F. T. and Turner, M. (2000). Sexual Victimization among College Women: Results from Two National-Level Studies. Washington, D.C.: National Institute of Justice, U.S. Government Printing Office.

Fisher, B. S., Sloan, J. J., Cullen, F. T., and Lu, C. (1998). Crime in the ivory tower: the level and sources of student victimization, *Criminology*, 36(3), 671–710.

Fremouw, W. J., Westrup, D., and Pennypacker, J. (1997). Stalking on campus: the prevalence and strategies for coping with stalking, *Journal of Forensic Science*, 42(4), 666–669.

Frieze, I. H. and Davis, K. (2000). Introduction to stalking and obsessive behaviors in everyday life: assessments of victims and perpetrators, *Violence and Victims*, 15(1), 3–5.

General Accounting Office (1997). *Campus Crime: Difficulties Meeting Federal Reporting Requirements*. Washington, D.C.: General Accounting Office.

Hall, D. M. (1998). The victim of stalking, in J. R. Meloy (Ed.), *The Psychology of Stalking: Clinical and Forensic Perspectives*. San Diego, CA: Academic Press.

Hindelang, M. S., Gottfredson, M., and Garofalo, J. (1978). *Victims of Personal Crime*. Cambridge, MA: Ballinger.

Holmes, D. A., Taylor, M., and Saeed, A. (2000). Stalking and the therapeutic relationship, *Forensic Update*, No. 60, 31–35.

Koss, M. P., Gidycz, C. A., and Wisniewski, N. J. (1987). The scope of rape: incidence and prevalence of sexual aggression and victimization in a national sample of higher education students, *Journal of Consulting and Clinical Psychology*, 55, 162–170.

Kurt, J. L. (1995). Stalking as a variant of domestic violence, *Bulletin of the Academy of Psychiatry and the Law*, 23, 219–223.

Langhinrichsen-Rohling, J., Palarea, R. E., Cohen, J., and Rohling, M. L. (2000). Breaking up is hard to do: unwanted pursuit behaviors following the dissolution of a romantic relationship, *Violence and Victims*, 15(1), 73–90.

Levitt, M. J., Silver, M. E., and Franco, N. (1996). Troublesome relationships: a part of human experience, *Journal of Social and Personal Relationships*, 13(4), 523–536.

Lion, J. R. and Herschler, J. A. (1998). The stalking of clinicians by their patients, in J. R. Meloy (Ed.), *The Psychology of Stalking: Clinical and Forensic Perspectives*. San Diego, CA: Academic Press.

Logan, T. K., Leukefeld, C., and Walker, B. (2000). Stalking as a variant of intimate violence: implications from a young adult sample, *Violence and Victims*, 15(1), 91–111.

Makepeace, J. M. (1981). Courtship violence among college students, *Family Relations*, 30, 97–102.

McAnaney, K. G., Curliss, L. A., and Abeyta-Price, C. E. (1993). From imprudence to crime: anti-stalking laws, *Notre Dame Law Review*, 68, 819–909.

McCreedy, K. R. and Dennis, B. G. (1996). Sex-related offenses and fear of crime on campus, *Journal of Contemporary Criminal Justice*, 12(1), 69–80.

Miethe, T. D. and Meier, R. F. (1994). *Crime and Its Social Context: Toward an Integrated Theory of Offenders, Victims, and Situations*. Albany: State University of New York Press.

Muehlenhard, C. L. and Linton, M. A. (1987). Date rape and sexual aggression in dating situations: incidence and risk factors, *Journal of Counseling Psychology*, 34(2), 186–196.

Mustaine, E. E. and Tewksbury, R. (1999). A routine activity theory explanation for women's stalking victimizations, *Violence against Women*, 5(1), 43–62.

Paludi, M. A. (1996). *Sexual Harassment on College Campuses: Abusing the Ivory Power*. Albany: State University of New York Press.

Pathé, M. and Mullen, P. E. (1997). The impact of stalkers on their victims, *British Journal of Psychiatry*, 170, 12–17.

Reaves, B. and Goldberg, A. L. (1996). Campus Law Enforcement Agencies: 1995. Washington, D.C.: Bureau of Justice Statistics, U.S. Government Printing Office.

Roberts, A. R. and Dziegielewski, S. F. (1996). Assessment typology and intervention with the survivors of stalking, *Aggression and Violent Behavior*, 1(4), 359–368.

Sampson, R. J. and Lauritsen, J. L. (1990). Deviant lifestyles, proximity to crime, and the offender-victim link in personal violence, *Journal of Research in Crime and Delinquency*, 27, 110–139.

Sampson, R. J. and Wooldredge, J. (1987). Linking the micro- and macro-level dimensions of lifestyle-routine activity and opportunity models of predatory victimization, *Journal of Quantitative Criminology*, 3, 371–393.

Sellers, C. S. and Bromley, M. L. (1996). Violent behavior in college student dating relationships: implications for campus service providers, *Journal of Contemporary Criminal Justice*, 12(1), 1–27.

Sinclair, H. C. and Frieze, I. H. (2000). Initial courtship behavior and stalking: how should we draw the line? *Violence and Victims*, 15(1), 23–40.

Spitzberg, B. H. and Rhea, J. (1999). Obsessive relational intrusion and sexual coercion victimization, *Journal of Interpersonal Violence*, 14(1), 3–20.

Spitzberg, B. H., Nicastro, A. M., and Cousins, A. V. (1998). Exploring the interactional phenomenon of stalking and obsessive relational intrusion, *Communication Reports*, 11(1), 34–47.

Student Right-to-Know Act and Campus Security Act of 1990 (Clery Act) (1992). 20 U.S.C § 1092(f).

Tjaden, P. and Thoennes, N. (1998). Stalking in America: Findings from the National Violence Against Women Survey (RIB). National Institute of Justice, U.S. Department of Justice, Washington, D.C.

Tjaden, P., Thoennes, N., and Allison, C. J. (2000). Comparing stalking victimization from legal and victim perspectives, *Violence and Victims*, 15(1), 7–22.

U.S. Bureau of the Census (1999). College Enrollment of Students 14 to 34 Years Old, by Type of College, Attendance Status, Age, and Gender: October 1970 to 1997. Washington, D.C.: U.S. Bureau of Census, U.S. Government Printing Office.

U.S. Department of Education (1997). National Center for Education Statistics, 1997 Integrated Postsecondary Education Data System, "Fall Enrollment Survey." Washington, D.C.: U.S. Department of Education, U.S. Government Printing Office.

Westrup, D. and Fremouw, W. J. (1998). Stalking behavior: a literature review and suggested functional analytic assessment technology, *Aggression and Violent Behavior*, 3(3), 255–274.

Zona, M. A., Palarea, R. E., and Lane, J. C., Jr. (1998). Psychiatric disorders and the offender–victim typology of stalking, in J. R. Meloy (Ed.), *The Psychology of Stalking: Clinical and Forensic Perspectives*. San Diego, CA: Academic Press.

About the Contributing Author

Bonnie S. Fisher, Ph.D.

Bonnie S. Fisher, Ph.D. is an associate professor in the Division of Criminal Justice at the University of Cincinnati and a senior research fellow at the Criminal Justice Research Center. Her most recent work examines the evolution, controversies, and future research efforts of the measurement of the sexual victimization of women. She recently completed two national-level studies funded by the National Institute of Justice and the Bureau of Justice Statistics that examine the extent and nature of sexual victimization and violence against college women, respectively.

Dr. Fisher is the author of *Campus Crime: Legal, Social and Political Perspectives* and more than 50 articles on topics that include college campus victimization, sexual victimization, and violence of female college students.

Acknowledgment

Many thanks are extended to Georgia Spiropoulos, M.A., for her research assistance and comments to earlier drafts of this chapter on campus stalking. Any mistakes, of course, are the author's.

The Dynamics of Campus Stalkers and Stalking: Security and Risk Management Perspectives

10

ROBERT L. JONES
GLENN S. LIPSON

Contents

Introduction

Stalking has captured the attention of the American public. We have all witnessed an explosion in awareness regarding the issues pertaining to stalking. A week does not pass without another breaking news story from somewhere about someone being stalked. College campuses large and small have not escaped the nefarious popularity of the stalking phenomenon. What was once seen as a benign anti-social behavior has erupted into an everyday occurrence dramatized by bold headlines and "film at eleven."

Just about everyone you talk to has either been stalked or knows someone who has been stalked. Across the American landscape, academicians, mental health professionals, prosecutors, defense attorneys, talk show hosts, the

0-8493-0811-9/01/$0.00+$1.50
© 2001 by CRC Press LLC

239

media, and self-proclaimed "experts" are talking and writing about stalking. High-profile stalking cases involving glamorous Hollywood celebrities such as Theresa Saldana, David Letterman, Madonna, Rebecca Lynn Schaeffer, Diana, Princess of Wales, Brad Pitt, Steven Spielberg, and others have made stalking the topic of the hour (see Chapter 2 by Dr. Ronald M. Holmes, this book).

This chapter is not a review of the latest stalking literature, nor is it a scientific study of campus stalking. Instead, this chapter is an examination of campus pursuit behaviors derived from actual campus law enforcement experience. The main goal of this chapter is to simply add to the existing body of knowledge concerning campus stalking. Information provided in this chapter should enable the reader to better understand and manage the various types of campus pursuit behaviors. Further, this chapter should encourage researchers to explore more closely the unique nature of campus pursuits.

After 20 years of managing hundreds of campus pursuit situations, we have discovered unique elements particular to campus stalking claims. Therefore, the information is best generalized to campus populations and should not be presumed to apply to other environments. For example, many of my colleagues hold the belief that stalking on campus is a common occurrence. There is the belief that stalkings occur more frequently on campus than in the general population.

Pursuit behaviors are very common on campus. "Stalking" when meaningfully defined is rare. The term "stalking" is used to describe only those pursuit behaviors that meet the definition of the crime and thus include a high level of fear for the pursued. The annoying and persistent pursuit of a relationship is often incorrectly identified as stalking.

In 1997, a study was conducted with two large samples of college students (Fremouw et al., 1997). Researchers found that 21% of the students in the first survey reported having been stalked. The researchers attempted to replicate the results in a second survey. This second survey found that 27% of the students questioned reported that they had been stalked. Averaging the two results the authors suggest that approximately 24% of the college students report having been victims of a stalker. Thus, nearly one quarter of the college population (combined male and female) reported they had been stalked. These data lead researchers to the conclusion that in the campus environment, "Stalking is not a rare phenomenon."

The results of the studies were not consistent with our campus experience. If these percentages were accurate, it would mean that more than 5000 students on our particular campus had at one time or another been stalked. This percentage suggests that the number of actual campus stalkings is very large.

These findings need to be further examined; upon closer scrutiny they appear biased by the survey's wording. For example, the survey asked, "Have you ever been stalked, defined as having someone knowingly, and repeatedly following, harassing or threatening you? Yes or No." The question defined stalking as any behavior involving repeated following, repeated harassment, or threats.

The word "or" preceding the word "threatening" turned almost any unwanted pursuit behavior into a stalking. Because stalking requires a credible threat component, the question should have addressed the person's experience of credible fear from an unwanted pursuit. If the respondents had been instructed that stalking must include a credible fear for your safety, the findings might have been significantly different. At our campus the campus stalking incidents are rare. The campus environment is unique in affording numerous social activities and multiple targets to transfer one's obsession. The sense that this person is the only one is less dramatic in a sea of more possibilities.

University and College Campus Pursuit

There are many different categories of pursuit behaviors. These typologies include simple pursuit, aggravated pursuit, obsessional, simple obsessional, love obsessional, erotomania, unwanted pursuit, romantic pursuit, obsessive relational intrusion, love sickness, obsessional followers, resentful stalking, predatory stalking, and criminal pursuit. In our experience four categories best describe the various reported campus pursuit-type behaviors (Zona et al., 1993, 1998; Mullen and Pathé, 1994; Lipson and Mills, 1998; Meloy, 1996). These are

1. Ordinary pursuit
2. Unwanted pursuit
3. Stalking
4. Reluctant (false) reporting victim

In simplistic terms, ordinary pursuit is normative, unwanted pursuit is undesirable, stalking is illegal, and the reluctant (false) reporting victim is problematic.

Ordinary Pursuit

Relationships develop often from the pursuit of intimacy. Most pursuit behaviors are culturally accepted and socially expected. Men and women pursue relationships with others. Evolutionarily men have pursued women in order to continue their lineage.

Young impressionable college adolescents are no exception. As part of their extracurricular activities they frequently seek intimacy and at times sexual partners. College is the first time for many students who are out from under the yoke of parental expectations. Furthermore, it is a time of unrestrained social experimentation. The excessive consumption of alcohol is often a normative experience. The thought of a standard bad time is lost and sexual exploration is desired and sought.

The typical campus environment is the testing ground for inexperienced male and female adolescents whose view of human relationships is limited at best. It is a place where the perception of what constitutes a successful relationship is often skewed by faulty and inaccurate television portrayals of "real life" relationships. When you combine these faulty perceptions with inexperience, innocence, idealism, naiveté, and then add a dash of rejection you have the perfect recipe for student awkwardness in their relationship pursuits.

The college campus is a place where males, in particular, learn, practice, and perfect their pursuit behavioral skills. The typical college adolescent in our society is in need of, and in search of, relationships. Indeed, the "college experience" is as much about the development of meaningful personal relationships as it is about academics. But, unlike formal academics where knowledge and skill are customarily acquired in a classroom or from a book, the development of acceptable social skills is found outside the classroom through a process of trial and error that sometimes can be vicious and cruel. This is the expectation, not the exception, and thus is an ordinary part of maturation.

Unwanted Pursuit

The majority of reported campus-stalking claims involve unwanted pursuit behaviors. These cases do not meet the legal definition of stalking because they lack a pursuer who is threatening the harassed individual. However, because the term "stalking" is so misunderstood, it is frequently misused to describe every unwanted advance, gesture, solicitation, strange e-mail, bizarre note, or letter; when "stalking" is used correctly it refers only to unlawful behavior.

The college experience is multi-faceted, and so are the relationships that develop. Included in the mix of relationships are friends, classmates, study partners, acquaintances, student teacher relationships, teaching assistants, and romantic partners. While the large majority of such relationships are positive, enriching, and fulfilling, a few do turn sour. Relationships that sour do not always result in the same resolution for all parties involved. Some people hold on longer to the belief the relationship is still salvageable; these individuals try to add some ingredient to restore the palatability of the relationship.

When someone desires another party out of his or her life *any* contact can be experienced as annoying and harassing. The typical campus unwanted pursuit involves a female student who is being pursued by another male student whom she (knowingly or unknowingly) had some sort of a relationship with. The insistent pursuer typically engages in one or more of the following behaviors *minus* any threat of violence or criminal act:

- Repeated telephone calls from the pursuer
- Unsolicited letter writing
- Unsolicited e-mail messages
- Unsolicited electronic pages
- Unsolicited sending or leaving gifts
- Notes on car or at residence
- Surveillance behaviors, both on foot or by car
- Unexpected appearances
- Contacting friends, family, or co-workers

While experience tells us that most unwanted pursuits do not lead to stalking or violence they can be extremely emotionally consuming and psychologically exhausting. Therefore, such behaviors should be taken seriously and managed to prevent escalation to a criminal stalking.

Typical campus unwanted pursuit has the following characteristics:

- A male pursues a female.
- Pursuit behaviors of this type stem typically from an existing or prior relationship (typically a romantic attraction).
- Whereas the pursuer is acquainted with the person being pursued, the person being pursued may not know this other individual very well.
- Pursuit behaviors of this type typically relate to some form of rejection (actual or perceived).
- Affection and/or anger toward the person being pursued typically motivates pursuit behaviors of this type.
- Pursuit behaviors of this type are less common than ordinary pursuit, but more common than campus stalking.

Campus relationships are complex undertakings involving social risk taking and significant emotional investments. While most relationships are positive experiences and can even flourish into lifetime partnerships, others are simply doomed to fail as the chemistry or timing is just not right. "Bad chemistry" is often the euphemism used for the belief that one has established intimacy with the wrong partner. Rejection for the socially inexperienced college adolescent can sometimes be difficult to manage for those who have limited life experiences.

The emotional and psychological fallout from a failed relationship can be devastating to the person being rejected. In addition to the already burdensome academic, social, cultural, and environmental baggage these young people carry, rejection can lead some to embark upon a course of serious and potentially dangerous unwanted pursuit behaviors to change an undesirable end to the relationship they have longed for. Very few of these cases rise to the level of criminal stalking.

Based on research and experience the closer the relationship the greater the potential for violence (Meloy, 1996). The typical young college adolescent (potential pursuer) has not had the time to establish a long-term "close" relationship. Intensity, however, can foster a deep bond and some of these relationships are earthshaking in terms of the newness of such intimacy. Nonetheless, the typical campus relationship does have a multi-year history of difficulties that would involve separations, extended family complications, children, mortgages, and financial problems. Therefore, the potential for violence resulting from campus pursuit behaviors is less when compared to the general population.

Stalking and Stalkers

So what is stalking? First, by definition, stalking is illegal and as stated should not be confused with unwanted pursuit behavior. Stalking is unwanted pursuit coupled with a credible criminal threat (e.g., vandalism, threats of violence, acts of violence) that causes the person being pursued to be fearful. Although all 50 states and the federal government have stalking statutes, there is still no agreed-upon universal definition of what constitutes stalking. For our purposes, we will use California Penal Code Section 646.9; it defines a stalker as:

> Any person who willfully, maliciously, and repeatedly follows or harasses another person and who makes a credible threat with the intent to place that person in reasonable fear for his/her safety, or the safety of his/her immediate family.

In spite of this clear definition, on campuses we have learned that stalking to one person is persistence to another, and that while tenacity may be flattering to a third person, it is rebuked and called stalking by someone else. Adding to the confusion is our national and local media which consistently use the term stalking indiscriminately. In the absence of a credible threat(s) (threats of violence, acts of violence) that causes the person being pursued to be fearful, what may very well be an outrageous unwanted pursuit cannot be referred to as stalking.

The perception that the majority of "stalkers" are people that lurk in the darkness and who are unknown to the victim is not only false for the general population, but also for the campus population. In truth, most pursuers are known to the person they are pursuing (Meloy, 1996). Typical campus stalking characteristics are

- Repeated annoying telephone calls (coupled with threats of violence)
- Unsolicited letter writing (coupled with threats of violence)
- Unsolicited e-mail messages (coupled with threats of violence)
- Unsolicited electronic pages
- Unsolicited sending or leaving gifts
- Notes on car or at residence (coupled with threats of violence)
- Surveillance behaviors, both on foot or by car
- Unexpected appearances
- Transmitting threats of violence via friends, family, or co-workers
- Acts of vandalism
- Acts of violence
- The closer the relationship (actual or perceived) the greater the risk of violence

Reluctant False Reporting Victim (RV)

Without question for campus authorities the most problematic cases involve a false victim. We describe in this chapter a different type of false victim. What is suggested is that there are different types of false reports. For example, the prototypical false victim deliberately files a report attempting to use the justice system to manipulate others. A reluctant (false reporting) victim (RV) does not want law enforcement involved. His or her (RV) report represents a capitulation to the wishes of others to involve the police. The (RV) does not initially view the police as an instrument to manipulate others or as a tool to strike back against someone.

The first widely disseminated and thorough analysis of false reports of stalking was studied by Mohandie et al. (1998) based in part on studies of the Los Angeles Police Department's (LAPD) database. The authors estimated that approximately 2% of all stalking cases involved false victims (Mohandie et al., 1998). On our campus, the nature of false reporting is very different. In the last 17 years, most (>50%) of the approximately 15 stalking cases reported to this University Police Department by students (eight females, seven males) have been reluctantly made false reports. We discovered in over half of our cases the reported occurrences simply did not happen. This number is so different from what has been generally expected that we felt the need to further interpret our numbers.

First, these findings refer to campus students' stalkings. These numbers do not include the considerable and quite numerous ordinary pursuit situations and/or unwanted pursuit cases involving students. And finally, it does not include university employees who have reported stalking situations.

In order to make sense of these cases they were reviewed individually. Across these cases a number of common features were found. As a caveat these numbers appear to be unique to the university setting. They have unique features that assist us in separating them from legitimate cases. What follows is a general description of factors that may lead a student to fabricate a fake report. A prototypical case will also be described to underscore the dynamics of this type of reluctant false reporting.

The first important variable is the unique nature of the university campus. The adolescent college student who finds him/herself in this new environment often is living away from home for the first time. The academic environment can be a pressure cooker. Successful students in their own high school find themselves competing with other accomplished classmates, upsetting their hard-won sense of where they fit in the pecking order. Not everyone can be at the top of his/her class and for some students being average or below is a new and unsettling experience. Their past triumphs frequently have fostered high expectations in their family and themselves. Their lackluster performance can lead to a collapse in self-confidence. Excuses are often sought to explain away academic difficulties. Blame can be projected upon roommates, sadistic professors, or a failed romantic relationship. Mounting family pressures to succeed, a sense of not fitting in, isolation, and symptoms of depression can result in someone reaching out for support and attention by fabricating a life story.

For some men and women they need a fantastic story in order to receive from their parents and others understanding and a lessening of expectations. Blaming a stalker is the "face-saving excuse" used by some individuals. One lie leads to another and soon at the insistence of well-meaning friends, roommates, and/or family members, the false victim reluctantly feels forced into filing a report.

The sincere concern of college students places enormous value on helping others in need. As a result, the "victim" is vigorously pushed to abandon any reluctance and file a report with authorities. Once a victim, others become attentive and supportive. Besides, a false report to the campus "cop" does not seem all that serious. Campus police are sometimes seen more benignly and with less power in general; making a false report seems less problematic.

The campus culture responds sympathetically to victims so much so that certain types of victimization provide the claimant with an immediate elevated social status. Such attention can be desirable and extremely valuable to those who are emotionally and/or psychologically in need. Thus, the attempt to explain away socialized academic problems is maintained by another reward of gaining the attention and caring involvement of others. For a while being a victim is not all that bad.

Sarah's Story: A Composite Illustration

Sarah leaves her history class and heads for the parking lot. The winter term was finally over; all that remained were final exams the following week.

Although it was not a particularly warm afternoon, beads of sweat began to form on her forehead as she walked away from the campus buildings into the parking lot. *Not again*, she thought. Sarah's pace quickened as she felt an anxiety rush; she fought back the urge to panic. *This is non-sense,* she thought, *everything's okay, just find the car.* Try as she may, she could not find her car. Everywhere she looked rays of light from the setting sun created shadows in and between the endless number of cars. The beads of sweat turned to a flood. Sarah not only felt her heart beat, but now she could hear it. She stopped, wiped her eyes, and tried to calm down. She scanned across the ocean of cars; she could see every car but hers.

Sarah forgot she had switched cars with her brother; she'd forgotten that her brother insisted she take his car instead. Sarah remembered hearing somewhere that "fear" was a gift, a sixth sense regarding pending danger, an instinctive physiological catalyst that would ignite the fight or flight response. Whatever the value of the gift, at that moment Sarah wanted nothing to do with it. All she wanted was to get in her car, lock the door, and feel safe. She replaced her walk with a walk-run. She again asked herself, *Where's the car?* She couldn't see him, but she sensed he was there. For several weeks, especially in public places, Sarah felt him watching her. At last, Sarah saw the car, just two more rows, just one more, *I made it.* Sarah carried her keys in her right hand, not only to get into her car quickly, but also to be used as a weapon if necessary. Sarah's momentary sigh of relief was replaced with horror when the key wouldn't go into the lock. She tried again, this time forcing the key into the lock, but it wouldn't turn. She again felt flushed with a new wave of panic; her hand started to shake as she mumbled, *Open, open, please open.* Safety was just one foot away; she could see it, but she could not reach it. She yelled at the keys, *What's the problem!*

The emotional roller coaster Sarah was on just entered another loop. She realized she had the wrong keys; her brother's keys were in her purse. She pulled the key out of the door lock and dropped the ring. She reached into her purse and to her amazement, she grabbed hold of the keys lying at the bottom with one quick swipe. She thought to herself, *No problem.* As she shoved the key into the door lock, she herself was violently shoved up against the car door. Like an electric shock, Sarah felt pain rush though her left temple as her head slapped against the window. From behind, he uttered the single word, *Look.* Sarah froze in place as a cold chill streaked through her body. It was him as she recognized the voice. Sarah saw a black glove wrapped around the handle of a gun as it rose up to her face. She remembered thinking it wasn't real, but she knew better. He then said, *Walk, don't scream and I won't hurt you.* Sarah had a thought, *If he's not going to hurt me, then why the gun?* In the next second, Sarah flashed upon all her self-defense training, and the many conversations she'd had with her father about what to do if she was ever confronted with such a situation. *Why should I trust a guy who is pointing a gun at me?* In the time it takes to swat a fly, she scanned the parking lot for help, she assessed her situation, and she weighed her options. But in the end, Sarah turned and walked as she was told. At that moment, for the first time ever, Sarah realized if she couldn't flee or fight, she could surrender.

Sarah was an average 19-year-old college student who came from an upper middle-income family. Everyone knew that when the time came she would go off to college. Her entire life had been in one way or another a series of small steps in preparation for college. She was an obedient child, she got good grades, and she stayed clear of drugs and marijuana. Like her parents, brother, and sister, Sarah was a high achiever, but unlike them, it wasn't easy. While they all thrived on challenges, Sarah struggled to meet the challenges. Although not Miss Congeniality, her friends described Sarah as having a nice personality. Boys did not play a significant role in her life, making the move to college an unencumbered one. Since moving away from home, Sarah had some encounters with alcohol; the "college experience" demanded it. Sarah's parents both worked outside the home and both had been successful by most measures.

In Sarah's world, college was a synonym for success. There had never been a question as to whether or not she would attend college; the only question was where. Her older brother was in graduate school and her younger sister was a high school senior ready for college.

Sarah could no longer see the gun, but she knew it was there. Although she remembered, "Guns don't kill; people do," guns had always scared her to death. The thought that the gun could go off at any moment causing a solid piece of metal to tear into her body was almost more than she could bear. Sarah flashed on all the television programs, movies, and news reports she had seen where people had been shot. She remembered the small non-descript entry wound that was always followed by a gaping exit explosion of flesh. After taking three or four steps, walking became a serious problem. She felt her legs weaken and her knees began to buckle. Sarah stumbled and fell to her knees between her brother's Jeep and the car parked next to it. Sarah was not going anywhere, not because she refused to move, but because she couldn't move.

Sarah could hear the words, *Hey, are you okay? Can you hear me? Don't move.* She was confused; the voice was different and words were out of context. Sarah said, *What?* The voice again said, *Are you okay? Let me help you.*

Jason could see someone moving on the ground between the cars way down the row of cars. He couldn't make it out, but something was there. Jason scanned the parking lot; there was no one in sight. As he got closer, the shadowed figure became clearer. It was a person. It was a girl. The girl was lying on the ground between two parked cars. He ran over to her and said, *Don't move, are you okay? Let me help you.*

Sarah understood the words, "Don't move." But, the words, "Are you okay? Let me help you" made no sense. Sarah thought, *What does he want me to do now?* He threatened me with a gun, he ordered me to move, now he's telling me not to move and to let him help. Sarah was simply dreaming, she thought; this was just a nightmare. When she opened her eyes she would be safe in her bedroom and everything would be fine. Wrong again.

Sarah whimpered as Jason fought to understand her. Jason looked around; there was still no one in sight, but he could see one of the campus emergency call boxes about six cars away. Sarah began to recover. It seemed like an eternity, but in real time it was probably no more than a few seconds. With Jason's help, she raised herself up and laid back against her brother's car. Sarah began to understand that Jason was someone else; he was there to help her, not to harm her. Jason remembered the call box. He told Sarah to sit still; he was going for help. Three minutes later, the campus police were on the scene and an investigation was launched into what happened to Sarah.

Weeks earlier, Sarah had told the police that *things* started to happen around the beginning of the quarter when she first found a note on her car. The note read, "Will you be mine?" Although she felt it was a "little creepy," she didn't think much of it and threw the note away. A few days later, she started to receive hang-up calls at her apartment. Again, Sarah thought nothing of the calls. Twice she used the *69 call-back feature, but the recorded message told her, "Although your call-back feature is working, we are unable to connect you at this time." Sarah had an unlisted telephone number, but she later learned that her telephone number had been listed in the campus student directory.

There was also the *Eagle's Nest* campus cafeteria incident. Sarah had been in the cafeteria for about an hour when she needed to use the restroom. She got up, took her purse, but left her books and materials on the table. She returned a few minutes later. She could see a piece of paper sticking out of one of her books. She pulled it out. The words, "You are so beautiful, I hope we will be together soon" were written in blue ink. Sarah gasped. She folded the piece of paper, bowed her head, and closed her eyes. *What's going on here?* Sarah opened her eyes and looked around the room. The entire room was filled with people, but no one appeared to be particularly interested in her. There were a few guys sitting by themselves, but she couldn't establish eye contact with any of them and they all appeared to be occupied with something else. There was no one she recognized. Sarah looked at the note again and thought there must be a clue there. She could not be certain, but the writing appeared to be the same as the note on her car. Being more irritated than scared, Sarah packed up her things and left. In an act of defiance, Sarah threw the note into the trash can as she walked out. Weeks later, Sarah would attribute her *snub* as the turning point in her nonexistent "relationship" with her pursuer. She concluded that this single act of defiance probably sent him over the edge.

Through the years, the campus police had investigated many similar types of unwanted pursuit cases involving the same types of behaviors. Not only was Sarah being stalked, but also the entire campus community was now being terrorized with the knowledge that a stalker was "out there." The campus newspaper had learned of the incidents and they had written several stories which had been splashed across the front page in the last few weeks. Editorials ran the gamut; wild-eyed speculation was the order of the day. Campus police were feeling the pressure to quickly solve the case. The pressure seemed to be equally divided between students and campus officials.

As the first officer arrived on the scene, Sarah was still shaking. He recognized Sarah, but he couldn't place the face. It wasn't until the second officer arrived that the picture started to emerge; Sarah was the student who was being stalked. Several weeks earlier at the insistence of Sarah's roommates, she had reluctantly called the police and filed a report about being stalked, and there was something about a red rose, but the officer could not remember the details. However, he did remember that there were several reports about Sarah.

The "red rose" incident occurred in the campus library at approximately 10:30 P.M. one night while Sarah was studying alone in one of the small cubicles. She left the cubicle to return a book to the stacks; she was gone no more than 60 seconds. When Sarah returned, a single long-stem dried red rose was lying on her chair. *Is this a death threat?* she thought. Sarah grabbed her things and ran and she didn't stop running until she was safe inside her apartment. Twenty minutes later, Sarah stopped shaking and was able to talk to her roommates. Fifty-five minutes later, the campus police were called for the first time.

Three days following the red rose incident, Sarah arrived to class a couple of minutes late. A friend who was concerned for her safety had escorted her to class. It was a large classroom with a theater-style configuration. The room was dark as she entered; her instructor had already started a film. Sarah stood in the back of the room waiting for her eyes to adjust to the darkness. She was unable to make out faces or individuals, but within a few seconds she could see a few empty seats near the left aisle. Sarah moved to one of the seats and sat down. She placed her purse on the floor and looked up at the screen. Thirty seconds later she heard someone walk in and take the seat behind her. She paid no more attention. About 5 minutes into the film, Sarah began to hear a rubbing type of sound coming from behind her. The noise was not loud, yet annoying, like someone was scratching an itch. The sound would stop and start up again. Sarah looked over her shoulder; all she could see was some guy sitting there. The noise stopped. One minute later, she heard a voice whispering something near her left ear. The voice said, "*Thank you, that was great.*" Sarah shrieked around in her seat just in time to catch a glimpse of the guy turn out of the seat behind her and almost run out of the room. After class, Sarah rushed to the campus police department and filed a report of the incident. Sarah was not able to provide much of a description, other than to say that she thought he appeared to be a college-age black male, about 6 feet tall with dark hair.

At this point, Sarah had related six separate incidents — (1) the note on her car, (2) the telephone hang-ups, (3) the cafeteria note, (4) the red rose at the library, (5) the classroom incident, and (6) the attempted abduction from the parking lot. Although the campus police had launched a full investigation, which included identifying/locating witnesses, conducting interviews, developing composite sketches, stakeouts, telephone traps, special escorts, and community press releases, the efforts to find the pursuer were not bearing fruit. To make matters worse, not only was Sarah becoming increasingly anxious about her own safety, but also she was under the impression that the campus police were not taking her seriously. Sarah made it very clear that she thought her stalker was going to hurt her and she didn't want to have to later say, "I told you so." While still seated next to her brother's car, Sarah could see the officers talking and she heard one of the them call for an ambulance. *Ambulance? I don't need an ambulance!* Sarah said, out loud. *I'm all right. Please, just call my brother.* At the police department the following day (with her parents sitting next to her), Sarah said, "I told you so!"

Sarah never saw her stalker again, and there were no more reported incidents. As Sarah's terror became to wane, campus terror had just begun. The fallout from Sarah's stalking was immediate, swift, and onerous. Expressions of anxiety, fear, and apprehension were apparent everywhere. Reports of suspicious persons quadrupled; the campus police were responding to calls everywhere. The campus escort service quickly became overwhelmed with calls for service. Even the "false" sense of security normally associated with campus life had been shattered; academic peace and tranquility had been wiped out. From every corner of campus, community members were downright scared.

The outside media eventually picked up the story. News crews with their video trucks and with telescoping antennas became a common sight around campus. Students, faculty, employees, administrators, or anyone with an opinion were 15-second sound bite targets for the five o'clock news. Campus officials were besieged by calls from concerned parents demanding action. College students of the new millennium generation are born into a culture of parent involvement. Parents were now actively immersed in every aspect of their kids' college lives and student safety was a high priority.

Based on the coverage of this case there were calls from state legislators looking for answers on behalf of their constituents whose children attended the school. There were even unsubstantiated reports that a few students had withdrawn for the remainder of the year. Campus life had been directly impacted. At first, a wave of paranoia swept the campus, leaving every black male as a potential stalking suspect. Moreover, Sarah became the rallying cry for a number of campus causes, special interest groups, and individuals who were dissatisfied with the campus administration, in general, and with the campus police in particular.

Certain campus groups seized upon this opportunity to exploit the difficulties the police had in order to promote their own political self-interest. There were calls for the campus police to be taken off the case and replaced with "real" cops. Opinions and views quickly circulated that the campus police were not capable of handling such an investigation.

The debate surrounding campus law enforcement was ignited once again. The officers found themselves not only involved in a criminal investigation, but they were also engulfed in a political struggle. As is normally the case in such emotionally charged situations, the criminal aspects of the case became subordinate to what should have been collateral political issues. What were no more than auxiliary issues began to take on a life of their own; events began to spiral out of control. Issues surrounding sexual harassment, gender differences, inclusion, and exclusion took on new meanings. This was a golden opportunity for the politically savvy. The police department's attempt to identify the black suspect fueled the long-standing debate concerning the issue of "racial profiling."

On a college campus, where tolerance is a doctrine touted as a "principle of community" and where the campus culture is supposedly rooted in the appreciation and value of difference, there is much hypocrisy. In truth, the typical college campus has little tolerance for politically incorrect individuals, groups, and/or their speech. While the flavor of the month may be not to offend anyone for any reason, at any time, such is not true for current political incorrectness.

In fact, the shortest distance between prominence and obscurity on a college campus is political shortsightedness. Notwithstanding the popular party line, a college campus is not a home for the celebration of difference, but a breeding ground for intolerance of political dissimilarities and the disdain for the establishment and/or institutions of authority. Tolerance on this particular campus proved to be more theoretically based than reality based. Once again, the winds of campus political correctness turned a criminal investigation into a political typhoon — this one named Sarah. Fear, anxiety, and paranoia quickly turned to anger and name-calling. In its wake, the paranoia was quickly replaced with campus-wide paralysis. Political carpetbaggers seized the moment to exploit community fears relating to social, ethnic, gender, and racial bias for their own partisan politics. The only vultures yet to become involved were the lawyers. They were, however, seen lurking in the background.

After a painstakingly thorough investigation lasting several months, investigators determined that the stalking of Sarah never happened — her reports were false. However, in the wake of typhoon Sarah, the campus laid in ruins. Hundreds of community members had been unnecessarily terrorized by Sarah's lies. Professional reputations had been maligned, friendships had been destroyed, and careers jeopardized. Although Sarah had to shoulder a great deal of the responsibility as to what happened, there are many others who greatly contributed to this arising situation.

Sarah's Composite Stalking Case Analysis

While Sarah's story is a composite example of the most frequently reported campus student-stalking scenario on our campus, it is nonetheless a false victim report. The value of Sarah's story lies in the fact that it is a composite example of a false victim student stalking report. As outrageous, unbelievable, and offensive as this may be to some, the fact remains that reported incidents of campus student stalking on our campus have been more likely to be false than true.

This revelation stems from a review of all the stalking cases reported to the University of California at San Diego Police Department (UCSD Campus) during the last 17 years. As previously discussed, the reader must not confuse stalking with unwanted pursuit behaviors which are frequently reported and which have a high degree of authenticity. Furthermore, these data only include those individuals who have knowingly made false reports; it does not include those who made reports and who, because of some emotional or psychological complications, honestly believed they were being stalked. While every alleged stalking case needs to be taken seriously, *"Things are not always as they appear."* The critical task, of course, is to know which cases are false.

False allegations involve all types of students for a myriad of reasons, but the literature and case histories suggest that the false reporting of stalking stems from adolescent immaturity, a lack of self-esteem, coupled with one or more of the following:

- An attempt to resurrect a failing personal relationship
- A need to punish and/or inflict revenge upon another person for some perceived wrong
- A need to deflect attention from personal problems and/or academic difficulties
- A need for attention and/or sympathy from family, friends, or a significant other

You might recall that Sarah's "stalking" began during the winter quarter of the academic year. While there is not enough data to draw any accurate or reliable conclusions as yet, it is nonetheless a notable fact that most of our false stalking reports were filed with campus law enforcement during the latter portion of the academic year, between January and June.

It is thought that the circumstances (personal problems, relationship difficulties, academic troubles, etc.) that eventually cause the RV to file a false report take several months to develop from the start of the academic year in September.

False stalking reports are typically filed by reluctant female college students who are high achievers. They are faced with academic difficulties and are under a great deal of pressure from their families to succeed academically. Since there is not a negative social stigma attached to being stalked, it can provide an easy excuse for the failure to thrive on campus. Because pursuit situations can be emotionally painful and sometimes physically threatening to stalking victims, we naturally feel empathy and compassion. But it is precisely this empathy, compassion, and attention that pressures the RV to file the false report.

Once reported to the police, the RV becomes tangled in a web of falsehoods which snowballs into an avalanche. Initially described unwanted pursuit behaviors rapidly progress to stalking. The investigator will quickly note that the descriptions of the pursuit behaviors are inconsistent with actual true stalking case histories. The RV's expressions of fear and vulnerability are not genuine and often transparent. This is probably due to the fact that the RV's responses, emotions, actions, and reactions are based upon the imperfect and inaccurate television portrayals of victims.

The RV will often create or manufacture evidence because verifiable independent corroboration from others is impossible to generate. The RV will inadvertently or accidentally destroy evidence that reportedly existed. The RV often finds excuses why anti-pursuit strategies recommended by law enforcement were not adhered to. While there may be a hint of a romantic pursuit, the reported incident(s) typically lack a rational and/or recognizable motive for the pursuit behavior. Incidents are never witnessed by an independent corroborating third party.

The experienced investigator knows that for the non-celebrity, non-public figure such as the typical college student, "stranger stalking" is still quite rare. Reliable data from the literature on stalking report that stalking, which is based upon an existing relationship, is by far the most common (Mohandie et al., 1998; Davis, 2000a). The reasons are obvious; most stalkings are the result of an established relationship which provides an explanation (motive) for the unwanted relentless pursuit, harassment, and stalking behavior. The authors believe that the fictional investigator and character, Sherlock Holmes, as created and developed by Sir Arthur Conan Doyle, said that a "motive is a detective's most powerful investigative tool." Absent is a reasonable motive for the reported incidents; it is possible for the RV to, by name, identify the stalker (excluded are cases that are obviously vindictive in nature and which target a former significant other).

We live in a society that is obsessed with reality-based television where those who have suffered and "survived" are viewed as champions and some-times become social icons. Reluctant victims who make false reports are no different. In order to maintain their victim status the energies exerted to maintain the illusion can cause serious emotional and psychological damage. The reluctant victim is not at risk from a non-existent pursuer; however, he/she is at significant risk from self-inflicted injuries. Their way out of their difficulties only creates more problems.

Reluctant (False) Victim Reporting Characteristics

The reluctant (false) victim reporting (RV) characteristics include:

- Most false reports are filed during the latter portion of the academic year.
- The RV typically files a report with campus law enforcement author-ities at the insistence of well-meaning family, friends, roommates, or co-workers.
- The more the reported incidents deviate from the norm, the more likely the report(s) are false.
- Reported incidents will *always* lack verifiable independent third-party corroboration.
- Other than to terrorize, there is no discerning motive for the "stalking" behavior.
- Reported incidents typically involve an unknown pursuer or at least a person that can't be identified (see also Dr. Joseph Davis, Chapter 17, this book).

A false report, whether reluctant or not, in different environments has a similar impact. First, the negative publicity can create a state of fear in a community. The political backlash can damage the reputations and support of agencies and individuals. Second, the investigation of a false claim can tie up law enforcement and other resources. In particular, mental health per-sonnel are either under-utilized or manipulated to make the alleged false victim's reports more believable. Third, civil litigation potentially may arise as individuals claim to be damaged by the course of events. Fourth, innocent individuals or groups can be wrongly accused (Zona et al., 1993, 1998; Mohandie et al., 1998).

Besides the reluctance of our false victims, the motivations and consequences of their actions are consistent with the individuals who falsely claim to have been raped. In these cases the suspect is often unknown and indeterminable. When incidents occur the claimant is always alone, but yet accessible to the perpetrator.

Finally, there are never any third-party witnesses. In false rape allegations the victim often has problems describing the assailant. Vigorous resistance is offered to no avail. The assailant is a total stranger. Often there is a report of phone calls and notes that cannot be produced (Aiken et al., 1995). A motivation for different types of false victims appears to involve finding a way to have their emotional needs met. Although false rape reports are rare, friends and family in the cases studied were seen as providing support and sympathy for the alleged victims. Their self-esteem is seen as another motive for potential false allegations (Aiken et al., 1995).

Conclusion

The dynamics (differences and similarities) in campus student stalkings are a fascinating area that needs to be further explored. Whether the distinction we are making between reluctant false victims and other types of false victims is a useful one will only be determined through research and application. It is a treatment adage that suggests that how a process begins is crucial to the understanding of what type of intervention is needed.

Although the consequences of false reports can often be the same, how they might be recognized sooner and prevented may be different if we better understand what brought the individual in contact with law enforcement. It is also the purpose of this chapter to suggest that at least at the campus where these data have been collected, stalking is not endemic.

Sharpening our understanding pertaining to what is happening on our college and university campuses ultimately will help us in the best allocation of our limited, but valuable, existing resources.

Bibliography

Aiken, A. A., Burgess, A. W., and Hazelwood, R. R. (1995). False rape allegations, in *Practical Aspects of Rape Investigation*, 2nd ed.(13, 219–238). Boca Raton, FL: CRC Press.

Davis, J. (August 2, 2000). Personal communication, Stalking, stalkers, and false victimization syndrome, San Diego, CA.

Davis, J. (2000a). Falsely Alleged Victimization Syndrome (FAVS). Unpublished paper and manuscript on False Victimology Case Research, San Diego, CA.

Fremouw, W. J., Westrup, D., and Pennypacker, J. (1997). Stalking on campus: the prevalence and strategies for coping with stalking, *Journal of Forensic Science*, 42(4), 666–669.

Lipson, G. S. and Mills, M. (1998). Stalking, erotomania and the Tarasoff cases, in J. R. Meloy (Ed.), *The Psychology of Stalking*, Vol. 13 (pp. 258–271). San Diego, CA: Academic Press.

Meloy, J. R. and Gothard, S. (1995). Demographic and clinical comparison of obsessional followers and offenders with mental disorders, *American Journal Psychiatry*, 152(2), 258–263.

Meloy, J. R. (1996). Stalking (obsessional following): a review of some preliminary studies, *Aggression and Violent Behavior: A Review Journal*, 1, 11–16.

Mohandie, K., Hatcher, C., and Raymond, D. (1998). False victimization syndromes in stalking, in J. R. Meloy (Ed.), *The Psychology of Stalking* (pp. 225–255). San Diego, CA: Academic Press.

Mullen, P. E. and Pathé, M. (1994) The pathological extensions of love, *Australian and New Zealand Journal of Psychiatry*, 284, 469–477.

Zona, M., Palarea, R. E., and Lane, J. C., Jr. (1998). Psychiatric disorders and the offender-victim typology of stalking, in J. R. Meloy (Ed.), *The Psychology of Stalking: Clinical and Forensic Perspectives*. San Diego, CA: Academic Press.

Zona, M., Sharma, K., and Lane, J. (1993). A comparative study of erotomanic and obsessional subjects in a forensic sample, *Journal of Forensic Sciences*, 65, 894–903.

About the Contributing Authors

Detective Sergeant Robert L. Jones

Detective Sergeant Robert L. Jones has been a California peace officer for more than 27 years. After obtaining his degree in business from San Jose State University in 1971, he began his law enforcement career as a deputy sheriff with the Santa Clara County Sheriff's Department. Seven years later, after having worked as a patrol deputy and supervisor in the county narcotics bureau, he left the department. In 1980, he found his way to the University of California Police Department in San Diego where he was assigned to the department's detective bureau. Two years later, he was placed in charge of the bureau, a position he has held for the last 18 years. In 1993, Sergeant Jones was selected to attend the FBI National Academy in Quantico, Virginia. In September 1993, he graduated from the 174th Session of the FBI National Academy and has been an active member in the FBI National Academy Associates.

In 1994, the growing number of instances of workplace violence around the country and on the university campus caused Sergeant Jones to initiate an extensive examination of the issues concerning campus workplace violence. In early 1995, he researched and drafted UCSD's "Zero Tolerance Policy" relating workplace behavior and he authored the UCSD Workplace Violence Employee Handbook. He established the UCSD Incident Management Group (IMG). To date, Sergeant Jones has participated in the assessment/management of more than 500 workplace violence situations, from minor unwanted pursuit cases to employee sabotage, stalking, and physical violence. In 1996, Sergeant Jones became a core member of the San Diego County District Attorney's Office Stalking Case Assessment Team (SCAT); he regularly participates in the risk assessment and threat management of serious stalking cases. In 1998, Sergeant Jones was a founding member of the San Diego Chapter of the National Organization of Association of Threat Assessment Professionals (ATAP). As an active member of the San Diego chapter, he continues to assist in the presentations of the bimonthly meetings. Although Sergeant Jones claims not to be an expert, he is a recognized authority on issues of workplace violence, stalking behaviors, and their assessment. He is a frequent lecturer on both topics.

Glenn S. Lipson, Ph.D., ABPP

Glenn S. Lipson, Ph.D., ABPP holds a Doctor of Philosophy degree in clinical psychology and is a psychologist engaged in private outpatient practice in San Diego, California. Dr. Lipson specializes in clinical and forensic psychology, assessment, and psychotherapy. He is a member of the Stalking Strike Force and Stalking Case Assessment Team. Dr. Lipson is an accomplished clinician, researcher, and author and is a recognized court expert in the field of forensic mental health and the law. He holds an adjunct professor appointment at the Professional School of Psychology in San Diego, California where he teaches pre-doctoral students in clinical inference. Dr. Lipson is a member of several professional organizations that include the Association for Threat Assessment Professionals (ATAP). He is also a diplomate of the American Board of Professional Psychology.

PART V

Threat Assessment and Safety Planning

Future Prediction of Dangerousness and Violent Behavior: Psychological Indicators and Considerations for Conducting an Assessment of Potential Threat *

11

JOSEPH A. DAVIS
LISA M. STEWART
ROBIN SIOTA

Contents

* Source: Future Prediction of Dangerousness and Violent Behavior: Psychological Indicators and Considerations for Conducting an Assessment of Potential Threat by Davis, J., Siota, R. L., and Stewart, L. *Canadian Journal of Clinical Medicine*, Edmonton, Alberta, Canada (research monograph). Copyright © 1999. Scope Communications. Reprinted with permission.

Introduction

No criminal act causes more concern to society than crimes that seriously injure or kill its citizens while at home or at work, and especially its children while at school or at play. Consequently, many people regard offenders who carry out these violent crimes with fear, believing involuntary commitment to a maximum security forensic mental health setting for an undetermined length of time (often longer than their original sentences), or their death, to be the only choice as an absolute precaution against future acts of violence. The issue of future dangerousness has led many threat assessment experts, as well as those in the judicial and law enforcement field, to debate heavily over the ability of the available clinical adult and juvenile population to predict the probability of future violent behavior or "dangerousness" of an offender.

This chapter will attempt to outline some of the methods used for assessing dangerousness and predicting future violence. Additionally, this chapter will also examine the limitations of threat assessment evaluations and violence prediction models and the conclusions drawn by researchers as well a variety of security personnel, social and behavioral scientists, psychiatrists, psychologists, criminologists, sociologists, and clinical social workers as practitioners who work in the field of threat assessment and risk evaluation. While there is no scientifically confirmed set of variables or any precise techniques for predicting the dangerousness of the violent offender, society and its legal system have called upon social and behavioral scientists, psychologists, psychiatrists, criminologists, and various security-conscious investigative personnel to do the impossible — to predict future behavior. That new breed — part diagnostician, part sleuth, part researcher, part analyst — is becoming known as "threat assessment specialist."

The American Law Institute's Model Penal Code (ALI-MPC) recommends the sentencing of career criminal, disturbed, dangerous, and multiple offenders to extended terms of imprisonment. In 1973, the ALI-MPC Task Force on Corrections of the National Advisory Commission on Criminal Justice Standards and Goals likewise recommended terms of 5 to 25 years for professional criminals, habitual felony offenders, and dangerous offenders.

In addition, Washington, D.C. enacted into law in 1970 a provision for pre-trial detention of a person charged with a dangerous crime if the government determines that no condition exists to reasonably assure the safety of the community. While laws and penal codes are being enacted to safeguard the populace against the dangerous offender, those whose jobs are to determine the dangerousness of individuals are divided on the issue of whether such predictions can accurately be made (Koerin, 1978).

It is apparent that while various therapeutic disciplines proceed from different points of reference in their determination of dangerousness, each ends up raising basically the same issues, namely, the concern with the identification of individuals demonstrating a dangerous state of mind or individuals whose future behaviors are likely to be threatening to either themselves or others by some definable standard, and the imposition of control and correction through some rehabilitative process. Each is looking for that one distinguishable, scientifically significant correlation between an organic, emotional, behavioral, or environmental element and the quantifiable outcome of dangerous behavior.

For the purpose of this chapter and the discussion of the methods of prediction to follow, the terms "psychopath," "sociopath," and "antisocial personality disorder" (ASPD) will be used interchangeably, as they stem from the same root. The original term "psychopathic personality disorder" was replaced by the term "sociopathic personality disorder" in the *Diagnostic and Statistical Manual of Mental Disorders* (DSM) I & II (1952, 1968). The term "sociopath" was then replaced with "antisocial personality disorder" in the DSM-III (1980), and has retained this designation in the following revisions: DSM-III-R (1987) and DSM-IV (1994). While the term "antisocial personality disorder" is not a direct re-definition of either psychopath or sociopath, each has built upon its predecessor to more fully define the emotional as well as the behavioral traits exhibited by the individuals diagnosed as such.

Violence Prediction and Threat Assessment

Dangerousness, as a consequence of behavior, is not a diagnostic category or medical classification. The issue of dangerousness is a clinical impression derived from a thorough and comprehensive analysis of data focusing on an individual's conduct in the past as well as the present, for the specific purpose of determining (or predicting) conduct in the future (Davis, 1994). Furthermore, the prediction of dangerousness is proposed solely for the purpose of predicting violent behavior and not for the purpose of diagnosing mental illness or disorder (Monahan, 1985). The prediction of dangerousness by clinicians has been requested for three main purposes: (1) in the area of risk assessment for the protection of potential victims; (2) in the area of threat assessment for the protection of the individual in question, i.e., dangerous person etc., from the consequences of his or her potential criminal actions; and (3) to answer the question as to restrict or not to restrict personal liberty (civil commitment, involuntary hospitalization, incarceration, etc.) due to questionable acts of conduct that rise to the threshold level of violence and dangerousness (Davis, 1994; Dietz, 1985).

Finally, the prediction of dangerousness also brings forward into a much larger public and political domain the issue of setting or establishing public policy, i.e., drafting legislation on public safety and community protection from the dangerousness individual, i.e., *Megan's Law* (derived from the case of 8-year-old Megan Kanka who was abducted and murdered by a paroled sex offender who lived in her residential community), which addresses sex offenders (called "290 registrants" in California), or California's *Three Strike Law* which focuses on repeat recidivist offender behavior or the control of "career criminal" conduct through long-term (lifelong) incarceration etc. Dangerousness is not only determined by the prediction of the offender's likelihood to violate others, but the likelihood of injury to self as well.

Unfortunately, to date, there does not seem to be a universally accepted definition of what constitutes a determination of dangerousness (Smith, 1971). Furthermore, there does not seem to be a recognized, cited, or agreed upon model (citing the case of *Daubert v. Merrill-Dow Pharmaceutical* and the *Test of General Scientific Acceptance*) in the disciplines of psychology, psychiatry, or criminology (scientific, quasi-scientific, or pseudo-scientific based) as to how to go about assessing and evaluating dangerousness (Davis, 1994). One definition of dangerousness is "the potential for inflicting serious bodily harm on another." The Model Sentencing Act, Section VI, further defines the dangerous offender as one who "is being sentenced for a felony; (a) in which he inflicted or attempted to inflict bodily harm; or (b) a felony which seriously endangered the life or safety of another and has been previously convicted of one or more felonies not related to the instant crime as a single criminal episode; and (c) the court finds that he is suffering from a severe mental or emotional disorder indicating a propensity toward continuing criminal activity of a dangerous nature" (Smith, 1971).

As is noted above, previous history as a violent offender is an integral part of the assessment of dangerousness. In the literature researched, all of the test samples consisted of previously convicted offenders. Only in the research on juveniles were any statistics of pre-conviction behavior given as predictive symptomology.

Purpose of Prediction of Violence and Dangerousness

Within the justice, correctional, and mental health fields, determinations of dangerousness are constantly being made. In ordering pretrial detention or setting bail, judges base their decision, in part, on an assessment of the danger the individual presents to the community. The length of an offender's sentence and his eligibility for parole are also contingent on the offender's history of violence and on predictions of future violent behavior. Criminal or civil commitments to mental institutions rest on psychiatrists' diagnoses and prognoses of future dangerousness (Koerin, 1978).

Formula for Scientific Prediction of Future Violence

Many professionals have attempted to develop valid and reliable techniques for predicting dangerousness. For the most part, historically, two methods of violence prediction have been used: the clinical case study (single or multiple case study) method and the statistical method that uses a factor analysis method. While it has been universally accepted by threat assessment specialists that human behavior (B) is a function of both personality factors (P) and situational (S) variables [B = (P + S)], psychiatrists, psychologists, and applied criminologists typically focus on the former at the expense of the latter in clinical threat assessments (Megargee, 1980).

Furthermore, researchers believe that situational and personality variables as well as behavioral factors associated with the assessment of threat includes pre-threat indicators (PTI). PTI, for the most part, give the threat assessment specialist an overall "credible threat indices" (threshold indicator of dangerous behavior). Therefore, a formula taking into consideration PTI would suggest [PTI = B + (P + S)] = CTI (credible threat indices [indicator]). Statistical analysis methods have in many cases included some situational variables in their predictive variables to also include PTI, B, P, and S (Davis, 1998).

Clinical Prediction of Violence and Dangerousness

Clinical assessment is described by Gottfredson (1971, as cited by Koerin, 1978) as a wide band procedure in which a broad range of information about the individual is gathered from sources such as interviews, social history, and projective testing.

In a research study by Kozol, Boucher, and Garofalo (1972) as cited by Koerin (1978), the cases sampled 592 convicted male offenders, a majority of whom had committed a variety of sexually related offenses with some involving extreme violence. Each was observed for a period of approximately 10 years. The threat criteria for evaluating dangerousness included: (1) previous attempts to inflict serious injury on another, (2) anger, (3) hostility, (4) displayed or suppressed resentment, (5) enjoyment of others suffering, (6) little or no compassion for others, (7) irritation with or rejection of authority, (8) sense of being a victim (victim mentality), (9) inability to tolerate frustration (low frustration tolerance), and (10) inability to delay satisfaction or control impulses.

The subjects were evaluated by at least two psychiatrists, two psychologists, and one clinical social worker. A detailed life history was completed for each subject. Each additionally underwent a battery of psychological tests that included an objective personality assessment. The clinicians obtained detailed descriptions of the actual assault, as perceived by the victim and as perceived by the offender. After evaluating all the data, the clinicians recommended that some of the subjects be released, while others were determined to need further psychiatric treatment.

The predictions they made were reasonably accurate. The recidivism rate for serious assault was 34.7% for those released against the research team's advice, as compared to only 8% serious assault recidivism by those released with the team's consent. It is important to note that 65% of those released against the research team's advice did not commit a violent assault.

A clinical study was conducted by Hodges (1971) as cited by Cohen et al. (1978) based on the Patuxent Correctional Center in Maryland. The researchers followed up on 447 "defective delinquent" (dangerous) offenders for 3 years. Hodges found that 81% of those recommended by the clinical staff for incarceration, who were not incarcerated by the court (the "untreated" group), committed another offense, although this was not necessarily a violent crime. Of those committed to the Patuxent Correctional Center, but later released against staff recommendation (the "partially treated" group), 71% committed a new crime. Only 37% of those committed and later released on the staff's recommendation (the "fully treated" group) were arrested for a new crime. This study predicted not only future dangerousness, but also non-dangerousness as well. The total accuracy of prediction in the Patuxent Correctional study was 60% overall.

The question to consider is whether the freedom of the 19% who were released against the staff's recommendation and didn't commit a new crime outweighs the additional incarceration of the unknown number of those 63% who were kept for treatment, who may not have committed a crime if released early. Also, a factor is the crimes committed by the 81% who were released and committed another crime. The study does not state how many of those new offenses were violent crimes.

Statistical Predictive Models of Dangerousness and Violent Behavior

Statistical prediction models and techniques have evolved with the objective to improve predictive accuracy. Numerous attempts have been made to devise statistical tables to predict parole success or failure or the probability that an individual will commit a future offense (violent or otherwise) once placed on conditional release back into the mainstream community.

The statistical method considers a narrower range of factors evaluated which specifically relate to criminal behaviors. Most researchers follow the procedure of establishing predictor variables, that is, what behavior is to be predicted and what procedure is to be used for classifying persons on the basis of behavior. Next, the characteristics expected to be closely related to the predicted behavior are selected and defined. The procedure is then tested on a representative sample of the target population to determine the relationships between the criterion categories of behavior and the predictor factors.

The statistical method is used by Hare and Hart (1994) in their clinical research on the association between psychopathy and crime, particularly violent crime. They describe their concept of psychopathy as similar to the category of antisocial personality disorder as described in the DSM-III,

DSM-III-R, and the DSM-IV (American Psychiatric Association, 1980, 1987, 1994).

Examining Violent Behavior

The procedure Hare and Hart (1994) used for assessing psychopathy in the criminal population is the revised version of the *Hare Psychopathy Checklist–Revised* or the *PCL-R* (see Table 11.1; Hare, 1991). The checklist or PCL-R is a 20-item symptom-based constructed rating scale. Each item is scored on the basis of a structured clinical interview with the subject, which also includes a thorough review of the subject's case history for background information (if any history is available to the interviewer, a *consent to release* must be secured in advance).

Each item on the PCL-R (see Table 11.1; Hare, 1991) is scored on a 3-point scale reflecting the degree to which it applies to the individual (0 = Does Not Apply; 1 = Uncertain, Applies Somewhat; 2 = Definitely Applies). The total score can range from 0 to 40 and represents the degree to which an individual resembles the prototypical psychopath. For diagnostic purposes, a score of 30 or above is considered to be indicative of psychopathy.

With respect to reliability and validity, Hart, Hare and Harper (1992), as cited by Hare and Hart (1994), report the internal consistency (alpha) for the PCL-R, aggregated over seven samples of male prison inmates from Canada, the United States, and England (n = 1192), was .87. The inter-rater reliability (intra-class correlation) was .83 for single ratings and .91 for the average of two ratings. Table 11.1 presents the PCL-R items with factor application codes and variable loadings.

Wong (1984), as cited by Hare and Hart (1994), analyzed the criminal records of a random sample of 315 male inmates from minimum, medium, and maximum security correctional institutions in Canada. Psychopaths were defined by a PCL-R score of at least 30 and non-psychopaths by a score of 20 or less.

Compared with the non-psychopaths, the psychopaths committed more than twice as many offenses per year (mean of 4.4 and 1.9, respectively), almost nine times as many institutional offenses (6.3 and 0.73), and had their first formal contact with the law at an earlier age (17.8 and 24.1). The researchers also found that psychopaths committed almost four times as many institutional offenses and engaged in significantly more threatening behavior and acts of violence than non-psychopaths.

Hart, Kropp, and Hare (1988), as cited by Hare and Hart (1994), administered the PCL-R to 231 male inmates prior to their release from prison on parole or mandatory supervision. Each subject's progress was followed until

Table 11.1 Items in the Hare Psychopathy Checklist–Revised (PCL-R)

1.	Glibness/superficial charm
2.	Grandiose sense of self-worth[a]
3.	Need for stimulation/proneness to boredom[a]
4.	Pathological lying
5.	Conning/manipulative[a]
6.	Lack of remorse or guilt[a]
7.	Shallow affect[a]
8.	Callous/lack of empathy[a]
9.	Parasitic life-style[b]
10.	Poor behavioral control[b]
11.	Promiscuous sexual behavior
12.	Early behavior problem[b]
13.	Lack of realistic, long-term goals[b]
14.	Impulsivity[b]
15.	Irresponsibility[b]
16.	Failure to accept responsibility for actions[a]
17.	Many short-term marital relationships
18.	Juvenile delinquency[b]
19.	Revocation of conditional release[b]
20.	Criminal versatility

[a] Loads on Factor 1.
[b] Loads on Factor 2.

Source: Hare, R. (1991). Reprinted with permission of Multi-Health Systems, 908 Niagara Falls Blvd., North Tonawanda, NY 14120-2060, (800) 456-3003 (as cited by Hare and Hart, 1994). For more information on the PCL, contact this citation and source or the author, Robert Hare, Ph.D., University of British Columbia, Vancouver, B.C.

(1) he had his release revoked, (2) he was convicted of a new offense, (3) he successfully reached the end of the period of supervised release, or (4) the end of the study period was reached. An unsuccessful release (failure) was defined as revocation or conviction for a new offense during the period of supervision. Overall, 46.3% of the releases, 56.4% of the mandatory supervisions, and 25.3% of the paroles ended in failure. The outcome: (0 = Success; 1 = Failure) was correlated .33 with the PCL-R. A series of regression analyses demonstrated that the PCL-R made a significant contribution to the prediction of outcome over and beyond that made by relevant criminal-history and demographic variables.

Psychopaths not only violated the conditions of release faster and more often than did non-psychopaths, but they also received more suspensions and presented more supervisory problems during the conditional release period. The tests associated with Hare's Psychopathy Checklist–Revised or PCL-R (Hare and Hart, 1994) strongly suggest that psychopathy per se is associated with an increased risk for criminal and violent behavior, or dangerousness, in male offenders.

Davis (1994) suggested that the prediction of future violence is an inexact science, if it is a science at all. He further suggests that threat assessment and the future prediction of dangerousness are more of an art than a science. Furthermore, he suggests that all threat assessments come with a host of potential caveats when trying to predict future human behavior given the parameters of such tasks. Particularly, when the question of violence is raised, an assessment of threat is not without its share of problems. Oftentimes, a threat assessment usually raises more questions concerning other variables of human behavior, i.e., false-positives, false-negatives, predictive validity and reliability, and non-violent behavior, than the threat assessment actually sets out to answer.

Formula for the Prediction of Future Violence and Dangerousness

Davis (1986) completed an unpublished research study involving a sample of court-ordered men (age range 18 to 65) referred for outpatient psycho-therapy to address aggression, communication skills, anger management, low stress tolerance, and marital discord. Each had been charged and convicted of domestic violence and assault. The outcome of the research suggested that threat assessment specialists and forensic mental health treatment providers evaluate carefully the threat time frame and any course of action taken by the person being evaluated.

Threshold of Violence and Violence Potential

What Davis (1995) calls threshold factor(s) or "TF," the threat assessment specialist must also include the most current outstanding elements involving situational (S), cognitive (C), behavioral (B), emotional (E), drugs and/or alcohol (D/A), and economic (Ec) issues (stressors) associated with the potential for violence (PV). To be relevant to any threat assessment, each factor or variable must reach a "threshold" of intensity to become an issue regarding the potential for violence and future dangerousness. In addition, the person's history of violence (H×V) must be included (if any) when that question is raised in the context of what he calls the "R-S-I-F" assessment factor (Recency–Severity–Intensity–Frequency). John Monahan, Ph.D., a distinguished professor at the University of Virginia, has conducted most of the pioneering research on the concept of dangerousness and the prediction of violence (1985). What he suggests when assessing for future violence is that one should consider and identify such variables (if any) as how recently violence was committed along with its severity, intensity, and frequency, therefore asking, what variables involving R-S-I-F are involved in the prediction of dangerousness?

Davis (1998) has further suggested bases upon the research of Monahan (1985) and others that in cases involving the assessment of threat and the prediction of potential future violence (prediction of dangerousness), that the threat assessment specialist examine carefully the elements of R-S-I-F. These factors, according to Monahan (1985), often surround certain areas of interview and inquiry that evaluate violence for prediction purposes such as threshold and potential escalation from a standpoint of *recency, severity, intensity, and frequency.*

Threat Assessment and Areas of Inquiry

As to the areas of inquiry within the context of a threat assessment, the specialist must concern him- or herself with a four-step procedure that must include the following:

1. How *recent* was the act or contact reported or threat statement made (verbally, physically, symbolically, electronically, or by paper communication)?
2. How *severe* was the act, contact, or statement of threat in question?
3. How *intense* was the act, contact, or statement of threat made? (Quantitatively scale the threat from 1 to 10, with a score of 1 being the lowest and 10 being the highest.)
4. How *frequent* was the action, contact, or statement made?

Thus, according to Davis (1995 and 1997), R-S-I-F used in the context of a threat index (Ti) or formula for the threat assessment specialist integrating such features and factors into an examination of threat potential might look something like the following:

Threat Assessment Legend

(S)   = Situational variable(s), i.e., loss of job, marital problems, etc.
(C)   = Cognition/thinking, i.e., delusional, hallucinating, paranoid, disoriented, etc.
(B)   = Behavior, i.e., erratic, eccentric, aloof, hyperactive, etc.
(E)   = Emotion, i.e., agitated, depressive, etc.
(Ec)   = Economic stressor(s), i.e., unpaid, taxes, overdue bills, etc.
(R)   = Recency of action(s), i.e., threats (verbal, physical, written, etc.)
(S)   = Severity of action(s), i.e., threats (verbal, physical, written, etc.)
(I)   = Intensity of action(s), i.e., threats (verbal, physical, written, etc.)
(F)   = Frequency of action(s), i.e., threats (verbal, physical, written, etc.)
(H×V) = History of violence (past 3 to 6 months, past year, past 5 years, etc.)
(TF)   = Threshold factor (assigned 1 to 10 scale) (0 to 3 = low; 4 to 6 = moderate; 7 to 10 = high)

(Ti) = Threat index (outstanding variables representing violent behavior)
(PvP) = Predictive violence potential (outcome)
(PV) = Potential for violence (outcome)
Σ   = The sum of the equation for the purposes of violence prediction
        and future threat

Threat Assessment Equation

$$S + C + B + E + D/A + Ec\ [RSIF + H \times V] \times TF\ (Ti) = Outcome$$

$$\Sigma\ (sum) + TF/Ti\ (outcome) = PvP$$

Predictive violence potential is the Σ (sum) = PvP

PvP (prediction of violence potential) = PV (potential for violence)

Threshold of Behavior and Violence

When such levels or thresholds of behavior involving poor impulse control, as well as certain aspects of cognition and emotion, reach a determined threat level, i.e., tolerance threshold, the threat assessment specialist must consider the potential that there is a high probability for acting out; also, if the person in question has two or more critical incidents of violence in as recent as 1 year, especially within 3 to 6 months or less from the date of the current threat assessment. Finally, when the person in question has a positive history for drugs, chemical abuse, and/or alcohol abuse accompanied with either a paranoid-type, borderline, or anti-social personality disorder, the potential for threat is enhanced for acting out (Davis, 1995; Steadman et al., 1994; Monahan, 1985; Megargee, 1980).

Monahan (1985), as cited in Ewing (1985), provided further insight into the clinical prediction of dangerousness, violence, and aggression by offering a reasonable guide to predicting violence behavior that should be asked by the evaluator of any case focusing on the issue regarding the propensity for violence and dangerousness. In his research on violence, human aggression, and dangerousness, Monahan (1985), as cited in Ewing (1985), suggested that 13 questions be used to screen for the purposes of making a prediction of violence or during a threat assessment when the question of dangerousness has been raised. See Table 11.2.

Proposed Traits of Violent Offenders

Various personnel with the Federal Bureau of Investigation (FBI) assigned to the Behavioral Science Unit in Quantico, Virginia have interviewed numerous

Table 11.2 Screening Questions for the Threat Assessment Evaluator

1. What events precipitated the question of the person's potential for violence being raised, and in what context did these events take place?
2. What are the person's relevant demographic characteristics?
3. What is the person's history of violent behavior?
4. What is the base rate of violent behavior among individuals of this person's background?
5. What are the sources of perceived stress in the person's background and current situation?
6. What cognitive and affective factors indicate that the person may be predisposed to maladaptively cope with stress in a threatening, violent, acting-out manner?
7. What cognitive and affective person may be predisposed to a nonviolent manner?
8. What is the likelihood that if a person coped in a violent way to stress in the past will they cope with stress in a similar way in the near or distant future?
9. In particular, who are the likely (targeted) victims of the person's violent behavior? How available are they?
10. What means does the person possess to commit acts of violence?
11. Am I giving a balanced consideration to the factors indicating the absence of violent behaviors, as well as to the factors indicating its occurrence?
12. Am I giving adequate attention to what I estimate as the base rate of violent behavior among persons in similar situations as the person being examined?
13. Other significant clinical or forensic variables involved in this case?

Source: Excerpted from *Psychology, Psychiatry, and the Law: A Clinical and Forensic Handbook* (p. 26). by C. P. Ewing (Ed.), 1985. Sarasota, FL: Professional Resource Exchange, Inc. Copyright 1985 by Professional Resource Exchange, Inc. Reprinted with permission.

career criminals who have perpetrated violent crimes such as assault, rape, homicide (serial, spree, and mass), and assassination. According to Brantley (FBI training handout, research date unknown), other FBI behavioral science personnel, and Davis (1999), certain traits, characteristics, and criminal typologies of offenders are used to psychologically profile and somewhat predict future behaviors of a like or similar subject carrying out future crimes of the same category or type. Brantley (research date unknown) as well as Davis (1999) offer some insight regarding violence indicators shared among many offenders. See Table 11.3.

An Exceptional Case Study Research on Violent Offenders

The National Institute of Justice (NIJ) funded a 5-year project and study that began in 1992. Completed by Fein and Vossekuil (1998), the researchers reported their findings in a Department of Justice publication titled *Protective Intelligence and Threat Assessment Investigations.* The publication highlighted what the researchers called the *Exceptional Case Study Project* (ECSP).

In the ECSP study and project, Fein and Vossekuil (1998) identified in a sample 83 persons who committed violent attacks of behavior from 1949

Table 11.3   Characteristics Shared among Violent Offenders

- Low frustration or low stress tolerance
- Poor impulse control or impulsive behaviors
- Emotional blunting or lability, dysphoric mood, or chronic depressive illness
- History of childhood abuse
- Social withdrawal or social isolation
- Hypersensitivity (jokes, ridicule, rejection, performance, lack of attention)
- Altered consciousness; delusions, orientation to self, place, time, and event
- Substance abuse, chemical or poly-substance abuse
- Threats of violence
- Defensive — externalizes and displaces blame onto others
- Takes little or no responsibility for his or her actions (consequences)
- Mental health problems requiring inpatient hospitalization (civil commitment)
- History of personal violence or violence in the family
- Odd, unusual, or bizarre behavior as well as "magical-type thinking"
- Somatic problems, conversion disorder, or hypochondriasis
- Obsessive and compulsive behaviors or ritualistic behaviors
- Fixation or preoccupation with themes of violence
- Behavioral triad (arson, animal torture, enuresis) to include school problems
- Paranoid personality features

Source: Excerpted from Brantley, A. (n.k.d.). FBI Academy, Behavioral Science Unit, Department of Justice, Quantico, Virginia. Training seminar handout on Criminal Behavior Traits and Violence. Research. Date of research is unknown.

Source: Excerpted from Davis, J. (1998). The Psychology behind Crime: A Primer to Understanding Criminal Behavior. Unpublished manuscript and notes. San Diego, CA.

to 1996. In their review of the data and literature from all of the reported 83 cases, they examined carefully the motives, targets of violence, plan of attack, style of communication, role of mental illness, and the key life experiences of the perpetrators. The researchers found a striking relationship that included various inadequate personality traits, dysfunctional behavioral characteristics, and unstable emotionality as well as a plethora of perceptual distortion and paranoid thinking patterns and styles among a majority of the individuals in the sample. In their examination of these cases as reported in ECSP, Fein and Vossekuil (1998) highlighted the following characteristics that were determined to be important in examining violence and dangerousness. The ECSP study reported the histories and characteristics of violent attackers and near-lethal approachers that included demographic data and traits. See Table 11.4.

Conducting a Threat Assessment Evaluation

Fein and Vossekuil (1998), in the ECSP study, provided guidance as to what areas to examine carefully when the issue of dangerousness surfaces. They

Table 11.4   Exception Case Examination of Violence

- Offenders and near-lethal approachers' ages ranged from 16 to 73 years
- Many in the sample (about 50%) had at least attended college or graduate school
- Many had histories of mobility and transitory behavior
- Many (about two thirds) were described to be socially isolated in their behavior
- Few in the sample were reported to have arrest crimes with weapons violations
- Few of the sample had criminal incarceration histories at the federal or state level
- Many had histories of weapons use, but many did not have formal weapons training
- Many had histories of explosive anger traits but only half had histories of violence
- Many had long histories of harassing other individuals
- Many had reported that they had an interest in attacking a public figure
- Many had reported interests in militant activities and radical ideas but few had been members of such groups or radical activities
- Many had clinical histories for serious depressive illness, desolation, or despair
- Many had been known to have attempted a self-destructive act such as suicide or to have at least considered suicide as an option at some time during the attack or near-lethal approach to an intended target
- Finally, the research reported that all had histories of grievances and resentments, frequently directed at a public official or popular figure

Source: Excerpted from *Protective Intelligence and Threat Assessment Investigations*, NIJ Funded Research, NCJ #170612, U.S. Government Report, as reported by Fein and Vossekuil (1998).

suggested that the threat assessment specialist entertain the following three areas of inquiry for the purposes of protective intelligence and security: (1) identifiers, (2) background information, and (3) current life situation and circumstances. Table 11.5 highlights these areas of inquiry for the purposes of protective intelligence and security.

Finally, Fein and Vossekuil (1998) highlighted some areas of interest worth additional inquiry, such as: (1) examining the interest in assassination; (2) examining communicated plans about attacking a public figure or official; (3) communicating an inappropriate interest in an official, especially where such comments that have been expressed imply a threat of attack; (4) visiting the physical site of the intended person's residence or place of employment; (5) approaching the intended person at his residence, place of employment, or in a social setting (excerpted from *Protective Intelligence and Threat Assessment Investigations* [1998], NIJ Funded Research, NCJ # 170612, U.S. Government Report, as reported by Fein and Vossekuil [1998]).

Davis (1998) also suggested that any contact that implies even a remote chance for any potential threat of violence delivered through unconventional means, i.e., electronically (e-mail, fax transmission, pager, cell phone, voicemail), or through conventional means, i.e., verbally or through written communication, is viable enough for an additional inquiry and investigation into the likelihood of a possible attack.

Table 11.5   Threat Assessment and Subject Characteristics

1. Name of individual and any aliases used
2. Birth date of individual
3. Social security number and/or military identification number
4. Current address and work address (if any)
5. Names and addresses of next-of-kin or close relatives
6. Physical description and current photograph (if available)
7. Samples of handwriting (if available)

Source: Excerpted from *Protective Intelligence and Threat Assessment Investigations* (1998). NIJ Funded Research, NCJ #170612, U.S. Government Report, as reported by Fein and Vossekuil (1998).

Threat Assessment and Subject Background

1. Education and training
2. Criminal history check
3. History of violent behavior (if any)
4. Military history
5. History of specialized training and use of weapons
6. Employment history
7. Mental health history to include involuntary hospitalization
8. History of grievances toward target individuals, groups, or businesses
9. Marital or relationship history
10. History of harassment behavior
11. History of interest in militant or extremist activities, ideas, or groups
12. Travel history in the U.S. and abroad (past year)

Source: Excerpted from *Protective Intelligence and Threat Assessment Investigations* (1998). NIJ Funded Research, NCJ #170612, U.S. Government Report, as reported by Fein and Vossekuil (1998).

Juvenile Predictors of Violent Behavior

Predictions of children's future behavior are often requested as aids in disposing of cases in juvenile, domestic, and family relation courts. Nine different studies identified 30 different factors as statistically related to violent behavior in children. The correspondence was judged sufficient to justify their use as predictors (Schlesinger, 1978).

Between January 1 and June 30, 1973, 122 juveniles were evaluated to see how many of the predictor factors were present in their cases, and which were the most prevalent. Of the 30 factors, 23 were present in the cases studied. Within these 23 factors, 240 incidents were noted. The three highest factors were (1) truancy, with 66 cases cited; (2) school misconduct, with 40 cases cited; and (3) fighting, with 20 clinical case studies cited. It is important to note that the predictions made in the studies done were for future violent behavior as a juvenile. Note that these juvenile factors may not be consistent or generalizable with predictions in the adult population for future

Table 11.6 Juvenile Predictors Identified by Research Studies

Investigator	Predictors
Bender	Abnormal EEG or other neurological condition
	Epilepsy (various types)
	Extremely unfavorable home life experiences
	Poor home life and living conditions
	Personal experiences with violent death
Cowden	Poor personality prognosis
	Poor institutional adjustment
Hellman and Blackman	Chronic enuresis, fire setting
	Cruelty to animals
Glueck and Glueck	Overly strict or lax discipline by either parent
	School retardation, school truancy
	School misconduct
Guze, Goodwin, and Crane	Sociopathy, alcoholism, drug dependency
von Hirsch	Known history of violence
	Original commitment for a violent offense
	Commitment for fourth or more time
	History of moderate or serious opiate use
	Referred to a psychiatrist on commitment
Wenk and Emrich	Violent admission offense
Justice, Justice, and Kraft	Fighting, temper tantrums
	Inability to get along with others
Sendi and Blomgren	Parental brutality
	Exposure to violence or murder
	Sexual inhibition
	Seduction by or perversion in parent
	Unfavorable home environment

Note: Where repetition of predictors occurs among authors, such overlap is eliminated from this list.

adult behavior. However, a threat assessment specialist must consider any previous act of violence or violent-type behavior for the purposes of predicting future dangerousness when assessing the juvenile's propensity to engage in lethal life-threatening and even non-lethal life-threatening behavior. Table 11.6 contains a summary of these clinical factors.

Previously, the most well-known childhood, adolescent, or juvenile symptomatic predictor is a "behavioral triad" consisting of (1) enuresis (chronic bedwetting), (2) fire setting, and (3) cruelty to animals (Ressler et al., 1988). This behavioral triad has been frequently reported, either individually or conjointly, as possible clinical psychopathological precursors to future adult violent crime. Justice, Justice, and Kraft (1974), as cited by Mesnikoff and Lauterbach (1975) in their review of the predictors of adult violence, acknowledge the persistent evidence for the triad of child behavior indicated above as correlates of later adult violence. However, the researchers asked whether that behavioral triad of childhood symptoms was enough to make a valid and reliable future prediction of violence and dangerousness. The researchers determined that the identifiers found in the behavioral triad were not enough. The research does, however, represent a good but limited beginning toward identifying antecedent behavior and a possible profile of potential adult violence or dangerousness to come in the future, particularly if the behavior is not professionally addressed via early mental health intervention with the child, adolescent, or juvenile.

The Justices and Kraft research (1974), as cited in Mesnikoff and Lauterbach (1975), identified four other early warning signs in children: (1) fighting, (2) temper tantrums, (3) aloneness, and (4) truancy/school failures. The researchers found that the latter signs were even more of a frequent predictor of adult violence than the original behavioral triad of enuresis, firesetting, and cruelty to animals.

Conclusion

In their monograph on the *Law of Homicide,* Wechsler and Michael (1937), as cited by Smith (1971), concluded that "all men agree that in general it is desirable to prevent homicide and bodily injury. While the unnecessary taking of life may be viewed as socially dangerous conduct, it does not follow that all persons who murder are necessarily dangerous." Studies have consistently indicated that upwards of 75% of all murders are committed by a relative, friend, acquaintance, or associate of the victim. Greenland (1971), as cited by Mesnikoff and Lauterbach (1975), states that these murders are usually impulsive, suggesting an explosion of built-up tension prior to the act of lethal violence. Thus, the potential for dangerousness of the offender would depend upon the likelihood of his or her again entering into a similar relationship under similar situations or contiguous-like circumstances.

Drawing clinical-forensic inferences from statistical analyses weighs heavily in the judicial decision that past misconduct alone is not a sufficient-enough basis for the label "dangerous," and thus does not always justify indefinite incarceration. In order to safeguard against the overprediction of dangerousness, i.e., false positives, it is suggested that offenders should be presumed not dangerous unless proved otherwise. Furthermore, the status and adequacy of treatment should be elevated and periodically reviewed by outside agents of the court. In addition, the offender must be confined only in a facility that meets reasonable standards of decency and human dignity.

Dangerousness cannot be predicted by professionals trained only in understanding psychodiagnosis and its related treatment modalities. Validating the existence for the potential for violence and future dangerousness is an outcome and conclusion reached by many mental health treatment providers and threat assessment specialists. However, the process by which each reaches that outcome and conclusion is not without its share of complexities.

The prediction of dangerousness is possible but complicated. It is the reliable level of threat assessment accuracy that is necessary to which its application is to be defined and validated. The current approaches to assessing threat and predicting future violence and dangerousness are still evolving. Some would have the clinician or threat assessment specialist err on the side of public safety, while others would insist on protecting the would-be rights of the offender.

How much is the potential elimination of an act of violence against one person's worth? The price for such elimination is very likely the restriction of another person's freedom. It is a perilous, narrow path between the requirements for a just social order and the expression of individual personal freedom. To properly balance social order and control vs. personal liberty is a complicated sociopolitical issue, not a clinical one per se, frequently addressed by our highest courts and legislative branches.

The threat assessment specialist should neither be given the opportunity nor attempt to usurp society's right to determine the risks it is willing to take in resolving the conflict between public safety and personal liberty (Cohen et al., 1978). Regardless of the need to allow courts and legislative branches to deal with the issue of public safety and personal liberty, individuals who evaluate human aggression as well as threats of violence will continue to find themselves challenged to make a complex decision to which they will ultimately be held accountable.

The person in the role charged with the task of evaluating threats of violence and aggression in public policy, who debates over security vs. liberty, should generally be that of an advocate for security for his or her patients, his or her community, and for others (Dietz, 1985).

Dietz (1985) debated further on the issue of public policy, liberty, and security by stating:

> I think we have a moral duty to the potential victims of those whom we evaluate. Like the legal duty that has been recognized in some jurisdictions, this moral duty does not require perfect prediction, only reasonable prudence in the exercise of professional judgment. (Dietz, 1985)

Bibliography

American Psychiatric Association (1980). *Diagnostic and Statistical Manual of Mental Health Disorders*, 3rd ed. Washington, D.C.: APA Press.

American Psychiatric Association (1987). *Diagnostic and Statistical Manual of Mental Health Disorders*, 3rd revised ed. Washington, D.C.: APA Press.

American Psychiatric Association (1994). *Diagnostic and Statistical Manual of Mental Health Disorders*, 4th ed. Washington, D.C.: APA Press.

Brantley, A. (n.k.d.). Criminal Behavioral Characteristics: Traits of Violent Criminals. FBI Academy, Behavioral Science Unit, Department of Justice, Quantico, VA. Public safety training handout from attendance at a seminar on criminal behavioral assessment. Research date is unknown.

Cohen, M. L., Groth, A. N., and Siegel, R. (1978). The clinical prediction of dangerousness, *Crime and Delinquency*, 24, 28–39.

Davis, J. (1986). Success from Violence and Violence Recidivism: Can We Successfully Treat Domestic Violence Offenders on an Outpatient Basis? A Clinical-Forensic Study of Male Abusers Court Ordered for Outpatient Treatment. Unpublished research, presented at the Virginia Psychological Association (VPA) and the Virginia Academy of Social Sciences (VASS) Annual Conference. This study was conducted with the approval of the Department of Mental Health, and Mental Retardation and Substance Services, Community Mental Health, Forensic Mental Health Outpatient Court Services, Virginia.

Davis, J. (1994). The Assessment of Threats and Prediction of Future Violence: Just How Accurate Can We Be? Unpublished paper presented to the Annual Conference of ACJS, Academy of Criminal Justice Sciences, San Diego, CA.

Davis, J. (1995). Mental Illness, Violent Crime and Public Policy: How Can We Prevent the Mentally Ill from Becoming Our Next Criminals? Violence research conducted on the subject of mental illness, justice, and mental health public policy, Vollmer Institute for Law, Justice and Policy Studies, Orange, CA.

Davis, J. (1997). The Potential Threat of Violence: A Formula for Threat Assessment Specialists. Presentation and workshop on stalking and potential violence, Annual Conference, Peace Officer Research Association of California (PORAC), Monterey, CA.

Davis, J. (1998). In the Mind of Stalkers: Stalking, Stalkers and Their Victims. Presentation to the International Association of Crime Analysts (IACA), Annual International Training and Continuing Education Conference, San Diego, CA.

Davis, J. (1999). *Psychology behind Crime: A Primer to Understanding Criminal Behavior.* Anaheim, CA: Pulse Custom Publishing.

Dietz, P. E. (1985). Hypothetical criteria for the prediction of individual criminality, in C. D. Webster, M. H. Ben-Aron, and S. J. Hucker (Eds.). *Dangerousness: Probability and Prediction, Psychiatry and Public Policy* (pp. 87–102). New York: Cambridge University Press.

Ewing, C. P. (1985). *Handbook for Forensic Psychiatry, Psychology and Law.* Sarasota, FL: Professional Resource Exchange, Inc.

Fein, R. A. and Vossekuil, B. (1998). Protective Intelligence Threat Assessment Investigations: A Guide for State and Local Law Enforcement. Research Grant # 170612, National Institute of Justice, U.S. Department of Justice, Office of Justice Programs, Washington, D.C.

Hare, R. D. (1991). *Hare Psychopathy Checklist.* New York: Mental Health Systems.

Hare, R. D. and Hart, S. D. (1994). Psychopathy, mental disorder, and crime, in S. Hodskins (Ed.), *Mental Disorder and Crime* (pp. 104–115). New York: Lexington Books.

Hare, R. D. and McPherson, L. M., (1984). Violent and aggressive behavior by criminal psychopaths, *International Journal of Law and Psychiatry*, 7, 35–50.

Hucker, S. J. and Ben-Aron, M. H. (Eds.) (1985). *Dangerousness: Probability and Prediction, Psychiatry and Public Policy* (pp. 53–64). New York: Cambridge University Press.

Koerin, B. (1978). Violent crime: prediction and control, *Crime and Delinquency*, 24, 49–58.

Megargee, E. L. (1980). The prediction of dangerous behavior, in G. Cooke (Ed.), *The Role of the Forensic Psychologist*, (pp. 189–215). Springfield, IL: Charles C Thomas.

Mesnikoff, A. M. and Lauterbach, C. G. (1975). Association of violent dangerous behavior with psychiatric disorders: a review of the research literature, *Journal of Psychiatry and Law*, 3, 415–445.

Monahan, J. (1985). Evaluating potentially violent persons, in C. P. Ewing (Ed.), *Psychology, Psychiatry and the Law*, (pp. 9–39). Sarasota, FL: Professional Resource Exchange, Inc.

Ressler, R., Douglas, J., and Burgess, A. (1988). *Sexual homicide: Patterns and Motives.* New York: Lexington Books.

Schlesinger, S. E. (1978). The prediction of dangerousness in juveniles: a replication, *Crime and Delinquency*, 24, 40–48.

Smith, C. E. (1971). Recognizing and sentencing the exceptional and dangerous offender, *Federal Probation*, 35, 3–12.

Steadman, H. J., Monahan, J., Robbins, P. C., Appelbaum, P., Grisso, T., Klassen, D., Mulvey, E. P., and Roth, L. (1994). From dangerousness to risk assessment: implications for appropriate research strategies, in J. Monahan (Ed.), *Prediction of Violence* (pp. 39–49). New York: Lexington Books.

About the Contributing Authors

Joseph A. Davis, Ph.D., LL.D.

An academic and research expert in the area of public safety psychology, and clinical-forensic psychology and trauma, the editor of *Stalking Crimes and Victim Protection: Prevention, Intervention, Threat Assessment, and Case Management* is Joseph Davis, Ph.D., LL.D., with a B.S. in psychology with honors, M.S. in psychology, Ph.D. in clinical psychology, and LL.D., Doctor of Laws, in law and public policy (honoris causa). Dr. Davis completed his post-graduate forensic mental health assessment, education, and training at the University of Virginia at the Institute of Law, Psychiatry and Public Policy in 1985. He is the executive director of the Institute of Law, Psychology and

Public Policy Studies and is a partner with The TAP Group, Inc. (threat assessment and prevention) in San Diego and Long Beach, California.

With adjunct faculty appointments at several major universities in California and abroad, he has published extensively over the past 17 years in five academic areas covering the disciplines of clinical-forensic, police/public safety psychology, criminology, traumatology, law, and public policy. Over the past 6 years, he has been the medical and allied health editor-in-chief and a member of the editorial advisory board to the *Canadian Journal of Clinical Medicine* in Edmonton, Alberta. In addition to devoting his time to university-level teaching and clinical research, he maintains a private office devoted to management and organizational consulting, training, research and development, critical incidents and trauma response, and public safety psychology. He is married and is the father of two daughters. A native of Virginia, he and his family reside in San Diego.

Lisa M. Stewart, M.A.

Lisa M. Stewart, M.A. is a 1998 graduate of the Forensic Psychology Graduate Program at the John Jay College of Criminal Justice in New York. She completed her externship at the Center for Applied Forensic-Behavioral Sciences in San Diego. She is currently a doctoral student in the clinical psychology program at the Fielding Institute in Santa Barbara, CA.

Robin Siota, Psy.D.

Robin Siota, Psy.D. completed her doctor of psychology degree program at Pacific University. Dr. Siota also completed her pre-doctoral internship in clinical and forensic psychology in San Diego. She is currently an independent consultant and clinical researcher in Southern California.

Minimizing Potential Threats and Risks to Stalking Victims: Case Management, Security Issues, and Safety Planning

12

BRUCE L. DANTO*

Contents

* Bruce L. Danto, M.D., an early pioneer in the field of forensic psychiatry and the psychology of stalking, passed away in Fullerton, California in 1998 before this chapter was published. Prior to his death, Dr. Danto authored this unpublished manuscript and provided a copy to the editor. Dr. Danto's wife, Joan Danto, MSW, L.C.S.W., who currently operates a private psychotherapy outpatient practice in Fullerton, California, has kindly granted permission to publish her husband's research.

0-8493-0811-9/01/$0.00+$1.50
© 2001 by CRC Press LLC

Introduction

In 1990, according to Melita Schaum and Karen Parrish (1995), 30% of female homicide victims were killed by ex-lovers or husbands. They presented the estimate made by many professionals who felt that 90% of these women were stalked before being murdered.

Most stalking incidents are not reported because only a few, those from the celebrity group, become national news. The average person might therefore be inclined to see this as a rare phenomenon.

Most people remember the case of Robert John Bardo, who was obsessed with actress Rebecca Lynn Schaeffer. His efforts to establish contact with her at the security gate of the television studio where she worked resulted in his being turned away.

After learning of her address through publicly available records, he went to her apartment and when she opened her door, shot her in the chest with his .357 magnum revolver. The only good that followed this tragic loss was the fact that Senators Barbara Boxer and Bob Krueger introduced legislation in Congress that made stalking a federal crime (interestingly, Senator Krueger had himself been a stalking victim).

This author is [was] Director of Forensic Science at West Coast Detectives. He and others in the field, like former LAPD Captain Robert Martin, who founded the Threat Management Unit (TMU) of the Los Angeles Police Department (LAPD), and Lieutenant John C. Lane have known for years about the problems of stalkers.

The police department has trained investigators to deal with these particular issues. According to California law, stalkers can be prosecuted under the stalking law, as well as the terrorism law, for making threats of death against a given victim.

Some of the people in this field who have studied the dynamics of stalkers include Gavin de Becker, a security expert, and Dr. Park Dietz, a nationally recognized psychiatrist and forensic mental health expert. Most people who have been involved with law enforcement do not see stalking as a new crime, even in terms of recent centuries, nor is it limited to any particular locality.

We know from victims that stalkers can engage in everything from phone harassment to vandalism, from sending letters and gifts to theft, from pursuit behavior to assault, rape, and even murder.

According to Schaum and Parrish (1995), stalking usually takes place between ordinary people, often former romantic partners or spouses. There is often a connection between domestic violence and stalking. Despite the public's overwhelming picture of stalkers in terms of celebrities or in terms of spouses or partners, however, the broad arena of remaining cases involves either casual acquaintances or random targets. They may involve co-workers at a place of employment.

The primary source of support for all those who have been victimized has to be the judicial system. It is a system that can bring order out of chaos and represents a necessary step in ensuring a victim's safety.

Unfortunately, there seems to be a great debate about whether or not personal restraining orders work. In the opinion of this author, they are a necessary ingredient in preparing the police to intervene, whether they stop the stalker in his activities or not.

Anatomy of a Stalking

A 47-year-old woman married a very handsome 32-year-old Hispanic male. Sometime after the marriage took place, she discovered that he was involved in drugs and was an enforcer in the drug business. She became concerned that this might disqualify her from working at her job for a large aircraft company, where she handled contracts for defense products.

He soon began to rape and abuse her. She filed a criminal complaint, and he was sent to a medium-security prison. While incarcerated, he wrote love letters to her, and she felt that he had learned something from the experience. Upon his release, she arranged to take a trip with him to Big Bear, a state park in southern California. When she was back in his area of control, however, he raped and beat her severely.

She had entered treatment with this author because she was emotionally falling apart, living in constant terror, and suffered a post-traumatic stress disorder (PTSD) from the abuse suffered at the hands of her husband. He wanted her to assume paying off the loan on the boat he had ordered, and he cashed in all of her credit cards to their limit so that she was tied up financially, legally, and emotionally. Subsequently, he was reincarcerated.

In her efforts to try to meet some new men, she went to a bar one evening, met a man who seemed nice, and as they were taking a walk down the street, he pulled her into an alley and attempted to rape her; further bruises and trauma resulted.

It was important to help her. Her husband was sending threatening letters from prison and was telling her that some inmates owed him favors and would kill her while he was still in custody. As a result, she was able to get a restraining order, and because this author was a part of the Association of Threat Assessment Professionals (ATAP), networking provided a contact with a California Department of Corrections (CDC) investigator. That contact led to restricting any letters that were sent to her. The writing of these letters amounted to an infraction, and he had to put in another year in prison.

In the meantime, with the reduction of employment in the aerospace industry, her job collapsed. She carefully planned to get a new social security number, moved to another state, and changed her name. She entered treatment with another psychiatrist in Florida and, at last word, is doing much better and certainly feels safer.

Her husband has been released from prison and is now on parole. An interesting feature of this case is the fact that he involved two other women in the same kind of target-like behavior and threatened to kill them, too.

Stalking Case Analysis

This case illustrates not only what the stalker was able to do, showing his intense rage toward women, but also what a therapist may have to do in order to deal with this kind of problem. This is not solely conventional treatment of PTSD. The author took photographs of injuries and was actively involved with the police and particularly the parole department, because after the offender had been released from prison and the couple made their ill-fated trip to Big Bear, it was necessary to report to the parole officer the amount of damage she subsequently sustained.

Issues of Safety and Security

Coming up with a reasonable security plan to protect her was also important. One of the problems in this case, for example, was the fact that the husband had aides whom he could call upon from prison to achieve his threats and keep her off-balance.

The note of caution struck by this case is that once they are out of the criminal justice system and complete the requirements of incarceration and parole, there is no way of stopping stalkers unless a new crime has been committed.

Another Stalking Case Illustration

In another case, a 51-year-old married female moved with her new husband into a mobile home park. In 1995, a neighbor began to harass the couple. Every night between 9 and 11 P.M., he threw rotten fruit as well as stones against their unit. He threatened to kill them and also made provocative gestures and remarks in regard to having sex with the woman. He also terrorized the other residents of the mobile home park.

A neighbor witnessed an attack, but by the time the police arrived to take a statement from her to use later in court proceedings, she denied having seen anything improper.

As the woman's therapist, this author urged contact with the police and was also successful in getting her to take out a personal restraining order, allowing her to set limits on the perpetrator.

Stalking as a Predatory Activity

Basically, stalking involves a repeated pattern of harassing or following another person. The element of threat made is personalized to a particular victim. These incidents are repetitive in nature and involve a commitment to a fixed pattern known as a course of conduct. One verbalized or written threat is not enough to establish a continuity of purpose.

Threats or threatening behavior are addressed by most state legislatures. What is important is that the victim feels threatened by the stalker's actions. Many states will require that a threat has to be credible and show intent or the ability or opportunity to carry out the threat.

Most cases involve women being victimized by male stalkers. Occasionally, a homosexual admirer will stalk a man or woman (an interesting example of this was the case of actress Sharon Gless). According to Schaum and Parrish (1995), Gavin de Becker has catalogued in his work more than 300,000 bizarre letters and gifts that have been sent to stars by obsessed fans. The messages range in value and size from five 1-cent postage stamps to a motorcycle. The writers give gifts pertinent to their particular victim, as well as some that are hard to explain, such as a disposable razor, a half-eaten candy bar, a tube of toothpaste, and a stone. Contents have also included animal feces, a facsimile bomb, and a syringe of blood.

The data presented by Dietz et al. (1991a), according to Schaum and Parrish (1995), involves observations that the presence of a threat provides no clear prediction; a written threat does not reliably predict contact. However, some writers express the desire for contact, and they are more likely to approach the stars. Those who mention sharing a special destiny or fate with the celebrity are also more likely to initiate personal face-to-face contact. Other predictors include:

- Mention of a specific date or place
- More than ten letters written to the celebrity
- Mention of a weapon
- Writing from more than one address
- Writing to the same celebrity for more than a year
- Attempting to telephone as well as make written contact

Celebrity personalities who are local rather than national are more likely to be ready targets. Dietz and colleagues found that the presence of a threat in and of itself does not serve as an accurate prediction of harm (1991b).

In a study done by Dr. Michael Zona of the U.S.C. School of Medicine, erotomania tends to make its first appearance in relatively young individuals. In young persons, the condition has a rapid onset (Zona et al., 1993). Zona notes that a few erotomanics have done well on psychiatric medication. He states that the medication, *pimozide*, is particularly useful in the treatment of the erotomanic disorder.

Zona, in his research, found that the group most likely to seek out celebrities were erotomanic stalkers. An erotomanic stalker is one who delusionally believes that the victim is in love with him. A celebrity may sing a song or play a particular part in a movie and the stalker becomes convinced that these are personal communications and that he is being directed to do certain things which the law would define as criminal (Zona et al., 1993).

Other stalkers are ones who are more psychopathic, people who relate to others by way of domination and intimidation and who use force and fear as means of controlling the defenseless-type person. Those who are psychopathic or personality disordered may don disguises. This type of stalker may feel less than whole; and feelings of being worthless or empty are found underneath the bravado of being a mastermind.

A Stalker Classification Schema

Danto (1990) classifies the types of stalkers by way of behavior. This system is appealing and logical because it helps to more accurately assess risk to the victim regardless of current psychiatric condition. It was developed in order to deal with different stalker profiles and establish a way of keeping them away from the target.

Meeting with stalkers in an undercover capacity also helps an investigator to look for signs of behavior. It is important to note that police and investigators ensure their own safety by employing established law enforcement techniques necessary to gauge the danger of imminent violence, such as reading a subject's body language.

The Fan — The first type is the fan. This stalker craves memorabilia from a star such as an autograph or photograph. He poses no threat of danger to the star.

The Erotomanic Worshiper — The erotomanic worshiper is one who adores the star and also feels the star loves him. He becomes a player in a fantasized romantic relationship.

The Obsessed Fan — The obsessed fan is one who has active fantasies about the victim and who wants to build a life around the importance of the victim. He can think of nothing else and may be psychotic or delusional. He is motivated by narcissism to direct everything in his fantasy toward his fulfillment.

The Controller — Another type is the controller. This stalker carries his focus beyond a romantic attachment and wants dominion over the life and career of the victim. He is a person who lives to thrive off the reflected achievement and power of the victim, because in his lifetime he has accomplished nothing.

The Violent Threatener — Another type of stalker is the violent threatener. The violent threatener is one who becomes angry at the star for not corresponding with him, but also because the star does not want to grant his wishes for romance and the need to control. A star's refusal to respond and acknowledge him produces a feeling of impotence, which then calls for a threat to become the tool of the impotent wrongdoer.

The Death Threatener — Another type is the death threatener. The death threatener is one who shows an early commitment to violence, and whether it is for reasonable or fantasized frustration, it may have reached the final point before he is ready to kill the celebrity or the target.

The Killer — The killer has gone through the previous stages. He is a stalker for whom reality testing has become very impaired, and he is convinced that a sacrifice of the victim is necessary, sometimes believing he is being directed by some other force. This person has already thought about and made plans to kill the victim.

This classification system has a high degree of practicality for the author, because it reflects on the degree of risk of violence. In profiling stalkers and the degree of risk and investigating them undercover, it has proven to be more effective than making formal diagnoses on people who have not as yet been examined (Danto, 1990).

Victim Risk and Case Management

Michelle Taylor, a stalking case and risk management specialist, described the points that are necessary to consider, and her summary was very good. She discussed the need to prosecute the stalker to ensure the victim's safety. She advised utilizing a temporary restraining order and police intervention and having a friend or representative threaten the stalker if he is known (Taylor, 1997).

These measures would be effective in thwarting further activity on the part of the stalker if he were not obsessed or obsessive-compulsively driven to achieve an impossible goal. Of course, if they were reasonable persons, they would not be stalking in the first place.

Ms. Taylor discusses several case management strategies and options that are available. These include:

1. Notifying those in a position to be alert to and detect communications or information such as letters or phone calls
2. Engaging the services of a private box service for all mail
3. Placing real property in a trust

4. Listing utilities under the name of a trust or a friend
5. Requesting that a code word be put on the victim's utility, bank, or other accounts
6. Avoiding giving out the victim's address to an employer, co-workers, or other acquaintances
7. Being careful to avoid being followed from predictable places (certainly, one example of this would be the action of the paparazzi in pursuing Princess Diana)
8. Requesting that phone numbers be unlisted
9. Answering telephones with the last four digits of the phone number, causing unfamiliar callers to believe that they are dealing with an answering service
10. Not providing personal information on the outgoing answering message
11. Establishing separate phone lines which are installed at a location other than the victim's residence
12. Carefully reviewing information the victim provides for public records, even with documents that may seem insignificant, such as pet licensing papers
13. Establishing security measures at the victim's residence
14. Increasing the victim's personal safety by learning self-defense

This author feels that a clear "no" must be given to the stalker so that he feels there is no possible chance of either a meeting or a future in this relationship. This may result in the stalker turning attention elsewhere, which does not necessarily mean an improvement except to this particular victim (Danto, 1990).

Taylor (1997) also advises that law enforcement intervention might be needed if the stalker does not give up his pursuit.

This author feels that contacting the police should be done early in the case in order to establish sufficient documentation for any necessary legal action. Records of all stalking behavior should be kept. All efforts to contact the victim should be documented, and copies of letters and messages left on answering machines should be preserved. Counting on the police to help protect a stalker victim cannot possibly be achieved without the presence of records. The criminal justice system is still doing too little to protect victims, but without records this author can assure the reader that nothing will be done.

This author advises that stalker-victim patients keep a duplicate set of records (so that the stalker cannot find and destroy evidence); most patients leave a second set of records with the therapist or another trustworthy person.

It is important to establish the boundaries involved in the act of stalking. Most victims can recall a time when unwanted attention began and then progressed from an annoyance to a dangerous intrusion. Initially, families may react as if there is nothing to get worried about. They may even assume that it is a kind of romantic jockeying for control of a relationship.

However, statements such as "I'm going to make you mine," "I am nothing without you," and "you belong to me" express the control urge that goes along with stalking, particularly in an obsessive state.

Stalking can begin small and become large, depending both on the victim's reaction and on how attractive the victim is to the stalker. An investigator cannot assume that stalker victims know their stalkers.

Stalkers prefer secrecy, and no mistake should be made — the stalker is a hunter or predator; he is like any other hunter in the woods during hunting season. However, for the stalker it is always hunting season.

Some of the mythology of stalking bears a similarity to that about rape victims. There has always been a basic assumption by some police and legislators that rape and stalker victims do something to get the juices flowing in the stalker and rapist. This is not the case, because the victim fundamentally is a fantasized object for the stalker.

The victim frequently is unaware of what there is about him or her that is so important to the stalker. In many cases, the stalker does not know either because it is essentially a transference kind of behavior, namely, taking feelings out on others that the stalker has toward an important figure in his life, perhaps his own parents.

Writings of Stalkers

The writings and verbal statements of stalkers will vary in quality of feelings communicated. They may use very humiliating kinds of swear language or choose words which express their rage or which reflect an emotional violence they are suffering. When specific threats are made, victims tend to melt into a plate of butter and are not in a position to handle this kind of situation. They need informed, sensitive, and compassionate security help (Dietz et al., 1991a).

Victim Analysis

An important skill for someone targeted by a stalker is the ability to effectively handle guilt and realize that one is not responsible for the whole crime of stalking. Anxiety and fear can be dealt with using physical exercise and counseling and continuing to fight for protection. The victim has to become an advocate for himself or herself; talking it out with others in the form of a support group may be helpful.

The author cautions that it is important to be selective in the choice of a therapist, counselor, social worker, clinical psychologist, or psychiatrist. Professionals must be chosen who are familiar with this kind of behavior; otherwise the client is likely to receive advice that is not only uninformed but dangerous.

Schaum and Parrish (1995) advise victims to minimize stress, particularly traumatic stress. Stress of this type has an overwhelming impact on victims, but in this author's experience, victims cannot help but be traumatized and terrified by any car waiting outside that does not look familiar when they leave for work. It is important to keep accurate records, because the function of the memory may be affected by extreme stress.

The victim may try to desensitize himself by regulating the flow of traumatic reality. Of course, extreme anxiety or stress can have an impact on physical functions ranging from gastrointestinal disorders to substance abuse, particularly alcohol; an individual may understandably want to get his mind on something else besides this primary source of pain, the stalking. Prolonged stress can also affect the autoimmune system so that unresolved infections or inflammations may arise (Danto, 1990; Davis, 1997).

In allowing oneself to become righteously angry, the victim of stalking has to safeguard against the anger becoming a debilitating force — the anger must not become directed inward. Care should be taken not to let anger become a way of jeopardizing his or her safety, or to escalate a situation into violence. There must also be an effort to prevent anger from creating a false sense of courage and security, almost a dare to the stalker to come after oneself.

For the victim who is somewhat naive or has not been out in the world to learn ways of coping with life, ongoing trauma may very well affect or influence one's sense of identity and self-image.

Treating the Victim of Stalking

Depression may be a severe consequence of prolonged stress along with anxiety, and may be seen in terms of crying spells, loss of sense of pleasure or interest in things normally enjoyed, decreased appetite, insomnia, or even sleeping too much. There may be an abnormal restlessness or a drop in physical activity, along with fatigue, feelings of worthlessness or guilt, diminished ability to concentrate or make decisions, and recurring thoughts of death and suicide, as well as a realistic fear of death as determined from the communications and references to death in those communications (Danto, 1990).

Approaches to Managing Stalking Cases

All contacts should be documented. If there are witnesses, it should be determined whether they are willing to testify in court. Law enforcement should be contacted religiously with each incident, and the victim should request the police to log each call.

An attorney or legal service should be contacted to explore all legal remedies, including a personal or other type of restraining order, and whether or not each individual incident will invite a criminal charge.

An attorney should send a registered letter to the stalker that he must cease and desist, as the victim is working with the police to secure his arrest if he continues to stalk. The victim should make himself or herself available to public service features or public advocacy programs. An effort should be made to contact politicians about the plight of being a victim. A free home security review from local police or security companies will help.

All neighbors who can become extra eyes and ears should be informed. If the victim is in possession of a photograph of a stalker, of course this should be given to everyone involved, especially neighbors.

If a stalker's vehicle is seen, there should be a procedure decided upon in which the victim can call a neighbor to see about getting the license number and an accurate description of the vehicle.

It is important to keep a camera readily available at all times. This author carries a Leica™ (camera), a small mini-camera, and it has come in handy on a considerable number of occasions.

A surveillance camera can either be rented or purchased and can be placed inside the home or apartment to film the areas around the doors and cars where stalkers like to leave gifts or letters. For those who can purchase television surveillance equipment, it is important to have a camera focused on the outside of the entrance door so that the caller can be fully viewed without employing a face-to-face contact before the victim feels comfortable. A home security alarm system is also important.

A peephole viewer is crucial, because before the door is opened, one can see who the caller is. In Rebecca Lynn Schaeffer's case, she opened the door and was shot before she knew what hit her. Had she had a simple peephole, she might have been able to completely escape her death.

During a crisis period, it may be necessary to rent a car and change the rental car frequently so that the stalker cannot get a fix on a vehicle. The victim should never walk alone at night, and it would be wise to have someone walk with the victim to his or her car from work or shopping, etc. When a victim leaves home, a security agent, if resources permit, can help ensure necessary security. Security arrangements should not involve guards who are paid $5 per hour.

Executive Protection

For executive protection, highly trained people are necessary, ones who have gone through a stint of training such as schools run by Dr. Richard Kobetz in Virginia, known as the Executive Protection Institute (EPI) or "Nine Lives." Gun-wielding ex-cops or private detectives are not suited well to a protective role. These persons, not infrequently, are unaware of what needs to be avoided in planning. The whole idea of being an executive protection specialist is to avoid armed confrontations.

A careful decision must be made as to whether or not a firearm is a reasonable approach to self-defense. In these cases, victims are frequently easily intimidated, rather passive, and easily manipulated by force. For all intents and purposes, these individuals are not assertive enough to use a firearm, mace, or stunguns. They are not usually candidates to be taught the art of self-defense with martial arts. This author has found it unrealistic and not necessarily beneficial to expect them to get a gun to use in their own defense. Safe use of a firearm is not automatic — anyone who has a gun for home protection must learn to fire it, get to know its function as a machine, and clean it. You cannot develop those skills with a gun in a box. Furthermore, guns must be made safe for children and everybody in the household. This involves a dilemma, however. State laws are now appearing that require all guns in a household to be in a locked state. This may compromise one's ability to use a firearm in a crisis — the target will certainly not patiently wait for you to unlock your weapon.

The advantages of a firearm must be reviewed with professionals who can help the victim decide whether that is the best way to go, and, if it is decided that it is beneficial, they can help one learn how to handle the firearm. In addition to the question of firearms, getting a dog can be beneficial. Carrying a mace canister should be considered, particularly if there is an air horn included. A car phone is of great help. Not only are portable phones important to ensure safety, but they are also crucial to establish contact with telephone company security so that calls can be traced where identifying information is not readily available. If this is done, even though calls may come from a phone booth, if there is a pattern of using the same phone booth, it is possible to apprehend the caller because a stakeout can be established.

The victim should make sure to maintain optimum health by getting rest and good nourishment. It cannot be emphasized enough that the victim should look for sources of either group or individual therapeutic support in terms of a mental health setting, either public or private.

One caution in particular should be taken, and that is not to threaten the stalker or seek retaliation of any kind, such as vandalizing the stalker's car. The victim should not threaten to kill a stalker. The best remedy is always a legal one. The computer and the police can be the best forms of retaliation.

It is important for the victim to strive for an emotional position where the stalker cannot arouse fear of death or ruling his life. The victim has to become action-oriented as suggested above with law enforcement, keeping records and looking for witnesses. Both criminal and civil legal issues should be explored.

Personal Safety and Security Training

Self-defense is an issue raised by Michelle Taylor (1997), but, again, there are pros and cons to the issue of having an armed victim. If at all possible, it would be best to have an armed executive protection specialist who is familiar with safety plans and whose skills will protect the victim. Stalkers do not always react well to temporary restraining orders, because they are tangible evidence of rejection. It will be important that victims be fully prepared to cooperate with the police, or efforts to protect them will be unsuccessful. The victim has to understand that the possibility of harm is great and personal, and that no useful purpose is served by interfering or failing to cooperate with any police agency involved.

Victim Assistance

Conspicuously missing from most papers and books dealing with stalkers are concern and guidelines for the role of the psychotherapist or specific psychiatric treatment. According to Joseph Davis (1997), his research on predatory stalkers, victimology, victim trauma from stalking, threat assessment, and case management suggests that stalking victims need to share their fears with someone who understands stalker conduct. Part of that sharing has to involve a therapist who is familiar with stalking and knows that victims suffer anything from a general or basic fear of harm.

Davis (1997) also suggests that stalking victims function with a diminished or decreased quality of life involving a host of psychosocial stressors; and that these accumulating stressors imposed on their life from the relentless pursuit from a stalker usually involve some aspect of acute stress syndrome or PTSD. The fears that come from a stalking pursuit will interfere with being able to experience pleasure, sleep, eating, sex, and freedom to leave one's home. Furthermore, Davis (1997) feels that a victim frequently become agoraphobic, irritable, angry, and resentful of not being able to strike back against someone who places his or her life in real or perceived danger (also see Chapter 14 by Collins and Wilkas, this book).

In contrast to many cases of psychotherapy, a professional treating a stalking victim must keep in mind that he/she may have to ensure the victim's feeling of security by leaving instructions with the office answering service that he/she be contacted at any hour regarding a change in the victim's state of mental health. Medications may be required to make it possible for the victim to survive either marked anxiety states or depression. The therapist should be familiar with the client's security arrangements and who to contact to get information in the event that he/she needs to be updated. Therapists may find it necessary to walk a patient to her car from a therapeutic appointment. Stalkers are discouraged by an unfamiliar person who is close to the victim.

If threats are coming from a prisoner, it would be important to network with someone who can contact, for example, the investigative division of the California Department of Corrections (CDC), since a prisoner's threat in itself constitutes a crime and will add more time to be served to the perpetrator's sentence.

Where to Get Help and Support

In the opinion of this author, it would be helpful to set up an 800 number, such as 1-800-ALERT98, for persons who are being stalked to call for information. In that way, the appropriate steps to follow would be readily available to victims. For this to be launched on a national level would, of course, require funding.

Ms. Sylvia Hayes, herself a stalker survivor in 1994, became active with an organization called *Stalker, Incorporated*. She became host of a live call-in radio program entitled, "The Spotlight on Safety Show," airing weekly on Station WERE in Cleveland, Ohio.

Her program offers advice on a local level to citizens of Ohio. The author doubts that a national radio show would be useful except to teach by example. In addition, whoever is handling the show should be familiar with laws regarding stalking, the advisability of firearms, and each state's law regarding personal restraining orders.

An alternative plan would be the promotion for statewide programs throughout the country so that local resources could be utilized. To follow the local- or state-level plan, an advisory board could be formed including mental health personnel familiar with stalking crimes, attorneys familiar with the law, and a judge who is familiar with sentencing guidelines. If an abuse center or safe home becomes a part of the program, then those who run them should be on the advisory board, i.e., spousal abuse shelters.

Conclusion

Characteristics of stalkers and victims were reviewed and practical measures of dealing with the interaction between these people were discussed. Psychological or psychiatric case management techniques and treatment considerations were also discussed, along with security measures.

Bibliography

Danto, B. L. (1990). *Prime Target.* Philadelphia: The Charles Press Publishers.

Davis, J. (1997). Personal communication, Threat Assessment and Stalker–Victim Case Management Issues, San Diego, CA.

Dietz, P., Matthews, D., Martell, D., Stewart, T., Hrouda, D., and Warren, J. (1991a). Erotomania, *New Statesman and Society*, 3, 31–32.

Dietz, P., Matthews, D., Van Duyne, C., Martell, D., Parry, C., Stewart, T., Warren, J., and Crowder, J. (1991b). Threatening and otherwise inappropriate letters to Hollywood celebrities, *Journal of Forensic Sciences*, 36(1), 185–209.

Schaum, M. and Parrish, K. (1995). *Stalked.* New York: Pocket Books.

Taylor, M. (1997). Personal communication, Stalker-Victim Case Management, Risk Assessment, and Security Issues, Los Angeles, CA.

Zona, M. A., Sharma, K. K., and Lane, J. C. (1993). A comparative study of erotomanic and obsessional subjects in a forensic sample, *Journal of Forensic Sciences*, 38(4), 894–903.

About the Contributing Author

Bruce L. Danto, M.D.

Bruce Danto, M.D., an early pioneer in the field of forensic psychiatry and the psychology of stalking, passed away in Fullerton, California in 1998 before his chapter was published.

Dr. Danto was the author of numerous papers, chapters, and books on criminal and forensic psychiatry. A fellow and diplomate in forensic psychiatry in several national organizations, he along with Dr. Thomas Streed co-operated *Death Investigation International*, a private agency devoted and dedicated to the investigation of equivocal death. Prior to his death, Dr. Danto appeared with Dr. Joseph Davis, Dr. John E. Douglas, Dr. Thomas Streed, and Dr. Jack Annon as a member of a 3-day "Mind Hunter Panel" that discussed many cases that included elements of stalking and stalkers. Dr. Danto authored this unpublished manuscript and provided a copy to the editor.

Dr. Danto's wife, Joan Danto, MSW, L.C.S.W., who currently operates a private psychotherapy outpatient practice in Fullerton, California, has kindly granted permission to publish one of his last remaining works on stalking and stalker behavior. This book, in part, is posthumously dedicated to the memory of Dr. Bruce L. Danto: mentor, colleague, and friend.

PART VI

Stalkers and Their Victims: Case Management Strategies

Case Management Strategies Regarding Stalkers and Their Victims: A Practical Approach from a Private Industry Perspective

13

JO ANN UGOLINI
KIM KELLY

Contents

Introduction

This chapter focuses on a practical approach to managing cases of unwanted pursuit, more commonly referred to as "stalking." The opinions and practices presented here have been derived from over a decade of experience managing such cases in the ever-growing sea of private industry "experts." The mere fact that an entire industry exists, complete with books and conferences dedicated to the topic, and that law enforcement and prosecutorial divisions are developed to deal solely with this issue is proof of the seriousness and complexity surrounding this not-so-unique behavior. The following information reflects an unconventional private industry spin on case management not generally afforded law enforcement or clinical practitioners, who are often limited in resources and by professional obligations and duty.

The first section of the chapter addresses the authors' theory of effective case management. The practical application of this theory will follow.

Case Management Theory

Frankly, the most effective way to manage stalking cases is to prevent them. This is best accomplished through education in prevention and early identification. Private citizens, professionals, public figures, corporations, and government agencies should be encouraged to engage in practices designed to detect, deter, and prevent stalking cases. Such practices might include confidentiality of personal information both personally and professionally, effective access control, and employee policies, procedures, and training addressing inappropriate behaviors and the importance of reporting it. Early identification becomes paramount in cases of stalking. Steps taken or not taken to manage a case early on can greatly impact the course and outcome of the case. Providing training and implementing policies that encourage early reporting, therefore, are important to case management. Once a case rises to a level that requires a case manager's involvement, the likelihood of it being resolved to the satisfaction of all involved parties is slim.

Prior to making recommendations in a case, a case manager must first completely understand the case and the dynamics involved. Such an understanding can only come from a thorough evaluation. An evaluation should address three important areas: the pursuer's intent, the pursuer's situation and ability to carry out harm, and the victim's vulnerability. Since danger-ousness is situational, it stands to reason that a death row inmate writing menacing letters to the President of the United States is of less concern then an angry former employee who recently acquired a weapon.

Developing a Working Relationship with the Client

Next, the case manager should be committed to developing a working rela-tionship with the client (victim). This begins with determining the goals of the victim(s) with regard to the outcome of the case. Equally as important, however, is to make certain that these goals are in line with your goals as case manager and the goals of other involved agencies. Though it seems the goal of victim safety/prevention of violence would be obvious, this is not always the case. White and Cawood (1998) as well as others have called for a better understanding among all parties involved of "the goals, perspectives, tools, and biases of these agencies or entities … as well as understanding how to communicate and collaborate on case issues and management." White and Cawood also call for "teamwork" and "a shared view of a case."

Common Goals of Case Management

Common goals for victims include: personal/family safety, peace of mind, making the pursuer "go away," stopping the pursuer's intrusive behavior, punishing the pursuer, "fixing" the pursuer, and avoiding liability/lawsuits.

Case manager goals generally coincide with the way they measure success, such as client satisfaction/safety (private industry), arrests (law enforcement), convictions (prosecutors), and improved mental health (clinicians).

Conflicts in Managing Cases

The occasional conflict between the victim's and case manager's goals tends to cloud and complicate the true essence of our work. A client who is inter-ested in punishing his pursuer will certainly balk at a recommendation to "do nothing," as will a corporate client hoping to avoid a wrongful termina-tion lawsuit when you recommend immediate termination, or when you suggest an unorthodox severance package.

The overall goal of a case manager should center on violence prevention. Assuming that the pursuer intends to physically harm the victim, physical violence cannot occur if the intended victim is not available to the pursuer. It would then follow that a case manager should undertake efforts to move the victim (figuratively and sometimes literally) away from the pursuer. Because victims often resist such actions, efforts are often turned to keeping the pursuer away from the victim through restraining orders, arrests, and incarceration. Each of these responses by their nature, however, can create an environment contrary to our goal. This is not to imply, however, that these measures are not warranted in some cases.

An experienced case manager knows that there are only two absolutes in case management: (1) Cases are dynamic and (2) though cases may seem similar and have similar circumstances, all cases are different and should be treated as such.

Case Illustration

To illustrate this point, consider a scenario whereby you are a "collision prevention expert" called in to prevent two trains from colliding. Each time you are called in, the situation is the same (two objects on a collision course), though the circumstances will likely be different. Would you reasonably offer the same solution such as derailing one train in favor of the other, for example, in every situation? What if one train hadn't even left the station yet? The prudent professional would more likely first conduct an evaluation of the situation to determine factors such as the location, speed, and direction of each train, their proximity to each other, any points between the two where you could divert one or the other train, the makeup of the cargo, and the likelihood of stopping both trains short of impact.

Once an evaluation is completed, you would likely begin to apply "best case scenario" strategies based on the seriousness of the situation. Unless the situation is urgent and the collision deemed unavoidable, it is not reasonable or responsible to use extreme measures before exhausting your options for diverting or stopping the objects without damage to either.

Focus on Situation, Not Controlling Behavior

Similarly, case management should focus on managing situations rather than controlling behavior. These efforts should focus on factors associated with the pursuer's intent, their situation, and the victim's vulnerability. If a threat assessment professional is called to evaluate a case, it is likely that the intent of the pursuer has not yet escalated to the point of unavoidable violence. Cases in which the pursuer has the initial intention to harm the victim are given other distinctions like sexual assault, assassination, and serial killings. Perpetrators of these types of crimes seldom intentionally make their presence and intentions known to the victim in advance.

The Evaluation of Stalker Motive and Intent

Based on their research, Wright et al. (1996) suggested that there are four main motives for stalking behaviors: infatuation, possession, anger/retaliation, and other (cases where the motive is unclear). Motivation, or intent, is best determined through evaluation of pursuer communications/behaviors and interviews of the victim and involved parties. Assessment of the seriousness of the situation (how close to impact the trains are) will dictate a case manager's course of action. In his book, *The Gift of Fear*, Gavin de Becker (1997) discusses the importance of evaluating the risk of violence by seeing the situation from the pursuer's perspective, especially on issues pertaining to four areas: justification, alternatives, consequences, and ability. Does the pursuer feel justified in using violence? Does the pursuer perceive any alternatives to violence to accomplish his goal? Are the consequences acceptable or even favorable? Does the pursuer feel he has the ability to successfully use violence? A case manager must be able to view the situation from the perspective of the pursuer to ensure an accurate evaluation.

Ongoing Monitoring of the Case

Case managers must continually monitor pursuer communications for evidence of changes or escalations in intent. Meloy (1997) proposes that there are certain events he terms "dramatic moments" in cases when the stalker, feeling humiliated or shamed, becomes enraged — increasing the risk of violence. Case managers should be constantly aware that their recommendations could actually perpetuate these "dramatic moments."

Knowing and continually monitoring a pursuer's intentions, then, is crucial to successful case management. This is why, in most cases, it is ill-advised to cut off all avenues for a pursuer to communicate to a victim. For example, an inmate's letters to a public figure may be disturbing, but they are not, in themselves, harmful. In fact, they are a valuable source of information about the inmate's intentions, situation, plans, etc. If and when that inmate talks of being released and traveling to see the public figure (because they will tell you), efforts can be taken to prevent the successful encounter — not to stop the letters. Inevitably the pursuer will continue to write and provide information about the failed encounter as well as future plans.

If managed properly, communications are more effective than investigative techniques for keeping track of pursuers and their intentions. They are also valuable evidence. It is imperative, however, that pursuers *not* receive a response or any indication that their communications are reaching the victim, unless that response is required by law (as in the case of a legal document).

Post-Intimate Case Management of Stalkers

In the case of post-intimate stalking cases, the stalking behavior is born out of the need to control the victim. These pursuers control the victim through fear and disruption of the victim's life (Hall, 1997). Because pursuer's communications such as letters and phone calls often do serve to frighten and annoy victims, case managers should work to reduce their impact on the victim, not eliminate them.

For example, a practitioner can recommend that a victim arrange to have a new phone line installed and move the existing line to an automatic voice-mail system. This allows the pursuer to continue to call, without the victim having anxiety and fear about answering the telephone. To further reduce this anxiety, the practitioner or a friend can frequently review and properly document the messages, so the victim does not have to. I've managed cases where a pursuer sent hundreds — even thousands — of disturbing communications to a celebrity without ever trying to make face-to-face contact. The impact on the celebrity was minimal because he was not exposed directly to the disturbing content.

A Pursuer's Situation and Ability to Carry Out Harm

Your investigation and review of the communications should have provided at least some historical and current information (or lack thereof) that gives you a fairly clear picture of the pursuer's current living situation. If not, it is important to devise ways to obtain this information in cases where your client is more vulnerable to potential harm and the risk is high. Key information to obtain includes the pursuer's location and proximity to the client, mobility, stability, family and social relationships, knowledge of the client's environment and schedule, and possession of weapons. A case manager should look for any significant changes in these areas and continue to closely monitor them. Any change that indicates degradation, for example, or appears to be an effort by the pursuer to get closer to the client should be considered significant.

Some practitioners believe one way to dissuade pursuers is to visit them at their places of employment, thereby embarrassing and humiliating them or making their behavior known to their employers. This tactic wrongfully assumes that the pursuer is reasonable enough to discontinue the pursuit in fear of losing his job. The unfortunate result is that often the pursuer either quits or is terminated from his employment and now has many more hours to concentrate on his stalking of the person who "ruined his life." Remember our goal is to create distance between the pursuer and the pursued.

Accordingly, a case manager should take steps to "prop up" a pursuer at all stages of a case — even during a court hearing. Focus should remain on the pursuer's inappropriate behavior, not on the pursuer personally. In the case of an angry former employee, the case manager can assist in helping him move on to other employment by utilizing outplacement services, for example. A mentally ill pursuer might be directed to a local shelter or an organization that will assist him in obtaining needed services. A creative case manager can find great ways to redirect pursuers without, where necessary, ever being linked to the client — which is imperative.

Reducing Targeted Victim Vulnerability

This is the area where a case manager can be most effective. Victims should first be encouraged to educate themselves on the dynamics of these cases and their responsibilities in managing them. Again, you should take time to ensure you have a shared goal for the outcome. Victims should be apprised of the results of your evaluation and all possibilities for managing the case, including those that the threat assessment professional recommends and why.

Williams et al. (1996) discussed the need for law enforcement agencies to make clear their limitations with regard to providing protection, whereby reducing their liability and preventing a victim's false sense of security. Private industry professionals assume much more liability and must be diligent in documenting all information and recommendations provided to a client. Clients must also be informed of possible risks associated with each case management option.

Work to Improve the Client's Situation

Next, efforts should be undertaken to improve the client's situation, making them less vulnerable to the pursuer. These efforts will include both physical security enhancements as well as changes in behavior. Though practitioners should always make "best case scenario" recommendations, we must also be prepared to remain flexible enough to work with clients who, for economic reasons, are not able to implement the ideal changes.

Depending on the seriousness of the case and your evaluation of the client's vulnerability, physical security recommendations might include improved access control at the home and, if applicable, the workplace. Because victims are frequently pursued (and attacked) at the workplace, it is pertinent that appropriate staff are all made aware of the situation and are involved in aspects of the management process. Victims are often reluctant, however, to take this step out of fear of losing their job.

Developing an Early Warning System

Issues of Victim Vulnerability

A system for early warning of visitors and possible breaches of home security are also valuable. This can be accomplished in a variety of ways including an advanced security system, watchful neighbors, or even dogs.

Victims are most vulnerable when in transition from one place to another (e.g., the house to the car, the parking lot to the door of the workplace, outside the courthouse, etc.). Practitioners should work with victims to first increase their awareness of these situations and then to create plans for making them safer. For instance, since a pursuer knows the victim will be appearing at his court hearing, efforts should be undertaken to have the victim arrive and depart the facility through a non-public area at an unsuspected time. If possible, similar arrangements should be made at the workplace with the victim's schedule, parking, and entry/departure. Plans should also be discussed for the victim getting safely into and out of the residence and other frequented locations.

Managing Victim Fear

Managing victim fear often presents a case manager with his or her greatest challenge. By the time you become involved in the case, the pursuer has engaged in a lengthy assault on the victim's psyche. In fact, victims often believe the pursuer to have extraordinary abilities or inside links to databases of information. This belief often results from the fact that the pursuer seems to always be able to get the victim's new telephone number or address. Or, the pursuer always seems to know the victim's schedule, where he or she has been or what he or she was wearing.

Victims also experience a variety of psychological repercussions such as insomnia, depression, anxiety, stress, feelings of futility, and helplessness. Though the incidence of violence in stalking cases is, statistically speaking, low, the damage experienced both personally and economically due to these psychological factors can be extensive.

Traumatic Stress from Stalking

Victim feelings of depression, ongoing stress, and helplessness are exacerbated when they get little or no support from family, friends, employers, and, sometimes, law enforcement and other agencies. Validating a victim's feelings is an important step in case management. To reduce anxiety, a case manager should educate the victim on ways pursuers obtain information and use it to make the victim feel powerless. Victims need to be shown that, though it takes time and much effort, these situations can improve and even be resolved (see also Chapter 14 by Collins and Wilkas, this book).

Working with victims also requires a certain level of trust. You will be recommending actions that may seem contrary to what they feel is appropriate. If they do not trust you, they will likely disregard or ignore some of the more difficult-to-implement suggestions. One way to develop trust is by thoroughly explaining to them what they can expect to happen with each step. For example, if you recommend the victim cut off all contact with her former boyfriend you must explain to her that it is very likely that he will cycle through a myriad of behaviors to incite a response such as pleading, claims of needing help, anger, intimidations, and threats. Once victims become better educated regarding the pursuer's manipulative behavior they tend to become more confident in dealing with it.

Victims most certainly have anxiety about face-to-face encounters with the pursuer. Case managers should take time to work with the victim to develop and practice plans to deal with a variety of possible scenarios. Because victims sometimes have the belief that the pursuer is omnipotent, it is helpful to have them enroll in some type of self-defense class.

The best type of class includes practice in real-life scenarios using full-contact apparatus. Victims also benefit from practicing verbal skills in confrontational situations. For some, this type of training can be life-changing.

It is important to point out that some victims of stalking respond more aggressively toward the stalker despite being educated about the likely negative repercussions of this stance. They often take an aggressive attitude and refuse to make any changes or behavior modifications — other than perhaps obtaining and carrying a firearm. These individuals respond to threats with counter-threats that can quickly escalate the situation. In my experience, these situations have been resolved in unfavorable ways. Even if a victim comes around to understanding the negative impact of this approach the mere fact this aggressive behavior was initiated has already raised the stakes.

Putting Theory into Practice

Practical Applications

There are essentially a finite number of options available to a case manager for dealing with cases of inappropriate pursuit. Differences, as well as controversies, in management styles generally come from the way these same options are applied and when.

The authors have listed the most commonly considered options below and organized them into category according to who would actively be involved in the action.

Victim Responses

- No detectable response/continued monitoring and documentation
- Direct confrontation to dissuade further contact
- Indirect confrontation (by a friend or family member)
- Return of written communications (unopened)
- Change of habits/behaviors to improve safety/avoid contact
- Relocation/"go into hiding"
- Conduct countersurveillance

Local Law Enforcement Remedies

- Police warnings/interview
- Anti-stalking laws
- Terrorist threat laws
- Telephone harassment laws
- Harassment laws
- Trespass laws
- Threat trespass laws
- Domestic violence/assault
- Emergency protective orders
- Release notification agreement
- Violations of parole/probation/court orders

Federal Law Enforcement Remedies

- Postal Service violations (threatening mail/pornography)
- Anti-stalking statute

Civil Remedies

- Stalking tort
- Corporate/individual restraining orders

Mental Health Agencies

- Involuntary psychiatric evaluations/holds
- Tarasoff warnings (duty-to-worn)
- Release notification agreement

As stated previously, each case should be evaluated and managed individually based on the circumstances presented at the time of a practitioner's involvement. With this in mind, it would be irresponsible to offer specific guidelines for implementing the above options. Considering the theories presented earlier in the chapter the authors will, however, make general comments about some of the options and situations where they have proven effective or ineffective.

Victim Responses and Support

In nearly all types of inappropriate pursuit, it is recommended that the victim cut off communication with the pursuer. This can be the most important and difficult step for a victim and practitioner to accomplish, especially when the victim shares custody of children with her pursuer or has been in a relationship with the pursuer for a long time. In these cases, the recommendation to cease communication often causes escalation of stalking behavior. As a result, victims sometimes feel the recommendation is ineffective and quickly responds to the pursuer. This response invariably takes a case back to square one.

Direct or indirect confrontation of the pursuer either by the victim or a representative is rarely an effective management tool. If the pursuer is reasonable enough to be talked out of his behavior, he would likely not be acting that way or would stop on his own. Because this option is more likely to worsen a case then help it, it should almost never be considered.

The value of continued monitoring and documentation of communications as well as changing the victim's situation and behaviors has already been discussed. These options not only serve to reduce the victim's vulnerability, but also assist in successful law enforcement intervention should it be warranted. They also carry very little risk of worsening the case.

Sometimes victims want or need to relocate. In those cases, the victim should receive recommendations for safeguarding the new residence address and telephone number. Generally speaking, however, victims often see relocation as undesirable, impractical, and costly. It should, however, be seriously considered in high-risk cases.

Countersurveillance of the pursuer is also a costly and, frankly, often unreliable option. If detected, it too can worsen a case dramatically. For this reason, it is only advisable for general information gathering (i.e., how the pursuer is spending his day) or, in serious cases, as a small part of a heightened facility access control program.

Local Law Enforcement Options

Victims and law enforcement agencies alike have historically been frustrated in dealing with inappropriate pursuers. Until the passing of anti-stalking laws, law enforcement agencies were limited in their ability to respond to stalking behaviors, which were not technically illegal. Generally speaking, law enforcement training is focused on responding to and investigating crime, not preventing it; hence the designation "law enforcement," not "crime prevention." In fact, the constitution guarantees our right to freely express ourselves within the confines of the laws. Stalkers, being of generally high intelligence, know their rights and use the system to their advantage.

In the absence of an actionable crime, law enforcement agencies attempt to assist victims by making contact with the pursuer and/or making suggestions to victims that will make police intervention possible (such as restraining orders). The Los Angeles Police Department's (LAPD) Threat Management Unit (TMU) has suggested their data illustrate that these interventions are effective in deterring stalkers (Williams et al., 1996).

It is our experience, however, that for every successful case involving some type of intervention, there are at least ten times that number of successes where police interventions were not applied. The opposite, however, is not true. Many cases which resulted in violence contained some type of police intervention or restraining order. This isn't to imply that the intervention *caused* the violence, only that it didn't necessarily prevent it.

Research on Stalking

In their *Third Annual Report to Congress* (U.S. Department of Justice, 1998), the Office of Justice Planning (OJP) reported that 19% of former stalking victims they polled believed their stalking ceased because they moved. Another 18% stated the belief their stalking ceased because the pursuer found a new love interest. Conversely, only 9% said they believed the stalking ceased because the stalker was arrested, 1% said the stalking stopped because the stalker was convicted of a crime, and less than 1% said the stalking stopped because they obtained a restraining order.

This finding supports the goal of creating distance, rather than controlling the pursuer's behavior (which, in the absence of an actionable crime, is what police interventions attempt to accomplish).

Restraining Orders and Case Management Issues

The controversy surrounding the use of restraining orders as a case management tool is pervasive among practitioners. Hall (1997), who does an excellent job of reviewing the merits as well as the limitations of restraining orders, points out that their true downfall lies in their lack of enforcement and the message that is then conveyed to the pursuer. Restraining orders also take us farther away from our goals of putting distance between the pursuer and the pursued and maintaining the pursuer's dignity. They also convey a certain type of vulnerability on the part of the victim.

Practitioners should carefully consider the use of restraining orders as a management tool. Victims often don't realize that obtaining one involves a civil lawsuit that will cost them money and require them to appear in court with the pursuer. If the victim decides to obtain a restraining order, she (or he) should be advised of the inherent risks before, during, and immediately after the court proceedings, as well as cautioned about being lulled into a false sense of security. It is our experience that restraining orders are most often effective and less risky when issued as a condition of probation in connection with a criminal conviction.

Other possible law enforcement interventions involve violations of a number of applicable laws, most of which are listed above (they may vary, however, from state to state). Practitioners should familiarize themselves with the elements for proving each and consult with local police and prosecutors to determine the likelihood for convictions. Arrests and convictions for trespassing are generally effective in sending a message to the pursuer that the victim will not tolerate intrusive behavior, but also in demonstrating a course of conduct and securing a stay-away order as a condition of probation.

Generally speaking, practitioners should consult with law enforcement and prosecutors in advance of pursuing criminal charges to determine the likely outcome of a proposed course of action. This approach requires the multi-agency collaboration and cooperation discussed earlier. Since we have already noted that a successful prosecution does not necessarily mean the end of the stalking behavior, the practitioner should weigh the benefits against the possible risks.

If a pursuer is incarcerated the practitioner should consider efforts to negotiate a release notification agreement with the facility. Caution should be exercised in cases where the incarceration has nothing to do with the victim since you run the risk of the pursuer learning of your contact with the facility. One can imagine the damage that can be caused if an inmate with a "love" interest in a celebrity learns that the celebrity made contact with his facility, especially if prior to your contacting the facility, your client was only one of several of the inmate's "love" interests.

Federal Law Enforcement Options

Though the passing of the federal anti-stalking statute gives practitioners a valuable option, it has been my experience that federal law enforcement agencies suffer from the same limitations as local law enforcement. Again, merits of a case should be discussed prior to getting their official involvement.

Mental Health Agency Options

Involving mental health agencies in case management is often a challenge. Since it is difficult to get a pursuer to voluntarily commit him- or herself for evaluation, case managers must have a close working relationship with mental health providers at local jails, county mental health facilities, shelters, and other related agencies. Though involuntary psychiatric holds and treatment generally last for a short period, they can be effective in de-escalating a pursuer at a critical point in the case and/or give a victim time to make some emergency changes in her situation. As with law enforcement, clinicians are becoming more and more educated and experienced in dealing with stalking behaviors.

Corporations can also make use of their employee assistance programs to work with both victims and pursuers. Victims or a practitioner acting on their behalf should make known to any clinician treating the pursuers their desire to be notified of information that might relate to their safety (as per the *Tarasoff* decision).

Conclusion

The recurrent message throughout this chapter is that stalking cases are most effectively managed by the continued monitoring and management of factors; that is, those factors that surround the stalking-victim situation rather than trying to control the pursuer's (stalker's) behavior. Successful case management also depends on a shared goal between all parties of interest involved and by exercising only management options that can take you closer to that goal.

In summary, the authors would like to make one final point, which, to our knowledge, has not been addressed in the professional literature. Case managers should also be aware of the long- and short-term effects of this type of work on them.

The negative effects of repeated exposure to high-stress situations in other professions has been well documented. The responsibility inherent in making high-stakes predictions, not to mention the regular interaction with individuals who are facing tremendous challenges, takes its toll. An additional burden is the requirement to, in a sense, work the same hours the pursuer "works."

Case managers must realize the impact this work can have on their emotional and physical health and undertake efforts to minimize that impact. A closer look at the tragic circumstances of our fallen colleagues should be enough incentive for the experts in "prediction" to pause and take notice of their own physical and mental wellness.

Bibliography

de Becker, G. (1997). *The Gift of Fear: Survival Signals That Protect Us from Violence.* Boston: Little, Brown.

Hall, D. (1997). The Victims of Stalking. Unpublished doctoral dissertation, The Claremont Graduate School, Claremont, CA.

Meloy, J. R. (1997). The clinical risk management of stalking: someone is watching over me, *American Journal of Psychotherapy,* 51(2) Spring, 174–189.

U.S. Department of Justice (July 1998). Stalking and Domestic Violence: The Third Annual Report to Congress under the Violence Against Women's Act. Office of Justice Programs, Washington, D.C.: U.S. Government Printing Office.

White, S. G. and Cawood, J. S. (1998). Threat management of stalking cases, in J. R. Meloy (Ed.), *The Psychology of Stalking: Clinical and Forensic Perspectives* (pp. 298–317). San Diego: Academic Press.

Williams, W. L., Lane, J. C., and Zona, M. (1996). Stalking and successful intervention strategies, *The Police Chief Magazine,* 104–106.

Wright, J. A., Burgess, A. G., Burgess, A., Laszlo, A. T., McCrary, G. O., and Douglas, J. E. (December 1996). A typology of interpersonal stalking, *Journal of Interpersonal Violence,* 11(4), 487–502.

About the Contributing Authors

Jo Ann Ugolini, M.B.A.

Jo Ann Ugolini, M.B.A. has over 12 years of experience in the field of threat assessment and risk management, having personally assessed and managed thousands of cases involving inappropriate pursuit. Ms. Ugolini spent the majority of her career with the office of Gavin de Becker, Inc., where she worked as assistant director of threat assessment and management and later as director of advanced training and artificial intuition systems.

She was a lead designer of many of Mr. de Becker's computer-assisted threat assessment software programs and was responsible for training representatives from *Fortune 500* companies and law enforcement officials at the federal, state, and local levels. Ms. Ugolini holds a Master of Business Administration degree (M.B.A.) and currently operates her own safety and privacy consulting business. Always dedicated to assisting and empowering victims, Ms. Ugolini offers consulting services to members of the general public affected by stalking at a significantly reduced rate through the Website: www.StalkingAssistance.com.

Kim Kelly, B.A.

Kim Kelly, B.A. was a federal agent for over 10 years specializing in crimes against the family (domestic violence and child physical and sexual abuse). In 1996, she was a national finalist in the prestigious Julie Y. Cross Award for Women in Federal Law Enforcement due to work in initiating legislation involving the registration of sex offenders on a federal level. She was also a member of The Violence Against Women Act Task Force, San Diego County Chapter. Over the last several years Ms. Kelly has worked on varying projects with Gavin de Becker, Inc., a prominent expert in the prediction of violence and best-selling author of *The Gift of Fear* (Little, Brown, 1997). She holds a Bachelor of Arts degree in behavioral science, with a minor in criminal justice, and has completed extensive master's level study in psychology.

Ms. Kelly is a member of the Stalking Strike Force and the American Professional Society on the Abuse of Children. She also developed, created, and manages the current Website: www.StalkingAssistance.com, a resource for individuals affected by the crime of stalking.

Stalking Trauma Syndrome and the Traumatized Victim

14

MELISSA J. COLLINS
MARY BETH WILKAS

Contents

Introduction

In this chapter, the authors propose that stalking trauma syndrome (STS) is a condition that can occur when a victim is subjected to repeated and persistent stalking behavior. In STS, a stalking victim experiences: (1) a cycle of crisis; (2) significant psychological effects, including helplessness and hopelessness, anxiety, depression, desperation, and loss of control as well as behavioral changes; and (3) recovery-based effective coping tools for stalking victims and their families.

Take a journey with the authors and vicariously observe and experience stalking behavior as it was once allowed in our American society ...

Observe an ex-boyfriend who, 2 years after an unpleasant end to a 1-year relationship, is still calling his former love 15 times a day and leaving her

0-8493-0811-9/01/$0.00+$1.50
© 2001 by CRC Press LLC

messages, writing her love letters and sending them to her daily, and delivering peach roses, her favorite flower, to her doorstep every week. *She must be flattered by all of the attention …*

Notice a former husband slashing the tires of his ex-wife's car, threatening in court to take their children away, and parking outside of her workplace every day, sometimes following her home. *It's a domestic situation, they will work it out …*

Watch a young woman fall into the delusional belief that a partner in a law firm, where she works as an assistant, is in love with her. See how she functions day-to-day as if they were a couple: she tells the other assistants of their "involvement," calls him at home and initiates intimate conversation, and begins using his surname as if it were hers. *But … she's just a secretary … she's harmless …*

That was then, but this is now. Such behavior is now considered criminal and falls under the crime of stalking. Stalking is when an individual intentionally and knowingly engages in repeated behavior directed toward another person, causing that person to fear for his or her safety or the safety of his or her immediate family. The behavior may or may not be accompanied by a direct or indirect threat. Although we are in a slow transition of acknowledging and treating stalking behavior as criminal, the public, advocates, and the criminal justice system are focusing on the issues and the momentum is building for change.

Stalking, Stalkers, and Their Victims

The appearance of stalking in our society is epidemic. In 1998, the U.S. Department of Justice (DOJ) released a report on "Stalking and Domestic Violence," including pages of compelling statistics about stalking in the United States. The following are some of those findings:

- Approximately 1.1 million women and 0.4 million men are stalked annually.
- An estimated 8% of women and 2% of men have been stalked at some time in their lives.
- 45% of female victims and 52% of male victims do not report their stalking to the police.
- 78% of victims are women and 87% of stalkers are men.
- Approximately 74% of stalking victims are between the ages of 18 and 39.
- Stalking cases last an average of 1.8 years. Cases involving intimate or former intimate partners last, on average, 2.2 years.

- Approximately 85% of stalking cases involve an intimate or previous intimate relationship between the stalker and the victim.
- Men are more likely to be stalked by strangers or acquaintances, 90% of whom are men. Women are significantly more likely to be stalked by an intimate or former intimate partner.

As of December 1999, all 50 United States and the District of Columbia have enacted anti-stalking laws. Anti-stalking laws vary greatly from state to state. For example, 26 states include "threatening the victim's immediate family," 2 states incorporate behavior referred to as "lying-in-wait," and 10 states address "stalking via electronic means" (National Center for Victims of Crime, 2000). States also vary on their criminal law provisions for stalking. In 32 states, stalking can be a felony on first conviction; in the other 18 states, stalking carries misdemeanor penalties for a first-time conviction, and repeat stalking is a felony in all but 2 of those states (U.S. Department of Justice, 1998).

Regardless of the differences existing in today's anti-stalking laws, after nearly two decades of effort, stalking is a crime, it is against the law, and tolerance for stalking behavior is declining. Despite all of the positive steps in the anti-stalking movement, there remains one inescapable element — the victim. Pappas (2000) concurs, adding that "even where attempts to criminalize stalking and to punish stalkers have been made, these efforts have often neglected the concerns of the victims of stalking" (p. 947). The ramifications of stalking behavior on the victim vary in each case. Nonetheless, stalking has a negative mental health impact on its victims (U.S. Department of Justice, 1998).

Stalking Trauma Syndrome

STS is a theory that can be related to post-traumatic stress disorder (PTSD), battered woman syndrome, and rape trauma syndrome; yet STS is a unique condition. According to the DSM IV-TR (American Psychiatric Association, 2000), the essential feature for PTSD is "the development of characteristic symptoms following exposure to an extreme traumatic stressor involving direct personal experience of an event that involves actual or threatened death or serious injury, or other threat to one's physical integrity" (p. 463).

Such traumatic events include military combat, natural or man-made disasters, and violent personal assaults. In STS, however, exposure to an extreme traumatic stressor is not a one-time, isolated event; rather, it can be a daily occurrence.

PTSD does not, in effect, recognize the consequences which spawn from the repeated and persistent victimization stalking presents. And, because stalking takes place in an uncontrollable environment, the unpredictability

of behavior bears even heavier on the victim. In other words, "events involving loss of control and violation of expectations for control have different
effects than do events that remind us of forces over which control was never
expected" (Baum et al., 1993, p. 279).

Lenore Walker's (1979) *The Battered Woman* contains two distinct elements:
a cycle of violence and symptoms of learned helplessness. The cycle of violence consists of three phases: tension-building phase, active battering phase,
and the calm, loving respite phase (Walker, 1979). STS posits a cycle of crisis,
rather than a cycle of violence. The cycle of crisis also includes three phases:
the crisis phase, the recovery phase, and the anticipation phase. In STS, there
is no active battering phase, but rather a crisis phase in which the victim
suffers repeated psychological trauma.

The element of learned helplessness in battered woman syndrome differs
from the element of helplessness in STS. Walker (2000) indicates that the
original meaning of learned helplessness was confused with being helpless.
She conveys that the intended meaning is "having lost the ability to predict
that what you do will make a particular outcome occur" (p. 116). Thus, when
a woman is repeatedly battered, yet unable to flee the traumatic situation
even when escape is apparent and possible, the result is learned helplessness.

A victim of battered woman syndrome is in a relationship with her abuser
and she actively tries to change the situation in order to stop the battering.
For example, a woman may attempt to have a perfect dinner ready, the house
clean, and the kids calmed down by the time her husband arrives home from
work. However, when the abuse persists, regardless of her efforts, and she is
continuously subjected to the cycle of violence, she loses the ability to predict
the success of her actions (Seligman, 1975) and learned helplessness ensues.

A victim of stalking, on the other hand, does not have an active relationship with the perpetrator and does not have the option of attempting to
behave a certain way in order to stop the perpetrator's actions. Furthermore,
he/she is subjected to an uncontrollable environment where escape is neither
apparent nor possible; walking away is not an option. Thus, the victim's
helplessness stems from the lack of ability to do anything about the situation
on his or her own accord.

Rape trauma syndrome (Burgess and Holmstrom, 1974) is a theory that
specifies and describes the trauma that victims of rape experience. Burgess
and Holmstrom's (1974) "The Rape Trauma Syndrome" depicts two phases:
the acute phase and the reorganization phase. The acute phase, which ensues
immediately after the offense and can persist up to several weeks, is characterized by disorganization, including both impact reactions and somatic reactions; the reorganization phase is a continuum of lifestyle adjustments and
long-term chronic traumatic effects (Foa and Rothbaum, 1998).

Although several of the resulting behaviors of rape trauma syndrome are
similar to STS, there are three distinct differences in relating these two conditions.

First, rape is a one-time, isolated trauma, whereas stalking involves persistent and prolonged victimization. Second, like rape, stalking is about power and control. However, a stalker's desire for power and control is an ongoing pursuit the victim must endure.

Finally, in STS, the psychological effects are usually experienced by the victim both during and after the trauma. In rape trauma syndrome, the psychological effects are experienced solely after the trauma.

The Cycle of Crisis

Stalking is a crime like no other. The type of victimization present in stalking does not appear to have a definite beginning or a definite end. There is actually a pattern of events which materializes in stalking cases. It is our goal to unveil this pattern so that the victims, criminal justice system workers, and advocates can begin to identify how to treat the psychological conditions that a normal person faces when being stalked.

Stalking usually begins with one event that is characterized as unwanted behavior. However, the effects of this event eventually multiply. The stalker repeats the harassing and threatening behavior in order to reinforce the impact on the victim and to give the appearance of power and control. In this, the person being stalked begins to believe that the stalker actually does have control over every element of his or her life. Although some threats exhibited by the stalker may seem benign, it is difficult to distinguish credible threats from dangerous warnings. Unfortunately, sometimes a stalker's threats are valid, and in these cases the victim may have to take extreme measures to ensure his or her own physical and psychological safety.

In STS, there is a cycle of crisis that occurs whereby the stalking victim is subject to repetitive harassment, threats and/or threatening behavior, and violence perpetrated by the stalker. The cycle of crisis consists of three phases: the crisis phase, the recovery phase, and the anticipation phase. The victim is unable to effectively recover due to the recurrent nature of the victimization and anticipation of subsequent new events.

The very element that sets stalking apart from other crimes is that there is a repetition of offenses, rather than one isolated event. We see this pattern employed by the stalker in the following example:

> Bob, a former boyfriend of 6 years, is stalking Susan, a 40-year-old flight attendant. Susan ended the relationship because Bob became extremely jealous and verbally abusive when Susan left on trips for work. Now, he makes it quite clear that he cannot accept the fact that the relationship is over. In fact, it seems that he does not have the capacity to end a relationship in a healthy way. So, for the next 2 years, he sends her a dozen "black roses"

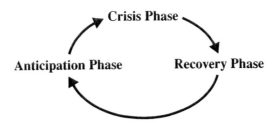

Figure 14.1 Cycle of crisis in stalking trauma syndrome.

every week. In addition, he calls her house, her friends, and even her parents. Bob sends e-mails containing threats that he will kill Susan. He occasionally spray paints her house, saying "you are a whore," or that "you will pay for this." Susan comes home from work to find broken windows and notes on her door. Bob shows up at her job, claiming that he is there on business, when he actually has no legitimate reason to be in the airport. He puts sugar in the gas tank of the car to destroy the engine. Susan expects something new to happen every day.

The recurrence of victimization taking place in the vignette is typical in stalking cases, although specific details and behaviors may vary. In stalking cases, the perpetrator engages in intimidation, physical aggression, and relentless threats of violence. The victims are forced to wait and try their best to handle the situation. However, they often feel like the situation is hopeless, that they are helpless against the attacks, and that the stalking will never end.

The routine that is created by the pattern of events induces the victim to remain in a state of heightened awareness for a longer period of time. This heightened state of awareness is present in STS through the cycle of crisis (see Figure 14.1). In this cycle, there is an initial crisis phase, which is prompted by the stalker's acts of harassment, pursuit, or attack. The crisis phase is followed by a short time of perceived peace, or the recovery phase. However, another strike is expected to follow shortly thereafter. We shall call the victim's anxiety or expectation of future attacks the anticipation phase. Here, the stalking victim tries to cope with what is occurring.

In Walker's (1979) cycle theory of violence, "the battered woman's attempts to cope with the minor battering incidents of the tension-building phase are the best she can do" (p. 58). In the cycle of crisis, the stalking victim uses effective or ineffective coping tools in response to the current incident or series of incidents perpetrated by the stalker. However, this cycle eventually precedes another crisis phase, or the next act perpetrated by the stalker.

The cycle of crisis is exemplified in the following vignette:

Paul is being stalked by Jimmy, a former co-worker. Paul was Jimmy's supervisor at a day-care center, and Jimmy feels vengeance because he believes that he was wrongfully fired and that Paul is responsible. Since then, Jimmy has become disruptive to Paul at work, and has tried to make it appear that Paul is a high-risk employee who should not work with children. Jimmy has attempted to cause problems in the office and link them to Paul. One day, Paul comes home to find a letter in his mailbox, which is threatening to notify management of a Website created by Jimmy to destroy Paul's reputation. This Website has nude photographs of Paul, and invites children to show up at his home address. These are not actual photographs of Paul; Jimmy has cropped a photo taken at an office Christmas party, and altered it by attaching Paul's profile to a nude photo of someone else. Nonetheless, it looks very real and could be damaging to Paul's reputation. Paul becomes disgusted, alarmed, feels a sense of extreme mistrust, and fears the loss of employment. He experiences the crisis phase. After he reads the letter, he goes in his house, tries to calms down, and attempts to make sense of what has occurred. This is a brief recovery phase. The next day, Paul spends the majority of time wondering what Jimmy will do next — will he show up at his job and post the Website on the employee bulletin board, as threatened in the letter? Paul cannot concentrate on any work project. He tries to cope with the situation. This is the anticipation phase of the cycle. However, nothing happens until the end of the day. When Paul returns home, he checks his computer and sees that Jimmy has left him 32 e-mail messages. These e-mail messages are all linked to the scandalous Website and have been forwarded to co-workers, his boss, and the parents of the children at the day-care center. Paul panics, begins to have shortness of breath, and suffers intense anxiety.

Here, he re-experiences the crisis phase.

"Stalking victims are subject to persistent, repetitive trauma, as opposed to most other victims of crime and victims of other traumatic events" (Mullen et al., 2000, p. 59). Stalking creates a scenario whereby each day there can be a new event. This reinforces the fact that the victim is forced to fear for his or her safety on a daily basis. Stalking victims often report a feeling of needing to continually look over their shoulder, wondering if the stalker will strike again. This existence of a cycle of crisis in which the stalking victim lives lends itself to the belief that the situation is unpredictable, uncontrollable, and that an end to the stalking is hopeless.

In case studies of stalking victims, Dziegielewski and Roberts (1996) have found that "most victims of stalking have been forced to encounter sustained abuse, which may end in serious and severe personal attack, resulting in the victim entering a crisis state" (p. 86). It is very difficult for the stalking victim to move beyond the crisis state because of the repetition of new attacks or crises.

Eventually, the recovery phase of the cycle of crisis is brief or non-existent. As the stalker becomes more relentless in his/her pursuit, the victim only experiences the crisis phase and anticipation phase again and again (see Figure 14.2).

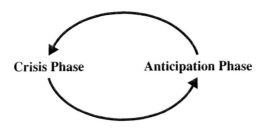

Figure 14.2 Cycle of crisis in stalking trauma syndrome without a recovery phase.

The target of stalking is unable to maintain peace, or enter the recovery phase because of the frequency of intrusive attacks and escalation of stalking. The victim's life is now consumed by constant alarm, fear, and hypervigilance. "The trauma associated with any type of victimization is magnified for those who continue to be threatened by their abuser. Victims who are stalked live in a constant state of fear" (Tellefsen and Johnson, 2000, p. 20).

Cycle of Violence in Stalking Cases

There are several elements that contribute to the duration of the cycle of crisis in a stalking case. The authors postulate that the most notable of these factors are (1) the length of a stalking episode, (2) the type of criminal justice response, (3) a victim's support system, and (4) presence of implied and/or direct threats. As we shall examine later in this chapter, these components may detract from the stalking victim's adaptive coping with the situation.

Because the normal length of a stalking episode is 1.8 years, the emotional effects that a victim experiences are prolonged (U.S. Department of Justice, 1998). If the length of a stalking case is extensive, we may assume that the victim has been subject to more frequent periods of crisis. For instance, in one scenario, a stalking victim may be pursued for 5 years before the victimization ends. This individual may believe that the pursuit will continue for another 5 years.

Thus, that victim may experience endless periods of crisis. In another case, the stalking may end after 3 months and the victim might be more adaptive because the cycle of crisis has been repeated less often. The prolonged length of any given stalking episode, combined with the lack of control, may add to the victim's belief that the events of the crime will continue forever.

The victim cannot always prove that all of what is occurring is actually the action of the stalker. For instance, a victim who receives harassing phone calls from a pay phone may find that it is difficult to prove that his/her stalker is the perpetrator. While the victim may not doubt that the calls are from his/her stalker, the criminal justice system requires a certain amount of proof for an investigation, an arrest, or a criminal court case to be effected. Social workers, police officers, and prosecutors may find it necessary to subject the victim to intensive questioning and seemingly place him/her under scrutiny. Unfortunately, this is usual and necessary in any criminal investigation.

Unlike other types of crime, it often seems like a victim of stalking assumes the role of proving his/her case against the stalker. Often, no one believes the victim. As a result, he/she may be questioned several times and begin to doubt him/herself. A consequence of this may be dropped charges, so that the victim does not have to endure more questioning and relive the trauma. As a result, the stalker may not fear the consequences of the victim's actions and may begin a more relentless pursuit. Like many other types of crime victims, at the time of intervention, the stalking victim is usually in crisis, and stalking has commonly escalated from being an annoyance, to being obsessional and dangerous (U.S. Department of Justice, 1998). Although a few phone calls may seem innocuous to an outsider, it is crucial that advocates, criminal justice system personnel, and others take the crisis state of a victim into consideration in order to minimize the impact of STS.

The support system that a victim has is intrinsic to his/her response and coping with the victimization. A network of family and friends that is supportive of the victim contributes to quicker recovery. A support system that minimizes the problem or blames the victim is a great deficit. In fact, "family and friends may also minimize the problem, which is often a contributory factor to an increased sense of isolation" (Bertrand, 1998, p. 1). They may even try to convince the victim that he/she is encouraging the behavior. As a result, the victim may disregard his/her own innate sense of fear, and place him/herself in more dangerous situations. Although all parties should consider the danger level involved, we suggest that the victim trust his/her instincts and refrain from self-doubt. While this is a difficult task, doubting oneself may become a contributing factor to feelings of helplessness and self-blame.

Stalking may involve implied or direct threats of violence. However, the trauma does not necessarily need to be an act of physical violence to affect the victim. "Even the threat of violence implicit in the actions of the stalker can disrupt major areas of the victim's life" (Harmon et al., 1998, p. 238). Examples of direct threats may include, "I will kill you," "You will pay for leaving me," or "I'm going to make you lose your job." In some cases the stalker employs the tactic of using implied threats. Implicit threats may communicate similar ideas that direct threats convey. For example, a perpetrator may elicit the same fearful response in a victim when saying "be careful driving tonight" as saying "I will run you off the road tonight." In this case, perhaps the perpetrator has run the victim off the road several times before, and the threat is understood although it is implied. In addition, the stalker may also have intimate knowledge of a victim's fears and therefore have no need to communicate a threat in a direct manner.

The impact on the victim's level of fear, however, remains the same in both instances. In fact, Mullen et al. (2000) found that many victims would have preferred a physical attack over the chronic psychological anguish.

Psychological Effects of Stalking on the Victim

To date, research in the field of stalking has largely been devoted to the psychiatric diagnoses, classification and typology, and threat level of a stalker. However, research on the psychological effects that stalking has on its victims is drastically limited (see Hall, 1998; Pathé and Mullen, 1997). Because stalking entails repeated victimization over a long period of time, the victim is compelled to fear for his/her safety, including the fear of serious bodily injury and death. Hall agrees that "Living in fear, especially over a prolonged duration of time, takes a toll on the quality of human life" (p. 136).

The authors have found the most common psychological effects suffered by victims to be helplessness, hopelessness, anxiety, desperation, and loss of control. All of these symptoms support the condition known as STS. Helplessness and the resulting hopelessness are the two key elements of STS. Many factors can contribute to this sense of helplessness, the most commonly reported ones being ineffective response from the criminal justice system, lack of resources, and a deficient support system.

In today's society, there is an assumption that we live in a fair and safe environment (Mullen et al., 2000), and that, if victimized by crime, we will be helped. For those victims that do reach out for assistance and are met with indifference, judgment, disbelief, condemnation, and neutrality, such expectations are hence extinguished. Along with being a victim of stalking comes a tremendous sense of vulnerability. Unfortunately, the notion of a stalking victim being treated poorly by the criminal justice system, not taken seriously by victim assistance organizations, and not believed by his or her own family and friends is not uncommon. Thus, with each effort being confronted with a virtual slap in the face, the victim ultimately feels a sense of helplessness.

Duration of Stalking Victimization

Stalking can last for weeks, months, even years. Thus, the prolonged exposure to persistent trauma combined with inefficient response from the criminal justice system, lack of resources, and a deficient support system results not just in a sense of helplessness, but ultimately in a sense of hopelessness. Because stalking creates an uncontrollable environment, those feelings are evermore exaggerated. The stalking victim must attempt to regain control in a seemingly hopeless situation. Many stalking victims state that they "just gave up trying to get help."

Others have reported taking measures on their own, like relocating or changing their names, but when their stalkers found them again and again, profound feelings of hopelessness and helplessness set in.

Anxiety, desperation, and loss of control are additional psychological effects to which a victim of stalking is exposed. Anxiety is a term used to describe a general nervousness an individual feels and can be attributed to a multitude of factors. In the case of stalking, a victim's anxiety is rooted in the unpredictability of behavior on the part of the stalker. This anxiety pervades the victim's life and affects his/her daily functioning.

Desperation, as applied to victims of stalking, is synonymous to a feeling of powerlessness. Victims frequently state that because they did not have solid proof that the perpetrator was, in fact, stalking them, the police repeatedly turned them away. In addition, they often hit a point where they feel they have exhausted the last of their resources and, thus, have no place left to turn. One victim conveyed, "I just walked around in a daze, praying the nightmare would end … I tried everything … I … I half hoped he would just kill me and get it over with."

One of the most commonly reported psychological effects of stalking is feeling a loss of control. One victim, who had been stalked for over a year by the brother of her former husband, remembers, "it did not matter what I said, what I did, who I talked to, where I turned … he just kept on and kept on and kept on." The sense of loss of control is even more profound when the stalker has opted to terrorize and traumatize the victim's family, especially children. One such victim, whose stalker wanted revenge for work lost 5 years prior, was overwhelmed by the loss of control he faced in not being able to protect himself or his family, all of whom had become targets of the stalker.

Victims of stalking also endure a multitude of behavioral changes, the most commonly reported being disruption in eating and sleeping habits, social isolation, and hypervigilence. In a study conducted by Pathé and Mullen (1997) of 100 stalking victims, sleep disturbance was most often experienced as nightmares and hyperarousal, and approximately half of their sample endured appetite disturbance in the form of weight loss. In addition, a large majority of the sample manifested hypervigilance, panic attacks, and jumpiness.

Not all victims experience all of the aforementioned psychological effects and behavioral changes, nor are they all experienced to the same degree. For example, some victims may experience symptoms only during the actual stalking episode. With each new strike, the victim can break down and may attest to feeling helpless, desperate, and a loss of control during the victimization. Yet, once the harassing behavior ceases, the victim can return to his/her safe environment and can begin to live his/her life as it was prior to the stalking experience.

On the other hand, there are victims who may throw themselves into survival mode during the active stalking behavior. They may only experience limited psychological effects and behavioral changes at the time. After the stalking subsides, however, the effects suffered by the victim may increase and feelings such as anxiety and loss of control may ensue.

It is most common that a victim reports experiencing psychological effects and behavioral changes both during and after the stalking ordeal. "When any kind of abuse stops, the damage doesn't just disappear, it becomes part of the person's baggage" (Greene, 1996, p. 1). Even though their perpetrators have presumably ceased to harass and terrorize them, many victims, even years later, still live in fear that their stalkers will find them and that their nightmares will begin all over again.

As one victim stated, "You know, my stalking ordeal ended several years ago … but, don't you think that I don't still look over my shoulder … to tell you the truth, I don't know what I would do if I saw my stalker again."

Coping with Stalking and Stalker Pursuit

We have discussed how stalking has an enormous impact on its victims. In response to this, stalking victims employ various coping mechanisms in order to manage their lives. However, this chapter suggests that the manner in which a victim copes with the situation has significant effects on his or her own survival, safety, and psychological consequence. Thus, the pertinent questions become: what are the effective coping tools that may assist victims in their time of crisis? What may we consider non-effective tools? And, how do victims overcome the cycle of crisis and STS and re-establish a sense of control in their lives?

The repetition of the cycle of crisis reinforces the belief that there is no end to stalking. The sheer recurrence of the cycle over long periods of time may cause a victim to feel as though he/she would like to retreat and hide. Furthermore, it challenges a sense of trust in others and justice in the world that the victim once possessed. "Stalking characteristically produces in the victim hypervigilance and a pervasive sense of mistrust in others" (Mullen et al., 2000, p. 58). The individual often displays behavioral changes such as loss of sleeping or eating. He or she may feel hopeless and helpless. The victim may feel a loss of control over his or her own life. It would seem likely that all stalking victims would retreat and give up, due to a perceived lack of solutions. Mullen et al. (2000) found that "over 75% of (stalking) victims reported feeling powerless in the face of repeated intrusions" (p. 60).

When faced with this crime, some victims do not overcome the cycle of crisis due to ineffective coping tools. We hypothesize that such coping mechanisms are more emotion-focused, or escape- and avoidance-focused (Lazarus and Folkman, 1984). An example of this type of coping tool may include a victim who stays at home, does not make others aware of the stalking, and uses drugs and alcohol to escape. While the stalking persists, the victim will continue to feel powerless and hopeless. The victim may also feel that his or her life will never be normal again. He or she perceives the cycle of crisis as unchangeable and inescapable. We suggest that the victim's perception of the situation affects how he or she will cope with future crises.

The crisis state of the victim is defined as the point at which the victim's coping mechanism fails (Dziegielewski and Roberts, 1996). The authors suggest that emotion-focused coping is an ineffective tool when dealing with the cycle of crisis present in STS. An individual who engages in such behavior may become clinically depressed.

Beck et al. (1987) found that the "pursuit of solutions" would be associated with lower levels of hopelessness. A depressed individual will not pursue solutions, and thus may put his safety at risk. Also, depressed individuals are more likely to retreat and less likely to seek assistance with the criminal justice system or an advocate. The key for stalking victims is to actively seek solutions and break the cycle of crisis. The victim must also believe that the stalking will end, seek professional assistance, and take tangible steps to ensure his/her own safety.

It is vital that the stalking victim can see that the situation will eventually come to an end. Once there is a shift in the victim's perception of the situation, he or she is able to begin active involvement and effective coping tools. Through this, the victim is able to regain a sense of control. It is notable that some effective coping measures may represent more aggressive steps toward safety. This may include criminal justice intervention, a change in employment, psychotherapy, relocation, or a change in identity. Mullen et al. (2000) found that more than a third of stalking victims in their study changed their job, school, or career in response to stalking, and that 40% moved their residence. These extreme measures are reflective of the level of interference that STS creates in a victim's life.

While effective coping tools will cease the cycle of crisis, they will also contribute to the victim's physical safety. The victim who notifies friends, family, and others of the situation gains a support system that will assist him in the time of crisis. Furthermore, the involvement of an advocate may help the victim to fight for his or her own survival, to believe that the victimization is not his or her fault, and to see alternatives and choices in each own particular situation.

The use of effective coping means may allow the victim to explore tangible and realistic safety plans, which, in turn, may deter the stalker. Some examples are getting a home security system, traveling with a companion, or

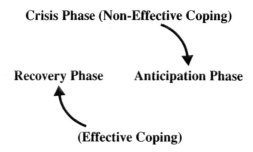

Figure 14.3 Cycle of crisis in stalking trauma syndrome with the effects of coping.

supplying a photo of the stalker to the security guards at the entrances of his/her place of business. In addition, the stalking victim may seek the assistance of the police department, file complaints against the stalker, or obtain a protective order against the stalker. While it is impossible for a stalking victim to directly control the actions of his or her assailant, we believe that action can be taken by the victim to increase personal safety.

The presence of these active steps assists the victim in a dual manner. First, the victim takes into account his or her safety. Second, the victim begins to see the situation as hopeful which affects the cycle of crisis (see Figure 14.3). Effective coping tools are present, which disrupt the progression of the cycle of crisis and enable the victim to make sense of what is occurring. The victim may then reorganize his/her life accordingly. Without effective coping tools, the anticipation phase of the cycle includes anxiety about the past crisis as well as anticipation of future harm. Even if any real threat of the stalker is removed, the victim may fear that future crisis is possible. The use of effective coping skills is resultant in a hopeful and definitive recovery phase.

The victim begins to feel that the stalker may be stopped by the involvement of the criminal justice system. The victim may succeed in reorganizing his or her life so the stalker cannot find him or her. He or she may also notify employers, friends, and family in order to regain a social support system. We hypothesize that these coping measures will minimize longer-term trauma to the victim as well as help ensure his or her safety. The person employing such strategies will become a survivor of stalking and STS will have less of an impact on the individual.

Bibliography

American Psychiatric Association (2000). *Diagnostic and Statistical Manual of Mental Disorders (4th edition-text revision).* Washington, D.C.: American Psychiatric Association.

Baum, A., Cohen, L., and Hall, M. (1993). Control and intrusive memories as possible determinants of chronic stress, *Psychosomatic Medicine, 55,* 274–286.

Beck, A. T., Rush, A. J., Shaw, B. F., and Emery, G. (1987). *Cognitive Therapy of Depression*. New York: Guilford Press.

Bertrand, D. (March 3, 1988). Battling the stalkers: activists and cops team up on awareness, *The Daily News*. p. QL11.

Burgess, A. W. and Holmstrom, L. L. (1974). The rape trauma syndrome, *American Journal of Psychiatry*, 131, 981-986.

Dziegielewski, S. F. and Roberts, A. R. (1996). *Crisis Intervention and Time-Limited Cognitive Treatment*. London: Sage Publications.

Foa, E. B. and Rothbaum, B. O. (1998). *Treating the Trauma of Rape: Cognitive-Behavioral Therapy for PTSD*. New York: Guilford Press.

Greene, C. (1996). Battered Women's Syndrome. Website: http://www.prisonactivist.org/ road/outside/cgreene-bws.html.

Hall, D. M. (1998). The victims of stalking, in J. Reid Meloy (Ed.), *The Psychology of Stalking: Clinical and Forensic Perspectives* (pp. 113–137). San Diego: Academic Press.

Harmon, R. B., Rosner, R., and Owens, H. (1998). Sex and violence in a forensic population of obsessive harassers, *Psychology, Public Policy, and Law*, 4(12), 236–249.

Lazarus, R. S. and Folkman, S. (1984). *Stress, Appraisal and Coping*. New York: Springer.

Meloy, J. R. (1998). *The Psychology of Stalking: Clinical and Forensic Perspectives*. San Diego: Academic Press.

Mullen, P. E., Pathé, M., and Purcell, R. (2000). *Stalkers and Their Victims*. Cambridge: Cambridge University Press.

National Center for Victims of Crime (2000). Laws and Public Policy: State Stalking Laws. Website: http://www.nvc.org/law/statestk.htm.

Pappas, D. M. (2000). Stopping New Yorkers' stalkers: an anti-stalking law for the millennium, *Fordham Urban Law Journal*, 27(31), 945–952.

Pathé, M. and Mullen, P. E. (1997). The impact of stalkers on their victims, *British Journal of Psychiatry*, 170, 12-17.

Seligman, M. E. P. (1975). *Helplessness: On Depression, Development, and Death*. San Francisco, CA: W. H. Freeman.

Tellefsen, L. J. and Johnson, M. B. (2000). False victimization in stalking: clinical and legal aspects, *New York State Psychologist Association Notebook*, 12(1), 20–25.

Tjaden, P. and Thoennes, N. (1998). Stalking in America: Findings from the National Violence Against Women Survey. Washington, D.C.: National Institute of Justice and Centers for Disease Control and Prevention, April 1998, under Grant. No. 93-IJ-CX-0012.

U.S. Department of Justice (1998). Stalking and Domestic Violence: The Third Annual Report to Congress under the Violence Against Women Act. Violence Against Women Grants Office, Washington, D.C.: Office of Justice Programs, U.S. Government Printing Office.

University of California, Davis (2000). Rape Trauma Syndrome: An Overview. Website: http://pubweb.ucdavis.edu/documents/RPEP/rts.htm.

Walker, L. E. (1979). *The Battered Woman.* New York: Harper and Row.

Walker, L. E. (2000). *The Battered Woman Syndrome,* 2nd edition. New York: Springer.

Additional Notes

1. Stalking Trauma Syndrome or STS is a new theory that the authors are introducing. It is not currently utilized in clinical practice as a diagnosis.
2. The victim quotes used in this chapter are taken from clients the authors worked with; this was not an empirical study. The names of these victims are not used in order to protect their privacy. The vignettes and interviews were not done solely for the work in this chapter, but through interviews of victims seeking assistance for stalking and stalking-related issues.
3. There is not one per se, agreed-on definition of stalking. This definition reflects various definitions found throughout stalking literature (see U.S. Department of Justice, 1998; Meloy, 1998; Mullen et al., 2000).

Anti-Stalking Resources on the World Wide Web

- Anti-Stalking Website: www.antistalking.com
- National Organization for Victim Assistance: www.try-nova.org
- National Center for Victims of Crime: www.ncvc.org
- Safe Horizon: www.safehorizon.org
- S.O.S. (Survivors of Stalking): www.soshelp.org
- The Stalking Sanctuary: www.stalkingvictims.com
- LAPD Threat Management Unit: A special law enforcement resource dedicated to the crime of stalking: 213/893-8339
- National Center for Victims of Crime: 800/FYI-CALL: 800/394-2255
- National Domestic Violence Hotline: 800/799-SAFE: 800/799-7223
- National Organization for Victim Assistance (NOVA): 800/879-6682
- Safe Horizon 24-Hour Crime Victims Hotline: 212/577-7777
- Survivors of Stalking (S.O.S.): 813/889-0767

About the Contributing Authors

Melissa J. Collins, B.A.

Melissa J. Collins, B.A. is a nationally recognized victim services specialist and expert on the victimology of stalking. She is known for her innovative and compassionate approach to providing services to crime victims, particularly victims of stalking. She is currently the coordinator of an anti-stalking program that provides practical assistance for victims of stalking in New York City. There, she has worked with stalking victims for over 5 years. Ms. Collins has been instrumental in designing numerous training protocols, advocacy policies, case management strategies, and counseling services available to stalking victims. Ms. Collins is a frequent speaker and trainer on the issue of stalking crimes and victims for local and national service providers, educational institutions, criminal justice agencies, conferences, and focus groups. She has been retained as an expert witness in civil litigation on stalking victim issues, and is a certified Federal Law Enforcement Trainer on domestic violence and stalking. She is the recipient of local awards, honoring her service to victims of stalking in New York City. Ms. Collins is a member of several professional organizations, including the New York Electronic Crimes Task Force and the American Psychological Association. She conducts collaborative research on stalking crimes and legal and victim issues in the New York metropolitan area.

Mary Beth Wilkas, M.A.

Mary Beth Wilkas, M.A. is a native of Chicago, Illinois with nearly a decade's worth of security and investigative experience. Ms. Wilkas received her B.S. in criminal justice from Indiana University in 1987 as well as a minor in Spanish language following intensive studies at the Universidad de Sevilla. She also holds a Master's degree in forensic psychology from John Jay College of Criminal Justice in New York City. Shortly after her college graduation, Ms. Wilkas moved to Seville, Spain, where she spent three years developing her career skills, pursuing a series of foreign courses, and establishing international relationships. She was recruited into the U.S. Secret Service (USSS) upon her return to the United States and began her career as a special agent in the Washington Field Office during the first Bush administration. Following her government service, Ms. Wilkas moved to Lima, Peru with the Organization of American States (OAS) with the mission of protecting the OAS ambassador during an international election observation. Later, she was recruited on a Department of State contract to protect the President of Haiti during a period of civil and political turmoil in Haiti.

In addition to working with various Fortune 500 companies, lending domestic and international protective services to senior executives and their families, Ms. Wilkas has worked for The Investigative Group, Inc., a global leader in investigative intelligence — headquartered in Washington, D.C. She was also contracted to lead an inquiry of illegal arms sales during the "Iraqgate" investigation. Ms. Wilkas is fluent in the Spanish language and culture. She has worked as a counselor in the stalking unit in the borough of Queens in New York City. Ms. Wilkas currently provides training and seminars around the country.

PART VII

Stalking the Stalker:
Prevention and Intervention

Developing a Model Approach to Confronting the Problem of Stalking: Establishing a Threat Management Unit

15

GREGORY S. BOLES

Contents

Introduction

California Penal Code § 646.9 was adopted in 1990 and was the first law in the United States to provide criminal penalties for stalking. The key elements of the anti-stalking model, California statute and law, are

- A course of conduct involving harassing or threatening behavior
- A credible threat, implicit or explicit, against the victim or the victim's family with apparent ability to carry out the threat
- Intent to place victim in fear for his or her own safety or that of immediate family
- Actual substantial emotional distress by the victim from the reasonable fear created by the course of conduct and threat

Simple stalking as defined above constitutes what in state practice is called a "wobbler" offense. That is, stalking may be treated at the discretion of the district attorney as either a felony or a 1-year misdemeanor. Stalking in violation of a court restraining order is always a felony, with a maximum sentence of up to 4 years.

Because stalking laws are so new in California and elsewhere, only a small number of police departments have established special units to respond to stalking complaints. The first such unit is that established by the Los Angeles Police Department (LAPD).

LAPD Threat Management Unit

The LAPD Threat Management Unit (TMU) was the first (and until recently, the only) police unit to specialize in handling stalking cases. The TMU was set up in 1990 as a result of meetings between the LAPD and entertainment industry representatives to discuss what to do after the famous Rebecca Schaeffer murder case involving a stalker. These meetings resulted in a commitment by the LAPD to establish a dedicated unit for responding to threats involving strangers. This was a new approach to an old problem of how to handle cases involving obsessive behavior that may contain elements of harassment or threatening behavior, often without, however, any *present* injury. As the LAPD notes:

> Unless a specific crime had been committed, police agencies have historically remained uninvolved in such cases, leaving the victim to deal with his/her problem. However, by the time such cases escalate, some victims have experienced tragic consequences before police intervention could be initiated (Threat Management Unit Guidelines, February 1999).

This brief quote includes two key elements of stalking cases: their continuing nature, which will typically continue into the future, and the role of the special stalking unit for homicide prevention.

Overview of TMU Responsibilities

To fill the void in police services that stalking complaints historically found, the TMU today is responsible for investigating serious threat cases in the city. This includes cases involving:

- Stalking
- Terroristic threats
- Public officials
- Workplace violence involving city workers

Other duties include training divisional detectives and other law enforcement personnel. The TMU supervisor spends approximately 10 hours each month providing training. This includes training for LAPD detectives, Peace Officer Standards and Training (POST), and training for other organizations, including the California District Attorneys Association. The TMU has trained the mayor's and other elected officials' staff about how to assess threats in letters, and it works with the city's threat assessment team on employee violence cases not accepted by the TMU. The TMU has also contributed to the city a workplace violence prevention policy and a workplace violence prevention protocol for police department employees.

TMU case investigations all involve similar tasks and problems. The most significant of these is threat assessment. It was this factor that led the unit to take over the elected official threat cases from the Criminal Conspiracy Section. The reason for this change in unit responsibility is that assassins rarely make explicit threats; specialized expertise is needed to assess the level of danger or seriousness of any implied threats. Other commonalties among TMU cases are the need to conduct surveillance (for some cases) and the need to take a proactive approach to prevent crime, in addition to reacting to crimes already committed. A final commonality is the use of community resources in investigations, to both prevent and investigate threats and other crimes.

TMU Staffing and Caseload

The TMU is composed of eight detectives and one supervisor, a significant expansion from the original three detectives and one supervisor. The TMU detectives range in rank from Detective II (equal to sergeant) to detective trainee. Most have a minimum of 10 years of law enforcement experience; and the TMU supervisor (rank of Detective III) has 24 years of law enforcement experience and has been with the TMU since 1992.

Most cases accepted by the TMU involve stalking. While workplace violence cases are increasing, they are still relatively rare (16 cases in 5 years). About 30% of the TMU's stalking cases come from the entertainment industry.

Each unit detective typically has 10 to 15 active cases. In the course of 1 year, the unit investigates about 200 cases. Of these, approximately 70% involve citizen complaints, the majority of which are related to domestic violence.

Case Referral and Acceptance

Cases are referred to the TMU from the Major Assault Crimes (MAC) units, patrol officers, the District Attorney, the City Attorney, the public (including victim service agencies), and the movie studios or other entertainment industry organizations. The TMU's officer-in-charge also reviews all police crime complaints involving stalking or terroristic threats to identify other cases for possible TMU involvement. Occasionally, the TMU also handles cases referred by the commanding officer of the Detective Services Group; this can occur where high-profile cases are brought to the attention of the commander (whether or not they fit the TMU's criteria for case acceptance).

Accepting Cases of Stalking and Credible Threat against Persons

Cases accepted by the TMU are those requiring the extra investigative and specialized resources available to the unit. For example, the stalking cases handled by the TMU are "long-term abnormal threat and harassment cases." The unit also accepts cases that have not yet reached the threshold of criminal behavior (e.g., "credible threat" or victim fear may be lacking). Although the harassing behavior in these cases may threaten to escalate into criminal stalking, a proactive response by the TMU detectives at this point may forestall more serious behavior and result in case termination without further formal action such as arrest.

The Case Management Process

When a case is received by the TMU, a case intake form is filled out. This is used to record such information as:

- Victim information (name, age, DOB, telephone numbers)
- Case information (crime location(s), detective name, date referred to TMU)
- Suspect information (name, address, description, etc.)
- Restraining order information (order number, termination date)
- DMV and related vehicle information
- Type of police report (crime, arrest, property)

The intake form is entered into an Access database, permitting cross-checks (e.g., prior stalking cases), case monitoring, and statistical summaries. Once the intake form is completed, the detective assigned to the case interviews the victim by telephone. A decision is then tentatively made by the detective to accept the case pending an in-person interview with the victim to assess victim credibility and willingness to cooperate. The final decision whether to accept the case or not is made by the TMU unit supervisor.

Regardless of whether or not the case is accepted, TMU detectives provide victims with safety information. This may include suggestions about varying their schedules, changing phone numbers, monitoring incoming phone calls, and informing others so they can also take precautions. Victims whose cases are accepted are also told to keep daily logs of all stalking-related incidents to build a paper trail to prove stalking occurred.

From case referral to case termination, stalking cases are handled by the TMU detectives on a vertical basis. The only exception to this rule is when a detective is out sick or on vacation; then another detective will temporarily step in to handle the case.

Accepting a Threat Management Case

Once a case is accepted, the detective assigned to the case will investigate and call the complainant every 7 days. If a case is designated inactive, detective calls will be made every 30 days. Similarly, if a case involves pre-stalking behavior (designated PEST cases, does not reach the level of serious threatening behavior), the assigned detective monitors the case by contacting the victim every 30 days. Another group of cases is considered "information only." These are cases that are outside the LAPD's jurisdiction or do not fit unit criteria for handling.

When a case is closed, the detective sends a letter telling the victim to contact the detective at once if the stalking reoccurs. Cases are closed through arrest, mental health intervention, self-resolved (suspect stops the stalking activity), or where the victim is uncooperative, making it impossible to prosecute or to increase victim safety.

In all cases where the stalker's identity is known, the TMU detective checks the suspect's criminal record, looks for wants and warrants, and reviews the Automated Firearms System for information about gun ownership. The detective will also review the Mental Evaluation Unit (MEU) files and ask for a hand search of the files in appropriate cases. A copy of the suspect's driver's license, booking, or other ID photo will also be ordered. If at all possible, the detectives will also contact the stalking suspect in person. In misdemeanor stalking cases, they may send the stalker a letter asking him to contact the detective, or may directly contact the stalker through phone or personal interview.

The TMU detectives may also encourage the victim to obtain a court protective order against the stalker or inform the victim's employer that they may also seek a protection order against work-site stalking incidents. Where an order is obtained, the detective will personally serve the court order on the suspect.

If an emergency arises, victims are told to call 911 and inform the operator that this is a TMU case. Police "first responders" have been instructed to contact the TMU detective via beeper, if necessary. The detective then informs the unit supervisor; however, very few emergencies actually require off-duty detectives to report in. In appropriate cases, detectives may act to divert suspects to a mental health agency for competency and dangerousness assessments.

Each stalking case is placed in a separate "stalking book." The stalking book is kept by the detective assigned to that case until the case is completed, whereupon the stalking book is placed in the TMU files. The stalking book contains a chronological record of all case activities and all paperwork associated with the case, including crime reports, evidence/property reports, follow-up and progress reports, detective notes, crime scene photos, newspaper clippings, and prosecution materials (see Appendix at the end of this book).

Threat Assessment and Case Management Training

One purpose of a specialized unit such as the TMU is to develop expertise among unit members in dealing with the crime of stalking and other threat crimes. This requires that the unit officers stay with the unit for a relatively extended period of time sufficient to both develop and use their expertise. Fortunately, staff turnover is not a major managerial concern with the TMU, since several of the detectives have been assigned to the unit for an extended period. However, the department does have a policy of rotating younger officers, several of whom may have to move to another unit to receive promotions.

A more serious problem is managing overtime. Managers are rated on how well they control overtime use. As a result, whenever special demands such as surveillance can be scheduled, officers will change their shift hours to minimize overtime. There is no LAPD policy against the use of flextime where the activity is scheduled (e.g., victim interview can only be done in the evening). Overtime is permitted, however, for emergency field work, such as looking for a dangerous suspect or completing the paperwork associated with an arrest. Long interviews that run over the scheduled work day may also be an authorized overtime activity. As a result, detectives may telecommute in order to complete the necessary paperwork. To ensure timely handling of case referrals, the first detective arrives at the TMU offices at 7 A.M. The day ends at 5 P.M.

Detectives are partnered to ensure officer safety. Thus, whenever a detective is sent on a field assignment (e.g., serve protective order, surveillance), he or she will be accompanied by a partner. This partnering is especially important when interviewing suspects because of their potential for unstable behavior. Partnering detectives also allows for consistency in case handling when a detective is not on duty because of sick leave, vacation, etc.

Celebrity Stalking Cases

Special managerial approaches are needed in Los Angeles to deal with celebrity stalking. Each detective in the TMU is responsible for liaison with three or four different movie–television studios. Liaison with shelter advocates is also needed to ensure that victims receive needed services.

Training new detectives assigned to the TMU is done through on-the-job training by assigning the new detective to team with an experienced detective. This is done for a period of 6 months to 1 year. At least twice a year, the TMU has "training days" when outsiders come in to talk to unit members. Typically this would include one academic and one tactical training day. The unit members are all receiving training on the use of the Internet in stalking crimes; this is being provided by SEARCH and a state DOJ course on Internet crime. TMU staff also attend meetings of the Association of Threat Assessment Professionals (ATAP).

Other Units Established to Handle Stalking Cases

Major Assault Crimes

MAC units are located in each of the LAPD's 18 geographical divisions. Among the duties of detectives assigned to MAC units are investigation of less serious or aggravated stalking cases and domestic violence assaults. But even simple stalking cases that cross division lines are assigned to the TMU.

Detectives newly assigned to MAC units receive training from the TMU; training is scheduled every quarter. Upon request, the TMU may also provide technical assistance to a MAC detective handling a stalking case.

A grant application has been submitted to the state to have two members of MAC in each division responsible for identifying stalking cases before they escalate. These detectives would try to use shelters for this purpose. The TMU will train shelter staff for this.

SMART Teams

The LAPD's System-Wide Mental Assessment Response Team (SMART) pairs a mental health professional and a law enforcement officer to conduct field assessments of suspects who display symptoms of psychiatric disorders. When officers respond to a call where the suspect may be mentally disordered, the officer can call the MEU to assist. The unit will dispatch a SMART team, relieving the officers and allowing them to respond to new calls for assistance. The SMART team will then determine whether the individual should be released, arrested, or be involuntarily sent to a 72-hour holding facility for assessment and treatment. The TMU detectives consider SMART to be a very important resource.

School Threat Assessment Teams

A recent LAPD and TMU initiative is the establishment of a partnership between the department and L.A. Unified Schools to create threat assessment teams in the schools that use the assessment techniques pioneered by the TMU. The plan is for each school to establish an assessment team comprised of a school official, a law enforcement officer, a mental health professional, and legal counsel. The purpose of the teams will be to identify and resolve bona fide threats of violence in the schools. The TMU will be responsible for providing technical expertise and training. As of this writing, the school threat assessment teams are being formulated. TMU and other training will be implemented in the near future.

Threat Management Unit Cases

To illustrate the investigative and legal issues facing TMU detectives, this section provides summaries of five cases handled by the TMU within the past few years.

Stalking Case Example One

The TMU took over the investigation of a residential burglary/stalking case originally handled by the LAPD's North Hollywood Division. The first incident in the case was a burglary of the victim's residence. The burglar bypassed several items of value in favor of taking undergarments from the victim's clothes hamper. Immediately following the burglary, the victim began receiving obscene telephone calls late at night. The caller graphically described his intent to return and rape the victim. Using phone trap records, the TMU detectives and officers from the North Hollywood Special Problem Unit staked out a pay phone identified by the phone trap. This surveillance led to the identification and arrest of a parolee with prior convictions for rape and residential burglary. The suspect was literally caught in the act of placing a call to the victim from the nearby pay phone. A subsequent search of the suspect's apartment resulted in the recovery of several items belonging to the victim.

The District Attorney's office filed charges of felony burglary, stalking, and receiving stolen property. At trial, the suspect was convicted on all counts. He was sentenced to a term of 60 years to life.

Stalking Case Example Two

In January 1995, TMU detectives were directly contacted by the father of a female victim, requesting their help in handling an aggravated stalking situation. The victim and the female suspect had maintained a love relationship off and on for 4 years. During that time, the suspect became increasingly violent, leading to their subsequent breakup. After the separation, the victim began to receive numerous hang-up and threatening phone calls. These calls then began to include threats to the victim's immediate family.

The victim's father was also the recipient of unordered magazines and advertising material from companies such as the Franklin Mint. The suspect also got herself arrested to be with the victim while the victim was in jail facing a forgery charge. After accepting the case, the TMU detectives instructed the victim on what she should do to help gather evidence of stalking (e.g., keep a log). With the evidence obtained from the victim, the TMU detectives obtained an arrest warrant for stalking against the suspect. The suspect subsequently pled guilty to stalking and was placed on probation. Upon release from jail, the suspect again began to terrorize the victim and her family. The suspect was immediately re-arrested by the TMU for violating probation. Probation was revoked by the court and a 1-year prison sentence was imposed.

Stalking Case Example Three

In November 1994, the TMU was assigned a case involving the stalking of the director of a then-popular television series. The victim was mailed death threats using cutout letters (e.g., "you will die"), mutilated dolls (cocktail swords stuck into the crotch of a "Ken doll" with its pants pulled down and red nail polish paint splashed on the doll; Figure 15.1), and envelopes full of feces. A possible suspect who had lived at the victim's home for a while was identified by the victim, but there was no physical evidence linking him to the crime. The detectives began to work off-duty hours conducting stakeouts of the suspect in an effort to link him with the crimes.

In May 1995, the detectives conducted surveillance of the suspect's car because he had no known address. This ultimately led to seeing the suspect approach the car carrying a package similar in appearance to those previously received by the victim. The suspect was then arrested while attempting to mail another package of feces to the victim (see Figure 15.2). The suspect

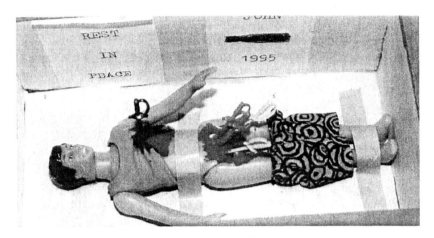

Figure 15.1 Mutilated "Ken" doll sent to a stalking victim; TMU 1994–1995 case.

Figure 15.2 Human feces sent to a stalking victim; TMU 1994–1995 case.

was charged by the L.A. District Attorney's Office with felony stalking and was convicted and sentenced to 2 years in prison.

Stalking Case Example Four

The suspect, a terminated employee of a national television network, was stalking and terrorizing a former co-worker. His behavior became so obsessive that the victim eventually obtained a court order against his behavior. Sometime thereafter, the victim's vehicle was burglarized and her identification badge taken. A few days later, the suspect's psychiatrist notified the TMU and the police mental health unit that the suspect had reported thoughts of kidnapping and killing the victim, then killing himself. A check of the automated firearms system showed that the suspect had eight firearms registered to him.

Based on this information, the TMU obtained a search warrant for his residence to look for firearms. The suspect was then civilly detained as a mental health risk under § 5150 of the state Welfare and Institutions Code (a.k.a. WIC Codes) and the search warrant was executed. During the search, the TMU recovered 16 weapons and numerous rounds of ammunition. The victim's identification badge, taken in the burglary of her car, was also found. Additional evidence was found that linked the defendant to child pornography. The District Attorney's office filed charges of stalking, burglary, and receiving stolen property. The suspect pled to the burglary charge and was sentenced to 2 years in prison.

Stalking Case Example Five

The TMU was contacted by a male model who reported that he was a victim of stalking by a former companion, a physician specializing in infectious diseases. The victim and the suspect had known each other for 18 months. When the suspect told the victim that his intentions were of a romantic nature, the victim did not want to become so involved. A friendship relationship continued for another year before the victim decided to end their relationship completely because of the suspect's attempts at possessiveness. The suspect began to harass the victim, placing numerous phone calls to the victim and threatening him with great bodily injury. The suspect then began to walk around the victim's neighborhood in disguise, enabling him to monitor the victim's activities and visitors. At one point the suspect, dressed as a woman, assaulted the victim outside his home.

A restraining order was obtained to prohibit this harassment, but the suspect continued to show up at locations that the victim frequented, sometimes traveling three times in one evening to different locations. The suspect also left cards and mementos at the victim's residence. After entering the case, the TMU detectives arrested the suspect in front of the victim's residence for stalking. At the time of the arrest, the suspect possessed binoculars and a flashlight, which he explained he needed to help him find a wallet he lost earlier that evening.

The L. A. District Attorney's Office eventually charged the suspect with stalking and making terroristic threats against the victim. After release from jail on bail, the suspect continued to violate the restraining orders of the court. The victim filed three additional crime reports alleging order violations, and the suspect was again arrested in front of the victim's residence. The original complaint was amended to include an additional count of stalking, and a bail revocation hearing was held at which a new bail was set at $500,000. Unable to make bail, the suspect remained in custody until trial. He was found guilty of stalking, but acquitted of terroristic threats. The court sentenced him to a term of 3 years in prison.

Conclusion

In many ways, the TMU is still a work in progress. The unit was established when stalking offenses were still not a criminal offense under the state Penal Code. Its original focus on stranger threats has expanded to include domestic violence stalking, workplace violence, and threats against government officials. It continues to receive ad hoc assignments to investigate criminal cases involving high profile victims that must be balanced against the need to protect many other citizens from serious threats. Most significantly, the TMU now has a parallel unit in the District Attorney's Office, whose existence may be expected to have an impact upon how the TMU operates.

At the same time that it is evolving, the unit operates within a professional structure. It has investigative and managerial protocols that govern the detectives' activities, while giving them flexibility to deal with a specialized and limited caseload.

It is also clear that TMU responsibilities go beyond simple case investigations. Because stalking crimes in Los Angeles far exceed the number of cases that the TMU can handle, the unit acts as a resource and model for other LAPD detective units. It is also a training resource both for the LAPD and for other criminal justice personnel around the state.

Most recently, the responsibilities of the unit were again expanded to include training for school threat teams. Because of other demands, the TMU does not, however, undertake many community education or public speaking events to foster increased victim awareness of stalking or encourage service agency referrals (as the L. A. District Attorney's Office does).

The "bottom line" is that just as stalking is itself a unique crime, so, too, the TMU is a unique unit within the LAPD. As the department, the TMU, and indeed the entire justice system learn more about stalking and stalkers, the more its responsibilities and its operating procedures will change.

The key point is that the TMU has been and continues to be a leader in responding to stalking crimes on a daily basis, while at the same time improving methods for responding to these crimes that can have devastating consequences for the victims unless promptly and effectively responded to by the justice system.

Bibliography

Boles, G. and Peters, G. (1999). Conference Presentation on Special Investigation Techniques: Threat Assessment and Case Management. Third Annual Stalking the Stalker Training Conference, San Diego, CA.

Los Angeles Police Department (February 1999). Threat Management Unit Guidelines, Los Angeles, CA.

Los Angeles Police Department (no known date). Threat Management Unit's Stalking Victim's Handbook, Los Angeles, CA.

Peace Officer Standards and Training (June 1996). *POST: Training Video on Stalking.* Sacramento, CA: California Peace Officer Standards and Training Division.

About the Contributing Author

Gregory S. Boles, LAPD (Det. III, ret.)

Detective Gregory S. Boles is a 25-year veteran of the Los Angeles Police Department. He was assigned as the assistant officer-in-charge of the department's Threat Management Unit (TMU). The TMU is the first law enforcement unit of its kind in the nation. TMU has responsibility for the investigation of long-term abnormal threat and/or harassment cases throughout the city of Los Angeles. In addition, the TMU is responsible for investigating threats made to the city's officials and high-level workplace violence cases involving city entities.

Detective Boles has supervised hundreds of stalking and threat investigations. He has appeared on *Good Morning America* and other network television programs in order to educate the public of the phenomenon of stalking. Detective Boles routinely provides instruction regarding threat management to personnel of the LAPD and other law enforcement agencies, in addition to private industry. He served as a consultant to the California Commission on Peace Officer Standards and Training (POST) for development of the state peace officers' curriculum on stalking.

Detective Boles retired from the LAPD in September 2000. He is now Director of Global Threat Management Services, Western Division, Kroll Associates, and Kroll Worldwide. Kroll Associates is an international security firm. Kroll's main office is located in Los Angeles, California.

Stalking the Stalker: Law Enforcement Investigation and Intervention

16

WAYNE MAXEY

Contents

Introduction

Stalking is not just a criminal justice problem, nor is it solely a mental health problem. To effectively deal with the stalking situation, I believe a multidisciplinary approach is necessary. Law enforcement officers, prosecutors, mental health professionals, and victim advocates need to work together as a team to achieve two primary goals:

1. Keeping the victim safe
2. Intervening and possibly stopping the stalking behavior

This chapter addresses law enforcement's role on the team. The author hopes that the following information will be helpful to officers and investigators who are charged with the responsibility of investigating a stalking situation. This author also hopes it will provide some insight to mental health professionals and victim advocates who also may deal with a stalker and/or the victim. As we learn about each other's process, techniques, and "job-specific" language, we increase our effectiveness as a team.

This chapter should serve as a guideline to the investigation of stalking situations. Each case should be evaluated individually. Not all cases will rise to the level of criminal prosecution or other traditional law enforcement intervention. But that does not mean we sit idly by. We may be able to develop case management strategies that move us closer toward our goals. I have included an interesting case we handled a few years ago in San Diego as an example to illustrate certain areas. As you will read, it was an exceptional case as it sped to its conclusion. But it started as many stalking cases do — somewhat benign in appearance, a low-grade misdemeanor case.

Stalking Cases and Law Enforcement

Law enforcement officers should reflect on the numerous times that they have responded to similar calls for service. The typical domestic relationship gone awry, the two parties are feeling rejection and expressing anger. In some cases one or both of the involved parties will develop a quest for revenge. My hope is that in the future, officers and investigators will look at these situations closer and ask, "what else is going on here?" And "what else can we do before things get violent?"

Law enforcement intervention usually begins when the victim calls to report an incident. The first responders (patrol officers or sheriff deputies) arrive to evaluate the situation, basically with two questions in mind:

1. Has a crime been committed?
2. Do I need to write a crime report and/or make an arrest?

Unfortunately, in many stalking situations, there are activities that do not qualify as crimes (i.e., leaving unwanted gifts, notes, cards, or letters for the victim).

The first responder may decide that there is no crime and, therefore, no need for further law enforcement intervention. Stalking cases can be very complex. If officers are not trained to recognize and further investigate these cases, they miss the opportunity to intervene in a potentially dangerous (and sometimes deadly) situation. Also, an officer's response (or lack thereof) may reinforce to the victim that there is nothing that can be done by law enforcement. In the future, the victim may be less inclined to report incidents.

In the best-case scenario, a first responder DOES recognize the situation as a potential stalking case. This chapter will address issues for the first responder and some ideas on conducting follow-up investigations, including assessing the stalker, gathering evidence and corroboration, victim management, and case management/intervention strategies.

The First Responder

Through this chapter, the first responder will be introduced to some of the complexities of stalking cases. Suggested guidelines for conducting the preliminary investigation are provided. Additionally, I urge officers to learn the applicable law(s) pertaining to stalking in their jurisdiction.

Routinely, officers and deputies are dispatched to calls for service. In addition to gathering information on the event that precipitated the call, the author suggests that the officer also ask, *What else is happening?*

Stalking cases involve patterns of conduct or behavior. It is common that there will be a series of activities that have been directed toward the victim, and the victim's family, friends, and co-workers. A short list of the frequent harassing behaviors associated with stalking follows:

- Sending cards and letters
- Sending harassing/annoying e-mails to victim
- Hang-up phone calls
- Leaving gifts for the victim
- Researching personal information about the victim
- Following the victim, or showing up at places the victim frequents
- Taking photographs of the victim
- Posting information about, or photos of, the victim on the Internet
- Sending in requests for the victim to receive magazine subscriptions and other products (i.e., Franklin Mint offerings, book clubs, record/CD clubs, etc.)

Responding officers should keep in mind that anytime there are harassing behaviors, there is a chance a stalking situation may be developing. Recognizing that some of the above-listed acts may not be crimes, officers should still try to document the incident in some fashion (such as a miscellaneous report, or by instructing the victim to write down and preserve for diary purposes the date/time/location, the officer's name, badge number, and call incident number). This may be the starting point of documenting a stalking situation.

Officers that respond to crimes should also document by filing crime reports or by other agency-approved methods. Some of the common crimes reported by stalking victims include:

- Vandalism of victim's property (especially to the victim's car)
- Threatening/harassing phone calls
- Threatening/harassing e-mail messages
- Violation of restraining or protection orders
- Burglary of victim's home
- Theft of victim's property (including pets)
- Wiretapping or eavesdropping
- Physical assaults of the victim (including sexual assault)

Once the first responder recognizes that a stalking situation is starting, the following should be considered in conducting the preliminary investigation:

- What other activities/incidents have occurred?
- Were law enforcement reports filed?
- If reports were filed, determine the reporting agency and obtain case numbers.
- What is the length of time the suspect has been directing activities toward the victim?

- Who else has the suspect acted out against? (victim's family, friends, co-workers, other victims)
- Is there a valid restraining/protective order in place?
- Has the suspect violated the order in the past? How? Were reports filed?
- Has the suspect been violent with the victim? How? Were reports filed?
- Has the suspect made threats? What exactly was said?
- Is the victim afraid of the suspect?
- Get specifics. How has the victim reacted to the activities? (Has the victim moved, changed phone numbers, taken self-defense courses, obtained a restraining/protective order, applied to carry concealed weapons, carried pepper spray, etc.) *Note:* The victim's state of mind is an important component in proving a stalking case in court proceedings.
- Is there any evidence that can be gathered? (See Evidence and Victim Corroboration section.)
- Who is the suspect? Obtain more than the usual identifying information (see Assessing the Stalker section).
- Document, document, document (remember that your report may be the first to start the paper trail to prove the course of conduct).

Stalking Case Example

The victim and the stalker met at a university and started a dating relationship. After only 3 months the victim tried to break off the relationship because the stalker had become controlling, attempting to isolate the victim from her friends and family. The stalker was moody, with outbursts of anger, and there was at least one incident of domestic violence. The stalker commented to the victim "you don't want to be my enemy," and then placed the victim in a chokehold causing minor injury. This incident was not reported to law enforcement. When the victim finally broke off the relationship, she began receiving threatening and harassing phone calls from the stalker. The victim called police and a report of harassing phone calls was made, but no additional follow-up investigation was conducted. A couple of days later, the victim came out of her home to find that the rear windshield of her car had been shattered by a brick, and that all four tires had been flattened. As the victim tearfully viewed the damage, she looked across the street to see a car similar in description to the stalker's car drive away. That night she received a voice mail from the stalker — "save your tears, I have more planned for you." The victim called the police to report the incidents.

If you were the first responder on this case what questions would you ask? What information would you write in your report? (Unfortunately, there was no follow-up investigation after the second reported incident, either.)

Follow-Up Investigations

In some jurisdictions the first responder may also conduct the follow-up investigation. Therefore, the following areas should be of interest to patrol officers and deputies, as well as investigators. A thorough, well-planned investigation should be conducted with the following areas to be considered:

- Assessing the stalker
- Victim issues/management
- Evidence and corroboration
- Case management/intervention decisions

Assessing the Stalker and Stalker Behaviors

The investigator (and the first responder) should learn as much as possible about the stalker. In addition to identifying information (name, date of birth, address, phone number, physical and vehicle descriptions, etc.), the following information should be considered:

- Prior threats/violence with current victim and/or any prior victims
- Prior stalking behaviors
- Criminal history (*Note:* an absence of a criminal history does not necessarily indicate that the suspect will not act out violently)
- Mental disorder or mental illness history
- Drug/alcohol abuse
- Weapons possession/use/access to/familiarity/or fascination with
- Has the suspect threatened/attempted suicide?
- Presence or absence of inhibitors (inhibitors are factors that may prevent the suspect from acting out violently, i.e., family, friends, job, health, reputation, etc.)
- Proximity to significant dates, such as anniversaries, holidays, birthdays, etc.
- Stalkers often acting out on significant dates or in response to certain events, such as the service of a restraining order, family court hearings, disciplinary actions taken at work, etc.

These factors can provide the framework for a more detailed assessment of the stalker. A thorough threat assessment process can be conducted by the multi-disciplinary team — the law enforcement officer, prosecutor, mental health professional, and victim advocates. Also, keep in mind that the assessment process is ongoing throughout the investigation and management of the case. The stalking situation is dynamic and may change rapidly, calling for re-evaluation of the assessment. The author thinks that law enforcement officers should strive to learn as much as possible about threat assessment techniques (just add that to the hundreds of other things you have to learn and master).

University of California at San Diego Associate Professor of Psychiatry and clinical researcher J. Reid Meloy, Ph.D., recently published the book, *Violence, Risk and Threat Assessment* (Meloy, 2000). This book is written, as its subtitle states, as a practical guide for mental health and criminal justice professionals.* Additional information on threat assessment by researchers such as Fein et al. (1995), Borum et al. (1999), Davis et al. (1999), Zona et al. (1993, 1996), Monahan (1985), Steadman et al. (1994), and Schlesinger (1978) also provide thorough information on the subject of assessing potential threats of violence in adults and juveniles (also see Chapter 3, this book, by Denise Emer, Ph.D., for more information on juvenile crime and stalking).

What do we do with the information gathered during the assessment process? Later in this chapter we will discuss some case management and intervention decisions.

Stalking Case Example (continued)

Remember when we left our case, two incidents had been reported to the police. Also, there was one domestic violence incident that was *not* reported. In conducting the follow-up investigation, would the details of this unreported incident be important? Of course they would be.

Also, if you were doing the follow-up and spoke with the victim in this case, you would have learned that days following the vandalism to her car, she was also receiving the following message on her pager: "187." That is the California Penal Code section for murder.

Thus, we do our traditional cop things such as running a criminal records check on our stalker and interviewing the victim and any others that have information about this suspect and the situation. *Well, in this case the suspect had been arrested for stalking and assault with a deadly weapon in an adjacent county a couple of years earlier.* How does this change the complexion of this case? What do you think the possibility is that the stalker will act out violently toward the victim?

We also contact the previous victim and learn as much about that case as possible. Are the same dynamics present in the instant case as there were in the previous case? Was a restraining order or protective order in place? If so, how did he react to the service of the order? Did he violate the order? How and when? We contact the investigator or officers that dealt with the previous case and try to determine: What worked well in dealing with that case?

---

* The following literature is very informative on threat assessment: "Threat Assessment: An Approach to Prevent Targeted Violence," (Fein et al., 1995); "Threat Assessment: Defining an Approach for Evaluating Risk of Targeted Violence," (Borum et al., 1999). I have also listed other recommended reading in the reference list.

What didn't work? Were there any warning signs to indicate that the stalker was getting ready to act out violently? What was the final disposition of the case? Is the suspect on probation or parole? Can we get him back into custody for violating the conditions of probation or parole?*

Victim Issues and Management

Law enforcement officers frequently respond to events where the victim has tangible, visible injuries such as cuts, bruises, broken bones, and stab and gunshot wounds. In stalking cases, these physical injuries may not be present. For the stalking victim, the injury is the *fear* of what *may happen*. This fear can be overwhelming. The responding officer should carefully evaluate the situation, acknowledge the legitimacy of the victim's fear, and recognize that the stalking behavior may indeed be the precursor of violence.

Law Enforcement's Role in Advising the Victim

What should law enforcement officers advise victims of stalking? First, the author feels it is very important that we let the victim know that we *cannot* guarantee their safety 24 hours a day/7 days a week. This is the reality in most cases. We do not want the victim to believe that since they have called law enforcement, that everything is going to be okay. The victim *must* be responsible for his or her own safety.

Most agencies have published brochures on safety tips for victims, or have on staff crime prevention officers that can work with victims on better securing their residences or workplace, and developing general safety plans. These resources should be considered and utilized as part of the victim management plan. The victim advocate on the team can be very helpful in preparing the safety plan.

Because the stalker may pose a serious risk to the victim, officers should be careful about the advice they give. Law enforcement officers should be cognizant of potential civil liability should a victim be subsequently harmed. With that said, there is certain advice that is generally safe to give to victims:

- Stop all contact with the stalker.
- Contact law enforcement to report incidents.
- Keep a diary or log of the activities, e.g., SCID (stalking critical incident diary) etc. The diary should include date, time, location, what occurred, who witnessed the event, name of officer(s) that responded, and incident/report case numbers.

---

* In the previous case, the defendant was allowed to plead guilty to a lesser offense — battery on a person, a misdemeanor simple assault, and the stalking count was dropped completely. What message did that send to the stalker?

- Save all evidence: notes, letters, cards, gifts, phone messages, e-mail messages.
- Do not have a third party (with the exception of law enforcement) attempt to intervene with the stalker.

Safety Planning Suggestions for the Victim

The victim can also consider the following:

- Obtain a restraining order. *Caution:* The restraining order may not be appropriate in every case. In fact, it may escalate the situation.
- Change phone number. Another option is to keep the current phone number and have an answering machine screen calls. The stalker may leave messages that could be of evidentiary value. If the victim can carry a cellular phone at all times, immediate contact with law enforcement is possible. One of our local cellular phone companies donated phones for us to issue to victims for this purpose.
- The victim should alter his or her routines. Do not use the same route while going to/from work or other activities. Do not park in the same location at home or work. If the victim continues the same routine day in and day out and the stalker knows that routine (or will learn the routine through surveillance), the stalker will know where and when to strike.
- Advise friends, family, neighbors, and co-workers of the problem. Stalkers can be very manipulative and may use those close to the victim as unwitting accomplices. If those close to the victim are not aware of the situation, they may give up phone numbers, addresses, or other information about the victim.
- Contact the phone company to get a trap installed on the phone so that hang-up or harassing calls can be traced.
- Avoid places/events the stalker knows the victim frequents.

Also, some additional safety suggestions are

- If the victim and the stalker have children in common, and family court orders require visitation, the victim should have a third party make the custody exchange. Again, it is important to **AVOID CONTACT**. If a third party is not available, arrange for the exchanges to take place at a police station or location where law enforcement can be present to preserve the peace.
- If the victim moves, try to have a roommate or relative put the bills in their name, not that of the victim. Utility, phone, and other service providers should be notified of the problem, and be requested to place a code word on the account for the victim. Stalkers have been known

to call the electric company posing as the victim and request that
service be cut off.
- Develop a safety plan. The officer, deputy, investigator, or victim advocate
  can assist in developing these plans. It is better for the victim to be
  prepared should the stalker locate him or her. "Advance scripting" can
  be helpful — for example, "if I am driving to work and see the stalker
  following me, I will get on the cellular phone and dial 911, and drive
  to the nearest police station which is located at _____." *

Victim Management

As previously mentioned, stalking is a long-term pattern of behaviors. And
unlike many crimes, the actions (or inaction) of the victim greatly impact
whether the situation will de-escalate, stay the same, or escalate. Of course,
our goals are to help the victim stay safe and deal with the situation, de-
escalate it, and eventually cause the behaviors to stop. Achieving these goals
can be challenging. One of the most important services the law enforcement
officer can provide is victim management. In addition to recognizing and
investigating the stalking case, the law enforcement officer can provide some
guidance on how to deal with the situation and educate the victim on the
psychodynamics of stalking.

The officer can also provide referrals to support groups or organizations
(enter the victim advocate from your team). This is not, however, just giving
the victim a brochure and leaving the scene — it has to be an ongoing process.
As the stalking ordeal continues, the victim may start to lose resolve and be
tempted to allow contact from the stalker. Remember, the stalker can be very
convincing and persuasive. If the investigator (or victim advocate) is there to
provide some reinforcement and support, we can stay on track toward our goals.

Additionally, establishing rapport with the victim early on provides for
open communications. In a lot of cases, the victim knows his or her stalker
better than anyone. What greater source of information can we get? Also,
through this education process the victim will know how to react (and not
react) to the stalker and how to call for help. He or she will be better prepared
to report and record incidents and keep any evidence that will help in managing or prosecuting the case. The victim is an important part of the team.

---

* Advance scripting can be used in various forms. For instance, the victim should script
out what he or she will say and do if he or she comes face to face with the stalker. This
should prevent what I call the "hominy factor." That is when the victim runs into the
stalker and is frozen in place, unable to move or speak except for repeating, "hominy,
hominy, hominy." This provides the stalker the perfect opening to make a last pitch for
reunification (or worse, act out violently on the victim). We suggest that whatever the
victim says to the stalker, that it be short, to the point, and be made while the victim is
getting distance away from the stalker. The victim should not get involved in a conversation
with the stalker, or agree to hear the stalker out, as this may signal that the victim is
conflicted and negotiations are again open.

Stalking Case Example (continued)

> In the example case the victim decided on her own to move from her apartment. She moved in with her mother and had the lease, utilities, and other information placed in mother's name. She even switched cars with her mother because the stalker knew what her car looked like. Good things, huh? The only problem was that the stalker also knew where she was attending another university for graduate studies. After approximately 8 weeks of no contact from the stalker, the victim started driving her own car. Unfortunately, the stalker had staked out the campus and followed the victim to her new home.

Evidence and Victim Corroboration

First responders often see the fresh results of the stalker's activities. Photographs of vandalized property, items left for the victim by the stalker, and other potential evidence should be documented, seized, and impounded. Additionally, this is the ideal time for the officer to educate the victim in evidence preservation. Victims may be so scared or upset with the stalker that they tear up threatening and obscene letters or cards, or erase threatening voice mail messages or delete e-mails. Stalking crime and evidence collection include:

- Letters, cards, and gifts sent to or left for the victim
- Phone answering machine message tapes
- Photos of vandalism or graffiti
- Fingerprints left by the suspect
- Phone records
- E-mails (saved on a disk and a printed copy)

Also, officers and investigators should be aware of items taken from the victim. If the opportunity arises to conduct a search of the suspect's home, vehicle, and workplace, these items can prove to be of excellent evidentiary value.

As mentioned in the previous section, the education process prepares the victim for future activities, and the victim, in turn, will be better prepared to preserve evidence for the responding officer.

Use of Search Warrants

The use of search warrants should be considered during every stalking investigation. Consult with your prosecutor, and follow your agency's policy and procedures for writing, obtaining, and the service of search warrants.

For suggested language in developing the search warrant, the author has provided a sample in Appendix 16.1.

Officers/investigators serving a search warrant should be alert for the following potential items of evidence:

- Photographs of the victim
- Photographs, diagrams, or drawings of the victim's home or workplace
- Writings, logs, diaries kept by the suspect that describe his/her stalking activities and thoughts/fantasies about the victim or other victims
- Personal items belonging to the victim
- Video or audio cassette tapes that might have information concerning the stalking, such as surveillance footage
- Books describing stalking techniques or having subject matter dealing with stalking, harassment, violence, or police procedures
- Any equipment that appears to have been used to "stalk" the victim, such as cameras, binoculars, video recorders, listening devices, etc.
- Personal computers containing diaries of the stalker, or yielding evidence that the stalker has used the Internet to research information about the victim*

Note: Patrol officers and deputies — this search warrant section is not just for the investigators. If your state statute makes provisions for "after-hours" telephonic search warrants, use them! Even if it is "zero dark-thirty," you were just with the victim, and you saw the fresh results of the stalker's handicraft; the stalker probably will not expect you to hit the door with a search warrant to recover the stuff he took from the victim, or the other great potential evidence.

---

* The stalker may use the technology to obtain information about the victim, or post photos, home addresses, and phone numbers of the victim on bulletin board systems or Websites. If the suspect has a computer, include it in your search warrant and seize it. There are software programs and hardware available only to law enforcement for the forensic analysis of computers. It is highly recommended that you take an expert in the seizure and analysis of computer evidence with you on the service of the search warrant. The National Cybercrime Training Partnership has published an excellent pocket-size guide to investigating online crime for law enforcement officers. Contact them at www.nctp.org. Also, the High Tech Crime Consortium or HTCC in Tacoma, Washington directed by Toby M. Finnie is also an excellent source of information on technology and cybercrime. Please contact them for more info at www.hightechcrimecops.org. For additional information on cyberstalking and electronic crimes, please see Chapter 8, this book, by Bonnie D. Lucks, M.A.

Stalking Investigation and Case Management Strategies

Stalking cases are unique in that they are usually not just a "one-time" event. Therefore, the author feels that stalking cases require "managing" and not just "responding-to after the fact" as we do in the traditional law enforcement sense. These are truly cases where we can be proactive! There are several areas of managing a stalking case: first, educating and providing support to the victim; second, we are assessing the stalker (which is an ongoing process throughout the case); and third, working as a team with the prosecutor, mental health professionals, victim advocates, and anyone else that is related to this particular case. So, what do we do? We develop intervention strategies.

Every Stalking Case Is Different

Each case is different. If SCAT has a case where all of the elements of the crime are present, and we have the evidence at hand, do we arrest and prosecute? Maybe so, but there may be other factors to consider.

In San Diego, we have managed cases that we felt were better served not to pursue through the traditional prosecution. In a companion chapter of this book, my colleague, Deputy District Attorney Kerry Wells, has detailed such a case. Then there are the cases where prosecution is *exactly* what the "doctor" ordered. Through prosecution, we get the stalker in custody. Now is a good time to discuss the "hook and book" aspect of case management.

When we are involved in the management of a stalking case and we put the "habeus grabbus" on the suspect, we recommend requesting "high bail." Check your local jurisdiction and agency policy for guidance, but you should be able to justify to a judge in certain cases that this is a serious situation and that the only way to keep the victim safe is to keep the stalker behind bars. One way of convincing the judge is to articulate that you remain current on research projects and their published results relating to stalking and threat assessment (having read this book and other sources, for example).* If you have a case where factors are present in the assessment of violence risk that lead you to believe that this situation will escalate and the stalker will strike out toward the victim, tell the judge. Also, articulate your experience in investigating similar crimes of stalking, domestic violence, threat assessment and assaults, etc. Your experience counts a great deal in this process. If

---

* One excellent source for training and education is the Association of Threat Assessment Professionals (ATAP). This association hosts an annual training conference each summer in Anaheim, California. The leaders in the field of threat assessment research and case management present the most up-to-date information at this conference. There are also chapters of the association throughout the country. For further information check out their Website at www.atap.cc. Also, the San Diego Stalking Strike Force has some training materials that can be shared with other law enforcement officers and their agencies.

presented with a set of facts that bring the pieces of the puzzle together, a judge is not going to risk having someone injured by a stalker released on bail.

Prosecuting the stalker may allow us to have some control on his/her future behavior, through conditions of probation or parole. Also, most people do not like jail. And having the potential to send them back if they violate probation or parole can be a great deterrent. We often see stalkers with some mental illness or character defect, and by putting them into the criminal justice system the court may order mandatory treatment and medication as condition of probation or parole. This is treatment that they most likely would not seek out on their own.

Covering All the Prosecutorial Bases

If we are going to prosecute the case, we need to make sure that we "cross the t's" and "dot the i's." Nothing can be worse than going forward on a case and having a jury acquit the stalker. This can reinforce to the stalker that what they have been doing is "okay" and that no one, especially the cops (who most people do not want examining their lives and actions), can do anything to them. Again, this is where the victims come into play — the victims must be able to articulate not only what the stalkers were doing, but what impact it had on their lives. Also, the evidence that is gathered in an investigation can help educate and persuade the jury that what the stalker was doing was not only illegal, but also very harmful and very impacting.

Use of Restraining Orders

Case Management Strategies and Potential Caveats

Now we will discuss some other possible interventions besides prosecution. First, and probably the most recognized, is the restraining order or protective order.* Temporary restraining orders (TROs) can be effective boundary-setting devices. The court sets the limits and if the stalker violates them, law enforcement can make an arrest. The author cautions to evaluate the case closely before recommending restraining or protective orders. The TRO may escalate the situation and may trigger a violent response by the stalker. If it is a situation where the victim knows the stalker very well, I ask the victim, "What is (stalker) going to do if you get a TRO?" If the victim replies, "Oh, he's (she's) going to kill me when he (she) hears about it," then maybe now is not the time to get a TRO. If we do decide to get one, we may take steps to make sure the victim is unavailable to the stalker on the day of service, and the day, the day before, and day after the court hearing to finalize the TRO. Remember earlier that we discussed significant dates? The TRO process

---

* This is an interesting study on domestic protection orders: "Domestic Protection Orders and the Prediction of Subsequent Criminality and Violence toward Protectees" (Meloy, 1997).

can produce those significant dates — tell the victim that this is a time to be especially alert.

To Use or Not To Use a Restraining Order

In deciding to recommend a TRO, one factor to consider is how are TROs enforced in your jurisdiction? If we are managing a serious case, we better be ready to react quickly and effectively if the TRO is violated. Another factor is how the suspect reacted to any previous TROs. Did the stalker violate the order? If the stalker violated that one (and believe it or not, we have had stalkers that had numerous TROs in their past), then chances are good he/she will violate this one.

In our cases, we try to be present at the "order to show cause" court hearing on the restraining order. This gives us a good preview of the stalker — does the stalker contest the order? Does the stalker have an attorney appear on the matter? Quite often, the stalker will represent himself. Some stalkers have narcissistic personalities. I have seen them swagger into court dressed in a suit and tie, carrying a briefcase, and hear them answer up, "(stalker's name) appearing for the defense your honor." What does the stalker say about the situation? It is my experience that the stalker will present as a reasonable and likable person who just cannot believe the victim has filed for this order.

The stalker usually goes on to assure the judge that he/she wants nothing to do with the victim, will not contact the victim in the future, and that the order is not necessary. *Note:* In the state of California, there are certain restrictions on obtaining and possessing firearms while being restrained under a TRO. This may be some of the motivation for the stalker not wanting the order issued. Consult your jurisdictions for laws concerning this issue. If we know the stalker has firearms, we may be successful in having the judge order the stalker to surrender them for the duration of the TRO. This is another useful intervention technique.

Sometimes, a sharp judge will read between the lines and indicate that he/she will indeed be issuing an order. The fast-thinking stalker will then ask the judge for mutual orders, claiming the victim is actually stalking him and he wants protection, too. Hopefully, the judge will not issue a mutual restraining order, because to do so only reinforces the stalker.

The "Knock and Talk" Strategy

Another intervention technique is the "knock and talk." Law enforcement goes to the stalker to tell him to stop the behavior. Use caution in utilizing this method. In cases of the "naive pursuer" (just someone who doesn't get the message) it may work well. We have successfully used it when the actions of the stalker are scary to the victim, but do not rise to level of credible threat for prosecution. We tell the stalker not only to stop the behavior, but admonish him that it is scaring the victim. Then if it continues or escalates to a prosecution, the stalker can't come into court and say, "Hey, I was just giving a pretty lady flowers, and asking her out." We have had this method abate the behaviors, but we also have had the conduct continue and we were able to make an arrest and successfully prosecute. But *use caution*. The stalker may think, "they can't touch me or they would have arrested me. I must be just on the line." The stalker then not only walks, but gleefully dances on this line, continuing to harass the victim.

Use of Surveillance Methods

The use of surveillance can prove helpful in some cases. However, it is labor intensive (if you have ever conducted a surveillance, you know that the more team members you have the less likely you will be discovered or lose the stalker). Still, a surveillance can be great for intelligence-gathering on the suspect, and it may present the opportunity to catch the stalker doing his dirty deeds toward the victim. If you are using surveillance as a protective measure, use caution. Inevitably, the team will lose the stalker at some point during the surveillance. If this happens, you better have a plan and way of letting your victim know that you lost the stalker, or some method of providing protection for the victim. Which leads to another problem — if you put a surveillance team on the stalker, or protective detail on the victim, when do you call it off? Surveillances cannot be conducted forever, 24/7. The use of significant dates or events may provide a framework for when and how to most effectively conduct these operations. Also, surveillance may not be appropriate in every case. What if your stalker is paranoid schizophrenic? (Yes, Mr. Stalker, we are following and watching you.) Do you want to risk possibly causing the stalker to act out in a "pre-emptive" strike against your victim because now he has proof that he is being followed?

Stalking Case Example (continued)

When we left off, our stalker had followed our victim from campus to her new residence. I would like to think that if we could have conducted a good follow-up investigation and assessment, we may have discovered that the stalker had this information.

> The stalker not only had the new home address, but he also made a couple of approaches to the house and figured a way to make his entry. One early morning, around 2:30 A.M., the victim was asleep in her bed when she was awakened by a loud popping noise. That noise was the stalker hitting her in the mouth with a ball-peen hammer. The victim sat up and screamed, and the stalker struck her again, this time causing a laceration under her right eye. The stalker fled the scene and the local area, but was captured by

police a few days later. The assault was reported by the media, and at a press conference arranged by the victim's attorney, the victim stated what we have heard too many times in years past — "what does he have to do, kill me before someone does something?"

But, this is not the end of this story. Usually, in the traditional cases we work, the suspect is arrested, he is in jail awaiting trial — everything is going to be okay, right? Well, in this case

> … the stalker approached his cellmate to arrange for a "hit man" to kill the victim. The stalker wanted the victim brutally murdered, and he wanted it done on Valentine's Day. The stalker provided the cellmate with the address and directions to the victim's home, as well as her work schedule. We were lucky this time, because the cellmate contacted our unit to report this request. We first relocated our victim and her family, and then started a separate investigation into the solicitation for murder. We hired a make-up artist from a local television production company and had our victim made up as if she had been shot in the head. We took the victim back to the old address and posed her as if she had just arrived home from work. We took several Polaroid photos as if the hit man had killed her. We then sent in one of our undercover investigators to the jail to meet with the stalker. He showed the stalker a Polaroid photo and asked if that was what he wanted done. The stalker affirmed that was what he wanted (all of this of course in the visiting room which we had wired for video and audio), and confirmed that the ownership of his car was the payment he had agreed to give the hit man. The stalker was convicted of the original stalking, burglary, assault with a deadly weapon, torture, and, in a separate trial, solicitation for the murder of the victim. He was sentenced to state prison where he will hopefully remain for a long time.

An exceptional case, of course, but remember it started as many stalking cases do.

Surveillance of the Suspect

The use of hidden cameras has also been successful in some cases. There are numerous devices available to law enforcement where the camera is hidden in clocks, smoke alarms, door-peephole cameras, etc. We had a case where the victim, on her own initiative, placed a video camera in the front window of her apartment. The camera captured the stalker leaving a note on her door. What great evidence!

Multidisciplinary Approach

Since these cases can be challenging and long-term, jurisdictions also may want to consider developing multi-disciplinary groups to address the problem. In 1994, Deputy District Attorney Kerry Wells founded the San Diego

Stalking Strike Force. At the time she was the chief of the District Attorney's Domestic Violence Unit (DVU), and was routinely taking to trial domestic murder cases. In a majority of these cases, there were stalking behaviors present before the murder.

Stalker Cases Needing More Attention

Recognizing that our criminal justice system in San Diego County was not recognizing the stalking activity or taking action in these cases, she started a professional group committed to making some changes. Members of the law enforcement agencies in the county (including state and federal agencies), prosecutors from the District Attorney's Office and the San Diego City Attorney's Office, mental health professionals, and victim advocates started work to change things.

One feature of our group is that we are not funded by a "big-bucks" federal grant, nor do the participants' agencies shell out money to support the Strike Force. It is all voluntary, with the agencies involved allowing (and in some cases encouraging) participation by their employees. We started out trying to determine how many stalking cases were being reported in the county. We found dismal figures — by comparing the figures to the numbers of domestic violence incidents in the county, we knew the crime of stalking was being underreported. We started training programs for law enforcement and prosecutors, and the victim advocates developed a handbook for victims and began offering other services.

Stalking Case Assessment Team (SCAT) Approach

In 1994, we started SCAT (Stalking Case Assessment Team), again a multi-disciplinary group that meets each month and serves as a forum to present stalking cases and to discuss and brainstorm possible management and intervention strategies. We feel that positive changes have occurred as a result of the Strike Force's efforts. In addition, along with key SCAT team members, we also developed a training manual for new team members. The manual is also used to train and educate new local police and sheriff department officers in training at the local San Diego Regional Police Officer Training Academy, other local law enforcement personnel, probation staff, and local judges on the crime of stalking, stalking behavior, evidence, victim assistance, and anti-stalking law legislation. An example of the *San Diego Strike Force Training Manual* (Wells, 1999) can be found in the Appendix at the end of this book.

These are just some suggestions for the investigation, management, and intervention portions of stalking cases. Be creative — do not limit yourself to only utilizing the traditional law enforcement tactics.

Conclusion

Stalking cases are unique and pose a challenge for law enforcement. The cases require a multi-disciplinary approach — law enforcement officers, prosecutors, mental health professionals, and victim advocates must work as a team to effectively manage them. From the first responder to the follow-up investigator, there are many aspects to learn about identifying, investigating, and managing stalking cases. They are truly the type of cases in which law enforcement can be proactive — before someone gets hurt. These cases are unlike any this author has investigated in his law enforcement career. They are quite challenging, but also very rewarding.

The stalker is usually bright and creative when it comes to finding methods of harassing and threatening the victim. With the widespread use and availability of computers, the Internet is fast becoming the "new tool of terror" for the stalker. Law enforcement must continue to strive for better education and training of our officers, and to utilize whatever technology and techniques we can develop to combat stalking on whatever field it may occur.

Bibliography

Borum, R., Fein, R., Vossekuil, B., and Berglund, J. (1999). Threat assessment: defining an approach for evaluating risk of targeted violence, *Behavioral Science and the Law*, 17, 323–337.

Davis, J., Siota, R. L., and Stewart, L. (1999). Future prediction of dangerousness and violent behavior: psychological indicators and considerations for conducting an assessment of potential threat, *Canadian Journal of Clinical Medicine* (Edmonton, AB, Canada) (research monograph), 6(3), 44–58.

Fein, R., Vossekuil, B., and Holden, G. (September 1995). Threat Assessment: An Approach to Prevent Targeted Violence, National Institute of Justice: Research in Action, 1–7. Washington, D.C.: U.S. Government Printing Office.

Meloy, J. R. (1997). Domestic protection orders and the prediction of subsequent criminality and violence toward protectees, *Psychotherapy*, 34(4), 447–457.

Meloy, J. R. (2000). *Violence, Risk and Threat Assessment*. San Diego: Specialized Training Services Publishers.

Mesnikoff, A. M. and Lauterbach, C. G. (1975). Association of violent dangerous behavior with psychiatric disorders: a review of the research literature, *Journal of Psychiatry and Law*, 3, 415–445.

Monahan, J. (1985). Evaluating potentially violent persons, in C. P. Ewing (Ed.), *Psychology, Psychiatry and the Law* (pp. 9–39). Buffalo, NY: Professional Resource Exchange, Inc.

Schlesinger, S. E. (1978). The prediction of dangerousness in juveniles: a replication, *Crime and Delinquency*, 24, 40–48.

Steadman, H. J., Monahan, J., Robbins, P. C., Appelbaum, P., Grisso, T., Klassen, D., Mulvey, E. P., and Roth, L. (1994). From dangerousness to risk assessment: implications for appropriate research strategies, in J. Monahan (Ed.), *Prediction of Violence* (pp. 39–49). New York: Lexington Books.

Wells, K. (September 1998). *Training Manual on Stalking*. San Diego, CA: San Diego Stalking Strike Force, San Diego District Attorney's Office.

Wells, K. (September 1999). *Training Manual on Stalking*. San Diego, CA: San Diego Stalking Strike Force, San Diego District Attorney's Office.

Williams, W. L., Lane, J., and.Zona, M. A. (February 1996). Stalking: successful intervention strategies. Alexandria, Virginia, *The Police Chief Magazine*.

Zona, M. A., Kaushal, K. S., and Lane, J. (1993). A comparative study of erotomanic and obsessional subjects in a forensic sample, *Journal of Forensic Sciences*, 38(4), 894–903.

Zona, M., Palarea, R., and Lane, J. (1998). Psychiatric diagnosis and the offender-victim typology of stalking, in J. R. Meloy (Ed.), *The Psychology of Stalking*, (pp. 69–84). San Diego, CA: Academic Press.

Additional References

Borum, R., Fein, R., Vossekuil, B., and Berglund, J. (1999). Threat assessment: defining an approach for evaluating risk of targeted violence, *Behavioral Sciences and the Law*, 17, 323–337.

de Becker, G. (1997). *The Gift of Fear: Survival Skills That Protect Us from Violence*. New York: Little, Brown.

Fein, R. A., Vossekuil, B., and Holden, G. (1995).Threat Assessment: An Approach to Prevent Targeted Violence, National Institute of Justice: Research in Action. Washington, D.C.: U.S. Government Printing Office.

Gross, L. (2000). *Surviving a Stalker: Everything You Need to Know to Keep Yourself Safe*. New York: Marlowe and Company.

Meloy, J. R. (Ed.) (1998) *The Psychology of Stalking: Clinical and Forensic Perspectives*. San Diego, CA: Academic Press.

Meloy, J. R. (2000). *Violence Risk and Threat Assessment*. San Diego, CA: Specialized Training Services.

San Diego Stalking Strike Force (2000). *Training Manual on Stalking*. San Diego, CA.

Spitzberg, B., Nicastro, N., and Cousins, A. (1998). Exploring the interactional phenomenon of stalking and obsessive relational intrusion. *Communication Reports*, 11(1), 34–47.

Tjaden, P. and Thoennes, N. (1998). Stalking in America: Findings from the National Violence Against Women Survey, National Institute of Justice Centers for Disease Control and Prevention: Research in Brief. Washington, D.C.: U.S. Government Printing Office.

Williams, W., Lane, J. C., and Zona, M. A. (February 1996). Stalking: successful intervention strategies, *The Police Chief*, 104–106.

Zona, M. A., Sharma, K. K., and Lane, J. C. (1993). A comparative study of erotomanic and obsessional subjects in a forensic sample, *Journal of Forensic Sciences*, 38(4), 894–903.

Appendix 16.1: Construction and Use of Search Warrants in Stalking Cases

During the investigation of stalking cases the use of search warrants is highly recommended. Contact your local prosecutor and refer to your agency's policies and procedures for writing and the service of search warrants. The following language can be used in the portion of the search warrant listing the property to be seized:

> ... for the following property to wit: including, but not limited to, any written material or photographs, phone books, phone bills, address books, diaries, letters, notes, receipts, or any other articles of personal property that tend to establish dominion and control, of (insert suspect's name); personal phone bills, cellular phone bills, pager bills, showing calls placed to (insert victim's name) residence or place of employment; all cameras, including disposable, 35mm, video, and Polaroid cameras; undeveloped film used in previously listed cameras; negatives of photographs, video footage or any picture or depiction of the (victim); and letters and written documents including but not limited to threats related to the stalking of (victim); address books, diaries, letters, notes, diagrams, drawings or maps of the victim's residence or workplace, writings, logs notes, diaries and memos maintained describing stalking activities, thoughts or fantasies about the victim; any books describing stalking techniques or dealing with stalking, harassment, etc.; any equipment that appears to have been used to stalk (victim), such as camera, binoculars, video recorders, listening devices, video or cassette tapes that might contain information on the stalking of (victim), such as surveillance footage; any property belonging to (victim), including ... insert specific items taken by the stalker.

Appendix 16.2: Writing the Search Warrant for Stalking Cases — Drafting Specific Language Requirements

The following language can be included in the section of the warrant describing the property to be seized:

> ... following property to wit: any papers, writings, documents, effects or other items bearing information about the following e-mail account(s) (for example, mickeymouse@aol.com) or derivations of those e-mail names; and any computing or data processing devices and associated peripheral equipment such as computer units, keyboards, central processing units, external drives and/or external storage, tape and/or disk, terminals and/or video display units and/or other receiving devices and peripheral equipment such as printer, automatic dialers, modems, acoustic couplers, associated telephone sets, and any other controlling devices; and computer or data processing software and the device and/or devices on which such software is stored such as hard disks, floppy disks, Jaz disks, Zip disks, integral RAM or ROM units, cassette tapes, magnetic tape reels, and any other permanent or transient storage devices; and any computing or data processing literature, printed or otherwise, list computer programs in which all or part make reference to computer journals, diaries, correspondence, memoranda, computer software, programs and source documentation, logs, operating instructions, flowchart, diagrams, historical data from (insert dates of activity) ...

About the Contributing Author

Wayne Maxey, B.S.

Wayne Maxey, B.S. is currently assigned as an investigator in the Stalking Unit of the Special Investigations Division, San Diego District Attorney's Office. He investigates and prepares for trial cases involving stalking, threats, and workplace violence.

He started his law enforcement career with the San Diego, California Police Department. He then joined the Chula Vista, California Police Department where he worked as a patrol officer, and then as an investigator in the Sex Crimes/Child Abuse Unit. He was transferred to the Crimes of Violence Unit where he investigated homicide, robbery, felony assaults, domestic violence, and stalking cases. He was promoted to sergeant and worked as a patrol supervisor.

Mr. Maxey is co-chair of the Stalking Strike Force, a multi-jurisdictional, multi-disciplinary group that was formed in 1994 to address the problem of stalking. He coordinates the Stalking Case Assessment Team, a group that investigates and manages difficult and ongoing stalking cases. He is the current president of the San Diego chapter of the Association of Threat Assessment Professionals (ATAP).

Obsession, Fantasy, and the Falsely Alleged Stalking Victim

17

JOSEPH A. DAVIS

To be, or not to be, that is the question …
— *Hamlet*, **Act III (William Shakespeare)**

Contents

Introduction

In terms of a legislative initiative that drafted a new legal statute, California lawmakers created a crime for the 1990s called "stalking." Since then, stalking has received a tremendous amount of professional attention from the criminal justice, law enforcement, and mental health professionals as well as public policy experts and victim advocates.

In 1990, California became the first state in the United States to legislatively pass an anti-stalking statute (Penal Code section 646.9). Since then, every state has enacted a similar or at least some type of anti-stalking or anti-harassment legislation. Also, since 1990, Penal Code section 646.9 has been amended in California several times.

The effect of these amendments has been to significantly broaden the definition of stalking to include what is referred to as "credible threat" and increase the category of people against whom that threat can be made. Herein lie many of the problems regarding stalking, stalkers, and stalker-victimization: those being, trying to define credible threat, stalking, stalker, and victim. To make matters even more difficult, categories regarding research on stalkers such as simple obsession, love obsession and erotomania seem to confuse those outside the forensic psychological, psychiatric, and applied criminological fields. Furthermore, these categories now include another convoluted typology that involves an invented or imagined stalking-victim claim and scenario.

Victimization Syndrome

The False Stalking Victim

From a study conducted by Zona et al. (1993) and colleagues in the Los Angeles Police Department, three types of stalkers were identified. However, in addition to the Zona typology of simple obsessional, love obsessional, and erotomanic, he suggested that another typology, although rare in comparison to the afore-mentioned, is found in some stalker and stalking case investigations which are unlike any other. The person in this type of stalker case alleges, over time, that he or she has been a victim of stalking (Zona et al., 1993; Mohandie et al., 1998). In the end, it is found in the convincing report or reports that the victim of the crime actually has not been a victim of stalking at all.

This type of victim has become known as the false stalking victim with false victimization syndrome (FVS) (Zona et al., 1993; Mohandie et al., 1998). Additionally, Davis (2000), in his research on false victimization, suggests that perhaps a more appropriate label or typology to identify and reference these individuals might be to use the "falsely alleged victim" and the "falsely alleged victimization syndrome," or FAVS, category.

A specific category and typology that is now being seen by experts who examine stalking cases is the infrequent case of the so-called FVS or FAVS. This psychological syndrome is rare and is found in a small percentage of stalker–victim-related investigations (Zona et al., 1993; Mohandie et al., 1998).

This chapter addresses the category of false victimization and the accom-panying victim syndrome and provides some psychological insight into this rare but seemingly occurring psychological phenomenon found in a small proportion of stalking-related cases.

False Victimization and Stalking

Since 1990, the crime of stalking has become an increasing problem for law enforcement, various medical specialists, nursing professionals, and mental health personnel. Among the cases that are nationally reported to be of a stalking nature, there now appears to be a growing (although small) number of cases that do not involve a true stalker–victim relationship, but actually a false victim–stalker relationship based on intellectual imagination, creativity, and fantasy.

On face value, the falsely alleged victim–stalker relationship appears to have all of the actual merits of a stalking crime. However, upon closer inspection, these cases of false victimization have no foundation suggestive of an unwanted stalking pursuit. FVS (Pathé et al., 1999; Wells, 1999; Mohandie et al., 1998; Zona et al., 1993) is a rare and infrequent occurrence found within the context of an unwanted stalking pursuit that involves someone who deeply desires to be placed in the role of a victim.

According to Davis (1998), the victim has an unmet psychological desire to be seen, attended to, and treated as a stalking victim. However, in FAVS cases, the victim (usually a female) chooses to carry out this fantasy within the context of falsely alleging and reporting to public safety (and even to mental health in some cases) that he or she is being terrorized, harassed, and pursued by a stalker in an unwanted advancement or relationship.

In short, the victim attempts to convince authorities that he or she is actually being pursued through the invention, usually predicated upon wishful fantasy, false scenarios, or claims involving a stalker. In fact, in FAVS or FVS cases, no actual stalker–victim relationship has ever existed in reality, only in fantasy. However, to the reporting victim, an elaborate scheme to falsely support a convincingly deceptive story that the crime of stalking is or has taken place does exist (Pathé et al., 1999; Davis, 1998, 1999a; Zona et al., 1998; Zona et al., 1993).

Prevalence of False Victims from Alleged Stalking Cases

According to Mohandie et al. (1998), the phenomenon of false victimization occurs in an estimated 2% of all nationally reported stalking and stalker case investigations. Furthermore, Mohandie et al. (1998) cited two case studies from the Los Angeles Police Department's (LAPD) Threat Management Unit (TMU) in 1993 and again in 1997.

In the 1993 case study, the LAPD's database showed that false victimization stalking cases occurred in 2 out of 102 cases or roughly a base rate of 1 in 50 or so in such cases. In a 1997 case study, the data revealed a total of 6 out of 341 cases (Mohandie et al., 1998). False victimization cases, according to the LAPD, were determined when the reporting victim actually confessed to not being stalked or when the investigators felt that the case was no longer credible from a stalking criminal investigative standpoint (Mohandie et al., 1998).

Stalking Fact or Fantasy?

The Alleging Victim of Stalking

Many stalking cases that this author has consulted on are quite complex, demanding, and time-consuming. False victim cases are of no exception. For the most part, all stalking cases from a psychological and investigative perspective place high cognitive, intellectual, and emotional demands on all personnel involved (Davis, 1999b; Davis and Emer, 1997).

FAVS is a relatively new and interesting phenomenon that mental health and law enforcement professionals are occasionally seeing that involves a "type of imagined unwanted pursuit" that on the surface level appears to have all the merit and foundation of any stalker case, but often reveals a psychological unveiling of twisted, distorted, and embellished confabulations or fabrications that is just as surprising to many agencies as it is to many of the people personally involved with the FAVS subject. To the new or untrained professional involved in a stalker–victim investigation, the process that this type of subject can place the hospital, clinic, agency, investigator, or victim advocate in can be quite stressful and overwhelming, often leading the aforementioned on a "wild goose chase" (Davis and Albrecht, 1999).

Investigating a False Victim Case

Being in the helping profession could place those who work with victims of stalking and related cases in a one-sided impressionable bias or myopic role; that is, regardless of the circumstances or situation, we truly want *to believe and help any victim involved in a crime*. However, in some very rare cases, the incident of stalking may *not* exist and is only *imagined* or feigned by the subject (Davis, 1999c).

In these cases, the alleged victim and subject are quite convincing and convincible to those who take their statement. A closer look at many of these cases has told me that such situations reveal some motive involving a secondary gain, i.e., attention, sympathy, extended services, mental health support, financial support or gain, etc. These are, in fact, instances of "believed stalking" (Pathé et al., 1999; Davis, 1998, 1999a; Davis and Emer, 1997).

Psychological Diagnostic Indicators of False Victims

According to those researchers who investigate stalking and false victimization (Pathé et al., 1999; Davis, 1999b; Mohandie et al., 1998; Zona et al., 1998; Zona et al., 1993), many false stalking victims present a diagnostic picture suggestive of a histrionic personality disorder. The histrionic personality from the DSM-IV, Cluster B, presents as a disordered character with many hallmark features (American Psychiatric Association, 1994). However, the desire to be the center of attention is first and foremost the central characteristic for making such a diagnosis (American Psychiatric Association, 1994). Another diagnostic indicator is the possession of a shallow but expressive emotionality and thought process which lack detail.

Although such outward presentations lack descriptive details, the histrionic personality is quite convincing and psychologically impressionistic (Zona et al., 1993, 1998). In fact, according to some researchers of false victim cases, the histrionic personality type may be so caught up in his or her fantasy and desire to be believed that self-destructive acts, behaviors, thoughts, and emotions may be found which are the "victim's" way to validate the seriousness of his or her story. These extreme actions or behaviors by the histrionic convince many professionals and only serve to increase the credibility of the false claims made by the alleging victim (Pathé et al., 1999; Davis, 1999c; Zona et al., 1998; Zona et al., 1993).

Furthermore, to the untrained investigator or interviewer, similar in scope to Munchausen's syndrome, Munchausen's syndrome by proxy (Munchausen's proxy by syndrome), FAVS can have a very perplexing, yet significant time-consuming impact and drain on any agency's services and their human resources. In addition to the histrionic personality and Munchausen types, the borderline personality disorder (BPD), also from the DSM-IV, Cluster B, may also present in some false victim cases (American Psychiatric Association, 1994).

False Stalking Victim Descriptors

When working with the "stalking victim," if you suspect a possible FAVS case, know what elements to look for, i.e., inconsistency in their statements, successive or subsequent interviews regarding the victim's stories seem to worsen, stories lack corroborating support and evidence, dates of recall for events lack consistency or credibility, etc. *Note:* Many FAVS cases take on an appearance of a theatrical quality (Pathé et al., 1999; Mohandie et al., 1998; Davis, 1998, 1999b; Zona et al., 1993).

Almost surreal-like, many FAVS *impressionists* alleging stalking victimization emotionally choreograph, psychologically dramatize, or manufacture or fabricate information to tell the investigator or interviewer what he or she wants to hear in that interview. Oftentimes, the interviewer or investigator as a follow-up measure to the interview session will literally find that the evidentiary trail of clues or events offered by the FAVS subject either have no reliable and valid connecting element, discernible beginning points or ending points, or lead investigative value (Davis and Albrecht, 1999). *Note:* Demand characteristics are often attributed to the authority figure (i.e., the interviewer such as a doctor, judge, investigator, detective, prosecutor, police officer, etc.) conducting the interview of the FAVS subject.

Many, if not all, FAVS subjects have low or poor self-esteem and often devaluate themselves in the presence of others. Given that low or poor self-esteem is a focal point for most of their neurosis or psychological dysfunction, the FAVS subject will want to over-please the interviewer or investigator (Davis, 1997a, 1998, 1999b).

The information provided by the overly cooperative FAVS subject is not only believable, but in some respects so dramatic to the investigator that it can appear quite unbelievable that so much could have happened to one person; you feel ambivalence as well as perplexed along with a sense of sorrow and compassion for the subject (this is the conscious ploy or the unconscious manipulative intent of many FAVS subjects). To make matters even more complex for the investigator or interviewer who is charged with the responsibility of getting inside the mind of the FAVS subject, the subject actually gets caught up in his or her pathologically weaved desire and fantasy to be unconditionally wanted by someone (anyone) who will pay attention to him or her (Davis and Albrecht, 1999).

Furthermore, part of the FAVS subject's desire is driven, in part, by psychodynamically driven origins that have evolved in the deepest recesses of his or her (most FAV subjects are female) psyche. Issues usually involving years of unmet needs, abandonment, unfulfillment, and disappointment at the conscious and, perhaps, the unconscious levels do contribute to an internally rich and creative fantasy life externalized by the FAVS subject by abreacting in the form of sympathy-seeking behavior (Davis, 1998, 1999c).

Therefore, the FAVS subject places him or herself in a socially acceptable role, that being one as the victim. Victims do get "good Samaritan" as well as professional attention (especially in the justice system) and rightfully so. However, when pathologically driven victim mentality is mixed with unmet desire of distorted unconscious or subconscious internal motives, the ingredients are right for false victimization and a pathologic personality in terms of development; the positive attention only continues to reinforce that motive per se (Davis and Albrecht, 1999).

Mohandie and colleagues (1998) suggested that the following 12 categories should be recognized and incorporated when suspecting a false victim case. The 12 categories can serve as checklist and reference from which the mental health professional as well as the law enforcement investigator can match against a presenting false victim reported case. They are

1. Initial attributions (first impressions as a overwilling victim)
2. Victim presentation (overly cooperative to help and do something to help)

3. Enlistment of others
4. Psychological data
5. Historical clues
6. Suspect problems
7. Motives
8. Reporting problems
9. Forensic-medical
10. Situational stressors (triggers)
11. Family dynamics
12. Intuition

Interviewing the False Victim of Stalking

When interviewing a potential FAVS case, it is imperative that you design your interview questions and queries beforehand around the dates, times, places, and events regarding stalking-stalker conduct as revealed by the subject. Remember, stalking is a form of unwanted pursuit that involves a repeat course of conduct following with some form of harassment of another person where a "credible threat" is often involved, suggesting an intent (explicit, implied, or other) to place that person in reasonable fear for his or her safety; in other words, a "repeated pattern and course of harassing conduct intended to frighten, intimidate or terrorize a targeted victim" (National Institute of Justice, 1993).

Finally, make careful observations (later transfer these observations to recorded notes) as to subject's mental status (mood, affect, hygiene, dress, orientation, perceptions, pre-occupations, mannerisms, rate of speech, thought content, etc.), eye contact, body language, or other non-verbal, behavioral, or physical reactions around the aforementioned disclosures. Furthermore, statement analysis as well as voice-stress analysis can also be key interview examining points when suspecting a FAVS.

Usually, since the many FAVS subjects are unusually over-cooperative (often appearing to go out of their way to help the investigator or interviewer), see if you can secure consent to audio and video record the initial as well any subsequent interviews. Doing so ensures a "second look" at the subject as to the aforementioned verbal, non-verbal, and mental state clues that are brought to the interview process (Davis and Albrecht, 1999; Davis, 1999b).

Many cases of stalking or false victimization that we want to place on our "wish list" to be moved to the "case closed" file never actually make that finite category. As my colleague, Dr. Steve Albrecht, CPP, a security and human resource management expert, states, "Stalking cases are never case closed, only case inactive." Therefore, stalking and false victim cases can remain open almost indefinitely (S. Albrecht, personal communication, 1998).

Conclusion

By definition, stalking and FAVS research have no conclusions. The research, to date, is an ongoing and evolving process, ever changing with each level of understanding. Those who understand it best are perhaps the false victims themselves.

Bibliography

Albrecht, S. (1998). Personal communication, San Diego, CA.

American Psychiatric Association (1994). *Diagnostic and Statistical Manual (DSM) of Mental Disorders* (Fourth Edition*)*. Washington, D.C.: American Psychiatric Association.

Davis, J. (1997a). A Developing and Psychological Threat Assessment Profile and Risk Analysis Regarding Those Who Stalk. Presentation, District Attorney of San Diego, 2nd Annual Stalking the Stalker Conference, San Diego, CA.

Davis, J. (1997b). Stalking and Stalkers: A Legal and Psychological Analysis. Course lecture and presentation, Thomas Jefferson School of Law, Course in Scientific Evidence and Expert Testimony, San Diego, CA.

Davis, J. (1998). Stalkers, Stalking and Their Victims: A Crime-Behavioral Analysis Perspective. Conference presentation, International Association of Crime Analysts (IACA), San Diego, CA.

Davis, J. (1999a). Stalker Typologies and Reciprocal Determinism: The Key to Performing an Accurate Assessment of Threat. Professional presentation, Association for Threat Assessment Professionals (ATAP), San Diego, CA.

Davis, J. (1999b). Stalkers, Stalking and Victimization: An Analysis of Those Who Stalk and Those Who Allege They Are Being Stalked. Presentation, District Attorney of San Diego, 3rd Annual Stalking the Stalker Conference, San Diego, CA.

Davis, J. (1999c). A Psychological Personality Assessment and Legal Analysis of Those Who Stalk. Professional seminar and presentation, San Diego State University, San Diego, CA.

Davis, J. (2000). The Falsely Alleged Victim of Stalking. The Baron Report. Fall/Winter. Website: www.Baroncenter.com.

Davis, J. and Albecht, S. (1999). Stalkers, Stalking, and Victim Assessment. Conference presentation, 25th Annual National Organization for Victims Assistance (NOVA) Conference, Los Angeles, CA.

Davis, J. and Chipman, M. A. (1997). Stalkers and other obsessive types: a review of and forensic psychological typology of those who stalk, *Journal of Clinical Forensic Medicine* (U.K.), 4, 166–173.

Davis, J. and Emer, D. (1997). Stalkers, Victims, and Stalking: Various Psychological Typologies. Conference presentation and workshop, Peace Officer Research Association of California (PORAC), Las Vegas, NV.

Hammell, B. F. (1996). Stalking: The Torment of Obsession: The STOP Program (Stalking Treatment Options Program). San Diego District Attorney Anti-stalking Case Conference, San Diego, CA.

Harmon, R., Rosner, R., and Owens, H. (1995). Obsessional harassment and eroto-mania in a criminal court population, *Journal of Forensic Sciences*, 40(2), 188–196.

Harmon, R. (1998). Anti-Stalking Legislation: A New Answer for an Age Old Problem. Conference presentation, Academy of Forensic Sciences 50th Anniversary meeting, San Francisco, CA.

Holmes, R. M. (1993). Stalking in America: types and methods of criminal stalkers, *Journal of Contemporary Criminal Justice*, 9, 317–327.

Jordan, T. J. (1995). The efficacy of the California stalking law: surveying its evolution, extracting insights from domestic violence cases, *Hasting's Women's Law Journal*, 6, 363–383.

Meloy, J. R. (1998). *The Psychology of Stalking*. San Diego, CA. Academic Press.

Mohandie, K., Hatcher, C., and Raymond, D. (1998). False victimization syndromes found in stalking, in J. R. Meloy (Ed.), *The Psychology of Stalking*, (pp. 9–84). San Diego, CA: Academic Press.

National Institute of Justice (1993). A Project to Develop a Model Anti-Stalking Code for States. Final summary report presented to the National Institute of Justice, 92, October. Washington, D.C.: U.S. Government Printing Office.

Pathé, M., Mullen, P. E., and Purcell, R. (1999). Stalking: false claims of victimisation. *British Journal of Psychiatry*, 173, 170–172.

Sullivan, C. A. (1996). Implementing an Anti-Stalking Multi-Agency Program in San Diego County. Unpublished Master's thesis research, San Diego, CA.

Walsh, K. L. (1996). Safe and sound at last? Federalized anti-stalking legislation in the United States and Canada, *Dickinson Journal of International Law*, 14, 373–402.

Wells, K. (1999). *The Stalking-the-Stalker Training Manual (Revised)*. District Attorney's Office, Special Operations Division, Stalking Strike Force, Stalking Case Assessment Team, San Diego, CA.

Williams, W. L., Lane, J., and Zona, M. A. (1996). Stalking: successful intervention strategies. Alexandria, Virginia, *The Police Chief Magazine*, February.

Zona, M. A., Kaushal, K. S., and Lane, J. (1993). A comparative study of erotomanic and obsessional subjects in a forensic sample, *Journal of Forensic Sciences*, 38(4), 894–903.

Zona, M., Palarea, R., and Lane, J. (1998). Psychiatric diagnosis and the offender-victim typology of stalking, in J. R. Meloy (Ed.), *The Psychology of Stalking* (pp. 69–84). San Diego, CA: Academic Press.

About the Contributing Author

Joseph A. Davis, Ph.D., LL.D.

Joseph A. Davis, Ph.D., LL.D. is a subject matter expert in the psychology of stalking, violent crime, and trauma. He is currently a partner with the TAP Group (Threat Assessment and Prevention), Inc., located in San Diego, Orange, and Los Angeles counties, California. Trained and educated in the academic disciplines of clinical-forensic psychology, law, and public policy, he is a clinical researcher and psychology, law, and public policy subject expert. A graduate of the University of Virginia's Institute of Law, Psychiatry, and Public Policy in 1985, Dr. Davis has written over 50 peer-reviewed papers and several books in the disciplines of psychology, criminology, traumatology, public policy, and law. For the past 6 years, Dr. Davis has been the medical and allied health editor-in-chief for the *Canadian Journal of Clinical Medicine* and a member of the journal medical advisory staff.

PART VIII

Anti-Stalking Laws and Prosecution as Problem Solver

Stalking Investigation, Law, Public Policy, and Criminal Prosecution as Problem Solver

18

NEAL MILLER

Contents

0-8493-0811-9/01/$0.00+$1.50
© 2001 by CRC Press LLC

Introduction

The Institute for Law and Justice (ILJ) under a grant from the National Institute of Justice is studying the status of stalking laws and their implementation in the United States.* This includes:

- Analyzing the stalking and related legislation in the 50 states
- Reviewing leading court decisions interpreting these laws
- Conducting a survey of police and prosecutor agencies across the country to determine how these laws are being implemented
- Undertaking field reviews in jurisdictions with innovative special anti-stalking efforts

While the first part of the study is simply to document what stalking laws have been enacted and how these laws have been interpreted by the courts, we have also found how difficult these cases are to investigate and prosecute.

The relative newness of the laws (first enacted in California in 1990) is part of the explanation for what we found, but not completely. Stalking cases are unique in many ways and their investigation and prosecution require new techniques that are specifically tailored for these cases. This means that stalking investigators and prosecutors must approach these cases from a problem-solving perspective. Each case can present idiosyncratic challenges requiring problem-solving approaches for identifying who the stalker is, gathering evidence to prove both the identity of the stalker and that a stalking has occurred, and proving these facts to a jury. Methods used with other types of crimes are often inadequate for stalking cases and new approaches must be developed.

This chapter details how the conclusions above were reached. First, the chapter describes the research findings for stalking law enactment and implementation. Next begins the analysis by first examining some critical background information on stalking, especially the unique elements that make up

---

* NIJ Grant number 97-WT-VX-0007.

the crime of stalking. We then look at the range of stalker and victim behaviors that together make up the crime of stalking. The next part discusses how the unique elements of stalking affect its investigation and prosecution. And finally the chapter examines the policy implications of the research findings.

Research Findings on Status of Stalking Laws and Their Implementation

The preliminary research findings on stalking laws, court decisions, field studies, training programs, and agency initiatives follow.

Stalking Legislation and Public Policy

The legislative review examined state laws relating to both the crime of stalking and such related crimes as violation of civil protection orders against stalking, harassment, terroristic threats, and invasion of privacy. In addition, the review examined state laws relating to warrantless arrest for stalking and requirements for stalking training.

As of November 1999, all 50 states' legislatures (and the District of Columbia) have enacted laws making stalking a crime. As more fully discussed in the Third Annual Report to Congress on Stalking and Domestic Violence (1998), these laws vary significantly in the specific behaviors outlawed and the penalties provided for their violation. In brief, most states' laws treat stalking as a felony offense. In 35 states, a conviction for a first stalking offense can be a felony; in 12 of these states, *any* first stalking offense is a felony. In the remaining 15 states, a repeat stalking conviction is a felony. Ten states provide enhanced felony penalties for harassment or stalking of a minor.

Twenty-seven states authorize civil protection orders against stalking, in addition to laws in every state providing for orders against domestic violence. Violation of a stalking protective order is a crime in 25 of these states and may be criminal contempt of court in the other 2 states. In only 5 states can a violation of the stalking order be treated as a felony; in many other states, however, repeat stalking in violation of a court order increases the crime level to aggravated stalking, which is a felony. In addition, repeat violations of a stalking order can be a felony in 8 states. In only 6 states does legislation provide for the entry of stalking protective orders into a special statewide registry for these orders. Thirty-five states also have registries for domestic violence protective orders; these orders often include anti-stalking provisions.

Stalking is one of several related crimes that infringe upon a victim's privacy and safety. Related crimes include harassment, terroristic threats, and invasion of privacy. The most serious of these offenses is the terroristic threat against the victim's person; terroristic threat laws are found in 35 states and the District of Columbia. Stalking differs from a terroristic threat in that in stalking, both the threat and the victim fear result from a *series* of acts, and the threat is for a future act. With a terroristic threat, a single act can constitute the threat; that threat must be one of imminent behavior and include the capacity to act on the threat. Harassment laws include simple harassment (25 states) and telephone harassment (43 states). Letter threat laws have been enacted in 20 states. The federal government has also enacted laws criminalizing interstate threats or harassment using the mail or electronic communications (including telephone).

In only 10 states where stalking can be a misdemeanor offense does state law authorize warrantless arrest for stalking, similar to that authorized for misdemeanor domestic violence. In the 12 states where stalking is always a felony, warrantless arrest is, of course, authorized where probable cause exists. In Mississippi, warrantless arrest for misdemeanor stalking is authorized where the stalking is against a spouse or ex-spouse.

Legislation in only 2 states (Minnesota and Nevada) requires law enforcement training in stalking. In comparison, 30 states require law enforcement training on domestic violence; this requirement may be administratively interpreted to include stalking.

Court Decisions

As of February 2000, our review identified over 400 stalking and related cases. Cases involving harassment issues were most prevalent (192 cases), followed by stalking (157 cases) and then threats (122 cases) (many cases involved multiple issues). Two state cases and 3 federal cases involved electronically transmitted threats.

While a few state stalking laws have been struck down as unconstitutional, this is a small minority. Where state stalking or related statutes were struck, the law typically lacked an "intent" requirement, either to create fear or an intent to do those acts that resulted in victim fear.

Double jeopardy claims were another common challenge, most often where there had been a previous finding of contempt of court. Rulings varied according to the factual differences among these cases as to whether the criminal offense and the contempt offense shared common facts to prove their cases.

Harassment laws that lack any "fighting words" restriction were the most vulnerable to constitutional challenge. But telephone harassment laws were not required to have such a limitation because of their focus on punishing invasions of privacy. For much the same reason, telephone harassment and threat laws commonly focus on the intent of the caller to harass or threaten, rather than the victim's response to these messages; a few states do not require actual fear to result. Harassment and threat laws also apply to situations where a third party intermediary to the communication is the one who informs the victim of the threat or harassing communication.

Statutory interpretation of threat laws lead some courts to equate reasonable fear with reckless behavior. Hence, specific intent to create fear is not required under this interpretation, merely a general intent to do the acts constituting reckless behavior, such that intent can be legally imputed ("should have known" analysis). Since a reasonable or prudent man test is used to judge reckless behavior, any resultant fear is also reasonable.

Despite the growing popularity of electronic communication, there are very few reported cases involving these mediums. Newspaper reports of e-mail stalking cases are, however, growing.

Implementation Efforts

Two sources of information were used to determine the extent of anti-stalking efforts. First, we conducted a national survey of police and prosecutor agencies. Second, we surveyed STOP-funded agencies to try to identify additional anti-stalking agencies, especially among non-justice system practitioners. Because of limitations of time, state agencies disbursing funds under other federal aid programs, most conspicuously the Victims of Crime Act, were not surveyed.

National Survey of Police and Prosecution Agencies

Law enforcement agencies (204) and 222 prosecutor offices in jurisdictions with a population over 250,000 were surveyed by mail in November 1998. The survey briefly asked what special efforts these agencies had undertaken against stalking, including special units, training, or written policies and procedures. We had about a 60% response rate to the first mailing. A second mailing was sent out to the non-respondents, resulting in an over 80% response rate.

The survey found:

- All but seven police agencies assign stalking cases to either their detective unit or to a specialized unit, most commonly the domestic violence unit, or to a combination of crimes-against-persons detectives and domestic violence investigators. A few agencies assigned stalking cases to their sex crimes unit. Only one law enforcement agency had a specialized stalking unit.
- Most prosecution offices similarly assign stalking cases to their domestic violence unit. A significant minority (15%) split stalking case duties between their domestic violence unit and another unit, usually the general trial unit. Another important pattern was for stalking to be handled by a special unit that is responsible for prosecution of domes-

tic violence, sex crimes, and specialized cases such as child or elder abuse. Seven offices have either a specialized stalking unit or an assistant or deputy prosecutor who specializes in stalking cases.

- Stalking recruit training for police is typically part of domestic violence training. About 13% of the agencies had specialized training in stalking independent of domestic violence, although several offered both types of training. Less than 15% of the police agencies offered no stalking training to recruits. Significantly, over one third provided no in-service stalking training to their officers. Slightly more than half reported in-service training on stalking is provided to all detectives or to special unit detectives.
- Most prosecutor offices (82%) provide some training on stalking. About 25% of the offices provide in-service stalking training to all their attorneys and 17% provide stalking training to new attorneys; most of these latter agencies provide both types of training. Over one third of the offices limit their in-service training to special unit prosecutors. Ten percent of the prosecutor offices said that the only stalking training their attorneys get is from outside training sources.
- Fifty-seven percent of police agencies have written policies and procedures for handling stalking cases, most often as part of their domestic violence protocols. Only 11 agencies have separate stalking protocols. A slightly smaller proportion (50%) of prosecutor offices said they had written policies for prosecuting stalking cases. Only six offices had separate stalking protocols, including one office with both.

The written comments provided by the respondents are very illuminating. They indicate, for example, that prosecutors in several states have significant problems with the statutory "credible threat" requirement. At the same time, some prosecutors in these same states did not report such problems. The reasons for this difference are not clear, but may be related to different methods for police/prosecution coordination in stalking cases. The need for training was expressed by many respondents and is implicit in the comments of others.

STOP Funding

A supplement to our agency survey was to telephone STOP state offices and ask them if they had funded any stalking projects. The STOP block grant program established by the Violence Against Women Act of 1994 explicitly provides for funding of stalking projects; stalking is one of seven legislative purpose areas specified in the act. Stalking has not been a priority for most of the state offices administering the STOP funds. A review of the financial reporting forms from the state STOP officials identified only 18 sub-grants that had possible stalking projects.

There is good reason, however, to believe that these reports significantly underestimate the number of STOP-funded projects that deal with stalking cases. These reports are based on sub-grantee project proposals; project activities are likely to vary considerably once they begin operations and have to meet victim demands. Because stalking cases are, in fact, much more numerous than many sub-grantees understood when submitting proposals, they are seeing many more stalking cases than originally estimated. The federal reporting program does not, however, track changes in project design or objectives.

To fill this information gap, we undertook a limited telephone survey of state STOP offices in about 40 states to:

- Verify the information provided that stalking was a project component
- Identify other projects that contain a stalking element, even if not officially reported as such

All but two of the offices called were cooperative in identifying anti-stalking initiatives. Once a stalking project was identified by state officials, further telephone calls were made to verify that stalking was an important project component. Not all states responded to the telephone survey. Nor were all state STOP offices able to identify funded stalking projects. Hence, the information reported here is not a census of STOP-funded stalking projects.

The telephone survey identified a total of 38 STOP-funded projects directed at stalking in 16 states. These include 7 projects to improve investigation of stalking, 9 projects to improve prosecution of stalking crimes, 12 projects to help victims of stalking, and 10 projects primarily providing training or developing protocols on stalking. See Appendix 18.1 for a complete listing.

Analytical Findings on Stalking and Stalkers

One of the first lessons of our research is that the term "stalking" is still not well understood in the criminal law context.

Stalking and Stalker Misperceptions

When asked about stalking activity:

- A prosecutor described a recent homicide case in which an investigator found a diary kept by the suspect, describing how he had followed the victim for nearly 1 year without the victim's knowledge.

- A STOP grants coordinator described how college men targeted specific vulnerable women to invite to a fraternity party at which they would be given date-rape drugs in their drinks.
- A police sergeant stated that proof of stalking includes showing that the suspect has taken action on his/her threats against the victim.
- An attorney filed a civil action based in part on the state anti-stalking law that claimed Websites' use of "cookies" to monitor site use is a "surveillance-like" scheme akin to stalking.

None of these four statements accurately refers to a stalking incident. They do, however, illustrate common misperceptions of what stalking penal laws prohibit. Thus, it is necessary in any discussion of stalking crimes to first define our terms. Otherwise there is a substantial risk that confusion will occur. As the above reports suggest, stalking, in common parlance (even among criminal justice professionals), is predatory behavior. For example, the lion stalks its prey or the hunter stalks the lion.

Stalking Addressed in Criminal Law

The crime of stalking involves much more than predatory behavior, although that is typically one element of criminal stalking. Most state penal codes define stalking as involving a pattern of willful or intentional harassing or annoying/alarming conduct such as repeat messages, following, vandalism, and other unwanted behaviors:

- Infliction of credible explicit or implicit threats against a victim's safety or that of her family.
- Actual and reasonable victim fear of the stalker resulting from this behavior.

This lengthy definition may be simplified to the three key prosecutorial elements that present the greatest difficulties of proof. These are

- The defendant's acts were willful or intentional behavior.
- Express or implied threats were expressed by these acts.
- Victim fear resulted.

Willful and Intentional Behavior

State stalking laws in most jurisdictions require that the prosecution show that the stalking behavior was intentional; that is, the stalker meant to perform those acts that constituted the stalking, such as following. In many of these states, the prosecution must also prove that the stalker intended to threaten the victim and to cause fear. Court decisions in several states have reduced the prosecutorial burden of proving intent to threaten and cause fear by holding that the defendant's actions were such that he knew or should have known that his actions would provoke perceptions of a threat and fear. Nonetheless, a common practice among police and prosecutors is to ensure that the stalker (where he is known) is made aware by the victim or her representative (e.g., a police officer) that his actions are not welcomed and that they provoke fear.

Legal Concept of Threat and Stalking

A threat under most states' stalking laws may be either explicit or implicit. In either instance, stalking threats, as distinguished from those covered by terroristic threat laws, do not require an immediacy to them; carrying out of the threat can lie in the indefinite near future. Implicit threats differ from explicit threats in not conveying by their very words a threat. Instead, a threat must be inferred by the victim based upon what the stalker says and does, taking into account any special knowledge that the victim has of the stalker, such as prior history of violence. Implicit threats must also meet a "reasonable person" standard to exclude oversensitive reactions from the law's reach. The reasonableness test must also be met by an explicit threat to forestall contentions that the threat was not serious, but merely intended to be a joke.

Issue of Victim Fear and Stalking

Stalker threat and victim fear in response to that threat are easy to separate where the stalking threat is explicit. But most stalking cases do not involve explicit threats. In cases where the threat is implicit in the stalker's actions, threat and fear are difficult to separate. Proof of one often also means proving the other, per the "reasonable person" standard. In these cases, one experienced stalking prosecutor with the San Diego District Attorney's Office notes that it is the context within which the harassing or stalking behavior occurs that provides the link between that behavior and victim fear.

For example, sending flowers as a gift may be stalking behavior, depending upon what actions have preceded the flower gift. In some cases, the threat against the victim may be obvious even where only implicit (as where the stalker places a nylon sex doll with a rope tied around its neck in the victim's bed). In other cases, more background information is needed, e.g., where the stalker uses the phrase "love forever" in conjunction with references to his prowess as a rifle sharpshooter.

The requirement in most jurisdictions for actual fear means that unless the victim is aware of being followed, simple predatory behavior does not constitute the crime of stalking. This prosecutor also points out that victim testimony about her fear may be corroborated by showing that actual behavioral changes occurred. In many cases, however, the victim's actions in response to the stalking may not match preconceptions about how victims are supposed to act; this can cloud the issue of victim fear.

A second lesson from the research is that there is no "typical" stalking case. Suspect behaviors vary widely. The only constant is a pattern of behaviors that together constitutes stalking behavior. Some case examples of stalking follow.

Illustrative Case of Stalking

Ms. X was involved in a dating relationship with GH, a fellow student at the University of California at San Diego. After 3 months together, Ms. X felt that he was trying to isolate her from her friends and family, and seemed controlling and demanding. Soon after Ms. X told GH their relationship was over, she found her car tires slashed and a brick thrown through the windshield. The vandalism was followed by threatening phone calls and messages on her pager citing the California penal code section for murder — "187." Ms. X went into hiding from him. A couple of months later, she was asleep in bed with her daughter when she was awakened by a loud popping noise — GH striking her in the mouth with a ball peen hammer. He fled the scene but was arrested days later. While awaiting trial, GH approached a cell mate to hire a "hit man" to kill Ms. X. Upon being told of this by an informant, the prosecutor's investigators staged a "murder." A makeup artist was hired to prepare Ms. X to appear as if she had been shot in the head. Polaroid photos were then taken of the "assassinated" Ms. X.

An undercover investigator then went to the jail and visited GH, who after seeing the photo, acknowledged that the murder is what he wanted. Charges were filled by the prosecutors in San Diego, and GH was convicted of stalking, burglary, assault with a deadly weapon, torture, and soliciting for murder. He received a prison sentence of 13 years to life.

Second Illustrative Case of Stalking

The victim, an 18-year-old female, sings in the church choir. She was seen performing with the choir by a total stranger who began to stalk her. Among other things, he sent pornographic pictures and videos to her home. With the pornography, he would add a message saying, "This is you and this is me." He also called her at home, making threats and playing the soundtrack from a pornographic movie. When he was arrested, he explained his actions as motivated by his being a "student of human nature." He said he simply wanted to see how she would react to his presents, and he would sit in the back of the church to see how she was holding up to his actions. The defendant was convicted of stalking and sentenced to 16 months in prison.

Third Illustrative Case of Stalking

The defendant had become fixated upon the victim, who refused to engage in a romantic relationship with him. After several years, the defendant began to pose as the victim on the Internet. He placed several sexually graphic "want ads" on Internet bulletin boards and in this way began to correspond with men while posing as the victim.

He then solicited the men to rape the victim, by claiming that he/she enjoyed rough sex and rape fantasies. As part of the solicitation, he provided the men with the victim's address, phone number, and other personal information. When the victim learned of these events from one of the men so solicited, she went to local police and was told there was nothing they could do. Eventually, the Federal Bureau of Investigation (FBI) referred her to the Los Angeles District Attorney's Stalking Assessment Team. After extensive investigation that included issuance of search warrants to Internet service providers to track the source of the Web postings, a felony stalking complaint was issued. The defendant eventually pled guilty and received a 6-year sentence to state prison.

What is Stalking Behavior?

What the stalker does and how the victim responds to the stalking behavior constitute the crime of stalking. To help investigators understand the crime of stalking, several typologies of stalkers and their relationship with their victims have been developed.

Stalker and Stalking Behaviors

Companion or "Crossover" Crimes

As the cases above illustrate, stalking encompasses a variety of threatening behaviors. The types of overt criminal behavior that stalkers engage in range from homicide and sexual assault at one end of the spectrum to petty vandalism and telephone harassment at the other. Typically, any single stalking case will involve several stalking-related offenses. These include, in addition to such serious offenses as those listed above, the following "crossover" crimes:

- Arson
- Assault
- Abduction

- Extortion
- Violation of court order
- Burglary/criminal trespass
- Theft of personal clothing
- Vandalism/destruction of property
- Cruelty to animals (pet mutilation or death)
- Wiretapping/mail tampering
- False reports to police (see Chapters 10 and 17, this book)
- Weapons violations

Some of these offenses standing alone are quite serious in and of themselves. Others appear to be relatively minor offenses. The serious stalking-related offenses will, of course, be treated seriously by law enforcement and prosecutors who are informed of their occurrence. But the lesser offenses, unless the officer or prosecutor is thinking about the possibility of stalking, may be given less attention than is needed.

Stalking and Stalker Typologies

In an effort to better understand the dynamics of stalking, researchers and practitioners both have collaborated to develop a variety of typologies of stalkers and of stalking behaviors. These include the following.

Psychological Motivations

One typology developed on the experiences of the Los Angeles Police Department's (LAPD) Threat Management Unit (TMU) focuses on the stalking relationship itself. Thus, this stalker typology distinguishes between three types of psychological motivations (Zona et al., 1993):

1. Simple Obsessional: Stalker and victim have a prior relationship (e.g., former intimate partners). The motivations for the simple obsessional relationship include a desire to lure the other person back into a relationship, anger at loss of control or feelings of mistreatment, and revenge for perceived wrongs.
2. Love Obsessional: The stalker and the victim have no prior relationship but the stalker, nonetheless, focuses on the victim as the object of love and adoration. Some stalkers suffer from a psychiatric disorder such as schizophrenia, while others are simply socially maladjusted. Stalking of public figures is a common subgroup of this category.
3. Erotomanic: The defining characteristic of this type of stalking is that the stalker believes that the victim is in love with him or her. Moreover, the stalker may perceive other parties as responsible for the victim's failure to acknowledge this love. Hence, spouses of the erotomanic's

victim may also become stalking victims because the stalker believes that removing the spouse would result in the victim's acceptance of the stalker.

A recent addition to this typology takes note of a small number of reported stalking cases that involve false victimizations: no one is stalking the "victim." This is sometimes called "false victimization syndrome." Motivations for this behavior range from psychiatric disorders to simple seeking of attention from another person or the authorities. When stalking laws were first implemented, most false stalking reports seemed to reflect the "victim's" desire for attention, to more serious psychological disturbances. More recently, as stalkers have become more familiar with these laws, false stalking reports have become part of the behavioral pattern of stalking itself whereby the stalker charges the victim with stalking him or her.

Other Stalker Motivation

Another typology for categorizing stalking is to look at key distinguishing features of the differing stalker motivations underlying the behavior, as well as victim–stalker relationship.

At least half of all reported stalking involves former intimate partners. In many of these cases, the stalking is an outgrowth of prior domestic violence. In these cases, the motivations for stalking may include stalking as a desire to continue the same control pattern that often underlies domestic violence itself; revenge for leaving the stalker; or mental illness resulting in an obsession.

Stranger Stalking

"Stranger" stalking is harder to describe. In some instances, the "stranger" stalker may actually be an acquaintance of the victim, such as a classmate in school or a prior patient or client of the victim. The stalker may even have had one or two dates with the victim. But no intimate relationship ever occurred between the two. In other instances, the stalker may indeed be a stranger, having become fixated on the victim without any personal relationship at all. Among stranger stalking of either type, the most common motivations are mental illness (see above) and revenge for a wrong whose fault is ascribed to the victim.

Motivation-based typologies focus on the reasons for the stalking. These can include the psychiatric illnesses that underlie erotomania and much of the love obsessional cases. More and more cases are being recognized where the motivation for stalking is revenge for real or perceived wrongs done to the stalker. Stalking may be an attempt to continue a pattern of control and abuse that led a domestic violence victim to leave the stalker.

Victim Behaviors

The way in which victims react to stalking presents yet another typology. One reason for extreme variance in victim behavior is that there is often a significant period of time between victim reporting of stalking and successful case resolution. This may result from inadequate law enforcement or prosecution response to an unfamiliar complaint. It may also occur as a consequence of the evidence collection process, which begins when the complaint is made. Only then can the agencies begin to document both the course of action constituting stalking behavior and the victim's resultant fear. During this interim period, the victim may have to cope with continued, ongoing stalking behavior as best she can, often without official support and advice.

As a result, many victims develop coping behaviors that may, on the surface, appear to undercut the seriousness of the threat faced by the victim and her fear of the stalker. One study of 128 stalking cases by a researcher working with the Sacramento District Attorney's Office found that victims' responses to stalking by former intimate partners consisted of four types of behavior (Dunn, 1999b). These were

1. Active resistance
2. Help seeking
3. Coping to reduce danger
4. Coping by complying with stalker's demands

Active resistance (self-help in facing stalker) included (declining order of frequency):

- Not letting defendant in
- Threatening to call 911
- Fighting/struggling
- Hanging up
- Logging or recording the stalker's behavior
- Yelling/swearing

Help-seeking behavior included:

- Calling police
- Insisting on prosecution
- Insisting on arrest
- Getting an escort
- Screaming

Victim coping strategies to minimize danger included:

- Screening phone calls
- Leaving the scene
- Staying with family or friends
- Hiding
- Changing phone number
- Moving within area
- Ignoring stalker
- Taking security measures

The most important of Dunn's findings (1999a) was the degree to which victims engaged in compliance behavior in an effort to appease the stalker in an effort to reduce the threats. Nearly one in five victims who had been stalked by former intimates exhibited some form of compliance behavior as a survival strategy. These included:

- Requesting case be dismissed
- Visiting defendant in jail
- Going places with defendant
- Recanting
- Continuing to have sex with stalker

Compliance behavior can complicate case outcomes by making it harder to prove that the victim is fearful of the stalker. Indeed, compliance can suggest to the naïve observer that the victim is encouraging or leading on the stalker. Moreover, victims of stalking by former intimates often have conflicting emotions toward the stalker who may be an "ex." Behavior reflecting both fear and love can muddy the image of victim innocence.

Stalking Investigation and Prosecution

The analysis of stalking investigation and prosecution is based upon fieldwork conducted in seven sites: three prosecutor offices, three law enforcement agencies, and one victim services agency. At each site, we interviewed experienced investigators and prosecutors in the specialized unit. In addition, we attended several specialized training sessions on stalking intervention and prosecution, where we talked with both the trainers and other stalking-experienced attendees.

Preliminary findings from these sites show some significant commonalties.

- Special stalking units develop necessary expertise in identifying, investigating, and prosecuting stalking crimes that is needed with what are essentially ongoing crimes.
- Staffing of special units is essentially still experimental. Often, central units share jurisdiction over stalking crimes with other agency units, taking only the most serious cases.
- Failure of non-special unit agency personnel to identify stalking behavior is a continuing problem. All of the special units devote considerable resources to training other criminal justice personnel and community education.
- Special unit staffs are highly qualified and motivated, often working unpaid overtime to handle both their caseload and community education/training.

The field review also showed that stalking cases present some unique case elements. These include the following:

1. They are hard to identify at the outset. Because stalking involves a course of conduct, complaints to law enforcement about a single incident do not reveal that stalking is occurring. Often, responding officers must probe the victim's description of what she is concerned about before the stalking nature of the complaint becomes clear.

2. Stalking is a prospective or future-looking crime, while most crime investigations deal with past crimes. Investigation of stalking typically requires collection of evidence of stalking only from the point when the victim reports the stalking to law enforcement; in most cases, the victim's report of prior stalking behaviors cannot be confirmed or corroborated by independent sources. Hence, proof of the stalking behaviors must come from future actions of the stalker. This further implies that the victim and the investigators must try to manipulate the stalker in his behaviors so as to facilitate the collection of evidence (e.g., encourage stalker conversation for taping in hope that threats will be made).

3. The victim's testimony may not be enough to prove stalking. Corroboration is often needed. Yet because the victim is often alone when the stalking occurs, direct corroboration may not be available. Hence, law enforcement is often dependent to some degree on the victim for evidence collection. This could include taped phone messages or conversations, or retaining letters, presents, etc. from the stalker.

4. Corroboration is also needed to prove the victim's state of mind: actual fear. This includes evidence that shows how the victim asked others for help in dealing with the stalker, such as having co-employees screen her calls at work, notifying apartment building personnel (e.g., door-men) of the stalking, proof of a change in telephone number, etc.

5. There is a need for threat assessment and management. At the same time that the investigation and prosecution are occurring, officials must also ensure victim safety. Thus, threat assessment and management are an integral part of the agencies' stalking response. This task is made especially complicated where the stalking suspect displays significant signs of mental illness, but not enough to warrant civil commitment (e.g., pathological jealousy).

6. It is necessary to distinguish between true and false victimization reports. As noted above, false victimization reports are difficult to distinguish in many instances; such common indicia of false reports, such as diminishing victim cooperation with the investigation, are not relevant in stalking cases. Whether the victim is seeking attention or trying to shift the blame, false victim reporters have significant incentives to keep telling their stories. And since all stalking cases are highly dependent on the victim to collect evidence, it will not be apparent until significant time has passed that there is no collaborative evidence.

7. Agency coordination is especially important. Cross-jurisdictional crime scenes are common when the victim, for example, works in one jurisdiction, lives in another, and shops in a third locality. Because stalking is an ongoing crime, steps must be taken to coordinate investigations across jurisdictional lines and to ensure that all agencies are made aware of the existence of the ongoing investigation. Stalking cases do not necessarily end with a conviction. Stalkers may continue their stalking behaviors while on probation and even while still incarcerated.

8. Investigative experience in dealing with these crime features is limited, resulting in the need to "make up" procedures and policies for evidence collection. Because stalking is a new crime, most agencies have yet to set policies or procedures for stalking investigation. Law enforcement must borrow methods from other crime investigation experience. But as noted above, most crimes are retroactive, looking at past events, not future actions. Hence, investigators must often create new investigative approaches to stalking.

Problem-Solving Stalking Investigations and Prosecution

Stalking investigations and prosecutions are often problematic because of staff inexperience with stalking cases and the absence of agency policies and procedures that might otherwise provide agency experience in lieu of personal expertise. As a result, investigators and prosecutors often need to develop new approaches to their cases. This occurs in two ways. Each stalking investigation has two major components — identifying and proving who the stalker is and proving a crime has been committed. The unique nature of stalking offenses complicates these tasks.

Identifying the Stalker

In many criminal cases, even the most serious, identification of the criminal is not a major responsibility of the investigation (e.g., family member or friend is the suspect). In many stalking cases, the identity of the stalker is unknown. Indeed, in many instances, there may not even be any suspects. Thus, the first task in a stalking investigation in these latter cases will be to develop a list of potential suspects. These may be gained from the victim, the victim's family, friends, and co-workers. Each possible suspect must be investigated and each alibi checked out.

Because stalking is an ongoing crime that continues to occur after law enforcement enters the case, it may be possible to use surveillance methods to help identify the stalker. Thus, law enforcement may post cameras at the victim's home that show the area around the residence. Or they may set up their own stalking team to follow the victim to see if any of the possible suspects appear in the area of the victim (while shopping, for example). Alternatively, law enforcement may set up a counter-stalking watch over a possible suspect to see if he engages in stalking behavior. In one case, law enforcement staked out the suspect's vehicle; when he appeared at the car, he was carrying an envelope addressed to the victim that contained a threatening note and feces. In another case, law enforcement used cameras to stake out a computer laboratory at a local university to identify who was using a specific machine determined to be the source of cyberstalking at the time threatening e-mail messages were sent to the victim.

Proving a Crime Was Committed

Proving that stalking occurred requires showing both that specific stalking acts occurred and that they resulted in victim fear. The primary source of evidence for proving both crime elements is the testimony of the victim herself. This testimony must be corroborated by other evidence such as the following:

- Testimony of victim's friends or co-workers who were present at a stalking event
- Documentary evidence such as letters or notes sent to the victim by the stalker
- Printout of e-mail messages sent to the victim

- Log of stalking events maintained by the victim noting time, date, and specific event occurrences
- Video evidence from a "stakeout" following the stalker, or of the victim showing the stalking, "following" behavior

Proof that the victim had a reasonable fear for her safety due to the stalking also begins with the victim's testimony. It too must be corroborated by testimony from:

- Victim's friends and co-workers about changes in victim's behavior, e.g., asking for an escort to go shopping or to the parking lot when leaving work
- Psychiatrist, psychologist, or other treatment professional offering expert testimony
- Security officials at workplace who had been informed of stalking occurrence
- Record of victim statements that are not limited by the hearsay rule (e.g., 911 tapes, police incident reports)
- Answering machine tapes; audio tapes of phone calls
- Pictures of stalker taken by victim (date and time stamped)
- Evidence gained through search warrants, including computer, stalker's diary, property of victim found at stalker's residence, pictures of victim taken by stalker, etc.
- Video-taped interview with stalker

Investigators must also separate out false from true victimization cases. Where such reports come from a need for attention, examination of the victim's background and presence of recent traumatic events may provide clues that false victimization is happening. Where the suspected stalker is filing reports against the victim, care is needed to ensure that these reports are properly handled, otherwise the victimization reports can be used to confuse matters at trial. One common investigative response is to have the victim keep notes on where she was during the day and to collect receipts from restaurants, shops, or parking lots to provide an alibi when needed. In addition to the problems discussed above, it should also be noted that stalking is one of the few personal crimes that can be committed on the Internet. Other such crimes include terroristic threat and harassment, both stalking-related offenses, as well as crimes such as solicitation of sex.

Threat Assessment and Case Management

The most important question in a stalking case is: How dangerous is the stalker likely to be to the victim? Protecting the victim is a higher priority than a successful prosecution. Hence, both law enforcement and prosecution will try to assess the degree of danger that exists both at the initial complaint and as the case continues. Typical factors considered in threat assessment include suspect's history of mental illness or violence; history of domestic violence; explicit threats of violence; vandalism or pet abuse; and/or increase in stalking activity.

Once the threat is assessed, the question arises as to how best to protect the victim. Each case must, of course, be assessed on its individual merits. Thus, in some cases, a simple "intervention" or warning interview will suffice; in others, a court injunction or protection order may be sought. In yet other cases, obtaining a civil order of protection may have the reverse effect of increasing the level of danger to the victim. Other common tactics used by law enforcement include providing the victim with an alarm system that will trigger police action at the home. Where this is done, more advanced systems will also ensure that the 911-dispatcher has access to descriptive information about any suspect and his vehicles. Victims will also be advised to take other actions such as changing phone numbers, varying routes to work, or renting a post office box for mail. In extreme cases, the victims will be aided in relocating their residence even out of the jurisdiction. In a number of states, laws now permit victims to protect their personal information on driver's licenses and even social security numbers.

Other Related Services

Either as part of threat management or just simply to provide needed counseling support, the victim should receive additional services. These include educating the victim about the nature of stalking and what she must do to help prove the case. A number of jurisdictions have developed brochures and other resources such as a formal log for recording stalking incidents. Victims must also be told of the importance of changing their behavioral patterns to reduce the likelihood of stalking incidents occurring. But only a few victim service agencies direct special attention to stalking victims, even in the context of domestic violence. Therapeutic services for stalking victims may also be made available, although such programs are rare.

Conclusion

At present, the implementation of stalking laws is limited to relatively few jurisdictions. Most of these programs use specialized staff who also serve as a resource for other agency personnel handling "spillover" stalking cases that are not handled by the core unit staff. By and large, a problem-solving approach to these cases is used by the best programs, in lieu of any routinized methods.

The goals should be to expand the numbers and responsibilities of specialized units handling stalking cases and to develop a methodology for investigation and prosecution that can be emulated by new stalking units. While problem-solving approaches will always be needed in some cases, many other cases could use the methods developed by the existing programs.

The key to achieving these goals is to motivate local agency policymakers to initiate special stalking units. This will require recognition on their part that stalking cases are

- More common than they think
- More dangerous than they appreciate
- Require specialized staff skills to investigate and prosecute

Because of widespread skepticism of research among local policymakers, national estimates of the numbers of stalking cases are not especially persuasive. Instead, policymakers must be pointed to the large numbers of serious stalking cases that special stalking units are presently handling in jurisdictions similar to that where these policymakers reside.

For example, Colorado Springs, Colorado reports handling about 40 serious stalking cases annually that are limited to domestic violence-related incidents. And the San Diego District Attorney's Office handles about 100 or more serious stalking cases annually, divided almost equally between domestic violence and stranger-related cases, with perhaps another 100 less serious cases handled by non-special unit prosecutors.

In Queens County, New York, Safe Haven advocates respond to between 250 and 300 stalking victims annually. And so on. In total, extrapolating from the experiences of the special anti-stalking units we have looked at and talked with, there are at a minimum 40,000 to 50,000 *serious* stalking cases each year. This statistic is not insignificant; it is three times the number of homicides and more than half of the number of forcible rapes.

Comparison of stalking cases to homicide and rape is not unjustified. At one level, many homicide cases, especially domestic homicides, often had a stalking component. This is the reason why stalking cases are so common among special units that are set up to deal with only the most serious threats to personal safety. At another level, the disruption in life that stalking can create for the victim can be just as serious as that from other personal injury crimes. Furthermore, because stalking is a continuing crime, its effects can continue to escalate until the victim requires extensive therapy, is forced to move the jurisdiction, spends thousands of dollars on safety equipment, etc.

Specialized expertise in investigation and prosecution of stalking cases can be developed even without specialized units. But this is not common, primarily because of the need for training in recognizing stalking cases. For example, a domestic violence investigation unit will necessarily be involved with cases that have a stalking element. Unless the unit staff are trained to look for patterns of behavior, rather than single incidents, the stalking will not be noticed. This problem is even more acute with stranger stalking that has not yet reached the stage of dire threats.

One way in which agencies can better deal with stalking crimes is to use funds available under the Violence Against Women Act of 1994 to develop new anti-stalking initiatives. The VAWA specifically includes stalking as a program focus area. And as we have seen, a number of jurisdictions have used their STOP and other federal dollars for this purpose. In other instances, the development of STOP-funded specialized domestic violence units has resulted in the unit staff being exposed to stalking for the first time as they work with victims.

What To Do and What Can Be Done

The major barrier toward any intervention is funding. Specialized staff means lower caseloads and so other staff will be required to pick up the cases that the new unit staff were formerly working on. It is not surprising, then, that so many new stalking units were started (and often continue) as pilot projects funded with federal grant money, especially those under the STOP program authorized by the VAWA. In a few instances, however, local funding was used to initiate a stalking effort and federal funds to supplement the locally funded initiative.

Regardless of how funded, specific actions needed include training. By and large most stalking victims are not receiving help from the justice system. We have heard numerous stories from all over the country of police officers refusing to take stalking complaints, even in jurisdictions where there are special stalking units or officers.

At all levels, the need for training is almost totally unmet. Meeting this need begins with state legislation requiring stalking training; only two states have such laws. While a few other state agencies such as California's Peace Officers Standards and Training Commission (POST) have developed special training programs for specialized officers, the largest need is for training patrol.

Based on the many training program materials we have reviewed to date, virtually no training focuses on the problem-solving view of stalking investigation and prosecution. Instead, the effort is limited to replicating the policies and procedures approach that has been used successfully with other crimes. But stalking is not completely subject to routinization of effort.

Stalking investigation is not limited to looking for evidence related to past crimes. Hence, techniques that work for investigating past crimes are not sufficient. Thus, stalking training must also focus on the problem-solving approach to investigation.

Training must go back to basics: How do I find out who is the stalker? How do I prove X is the stalker? This entails a mindset that is willing and anxious to innovate. And that is often what is needed.

Community Education

Community education is also needed. While television and the movies may vividly illustrate the dangers of stalkers, dramatizations about how the justice system handles these cases are missing. If few law enforcement officers know about stalking crimes, virtually no stalking victims understand that what is being done to them is a crime. The result is that only a small proportion of stalking cases are reported by victims. Instead, they might complain of harassment or violations of an order of protection. The stalking component is only revealed when a homicide results. In most jurisdictions, nobody, other than a few domestic violence service agencies and shelters, is telling victims to file stalking complaints.

In a few jurisdictions, these agencies are very aggressive and the authorities might see dozens or even hundreds of stalking cases. But such success is the exception, not the rule; and even then the number of justice agencies that handle a significant number of stranger stalkings is very low. Yet these cases are far more common than supposed, based on the experience of several specialized stalking units that aggressively respond to these cases. Victims need to be made aware of the stalking laws, and it is the responsibility of the justice agencies to take on the task of community education about stalking.

Justice system responses to stalking were nonexistent a decade ago. Today, there are a few jurisdictions that might be cited as having exemplary responses; in others, significant efforts are underway to improve their response to stalking. Even in the "best" jurisdictions, many gaps remain, especially in providing counseling and services to stalking victims.

Despite these problems, we are seeing steady improvement. And if the threshold of success in the effort to effectively help stalking victims has not yet been reached, it is in sight.

Appendix 18.1: STOP Sub-Grantees Identified by Survey State

State	Grantee	Description/Activity
Arizona	Mt. Graham Safe House	Provides services to domestic violence victims, including those who have been stalked by their abuser; advocates attend state POST training on stalking
California	San Diego District Attorney's Office	The stalking prosecution unit includes one attorney and one investigator assigned to vertically handle all domestic violence-related stalking cases; complements existing unit staff assigned to stranger stalking cases
	Los Angeles County District Attorney's Office	The stalking prosecution unit includes two attorneys and one investigator assigned to vertically prosecute most serious stalking cases in county
	Alameda County District Attorney's Office	Stalking prosecution team to vertically prosecute stalking cases in county and to coordinate state efforts to collect data about stalking protection orders
	San Joaquin County District Attorney's Office	Establish part-time stalking prosecution unit and assign one probation officer for intensive supervision of stalkers on probation
	San Francisco District Attorney's Office	Establish stalking prosecution team to vertically prosecute all stalking cases in the county
	California District Attorneys Association	Multidisciplinary training program, including stalking seminar and stalking as part of domestic violence training
	Peace Officer Standards and Training Commission	Training of law enforcement using previously developed multi-media stalking training unit as part of training for first responders (40 sessions), detectives (5 sessions), and sexual assault first responders (20 sessions)
Colorado	Ending Violence Against Women	Coalition of state prosecutors, sheriffs, and coalitions against domestic violence and against sexual assault; sponsors statewide training on violence against women issues, including stalking
	AMEND	Statewide training
	Project PAVE	Provides group counseling to domestic violence/stalking victims; individual counseling also provided; prevention education in schools includes stalking in curriculum
	Violence Prevention Coalition (Durango)	Developing protocols for risk assessment, victim logs, employers, and other system professionals

State	Grantee	Description/Activity
	Project Safeguard (Denver)	Assist with gaining orders of protection for domestic violence victims, including stalking victims (30% estimate), and provide services such as name change and safety planning
	Douglas County Sheriff	Domestic violence investigative unit also handles all stalking cases
	18th Judicial District Fast Track Prosecution	Stalking included in fast track prosecution program; special emphasis on training for CJ personnel, volunteers, and community in recognizing stalking and implementing new stalking law; and on tracking stalking defendants' locations through pretrial release Emergency Protection Program using beepers and mandatory call-backs
Connecticut	Sexual Assault Coalition and POST	Develop sexual assault and stalking training materials; POST delivers training
Delaware	Wilmington Police Department	Provide victim advocate services to victims of violence against women, including stalking
Georgia	Athens/Clarke County Police Department	Establish special investigative unit for domestic violence crimes where no arrest was made, including protective order violations and stalking
	Richmond County Sheriff	Improve investigation of stalking related to domestic violence or sexual assault offenses through enhancement in staffing of special investigative unit
Iowa	Iowa State Police	Developed a protocol/form for victims to fill out for police and prosecutor; held series of workshops
Michigan	Prosecuting Attorneys Association of Michigan	Multidisciplinary domestic violence training that includes stalking component
	Council Against Domestic Assault (Ingraham County)	Provides help to women seeking court protection orders against stalking and domestic violence; coordinates with prosecutor's victim witness unit and receives police reports on order violation complaints where no arrest made
Mississippi	Lamar County District Attorney's Office	Prosecutor assigned to handle domestic violence and stalking cases; also provides technical assistance to other prosecutors
Nevada	Elko County Sheriff's Office	Purchase of surveillance camera to help in stalking investigations
New York	New York City Police Department	Special units for stalking investigation established in two precincts
Ohio	Huron County Department of Human Services	Develop protocols for investigation and prosecution of stalking and to provide assistance for stalking victims; provide training and community materials on stalking prevention

State	Grantee	Description/Activity
	Southeast, Inc.	Provide advocate services for victims of stalking to help with evidence collection, assist in gaining protection orders, provide short-term counseling, arrange referrals for psychiatric assessment and counseling
	Rocky River Municipal Court	Establish support group for stalking victims
	Youngstown Police Department	Hired full-time investigator for stalking cases
Oklahoma	District Attorney for District 10	Victim advocate helps domestic violence and stalking victims with orders of protection
Oregon	Lane County Prosecutor Protective Order Clinic	Assists victims with applications for orders of protection against domestic violence and stalking
	Clatsop County Women's Resource Center	Funds court advocate who assists domestic violence/stalking victims in obtaining stalking orders of protection
	Sexual Assault Support Services	Provides legal advocacy and other services to stalking victims, presently numbering about 16 per month; works with legal services agency and law school clinic to assist with civil protection orders and university hearing process
Virginia	Chesterfield County District Attorney	Prosecutor assigned to domestic violence and stalking cases
	Winchester Women's Shelter	Developed stalking kits for victims, including cell phones, tape recorders, etc.
	Roanoke County Police Department	Held workshop on stalking
	Henrico County (Richmond) Police Department	Special domestic violence unit has one officer assigned to all stalking cases (about 20 per year); officer also does training for own (recruit, in-service), local, and regional agencies
West Virginia	Cabell County District Attorney Violence Against Women prosecutor	One attorney assigned to violence against women cases spends 25% of time on stalking; conducts training

State Stalking Legislation: Felony or Misdemeanor Penalties

State	Cite	Felony — First Offense	Felony or Misdemeanor	Misdemeanor — First Offense	Felony — Second Offense	Felony — Third Offense
AL	13A-6-90	✔				
AK	11.41.260		✔			
AR	5-71-229	✔				
AZ	13-2923	✔				
CA	PC 646.9		✔			
CO	18-9-111	✔				
CT	53a-181c		✔			
DE	11 § 1312A	✔				
FL	784.048		✔			
GA	16-5-90,z 91		✔		✔	
HI	711-1106.4			✔	✔	
ID	18-7905			✔	✔	
IL (ILCS)	720 ILCS 5/12-7.3	✔				
IN	35-45-10-5	✔				
IA	708.11		✔			
KS	21-3438	✔				
KY	508.130-.150		✔			
LA	14:40.2		✔		✔	
ME	17-A § 210-A			✔		✔
MD	Art 27 § 124	✔				
MA	Ch. 265 § 43	✔				
MI (MSA)	MSA 28.643(9)(3)		✔		✔	
MN	600.749		✔			
MS	97-3-107			✔	✔	
MO	565.225		✔		✔	
MN	45-5-220			✔	✔	
NE	28-311.03, .04			✔	✔	
NV	200.575		✔		✔	
NH	633:3-a			✔	✔	
NJ	2C:12-10		✔		✔	
NM	30-3A-3, 3.1		✔		✔	
NY	PL 120.40-.60		✔			
NC	14-277.3			✔	✔	
ND	12.1-17-07.1		✔		✔	
OH	2903.211		✔		✔	
OK	21 § 1173		✔		✔	
OR	163.732			✔	✔	
PA	18 PCSA § 2709		✔		✔	
RI	11-59-2			✔	✔	
SC	16-3-1720		✔		✔	
SD	22-19A-2		✔		✔	
TN	39-17-315			✔	✔	

State Stalking Legislation: Felony or Misdemeanor Penalties (continued)

State	Cite	Felony — First Offense	Felony or Misdemeanor	Misdemeanor — First Offense	Felony — Second Offense	Felony — Third Offense
TX	PC § 42.07			✔	✔	
UT	76-5-106.5		✔		✔	
VT	13 § 1061-63	✔				
VA	18.2-60.3			✔		✔
WA	9A.46.110		✔		✔	
WV	61-2-9a			✔		✔
WI	940.32		✔		✔	
WY	6-2-506		✔		✔	

Bibliography

Alldridge, P. (1994). Threat offenses — a case for reform, *Criminal Law Review*, No. 3, 176–186.

Allen, M. J. (1996). Look who's talking: seeking a solution to the problem stalking the stalker, *Web Journal of Current Legal Issues*, 4. Website: http:// www. newcastle. ac.uk /~nlawwww /1996/issue4/allen4.html.

American Prosecutors Research Institute (1997a). *Mission Possible: Stopping Stalkers* [a comprehensive training curriculum]. Alexandria, VA.

American Prosecutors Research Institute (1997b). *Stalking: Prosecutors Convict and Restrict*. Alexandria, VA. Annotation: Validity, construction, and application of stalking statutes, *American Law Review*, 29(5), 487.

Attinello, K. L. (July 1993). Anti-stalking legislation: a comparison of traditional remedies available for victims of harassment versus California Penal Code section 646.9 (California Anti-Stalking Law), *Pacific Law Journal*, 24(4), 1945–1980.

Bachman, A. and Coker, A. L. (1995). Police involvement in domestic violence: the interactive effects of victim injury, offender history of violence and rage, *Violence and Victims*, 10(2), 91–106.

Bachman, R. and Saltzman, L. (August 1995). Violence against women: estimates from the redesigned survey, in *Bureau of Justice Statistics Special Report*. Washington, D.C.: U.S. Department of Justice, Bureau of Justice Statistics.

Baker, D. (December 1995). When cyber stalkers walk, *ABA Law Journal*, 50–54.

Barton, G. (April 1995). Taking a byte out of crime: e-mail, harassment and the inefficacy of existing law, *Washington Law Review*, 70, 465.

Baty, J. A. (Fall 1996). Alabama's stalking statutes: coming out of the shadows, *Alabama Law Review*, 48, 229.

Benson, K. (September 1994). Stalking stopped in its tracks, *Police*, 18(9), 36–39, 75.

Bernstein, S. E. (1993). Living under the siege: do stalking laws protect domestic violence victims? *Cardoza Law Review*, 15, 525–567.

Birmingham, L.N. (Winter 1994). Closing the loophole: Vermont's legislative response to stalking, *Vermont Law Review*, 18(2), 477–527.

Borum, R. (1999). Threat assessment: defining an approach for evaluating risk of targeted violence, *Behavioral Science and the Law*, 17(3), 323–337.

Bouchard, K.J. (Winter 1997). Can civil damage suits stop stalkers? *Boston University Public Interest Law Journal*, 6, 551.

Boychuk, M. K. (Winter 1994). Are stalking laws unconstitutionally vague or over-broad? *Northwestern University Law Review*, 88, 769.

Bradburn, W. E. (1992). Stalking statutes: an ineffective legislative remedy for rectifying perceived problems with today's injunction system, *Ohio Northern University Law Review*, 19, 271.

Bradfield, J. L. (1998). Anti-stalking laws: do they adequately protect stalking victims? *Harvard Women's Law Journal*, 21(1998), 229–266.

Brewster, M. P. (1998). An exploration of the experiences and needs of former intimate stalking victims. Westchester University (available from National Institute of Justice, Rockville, MD).

Buckley, M. (1994). Stalking laws — problem or solution? *Wisconsin Women's Law Journal*, 9(23), 23–66.

Burgess, A. W., Baker, T., and Halloran, H. (December 1997). Stalking behaviors within domestic violence, *Journal of Family Violence*, 12(4), 389–403.

Carlson, M. J., Harris, S. D., and Holden, G. (1999). Protective orders and domestic violence; risk factors for re-abuse, *Journal of Family Violence*, 14, 205–226.

Carmody, C. (September 1994). Stalking by computer, *ABA Law Journal*, 80(9), 70.

Chaudhuri, M. and Daly, K. (1992). Do restraining orders help? Battered women's experience with male violence and legal process, in E.S. Buzawa and C.G. Buzawa, (Eds.), *Domestic Violence; the Changing Criminal Justice Response*. Westport, CT: Greenwood.

Church, E. J. (October 1998). But I still love you! Obsessive love, stalking, and the pursuit of remedies, *The New Mexico Trial Lawyer*, 26(9), 1, 203–212.

Clede, B. (September 1993). Monitoring stalkers: keeping track inexpensively, *Law and Order*, 41(11), 78–79.

Coleman, F. L. Stalking behavior and the cycle of domestic violence, *Journal of Interpersonal Violence*, 12(3), 420–432; Comment: the formation and viability of anti-stalking laws, *Villanova Law Review*, 39(1994): 1387.

Copelan, D. (Winter 1994). Is Georgia's stalking law unconstitutionally vague? *Mercer Law Review*, 45(2), 853–863.

Cordes, R. (May–June 1993). A deputy's hunch stops a wife stalker, *Sheriff*, 45(3), 29, 32.

Cordes, R. (October 1993). Watching over the watched: greater protection sought for stalking victims, *Trial*, 29(12), 12–13.

Crowley, R. R. (October 1995). Crimes against the person: provide two additional means by which aggravated stalking statute may be violated, *Georgia State University Law Review*, 12, 105.

Cyberstalking (August 1999). A New Challenge for Law Enforcement and Industry. A Report from the Attorney General to the Vice President. Website: http://www. usdoj.gov/ag/cyberstalkingreport.htm.

David, J. W. (1994). Is Pennsylvania's stalking law constitutional? *University of Pittsburgh Law Review*, 56, 205.

Davis, J. A. and Chipman, M. A. (1997). Stalkers and other obsessional types: a review and forensic psychological typology of those who stalk, *Journal of Clinical Forensic Medicine*, 4, 166–172.

Deirmenjian, J. M. (1999). Stalking in cyberspace, *Journal of American Academy of Psychiatry and the Law*, 17(3), 407–413.

Delaware Statistical Analysis Center (1996). *Domestic Violence in Delaware in 1994; An Analysis of Victim to Offender Relationships with Special Focus on Stalking.* Dover, DE.

Diacovo, N. (1995). California's anti-stalking statute: deterrent or false sense of security, *Southwestern University Law Review*, 24, 389.

Domestic Violence and Stalking: The Second Annual Report to Congress Under the Violence Against Women Act (1997). Washington, D.C.: U.S. Department of Justice, U.S. Government Printing Office.

Dunn, J. (1997). No place to hide: violent pursuit in public and private, in *Perspective on Social Problems*, Vol. 9 (pp. 143–168). Greenwich, CT: JAI Press.

Dunn, J. (1999a). What love has to do with it: the cultural construction of emotions and sorority women responses to forcible interactions, *Social Problems*, 46, 440–459.

Dunn, J. (1999b). Forceful Interaction: Social Construction of Coercive Pursuit and Intimate Stalking. Ph.D. doctoral dissertation, University of California at Davis.

Dvorchak, R. J. (1993). *Someone Is Stalking Me: A True Story of Marriage, Murder and Deadly Delusions in the Michigan Heartland.* New York: Dell Publishers.

Dziegielewski, S. F. and Roberts, A. R. (1995). Stalking victims and survivors; identification, legal remedies, and crisis treatment, in A.R. Roberts (Ed.), *Crisis Intervention and Time-Limited Cognitive Treatment*. Thousand Oaks, CA: Sage Publications.

Emerson, R.M. and Ferris, O. K. (August 1998). On being stalked, *Social Problems*, 45(3), 289.

Evans, R. (1994). Every step you take; the strange and subtle crime of stalking, *Law Institute Journal*, 68, 1021–1023.

Fahnestock, J. (1993). All stock and no action: pending Missouri stalking legislation, *University of Missouri–Kansas City Law Review*, 783.

Faulkner, R.P. and Haosi, D. H. (Winter 1994). And where you go I'll follow: the constitutionality of antistalking laws and proposed model legislation, *Harvard Journal on Legislation*, 31(1), 1–62.

Fein, R. A., Vossekuil, B., and Holden, G. (September 1995). Threat assessment: an approach to prevent targeted violence, in *Research in Brief*. Washington, D.C.: U.S. Department of Justice, National Institute of Justice, U.S. Government Printing Office.

Fink, M. (1999). *Adolescent Sexual Assault and Harassment Prevention Curriculum.* Holmes Beach, FL: Learning Publications.

Flynn, C. P. (1993). New Jersey anti-stalking law: putting an end to a 'fatal attraction,' *Seton Hall Legislative Journal,* 18, 297.

Fremouw, W. J., Westrup, D., and Pennypacker, J. (July 1997). Stalking on campus: the prevalence and strategies for coping with stalking, *Journal of Forensic Sciences,* 42(4), 666.

Fritz, J. P. (Summer 1995). A proposal for mental health provisions in state anti-stalking laws, *The Journal of Psychiatry and Law,* 23, 295.

Gargan, J. (February 1994). Stop stalkers before they strike, *Security Management,* 38(2), 31–32.

Gerberth, V. J. (October 1992). Stalkers, *Law and Order,* 40(10), 138–143.

Gilligan, M. J. (Fall 1992). Stalking the stalker: developing new laws to thwart those who terrorize others, *Georgia Law Review,* 27(1), 285–342.

Gondolf, E.W., McWilliams, D., Hart, J. B., and Stuehling, J. (1994). Court response to petitions for civil protection orders, *Journal of Interpersonal Violence,* 9, 503–517.

Goode, M. (1995). Stalking: crime of the nineties? *Criminal Law Journal,* 19 (1), 27.

Goodnough, D. (2000). *Stalking: A Hot Issue.* Berkeley Heights, NJ: Enslow.

Goom, S. (1997). Whether committed by words alone — letters inducing fear of violence — whether apprehension of "immediate" violence, *Criminal Law Review,* 576–578.

Great Britain Home Office (1996). *Stalking: The Solutions: A Consultation Paper.* London, England.

Greenberg, S. (Spring 1997). Threats, harassment, and hate on-line: recent, *Boston University Public Interest Law Journal,* 6, 673.

Gregson, C. B. (1998). California's anti-stalking statute: the pivotal role of intent, *Golden Gate University Law Review,* 28, 221–263.

Guy, R. A., Jr. (May 1993). Nature and constitutionality of stalking laws, *Vanderbilt Law Review,* 46(4), 991–1029.

Haggard, T. R. (March 1997). The South Carolina anti-stalking statute: a study in bad drafting, *South Carolina Lawyer,* No. 5, 13.

Hall, D. M. (1998). The victims of stalking, in J.R. Meloy (Ed.), *The Psychology of Stalking.* San Diego, CA: Academic Press.

Hankins, J. L. (Spring 1993). Criminal anti-stalking laws: Oklahoma hops on the legislative bandwagon, *Oklahoma Law Review,* 46, 109.

Harmon, B. K. (1994). Illinois' newly amended stalking law: are all the problems solved? *Southern Illinois University Law Journal,* 10, 165.

Harmon, R. B., Rosner, R., and Owens, R. (1995). Obsessional harassment and erotomania in a criminal court population, *Journal of Forensic Sciences,* 40(2), 188–196.

Hendricks, J. E. and Spillane, L. (October 1992). Stalking: what can we do to forestall tragedy? *The Police Chief,* 60(12), 4.

Holmes, R. M. (December 1993). Stalking in America: types and methods of criminal stalkers. *Journal of Contemporary Criminal Justice*, 9(4), 17–327.

Hueter, J. A. (January 1997). Lifesaving legislation: but will the Washington stalking law survive constitutional scrutiny? *Washington Law Review*, 72(1), 213–240.

Infante, C. (May 1994). The new stalking law, *Arkansas Lawyer*, 28 (Fall 1994), 30; Investigations, *Law and Order*, 42(5), 89.

Johnson, D. L. (September 1994). A team approach to threat assessment, *Security Management*, 38(9), 73.

Jordan, T. (Summer 1995). The efficacy of the California stalking law: surveying its evolution, extracting insights from domestic violence cases, *Hastings Women's Law Journal*, 6(2), 370–383.

Kace, J. H. (September 1994). Aftermath of seeking domestic violence protective orders: the victim's perspective, *Journal of Contemporary Criminal Justice*, 110(3), 204–219.

Keenehan, D. and Barlow, A. (1997). Stalking: a paradoxical crime of the nineties, *International Journal of Risk, Security and Crime Prevention*, 2, 291–300.

Keilitz, S., Hannaford, P. L., and Efkeman, H. S. (1992). Civil Protection Orders: The Benefits and Limitations for Victims of Domestic Violence, Grant No. 93-IJ-CX-0035.

Kienlen, K. K. (1998). Developmental and social antecedents of stalking, in J.R. Meloy (Ed.), *The Psychology of Stalking*. San Diego, CA: Academic Press.

Kienlen, K. K., Birmingham, D. L., and Reid, J. R. (1997). A comparative study of psychotic and nonpsychotic stalking, *Journal of American Academy of Psychiatry and the Law*, 25(3), 317–334.

Klein, M. (1998). Stalking situations, *American Demographics*, 20(3), 32.

Kolb, T. V. (1994). North Dakota's stalking law: criminalizing the crime before the crime, *North Dakota Law Review*, 70, 159.

Kong, R. (1996). Criminal harassment, *Juristat*, 16(12), Statistics Canada: Canadian Centre for Justice Statistics, 1–13.

Kowalski, S. K. (1994). Michigan stalking law: is it constitutional? *Michigan Bar Journal*, 73, 926.

Krueger, K. (Winter 1995). Panel presentation on stalking, *University of Toledo Law Review*, 25, 903.

Kurt, J. L. (1995). Stalking as a variant of domestic violence, *Bulletin of the American Academy of Psychiatry and the Law*, 23(2), 219–230.

Lardner, G., Jr. (1995). *The Stalking of Kristin: A Father Investigates the Murder of His Daughter*. New York: Onyx.

Lawson-Cruttenden, T. (1996a). Is there a law against stalking? *New Law Journal*, 6, 418–420.

Lawson-Cruttenden, T. (1996b). The government's proposed stalking law — a discussion paper, *Family Law*, 26, 755–758.

Lawson-Cruttenden, T. and Hussain, B. (1996). Psychological assault and harassment, *New Law Journal*, 146(6759), 1326–1327.

Lee, R. K. (1998). Romantic and electronic stalking in a college context, *William and Mary Journal of Women and the Law*, 4, 373–466.

Lindsey, M. (1993). *Terror of Batterer Stalking: A Guideline for Intervention*. Littleton, CO: Gylantic Publishing.

Lingg, R. A. (Spring 1993). Stopping stalkers: a critical examination of anti-stalking statutes, *St. John's Law Review*, 67(2), 347–381.

Los Angeles Police Department (February 1999). *Threat Management Unit Guidelines*. Los Angeles.

Los Angeles Police Department Threat Management Unit (n.k.d.). *Stalking Victim's Handbook*. Los Angeles.

MacFarlane, B. A. (1999a). People who stalk people. I, *The Advocate*, 57, 201–216.

MacFarlane, B. A. (1999b). People who stalk people. II, *The Advocate*, 57, 353–377.

Manitoba Law Reform Commission (1997). *Stalking*. Winnipeg.

Marks, C. A. (Summer 1997). The Kansas stalking law: a "credible threat" to victims; a critique of the Kansas stalking law and proposed legislation, *Washburn Law Journal*, 36(3), 468–498.

McAnaney, K., Curliss, L A., and Abeyta-Price, A. E. (April 1993). From imprudence to crime: anti-stalking laws, *Notre Dame Law Review*, 68(4), 819–909.

McCann, J. T. (1995). Obsessive attachment and the victimization of children: can anti-stalking legislation provide protection? *Law and Psychology Review*, 19, 93.

McCann, J. T. (1998). Risk of violence in stalking cases and legal case management, *Pennsylvania Bar Association Quarterly*, 69(3), 117–122.

McFarlane, J. M. (1999). Stalking and intimate partner femicide, *Journal of Homicide Studies*, 3(4).

Meloy, J. R. (Summer 1996). Stalking (obsessional following): a review of some preliminary studies, *Aggression and Violent Behavior*, 1(2), 147–162.

Meloy, J. R. (1997). A case study of stalking: "All I wanted was to love you," in J. R. Meloy et al. (Eds.), *Contemporary Rorschach Interpretation* (pp. 177–190). Mahwah, NJ: Lawrence Erlbaum Associates.

Meloy, J. R. (1998). The psychology of stalking, in J. R. Meloy (Ed.), *The Psychology of Stalking*. San Diego, CA: Academic Press.

Meloy, J.R. and Cowett, J. Y. (1996). Domestic protection orders and the prediction of subsequent criminality and violence toward protectees, *Psychotherapy*, 34, 447–458.

Michigan Legislature (1995). *Domestic Violence, Stalking, Date Rape: An Information Guide*. Lansing, MI: The Legislature.

Milano, S. M. (1995). *Defending Our Lives: Protecting Yourself from Domestic Violence and Stalking*. Chicago: Noble Press.

Miller, R. N. (January 1997). Stalk talk: a first look at anti-stalking legislation, *Washington and Lee Law Review*, 71, 213.

Milton, J. and Jankins, J. (Spring 1993). Criminal law: criminal "anti-stalking" laws: Oklahoma hops on the legislative bandwagon, *Oklahoma Law Review*, 46, 49.

Mohandie, K., Hatcher, C., and Raymond, D. (1998). False victimization syndromes in stalking, in J. R. Meloy (Ed.), *The Psychology of Stalking*. San Diego, CA: Academic Press.

Monaghan, P. (March 1998). Beyond the Hollywood myths: researchers examine stalkers and their victims, *Chronicle of Higher Education*, 44(26), A17.

Montesino, B. (1993). I'll be watching you: strengthening the effectiveness and enforceability of state anti-stalking statutes, *Loyola of Los Angeles Entertainment Law Journal*,13, 545–586.

Morin, K. S. (Winter 1993). The phenomenon of stalking: do existing state statutes provide adequate protection? *San Diego Justice Journal* 1(1), 123.

Morville, D. A. (1993). Stalking laws: are they solutions for more problems? *Washington University Law Quarterly*, 71, 921.

Moses-Zirkes, S. (1998). Psychologists question anti-stalking laws' utility, *APA Monitor*, 23(10), 53.

Mullen, P. E., Pathé, M., and Purcell, R. (2000). *Stalkers and Their Victims*. New York: Cambridge University Press.

National Criminal Justice Association (October 1993). Project to Develop a Model Anti-Stalking Code for States. Washington, D.C.: U.S. Department of Justice, National Institute of Justice, U.S. Government Printing Office.

National Criminal Justice Association (June 1996). *Regional Seminar Series on Implementing Antistalking Codes*. Washington, D.C.: U.S. Department of Justice, Bureau of Justice Assistance, U.S. Government Printing Office.

Nehilla, T. J. (Summer 1995). Applying stalking statutes to groups — a first amendment freedom of speech analysis, *Dickinson Law Review*, 99, 1071.

Nicastro, E. M., Cousins, A. V., and Spitzberg, B. H. (2000). The tactical face of stalking, *Journal of Criminal Justice*, 28, 69–82.

O'Reilly, G. W. (Summer 1993). Illinois' stalking statute: taking unsteady aim at preventing attacks, *John Marshall Law Review*, 26(4), 821–864.

Palarea, R. E., Zona, M., Lane, J. C., and Langhinrichsen-Rohling, J. (1999). The dangerous nature of intimate relationship stalking: threats, violence, and associated risk factors, *Behavioral Science and the Law*, 17(3), 269–283.

Pappas, D. M. (1996). When a stalker's hot pursuit turns coldly calculated chase in Minnesota: how specific need expressions of intent be or do actions speak louder than words? *Hamline Law Review*, 20(2), 371–393.

Pathé, M. and Mullen, P. E. (January 1997). The impact of stalkers on their victims, *British Journal of Psychiatry*, 170, 12–17.

Pathé, M., Mullen, P. E., and Purcell, M. (1999). Staking: false claims of victimisation, *British Journal of Psychiatry*, 173, 170–172.

Patton, E. A. (Winter 1994). Stalking laws: in pursuit of a remedy, *Rutgers Law Journal*, 25(2), 465–515.

Phipps, M. P. (September 1993). North Carolina's new anti-stalking law: constitutionally sound, but is it really a deterrent? *North Carolina Law Review*, 71(6), 1933–1953.

Pilon, M. (1993). *"Anti-Stalking" Laws: The United States and Canadian Experience.* Ottawa: Library of Parliament, Research Branch.

Poling, B. E. (1994). Stalking: is the law hiding in the shadows of constitutionality? *Capitol University Law Review*, 23, 279.

Proctor, M. (September 1995). Stalking: a behavioral overview with case management strategies, *Journal of California Law Enforcement*, 29(3), 63–69.

Riggs, S. M., Romano, J., Starkweather, J., and Waaler, B. (December 1997). *Domestic Stalking: Prevalence, Protection and Policies.* Williamsburg, VA: College of William and Mary, Center for Public Policy Research.

Roberts, A. R. and Dziegielewski, S. F. (Winter 1996). Assessment typology and intervention with the survivors of stalking, *Aggression and Violent Behavior*, 1(4), 359–368.

Roscha, N. (Winter 1994). The anti-stalking law of Ohio: will it pass constitutional muster? *University of Dayton Law Review*, 19(2), 749–781.

Ross, E. S. (Spring 1993). E-mail stalking: is adequate legal protection available? *The John Marshall Journal of Computer and Information Law*, 13(3), 405.

Salame, L. (Spring 1993). A national survey of stalking laws: a legislative trend comes to the aid of domestic violence victims and others, *Suffolk University Law Review*, 27(67), 67–111.

Samuels, A. (1997). Stalking defined, *Statute Law Review*, 18(3), 244–249.

Sanford, B. S. (May 1993). Stalking is now illegal: will a paper law make a difference? *Thomas M. Cooley Law Review*, 10(2), 409–442.

Saunders, R. (1998). The legal perspective on stalking, in J. R. Meloy, (Ed.), *The Psychology of Stalking.* San Diego, CA: Academic Press.

Saxl, M. V. (1998). The struggle to make stalking a crime: a legislative road map of how to develop effective stalking legislation in Maine, *Seton Hall Legislative Journal*, 23(1), 57–100.

Schell, B. H. (2000). *Stalking, Harassment, and Murder in the Workplace: Guidelines for Protection and Prevention.* Westport, CT: Quorum Books.

Schelong, K. M. (Fall 1994). Domestic violence and the state: responses to and rationales for spousal battering, marital rape and stalking, *Marquette Law Review*, 78, 79.

Schwartz-Watts, D. and Morgan, D. W. (1998). Violent versus nonviolent stalkers, *Journal of the American Academy of Psychiatry and the Law*, 26, 241–245.

Schwartz-Watts, D., Morgan, D. W., and Barnes, C. J. (1997). Stalkers: the South Carolina experience, *Journal of the American Academy of Psychiatry and the Law*, 25(4), 541–545.

Scocas, E. (1994). *Domestic Violence in Delaware: An Analysis of Victim to Offender Relationships.* Dover, DE: Delaware Statistical Analysis Center.

Sheetz, M. (2000). Cyberpredators: police Internet investigations under Florida Statute 847.0135, *University of Miami Law Review*, 54, 405–449.

Shields, J. M. (March/April 1998). Harassment: a simple charge, with a complicated application, *State Law Journal*, 70(3), 10–16.

Sloan, C. O. (Winter 1994). Standing up to stalkers: South Carolina's antistalking law is a good first step, *South Carolina Law Review*, 45(2), 383–427.

Sneirson, A. M. (1995). No place to hide: why state and federal enforcement of stalking laws may be the best way to protect abortion providers, *Washington University Law Quarterly*, 73, 635.

Snow, R. L. (1995). *Stopping a Stalker: A Cop's Guide to Making the System Work for You*. New York: Plenum Press.

Sohn, E. F. (May–June 1994). Anti-stalking statutes: do they actually protect victims? *Criminal Law Bulletin*, 30(3), 203–241.

Spence-Diehl, E. (1999). *Stalking: A Handbook for Victims*. Holmes Beach, FL: Marketing Manager Learning Publications.

Spitzberg, B. H. (1997). Intimate violence, in W. R. Cupach and D. J. Canary (Eds.), *Competence in Interpersonal Conflict* (pp. 174–201). New York: McGraw-Hill.

Stalking and Domestic Violence (1998). The Third Annual Report to Congress Under the Violence Against Women Act. Washington, D.C.: U.S. Department of Justice.

Stalking: Telecourse Reference Guide (1996). California Commission on Peace Officer Standards and Training (POST), Sacramento, CA.

State Justice Institute (1996). Validity and Use of Evidence Concerning Battering and Its Effects in Criminal Trials: Report Responding to Section 40507 of the Violence Against Women Act. Alexandria, VA.

Stearns, H. M. (1995). Stalking stuffers: a revolutionary law to keep predators behind bars, *Santa Clara Law Review*, 35, 1027.

Steinman, L. I. (August 1993). Despite anti-stalking laws, stalkers continue to stalk: are these laws constitutional and effective? *St. Thomas Law Review*, 6, 213.

Strikis, S. A. (August 1993). Stopping stalking, *Georgetown Law Journal*, 81, 2771.

The domestic violence pendulum: has it swung too far? Are harassment charges now being used as a sword rather than a shield? *Seton Hall Law Review*, 29(342), 342–366.

Thomas, K. R. (1992). Anti-Stalking Statutes: Background and Constitutional Analysis. Washington, D.C.: Congressional Research Service, Library of Congress, U.S. Government Printing Office.

Thomas, K. R. (March–April 1993). How to stop the stalker: state anti-stalking laws, *Criminal Law Bulletin*, 29(2),124–136.

Tjaden, P. and Thoennes, N. (November 1998). Prevalence, incidence, and consequences of violence against women: findings from the National Violence Against Women Survey, NIJ Research in Brief. Washington, D.C.: U.S. Government Printing Office.

Tjaden, P. and Thoennes, N. (1998). Stalking in America: findings from the National Violence Against Women Survey, NIJ Research in Brief. Washington, D.C.: U.S. Government Printing Office.

Tolhurst, K. W. (Fall 1994). A search for solutions: evaluating the latest anti-stalking developments and the National Institute of Justice model stalking code, *William and Mary Journal of Women and the Law*, 1(1), 269.

Tucker, J. T. (1993). Stalking the problems with stalking laws: the effectiveness of Florida Statutes section 784, 048, *Florida Law Review*, 45(4), 609–707.

Turl, P. (1994). Stalking is a public problem, *The New Law Journal*, 144(6647), 632.

U.S. Congress (September 19, 1992). Senate Committee on the Judiciary. Anti-Stalking Legislation: Hearing before the Senate Judiciary Committee. 102nd Congr., 2nd Session, Report 102–1073. Washington, D.C.: U.S. Government Printing Office.

U.S. Congress (September 29, 1992). Senate Committee on the Judiciary. Anti-Stalking Legislation: Hearing on S.2922, a Bill To Assist the States in the Enactment of Legislation to Address the Criminal Act of Stalking Other Persons. 102nd Congr., 2nd Session, Report 102–1073. Washington, D.C.: U.S. Government Printing Office.

U.S. Congress (March 17, 1993). Senate Committee on the Judiciary. Anti-Stalking Proposals: Hearings before the Committee on the Judiciary on Combating Stalking and Family Violence. 103rd Congr., 1st Session, Report 103–206. Washington, D.C.: U.S. Government Printing Office.

Varn, R. J. and McNeal, C. (1993). Point/counterpoint. Are anti-stalking laws fatally flawed? *State Government News*, 36(8), 9.

Walker, J. M. (1993). Anti-stalking legislation: does it protect the victim without violating the rights of the accused? *Denver University Law Review*, 71(1), 273.

Walker, L. E. (1998). Stalking and domestic violence, in J. R. Meloy (Ed.), *The Psychology of Stalking*. San Diego, CA: Academic Press.

Wallace, H. (Spring 1995). Stalkers: the constitution and victim remedies, *Criminal Justice*, 10(1), 16–19.

Wallace, H. (1995). A prosecutor's guide to stalking, *The Prosecutor*, 29(1), 26–30.

Wallace, H. and Kelty, K. (1995). Stalking and restraining orders: a legal and psychological perspective, *Journal of Crime and Justice*, 18(2), 99–111.

Wallace, J. H. and Silverman, J. (1996). Stalking and post traumatic stress syndrome, *Police Journal*, 69(3), 203–206.

Walsh, K.L. (Winter 1996). Comment: safe and sound at last? Federalized anti-stalking legislation in the United States and Canada, *Dickinson Journal of International Law*, 14, 373.

Ward, C. (June 1994). Minnesota's anti-stalking statute: a durable tool to protect victims from terroristic behavior, *Law and Inequality: A Journal of Theory and Practice*, 12(2), 613–647.

Warner, P. K. (1988). Aural assault: obscene telephone calls, *Qualitative Sociology*, 11, 302–318.

Wattendorf, G. E. (March 2000). Stalking-investigation strategies, *FBI Law Enforcement Bulletin*, 10–14.

Way, C. R. (June 1994). The criminalization of stalking: an exercise in media manipulation and political opportunism, *McGill Law Journal*, 39(2), 379.

Welch, J. M. (1995). Stalking and anti-stalking legislation: a guide to the literature of a new legal concept, *RSR: Reference Services Review*, 213(3), 53.

Wells, K. (August–October 1996). California's anti-stalking law a first, *Law Enforcement Quarterly*, 1–12.

Wells, K. (November 1996–January 1997). Stalker interviews are crucial, *Law Enforcement Quarterly*, 9–12, 31.

Wells, K. (July 1997). Stalking: the criminal law response, *Criminal Law Review*, 7(7), 463–470.

Westrup, D. (1998). Applying functional analysis to stalking behavior, in J.R. Meloy (Ed.), *The Psychology of Stalking*. San Diego, CA: Academic Press.

Westrup, D. (May 1999). The psychological impact of stalking on female undergraduates, *Journal of Forensic Science*, 44(3): 554–557.

Westrup, D. and Fremouw, W. J. (1998). Stalking behavior; a literature review and suggested functional analytic assessment technology, *Aggression and Violent Behavior; A Review Journal*, 3, 255–256.

Wexler, S. (1998). Crime of stalking, *Law Enforcement Technology*, 25(6), 34–37.

White, S. G. and Cawood, J. S. (1998). Threat management of stalking cases, in J. R. Meloy (Ed.), *The Psychology of Stalking*. San Diego, CA: Academic Press.

Wickens, J. C. (Spring 1994). Michigan's new anti-stalking laws: good intentions gone awry, *Detroit College of Law Review*, No. 1, 157–209.

Williams, W. L., Lane, J. C., and Zona, M. (February 1996). Stalking, successful intervention strategies, *The Police Chief*, 62(2), 24–26.

Wills, C. (1997). Stalking: the criminal law response, *Criminal Law Review*, 463–470.

Wisconsin Department of Justice (1996). *Report of 1996 Arrests for Stalking and Harassment in Wisconsin*. Madison, WI.

Wright, C. (1999). *Everything You Need to Know about Dealing with Stalking*. New York: Rosen Publishing.

Wright, J. A., Burgess, A. G., and Douglas, J. E. (September 1995). Investigating stalking crimes, *Journal of Psychosocial Nursing and Mental Health*, 33(9), 38.

Wright, J. A., Burgess, A. G., Burgess, A. W., and Laszlo, A. T. (December 1996). A typology of interpersonal stalking, *Journal of Interpersonal Violence*, 11(4), 487–502.

Zona, M. A., Sharma, K., and Lane, J. (April 1993). Comparative study of erotomanic and obsessional subjects in a forensic sample, *Journal of Forensic Sciences*, 38(4), 894–903.

Zona, M. A., Palarea, R. E., and Lane, J.C. (1998) Psychiatric diagnosis and the offender-victim typology of stalking, in J. R. Meloy (Ed.), *The Psychology of Stalking*. San Diego, CA: Academic Press.

About the Contributing Author

Neal Miller, J.D.

Neal Miller, J.D. is a principal associate with the Institute for Law and Justice (ILJ). Mr. Miller has nearly 30 years of policy-research experience with criminal justice. In the field of corrections, his work has ranged from drafting prison reform legislation for the Congress, to studies of local needs for new jails, to analyzing the numbers of persons with arrest records in the labor force for the U.S. Department of Labor. Recent court studies have included studies of prosecutorial policies in seeking juvenile waiver to adult court, the use of juvenile records as a factor in adult sentencing, and a study of attorney forum selection in civil law diversity cases. Other major studies have focused on gang crime and drugs in the workplace.

Most recently, Mr. Miller has worked on three major National Institute of Justice-funded studies of police and prosecutor initiatives relating to domestic violence, including national evaluations of the federal STOP block grant program and the discretionary funded Arrest Policies program. A third study is an examination of the implementation of state stalking legislation, from which his work here was derived. Mr. Miller has had over 50 books and articles published. His most recent work is a Compendium of Criminal Defense Standards, developed for the Bureau of Justice Assistance of the U.S. Department of Justice.

Prosecuting Those Who Stalk: A Prosecutor's Legal Perspective and Viewpoint

19

KERRY WELLS

Contents

Introduction

Prior to 1990 victims of stalking were often left to fend for themselves in the face of harassing and threatening behavior. Unless the stalker physically hurt them (or committed some other crime such as kidnap, rape, robbery, etc.) police officers' hands were essentially tied because no "crime" had been committed. Much to the consternation of well-intentioned officers, a common refrain heard from such victims was "What do I have to do — wait until he kills me?" But in 1989, the shocking murder of actress Rebecca Lynn Schaeffer by an obsessed fan, Robert John Bardo, and the senseless murder of three other women who had been stalked in Southern California changed the course of harassment laws forever.

California became the first governmental entity in the world to recognize the crime of stalking. In passing Penal Code section 646.9 the legislature took the unprecedented position that constitutionally protected freedom of movement and speech can be restricted where the intent and effect of such "freedom" is to terrorize another. Law enforcement, for the first time, was given a tool to intervene and protect victims before their fears became a reality and they were actually injured or killed.

The California stalking statute provided a model for other states, which quickly followed in drafting similar stalking legislation. Most states have the same basic core elements of stalking; that is, harassment and credible threat, but there are significant differences in the areas of the required intent on the part of the stalker and in the penalty or punishment imposed. For purposes of this chapter, the California statute will be discussed to illustrate the various legal issues raised by existing stalking laws.

While initially the drafting of the California 646 statute left some loopholes that allowed certain types of egregious behavior to go uncharged, the statute presently reads as follows:

> Any person who willfully, maliciously, and repeatedly follows or harasses another person and who makes a credible threat with the intent to place that person in reasonable fear for his or her safety, or the safety of his or her immediate family, is guilty of the crime of stalking.

The statute then further defines these terms and elements as follows.

Harassment

"Harasses" means a knowing and willful course of conduct directed at a specific person that seriously alarms, annoys, torments, or terrorizes the person, and that serves no legitimate purpose. This course of conduct must be such as would cause a reasonable person to suffer substantial emotional distress, and must actually cause substantial emotional distress to the person.

Course of Conduct Crime

A "course of conduct" means a pattern of conduct composed of a series of acts over a period of time, however short, evidencing a continuity of purpose. Constitutionally protected activity is not included within the meaning of "course of conduct."

Concept of Credible Threat

A "credible threat" means a verbal or written threat, including that performed through the use of an electronic communication device, or a threat implied by a pattern of conduct or a combination of verbal, written, or electronically communicated statements and conduct made with the intent to place the person that is the target of the threat in reasonable fear for his or her safety, or the safety of his or her family, and made with the apparent ability to carry out the threat so as to cause the person who is the target of the threat to reasonably fear for his or her safety or the safety of his or her family. It is not necessary to prove that the defendant had the intent to actually carry out the threat. The present incarceration of a person making the threat shall not be a bar to prosecution under this section.

It came as no real surprise that such a new and relatively complex crime would quickly face constitutional attack. Early challenges focused on the alleged vagueness of the language used to define the terms. In *People v. Heilman* (1994) 25 Cal. App. 4th, for example, the court held the term "repeatedly" was not unconstitutionally vague, given its common sense meaning of "more than one time." Other unsuccessful constitutional attacks have occurred in *People v. McClelland* (1996) 42 Cal. App. 4th 144 (challenging the vagueness of subsection (b) which applies when a restraining order is in effect), *People v. Tran* (1996) 47 Cal. App. 4th 253 (challenging the terms "harasses" and "serves no legitimate purpose"), *People v. Falk* (1997) 52 Cal. App. 4th 287 (challenging the term "safety"), *People v. Ewing* (1999) 76 Cal. App. 4th (challenging "alarm," "annoy," "torment," and "terrorize") and *People v. Borrelli* (2000) 77 Cal. App. 4th 703 (claiming the statute was overbroad and impinged upon First Amendment rights). Several other states, including Florida, Georgia, Oklahoma, and Virginia, have also upheld the constitutionality of their stalking statutes.

Court decisions have additionally begun to clarify the terms and definitions used in these statutes which have proved instructive on the type and level of proof required for prosecution and conviction of stalking. The most common legal issues faced by police and prosecutors are discussed below.

Course of Conduct and the Issue of Harassment

There are several issues to consider when determining whether a suspect's behavior constitutes legal harassment. First, has there been a series of acts committed? Second, have these acts targeted a specific person? Third, have the acts resulted in the required effect on the victim (i.e., fear)? And fourth, would the acts cause a reasonable person to be so affected?

It is clear that harassment by its very nature requires more than one act. While most states do not specify a particular number, the course of conduct required to constitute stalking is typically defined as a series of acts over a period of time, however short, evidencing a continuity of purpose. In California, case law has held that the time period involved can be as short as 1 day (*People v. McCray* (1997) 58 Cal. App. 4th 159). This refutes the common view that stalking must go on for weeks or months in order to be prosecutable. Recognizing that law enforcement can step in much earlier than that is obviously helpful in controlling situations that are likely to escalate.

If there has been a series of acts committed, the next question is whether there is a specific victim who has been targeted. For example, if the suspect stands in front of the doorway to a bank and harasses everyone who attempts to enter because he believes the bank's interest rates are too high, this would not constitute stalking. There is no "specific" victim. Neither would it be stalking when a young man indiscriminately harasses an entire neighborhood by loudly and dangerously driving through the streets. The crime of stalking contemplates the targeting of only one particular person.

If there has been behavior directed at a specific person, another important issue is showing how that behavior affected that person. It is not enough that the conduct is simply annoying or bothersome. Most states require that the stalker's acts must place the victim in fear for his/her safety. In California, the victim must not only be fearful but must also suffer from "substantial emotional distress" as a result of the stalking. This has been defined as something more than everyday mental distress or upset. The phrase "entails a serious invasion of the victim's mental tranquility" requires proof of the severity, nature, or extent of the distress (*People v. Ewing* (1999) 76 Cal. App. 4th 199, 210).

In addition, it is not enough that the victim was actually terrorized by the stalker's acts. The conduct must be such as would cause a reasonable person to feel the same. There is thus both a subjective and objective quality to the analysis of the stalker's conduct and the resulting fear. Of course, in order for jurors to make the determination of whether it was reasonable for the victim to be afraid, they are entitled to know all the information the victim was aware of that contributed to that fear. If, for example, one of the reasons the victim believed the defendant was capable of carrying out his threats was because he had assaulted her in the past, or she was aware of other violent behavior on his part against others, this evidence is relevant and admissible on that issue (*People v. Garrett* (1994) 30 Cal. App. 4th 962).

One question that is frequently raised regarding the definition of harassment is what specific types of conduct qualify. Most stalking statutes do not delineate any particular type of acts that are precluded, such as phone calls, letters, approaches, unwanted gifts, etc. The definition of "course of conduct" is, of necessity, broad and imprecise because there are, in fact, unlimited possibilities as to what might constitute harassing behavior.

Stalkers are limited only by their own imaginations, and what may be otherwise innocuous behavior can, depending on the circumstance, become terrifying. In one example, the suspect, who was a stranger to the victim, left pennies on her doorstep whenever he came to her front door. She had repeatedly told him to leave her alone and his presence at her house frightened her. When she came to work one day to find a penny on her desk, something that would probably go unnoticed by most people, she was terrified. She realized he had found out where she worked and had gained access to her office. It is important to recognize that in stalking prosecutions context is crucial. Almost anything can be harassing, depending on the context of the conduct and the surrounding circumstances. Frequently conduct that is not in itself illegal can constitute stalking when the entire context of the activity is evaluated.

The Issue of a Credible Threat

The majority of stalking statutes require some level of threat to be conveyed to the victim. Threats can be broken down into two categories: express and implied. Expressed threats are those that are stated directly, either verbally or in writing. "The next time I see you, you're a dead woman!" Express threats are common in stalking cases. Originally the California statute required an express threat of "death or great bodily injury." This requirement, however, was unrealistically stringent because many serious threats are not so explicit. Fortunately, the language of the statute was loosened in 1994 to allow the threat to be simply against the "safety" of the victim.

There is no requirement that the prosecution must prove the stalker actually intended to carry out the threat. It must only be proved that the defendant intended to place the victim in fear. In recognition of the fact that stalkers often continue to threaten their victims from their jail cells, a provision was added to the California statute in 1994 to provide that incarceration at the time of the threat is not a bar to prosecution. Indeed this is a common tactic of stalkers that can serve as the basis for additional charges.

In California, the threat may now be made against the victim or a member of the victim's "immediate family." Again, it is not uncommon for the stalker to attempt to terrorize his victim by threatening those he knows are close to her. This, in fact, is often the most effective way to induce fear.

Implied threats are also common. Implied threats can be either verbal ("Heaven awaits us both") or by conduct alone. Some conduct is more directly threatening than others. Sending a bullet to the victim with her initials etched into it, for example, sends a pretty unequivocal and clearly sinister message. But in California the threat can be implied simply by a "pattern of conduct."

Persistent pursuit of a victim despite being warned off by the victim, the courts, or the police may be sufficient to constitute credible threat, especially in the situation where the suspect has been put on notice that his behavior frightens the victim. In some states, such as Michigan and Oklahoma, evidence that the defendant continued to engage in a course of conduct after having been requested to discontinue contact gives rise to a rebuttable presumption that the conduct caused the victim to feel fear.

The intent of the stalker when making the threat is also relevant. In many states the stalker's conduct must not only place the victim in fear, it must be intended to do so. This element of specific intent to cause fear can raise difficult issues in some types of stalking cases. For example, when a delusional person truly believes that the victim is in love with him and desires his attention, it may not be possible to prove a specific intent to cause fear despite the terrifying nature of his pursuit. In California, the lack of such intent is a complete defense to the crime.

Working with Police on Stalking Cases

When a victim calls the police to report she is being stalked the usual procedure is for an officer to contact the victim, take a report regarding the allegations, and then determine how to proceed with the investigation.*

Depending on the police agency, this investigation might be conducted by the first responding officer or it might be turned over to a follow-up investigator. In either case, there is no question that most stalking cases require a significant amount of investigation.

Stalking usually involves numerous incidents, each of which may have several witnesses who need to be interviewed. But this is just the start. Stalking investigations can become quite complex. Is a surveillance necessary? Should a search warrant be obtained? What physical evidence needs to be gathered? Should the defendant be interviewed? These are just some of the questions that need to be addressed.

---

* Several states do not require proof of specific intent, provided that the stalker intended to do the act that caused fear. In these states the intent element of the crime is met if the victim had reasonable cause to feel frightened.

It is absolutely critical, in my belief, that the investigating officer contact the prosecutor who will be handling the case at the earliest possible stage of the investigation in order to discuss these various issues together. In San Diego, we have found it extremely effective to utilize a team approach to the handling of stalking cases. This approach differs from the traditional separation of responsibilities where police officers first investigate the case, then turn it over to the prosecutors to prosecute it in court. With the team approach an investigator, a victim advocate, and a prosecutor work together from the very beginning — the sooner the better. There are several advantages to this approach.

First, simply put, stalking cases are tough. Difficulties arise for a whole range of reasons including the long-term nature of the crime, the cross-jurisdictional issues that are frequently present, and the fact that many stalkers are extremely manipulative and calculating. Suffice it to say, catching the stalker in a manner that provides good, solid evidence for a successful prosecution is no easy task. Putting three trained, experienced heads together to identify the issues and develop a plan of action is always a more effective strategy than trying to go it alone.

Second, the prosecutor is on board with prosecution when the arrest is made. This is crucial. If a stalker is going to be arrested and placed into custody, it is vitally important that it should be on a case that will be issued by the prosecution. If not, and the stalker is released shortly after arrest because the prosecutor didn't feel there was enough evidence to file charges, one of two things will likely happen, and they are both bad: the stalker will either be angry at the victim for having had him arrested, or he will be empowered — he beat the system. The message he gets under these circumstances is "I can get away with what I've been doing — nobody can stop me."

Both of these situations significantly increase the danger to the victim, which is obviously something we want to avoid. The way to avoid this is by having communication between the prosecutor and investigator before the defendant is arrested. If both have been working together on the case, discussing the evidentiary issues, developing the proof, and making sure the evidence is sufficient to prosecute, the officer will not be faced with the situation (that occurs not infrequently otherwise) of having the case rejected by an unfamiliar prosecutor who has simply reviewed the cold paper file.

Third, protection of the victim is more effective with a team approach. We know that, unfortunately, stalking cases can be very long term. Despite arrest and prosecution the conduct may continue. Working as a team continues to provide support to the victim, as well as an immediate response from law enforcement should additional stalking occur. For example, if the victim receives another threat after the defendant is released from jail, she knows exactly who to call. In our unit, our investigator carries a 24-hour pager and can respond to our victims immediately. Once the suspect is re-arrested the prosecutor, who is already intimately familiar with the case, can immediately seek appropriate action, such as a revocation of probation. In our stalking unit we keep a case "for life." Once it is assigned to an investigator and prosecutor it is theirs forevermore. This continuity is very effective. As long as the stalker is focused on our victim, we want to be focused on him.

Fourth, other victim needs are more effectively addressed. Victims have many different needs when they are living through this type of terror and victimization. One of the stresses that many prosecutors feel when they first begin handling stalking cases is the difficulty of addressing not only all of the issues surrounding the actual prosecution of the case in court, but trying to help the victim with all of her various needs, such as emotional issues, safety planning, employment and housing issues, responsibility for saving/gathering evidence, etc.

The assistance of a victim advocate in this regard is invaluable. It allows prosecutors the time they need to focus on the issues they are specifically trained to handle, but does not ignore the crucial issues facing the victim. In the same regard the investigator can focus on the specific investigative needs of the case that have been identified.

Asking police investigators to contact the prosecutor at the start of their investigation rather than the end is somewhat controversial. I have found that some investigators and agencies are resistant to this idea because they feel it interferes with their duties and decision making. One detective once said to me, "Prosecutors are lawyers, not cops. Why should I want one mucking up my investigation?" The answer is simple: because it can make the investigation one that has a significantly better chance of leading to a successful conviction. And that's the goal, right? The idea is not to have the prosecutor tell the police officer how to investigate the case — it is true, they are not trained investigators. But they do know the legal issues they will face in court, the likely arguments that will be made by the defense lawyer, the common defenses and excuses used by defendants, and the weight that various pieces of evidence will have with a jury or judge. This information can be incredibly useful in guiding the investigation and developing the scope of the evidence so that there are no holes in the case.

Vertical Prosecution of Stalking Cases

An important component of the team approach to handling stalking cases is the advantage of having one prosecutor involved from start to finish. This is often called vertical prosecution and has been used as a successful technique in cases involving child victims, sexual assault, domestic violence, and elder abuse. There are several advantages to vertical prosecution, including the consistency of one attorney providing information to both the investigator and the victim, and allowing the victim to deal with only one knowledgeable person throughout the process. Nothing is more frustrating to victims than having to repeat their story over and over each time a different attorney touches the case. Stalking stories are long stories! Reliving them is emotionally draining, to say the least.

The vertical prosecutor ideally handles every court hearing that occurs on each case assigned to them. This includes arraignments, bail reviews, disposition hearings, probable cause hearings, trial, and sentencing. The vertical prosecutors in our unit also, as mentioned, work closely with the investigator and personally interview the victim before issuance of the case. Under these circumstances, that prosecutor knows every aspect of the case.

In contrast, it is nearly impossible for another prosecutor who has just recently been given a case in order to handle one aspect of it (such as a bail review) to be familiar with all its nuances and information. Stalking cases are usually big files. I have had many a stalking defendant try to manipulate the system by giving false information to his counsel or the court, hoping it will slide by unnoticed. At one bail review, for example, the defense attorney argued that his client was a long-term resident of his community, well liked by friends, family, and neighbors. The attorney had received this information directly from the defendant. In fact, however, the defendant's family had him arrested several times for being violent and his landlord had evicted him for terrorizing his neighbors. It was only because I had been working with the detective for several weeks on the case and had personally interviewed the victim that I knew this information. It was not otherwise something that was part of the case file. As it turned out, being able to rebut the defendant's false assertions was extremely valuable on the issue of setting appropriate bail. And you can rest assured that had I not continued to appear on that case, the defendant would have attempted the same argument somewhere else down the line.

In another case the defendant, who was seeking probation, told the judge at his sentencing hearing he no longer had any animosity toward the victim and just wanted to get on with his life. Interestingly, at his preliminary hearing only a month earlier he had repeatedly called the victim a "bitch" under his breath while she testified. His attitude and demeanor were so obvious and disturbing that his frustrated attorney had to repeatedly tell him to knock it off. This snapshot of his personality showed not only his continuing hatred of the victim, but his inability to control himself under circumstances where control was obviously to his benefit. This was very enlightening information that might not otherwise have made it to the judge had a different prosecutor been handling the sentencing.

While I am an advocate of vertical prosecution on all sorts of cases, there is no type of case where it is more important than stalking. Again, it all comes back to the long-term nature of this crime. Just because the stalker is prosecuted and sentenced to probation, jail, or prison doesn't necessarily mean the stalking will stop. Our experience is that it frequently continues. We spend a significant amount of time seeking the revocation of previously sentenced defendants who were granted probation. There is no question that if you want to be effective at a revocation hearing, you have to know the case — not only the facts of what the defendant did, but the history of what the court has previously done. I have had several cases where the judge has given a specific admonishment to the defendant at the time of sentencing that later became very important. One example occurred when a judge warned a probationer that if he had any more contact with the victim of any sort and for any reason he would send him to prison.

The admonishment was obviously designed to provide the strongest possible incentive to the defendant to leave the victim alone and the judge made it very clear what was expected in order for the defendant to stay out of custody. Several months later the defendant was back before the court because he had phoned the victim to tell her he still loved her. This hearing, however, was before a different judge. Unfortunately there was no notation in the court file regarding the sentencing judge's warning. Obviously, the defendant wasn't about to remind the court. In fact, the defense argued that the phone call was innocuous and certainly didn't justify a commitment to prison. Without knowledge of the sentencing judge's warning, a new judge might be persuaded to give the defendant another chance. A vertical prosecutor, who is aware of the prior admonition, can thus prevent the defendant's attempted manipulation of the system and ensure he suffers the appropriate consequences for a violation of the court's order.

Vertical prosecution is unquestionably advantageous to the prosecution of stalking cases. It provides for continuity in the treatment of defendants and ensures that the case is handled fairly but aggressively. It should be encouraged whenever possible.

The Issuing Decision

Victim Safety Is Always First

Deciding whether or not to file charges for any crime always involves the consideration of evidentiary issues. Is there sufficient evidence to prove the crime to a jury beyond a reasonable doubt? On this issue the same general evaluation of the evidence applies to stalking cases as it does to any other case. But stalking cases raise additional concerns. Our philosophy about filing cases differs somewhat from the traditional analysis. I believe that the primary issue must be the safety of the victim — not just "can the case be proved."

Assume, for example, that an ex-boyfriend who has a history of violence against the victim has told her if she ever presses charges against him he will kill her. This victim might understandably be reluctant to pursue a case against her stalker even though he continues to terrorize her. Should the prosecutor pursue it anyway? If the evidence is sufficient to prove a stalking case (or any other crime) should the defendant be charged despite a possible increased risk to the victim? It certainly doesn't seem fair for him to get away with his terrorist activity without any consequence whatsoever.

A well-known security consultant, Gavin de Becker, has a sign on his desk that says, "Do not come here for justice." His goal when he represents someone who is being stalked is to reduce the risk of the target being harmed — not necessarily to obtain justice against the pursuer. Sometimes this means simply not responding to the stalker in any way. He calls the concept "detach and watch," which essentially means detaching from the situation so as not to increase the chance of a violent response. The opposite of this is to "engage and enrage." Arrest and prosecution is a form of engagement; so is getting a restraining order, suing for harassment, or even sending the police to tell the suspect to cease and desist. All of these responses have the potential of enraging the stalker to the point where he might act out violently. He might actually do what he has threatened to do.

While de Becker is a private consultant who has a different focus than law enforcement, I believe that prosecutors should also be careful to look at the big picture when evaluating a stalking case. What is the goal of prosecution — to punish a misbehaving defendant or to protect the victim? While usually the goal is twofold, in stalking cases I believe the primary consideration should be the latter.

As a practical matter, in my experience the result of such a "big picture" analysis usually results in a decision to prosecute. But there have been some circumstances where we have declined to file an otherwise prosecutable case because we felt it was in the best interest of the victim's safety.

One example was a domestic relationship case where the defendant had stalked the victim for several months following the break-up of their relationship. The case was definitely provable as there were numerous tape recordings of his harassing and threatening phone calls, but his conduct had involved no actual violence and he had no criminal history of violence. He did, however, have an outstanding felony warrant that had recently been issued for a drug offense. When he learned of the existence of the warrant he fled California to avoid being picked up and incarcerated. Our information was that he had traveled to and was living in Florida.

We could have aggressively pursued him — filed a case, obtained a warrant that was put into the NCIC system, sought his arrest in Florida, and extradited him for prosecution.* This, of course, would have meant an all-expense-paid trip by the government that brought him right back to the victim's doorstep. If he was capable of making bail, he could have shown up at her house within the hour.

If we did nothing, however, we knew that he had a continuing and strong incentive to stay out of California — his drug warrant. Keeping a distance of 3000 miles between this defendant and his target was the safest thing we could do for her. We did not file the case. Since that time she has had no contact from him and is beginning again to feel safe.

In making a discretionary call like this there are several things to consider. First, what does the victim think? I believe this is a decision that should be made only after discussion with the victim.

Often the victim's instincts about the dangerousness of the defendant and the buttons that will provoke him are very accurate. While prosecutors are not bound by the desires of a victim in determining whether to prosecute or not, I believe the opinion of a stalking victim should be carefully considered — it is, after all, her life that is on the line.

Second, a close analysis of the defendant and his background is also important. Clearly, it is important to prosecute a defendant who has a history of violence or is otherwise a significant threat to the safety of others. It was certainly possible that the decision not to prosecute the stalker in the above example could have placed other potential victims in Florida at risk. What about the next girlfriend that dumps him, for example? But, as a practical matter, unless you can keep a defendant in custody for a significant amount of time, the possibility of future victims is a risk regardless.

Third, the chance of conviction and potential sentence is relevant to the analysis. If the case is weak, the upside of a possible conviction may be outweighed by the downside of significantly increasing the defendant's anger toward the victim while at the same time having him walk away from the charges empowered after having "beaten the rap." Similarly, if the result of a conviction will only be a short period of incarceration at best, it is a real possibility that an aggressive prosecutor might very well win the battle in court but lose the war of actually protecting the victim.

These are all difficult decisions and there are no easy answers. The point is that prosecutors should at least be aware of the various issues that exist and take the time to carefully evaluate each case on its own set of circumstances before blindly jumping into the courtroom arena with a "Tarzan" yell.

---

* NCIC stands for the National Crime Information Center. It is an FBI-maintained national database of criminal history, as well as other information such as the restraining order registry.

Interviewing the Victim

While many criminal cases are issued after simply reviewing the investigative reports to determine if the evidence appears sufficient, it is important for stalking prosecutors to *personally* interview the victim before filing charges. The time crunch of most busy prosecutors' offices often makes this difficult, but it is an extremely valuable tool in the evaluation and development of a case. It bears repeating: stalking cases are complex. They frequently involve numerous contacts by the stalker, sometimes numbering in the hundreds. These "contacts" can consist of a range of activity from phone calls to letters, gifts, assaults, break-ins, following, etc. Even if the victim has been previously interviewed by a competent investigator, I have never handled a case where more information didn't come out with a follow-up interview by the prosecutor. In fact, once I begin working a case, it is a frequent occurrence that every time I talk to a victim I learn something new. This isn't because the victim is holding back or previous interviews were not well conducted. It is simply a function of the nature of the crime. When there has been a long course of conduct involving numerous incidents it is often difficult to remember every detail of what happened.

Unless the right question is asked, or something jogs the victim's memory, or you are lucky enough to have a victim who has been keeping a detailed log of events, facts just continue to dribble out the more you talk to her. Thus, pre-issuance interviews almost always assist in flushing out important facts that a prosecutor knows will be relevant to the presentation of the case.

These interviews also give the prosecutor an opportunity to learn other information about the defendant, perhaps inadmissible at a trial, but very relevant for bail settings, sentencings, and safety planning with the victim. Victims often are a wealth of information regarding the defendant's mental health history, drug or alcohol abuse, violence tendencies, controlling behavior, etc. They often are aware of prior unreported "bad acts" of the defendant that can be relevant in proving the victim's fear.

Interviewing victims pre-issuance can also head off issues that might otherwise catch a prosecutor unaware. I have found it to be a useful tactic to ask a victim, "What will [your stalker] say about you?" It is not unusual for stalkers to project their pernicious attitudes and misdeeds upon their victims. And the victims have often heard the accusations before. It is helpful to be prepared to rebut the assorted distortions that he is sure to claim about her. Sometimes, too, there are legitimate credibility issues with the victim that need to be flushed out up front. Is the victim a drug user? Does she have a criminal history? Has she continued to see the defendant despite his stalking behavior, etc.? Having an open and frank discussion with the victim about these potential issues is very productive. If the prosecutor is aware of them ahead of time they frequently can he headed off at the pass. Nothing is worse for the case than "surprises" that are learned for the first time when the victim is on the stand testifying.

And finally, talking with the victim early on is a means of determining the degree of threat the defendant poses to her so that the prosecutor can press for an appropriate disposition of the case. Safety planning can begin, if it hasn't already, depending on the eventuality of the defendant being released from custody. The victim can be educated about what to expect from the court process and from the stalker.

It is our position on the "SCAT team" that the stalking victim is also a member of the team that is working together to address this problem. The victim must understand that it is her responsibility to cooperate with the prosecution, make safety changes, and assist in gathering evidence as the stalking continues. The fact is, victim assistance and cooperation are crucial to an effective prosecution and management of the case.

How Strong Should the Case Be?

Rule #1: Don't Issue the Case Unless You Can Prove It

Putting aside victim safety issues, the determination of whether to file charges depends on the quality and strength of the evidence. As with all types of cases, there is always a range of evidence. Some cases are very strong (we call them "slam dunks"). These are cases where there is strong corroboration of the stalking behavior in the form of independent witnesses, tape recorded or written threats, admissions from the defendant, etc. The chance of conviction in such a case is generally very high and the majority of these cases result in a plea of guilty.

Cases on the other end of the spectrum are frequently what we call "one on one" cases. These are cases where the victim reports that something has occurred but the defendant denies it and there are no independent witnesses to confirm either side. Without some corroboration, it is very difficult (if not impossible) to prove a "one on one" case to a jury beyond a reasonable doubt. This is obviously very frustrating to legitimate victims. They have truly been victimized but because there is no corroboration "no one will do anything about it."

Between the two extremes are all the other cases that have varying degrees of proof and which require the prosecutor to make a judgment call regarding issuance. My belief is that the evidence in a stalking case should be quite strong — not necessarily slam dunk — but definitely strong, before the case is filed. Simply put, if we are going to arrest and prosecute a stalker, then we should be pretty darn sure we are going to get a conviction. The reason, again, is victim safety.

As previously mentioned, there is no one more dangerous and empowered than a stalker who has beat the system. When that stalker walks out the courthouse door after just having successfully convinced a jury that he is "not guilty" — watch out. His victim is seriously at risk.

Rule #2: Don't Give Up! "Monitor" All Cases

It is important to recognize that just because the evidence is not strong enough to initially issue the case, does not mean that we can do nothing for the victim. In these situations (where we believe the victim is truly being stalked) we have developed a procedure of opening "monitor" cases. Our stalking unit will open an internal case file in which we continue to investigate the facts while providing assistance and guidance to the victim. This concept of monitoring a potential "future" case is fairly unusual in prosecutors' offices. Traditionally, cases are presented to the prosecution by the investigating agency to review for issuance. The prosecutor either decides to issue the case, or if the evidence is insufficient rejects it — end of story (of course, if new evidence is uncovered the case can be resubmitted). But stalking cases are different. They are not just one-time incidents where the evidence is either there or it isn't. A burglary, for example, happens and it's done. There are either fingerprints at the scene or there aren't. Rapes, robberies, assaults, even murders are also essentially one-act crimes that are committed and then done.

In contrast, stalking, by definition, is never a one-act crime. It always involves a continuum of conduct. And for that reason, just because the case is not issuable on one day (because the evidence is insufficient) does not mean it won't become issuable the very next day (when the stalker makes a threat in front of several people). The nature of the beast of stalking is that the strength of the evidence, as well as the degree of threat posed to the victim, can change in an instant. We must be prepared to respond swiftly and purposefully when it does.

As we monitor a case we generally work with the police agency to provide investigative assistance. This can mean any number of things, including coordinating a surveillance, putting cameras in the victim's home, or analyzing physical evidence. If proof of the stalking can be developed by the continuing investigation a "monitor" case frequently then becomes an issued case and a prosecution proceeds.

Victim Assistance through Education

Whether a criminal case has been issued or we are simply monitoring the stalker, one important goal of handling these cases is to educate the victim.

We have found that victim education is absolutely crucial in several areas. The first and foremost is safety. Safety advice to victims encompasses both short-term and long-term concerns. (For detailed specific safety recommendations see the Victim Advisory Form.) Short-term issues can involve, for example, whether the victim should leave her home immediately and go somewhere where she is not accessible to her stalker. These concerns depend to a large degree on the specific present situation. If, for example, the stalker has threatened, "If you get a restraining order I'll kill you," then the day he is served with that order is a time when she is obviously very vulnerable and immediate safety issues must be addressed. Victims must be aware that the degree of threat posed by the stalker is situational and fluid.

Victims also need to understand that, in addition to immediate safety issues, they may be in this for the long haul. It is an unfortunate fact that some stalking cases can go on for years. We have seen several cases where the stalker's obsession with the victim has lasted over 10 years and the end is not yet in sight. Not surprisingly, victims don't like to hear this. It's downright depressing. I sometimes feel like the doctor who has to tell a patient she's been diagnosed with cancer. It's a pretty terrifying diagnosis — not an easy one to make, not an easy one to hear. But like cancer, I try to explain to victims that, though scary, the diagnosis is not necessarily a death sentence. We have come a long way in understanding and treating the problem. Some courses of treatment can be very successful and may result in permanent and complete remission. Sometimes, however, more than one course of action is needed to eradicate the problem. Unfortunately this is an area where there can be no guarantees.

Safety Planning

In discussing safety issues with a victim, it is vitally important to emphasize that all safety decisions must be made by the victim herself. Victims need to understand that neither the prosecutor nor the police can physically protect them from their stalker; nor can we accurately predict whether a particular stalker might make good on his threats to harm her.

The prediction of future violence is a crapshoot at best, and the inability of even the most experienced and trained threat assessment experts to correctly forecast dangerousness should be carefully explained.

A portion of a form that we have victims review and sign in our monitor cases is as follows:

Victim Advisory Form

The Stalking Unit of the District Attorney's Office has opened a monitor case on your behalf in response to information from you that you are being harassed or threatened by someone. No criminal charges have been filed against your perpetrator at this time. This could be because of evidentiary or other reasons, including safety considerations.

The purpose of monitoring your case is to assist you in evaluating, investigating, and managing your case. In this regard our assistance is advisory only and you are under no obligation to act according to any advice given or to cooperate with our office in monitoring the case (see 1–7 Key Points below).

PLEASE READ CAREFULLY:
IT IS IMPORTANT THAT YOU UNDERSTAND
THE FOLLOWING INFORMATION

1. The Stalking Unit cannot protect you from violence from your stalker. While we may offer advice and assistance regarding safety options, the primary responsibility for your safety rests with you. We can provide you with a list of various security recommendations that you may want to consider. We may also recommend that certain safety precautions or other actions be taken, but the decision is always yours.

2. It is impossible to predict whether a stalker will act out violently towards a victim. There are certain "red flags" which may suggest an increased potential for violence, but the presence or absence of these factors does not necessarily predict actual violence and we have no control over how a suspect chooses to act. We cannot place your suspect under surveillance for any length of time or track his/her movements.

3. While stalking is a felony in California, we cannot guarantee that your stalker will ever be prosecuted, or that if he/she is prosecuted, he will remain in custody. Stalking is a difficult crime to prove and generally requires independent proof of harassment and credible threat. Sometimes prosecution may even make the problem worse by increasing the stalker's anger towards you. The decision to prosecute or not is made by the District Attorney's Office. The fact that the stalker is being prosecuted or is in custody does not necessarily mean you are safe. Please remember we have no control over the suspect's ability to make bail and cannot guarantee he/she will comply with court orders if released from custody. You must continue to be vigilant about your safety.

4. Our office is not routinely notified if a suspect is released from jail. It is your responsibility to contact the jail and request notifications. You will be given a warning about release only a very short time before it occurs.

5. Stalking is a problem for which there are no easy answers or solutions. It is also a problem that may be very long term. It may require you to make significant changes in your life or lifestyle in order to increase your safety. We cannot guarantee that whatever changes you make will stop the stalking. We cannot guarantee that our assistance will make the situation any better.

6. If you decide to obtain a Restraining Order you should know that the restraining order will not necessarily protect you. Sometimes restraining orders actually incite the stalker to act out violently. This is a time to be especially careful about your safety.

7. If you are in immediate danger from your stalker, call 911. It is recommended that you carry a cell phone with you at all times for that purpose. No one from the Stalking Unit is able to respond to emergency calls so contacting the police first, and immediately, is important.

Purpose of Informing the Victim

This form is not intended to scare victims, but it is intended to present a dose of reality regarding what a victim may be facing. I believe law enforcement's role in the community should include providing general advice and guidance to victims on various protection issues, but we cannot *guarantee* the safety of any particular victim and to do so opens up areas of potential civil liability if that victim is subsequently harmed. This is an area of law that is not black and white.

One California case that is particularly noteworthy is *Wallace v. City of Los Angeles* (1993) 12 Cal. App. 4th 1385. In that case, a young woman witnessed a murder. The investigating police detective obtained a written pre-trial statement from her and her identity as a witness was made known. She received threatening phone calls and told the detective that she feared the defendant. The detective said he would relocate her if the threats continued and he promised to alert her if she was in danger. In summary, he minimized the danger to her even though he knew, but did not tell the witness, that the defendant was a suspect in several other murder cases and had threatened witnesses in the past. A few days before trial the witness was tragically murdered. The Court of Appeal found (1) a special relationship was created when the detective enlisted the young woman as a witness, which (2) required him to warn her of the unforeseen dangers she faced, and (3) he was not entitled to immunity for his actions.

The present status of both state and federal case law suggests the following action by an investigator or prosecutor *may* create civil liability:

- Failing to honor express or implied promises to provide warnings or protection
- Making statements which minimize the actual peril faced by the victim or witness who then detrimentally relies on such statements
- Placing an unprotected victim or witness in close proximity to someone who poses a foreseeable threat to that victim or witness
- Requesting that a citizen perform an official function which involves a foreseeable risk

- Seeking out and presenting a person as a prosecution witness against a defendant who is known to threaten witnesses

Clearly all of these issues are potential occurrences in a stalking case. For these reasons, prosecutors and officers should never promise a victim that they can protect her from a stalker and they must be very clear that, while various safety options exist, the decision of which ones to utilize must rest with the victim. Another important area of victim education involves explaining the importance of cutting off all contact with the stalker. While specific safety recommendations need to be tailored to each specific case, one piece of general advice that we give to all victims we work with is **STOP ALL CONTACT WITH THE STALKER — NOW AND FOR GOOD!**

Too many victims who have once had a relationship with the suspect are concerned about "letting him down easily." This leads to a difficulty in saying, "leave me alone" and really meaning it. Stalkers can be very manipulative with their victim's feelings. A frequent request, for example, is "Just meet with me one more time so I can put some closure on this relationship." Unfortunately "one more time" rarely means what the words say, and the stalker simply uses this meeting to continue to negotiate some form of continued contact.

It is important that victims not fall for these types of manipulations. They need to be strong. They also need be very direct and firm about cutting off all contact. We have seen many victims who have repeatedly told their stalkers they don't want to talk to them anymore. But they are, of course, still talking to them. It may also be giving mixed messages, i.e., the stalker thinks to himself or herself, "if she really doesn't want to talk to me then why did she open the door?" (Stalkers don't necessarily think like other reasonable people.) If after leaving 40 phone messages on the victim's answering machine she finally returns the call in frustration to demand that he stop, the lesson he has learned is that persistence works. He got another chance to plead his case. And even negative contact is better than none at all.

I find that many stalkers have a lot in common with 2-year-old children. They cannot control their anger and tend to throw temper tantrums when frustrated. I learned early on with my toddler children that responding with anger to the tantrum was useless — it just amped up the volume of the tantrum. Trying to respond with reason was equally ineffective. Someone in the throes of a tantrum is simply incapable of listening to reason — the rational part of his brain, if it exists, has simply been switched off. The only course of action that ever worked for me was to simply ignore the tantrum. If my child decided to have a screaming fit I simply turned around and walked out of the room. It was amazing how quickly the screaming subsided when there's no one around to hear it or react to it.

While this comparison obviously oversimplifies the often complex psychiatric "stuff" going on inside the mind of a stalker, there is no question that many stalkers see negative responses from their victims in some sort of twisted, positive way. Even if the victim is screaming at them "leave me alone!" he is thinking "she really doesn't mean it, after all she did agree to meet with me."

Cutting off all contact with the defendant cannot be over-emphasized, but it is a concept that sometimes must be repeated over and over to a victim before it sinks in. We carefully explain that no contact means what the words say — no contact of any sort. No response to letters or e-mails, no answering the phone, no "one last time" meetings. We tell victims very specifically: if he shows up at work, don't go outside to talk to him and appease him. If he pounds on your door, don't answer it or respond. Call the police. We recommend that the victim make one final communication that clearly states she wants no contact, and then stick to it. Draw a line in the sand and don't step over it. Sometimes a restraining order serves as a well-drawn line. It is an unequivocal communication of the victim's desires to be left alone. And it has the stamp of a judge on it for emphasis!

Not only does continued contact with the stalker encourage continued stalking behavior, it can also prevent a successful prosecution for stalking. If the victim continues to have consensual contact with the stalker it is very difficult to prove that she is truly fearful of him. While victims may feel that it is safer to just "give him what he wants" rather than suffer the consequences of his wrath, the reality from a prosecution standpoint is that this type of accommodating behavior weakens the case. Many jurors who have never been in this type of situation will not understand or be sympathetic to this type of victim response.

Finally, one of the most important elements of victim education is teaching them the significance of keeping physical evidence and documenting the defendant's conduct in order to make the case provable. This is simply something that doesn't occur to many victims. They might, for example, be so upset at receiving a threatening letter that they immediately destroy it. Or they erase the disgusting messages left on their answering machine because they are so disturbing to listen to. Once we begin monitoring a case the victim knows to call us as soon as any further conduct occurs so that we can seize the evidence. We also provide them with a victim notebook that includes incident and phone logs to assist them in keeping track of any continuing activity, including a detailed description of the incident, the names of any witnesses, and the existence of any physical evidence. There is no question that victim education is often the key to ultimately developing a prosecutable case.

Being Creative

Most people have a pretty distinct picture in their minds of what "stalking" is. Popular media have done much to establish the common view that stalking consists of the persistent, scary pursuit of another person for either "love" or revenge. To most people there are basically two kinds of stalkers: obsessed fans of celebrities or rejected lovers who will not let the relationship go.

But, in fact, the category of people who might be legal stalkers is much broader. Most stalking statutes do not require any particular type of relationship between the parties; nor do they prohibit specific types of conduct or necessitate any specific motivation for the conduct (other than an intent to cause fear). The definition of "harassment" is, of necessity, very broad, and for that reason there are all sorts of possibilities of who might qualify for prosecution.

Many times police officers are faced with situations that their instincts tell them are dangerous and escalating but the behavior doesn't fit into a standard crime mold. Interestingly enough, many of these difficult "fringe" cases can be prosecuted as stalking cases.

Stalking Case Scenario One — The Neighborhood Terrorist

The neighborhood bully, who harasses and terrorizes the people who live around him, presents unique challenges for law enforcement. Not only is such a person hard to control, since he is often acting on his own property, but the dynamics of group victimization can become a cop's worst nightmare. These cases can go on for years and can impact a large number of people. In addition, the tragedy of these situations is that if law enforcement does not effectively step in to control things, the victims may be tempted to take the law into their own hands. Vigilante justice is then very likely to turn the victim into the criminal.

One such case that our Stalking Unit handled took place in the town of Jamul, located about 30 miles east of downtown San Diego. Jamul is a rural community where people often own several acres of land and the atmosphere is generally quiet and peaceful. But despite the open space and beauty of the area, one particular neighborhood in Jamul became the site of an unlikely neighborhood terrorist.

Linda, age 17, lived with her 58-year-old grandmother. The grandmother also lived with her daughter and grandchild in an unkempt home on a plot of land that had been owned by her family for many years. But despite her age and relative frailness, she had successfully harassed and terrorized the entire neighborhood, both young and old, for years.

Complaints regarding her behavior had been reported to the Sheriff's Department for over a decade. These complaints became so frequent that the officers started calling them "another crazy Linda call." Some of her bizarre behavior included: walking down the middle of the street refusing to move for traffic, screaming obscenities at people in their cars as they tried to drive around her, standing naked in her front yard, stealing neighbors' pets and hiding them in her house, and setting bonfires in her front yard. Parents of young children became concerned when she would scream at and threaten the children as they walked by her home on their way to school, calling the girls "whore" and other horrible epithets. The parents ultimately had to devise an alternate route for the school children so they could avoid this harassment. Most of this harassing behavior resulted in calls to the police, but often the conduct in itself was not criminal and the police felt there was little they could do. But there were other acts by Linda that were definitely criminal. She threw rocks at people who drove by the house. On one occasion she grabbed an elderly neighbor around the neck and attempted to strangle her. On another, she threatened to kill one neighbor's son, leaving numerous vile messages on his answering machine.

For a while, she targeted a particular family whom she apparently thought was "squatting" on her property. She would break into their home, go through their drawers, steal food from the kitchen, and rip up their photographs. If the occupants of the house tried to confront her she "went nuts," screaming obscenities and threatening to kill them.

These neighbors ultimately obtained a restraining order to keep her away. Other neighbors ended up selling their homes and moving because the harassment was simply too stressful.

In 1996, Linda began targeting another couple, Mr. and Mrs. Brown, a very likable elderly couple who were looking forward to enjoying their retirement years. Unfortunately they had the misfortune of buying the piece of property right next door to Linda. At the time of the purchase it was simply a plot of land that they intended to build their retirement home on. Unfortunately this plot had once belonged to Linda's father before he sold it years earlier. Linda could not be dissuaded from her belief that she owned this land and hence she was determined to drive the "squatters" off her property.

Her harassment of the Browns quickly became almost unbearable. She constantly screamed vulgar obscenities at her new neighbors, threatened violence, and came unannounced onto their property and into their home. She assaulted Mrs. Brown once with a coffee pot and demanded she get off "her f__ing property!" She even once tried to walk off with their 2-year-old granddaughter and then threatened to kill the child when Mr. Brown stopped her.*

---

* They initially lived in a mobile home on the property while the house was being built and ultimately moved into the completed home. Whether a victim should obtain a restraining order or not depends on the specific circumstances of each case. While many officers believe that all victims of harassment should be advised to pursue a restraining order, this type of "knee-jerk" advice may actually cause more harm than good. There are numerous documented cases where the obtaining of a restraining order escalated the situation and precipitated violence against the victim. We therefore believe that before such advice is given the circumstances of each case must be carefully evaluated.

The stress on Mr. and Mrs. Brown was tremendous and Mrs. Brown began having physical problems that required her to see a doctor. The Browns frequently called the police when the harassment occurred but were told the only thing they could do was get a restraining order. It wasn't until Linda came onto their property and took a swing at Mr. Brown with a garden hoe, nearly cracking his head open, that our Stalking Unit was contacted by the Sheriff's Department wondering if we could assist them on this case.

At first glance, this certainly didn't seem like a traditional stalking case. In fact, no one over the years had identified this behavior as stalking or called Linda a stalker. But a close analysis of the activity she had been engaging in revealed that the elements of the crime were there. There was no question that Linda had engaged in a course of conduct that was harassing to her next-door neighbors, and it was equally evident she had made a credible threat in both words and deed. In addition, the victims were clearly fearful and suffering substantial emotional distress. I filed a felony case against Linda charging her with two counts of stalking on Mr. and Mrs. Brown and one count of assault with a deadly weapon.

Stalking Case Scenario Two
— An Obsessed Psychiatric Patient

Karen is an intelligent young woman who has a long history of mental health problems and has been diagnosed with a borderline personality disorder. She has attempted suicide on numerous occasions over the years. Many of her attempts have been extremely histrionic and have placed other innocent lives at risk. They include, for example, pouring lighter fluid on her body and threatening to light herself on fire, threatening to jump off a building, and injecting herself with phenobarbitol before driving through the streets and freeways. For these reasons, Karen was well known to the law enforcement community in San Diego County.

For several years, Karen had been treated by a series of psychologists, the last of which was Dr. Moore, a female therapist who worked at a small mental health clinic in the heart of the city. Karen's treatment with Dr. Moore was placed in jeopardy, however, when she expressed an interest in finding out the therapist's home address and requested to visit her there. Dr. Moore explained to Karen that this request was inappropriate and visiting her home would violate treatment boundaries that would not be tolerated. Karen ignored the warning. She researched and found the doctor's address on the Internet and she then began driving by Dr. Moore's home. When Dr. Moore discovered this she terminated treatment and referred Karen to another therapist.

Angered by this "rejection," Karen began calling Dr. Moore pleading with her to take her back as a patient. The doctor refused. In response, Karen began threatening to kill herself on the doctor's front doorstep if she didn't give in to her demands. Dr. Moore, who had two young children, began to fear for her family's safety. After several days of threats and demands, Karen finally forced her way into the doctor's office armed with a .22 caliber handgun. She barricaded herself inside the room along with the doctor, pulled the phone out of the wall, and carefully loaded one bullet into the chamber of the gun. She then began playing "Russian Roulette." She put the gun in her mouth and pulled the trigger once, then twice, as Dr. Moore pleaded with her to put the gun down. On the third firing of the gun she shot herself in the head to the horror of Dr. Moore.

Amazingly, Karen survived this shooting. She was treated at the hospital for several days. Upon her release, however, she immediately began attempting to re-contact the doctor. She made numerous harassing phone calls and threats to kill herself, emphasizing she would "not die alone." She lamented that the gun she had used had not been of strong enough caliber and stated that she would try again. By this time, Dr. Moore was very concerned for the safety of herself and her family. She knew Karen was unstable and discussed the issue with her supervisors at the clinic as well as with various law enforcement officers. There seemed to be a general impression that because Karen had mental problems there was little the police could do. Feeling increasingly vulnerable, Dr. Moore ultimately obtained a restraining order and hired round-the-clock private security.

Karen, in the meantime, traveled to Arizona where she purchased another gun. Two days later she appeared again at Dr. Moore's clinic seeking her out. She brandished the .45 caliber gun and terrorized the entire clinic. After approximately 30 minutes Karen was finally convinced by the clinic director to relinquish the gun. She was taken into custody by the police but was transported to the hospital for a 72-hour psychiatric hold instead of to jail. No criminal charges were pursued.

Upon her release from the hospital 3 days later she wasted no time in continuing her plan to kill herself in front of Dr. Moore. She immediately returned to Arizona and this time purchased a .357 Magnum. Gun number three!

Within a few days she was again seen driving by the doctor's clinic. Private security personnel notified the police and Karen was chased as she circled the city and ultimately returned to the front of a clinic. There, as she sat in her car pointing the gun in all directions and putting it in and out of her mouth, she threatened to shoot herself in the head unless she could talk to Dr. Moore. A 20-minute standoff resulted, involving numerous police officers, before she finally surrendered. Again she was taken to the hospital for a psychiatric hold.

Our unit became involved in this case when, shortly after this last incident, we were invited to a PERT meeting to discuss "what to do about Karen." It was an interesting meeting of about 20 people, all of whom had some contact with Karen over the years. There were numerous mental health practitioners there, several police officers, several PERT members, the victim and other therapists from her clinic, my investigator, and myself.

What struck my investigator and me immediately, as we sat around the table discussing the case, was the different perspective that many of the therapists had regarding how to deal with Karen. One of the first comments made was something along the lines of "It's clear that we are not meeting the treatment needs of Karen; we need to do a better job of helping her."

About the only therapist in the room who didn't have quite as altruistic a viewpoint as this was Dr. Moore, who understandably was tired of being terrorized by this woman. In hindsight it seems absolutely reasonable that the therapists in the room would view Karen as a patient who needed help — she was indeed that. But she was also a criminal. From our perspective she was a woman who had been getting away with committing insidious crimes for quite some time, always falling back on the excuse that she was suicidal and needed "help." There was no dispute in the room that day that this woman was very bright and knew exactly what she was doing. There was also no dispute that she was clever and manipulative. But to us her guile had grown tiring and increasingly more dangerous. In our view, since it was clear that the mental health system, despite its sincere efforts, had been unsuccessful in controlling her behavior, it was time for the criminal justice system to step in.

I prosecuted Karen for felony stalking, as well as weapons and restraining order violations. She ultimately pled guilty to these counts.

Non-Traditional "Crazy" Stalkers — Does Prosecution Work?

I happen to think that it's redundant to refer to a stalker as "crazy." All stalkers are crazy to some degree. If they were normal, reasonable people they wouldn't be engaged in such obsessive, unreasonable behavior. So basically, dealing with mentally ill defendants comes with the territory when you prosecute stalkers. Obviously there is a wide range of types and degrees of mental illness, so the answer to the question posed above is "it depends." In many cases, people who engage in extreme harassing behavior, such as Karen and Linda in the above scenarios, have been in and out of the mental health system for years without much success. But does prosecuting them make things any better? The answer may have a lot to do with their specific psychiatric diagnosis.

If a stalker's mental illness is such that it can be controlled by medication (such as bipolar disorder) then I believe the probability of successfully controlling his or her behavior is significantly increased by prosecution. The reason is relatively simple. Even people suffering from mental illness don't like jail. The advantage of dealing with this type of offender in the criminal justice system, as opposed to the mental health system (as it exists today), is that you can force them to not only get treatment but to take their medication as well. You do this by holding the threat of custody over their head if they don't. "Crazy" or not, the threat of going back to jail is a significant motivator for many people.

It is therefore our goal in prosecuting these types of cases to get the defendant on felony probation if at all possible. This allows the court to impose strict probation conditions that must be adhered to or the defendant faces the sound of clanging doors again. We have found this to be a very effective way to ensure that the defendant remains in treatment and thus poses no continuing threat to the victim. It is for this reason that I believe prosecution of mentally ill defendants is not necessarily inconsistent with having compassion for their situation. I have seen more than a few cases where a defendant lived under the cloud of mental illness for years, with all of its attendant legal and social problems, and it wasn't until the threat of jail or prison forced them to address their illness that their lives were turned around. For the first time in many years they had the opportunity to become productive members of the community.

Linda was one of those defendants. She was crazed, delusional, irrational, angry, abusive, and violent when she was arrested and charges were filed. Eight months later, at her sentencing hearing, I saw a dramatic change. During her stay in jail she had become stabilized on medication and she was an entirely different person. She had become reasonable and rational. She recognized that she was seriously mentally ill and needed lifelong treatment and medication. She was sincerely remorseful for what she had put her neighbors through over the years.

Linda was placed on 5 years probation with orders to have no contact with the victims, remain on her medication as prescribed by her psychiatrist, and receive regular psychotherapy as recommended by her psychologist. Since her sentencing date, which has been 2 years now, there have been no further problems with "crazy Linda." She is living on her own and is described by her probation officer as a "model probationer." She is taking her medication and attending group and individual therapy. For the first time in almost two decades she feels in control of her life and is happy. While she obviously did not like her time in jail she has actually expressed gratitude for being prosecuted. And although there is always the possibility of a relapse we consider this prosecution a real success story.

Karen is a different story — but she also has a significantly different diagnosis. Personality disorders are unfortunately not treatable with medication. Nor is there any form of psychotherapy that is known to "cure" this sort of mental illness.

It has been our experience that defendants with personality disorders are much more difficult to control or predict. When we see a defendant who has been diagnosed with strong narcissistic and borderline features we know we are in for a struggle. Our antennae also go up regarding this type of defendant's potential dangerousness.

Karen was also placed on probation after serving a full year in local custody. It was hoped that a year in jail would assist in breaking her obsession with killing herself and doing it in front of Dr. Moore. It didn't. After being released from jail she was ordered to live in a board and care facility and to be on electronic monitoring because the court was still concerned about her potential dangerousness. It was only a short time after release from this facility that she was again arrested. She had approached a teenage boy and attempted to buy a gun from him so that she could kill herself. She mentioned that she was going to do it in front of her therapist. We initiated probation revocation proceedings and her probation was revoked. She was then sentenced to over 4 years in state prison.

Unfortunately, with this type of defendant it is much more difficult to gauge the "success" of criminal intervention. It is simply impossible to predict how long a particular obsession will last, or ascertain how determined an obsessed person is to eventually get to his or her victim. But one measurement of success is certainly the degree of protection that has been afforded the victim. In Karen's case the victim has been safe for at least as long as the defendant was incarcerated, and she has also been able to relocate in order to ensure her continued safety. Only time will tell whether Karen will ever cease in her persistent desire to traumatize others with her suicidal gestures and attempts.

Being creative about what types of conduct can be prosecuted as "stalking" is something to be encouraged throughout our law enforcement system. Police officers, prosecutors, and judges alike need to broaden their understanding of this crime so as to best utilize its protections for all members of the community who are victimized by the bullies of the world. There is no legal reason why the statute cannot apply to harassment situations between co-workers, parents and children, students and teachers, business partners, etc. While it is not recommended that charges be filed on factually borderline cases or ones with weak evidence, when unlawful harassment is occurring and the other elements of the statute exist, the stalking law may provide an effective tool to address what have previously been problematic and potentially dangerous situations.

Conclusion

Prosecuting stalking cases is fascinating work. These cases are complex, often long term, and can be all-consuming. They are certainly never boring. Stalkers never cease to amaze us with their sick creativity and twisted determination. It is hugely regrettable that their energies cannot be focused on less malevolent endeavors. But while these cases are interesting on an intellectual level, there is nothing abstract about these guys. We can never forget that the menace they present is very real to the victim. And because these defendants are so scary, the pressure on those who are evaluating these cases to make the right management decisions can sometimes seem monumental. Any misstep may have tragic results.

However, police officers and prosecutors across the country are accepting this challenging task. They are educating themselves about the dynamics of obsessive behavior and the intricacies of stalking investigations. Specialized units to assist stalking victims and aggressively prosecute stalkers are cropping up in jurisdictions across the country. Because of the hard work of so many dedicated professionals victims no longer have to feel as though the system has forsaken them. We have a unique opportunity to give them control over their lives again.

Aggressive prosecution of stalkers sends a forceful message to the perpetrator and the community that this type of terroristic activity will not be tolerated. It is a huge step toward increasing the safety of our individual victims and society as a whole. The tide is turning. No longer will we allow control freak psychopaths to terrorize at will. It is time to stalk the stalker.

Bibliography

People v. Borrelli (2000) 77 Cal. App. 4th, 703

People v. Ewing (1999) 76 Cal. App. 4th, 199

People v. Ewing (1999) 76 Cal. App. 4th, 210

People v. Falk (1997) 52 Cal. App. 4th, 287

People v. Garrett (1994) 30 Cal. App. 4th, 962

People v. Heilman (1994) 25 Cal. App. 4th, 256

People v. McClelland (1996) 42 Cal. App. 4th, 144

People v. McCray (1997) 58 Cal. App. 4th

People v. Tran (1996) 47 Cal. App. 4th, 253

Wells, K. (September 1999). *Training Manual on Stalking.* San Diego Stalking Strike Force. San Diego, CA: Office of the San Diego District Attorney's Office.

Recommended Reading List

Borum, R., Fein, R., Vossekuil, B., and Berglund, J. (1999). Threat assessment: defining an approach for evaluating risk of targeted violence, *Behavioral Sciences and the Law*, 17, 323–337.

de Becker, G. (1997). *The Gift of Fear: Survival Skills That Protect Us from Violence.* New York: Little, Brown.

Fein, R., Vossekuil, B., and Holden, G. (1995). Threat Assessment: An Approach to Prevent Targeted Violence. National Institute of Justice: Research in Action. Washington, D.C.: U.S. Government Printing Office.

Gross, L. (2000). *Surviving a Stalker: Everything You Need To Know To Keep Yourself Safe.* New York: Marlowe and Company.

Meloy, J. R. (Ed.) (1998). *The Psychology of Stalking: Clinical and Forensic Perspectives.* San Diego, CA: Academic Press.

Spitzberg, B., Nicastro, A., and Cousins, A. (1998). Exploring the interactional phenomenon of stalking and obsessive relational intrusion, *Communication Reports*, 11, 34–47.

Tjaden, P. and Thoennes, N. (1998). *Stalking in America: Findings from the National Violence Against Women Survey.* National Institute of Justice Centers for Disease Control and Prevention Research in Brief. Washington, D.C.: U.S. Government Printing Office.

Williams, W., Lane, J., and Zona, M. A. (1996). Stalking: successful intervention strategies, *The Police Chief*, Alexandria, VA, 104–106.

Zona, M. A., Sharma, K. K., and Lane, J. (1993). A comparative study of erotomanic and obsessional subjects in a forensic sample, *Journal of Forensic Sciences*, 38(4), 894–903.

About the Contributing Author

Kerry Wells, J.D.

Kerry Wells, J.D. currently heads the Stalking Unit of the Special Operations Division, San Diego District Attorney's Office. She has been a prosecutor for the past 20 years after graduating magna cum laude from Whittier College School of Law. She was one of the original attorneys chosen to prosecute child abuse cases when the District Attorney's Office first established a Child Abuse Unit in 1985. In 1989, she became chief of the newly established Domestic Violence Unit. Under her direction this unit became the largest specialized domestic violence unit in the state. She developed innovative protocols for the prosecution of domestic violence that have been nationally recognized.

Ms. Wells has lectured extensively throughout the state and the nation on the subjects of domestic violence, child abuse, and stalking. In 1998, she taught trial tactics at the National College of District Attorneys in Columbia, South Carolina. She is probably best known for the prosecution of Elizabeth Broderick, who murdered her ex-husband and his wife after stalking them for several years. This case received international attention and was one of the first cases covered live, gavel-to-gavel, by *Court TV*. A subject of books and made-for-television movies, this case led to Ms. Wells' interest in the much neglected and misunderstood crime of stalking. In 1994, Ms. Wells founded the Stalking Strike Force, which has as its goals increased education and awareness of the crime of stalking and an improved multi-disciplinary approach to stalking. She is an active member of the San Diego Chapter of the Association of Threat Assessment Professionals (ATAP).

PART IX

Stalking in the Workplace: Risk Management Issues

Workplace Violence and Unwanted Pursuit: From an Employer's Perspective

20

REGINA A. PETTY
LOIS M. KOSCH

Contents

0-8493-0811-9/01/$0.00+$1.50
© 2001 by CRC Press LLC

Introduction

Every day in America, three people die at work as a result of a violent act (1996 National Census of Fatal Occupational Injuries). Violence is the leading cause of death for women at work (de Becker, 1997). Of managers surveyed in 1999, 57% reported that a violent incident had occurred in their workplace between January 1996 and July 1999 (Society for Human Resource Management, 1999*) and there were about 2 million assaults and threats of violence against Americans at work each year according to the U.S. Department of Justice (1997). Workplace violence includes fights, assaults, harassment threats, stalking, telephone harassment, inappropriate communications, graffiti, and rape. Experts agree that violent episodes at work, no matter what the degree of injury, can have a significant adverse effect on employees resulting in elevated stress levels, fear, and reduced productivity. The problem is widespread and can occur in any workplace setting from the post office to the law office. Crime in the streets has now become crime in the suites.

As it has become the most important security threat for America's largest corporations (Pinkerton's Inc., 1999), employers are faced with the challenge of attempting to reduce the risk of workplace violence. They are motivated not only by a desire to protect employees from injury, but also to avoid legal liability (Kinney, 1993).** This chapter addresses the following: (1) an

---

* According to the survey, only 2% of workplace incidents include either shooting or stabbing. The rest included verbal threats (41%) and pushing and shoving (19%). The following were cited as violent behavior: personality conflicts (55%), family or marital problems (36%), and work-related stress (24%).
** The costs associated with workplace violence are enormous. They include medical and legal costs and lost productivity. In 1993, the National Safe Workplace Institute estimated that incidents cost employers between $250,000 per occurrence for a serious incident and $10,000 for a lower-severity incident. Its study estimated that the total cost to employers for workplace violence was about $4.2 billion in 1993 alone.

employer's legal obligation to provide a safe working environment; (2) various legal theories which have been advanced in an attempt to impose liability upon employers for injuries sustained as a result of workplace violence in actions brought by employees and third parties; and (3) tools which may help to decrease the risk that a violent act will occur in the workplace. The scope of an employer's legal liability arising from workplace violence is an emerging issue.

Employers' Legal Obligation to Provide a Safe Workplace: Statutory Overview

The Federal Occupational Safety and Health Act (Fed-OSHA) requires employers to provide employees with a place of employment which is "free from recognized hazards that are causing or are likely to cause death or serious physical harm ... to employees" (29 U.S.C. § 654(a)(1)). This includes the obligation to do everything reasonably necessary to protect the life, safety, and health of employees. Employers must take affirmative steps to prevent employee injuries.

Employees may not sue their employers based solely on OSHA violations. Nonetheless, employers who fail to comply with OSHA may be fined by the government anywhere from $25,000 to $70,000 (29 U.S.C. § 666(a)–(e)). Criminal penalties may also be imposed (29 U.S.C. § 666(e)). An employer's failure to eliminate serious recognized hazards from its workplace has been recognized as a violation of OSHA's General Duty Clause.* For example, OSHA cited the employer for failing to furnish a workplace free from violence where security measures were not taken to minimize or eliminate employee exposure to assault and battery by tenants of the apartment complex where they worked (*Secretary of Labor v. Megawest Financial, Inc.*, 1995). The Occupational Safety and Health Review Commission found that workplace violence may constitute a General Duty Clause violation if four elements are established: (1) the existence of a hazard that poses a "significant risk" to employees; (2) recognition of that hazard by the employer; (3) the hazard was likely to cause death or serious harm; and (4) feasible means existed to eliminate or materially reduce the hazard (*Secretary of Labor v. Megawest Financial, Inc.*, 1995). The duty to recognize an existent hazard may in part

---

* The General Duty Clause is contained in Section 5 of OSHA and states:
  (a) Each employer — shall furnish to each of his employees employment and a place of employment which are free from recognized hazards that are causing or likely to cause death or serious physical harm to his employees;
  (1) shall comply with occupational safety and health standards promulgated under this chapter.

depend on the type of workplace and any historical association it may have with a risk of violence.

In addition, at least six states, California, Washington, Oregon, Hawaii, Texas, and Florida, have their own OSHA guidelines and materials articulating employer obligations to protect workers (CA Lab. Code § 6400 et al., 1997). Violations may result in civil* or criminal sanctions.** Most often the state agency attention and corresponding inspections are directed toward the retail and health-care industries,*** although they are likely to investigate any workplace where a death or serious injury has occurred. For instance, Hawaii's State Occupational Safety and Health Division investigated Xerox Corporation after Byran Uyesugi killed seven of its employees in a workplace shooting in November 1999. The purpose of the investigation was to determine if Xerox did everything it could to prevent the shootings (Kua, 2000).****

At least one federal district court has found a "well-defined dominant public policy of workplace safety" (*G.B. Goldman Paper Co. v. Paperworkers Local 286*, 1997). The court noted that the issue of workplace safety had "prominently manifested itself on federal and local agendas" (957 F. Supp. at 619). For instance, concern about violence in the workplace prompted the Labor Department to issue guidelines to prevent and reduce workplace violence in health-care and social service industries (where almost two thirds of all nonfatal workplace violence occurs).

Judicial Developments

There is a small but growing body of case law that addresses employer liability for workplace violence. Cases often turn on their specific facts. This is a developing area of the law and there are few hard and fast rules. For the most part, however, injured employees and heirs of employees killed by workplace violence will be restricted to recovery through the workers' compensation system. Employees may succeed in avoiding workers' compensation preemption by

---

* For instance, California Labor Code section 6400 requires employers to provide a safe and healthful place of employment for employees.

** California Penal Code section 387 (California Corporate Criminal Liability Act of 1989) provides that corporations and managers may face criminal sanctions for failing to disclose concealed hazards for which there is a substantial probability of death, great bodily harm, or serious exposure.

*** The California Department of Industrial Relations, Division of Occupational Safety and Health (DOSH), conducted most of its workplace violence inspections in the retail and health-care sectors from 1993 to 1996 according to the *Journal of Occupational and Environmental Medicine*.

**** As of press time, the investigation was ongoing. However, the state agency noted in the cited news article (Kua, 2000) that Xerox had a reputation in the business community of "doing the right thing by their employees," stating further that it was "unlikely" that the agency would find that Xerox had done anything wrong.

alleging that the employer ratified its employee's violent behavior or that the violence resulted from the employer's intentional act.

Employee Eligibility for Workers' Compensation Benefits

Most employee-victims of workplace violence will be eligible for workers' compensation benefits. In some states employers have a duty to notify employee victims of crimes which occur on the employer's premises that the employee is eligible for workers' compensation benefits for injuries, including psychiatric injuries, resulting from the crime.* This often includes employees who are injured by a violent act which is committed at the workplace by a *non-employee* (*Murphy v. Worker's Compensation Appeals Board*, 1978). Violent acts committed by third parties do not always give rise to *civil* liability (*Arendell v. Auto Parts Club, Inc.*, 1994).

Worker's Compensation as an Exclusive Remedy

While injuries caused by workplace accidents are normally compensated exclusively within the workers' compensation system, certain types of intentional employer misconduct are beyond the boundaries of the employment relationship and thus may subject the employer to civil liability to the employee. This is known as the *intentional tort exception to the workers' compensation exclusive remedy rule*. This exception is recognized in many states. This exception will allow the employer to be sued in court instead of in the workers' compensation administrative forum. Usually a civil action will expose the employer to greater potential damages than an action within the workers' compensation forum. Thus, it is usually preferable for an employer to defend an action in the workers' compensation system.

However, it can be very difficult for an employee to establish sufficient evidence to invoke the exception. It requires a very high threshold showing, as is demonstrated by cases involving very reckless employer conduct that was still found to be within the workers' compensation exclusive remedy rule (*Arendell v. Auto Parts Club, Inc.*, 1994 and *Pichon v. Fairview Development Center*, 1996).

While some courts have recognized the widespread presence of violent crime, they are hesitant to hold employers responsible for public safety. For instance, in one California case the court noted, "unless crime in the workplace is highly foreseeable, employers cannot reasonably be expected to insure

---

* California Labor Code § 3553, which provides: Every employer subject to the compensation provisions of this code shall give any employee who is a victim of a crime that occurred at the employee's place of employment written notice that the employee is eligible for workers' compensation for injuries, including psychiatric injuries, that may have resulted from the place of employment crime. The employer shall provide this notice, either personally or by first-class mail, within one working day of the place of employment crime, or within one working day of the date the employer reasonably should have known of the crime.

against it" (*Muller v. Automobile Club of Southern California*, 1998).* The court further noted that there is a certain risk of crime in any workplace to which the general public has access.

In the *Arendell v. Auto Parts Club, Inc.* (1994) case, the court stated, "[t]here is no fundamental public policy requiring a retail employer to provide adequate store security; to the contrary there is a "well established policy" against forcing landowners to insure public safety" (see all *Arendell v. Auto Parts Club, Inc.*, 1994).

On the other hand, some courts have recognized a growing public policy condemning workplace violence. In *Columbia Aluminum Corp. v. United Steelworkers of America, Local 8147* (1995), the federal district court noted that the Department of Occupational Safety and Health had issued citations to employers for failing to protect workers from workplace violence. Moreover, where employers expressly agree to protect employees, they may be found legally responsible for their failure to do so (*Slager v. Commonwealth Edison Co.*, 1992).

An employee may avoid the exclusive remedy of workers' compensation if he can show that the employer ratified the violent employee's conduct. By ratifying conduct, an employer becomes a joint participant in the wrongful conduct (*Iverson v. Atlas Pacific Engineering*, 1983). Ratification occurs when an employer is aware of an employee's serious misconduct and fails to take any steps to stop the behavior and/or discipline the employee when the employer's conduct rises to the level of intentional misconduct (*Iverson v. Atlas Pacific Engineering*, 1983).

This theory is demonstrated in the three cases described below. In *Herrick v. Quality Hotels, Inns and Resorts, Inc.* (1993), in the course of firing a hotel security guard, the hotel's director of security threatened the guard with a gun. The guard sued his former employer for intentional infliction of emotional distress. The appellate court found that the action was not barred by the exclusive remedy provisions of workers' compensation law because the director's threat constituted a physical assault.** A physical assault is an

---

* In the case of *Muller v. Automobile Club of Southern California*, the plaintiff, a claims adjuster for AAA, was the recipient of a series of angry and threatening calls from an insured. She was terminated after developing a stress disorder and filed a lawsuit alleging various discrimination and contract causes of action along with a claim that she was subject to retaliation for expressing her fear of the insured. The court, finding no retaliation and affirming summary judgment for the employer, stated that the voicing of a fear about one's safety in the workplace does not necessarily constitute a complaint about unsafe working conditions pursuant to Labor Code section 6310 (prohibiting retaliation for filing of complaint).

** California Labor Code section 3602(b)(1) provides:

(b) An employee, or his or her dependents in the event of his or her death, may bring an action at law for damages against the employer, as if this division did not apply, in the following instances:

(1) Where the employee's injury or death is proximately caused by a willful physical assault by the employer.

exception to the workers' compensation laws; the exclusive remedy provisions of those laws were inapplicable and the guard was able to file his lawsuit against his former employer in court. Moreover, the appellate court said the director's conduct was ratified by the hotel manager who was aware the director kept guns on the property in violation of hotel policy and was aware the director had previously been arrested for physical assault on another employee and yet had failed to take any disciplinary action.

On May 3, 1999, a North Carolina jury awarded $7.9 million to the families of two men killed when a fired worker went on a shooting rampage at a tool distribution plant. The families successfully claimed that the companies failed to adequately protect the men from a known threat of violence. The key issue at trial was whether the employer properly protected employees from the gunman, who was fired 2 days earlier because of a string of violent incidents. The gunman had previously threatened that if fired he would come back and "take management with me" (North Carolina Employment Law Letter, 1999).

In August 1999, the widow of a man slain by Mark Barton during his July 1999 shooting spree at two Atlanta day-trading firms filed suit against the All-Tech Investment Group, Barton's estate, the owners of the building where All-Tech's office was located, and the building's security company. The widow's attorney alleged that All-Tech had a responsibility to run background checks on its day traders and should have discovered that Barton was a "volatile individual." The attorney indicated that such a check was especially important given that Barton worked in a "pressure environment," created by the employer (Victim's Wife Sues Day-Trading Firm, 1999).

As discussed herein, some employees and heirs of employees have successfully sued employers in court for injuries and death arising out of workplace episodes, despite the constraints of the workers' compensation system. The theories developed in the cases that follow demonstrate that employee-victims will not always be limited to remedies provided by the workers' compensation system.

Employer Duty to Warn

Employers have a duty to warn employees of a foreseeable risk of harm, especially where a particular, identifiable employee is threatened (*Duffy v. City of Oceanside*, 1986). The duty to warn may arise where an employer hires a person with history of violence who later forms social relationships or has unpleasant altercations with other employees. For instance, a city hired a parolee who had also spent time in a mental hospital following convictions for kidnapping, rape, and sexual assault. A female employee complained she had been sexually harassed by the parolee. Despite her reports, she was never informed of the parolee's background or warned to avoid contact with him.

Later, the two employees became friendly. Although the city was aware of the friendship, it never cautioned the female employee. The parolee eventually kidnapped and killed her. The appellate court ruled that her children alleged sufficient facts to proceed in a lawsuit against the city, that a jury could conclude that the city should have alerted the victim to the parolee's past criminal conduct, and the failure to warn was a substantial factor in causing her death. The court noted that because of the female employee's prior sexual harassment complaint and the male employee's criminal history, the "threat" of harm to the female employee was reasonably foreseeable.

In a Minnesota case, *Yunker v. Honeywell, Inc.* (1993), employee Landin was rehired by Honeywell following imprisonment for the strangulation of a co-employee. He had several confrontations with co-workers and was the subject of sexual harassment complaints. Landin developed a romantic interest in a female employee. When she rebuffed him, he began threatening her life. The female employee complained to Honeywell about Landin's harassment and threats. Landin quit Honeywell and, shortly thereafter, killed the female employee in her driveway with a close-range shotgun blast. The appellate court ruled that Honeywell owed a legal duty of care to the female employee which arose from its continued employment of Landin despite his troublesome conduct. Thus, the slain employee's heirs were entitled to a trial on their claim for negligent retention and for determination of whether its failure to terminate or discipline Landin proximately caused the female employee's death.

Domestic Violence

Foreseeability of danger may also be easy to establish where workplace violence arises from domestic conflict or stalking behavior of which the employer is aware. In a Texas case, *La Rose v. State Mutual Life Assurance Co.* (1994), Francesia LaRose's family successfully sued her employer in a wrongful death action. The family alleged that the employer failed to adequately protect La Rose after her former boyfriend phoned her supervisor and said that if she was not fired, he would come to the office to kill her. The following day, the ex-boyfriend walked right past the security guard in La Rose's office building (who allegedly had photos of him) and shot her to death.

Employers should be especially concerned about domestic violence spilling over into the workplace. It is conceivable that an employer who is aware that an employee is a victim of domestic violence may be liable for an intentional tort where the employee is threatened at work and the employer fails to act to protect the employee from harm.

This may expose the employer to liability outside the workers' compensation system. Moreover, at least two courts have found that victims of violence at work could not recover under the workers' compensation system when their injuries did not arise in the course of their employment, but rather were the result of private disputes such as workplace violence. However, the courts allowed the employees to proceed against their employers in court based on other legal theories. In *Arceneaux v. K-Mart Corp.* (1995), the employee's husband shot her during her lunch break inside the store. The court allowed her to sue K-Mart for negligence for failing to provide adequate security. In *Velasquez v. Industrial Comm'n.* (1978), two employees were shot by a co-worker following a personal dispute.

However, courts have not uniformly held employers liable in these instances. For example, a Georgia court found an employer not liable to an employee who was attacked by her boyfriend in its parking lot (*Griffin v. AAA Auto Club South, Inc.*, 1996). The court found that the employee assumed the risk of her boyfriend's attack when she failed to request an escort. Similarly, a Texas court found a hospital not liable when a man shot his wife while she was working there, despite the fact that there was some evidence that the attack was foreseeable (*Guerrero v. Memorial Medical Center*, 1997). The outcome of these types of cases will often depend on their specific facts.

Tort Theories

Negligent Hiring, Negligent Retention, and Negligent Supervision

Many states recognize that an employer may be liable for negligently hiring, supervising, or retaining an unfit employee.

Negligent Hiring

Negligent hiring occurs when the employer knew or should have known that hiring the employee created a particular risk or hazard and that particular harm materializes (see, generally, *Yunker v. Honeywell, Inc., supra* et al.) This should be a significant concern for employers who hire workers who go into private homes such as meter readers, cable TV installers, phone repair personnel, carpet cleaners, and home health-care or day-care workers. A criminal background check should be standard for persons hired for these types of positions.

A Massachusetts jury recently awarded $26.5 million in compensatory and punitive damages against a home health-care program after its employee, a home health aide, beat and stabbed to death a 32-year-old quadriplegic and his 77-year-old grandmother. The employer never performed a criminal background check which would have revealed six larceny-related convictions. Moreover, had it checked, the employer would have learned that the employee provided false information about his employment history and education (*Ward v. Trusted Health*).

An employer may be sued even where the employee was acting contrary to company policy. In an Illinois case, the court allowed a negligent hiring claim by a hitchhiker assaulted by a truck driver. The court allowed the case to proceed against the truck driver's employer even though it had instructed the driver not to pick up hitchhikers (*Malorney v. BSL Motor Freight, Inc.*, 1986).

Avoiding Liability

An employer may be able to defend such an action by showing a policy and practice of carefully reviewing and verifying all information provided on applications and resumes and conducting background checks appropriate to the position before making an offer. The background check should include a search of criminal, civil, and family law filings in every county and state the applicant is known to have lived. Such a search should turn up any record of criminal charges and any restraining orders issued for stalking-type activity. If the applicant's record is less than exemplary, the employer should consider the duties of the position, the amount and type of interaction this position has with other employees and the public, and whether the position will provide the applicant with an opportunity to repeat any past violent or inappropriate behavior.

Get the applicant's written consent to check references and a waiver of claims against you and those contacted. It is a good practice to document all of your inquiries, even if you do not obtain much information. Similarly, an employer should implement and enforce clear policies outlining acceptable and unacceptable conduct for such employees. While such policies may not protect a company from the filing of a lawsuit, they are useful in ultimately defending the action.

Negligent Retention/Negligent Supervision

Negligent retention or supervision occurs when, during the course of employment, an employer becomes aware or should become aware of an employee's tendency toward violence and fails to take further action such as investigation, discharge, or reassignment, in order to prevent injury to others (see, generally, *Hoke v. May Department Stores* (b), 1995 et al.). Such liability is based on the *employer's conduct* without any consideration of whether the employee was acting within the course and scope of employment (*Evans F., supra*).

In California, the families of three slain sightseers recently alleged negligent hiring and negligent retention theories when they sued the owners of The Cedar Lodge near Yosemite National Park. The complaints allege the lodge endangered the three women by assigning them to an isolated room and failing to properly check the background of its employee Cary Stayner, a handyman, who is accused of the serial killings.

The Complaint alleged that the lodge was at fault because it kept Stayner on staff despite the fact that it should have known he acted in an "unusual, bizarre or violent manner" on prior jobs. The suit also alleges that the lodge improperly supervised Stayner after it laid him off, but allowed him to continue to live on the premises (Hanley, 1999).

Avoiding Potential Liability

An employer's best defense is to thoroughly investigate any information it receives which indicates that an employee may pose a threat to the safety of others. The employer must follow up such investigation with any steps necessary to protect employees and third parties. This may include placing the dangerous employee on suspension or a medical leave of absence or terminating such employee. Employers should take all such threats seriously.

Intentional Infliction of Emotional Distress

In the employment context, a claim for intentional infliction of emotional distress is demonstrated by a showing that (1) the employer engaged in extreme and outrageous conduct; (2) the employer intended to cause, or recklessly disregarded the probability of causing, emotional distress; (3) the employee's severe emotional suffering; and (4) emotional distress that was caused by the employer's conduct (*Heller v. Pillsbury Madison & Sutro* and *King v. AC&R Advertising, Inc.*, 1995).

This theory was successfully employed by an employee against the residential care facility where she worked. The employee phoned her manager for help after she was seriously attacked by one of the residents. Despite the fact that she was the only employee on duty at the time, her manager ignored her cries for help because he believed his return to the facility would only reinforce the resident's violent behavior.

An Oregon appellate court upheld a $1.5 million jury award noting that the manager knew the employee was distressed when she phoned, yet he chose to leave her alone with the person who had attacked her (*Holland and Hart*, 1999).

Avoiding Liability: An Oregon Case

The Oregon case is a classic example of bad facts making bad law. Obviously, employers must respond immediately to employees who may be in imminent danger and the worker in the Oregon case should have been promptly assisted by management, police, and medical personnel. These types of situations may be avoided by implementing and enforcing policies and procedures that address risks peculiar to your workplace and with management training so key personnel respond appropriately in emergency situations.

Liability for Inaccurate Job References

Employers risk legal action when they provide good job recommendations for persons known to have histories of violence, inappropriate sexual behavior, or other serious workplace misconduct. A Florida appellate court allowed victims of workplace violence to seek punitive damages against the

perpetrator's former employer where the employer had endorsed the perpetrator in a letter of recommendation (*Allstate Insurance Co. v. Jerner*,
1995). In California, the court allowed a similar action by a minor student
molested by her school vice principal. The principal's former employer
provided him with a glowing letter of recommendation despite the fact that
he had also molested students at that school (*Randi W. v. Livingston Union
School District* (a), 1997). The court said that ordinarily a recommending
employer should not be held accountable to third persons for failing to
disclose negative information. Nonetheless, the court found it appropriate
to impose liability when the recommendation letter amounts to "an affirmative misrepresentation presenting a foreseeable and substantial risk of
physical harm to a third person" (*Randi W. v. Livingston Union School
District*, 1997 [at 1070]).

Avoiding Liability Altogether

Because of liability concerns, employers routinely decline to provide much,
if any, information about former employees. However, should an employer
decide to write a letter of reference or recommendation, it must be accurate.
Do not write letters that unjustifiably praise a troubled employee in an
attempt to "pawn off" that employee on someone else.

Premises Liability Based on Employer's Failure to Provide Adequate Security

Employees have not been successful in suing their employers on a premises
liability theory when they are assaulted by unknown criminal assailants. In one
such case two employees of an auto parts store injured during a robbery sued
their employer for failure to provide adequate security despite a known crime
risk. The store where the employees worked had previously been a target for
criminal activity. In addition, the employees had complained about lack of
security, to no avail. While the court acknowledged that the employer's conduct
was negligent or even reckless, it would not fall outside workers' compensation
exclusivity unless it rose to the level of "intentional misconduct." To show
"intentional misconduct" an employee must allege and prove that the employer
acted deliberately with the specific intent to injure the employee (*Arendell v.
Auto Parts Club, Inc.*, 1994).

Thus, unless the intentional tortious conduct is attributable directly to
the employer based on respondeat superior or ratification, a employee will
likely be limited to workers' compensation remedies. Where an act of violence
is committed by an unknown third party, it is unlikely that an employee will
be able to show the employer intentionally intended to injure the employee
or that the employer ratified the violent behavior.

Foreseeable Risks and Civil Liability

While an employer may not be liable to employees injured by criminal acts, it may be liable to third parties where criminal assaults are foreseeable and inadequate steps are taken to ensure public safety (*Ann M. v. Pacific Plaza Shopping Center*, 1993 et al.). In a recent decision, a California Court of Appeal found that the County of Los Angeles owed a duty to take reasonable steps to provide security measures against foreseeable criminal activity in the Central Civil Courthouse building in downtown Los Angeles. While waiting in a courthouse hallway for a hearing in connection with the dissolution of her marriage, Eileen Zelig was fatally shot by her ex-husband in front of the couple's 6-year-old daughter. The court allowed a lawsuit brought by the Zelig children against the County of Los Angeles to proceed (*Zelig v. County of Los Angeles*, 1999 and *Vaughn v. Granite City Steel*, 1991).*

Contract Theories of Liability

Employers who have adopted and implemented a workplace violence prevention program will be able to cite such policies in defense of any lawsuit arising from a violent incident. Above all, such programs can help save lives.

An implied contract may be inferred from the language in a company's policy manual (*Foley v. Interactive Data Corp.*, 1988).** If an employer has a policy addressing workplace safety or harassment issues, it could be used as the basis for an action for breach of implied contract. Nonetheless, it is strongly suggested that employers implement and enforce a workplace safety and violence policy.

Employer's Failure to Obtain a Restraining Order

Some states have enacted legislation allowing employers to obtain civil harassment restraining orders (see California's Workplace Violence Safety Act). Theoretically, an employee could argue the employer was negligent for failure to obtain a restraining order to keep a perpetrator out of the worksite. However, California law specifically states that the enactment of laws which allow employers to obtain restraining orders against workplace violence **does not** increase the employer's duty to provide a safe workplace. The California statute states, "[n]othing in this section shall be construed as expanding, diminishing, altering or modifying the duty, if any, of an employer to

---

* In *Vaughn v. Granite City Steel*, the court awarded $415,000 in a wrongful death action where an employee was fatally shot in the employer's parking lot, and the evidence showed that security was "grossly inadequate."
** In *Foley v. Interactive Data Corp.*, the California Supreme Court recognized that implied contracts may be inferred from language contained in company policies or handbooks.

provide a safe workplace for employees and other persons" (California's Workplace Violence Safety Act, § 527.8(k)).

Employer Civil Liability to Employee Perpetrators

An employer must also be sensitive to the rights of an employee who has committed a violent act or whose behavior gives rise to concerns about violence. The employer's handling of the violent or threatening employee is another source of potential claims against the employer. Possible claims from these employees may include defamation, wrongful termination, invasion of privacy, and discrimination on the basis of disability pursuant to the Americans with Disabilities Act (ADA) and corresponding state laws. For instance, an employer who attempts to warn others of an employee's threats may then face a defamation or invasion of privacy claim from the employee who made the threats.[*] A right to privacy has been recognized in 48 of 50 states (Schmitt, 2000).

Protections Afforded to Employee under ADA

Employers must be mindful that employee misconduct may be attributable to a medical condition such as a psychological or physiological disorder. Thus, it is possible that an employee who suffers an adverse employment action as a result of engaging in or threatening violent behavior in the workplace will file a claim of disability discrimination under the ADA (42 U.S.C. § 12101 et seq.) and/or state laws that provide similar protection (see, e.g., California Fair Employment and Housing Act [FEHA] et al.). The ADA governs employers with 15 or more employees.[**] The ADA prohibits discrimination against qualified individuals with known physical or mental disabilities. A disability is defined to include one or more of the following:

1. A physical or mental impairment that substantially limits one or more of the major life activities of such individual
2. A record of such impairment
3. Being regarded as having such an impairment (see Americans with Disabilities Act [a])

A variety of mental disorders have been found to constitute a disability, including depression, schizophrenia, post-traumatic stress disorder, compulsive gambling, borderline personality disorder with obsessive compulsive

---

[*] Such statements may be privileged under state law and thus will not sustain a cause of action for defamation.

[**] State laws may apply to employers with fewer than 15 employees. See, e.g., California Fair Employment and Housing Act (FEHA), Government Code section 12900 et seq., Illinois Human Rights Act, Illinois Compiled Statutes, 775 ILCS 5/1-101 et seq.

features, bipolar disorder, explosive personality disorder, and anxiety disorder (Thompson, 1995).

When dealing with what appears to be an employee's emotional problem, an employer is at most risk of violating the third type of disability, the perceived disability. For example, when an employer disciplines an employee for making an inappropriate threat an employee may allege that he was discriminated against for being perceived as having a disability which would make him capable of carrying out his threat (see, e.g., *Stradley v. Lafourche Communications, Inc.,* 1994). Similarly, employers who refer an employee who is exhibiting disturbing or unusual behavior for a psychological fitness-for-duty examination are also potentially at risk of a complaint alleging it "regarded" the employee as having a disability. The court in *Cody v. Cigna Healthcare* (1998) rejected this approach. That case involved a nurse who suffered from anxiety and depression. Her co-workers observed her "sprinkling salt in front of her cubicle to keep away evil spirits," staring into space and "drawing pictures of sperm." The court found Cigna's offer of paid medical leave and requirement that she see a psychologist did not indicate that it believed she suffered from an impairment. The court noted that "[e]mployers need to be able to use reasonable means to ascertain the cause of troubling behavior without exposing themselves to ADA claims ..." (*Cody v. Cigna Healthcare,* 1998 (at 599)). However, simply terminating employees based on unfounded fears of violence or because of inaccurate stereotypes may result in ADA liability (*Lussier v. Runyon,* 1994). Employers in these situations are strongly advised to consult with legal counsel to develop a strategy that will assist the employee and reduce the employer's risk of liability.

An employee is a "qualified individual" under the ADA if he or she can perform the essential functions of a position with or without reasonable accommodation (Americans with Disabilities Act [b]). Thus, an employer may have to investigate whether a known mental disability may be accommodated without undue hardship before an employee is terminated for violent behavior. An individual with a mental disability is not "otherwise qualified" if he engages in conduct that would disqualify someone who is not protected by the ADA. For instance, a federal district court in New York found that the FBI legally terminated a communications operator with bipolar disorder who experienced "substantial breaks from reality" rendering him unqualified to handle classified information (*Hogarth v. Thornburgh,* 1993).

Importantly, an employee may not be terminated or otherwise disciplined *because of* his or her disability. However, many courts have held that employers may lawfully discipline or terminate an employee with a claimed mental disability which causes the employee to exhibit violent behavior. Unfortunately, the judicial decisions in this area have not been uniform and it is very difficult to predict how a court might rule in any particular case (see, e.g., *Hindman v. GTE Data Services, Inc.*, 1994a and *Hindman v. GTE Data Services, Inc.*, 1995*).

The Florida case of *Hindman v. GTE Data Services, Inc.* illustrates the dilemmas involved in attempting to prevent workplace violence without running afoul of the ADA. There, the employer terminated Hindman when it discovered that he had brought a loaded gun to work. This violated strictly enforced company policy. Prior to his discharge, Hindman had been diagnosed with a chemical imbalance. However, this was never communicated to the employer. After the termination decision was made, Hindman's attorney notified GTE of the diagnosis and requested that GTE delay any decision regarding Hindman's employment because he was being admitted to the hospital due to his condition. GTE terminated him anyway and was sued for violation of the ADA. In his complaint, Hindman alleged that the chemical imbalance caused him to possess the firearm on the employer's property.

GTE moved for summary judgment arguing that Hindman's chemical imbalance did not constitute a disability under the ADA and, even if it did, Hindman was not otherwise qualified to perform the essential functions of his job because he was unable to abide by company policy prohibiting firearms at work. The district court denied the motion noting that Hindman's poor judgment in bringing a firearm to work was directly tied to his disability. The court also questioned whether there was an accommodation that GTE could have made which would have allowed Hindman to continue working. The court was critical that GTE had not even considered trying to accommodate Hindman's disability and that it had ignored a request from Hindman's attorney to hold off making a decision while Hindman sought treatment (*Hindman v. GTE Data Services, Inc.*, 1994b).

However, at the time of trial, on GTE's motion a different district court judge granted judgment as a matter of law in GTE's favor because there was no evidence that information regarding Hindman's disability was ever communicated to his employer until after the decision to terminate had been made (*Hindman v. GTE Data Services, Inc.*, 1995). GTE's initial loss in this case was very unusual because courts have almost uniformly held that employers do not have to excuse misconduct, even where it is caused by a disability.

In general, an employer does not violate the ADA by terminating an employee for unacceptable conduct, including threatening other employees, even if the conduct is directly related to a disability.

Employer Defenses to ADA Claims Raised by Violent Employees

There are several affirmative defenses available to employers who terminate employees who have threatened or actually engage in violent behavior and

---

* Where two different judges in the same district ruled differently on this issue *in the same case.*

are then faced with the claim "my disability made me do it" in a complaint for discrimination and violation of the ADA.

First, the employee is unable to perform the essential functions of the job and no reasonable accommodation exists which would enable the employee to perform the essential functions of the job. Often violent or threatening behavior can help an employer to demonstrate that an employee cannot make the factual showing needed to sustain an ADA action. The employer can point to the offending conduct to show the employee is not a "qualified individual" because he is incapable of performing the job requirements without posing a threat to the workplace.

Second, the employee would create a direct threat to the safety of himself or others and there is no reasonable accommodation that would reduce or eliminate the danger (29 CFR 1630.2(r)). For example, in *Lassiter v. Reno* (1995), the direct threat defense was successfully asserted to disqualify a U.S. Marshal with a delusional paranoid personality from carrying a gun, an essential job function. The assessment that someone poses a direct threat is based on an individualized assessment of the individual's present ability to safely perform the essential functions of the job. This assessment is to be based on a reasonable medical judgment and objective evidence. To complicate matters further, the EEOC's regulations interpreting the ADA state that an employer may not deny an employment opportunity to an individual with a disability merely because of a "slightly increased risk" (Appendix, 29 CFR § 1630.2(r)). Thus, there must be a high probability of substantial harm. To make matters even more difficult, the EEOC states that an employer may refuse to hire a person with a history of violence only when the employer can prove that the person poses a direct threat to health or safety. This is an onerous burden under the ADA. To meet this burden the employer would have to demonstrate that the employee poses a serious risk of imminent bodily harm to himself or others. In addition, the EEOC regulations indicate that an individual does not pose a "direct threat" simply by virtue of having a history of psychiatric disability or being treated for psychiatric disability (see EEOC Enforcement Guidance).

Despite the nearly impossible burdens imposed by the EEOC and the ADA in demonstrating "direct threat," the courts have almost uniformly held that actual direct threats or acts of violence are not protected by the ADA, even when caused by a physical or mental disability.

A third affirmative defense is available: as in every disability discrimination case, the employer may argue that the employee's condition does not rise to the level of a disability under the ADA. The ADA defines disability to include (1) a physical or mental impairment that substantially limits one or more of the major life activities; (2) a record of such impairment; or (3) the individual regarded as having such an impairment.

ADA Analysis When Evaluating Termination of Violent or Potentially Violent Hire

1. Does the employee have a physical or mental disability which is potentially protected by the ADA *and* which is known to the employer or decision maker?
2. If the answer is "yes," is the employee able to perform the essential functions of his or her job?
3. If the answer to (2) is "no," is there an accommodation the employer can make which will not impose an "undue hardship" on the employer and will allow the employee to continue to perform his or her job?
4. Does the employee pose a "direct threat" to the health and safety of others or a high probability of causing substantial harm to others?
5. If the answer is "yes" or "inconclusive," is a fitness-for-duty examination warranted?

Liability to Third Persons for Violent Acts Committed by Employees

The Respondeat Superior

In some states, an employee's willful, malicious, and even criminal torts may fall within the scope of his or her employment resulting in employer liability for the conduct, even though the employer has not authorized the employee to commit the crimes or intentional torts. Whether the employer will be responsible for the employee's acts depends, at least in part, on the connection between the employee's job duties and the improper conduct (*Lisa M. v. Henry Mayo Newhall Memorial Hospital*, 1995). For instance, in *Lisa M. v. Henry Mayo Newhall Memorial Hospital*, the California Supreme Court found the defendant hospital was *not liable* under the doctrine of respondeat superior for sexual battery committed by an ultrasound technician on a patient. The court concluded that the connection between the technician's employment and duties and his independent commission of a deliberate sexual assault was too attenuated, without proof of the hospital's negligence, to support allocation of plaintiff's losses to the hospital as a cost of doing business.

A contrary result was reached in *Mary M. v. City of Los Angeles* (1991). There, a woman raped by a police officer brought a personal injury action against the city which employed the officer. The court held that the city could be held liable on a theory of respondeat superior when an on-duty police officer misused his authority by raping a woman whom he had detained. The evidence in this case supported a finding that the officer was acting within the course of his employment.

However, in *Farmer's Insurance Group v. County of Santa Clara* (1995), the court noted that if the employee's tort is personal in nature, his mere presence at his place of employment and his attendance to occupational duties prior to or subsequent to the offense will not give rise to a cause of action against the employer under the doctrine of respondeat superior. If losses do not foreseeably result from the conduct of the employer's enterprise then they are not fairly attributable to the employer as a cost of doing business.

Numerous other cases have held that acts undertaken solely for the employee's personal gratification (such as sexual assaults) which have no purpose connected to employment do not give rise to employer liability on a vicarious liability theory (*Doe v. Capital Cities*, 1996 et al.).

Liability to Third Parties

An employer may also be liable to third parties (i.e., persons other than employees) on general negligence theories, including negligent hiring, supervision, and retention (*Hoke v. May Department Stores* (a), 1995). For example, an Oregon department store was sued for negligence by a customer who was sexually assaulted by a security guard who detained her to conduct a shoplifting investigation. The store was found to be liable to the customer for damages. In addition, the California Supreme Court has found that an employer may be held liable for negligent misrepresentation and fraud for providing a positive recommendation for a former employee who the employer knew had molested several students (*Randi W. v. Livingston Union School District* (b)).

Threats of Violence and "Good Cause" for Discipline or Termination

Courts have held that a threat of violence provides "good cause" for termination of an employee, thereby providing employers with a defense to wrongful termination claims brought by these individuals. Some courts have said that threatening, aggressive, or violent conduct makes a person "unqualified" for his position and thus not covered by the ADA. This is the case even where the offensive behavior is caused by a mental or physical disability.

In one California case, discharge from employment was an appropriate penalty for an employee's threats to kill her supervisor. In another case the employer prevailed on plaintiff's claims for discrimination under Title VII, the ADA and California law (*Davis v. Civil Service Com.*, 1997 and *Vagas v. Gromko*, 1997), where the court found that the employee's threats to kill his supervisors were a non-discriminatory reason for discharge. In another case, *Crawford v. Runyon* (1996), a U.S. Postal Service employee was appropriately terminated for threatening to kill his immediate supervisor even though he claimed to suffer from depression and stress-related mental disorders. In an Illinois case, a federal appeals court found that the employee was terminated, not based on her illness (depression and delusional paranoid disorder), but because she threatened to kill another employee. The court found this to be a lawful termination (*Palmer v. Circuit Court of Cook County*, 1997). In *Hamilton v. Southwestern Bell* (1998), the Federal Court of Appeals said, "The ADA does not insulate emotional or violent outbursts blamed on an impairment." In *Palmer v. Circuit Court of Cook County* (1997), a different court noted that forcing an employer to retain an employee who had made threats would "place the employer on a razor's edge — in jeopardy of violating the Act if it fired such an employee, yet in jeopardy of being deemed negligent if it retained him and he hurt someone." In both the Hamilton and Palmer cases, the courts found for the employer. The courts found the employers justified in terminating employees who made threats of violence and found that the employees were not protected by the ADA although they claimed their behavior was linked to a disability. The weight of legal authority holds that employers are entitled to terminate employees for acts of misconduct even when they are related to a disability (see *Collings v. Longview Fibre Co.*, 1995).

Discharge in Light of Collective Bargaining Agreement

A threat or an act of violence may not always provide sufficient "just cause" for termination or discipline in a workplace governed by a collective bargaining agreement. Improper application of a "just cause" standard when imposing discipline in response to a violent incident in a union environment might result in an arbitrator's reinstatement of an employee terminated by the employer in connection with a violent incident. Approximately 95% of collective bargaining agreements contain grievance and arbitration provisions, and approximately 80% of the agreements specifically require the employer to have "just cause" for discharging or disciplining an employee (see *Pugh v. See's Candies, Inc.*, 1981). There are distinct remedies to set aside or reduce employer-imposed discipline, and corresponding damage measures such as reinstatement and back pay. Recent studies indicate that union employers may have to pay closer attention to subjective factors employed in discharging or disciplining an employee. The nature of a specific grievant's involvement in a workplace fight, the severity of the incident, and the employer's consistent application of its own procedures are all factors which could impact an arbitrator's review of the employer's decision under a collective bargaining agreement and may constitute mitigating circumstances that warrant setting aside or reducing employer-imposed penalties (Robertson, 1998).

Additional cautionary measures mandated by a collective bargaining agreement create a potential stumbling block for employers seeking to embrace a "zero tolerance" standard in responding to workplace violence. A union employer may instead need to impose penalties that are commensurate with severity of the incident and the role the employee played. Moreover, employer discipline might be set aside or reduced where it failed to take proactive measures to prevent fights from occurring in the workplace.

Proactive Measures: Employer Steps to Prevent Possible Episodes of Workplace Violence

1. Research workplace violence counselors, security consultants, and legal counsel with experience in workplace violence matters before you have a problem, so that you immediately know who to call when the need arises.
2. Gun control: be aware of local gun control laws.

More than 30 states now have liberalized concealed weapons laws and 12 others grant licenses at the discretion of law enforcement offices, making it easier than ever for ordinary people to legally carry concealed weapons. However, no state law prohibits an employer from barring weapons in the workplace. An explicit company policy banning weapons is advisable. Employers in one of the more liberal concealed weapons states should consider requiring that each employee provide written acknowledgment of receipt of the company weapons policy so no employee can try to claim he was unaware of the policy.

3. Take steps to improve the security of the physical plant that may include a professional security audit.

Conduct workplace violence sensitivity training. Consider hiring an investigator to perform background checks on applicants including criminal, educational, motor vehicle, and other public records if such a check is appropriate to the position applied for and is performed uniformly on all persons who apply for the same or similar positions.

4. Develop and enforce a workplace violence policy.

The two most important elements of a workplace violence policy are (1) that it set forth zero tolerance for any type of violent behavior, including threats; and (2) that it provide a procedure for confidential reporting of such incidents. The policy should clearly identify inappropriate employee behaviors, unacceptable actions, sanctions for violations, and intervention opportunities for managers and supervisors. It should encourage employees to report any type of uneasiness either with a co-worker or someone outside the company. The policy should state that all complaints will be investigated.

All complaints should be handled on a confidential basis and should be investigated promptly and thoroughly. If you obtain employee medical information in the course of conducting the investigation, remember that all such information must be kept in the strictest confidence.

5. Always act promptly to investigate reports of violence, threats of violence, or threatening speech or conduct. Address the issue head on and take remedial and corrective action where warranted.
6. Consider implementing a plan to educate employees on domestic violence.

As illustrated throughout this chapter, domestic violence often spills over into the workplace. Some employers have responded to this threat by taking proactive steps to educate employees on the issue of domestic violence and offering employees a few hours off work where needed to obtain restraining orders or attend court hearings. For example, Target Stores sponsored educational workshops and distributed information about domestic violence to its employees. Marshall's Stores places domestic violence hotline numbers in women's restrooms along with the company's Employee Assistance Program (EAP) number. Liz Claiborne, Inc. includes domestic violence information and referral phone numbers with all employee paychecks (Robertson, 1998). Polaroid's domestic violence policy outlines various steps the company will take, including seeking restraining orders to keep perpetrators away from the worksite and relocating domestic abuse victims to help them escape their abusers (Robertson, 1998, p. 658).

Some companies even offer basic information on such things as how to go about actually obtaining a restraining order. Typically a manager or member of human resources is tasked with developing expertise in this area and then becomes a resource for any employee in need of such assistance. Raising awareness of the domestic violence issue and providing employees with information and support may reduce the likelihood that a domestic situation will erupt at work. It may also encourage employees to notify company management when they are faced with an abusive situation. If the employee feels she is in a supportive environment, or one in which she can obtain critical information and other help, she is much more likely to share the information than attempt to hide it. If the employer is aware of the problem it is certainly in a much better position to take remedial safety measures to protect the work force.

7. Consider obtaining a civil harassment restraining order.

In most states, a victim of threats, violence, or of stalking may obtain a restraining order (California Code of Civil Procedure (a)). Restraining orders are usually issued with a limited evidentiary showing so that the process may be handled without an attorney. Court forms or victim assistance projects may be available to assist the petitioner.

In some states, an employer may obtain a restraining order of its own that will prohibit harassing conduct by a perpetrator and order the perpetrator to "stay away" from the workplace and/or the victim (California Code of Civil Procedure (b)). An employer may even obtain a restraining order without the cooperation of the victim. However, the evidentiary showing required for an employer restraining order may be higher (*Scripps Health v. Marin*, 1999).

Even public entities have been able to enforce restraining orders to bar members of the public. For instance, Oregon State University (OSU) obtained a restraining order to exclude Robert Souders from campus after two female students filed complaints against him for stalking (*Souders v. Lucero*, 1999). Souders unsuccessfully sued the school under federal law. He alleged that he could not be barred from a university campus that was open to the public. The court found that although the campus was open to the public, "it does not follow that the university must allow all members of the public onto its premises regardless of their conduct" (*Souders v. Lucero*, 1999, at 1044). The court also noted that the school had a duty to protect its students by imposing reasonable regulations on the conduct of those who came onto campus and that the exclusion order was not directed toward constitutionally protected conduct.

8. Allow employees time off to obtain civil harassment restraining orders. Assist victim in obtaining restraining order against a co-worker. Such time off is now required by some state laws (California Labor Code § 230(c)).

In 1997 federal lawmakers attempted to pass the Battered Women's Employment Protection Act. The law would have required employers to provide employees with job-protected time off work to address domestic violence issues, including to seek legal assistance and attend court appearances. That law died on committee, but has since been incorporated into the Violence Against Women Act of 2000. In connection with the proposed 1997 legislation Congress made various factual findings including the following:

• Violence against women dramatically affects women's workforce participation, insofar as one quarter of the battered women surveyed had lost a job due at least in part to the effects of domestic violence, and over one half had been harassed by their abuser at work.

- 49% of senior executives surveyed said domestic violence has a harmful effect on their company's productivity, 47% said domestic violence negatively affects attendance, and 44% said domestic violence increases health-care costs, and the Bureau of National Affairs estimates that domestic violence costs employers between $3 billion and $5 billion per year. (See 143 Cong. Rec. S1659-03, S1678 [Daily Ed. February 26, 1997].)

Bibliography

1996 National Census of Fatal Occupational Injuries.

Allstate Insurance Co. v. Jerner, 650 So. 2d 997, 999 (Fla. Dist. Ct. App. 1995).

Americans with Disabilities Act (a), 42 U.S.C. § 12202(2); 29 C.F.R. § 1630.2(g).

Americans with Disabilities Act (b), 42 U.S.C. § 12111(8); 29 C.F.R. § 1630.2(m).

Ann M. v. Pacific Plaza Shopping Center, 6 Cal. 4th 666 (1993); *Issacs v. Huntington Memorial Hospital,* 38 Cal. 3d 112 (1985); *Taylor v. Centennial Bowl, Inc.,* 65 Cal. 2d 114 (1966); *Lopez v. McDonald's Corporation,* 193 Cal. App. 3d 495 (1987).

Arceneaux v. K-Mart Corp., No. CIV.A.94-3720, 1995 WL 479818 (E.D. LA. 1995).

Arendell v. Auto Parts Club, Inc., 29 Cal. App. 4th 1261 (1994).

Arendell v. Auto Parts Club, Inc., 29 Cal. App. 4th 1261 (1994); *Pichon v. Fairview Development Center,* 1996 WL 875080 (Cal. App. 4th Dist.).

Arendell v. Auto Parts Club, Inc., 29 Cal. App. 4th at 1265 (1994); see also *Ann M. v. Pacific Plaza,* 6 Cal. 4th 666 (1993) (building owner not required to provide security guards in common areas to protect employees of tenants); *Nicole M. v. Sears, Roebuck & Co.,* 76 Cal. App. 4th 1238 (1999) (Sears not liable for attempted sexual assault in parking lot).

CA Lab. Code § 6400; WA ST 49.17.050; O.R.S. § 654.003; HI ST § 396-1; Fla. Stat. § 812.173 (1997).

California Code of Civil Procedure (a), § 527.6.

California Code of Civil Procedure (b), § 527.8.

California Fair Employment and Housing Act (FEHA), Government Code § 12900 et seq.; Illinois Human Rights Act, Illinois Compiled Statutes, 775 ILCS 5/1-101 et seq.; Missouri Human Rights Act, VIA.M.S. § 213.020 et seq.; Pennsylvania Human Relations Act (PHRA) 43 P.S. § 951.

California's Workplace Violence Safety Act, Code of Civil Procedure § 527.8.

Cody v. Cigna Healthcare, 139 F. 3d 595 (8th Cir. 1998).

Collings v. Longview Fibre Co., 63 F. 3d 828 (9th Cir. 1995).

Columbia Aluminum Corp. v. United States Steelworkers of America, Local 8147, 922 F. Supp. 412, 420 (E.D. Wash. 1995).

Crawford v. Runyon, 79 F. 3d 743 (8th Cir. 1996); see also *Jones v. American Postal Workers Union*, 192 F. 3d 417 (4th Cir. 1999) (employee terminated in response to threat to kill supervisor could not pursue ADA action claiming his misconduct was caused by a mental disability).

Davis v. Civil Service Com., 55 Cal. App. 4th 677 (1997); *Vagas v. Gromko*, 977 F. Supp. 996 (N.D. Cal. 1997) (granting employer's motion for summary judgment).

de Becker, G. (1997). *The Gift of Fear: Survival Signals That Protect Us from Violence* (p. 9). Boston: Little, Brown.

Doe v. Capital Cities, 50 Cal. App. 4th 1038 (1996); *Jeffrey E. v. Central Baptist Church*, 197 Cal. App. 3d 718 (1988); *Rita M. v. Roman Catholic Archbishop*, 187 Cal. App. 3d 1453 (1986); *Alma W. v. Oakland Unified School Dist.*, 123 Cal. App. 3d 133 (1981).

Duffy v. City of Oceanside, 179 Cal. App. 3d 666 (1986).

EEOC Enforcement Guidance: The ADA and Psychiatric Disabilities, Washington, D.C.

Evan F., supra, 8 Cal. App. 4th at 843.

Farmer's Insurance Group v. County of Santa Clara, 11 Cal. 4th 992 (1995).

Foley v. Interactive Data Corp., 47 Cal. 3d 654, 681–682 (1988).

G. B. Goldman Paper Co. v. Paperwokers Local 286, 957 F. Supp. 607, 619 (E.D. Pa. 1997), focusing on Section 5 of OSHA.

Griffin v. AAA Auto Club South, Inc., 470 S.E. 2d 474, 477 (Ga. Ct. App. 1996).

Guerrero v. Memorial Medical Center, 938 S.W. 3d 789 (Tex. App. 1997).

Hamilton v. Southwestern Bell, 136 F. 3d 1047, 1052 (5th Cir. 1998).

Hanley, C. (October 28, 1999). Yosemite-area hotel sued by victims' kin for wrongful death: in lawsuit families question security at lodge, room assignment for three tourists, *San Jose Mercury News*, 5B.

Heller v. Pillsbury Madison & Sutro, 50 Cal. App. 4th 1367, 1388; *King v. AC&R Advertising, Inc.*, 65 F. 3d 764, 769 (9th Cir. 1995) (citations omitted).

Herrick v. Quality Hotels, Inns and Resorts, Inc., 19 Cal. App. 4th 1608 (1993).

Hindman v. GTE Data Services, Inc., 1994a WL 371396 (M.D. FL) and *Hindman v. GTE Data Services, Inc.*, 1995 WL 128271 (M.D. FL).

Hindman v. GTE Data Services, Inc., 1994b WL 371396 (M.D. FL); 3 A.D. Cases 641.

Hindman v. GTE Data Services, Inc. 1995 WL 128271 (M.D. FL). 29 CFR 1630.2(r).

Hogarth v. Thornburgh, 833 F. Supp. 1077 (S.D. NY. 1993).

Hoke v. May Department Stores (a), 891 P. 2d 686 (Or. App. 1995).

Hoke v. May Department Stores (b), 891 P. 2d 686 (Or. App. 1995), cert. Denied, 511 U.S. 1137 (1994) (involving injury to customer, not employee); *Moses v. Diocese of Colorado*, 863 P. 2d 310 (Colo. 1993); *Yunker v. Honeywell, supra*, 496 N.W. 2d 419.

Holland, J. and Hart, D. (December 1999). What should you be doing to protect your workplace? *Idaho Employment Law Letter.*

Iverson v. Atlas Pacific Engineering, 143 Cal. App. 3d 219 (1983); California Labor Code section 3601(a).

Kinney (September 1993). Breaking Point, The Workplace Violence Epidemic and What To Do About It. National Safe Workplace Institute.

Kua, C. (June 15, 2000). State checks to see if Xerox could have prevented deaths, *Honolulu Star-Bulletin.*

La Rose v. State Mutual Life Assurance Co., No. 9322684 (215th Dist. Ct., Harris City, TX. 1994).

Lassiter v. Reno, 885 F. Supp. 869 (E.D. VA. 1995).

Lisa M. v. Henry Mayo Newhall Memorial Hospital, 12 Cal. 4th 291 (1995).

Lucero, M. A. and Allen, R. E. (August 1998). Fighting on the job: analysis of recent arbitration decisions, *Dispute Resolution Journal,* 53, 50.

Lussier v. Runyon, 3 A.D. cases 223 (D. ME. 1994) (brought under the Rehabilitation Act, not the ADA).

Malorney v. BSL Motor Freight, Inc., 496 N.E. 2d 1086-89. (Ill. App. Ct. 1986).

Mary M. v. City of Los Angeles, 54 Cal. 3d 202 (1991).

Muller v. Automobile Club of Southern California, 61 Cal. App. 4th 431, 451 (1998).

Murphy v. Worker's Compensation Appeals Board, 86 Cal. App. 3d 996 (1978).

North Carolina Employment Law Letter, May 5, 1999; $7.9 million awarded in workplace shooting, *Los Angeles Daily Journal,* May 6, 1999.

Palmer v. Circuit Court of Cook County, 117 F. 3d 351 (7th Cir. 1997).

Palmer v. Circuit Court of Cook County, 117 F. 3d 351, 352 (7th Cir. 1997), cert. denied, 522 U.S. 1096 (1998).

Pinkerton's Inc. (1999). Top security threats facing corporate America, 1999 Annual Survey.

Pugh v. See's Candies, Inc., 116 Cal. App. 3d 311, 321, note 5 (1981).

Randi W. v. Livingston Union School District (a), 14 Cal. 4th 1066 (1997).

Randi W. v. Livingston Union School District (b), *supra,* note 49.

Robertson, J. C. (1998). Addressing domestic violence in the workplace: an employer's responsibility, *Law & Justice,* 16, 633, 656–657.

Schmitt, J. (2000). Escaping the Privacy Bind: An Outline for Employers, 11 Andrews Sex Harassment Litig. Rep. 3.

Scripps Health v. Marin, 72 Cal. App. 4th 324 at n. 9 (1999).

Secretary of Labor v. Megawest Financial, Inc., 1995 WL 383233 (June 19, 1995).

Slager v. Commonwealth Edison Co., 595 N.E. 2d 1097, 1104 (Ill. App. Ct. 1992) (injury to striking worker); *Circle K. Corp. v. Rosenthal,* 574 P. 2d 856, 858 (Ariz. Ct. App. 1977) (convenience store employee injured by third party).

Society for Human Resource Management (1999). Workplace Violence Survey.

Souders v. Lucero, 196 F. 3d 1040 (9th Cir. 1999).

Stradley v. Lafourche Communications, Inc., 869 F. Supp. 442 (E.D. LA. 1994).

Thompson, F. (Fall 1995). Psychiatric disorders, workplace violence and the Americans with Disabilities Act, *Hamline Law Review*, p. 36.

U.S. Department of Justice (1997) National Crime Victimization Study.

Velasquez v. Industrial Comm'n., 581 P. 2d 748 (Colo. Ct. App. 1978).

Victim's wife sues day-trading firm, *Los Angeles Daily Journal*, August 18, 1999.

Ward v. Trusted Health, No. 94-4297 (Suffolk Super. Ct., MA).

Yunker v. Honeywell, Inc., 496 N.W. 2d 419 (Minn. App. 1993).

Yunker v. Honeywell, Inc., supra, 496 N.W. 2d 419; *Evan F. v. Hughson United Methodist Church*, 8 Cal. App. 4th 828, 836–837 (1992); *Rita M. v. Roman Catholic Archbishop*, 187 Cal. App. 3d 1453 (1986).

Zelig v. County of Los Angeles, 73 Cal. App. 4th 741 (1999); Accord, *Vaughn v. Granite City Steel*, 576 N.E. 2d 874 (Ill. App. Ct. 1991).

About the Contributing Authors

Regina A. Petty, J.D.

Regina A. Petty, J.D. is a partner in the law firm of Wilson, Petty, Kosmo & Turner, LLP in San Diego, CA. She specializes in representing management in all aspects of employment law, including advising on workplace violence cases and related issues.

Lois M. Kosch, J.D.

Lois M. Kosch, J.D. is an attorney in the law firm of Wilson, Petty, Kosmo & Turner, LLP in San Diego, CA. Ms. Kosch specializes in representing management in all aspects of employment law, including advising on workplace violence cases and related issues.

PART X

Educating and Training Those Who Stalk the Stalker

Staying One Step Ahead of Stalkers and Stalking Crimes: Personnel Development, Training, and Ongoing Education

21

JOSEPH A. DAVIS

Contents

Introduction

Training cannot be overemphasized and reinforced enough in terms of significant importance on new and existing agency or departmental personnel. If you are a single investigator in a law enforcement division, part of an investigative unit, or a victim services professional, or if you are planning to develop an internal team, a public safety multidisciplinary team, or are currently directing a team already in operation, remaining focused and updated can be accomplished through professional training (Davis, 2000a).

Because of the current emphasis being placed on research funding and grant opportunities designed to unravel the mysteries of stalking, stalkers, and their victims, changes that are taking place at the state and federal levels will have an impact at the local level (Wells, 1999; Sullivan, 1996).

0-8493-0811-9/01/$0.00+$1.50
© 2001 by CRC Press LLC

Importance of Training for New and Existing Personnel

It must be continuously emphasized that stalking, as a recognized criminal act (and related conduct), is not new as a predatory-type behavior. However, stalking as a course of conduct crime is relatively new in terms of statutes, laws, and federal and state legislation (Maxey, 1999). In addition, many current stalking-type training programs designed to address this complex issue and, quite frankly, convoluted matter focus not only on a myriad of recent successes, but also on all of the inherent problems, failures, and caveats that have surfaced within the last decade: i.e., revisiting the concept of dangerousness and future prediction of violence, non-standardized approaches to conducting risk analyses and threat assessments, physical security issues, traditional vs. contemporary investigation approaches, terrorist threats, surveillance and technology, evidence gathering, constitutional issues of search and seizure, restraining orders, prosecution strategies, and bail reform regarding would-be potential repeat stalkers (Wells, 1999; Sullivan, 1996).

Annual, ongoing quarterly, or even monthly training to at least cover updates is necessary. Unfortunately, many of us who are involved in stalking research, stalker–victim research, relationship, relational, and communication research, as well training program development and service delivery to law enforcement personnel and the public have additional ground to break, not only on the issue of stalking, but also on some very specialized cases which we have examined — such as false victimization syndrome (FVS), falsely alleged victimization syndrome (FAVS), and inappropriate electronic pursuit via the Web, a.k.a. cyberstalking (Davis, 2000b).

Strike Force Concept

Multidisciplinary Case Assessment Team Approach

Most training programs are predicated (or at least should be) on empirical, demographic, as well as case study research from a variety of academic and professional disciplines. In 1994, due to the foresight of a few individuals, notably, Kerry Wells, Wayne Maxey, and Greg Peters (with additional assistance along the way by DA personnel like Peter Gallagher, Denise Vedder, Jacque Young, Fiona Kahlil, and Bonita F. Hammell*), the District Attorney's

---

* *Note:* Dr. Bonita F. Hammell died March 24, 1998 at the age of 48. She was a vital and integral part of the Stalking Strike Force, Stalking Case Assessment, and Stalking Strike Force Public Safety Training Team. Her work has left an indelible impression on the legacy of the team and on many of the current members. In part, her legacy continues to thrive through the existing team. Many members who remain had the opportunity to work and present with her the Annual "Stalking the Stalker" Training Conferences. Dr. Hammell is also credited, along with Mr. Wayne Maxey, as being instrumental as the first secretary in helping to establish the first ATAP Chapter in San Diego.

Office of San Diego launched a special operations unit (special ops) specifically designed to address stalking and many of the related or "crossover crimes" often seen in stalking–stalker cases. Thus, in 1994, the San Diego Stalking Strike Force and accompanying Stalking Case Assessment Team (SCAT) were developed to exclusively address stalking conduct, security issues, threat assessment, risk analysis, prosecution strategies, victim service needs, and, of course, the countywide training needs of local law enforcement (Wells, 1999; Maxey, 1999).

The training component, as part of the Stalking Strike Force and SCAT's Special Operations as a public service, has since expanded to include an annual "Stalking the Stalker" Conference. This is a statewide POST recognized conference and is a certified training venue for law enforcement.

The Strike Force's training program also provides out-of-state public safety and judicial training for judges and other DA personnel around the country, the most recent being a "stalking the stalker" training program venue held in London, England to the United Kingdom law enforcement personnel, i.e., Scotland Yard (Maxey, 1999; Wells, 1999).

Training Research and Development

In addition to stalking case assessment, investigations, case management, victim services, prosecution, law enforcement case consultation, public safety, and community training, SCAT has been busy researching and developing training materials to inform professionals across many disciplines and the public about stalking laws, stalker conduct, and victim services (Maxey, 1999). Part of this chapter has integrated the SCAT teams' research efforts to date and will provide the reader with content excerpted from the 1999 training manual (with kind permission granted for use by DDA Kerry Wells, Co-chair, Stalking Strike Force and SCAT, 1999).

Multidisciplinary Approach to Case Analysis and Case Management

An obvious commonality among all effective teams is shared interest, group cohesion, and dedication to a worthy cause. The Stalking Strike Force and SCAT have been effective since 1994 by using a multidisciplinary team approach. Utilizing the above formula of commonality, shared interest, cohesion, and dedication, using existing DA prosecutors, investigative and victim services personnel teams, along with many highly dedicated local professionals from various professions or disciplines such as law enforcement, probation, parole, U.S. Secret Service, FBI, mental health private practice, private law practice, clinical and empirical research, psychology, psychiatry, communication, applied criminology, security administration, victim services, etc., has benefited local law enforcement and the community by examining new and existing stalker–victim cases monthly. The service is one provided to public safety and to the public; there is no charge — only tremendous benefit (Sullivan, 1996; Maxey, 1999).

One of the first of its kind in the country since the inception of the Stalking Strike Force, the SCAT team has addressed hundreds of cases since 1994 and has assisted numerous other DA offices in the state, around the country, and abroad with their stalking, stalker, and stalker–victim cases (see Appendix, excerpted with permission from the *Stalking Strike Force and SCAT 1999 Training Manual*).

Bibliography

Davis, J. (1996). *Elements of Psychological Personality and Behavioral Assessment.* Anaheim, CA: Pulse Customized Publishing.

Davis, J. (1997). A Psychological and Legal Analysis of Those Who Stalk. Unpublished manuscript, San Diego, CA.

Davis, J. (March 1997). Developing a Threat Assessment and Risk Analysis of Those Who Stalk. District Attorney of San Diego, Second Annual Stalking the Stalker Conference presentation. San Diego, CA.

Davis, J. (October 1999). Stalker Typologies, Geographic Encounter Profiles (GEP), Crime and Intelligence Analysis: Examining the Mobility Patterns of Stalkers, and Victim Selection and Engagement. Conference presentation, Third Annual Stalking the Stalker Conference, District Attorney Office, San Diego, CA.

Davis, J. (December 1999). Reciprocal Determinism: The Key to Understanding Stalkers and Conducting an Assessment of Threat. Presentation, Association for Threat Assessment Professionals (ATAP), San Diego Chapter, San Diego, CA.

Davis, J. (2000a). Workplace violence and stalking: strategies for targeted victim and employee/employer safety planning, *The Baron Center Newsletter and Update — News You Can Use.* Website: www.BaronCenter.com.

Davis, J. (2000b). The falsely alleged victimization syndrome (FAVS): a psychological campaign for attention via stalking, *The Baron Center Newsletter and Update — News You can Use.* Website: www.BaronCenter.com.

Davis, J. (2000c). Falsely alleged victimization syndrome (FAVS): "To be or not to be … that is the question" (quote from the play, *Hamlet,* Act III by William Shakespeare, *circa* 1600s), In peer review for publication, San Diego, CA.

Davis, J. and Chipman, M. A. (1997). A forensic psychological typology of stalkers and other obsessive types, *Journal of Clinical Forensic Medicine U.K.,* 4, 166–172.

Maxey, W. (1999). Personal communication with co-director, Stalking Strike Force and SCAT, San Diego, CA.

Sullivan, C. A. (1996). Implementing an Anti-Stalking Multi-Agency Program in San Diego County. Unpublished Master's thesis, National University, San Diego, CA.

Wells, K. (1999). Personal communication with co-director, Stalking Strike Force and SCAT, San Diego, CA.

About the Contributing Author

Joseph A. Davis, Ph.D. LL.D.

An expert in the area of public safety psychology, the editor of *Stalking Crimes and Victim Protection: Prevention, Intervention, Threat Assessment, and Case Management* is Joseph Davis, Ph.D., LL.D. Dr. Davis holds a B.S. in psychology with honors, M.S. in psychology, a Ph.D. in clinical psychology, and a LL.D., Doctor of Laws, in law and public policy (honoris causa). Dr. Davis completed his post-graduate forensic mental health assessment, education, and training at the University of Virginia at the Institute of Law, Psychiatry, and Public Policy in 1985. He is the executive director of the Institute of Law, Psychology, and Public Policy Studies and is a partner with The TAP Group, Inc. (threat assessment and prevention) in San Diego and Long Beach, California. With adjunct faculty appointments at several major universities in California and abroad, he has published extensively over the past 17 years in five academic areas covering the disciplines of clinical-forensic, police/public safety psychology, criminology, traumatology, law, and public policy. Over the past 5 years, he has been the medical and allied health editor-in-chief and a member of the editorial advisory board to the *Canadian Journal of Clinical Medicine* in Edmonton, Alberta.

In addition to devoting his time to university-level teaching and clinical research, he maintains a private office devoted to management and organizational consulting, training, research and development, critical incidents and trauma response, and public safety psychology. He is married and is the father of two daughters. A native of Virginia, he and his family reside in San Diego.

KERRY WELLS
WAYNE MAXEY

Contents

* Since its inception in 1994, the San Diego Stalking Strike Force developed a training manual for its new Stalking Case Assessment Team (SCAT) members. The training manual, to date, has gone through several revisions resulting from existing team member experiences, updates in legislation, legal changes regarding the crime of stalking, i.e., use of restraining orders, law enforcement intervention, prosecution, etc., and new research published in the field regarding safety planning, risk management, security, victimology, treatment and evaluation, mental health, threat assessment, investigations, stalking, and stalker behaviors. The manual is included here with the kind permission of Ms. Kerry Wells and Mr. Wayne Maxey.

Introduction

Nationwide, it is estimated that 1 in 12 women will be victims of stalking at some point during their lives. At any one time, it is estimated that 200,000 women are being stalked in the United States. But stalking is not gender specific. Men make up a smaller but equally victimized group. It is estimated that 1 in 45 men will be victims of stalking at some point during their lives (National Institute of Justice, Centers for Disease Control and Prevention, 1998; "Stalking in America: Findings from the National Violence Against Women Survey" (Tjaden and Thoennes, 1998).

In 1990, California became the first state in the nation to pass an anti-stalking statute (Penal Code section 646.9). Since then, every state has enacted some sort of anti-stalking or anti-harassment legislation. Also since 1990, Penal Code section 646.9 has been amended in California several times. The effect of these amendments has been to broaden the definition of "credible threat" and increase the category of people against whom the threat can be made.

Elements of Stalking

Penal Code section 646.9 defines stalking as:

> Any person who willfully, maliciously, and repeatedly follows or harasses another person and who makes a credible threat with the intent to place that person in reasonable fear for his or her safety, or the safety of his or her immediate family.

Harassment as an Element of Stalking

"Harasses" means a knowing and willful course of conduct directed at a specific person that seriously alarms, annoys, torments, or terrorizes the person, and that serves no legitimate purpose. This course of conduct must be such as would cause a reasonable person to suffer substantial emotional distress and must actually cause substantial emotional distress.

Course of Conduct Crime

"Course of conduct" means a pattern of conduct composed of a series of acts over a period of time, however short, evidencing a continuity of purpose. Constitutionally protected activity is not included within the meaning of "course of conduct."

Credible Threat from Stalking

"Credible threat" means a verbal or written threat, including that performed through the use of an electronic communication device, or a threat implied by a pattern of conduct or a combination of verbal or written statements and conduct made with the intent to place the person that is the target of the threat in reasonable fear for his or her safety or the safety of his or her family and made with the apparent ability to carry out the threat so as to cause the person who is the target of the threat to reasonably fear for his or her safety or the safety of his or her immediate family.

It is not necessary to prove that the defendant had the intent to actually carry out the threat.

"Immediate family" includes any spouse, parent, child, any person related by consanguinity or affinity within the second degree, or any other person who regularly resides in the household, or who, within the prior six months, regularly resided in the household.

The present incarceration of the person making the threat is not a bar to prosecution for stalking.

Punishment for the Crime of Stalking

The first offense of stalking (where there is no restraining order) is a felony wobbler, i.e., can be charged as either a misdemeanor or a felony (Penal Code section 646.9(a)).

If a restraining order is in effect at the time, the crime is a non-reducible felony with a sentencing range of 2, 3, or 4 years (Penal Code section 646.9(b)). Upon a second or subsequent conviction, whether involving the same or different victim, the punishment is also 2, 3, or 4 years (Penal Code section 646.9(c)).

If probation is granted the defendant must participate in a counseling program unless the court finds "good cause" not to impose such a condition.

The court can also order a restraining on behalf of the victim that may be valid for up to 10 years (Penal Code section 646.9(h)).

Other Statutes Related to Stalking

In addition to Penal Code section 646.9, there have been several other recent additions to the law which investigators should be aware of when evaluating and handling a stalking case.

- Penal Code section 166(b)(1) now provides that any person who is guilty of contempt by violating an order of the court (i.e., no-contact order), who has previously been convicted under Penal Code section 646.9, is guilty of a misdemeanor punishable by 1 year in the county jail. A violation of this section can occur by contacting a victim by phone, mail, or directly, and incarceration of the defendant is no defense.
- Penal Code section 12021(c) prohibits any person who has been convicted of stalking within the previous 10 years from owning or possessing a firearm.
- Civil Code section 1708.7 establishes a tort of stalking which subjects a stalking defendant to liability for general damages, special damages, and punitive damages. (While investigators will not directly use this statute it is important to advise the victim that one option is a civil suit under this section.)

- Code of Civil Procedure section 527.8 allows an employer to obtain a restraining order against someone who is stalking or harassing one of their employees.
- Vehicle Code section 1808.21 provides that stalking victims may request confidentiality of their DMV records.

Legal Watch and Updates
(California, Department of Justice, 2000):
Crime of Stalking (Statute Amendments and Assembly Bills)

Code of Civil Procedure 1277-1278;

Government Code 6205.5, 6206.4-6206.7, 6208, 6210

Code of Civil Procedure 1277-1278; Government Code 6205.5, 6206.4-6206.7, 6208, 6210 are amended to provide that when a participant in the "Address Confidentiality for Victims of Domestic Violence Program" brings a petition for a name change, the petition, court order, and order to be published shall indicate that the name is confidential and on file with the Secretary of State. The Secretary of State must keep name changes confidential and requires that program participants notify the Secretary of State's Office of name changes within 7 days of the name change.

The program is renamed the "Address Confidentiality for Victims of Domestic Violence and Stalking" and adds victims of stalking to the program. Enrollees may use the address provided by the Secretary of State for voting, scholarly and political research, governmental purposes, and service of process. The address provided by the Secretary of State's Office may also be substituted for official records including birth, death, and marriage (SB 1318, AB 205).

Penal Code Section 3058.61

Penal Code Section 3058.61 is added to the Penal Code to require that the Department of Corrections, at least 45 days prior to the release date, notify the sheriff or chief of police, or both, and the district attorney of the county where the offender was convicted and the county into which a person convicted of stalking is to be paroled or released following a period of confinement on a parole revocation without a new commitment (SB 590). Existing law already requires the CDC, county sheriff, or local department of corrections to notify victims or their representatives of the release of a person convicted of stalking or a felony offense involving domestic violence.

Persons convicted of stalking on parole cannot be returned to a location within 35 miles of the victim's residence or place of employment upon the victim's request and if the DOC or Board of Prison Terms finds there is a need to protect the victim's life, safety, or well-being (SB 580).

Penal Code 3071

Penal Code 3071 is added to require that the DOC implement by January 1, 2002 stalking instructions for parole officers to include management of stalking parolees and notifying and interacting with victims (SB 1539).

Penal Code 13519.05

Penal Code 13519.05 is added to require that POST implement by January 1, 2002 a course or courses of instruction for training law enforcement officers in handling stalking complaints and guidelines for law enforcement response to stalking. Both shall stress enforcement of criminal laws, availability of civil remedies and community resources, and protection of the victim.

Training presenters shall include experts with expertise in direct services to stalking victims. Completion of training may be by telecommunication, video training, or other instruction (SB 1539).

Penal Code 1050

Penal Code 1050 is amended to provide for trial precedence over all other criminal and civil cases for death penalty cases where both sides announce they are ready. The same statute also provides for a single good cause continuance not to exceed 10 court days for cases of murder, stalking, child abuse, domestic violence, and career criminal where the assigned prosecutor is participating in another trial, preliminary hearing, or motion to suppress (AB 2125).

Vehicle Code 1808.21

Vehicle Code 1808.21 is amended to suppress vehicle registration and driver's license record information from any person except a court, law enforcement agency, or governmental agency, upon request of a person who is a stalking victim or is the subject of threats of death or great bodily injury. The person must submit verification that is acceptable to DW establishing his or her status.

Records are ordinarily suppressed for 1 year; 60 days before the 1-year period ends, DW must notify the subject. The suppression can continue for two additional 1-year periods upon submission of a letter indicating that the person continues to have a reasonable belief he or she is in danger of stalking or threat of death or great bodily injury (SB 2072).

Code of Civil Procedure 223

Code of Civil Procedure 223 is amended to authorize voir dire questioning of prospective jurors at trial by counsel for all parties. The court can impose reasonable restrictions and questioning is only to aid in exercises of challenges for cause (AB 2406).

Penal Code 646.9 and 646.93 Amended; 646.94 Added

Penal Code 646.9 and 646.93 are amended and 646.94 is added to increase the punishment for a second conviction of stalking to 2, 3, or 5 years in prison. Conviction for stalking where there is a prior felony conviction for PC 273.5, 273.6, or 422 is 2, 3, or 5 years in prison or up to 1 year in jail, a $1000 fine, or both (PC 646.9(c)(1)) (AB 2425).

Penal Code 646.93 is amended to require the sheriff to designate a telephone number for the public to inquire about jail and bail status, and scheduled release dates of persons arrested for stalking. The sheriff does not have to establish a new number for this purpose. Victim resource cards must specify the designated phone number. Existing resource cards can be used until supplies are exhausted before cards with the designated number must be provided. In counties where an arrestee is not incarcerated in a jail operated by the sheriff and in counties without a Victim Notification System (VNE), a telephone number shall be available for the public to inquire about jail and bail status, and scheduled release dates of persons arrested for stalking. The sheriff does not have to establish a new number for this purpose.

Victim resource cards must specify the designated phone number. Existing resource cards can be used until supplies are exhausted before cards with the designated number must be provided. If an arrestee is transferred to another facility, the transfer date and new facility location shall be made available through the designated telephone number. Resource cards issued pursuant to Penal Code section 264.2 shall list the designated telephone number (AB 2425).

Penal Code 646.94 is added, contingent on a budget appropriation, to ensure that the Department of Corrections places stalkers deemed to pose a high risk of committing a repeat stalking offense in an intensive and specialized parole supervision program (AB 2425).

Other Crimes (Crossover Crimes) Associated or Seen with Stalking

Threatening or harassing phone calls (Penal Code section 653)
Vandalism (Penal Code section 594)
Terrorist threats (Penal Code section 422; see below)
Threatening a witness (Penal Code section 136.1)

Peeping (Penal Code section 647(h))
Trespass, trespass threat (Penal Code section 601/602)
Violating restraining order (Penal Code sections 273.6, 166.4)
Violence offenses (Penal Code sections 242/243, 273.5, 245, 417)
Other violent offenses (Penal Code sections 207, 664/187, etc.)
Theft offenses (Penal Code sections 484/488, 459, 475, VC10851)
Cruelty to animals (Penal Code section 597)
Arson (Penal Code section 451)
Phone tapping (Penal Code sections 631/632)

Terrorist Threats Related to Stalking

Probably the most common companion crime to stalking is "terrorist threats." Many stalking cases will also include threats that can be independently charged and prosecuted under Penal Code section 422.

Penal Code section 422 defines the crime of terrorist threats as:

> Any person who willfully threatens to commit a crime which will result in death or great bodily injury to another person, with the specific intent that the statement is to be taken as a threat, even if there is no intent of actually carrying it out, which, on its face and under the circumstances in which it is made is so unequivocal, unconditional, immediate, and specific as to convey to the person threatened a gravity of purpose and an immediate prospect of execution of the threat, and thereby causes that person reasonably to be in sustained fear for his or her own safety or for his or her immediate family's safety.

The significant difference between this crime and stalking is that Penal Code section 422 does not require repeated conduct. One threat will do. It does require, however, that the threat be of death or great bodily injury, that it be "unconditional" and "immediate," and that it causes "sustained" fear on the part of the victim.

Case law has helped define these terms. Several cases have held that a threat can violate Penal Code section 422 even though it is "conditional" (e.g., "If you testify, I'll kill you."). These cases have held that conditional threats are true threats (despite technically conditional language) if their context and the surrounding circumstances reasonably convey to the victims that they are intended (*People v. Bolin* (1998); see also *People v. Brooks* (1994); *People v. Stanfield* (1995); *People v. Gudger* (1994); *People v. Melhado* (1998)).

"Sustained" fear was defined in *People v. Allen* (1995) as "a period of time that extends beyond what is momentary, fleeting, or transitory." In that case 15 minutes was sufficient.

In addition, a terrorist threat can qualify under Penal Code section 422 even though it was made to a third party and not directly to the victim. It is sufficient if the suspect intended the third party to act as an intermediary (in *People v. David L.* (1991) 234 Cal. App. 3d 1655).

People v. Teal (1998) held that Penal Code section 422 does not require certainty by the threatener that his or her threat has been received. If one broadcasts a threat intending to induce sustained fear, 422 is violated if the threat is actually received and induces sustained fear whether or not the threatener knows the threat has hit its mark.

Cited California Cases Involving Stalking Laws

Presently there are several cases that have interpreted California's stalking statute. In *People v. Heilman* (1994, 391) the defendant challenged the constitutionality of Penal Code section 646.9 claiming the term "repeatedly" was too vague. The court rejected the claim finding that "repeatedly" is a word of such clear understanding that its meaning is not vague. "It simply means the perpetrator must follow the victim more than one time" (*People v. Heilman*, 1994, 400).

In *People v. Carron* (1995), the court held that the crime of stalking does not require an actual intent to kill or cause great bodily injury. It only requires an intent to make a "credible threat" so as to place the victim in fear (Penal Code section 646.9 was amended to reflect this as well in January 1996).

In *People v. McClelland* (1996) the court found that ramming a car into the victim's house, calling her and her family members vile names, stating "Fire bomb at 6:00 o'clock," and throwing what appeared to be an explosive device at the house was sufficient evidence of harassment and credible threat.

In *People v. Tran* (1996) the court held that the phrase "and serves no legitimate purpose" within the definition of "harassment" is not unconstitutionally vague. Whether the defendant's actions served a "legitimate purpose" is an objective (reasonable person) standard, not determined by the defendant's own view of his conduct.

In *People v. Falk* (1997) the court held that a defendant's obsessive desire to engage in sexual acts with the victim (a stranger) and be with her "for eternity" was sufficient evidence of "credible threat."

In *People v. Kelley* (1997), the court found that a prosecution for stalking does not violate the double jeopardy clause (or Penal Code section 654) despite the defendant having been previously convicted of violating a restraining order, when the harassment continues after the TRO conviction.

In *People v. McCray* (1997), the court held that a single series of acts committed over the course of one day was sufficient to constitute "harassment" under the stalking statute (see also *People v. Halgren* (1997); *People v. Gams* (1997)).

Psychological Makeup and Typologies of Stalkers

It is important for officers and investigators to recognize there is no one particular profile for a stalker (Davis and Chipman, 1997). Some studies (Davis and Chipman, 1997; Zona et al., 1993) suggest that "stalkers" come from all walks of life. They can be male or female. Many boast of having above-average intelligence. Some have prior criminal records, many do not. Some have diagnosable mental illnesses while others may be simply socially maladaptive. Domestic violence "stalkers" often are not mentally ill but may have very dependent and/or controlling personalities. A common diagnosis for relationship stalkers is a DSM-IV Axis-II (American Psychiatric Association, 1994), narcissistic personality disorder or borderline personality disorder. Some stalkers' obsessions are aggravated by drug usage but others eschew drugs all together (Davis et al., 1999).

The relationship between stalker and victim can include past intimates, acquaintances, co-workers, or complete strangers. Stalkers can be motivated by anger, revenge, jealousy, or absolute fantasy or delusion (Zona et al., 1993; Meloy, 1998).

According to the research by Michael Zona et al. (1993), stalkers can be generally classified and categorized as follows:

1. Simple Obsessional: This type of stalker is the most common. It is usually a male who knows the victim as an ex-spouse, ex-lover, or former boss, and who begins a campaign of harassment against them. The stalking activities begin either after the relationship has gone bad or there is a perception of mistreatment.
2. Love Obsessional: This stalker is a stranger to the victim but is obsessed and thus mounts a campaign of harassment to make the victim aware of the stalker's existence. This type of person often "stalks" a celebrity or public figure, but can also become obsessed with the bank teller or grocery store clerk.
3. Erotomania: This stalker is usually female and falsely believes that the victim is in love with her and, but for some external influence, they would be together. The victim is often someone famous or rich or in a position of power such as an employer, movie star, or political figure. In this situation, those who are close to the victim (i.e., a spouse or lover who is perceived as being "in the way") may be the most at risk.
4. False Victimization Syndrome: This is a rare occurrence but involves someone who consciously or subconsciously desires to be placed in the role of a victim. Therefore, false victims establish a complex tale of being stalked which is, in fact, false.

Source: Zona, M., Palarea, R., and Lane, J., Jr. (1998). Psychiatric diagnosis and the offender-victim typology of stalking, in J. R. Meloy (Ed.), *Psychology of Stalking: Clinical and Forensic Perspectives*. San Diego, CA: Academic Press.

Source: Davis, J. (in press). Stalking, obsessive fantasy and falsely alleged victimization syndrome (FAVS) … or, false victimization: "To be or not to be, that is the question" (quote from the play, *Hamlet*, Act-III by William Shakespeare), *Canadian Journal of Clinical Medicine*, Edmonton, AB.

Source: Mohandie, K., Hatcher, C., and Raymond, D. (1998). False victimization syndromes found in stalking, in J. R. Meloy (Ed.), *Psychology of Stalking Clinical and Forensic Perspectives*, San Diego, CA: Academic Press, chap. 2, 9–84.

Recognizing a Stalking Case

Any time a victim reports any type of "harassing" behavior, the responding officer should be thinking about the possibility of stalking. Additional inquiry must be made to determine whether this is an isolated incident or repeated conduct. *Note:* It is not uncommon for a victim to put up with harassing behavior for some time before finally calling the police. Therefore, whenever a report is made you can assume the likelihood of prior behavior.

Remember: Victims of stalking can be either male or female. If the victim expresses a fear of the suspect these fears should be taken seriously and a detailed inquiry made to determine the origin of the fear. Male victims, in particular, feel that their fears are often minimized by law enforcement, which leads to a reticence to report continuing conduct.

Common "harassing" behavior includes:

1. Vandalism
2. Annoying or threatening phone calls
3. Following or other violations of restraining orders
4. Actual assaults
5. Sending unwanted letters
6. Showing up at the victim's home or workplace
7. Attempting to obtain private information about the victim from others
8. Leaving "gifts" for the victim
9. Disabling the victim's car
10. Taking mail from the victim's mailbox
11. Entering the victim's home when the victim is not there
12. Taking photographs of or "spying" on the victim
13. Reporting the victim to authorities for crimes that did not occur

When inquiring about prior behavior officers should always determine whether any prior police reports have been made and in which jurisdiction. You should also ask whether any friends or members of the victim's family have filed reports (often stalkers target others who are close to the victim as well as the victim).

Any time the suspect has engaged in "more than one" incident of some type of harassment, the case should be evaluated as a potential stalking case.

DON'T FORGET: "Stalkers" come in all shapes and sizes. Do not assume that because the "suspect" is a doctor, judge, teacher, etc. that the allegations are untrue. In fact, statistically, "stalkers" tend to be more intelligent and better educated than the average criminal population.

Investigating a Stalking Case

There are actually two parts to any stalking investigation:

1. Learning as much as possible about the stalker and his/her method of operation (assessing the stalker)
2. Establishing corroboration of the stalking conduct (gathering evidence)

Assessing the Stalker

Information that should be documented includes:

- Any prior threats made
- Any actual pursuit or following of the victim
- Any history of violence against the victim or others
- Information regarding the suspect's tendency toward outburst or rage
- Prior mental illness history
- Substance abuse problems
- Possession or knowledge of or fascination with weapons
- Any history of TRO violations

In addition, every stalking investigation should include a thorough research of the suspect's prior criminal history and/or prior contacts with law enforcement.

Gathering Evidence (Proof) of the Stalking Conduct

Search warrants.   Serving a search warrant on the suspect's residence and vehicle can be an invaluable tool in obtaining evidence to support the charge of stalking and in providing pertinent information about the stalker.

Items to be alert for when serving warrants include:

- Any photographs of the victim (many times these will have comments or drawings on them)
- Photographs, diagrams, or drawings of the victim's home or workplace
- Writings, logs, or diaries kept by the suspect that describe his stalking activities or thoughts/fantasies about the victim or other victims
- Personal items belonging to the victim

- Video or cassette tapes that might have information concerning the stalking, such as surveillance footage
- Books describing stalking techniques or having a subject matter dealing with stalking, harassment, or violence
- Any equipment that appears to have been used to "stalk" the victim, such as cameras, binoculars, video recorders, etc.

Items from the victim.   It is also important to seize any tangible items of evidence from the victim that substantiates the stalking behavior.

Evidence to be alert to seize include(s):

- Any taped phone messages
- Any letters or notes written by the suspect to the victim
- Any objects sent to the victim or left for the victim

Obtaining corroboration.   Corroborative evidence of the stalking conduct is key to any successful prosecution for stalking. Investigators should:

- Photograph any items vandalized, damaged, written on, etc.
- Check for fingerprints on vandalized items or other objects sent to or left for the victim.
- Advise the victim to put a trap on her phone.
- Obtain phone records from the victim and suspect's residence.
- If the victim's phone is not set up to record messages or conversations have the victim obtain such a machine.
- For any incident of harassment, determine whether other witnesses were present and interview them. Often friends, family members, co-workers, employees, etc. have information regarding the suspect's behavior. This corroboration is crucial.
- Research the defendant's whereabouts during the times of alleged acts to deter "alibi" defenses.
- On serious cases, consider surveillance of the defendant. This may be particularly useful in a case where there appears to be a pattern to the defendant's conduct.

Proof of the victim's state of mind.   A stalking case requires proof not only of the defendant's conduct, but of the victim's state of mind. The crime of stalking requires that the victim actually suffer "substantial emotional distress" because of the stalker's conduct. It is therefore important to document any evidence of the victim's response to the harassment. For example, has the victim:

- Moved to a new location?
- Obtained a new phone number?

- Put a trap on the phone?
- Told friends, co-workers, family of the harassment?
- Told building security?
- Given photos of defendant to security?
- Asked to be escorted to the parking lot and work site?
- Changed work schedule or route to work?
- Stopped visiting places previously frequented?
- Taken self-defense courses?
- Bought pepper spray or mace?
- Purchased a firearm?
- Put in an alarm system?
- Hired a bodyguard?
- Acquired a guard dog?

Assessment of Potential Threat and Future Dangerousness

Law enforcement has traditionally become involved after a crime has occurred with the primary focus of identifying the perpetrator and establishing evidence of the crime. Investigators in stalking cases, however, have a unique opportunity to act in a proactive way and prevent future harm to a victim. Assessing the potential threat posed by a suspect is an important step toward that goal.

Source: Fein, R., Vossekuil, B., and Holden, G. (September 1995). Threat Assessment: An Approach to Prevent Targeted Violence. Washington, D.C.: National Institute of Justice, U.S. Government Printing Office.

Source: Fein, R. and Vossekuil, B. (1998). Protective Intelligence and Threat Assessment Investigations. NIJ Funded Research, NCJ #170612.

Source: Monahan, J. (1985). Evaluating potentially violent persons, in C. P. Ewing (Ed.), *Forensic Psychology, Psychiatry and the Law.* Sarasota, FL: Professional Resources.

The distinction between making a threat and posing a threat is important.

- Some people who make threats ultimately pose threats.
- Some people who make threats do not pose threats.
- Some people who pose threats never make threats.

The primary objective of a risk assessment investigation is to gather as much information as possible on both the suspect and the victim/target.

Intelligence Gathering and Information about the Suspect

Multiple sources of information should be consulted to learn about the suspect's behavior, interests, and state of mind at various points in time. These can include:

- Personal interviews with the suspect (see "Stalking Suspect Interviews")
- Material created or possessed by the suspect such as journals, letters, books, magazines, or other items collected by him
- Interviews with people who know or have known the suspect, such as friends, family, co-workers, supervisors, neighbors, landlord, previous victims, etc.
- Any public records, such as police, court, probation, or corrections records, mental health records, or social services records

Information about the Target

To prevent violence the threat assessment investigator also requires information about the victim or targeted individual.

- Is the victim well known to the suspect? Does the suspect know about the victim's work, home, personal lifestyle, patterns of living, daily comings and goings?
- Is the victim vulnerable to attack? Does the victim have resources to arrange for physical security? What can change about the victim's lifestyle that could make attack by the suspect more difficult or less likely?
- Is the victim afraid of the suspect? Is that degree of fear shared by the victim's friends, family, and colleagues?
- How sophisticated or naive is the victim about the need for caution? How able is the victim to communicate a clear and consistent "I want no contact with you" message to the suspect?

Will He/She Strike?

Using the above information obtained throughout the investigation, the investigator must then seek to determine whether the suspect appears to be moving toward or away from an attack.

Studies show that violence is the product of an interaction of several factors that can be situational, environmental, physical, or psychological (or in some combination):

- The individual who is outwardly focused and takes violent action
- A stimulus condition that leads the subject to see violence as an option or solution to his problems
- A triggering event (internal or external)
- A setting that facilitates, potentiates, or permits the violence
- A present set or combination of circumstances that are comfortable and familiar to the stalker that has proven to be successful in the past (e.g., intimidating the victim at a specific time, event, location, etc.)

Source: Davis, J. (December 1999). Personality Psychology, Trait Theory, Behavioral Contiguity and Reciprocal Determinism: The Key to the Assessment of Potential Threat. In-service presentation, Association for Threat Assessment Professionals (ATAP), San Diego, CA.

Source: Davis, J., Siota, R. L., and Stewart, L. (1999). Future prediction of dangerousness and violent behavior: psychological indicators and considerations for conducting an assessment of potential threat, *Canadian Journal of Clinical Medicine* (research monograph).

Source: Monahan, J. (1985). Evaluating potentially violent persons, in C. P. Ewing (Ed.), *Forensic Psychology, Psychiatry and the Law*. Sarasota, FL: Professional Resources.

Source: Fein, R. and Vossekuil, B. (1998). Protective Intelligence and Threat Assessment Investigations. NIJ Funded Research, NCJ #170612.

Factors which suggest a high risk to the victim include:

- Present threats to kill the victim
- Past threats to kill this victim or other victims
- Use of weapons such as guns, knives, or other potentially lethal weapons
- Possession of lethal weapons
- Degree of obsession, possessiveness, or jealousy regarding the victim
- Violations of a restraining order with demonstration of little concern for the consequences of arrest and jail time
- Past incidents of violence — against the victim
- Access to the victim and/or the victim's family members
- Hostage-taking
- Depression or threats of suicide
- Other mental illness of the stalker
- Drug usage
- History of prior stalking victims

Source: Fein, R., Vossekuil, B., and Holden, G. (September 1995). *Threat Assessment: An Approach to Prevent Targeted Violence*. Washington, D.C.: National Institute of Justice, U.S. Government Printing Office.

Source: Fein, R. and Vossekuil, B. (1998). Protective Intelligence and Threat Assessment Investigations. NIJ Funded Research, NCJ #170612, Washington, D.C.

Stalking Suspect Interviews

Suspect interviews can be extremely important in assessing the dangerousness of the suspect and in obtaining information that will ultimately help prove a stalking case. For this reason these interviews should be videotaped whenever possible. Body language, gestures, voice tones, eye contact, etc. are all very important aspects in evaluating the stalker. These videos can be viewed later by a mental health expert for input, and can be valuable evidence in a subsequent prosecution.

Interviews should only be conducted after the suspect's background has been thoroughly researched. It can be very helpful to catch the suspect off guard when he realizes how much you know about him and his conduct.

BE AWARE: Stalking suspects can be very intelligent, manipulative, and cunning. They often are very good liars. They will commonly attempt to deny or rationalize their behavior or try to "outsmart" the investigator.

The goal of the interview should be twofold: to gather as much information as possible about the suspect's thinking, behavior patterns, and activities regarding the victim, and to encourage change in his behavior. By showing an interest in the suspect's life that is neither unduly friendly nor harsh, an investigator can increase the likelihood that the suspect will share valuable information.

CAVEAT: Investigators should be aware that in some cases interviewing the suspect may serve to intensify his interest in the victim. For example, someone who has written numerous letters to a stranger victim professing undying love for her (but who has not engaged in other behavior) may have his interest stimulated by an interview. Without an interview, his interest might dissipate on its own.

Other suspects may be "pushed" into action by police contact. A desperate or suicidal ex-partner who feels abandoned by the victim may sense that time is running out and be provoked into more extreme "action." Precautions must always be taken regarding these possibilities whenever a suspect interview occurs.

Types of Interventions and Approaches to Case Management

How an investigator handles a particular stalking situation generally depends on the type of stalking that is occurring and the level of risk presented to the victim. For example, often love-obsessional stalkers (i.e., someone focused on a celebrity) will cease their activity when simply confronted by police intervention. However, intervention in other cases can serve only to aggravate the situation.

Case management involves developing a plan that moves the suspect away from regarding violence against the victim as a viable option. Management may require the investigator to draw on resources connected to the suspect but not traditionally used by law enforcement, such as friends, family, associates, employers, mental health, and social service staff. All of these contacts may be used in seeking to aid the suspect to formulate more appropriate goals.

While vigorous prosecution may be the best way to prevent violence and minimize harm to the victim, it is also true that legal sanctions alone may not deter a person who desperately desires revenge or is prepared to die to achieve his objective.

Consultation with a mental health or behavioral sciences expert can be invaluable to the investigator when it appears the suspect may suffer from some sort of mental illness or whose behavior is extreme.

Specific Stalking Suspect Intervention Techniques

Detective or Investigator Contact

This type of contact is most appropriate in cases that have yet to involve criminal violations or involve very low-grade activities. It can include contact by mail, telephone, or in person. Oftentimes, a face-to-face visit at the suspect's workplace or residence may be all it takes to have a deterrent effect on the inappropriate behavior. This type of contact can also occur by way of a scheduled interview at the police station.

These types of initial contacts appear to be most successful with the "simple obsessional" case where the suspect and victim have had some prior relationship. In this type of case the suspect is less likely to be severely mentally ill and thus more likely to understand the potential consequences of his continued harassment.

Protective Orders/Temporary Restraining Orders

The second option for intervention usually involves having the victim obtain a restraining order against the suspect. This option is not without controversy. It is recognized that restraining orders may not be effective in actually protecting a victim and may instead "provoke" the stalker. Historically, however, this has had much to do with the fact that law enforcement has done little to respond to restraining order violations.

The primary advantage to having a restraining order against the suspect is that it allows him to be immediately arrested when a violation occurs. It is thus vitally important that when a police agency is attempting to utilize such orders as part of an overall intervention plan, the involved personnel be prepared to respond quickly to each violation. Only then is there a demonstration that the "system" is determined to sanction the suspect in order to control his behavior.

A second advantage to obtaining a restraining order is that it allows for enhanced charging of the stalking charge so as to have a more significant "hold" over him.

Arrest and Detention

The third type of intervention involves actual arrest and detention. Arrest and subsequent incarceration should not only impress upon the suspect the seriousness of his conduct, but also give the victim a measure of safety for at least some period of time. Spending time behind bars can have a sobering effect on many who have never experienced the pleasures of incarceration before. It also provides a glimpse of what lies ahead should the person choose to continue the harassing behavior.

Investigators should be cognizant of the fact that stalkers often attempt to continue their harassment from behind bars, intimidating the victim through phone contacts, letters, third person threats, etc. Victims must be advised of this and investigators should be prepared to document and corroborate any such activity.

Mental Health Agency Assistance Options

One option available to the police is the involuntary commitment of an individual who, because of a mental disorder, represents a danger to himself or others. Welfare and Institutions Code section 5150 allows an officer to commit such a person for a 72-hour treatment and evaluation. This commitment can be extended following a probable cause hearing and request by the treating physician for a period of 14 days. Utilizing this option, when appropriate, has two primary advantages: it takes the victim out of harm's way for some period of time so that she can provide for her safety, and it provides for some treatment and evaluation of the suspect which may diffuse the immediate situation.

Prosecution Approach

Successful prosecution for stalking depends on the concerted team effort of investigators, consultants, prosecutors, and the court system. For those suspects who clearly "do not get the picture" and thus present a continuing risk to the victim, vigorous prosecution for their criminal conduct is the only option. The goal of any such prosecution is to ensure conviction so that maximum controls can be placed on the defendant, thus increasing the safety of the victim.

Victim Impact Concerns

Most often, the criminal justice system measures crime by tangibles such as broken bones, stab wounds, gunshot holes, etc. The greater the injuries, the greater the charges, the more important the case. Stalking is different, because quite often nothing physically has happened to the victim yet. This makes the crime more difficult to assess and, consequently, it is taken less seriously than other crimes.

For the stalking victim, however, the fear that something will happen is overwhelming. Stalking victims never feel safe. They are waiting for "something" to happen. Frequently the stalker has permeated several aspects of the victim's life. He has been around her house, in the parking lot at her job, followed her to the cleaners, found her in the library, etc. She cannot feel safe anywhere; she's always looking over her shoulder to see if he is there.

To further complicate stalking cases, many people believe that stalking victims are merely paranoid and not in any real danger. Some even think that stalking is a form of flattery. Others blame the victim, wondering what she's done to encourage the stalker or why she can't stop the stalker's behavior.

Because of all these perceptions, the stalking victim may feel very isolated from family, friends, co-workers, and the criminal justice system. Because nothing may have "happened" to her yet, no one may help her. She is further isolated from support systems if she has moved or changed jobs as a way of protecting herself. She may also feel guilty that she has put family members or friends in possible danger if the stalker has made threats against them or she is concerned that he will.

Acknowledging the legitimacy of the victim's fear and recognizing that stalking behavior can indeed be the precursor of significant violence are a critical first step in any stalking investigation.

Advising the Stalking Victim

It is important to point out that generalizing about what a stalking victim should do in any particular case is not only ill-advised but can be dangerous. Not all "stalkers" are the same, nor are they necessarily "predictable." All stalking victims are afraid of their stalkers whether they have been expressly threatened with harm or not. But the degree to which the stalker actually poses a threat to the victim is often difficult to assess and can depend on numerous variables. With that said, it is generally agreed that the "domestic violence" stalker (simple obsessional) may pose the highest risk of all to the victim.

Gavin de Becker, an expert on security and stalking behavior, emphasizes that each case must be looked at individually and the circumstances evaluated carefully. He advises that in many cases intervention itself (i.e., obtaining a restraining order and prosecution) may be the aggravating factor that leads to violent retaliation. Other experts feel the victim's best option is to immediately get a restraining order. In any event, investigators must be very sensitive to the fact that by pursuing an investigation of the stalker in any manner the victim may be significantly increasing the level of danger to her.

Civil Liability Issues

Because any stalker may pose a serious risk to the victim, investigators must be very careful about the advice given to the victim and cognizant of potential civil liability should the victim be subsequently harmed. This is an area of the law which is not black and white.

One case in particular is noteworthy: *Wallace v. City of Los Angeles* (1993). In that case, a young woman witnessed a murder. The investigating police detective obtained a written pre-trial statement from her and her identity as a witness was made known. She received threatening phone calls and told the detective that she feared the defendant. The detective said he would relocate her if the threats continued and he promised to alert her if she was in danger. In summary, he minimized the danger to her even though he knew, but did not tell the witness, that the defendant was a suspect in several other murder cases and had threatened witnesses in the past. A few days before

SAN DIEGO COUNTY STALKING STRIKE FORCE

STALKING CASE ASSESSMENT TEAM (SCAT)
(619) 515-8900

THREAT ASSESSMENT WORKSHEET

SCAT Key Case # _____

Law Enforcement Agency: _____ L.E. Case#: _____

Name of L.E. Detective: _____ Date completed: _____

Detective's telephone #: _____ pager #: _____

Law Enforcement Case report(s) attached: Yes _____ No _____

Suspect's Name: _____ aka: _____

Race: _____ Age: _____ DOB: _____ Ht: _____ Wt: _____ Hair: _____ Eyes: _____

DL#: _____ SSN: _____

Residence Address: _____ Tel#: _____

Name of Business: _____ Tel#: _____

Business Address: _____

Suspect's Vehicle: (Year) _____ (Make) _____ (Model) _____

Style: (2dr/4dr) _____ Color: _____ Vehicle Lic.#: _____ State: _____

Suspect's relationship to victim: (The closer the relationship, the greater the threat).

_____ spouse   _____ former spouse

_____ dating relationship   _____ former dating relationship

_____ friend   _____ acquaintance

_____ co-worker   _____ relative

_____ professional acquaintance   _____ unknown person   _____ other _____

Victim's Name: _____ DOB: _____

Residence Address: _____ Tel#: _____

Name of Business: _____ Tel#: _____

Business Address: _____

(SCAT 3/00)

---

trial the witness was murdered. The court of appeal found (1) a special relationship was created when the detective enlisted the young woman as a witness, which (2) required him to warn her of the unforeseen dangers she faced, and (3) he was not entitled to immunity for his actions.

The present status of both state and federal case law suggests the preceding action by an investigator may create potential liability.

ASSESSMENT FACTORS: (Do not leave blank. Write either NA, None, or Unk).

1.   VEILED/SPECIFIC THREATS OF VIOLENCE:

   _____

   _____

   _____

   _____

2.   ACTS OF VIOLENCE AGAINST VICTIM:

   _____

   _____

   _____

3.   FITS OF RAGE, DISPLAYS OF ANGER, EMOTIONAL OUTBURSTS:

   _____

   _____

   _____

4.   HISTORY OF VIOLENCE:

   ____   documented (criminal history – see attached)

   _____

   _____

   _____

   ____   undocumented

   _____

   _____

   _____

5.   ANNOYING / THREATENING TELEPHONE CALLS:

   ____   residence

   _____

   _____

   ____   workplace

   _____

   _____

6. UNSOLICITED AND/OR THREATENING CORRESPONDENCE:

_____

_____

7. PROTECTIVE ORDER: Yes ___ No ___   DESCRIBE VIOLATIONS:

_____

_____

_____

8. SUBSTANCE ABUSE PROBLEMS:

_____

_____

_____

9. ACTS OF VANDALISM:

_____

_____

_____

10. FASCINATION WITH WEAPONS (guns, knives):

_____

_____

_____

11. FIREARMS – OWNERSHIP: (If registered, write reg.)

_____

_____

_____

12. THREATS OF SUICIDE OR MURDER/SUICIDE:

_____

_____

_____

13.   OTHER INFORMATION:

_____
_____
_____
_____
_____
_____
_____
_____
_____
_____
_____
_____
_____
_____
_____
_____

CONTINUE TO NEXT PAGE

OFFENDER'S CRIMINAL JUSTICE FACT SHEET

Driver's License: (L1)

_____

_____

Local PD files:

_____

_____

ARJIS: (MOI11) (FI's, traffic, pawns, arrests, crime reports, etc.)

_____

_____

Local Wants & Warrants: (MA09)

_____

_____

State/Federal Wants & Warrants: (QW)

_____

_____

Local Criminal History: (RI01)

_____

_____

Gun Registration: (QG – SUN System)

_____

_____

Local Pending Cases: (DA09) (City Attorney, D.A.'s Office)

_____

_____

Local Citations: (MC21)

_____

_____

County Probation: (PR09)

_____

_____

State/Federal Criminal History: (DOJ Criminal History)

_____

_____

SAN DIEGO COUNTY STALKING STRIKE FORCE

STALKING CASE ASSESSMENT TEAM (SCAT)

RECOMMENDATION SHEET

SCAT Case #
Date presented:

Team members present:

_____   _____
_____   _____
_____   _____
_____   _____
_____   _____

Recommendations:

_____
_____
_____
_____
_____
_____
_____
_____
_____
_____
_____

Follow Up:

_____
_____
_____
_____
_____
_____
_____

SCAT (3/00)   6.

Bibliography

Davis, J. (1999). Personality Psychology, Trait Theory, Behavioral Contiguity and Reciprocal Determinism: The Key to the Assessment of Potential Threat. In-service presentation, Association for Threat Assessment Professionals (ATAP), San Diego, CA.

Davis, J. and Chipman, M. A. (1997). Stalkers and other obsessional types: a forensic psychological typology of those who stalk, *Journal of Clinical Forensic Medicine, U.K.*, 4, 166–172.

Davis, J., Siota, R. L., and Stewart, L. M. (1999). Future prediction of dangerousness and violent behavior: psychological indicators and considerations for conducting an assessment of potential threat, *Canadian Journal of Clinical Medicine*, 6(3), 44–58.

Fein, R. A., Vosskuil, B., and Holden, G. A. (1995). Threat assessment: an approach to prevent targeted violence, National Institute of Justice — *Research in Action*, September 1–7.

Fein, R. and Vossekuil, B. (1998). Protective Intelligence and Threat Assessment Investigations, NIJ Funded Research, NCJ #170612.

Meloy, J. R. (1998). *The Psychology of Stalking: Clinical and Forensic Perspectives.* San Diego, CA: Academic Press.

Mohandie, K., Hatcher, C., and Raymond, D. (1998). False victimization syndromes found in stalking, in J. R. Meloy (Ed.), *Psychology of Stalking*, San Diego, CA: Academic Press, chap. 2, 9–84.

Monahan, J. (1985). Evaluating potentially violent persons, in C. P. Ewing (Ed.), *Forensic Psychology, Psychiatry and the Law*, Sarasota, FL: Professional Resources.

People v. Allen (1995) 33 Cal. App. 4th, 1149.

People v. Bolin (1998) 18 Cal. App. 4th, 297.

People v. Borrelli (2000) 77 Cal. App. 4th, 703.

People v. Brooks (1994) 26 Cal. App. 4th, 142.

People v. Carron (1995) 37 Cal. App. 4th, 1230.

People v. Ewing (1999) 76 Cal. App. 4th, 199.

People v. Ewing (1999) 76 Cal. App. 4th, 210.

People v. Falk (1997) 52 Cal. App. 4th, 287.

People v. Gams (1997) 52 Cal. App. 4th, 147.

People v. Garrett (1994) 30 Cal. App. 4th, 962.

People v. Gudger (1994) 29 Cal. App. 4th, 310.

People v. Halgren (1997) 52 Cal. App. 4th, 1223.

People v. Heilman (1994) 25 Cal. App. 4th, 256.

People v. Kelley (1997) 52 Cal. App. 4th, 568.

People v. McClelland (1996) 42 Cal. App. 4th, 144.

People v. McCray (1997) 58 Cal. App. 4th, 159.

People v. Melhado (1998) 60 Cal. App. 4th, 1529.

People v. Stanfield (1995) 32 Cal. App. 4th, 1152.

People v. Teal (1998) 61 Cal. App. 4th, 277.

People v. Tran (1996) 47 Cal. App. 4th, 253.

Wallace v. City of Los Angeles (1993) 12 Cal. App. 4th, 1385.

Wells, K. (1996). California's anti-stalking law — a first, *Law Enforcement Quarterly*, August–October, 9–12.

Wells, K. (1997). *Training Manual on Stalking* (revised edition). San Diego, CA: San Diego District Attorney Office, Special Operations Division, Stalking Strike Force, Stalking Case Assessment Team.

Wells, K. (September 1999). *Training Manual on Stalking*. San Diego, CA: San Diego Stalking Strike Force, Stalking Case Assessment Team.

Zona, M. A., Kaushal, K. S., and Lane, J. (1993). A comparative study of erotomanic and obsessional subjects in a forensic sample, *Journal of Forensic Sciences*, 38(4), 894–903.

Selected Bibliography

American Medical Association (1992). *Diagnostic and Treatment Guidelines on Domestic Violence*. Washington, D.C.

American Psychiatric Association (1994). *Diagnostic Criteria from DSM-IV*. Washington, D.C.: American Psychiatric Association.

Clarke, J. W. (1990). *On Being Mad or Merely Angry: John W. Hinckley, Jr. and Other Dangerous People*. Princeton, NJ: Princeton University Press.

Davis, J. and Chipman, M. A. (1997). Stalkers and other obsessional types: a forensic psychological typology of those who stalk, *Journal of Clinical Forensic Medicine, U.K.*, 4, 166–172.

Davis, J., Siota, R. L., and Stewart, L. M. (1999). Future prediction of dangerousness and violent behavior: psychological indicators and considerations for conducting an assessment of potential threat, *Canadian Journal of Clinical Medicine*, 6(3), 44–58.

Dietz, P., Matthews, D., Van Duyne, C., Martell, D., Parry, C., Stewart, T., Warren, J., and Crowder, J. (1991). Threatening and otherwise inappropriate letters to Hollywood celebrities, *Journal of Forensic Sciences*, 36(1), 185–209.

Fein, R. and Vossekuil, B. (1998). Protective Intelligence and Threat Assessment Investigations, NIJ Funded Research, NCJ #170612.

Fein, R. A., Vossekuil, B., and Holden, G. A. (1995). Threat assessment: an approach to prevent targeted violence, *National Institute of Justice — Research in Action*, September 1–7.

Geberth, V. (October 1992). Stalkers, *Law and Order*, 40(10), 138–143.

Goldstein, R. L. (1987). More forensic romances: De Clerambault's syndrome in men, *Bulletin of the American Academy of Psychiatry and Law*, 15, 267–274.

Hammell, B. F. (1996). Stalking: The Torment of Obsession: The STOP Program (Stalking Treatment Options Program). San Diego District Attorney Anti-Stalking Case Conference, San Diego, CA.

Harmon, R. (1998). Anti-Stalking Legislation: A New Answer for an Age Old Problem. Conference presentation, American Academy of Forensic Sciences 50th Anniversary meeting, San Francisco, CA.

Harmon, R., Rosner, R., and Owens, H. (1995). Obsessional harassment and erotomania in a criminal court population, *Journal of Forensic Sciences*, 40(2), 188–196.

Holmes, R. M. (1993). Stalking in America: types and methods of criminal stalkers, *Journal of Contemporary Criminal Justice*, 9, 317–327.

Johnson, P. (1993). When creeps come calling, *Law Enforcement Quarterly*, February–April, 9–10, 32.

Meloy, J. R. (1992). *Violent Attachments*. Northvale, NJ: Jason-Aronson Publishers.

Meloy, J. R. (1998). *The Psychology of Stalking: Clinical and Forensic Perspectives*. San Diego, CA: Academic Press.

Menzies, R. P., Federoff, J. P., Green, C. M., and Isaackson, K. (1995). Prediction of dangerous behavior in male erotomania, *British Journal of Psychiatry*, 166, 529–536.

Mohandie, K., Hatcher, C., and Raymond, D. (1998). False victimization syndromes found in stalking, in J. R. Meloy (Ed.), *Psychology of Stalking*, San Diego, CA: Academic Press, San Diego, chap 2, 9–84.

Monahan, J. (1985). Evaluating potentially violent persons, in C. P. Ewing (Ed.), *Forensic Psychology, Psychiatry and the Law*. Sarasota, FL: Professional Resources.

Monahan, J. and Steadman, H. (Eds.) (1994). *Violence and Mental Disorder: Developments in Risk Assessment*. Chicago, IL: University of Chicago Press.

Monahan, J., Appelbaum, P., Mulvey, E., Robbins, P., and Lidz, C. (1994). Ethical and legal duties in conducting research on violence: lessons from the MacArthur Risk Assessment Study, *Violence and Victims*, 8, 380–390.

Morin, K. (1994). The phenomenon of stalking: do existing state statutes provide adequate protection? *San Diego Justice Journal*, 1, 123.

National Institute of Criminal Justice (1993). A Project to Develop a Model Anti-Stalking Code for States. Final summary report presented to the National Institute of Justice. Washington, D.C.: U.S. Government Printing Office.

Silver, E. and Banks, S. (submitted for publication). Calibrating the Potency of Violence Risk Classification Models: The Dispersion Index for Risk (DIFR).

Silver, E., Mulvey, E., and Monahan, J. (1999). Assessing violence risk among discharged psychiatric patients: toward an ecological approach, *Law and Human Behavior*, 23, 235–253.

Steadman, H., Monahan, J., Robbins, P., Appelbaum, P., Grisso, T., Klassen, D., Mulvey, E., and Roth, L. (1993). From dangerousness to risk assessment: implications for appropriate research strategies, in S. Hodgins (Ed.), *Crime and Mental Disorder*. (pp. 39–62). Newbury Park, CA: Sage Publications.

Steadman, H., Mulvey, E., Monahan, J., Robbins, P., Appelbaum, P., Grisso, T., Roth, L., and Silver, E. (1998). Violence by people discharged from acute psychiatric inpatient facilities and by others in the same neighborhoods, *Archives of General Psychiatry*, 55, 393–401.

Steadman, H., Silver, E., Monahan, J., Appelbaum, P., Robbins, P., Mulvey, E., Grisso, T., Roth, L., and Banks, S. (in press). A classification tree approach to the development of actuarial violence risk assessment tools, *Law and Human Behavior*.

Williams, W. L., Lane, J., and Zona, M. A. (1996). Stalking: successful intervention strategies. Alexandria, Virginia, *The Police Chief Magazine*, February, 104–106.

Zona, M. A., Kaushal, K. S., and Lane, J. (1993). A comparative study of erotomanic and obsessional subjects in a forensic sample, *Journal of Forensic Sciences*, 38(4), 894–903.

Recommended Reading and Reference List

Borum, R., Fein, R., Vossekuil, B., and Berglund, J. (1999). Threat assessment: defining an approach for evaluating risk of targeted violence, *Behavioral Sciences and the Law*, 17(3), 323–337.

de Becker, G. (1997). *The Gift of Fear: Survival Skills That Protect Us from Violence*. New York: Little, Brown.

Fein, R. A., Vossekuil, B., and Holden, G. (1995). Threat assessment: an approach to prevent targeted violence, *National Institute of Justice: Research in Action*. Washington, D.C.: U.S. Government Printing Office.

Gross, L. (2000). *Surviving a Stalker: Everything You Need to Know to Keep Yourself Safe*. New York: Marlowe and Company.

Meloy, J. R. (Ed.) (1998). *The Psychology of Stalking: Clinical and Forensic Perspectives*. San Diego, CA: Academic Press.

Meloy, J. R. (2000). *Violence Risk and Threat Assessment*. San Diego, CA: Specialized Training Services.

Spitzberg, B., Nicastro, A., and Cousins, A. (1998). Exploring the interactional phenomenon of stalking and obsessive relational intrusion, *Communication Reports*, 11(1), 34–47.

Tjaden, P. and Thoennes, N. (1998). *Stalking in America: Findings from the National Violence Against Women Survey*. National Institute of Justice, Centers for Disease Control and Prevention, Research in Brief, Washington, D.C.

Williams, W., Lane, J., and Zona, M. A. (1996). Stalking: successful intervention strategies, *The Police Chief*, Alexandria, VA, 104–106.

Zona, M. A., Sharma, K. K., and Lane, J. (1993). A comparative study of erotomanic and obsessional subjects in a forensic sample, *Journal of Forensic Sciences*, 38(4), 894–903.

About the Contributing Authors

Kerry Wells, J.D.

Kerry Wells, J.D. currently heads the Stalking Unit of the Special Operations Division, San Diego District Attorney's Office. She has been a prosecutor for the past 20 years after graduating magna cum laude from Whittier College School of Law. She was one of the original attorneys chosen to prosecute child abuse cases when the District Attorney's Office first established a child abuse unit in 1985. In 1989, she became chief of the newly established Domestic Violence Unit. Under her direction this unit became the largest specialized domestic violence unit in the state. She developed innovative protocols for the prosecution of domestic violence that have been nationally recognized.

Ms. Wells has lectured extensively throughout the state and the nation on the subjects of domestic violence, child abuse, and stalking. In 1998, she taught trial tactics at the National College of District Attorneys in Columbia, South Carolina. She is probably best known for the prosecution of Elizabeth Broderick, who murdered her ex-husband and his wife after stalking them for several years. This case received international attention and was one of the first cases covered live, gavel-to-gavel, by *Court TV.* A subject of books and made-for-television movies, this case led to Ms. Wells' interest in the much neglected and misunderstood crime of stalking. In 1994, Ms. Wells founded the Stalking Strike Force, which has as its goals increased education and awareness of the crime of stalking and an improved multi-disciplinary approach to stalking. She is an active member of the San Diego Chapter of the Association of Threat Assessment Professionals (ATAP).

Wayne Maxey, Ba.S.

Wayne Maxey is currently assigned as an investigator in the Stalking Unit of the Special Investigations Division, San Diego District Attorney's Office. He investigates and prepares for trial cases involving stalking, threats, and work-place violence. He started his law enforcement career with the San Diego, California, Police Department. He then joined the Chula Vista, California, Police Department where he worked as a patrol officer, and then as an investigator in the Sex Crimes/Child Abuse Unit. He was transferred to the Crimes of Violence Unit where he investigated homicide, robbery, felony assaults, domestic violence, and stalking cases. He was promoted to sergeant and worked as a patrol supervisor. Mr. Maxey is co-chair of the Stalking Strike Force, a multi-jurisdictional, multi-disciplinary group that was formed in 1994, to address the problem of stalking. He coordinates the Stalking Case Assessment Team (SCAT), a group that investigates and manages difficult and ongoing stalking cases. He is the current president of the San Diego Chapter of the Association of Threat Assessment Professionals (ATAP).

Index